# Routledge Handbook of Islam in the West

Islam has long been a part of the West in terms of religion, culture, politics and society. Discussing this interaction from al-Andalus to the present, this *Handbook* explores the influence Islam has had, and continues to exert; particularly its impact on host societies, culture and politics.

Highlighting specific themes and topics in history and culture, chapters cover:

- European paradigms
- Muslims in the Americas
- Cultural interactions
- Islamic cultural contributions to the Western world
- Western contributions to Islam

Providing a sound historical background, from which a nuanced overview of Islam and Western society can be built, the *Routledge Handbook of Islam in the West* brings to the fore specific themes and topics that have generated both reciprocal influence and conflict.

Presenting readers with a range of perspectives from scholars based in Europe, the USA and the Middle East, this *Handbook* challenges perceptions on both Western and Muslim sides and will be an invaluable resource for policy-makers and academics with an interest in the history of Islam, religion and the contemporary relationship between Islam and the West.

**Roberto Tottoli** teaches Islamic studies at the University of Naples L'Orientale, where he is currently director of the Department of Asia, Africa, and the Mediterranean. He has published studies on the biblical tradition in the Qur'an and Islam (*Biblical Prophets in the Qur'an and Muslim Literature*, Richmond, 2002; *The Stories of the Prophets of Ibn Mutarrif al-Tarafi*, Berlin, 2003) and the medieval Islamic literature. He also dealt with the aspects and dynamics of contemporary Islam, editing the volume *Le Religioni e il mondo moderno. III. Islam* (Torino, 2009).

# Routledge Handbook of Islam in the West

Edited by
*Roberto Tottoli*

LONDON AND NEW YORK

First published 2015
by Routledge
2 Park Square, Milton Park, Abingdon, Oxon OX14 4RN

and by Routledge
711 Third Avenue, New York, NY 10017

*Routledge is an imprint of the Taylor & Francis Group, an informa business*

*British Library Cataloguing in Publication Data*
A catalogue record for this book is available from the British Library

*Library of Congress Cataloging in Publication Data*
Routledge handbook of Islam in the West / edited by Roberto Tottoli.
pages cm
Includes bibliographical references and index.
1. Muslims–Non-Muslim countries. 2. East and West. 3. Civilization, Western–Islamic influences. 4. Islam–History. I. Tottoli, Roberto.
BP52.5.R68 2014
297.09182'1–dc23
2013043513

ISBN: 978-0-415-69132-1 (hbk)
ISBN: 978-1-315-79427-3 (ebk)

Typeset in Bembo
by Taylor & Francis Books

Printed and bound in the United States of America by Publishers Graphics, LLC on sustainably sourced paper.

# Contents

Contents

# List of figures and tables

**Figures**

**Tables**

# List of contributors

**Tahir Abbas** is Professor of Sociology at Fatih University in Istanbul, Turkey. He is author of *Islamic Radicalism and Multicultural Politics* (2011), editor of the four-volume *Islam and Education* (2010), and co-editor of *Honour, Violence, Women and Islam* (with M.M. Idriss, 2011). He is a specialist in the area of Muslim minorities and ethnic studies in the West. He is currently completing a critical observational perspective on the Muslim world and Muslim minorities in the West, and a monograph on comparative Islamisms based on research and study visits carried out in Turkey, Pakistan, and Indonesia.

**Stefano Allievi**, Ph.D., is Professor of Sociology at the University of Padua. He specializes in migration issues, sociology of religion, and cultural change, and has particularly focused his studies and research on the presence of Islam in Europe. He has published extensively on these issues in different languages (www.stefanoallievi.it).

**Elisa Banfi** is currently Postdoctoral Research Assistant at the Institute for Citizenship Studies (InCiTe) at the University of Geneva.

**Herbert Berg** is Professor of Religion specializing in Islam in the Department of Philosophy and Religion at the University of North Carolina, Wilmington. His research focuses on Islamic origins and on African American Islam. His publications include *Elijah Muhammad and Islam* (2009) and *The Development of Exegesis in Early Islam* (2000).

**Patrick D. Bowen,** a recent graduate of the University of Denver-Iliff School of Theology Joint Ph.D. Program in Religious Studies, is the author of over a dozen articles and book chapters concerning Islam in the West. His forthcoming three-volume book is entitled *A History of Conversion to Islam in the United States*.

**Sylvia Chan-Malik** is Assistant Professor of American and Women's and Gender Studies at Rutgers University, New Brunswick. Her research examines the intersections of race, religion, gender, and sexuality, with a specific focus on the history of Islam in the United States. Her current book project is titled *Insurgent Traditions: Race, Gender, and Islam in the United States, 1923–2013*.

**Nathalie Clayer** is Professeur at the EHESS and a senior research fellow at the CNRS (Paris). She has published on religion, nationalism, and the state-building process in the Balkans and the Ottoman Empire. Publications include *Aux Origines du nationalisme albanais* (Paris, 2007) and, with Xavier Bougarel, *Les Musulmans de l'Europe du Sud-Est (XIXe–XXe siècles)* (Paris, 2013).

**Ghaliya Djelloul** is a Ph.D. candidate at CISMOC and teaching assistant at the Université Catholique de Louvain. Her research covers intersections between gender and Islam, and her latest publication is: *Parcours de féministes musulmanes belges* (2013).

**Adis Duderija** received his Ph.D. from the School of Social and Cultural Studies at the University of Western Australia in 2010. Dr. Duderija is currently Visiting Senior Lecturer at the University of Malaya, Malaysia. He has authored a number of works on Western Muslim identity construction and contemporary Islamic reform and hermeneutics. He is the author of *Constructing a Religiously Ideal "Believer" and "Woman" in Islam: Neo-Traditional Salafi and Progressive Muslim Hermeneutics* (2011). He is also the editor of *Maqasid Al Shari'ah and Contemporary Muslim Reformist Thought: An Examination* (forthcoming).

**Salua Fawzi** is currently a Ph.D. candidate at McGill University at the Institute of Islamic Studies. Her research focuses on Muslim American young adults, with a particular emphasis on their involvement in Muslim Student Associations and how this shapes their understanding of religious orthodoxy, authority, and praxis.

**Johan Fischer** is an Associate Professor in the Department of Society and Globalization, Roskilde University, Denmark. His work focuses on modern Islam and consumer culture in Southeast Asia and Europe. More specifically, Johan explores the interfaces between class, consumption, market relations, Islam, and the state in a globalized world. A central focus in this research is the theoretical and empirical focus on the proliferation of *halal* commodities on a global scale.

**Francesca Forte** gained her Ph.D. in Philosophy in 2008. From 2010 to 2013 she held a two-year research fellowship at the Department of Philosophy, University of Milan. Her research interests include: Islamic philosophy (in particular Averroè and latin translations of Arabic texts), the relationship between Islam and human rights, and the matter of history in contemporary Islamic thought. Currently she teaches Islamic studies in the class of religious sciences at Bruno Kessler Foundation, Trento.

**Marco Gallo** graduated from the Faculty of Philosophy and Letters at the University of Rome La Sapienza. He has been living and working in Buenos Aires for over two decades, where he is Pontifical Chair John Paul II Benedict XVI Francis at the Catholic University of Buenos Aires. He has written contributions and articles on interreligious dialogue, with a particular focus on Islamic–Christian relations.

**Mercedes García-Arenal** is a Research Professor at the Centro de Ciencias Humanas y Sociales, CSIC, Madrid. Her first book was *Inquisición y Moriscos: los procesos del Tribunal de Cuenca* (Madrid, 1978). The most recent, with Fernando R. Mediano, *Un Oriente español. Los moriscos y el Sacromonte en tiempos de Contrarreforma* (Madrid, 2010), now in a revised version in English, *The Orient in Spain: Converted Muslims, the Forged Lead Books of Granada and the rise of Orientalism* (Leiden, Brill, 2013); and, with Gerard Wiegers (eds.) *A Mediterranean Diaspora: The Expulsion of Moriscos from Spain* (Leiden, Brill, 2014).

**Miriam Gazzah** is currently a postdoctoral fellow at the Amsterdam Institute for Social Science Research (AISSR), working within the research program "Islamic Cultural Performances: New Youth Cultures in Europe." Her research interests include: European-Muslim youth, popular culture, music, and Islam. In 2008 she obtained her Ph.D. at the Radboud University in Nijmegen. Her thesis is entitled *Rhythms and Rhymes of Life: Music and Identification Processes of Dutch-Moroccan Youth*.

**Kambiz GhaneaBassiri** is Associate Professor of Religion and Humanities at Reed College. He is the author of numerous publications on Islam in America, including *A History of Islam in America: From the New World to the New World Order* (2010).

**Juliane Hammer** is Associate Professor of Religious Studies and Kenan Rifai Scholar of Islamic Studies at the University of North Carolina at Chapel Hill. She is the author of *Palestinians Born in Exile* (2005) and *American Muslim Women, Religious Authority, and Activism: More than a Prayer* (2012), and the co-editor of *A Jihad for Justice: Honoring the Work and Life of Amina Wadud* (with Kecia Ali and Laury Silvers, 2012) and of *The Cambridge Companion to American Islam* (with Omid Safi, 2013). She is currently working on research projects focused on American Muslim efforts against domestic violence and Islamic/Muslim marriage and family in discourse and practice in the United States.

**Karim H. Karim** is a Professor and the Director of the Centre for the Study of Islam at Carleton University in Ottawa, Canada. He has served previously as Director of Carleton's School of Journalism and Communication and the Institute of Ismaili Studies in London, and has been a Fellow of Harvard University's Center for the Study of World Religions. He holds degrees in Islamic Studies and Communication Studies from Columbia and McGill universities. Dr. Karim has been a distinguished lecturer at venues in North America, Europe, and Asia. He won the inaugural Robinson Prize for his book *Islamic Peril: Media and Global Violence*. Karim is currently working on a three-volume series of books on Western–Muslim relations.

**Francesco Alfonso Leccese**, Ph.D. in Studies on Near East and Maghreb (University of Naples L'Orientale, 2007), is Adjunct Professor of Culture and Society of the Arab Language Countries at the University of International Studies of Rome and Research Fellow at the Department of Political and Social Sciences at the University of Calabria. He is a specialist in contemporary Sufism with a focus on the Arab world and has written articles in journals, including *Oriente Moderno* and *Annual Review of Islam in Africa*. He is currently working on non-ethnical transnational Sufi networks.

**Mark Lindley-Highfield of Ballumbie Castle** is an Associate Lecturer and Research Affiliate in the Department of Religious Studies at the Open University. He is a social anthropologist by training and was educated at the universities of Oxford, Aberdeen, Edinburgh, and the Open University. Mark has carried out a prolonged period of fieldwork studying the motivations for religious conversion to Islam and Anglican Christianity in Mexico.

**Brigitte Maréchal** is Director of the CISMOC (Centre for Interdisciplinary Research on Islam in the contemporary World) at IACCHOS Institute and Professor at the Université Catholique de Louvain. Her publications include: *Muslims in the Enlarged Europe* (2003), *Les Frères musulmans en Europe* (2009), and *Yearbook of Muslims in Europe* as co-editor.

**Luca Mavelli** is a Senior Lecturer in Politics and International Relations at the University of Kent. His research focuses on questions of secularity, postsecularity, security, and political violence in international relations. He is the author of *Europe's Encounter with Islam: The Secular and the Postsecular* (Routledge, 2012), and has co-edited and contributed to the 2012 Special Issue of the *Review of International Studies* on "The Postsecular in International Relations." His articles have appeared, among others, in the *European Journal of International Relations*, *Millennium: Journal of International Studies*, and the *Journal of Religion in Europe*.

**Kathleen Moore** is Professor and Chair of the Religious Studies Department at the University of California Santa Barbara. Moore teaches courses on Islam in America and Muslim diasporas and the law. Her most recent book, *The Unfamiliar Abode: Islamic Law in the United States and Britain*, was published in 2010. The book provides an account of new forms of Islamic legal knowledge in diasporic networks. She is co-author of a book titled *Muslim Women in America: Challenges Facing Islamic Identity Today*, and has written several articles on American Muslims and the law. She is currently writing a book on Islam, Feminism and the Law: Difference in Diaspora, about anti-essentialism, religion, and justice seen through the lens of Muslim women in diaspora.

**Annliese Nef** is currently Maître de Conférences at the University Paris 1-Panthéon. After dedicating her Ph.D. to Norman Sicily, she is now studying Islamic Sicily. She is author of *Conquérir et gouverner la Sicile islamique aux XIe et XIIe siècles* (Rome, 2011) and editor of *A Companion to Medieval Palermo* (Leiden, 2013).

**Gian Maria Piccinelli** is Professor of Islamic Law and Private Comparative Law, and Director of the "Jean Monnet" Department of Political Sciences at the Second University of Naples. He has written several comparative essays on Islamic contemporary legal systems, with special regard to civil, commercial, and banking law. He has directed and collaborated in several scientific research projects concerning Islamic Law, the Legal Systems of Arab and Mediterranean Countries, and the Euro-Mediterranean Partnership.

**Eric R. Roose** is a cultural anthropologist and an art historian with an ongoing interest in the comparative iconology of modern religious architecture. Between 2009 and 2012 he was a postdoctoral fellow, funded by the Cultural Dynamics Programme of the Netherlands Organisation for Scientific Research, at the Amsterdam Institute for Social Science Research.

**Uriya Shavit** is a Senior Lecturer at the Department for Arabic and Islamic Studies and the Program in Religious Studies at Tel Aviv University. He is the author of *The New Imagined Community: Advanced Media Technologies and the Construction of National and Muslim Identities of Migrants* (2009), *Islamism and the West: From "Cultural Attack" to "Missionary Migrant"* (2013), and numerous articles on Muslim minorities in the West. His studies of the religious law of Muslim minorities are supported by the Israel Science Foundation (Grant 627.11).

**Roberto Tottoli** teaches Islamic studies at the University of Naples L'Orientale, where he is currently Director of the Department of Asia, Africa, and the Mediterranean. He has published studies on the biblical tradition in the Qur'an and Islam (*Biblical Prophets in the Qur'an and Muslim Literature*, Richmond, 2002; *The Stories of the Prophets of Ibn Mutarrif al-Tarafi*, Berlin, 2003) and the medieval Islamic literature. He also dealt with the aspects and dynamics of contemporary Islam, editing the volume *Le Religioni e il mondo moderno. III. Islam* (Torino, 2009).

**Anna Triandafyllidou** is Professor and Director of the Cultural Pluralism Research Area at the Global Governance Programme of the European University Institute (Robert Schuman Centre for Advanced Studies) in Florence, Italy. She has been a Visiting Professor at the College of Europe in Bruges since 2002, and Editor in Chief of the *Journal of Immigrant and Refugee Studies*.

**Alessandro Vanoli** teaches History of the Mediterranean at the University of Bologna. His research is focused on the history of the West Mediterranean and the relationship between Islam, Judaism, and Christianity in the Iberian Peninsula and in Sicily during the Middle Ages. His publications include *La Sicilia musulmana* (Bologna, 2012); *La Reconquista* (Bologna, 2009); *La Spagna delle tre culture. Ebrei, cristiani e musulmani tra storia e mito* (Rome, 2006).

**Iyad Zahalka** currently serves as the chief Qadi of Jerusalem. His Ph.D. dissertation discussed *fiqh al-aqalliyyat al-muslima* and the Arab minority in Israel. He has published a number of articles on Islamic law in academic compilations and two textbooks in Hebrew and Arabic on the *shari'a* courts in Israel.

# Introduction

## Islam in the West: histories and contemporary issues of the Western *umma*

### *Roberto Tottoli*

The question of the history of the presence of Muslims and Islam in Europe and America is no doubt a sensitive point in contemporary Western societies. It deals with history and identity, and the West and the Islamic world as conceptual frameworks. As such, it touches on various debates about the moving borders, the supposed essence and the intersection between the West and the Islamic world. The idea of this book originated in the aftermath of September 11th, and reflects on the new perception of Muslim presence in the West, which has developed in the decade since. It also relates to the European polemics of some years ago about a European constitution and a mention therein of Europe's Christian roots. This book does not deal with some supposed Islamic roots within the Western world, but aims to show that the past and present history of Europe and America attests that Islam has made a significant impact, which is testimony to a Muslim community, or Muslim communities, in the West today. These constitute a sort, as I mentioned in the title, of outer and Western *umma* which interrogates and interrelates with the Islamic community living in the Muslim world and, along with this, with the Western societies in which the Muslims live and act.

Many studies coming from various disciplines have analyzed the physical numbers of Muslims in Europe and the Americas today, and have discussed many aspects of this in relation to social dynamics, specific national organizations, various juridical questions, and also the topic of the religious discourses. Along with this, Islamic studies have produced new outlines and approaches to the historical episodes connecting Islam to the West, such as from the most famous cases of Muslim Spain and the Ottoman Balkans, to the complex history of the diffusion of Islam in North and South America after the European colonization. The two perspectives of the past historical cases and the many challenges of the contemporary Muslim Western communities are put together here in order to comprehensively consider some of the many points relating to the complex question of Islam in the West.

## The two conceptual frameworks

We are perfectly aware that a first problem arising is in the title itself and the problems connected to the definition of the terms used. Islam and West are two differing concepts, one

1

relating to a religion and pointing to a religious community and the second a geographical entity or supposed space. The question is complicated by the fact that, although according to today's perception the two terms are accepted as referring to two well-known realities, the concepts themselves had not always been the same throughout history and may not perfectly reflect the situation at different times and places. The juxtaposition of the two concepts, of Islam "and" the West, has been a popular subject. It has been made by a few fortunate essays (cf., for example, Daniel 1960; Lewis 1993) and by many other subsequent successful titles. However, the subject we are dealing with here, the interaction between the two supposed different entities, of Islam in the West, is more nuanced and complicated. The question of Islam and Muslims "in" the West is different though apt to be declined in different ways. This is, for instance, attested by other works, such as the essays collected by M. Farrar et al. (2012) bearing the title *Islam in the West*, conceived in the realm of multiculturalism and as made explicit in the opening pages of the introduction of the editors, dealing with the relationships between Muslims and Western societies.

The concept of a religious community in another society or societies in a defined space relates to several problems on the proper meaning of all this (geographical, cultural, political?). However, the title as such, with all its limits, creates a challenge, to which this volume will try to respond. Before we delve any further, a few words are indeed necessary to better understand the two terms (Islam, West) so as to give a proper definition of their use in the perspective of this volume.

As a matter of fact a concept like that of an Islam in the West makes sense once we define what we mean by "Islamic world." Though at first sight the definition appears simple and clear cut, this is not the case. The concept itself emerged in Western thought quite late (Haneda 2007). But it cannot be denied that a classical Islamic world is conceived as covering the places and countries where today there is a majority of Muslims. However, it is not straightforward to decide where to draw the line. First of all, the idea of Europe, then of Christendom, does not correspond to today's perceptions of the West. The border given by the Mediterranean is somehow distorted by the contemporary perception of the sea as a much more definite division than earth, but this was not the case in the past (cf. on this point Dakhlia and Kaiser 2013: 7–31). Further, when we come to some European regions and places removed from the current Mediterranean Sea, things get complicated. The presence of Muslims in Eastern Europe is not only connected to recent immigration but also to the historical presence going back in some cases to Ottoman rule and even before. For all these reasons, although the Muslim perspective of what constitutes the Islamic world today may mostly coincide with what Europeans and Americans consider as such, some little differences connected to sensitive points still exist. Muslim Spain is, for instance, usually included in the abode of Islam according to classical theory, and the position of other territories in the past under Muslim rule is from time to time recalled by Muslims who in this way aim to re-discuss borders and the presence of Muslims in specific places.

Muslim classical theory has indeed elaborated and defined a concept of a specific space inhabited by Muslims and above all under Muslim rule. That is the conception of the *dar al-islam* ("the abode of Islam"), which finds a self-definition in a counteracting *dar al-harb* or *dar al-kufr* ("the abode of the war," "the abode of misbelief"), also including a middle position in the *dar al-sulh* ("the abode of the treaty"), which is of no relevance in our perspective since it still characterizes the outer world with respect to Islam. Recent studies have underlined how these concepts emerged and found their definitive diffusion at least two centuries after the origin of Islam (cf. Calasso 2010). Notwithstanding this, the expression of the theory in the classical period with a more or less stable and consistent part of the world under Muslim rule and inhabited by most of the Muslims attests to the strong theological relevance of the concept of a place for Islam and Muslims. There can be no doubt about this, and the rich literature dedicated to geographical descriptions and travels in this abode of Islam attests to a fundamental unity and consequently a self-perception as a realm distinct from an outer world (see, for example, Miquel 1967–88). This is true even if in the geographical works the concept *dar al-islam/dar al-harb* does not constitute the reference framework (Miquel 1967–88, II: 533) and the interaction between the Muslim realm and the outside appears frequent and constant. The scant mention of these expressions in geographical and travel literature is not surprising, and attests to how the concept was predominantly theological and juridical, rather than geographical. It is in the realm of positive law that the terms make sense, when it is defined what a Muslim should do when finding himself outside the abode of Islam and thus without a Muslim rule permitting him to accomplish all that he needs in terms of religious duties. Though in juridical literature the historical situation during the Middle Ages attests to a much more complex situation in the question of Muslims residing outside the *dar al-islam* than the simple dichotomy (Abou El Fadl 1994), it is beyond doubt that Muslim theory has defined a Muslim world, inhabited by Muslims. There is no doubt, for the sake of this, that there are realms defined as Islam and an outer world, which includes the West, so that it makes sense from the Muslim perspective to deal with those Muslims who found their way outside this abode of Islam.

The other concept, i.e. the West, reflects similar dynamics in its formation and definition. The famous criticism by E.W. Said (1978), who spoke in terms of an image of the Orient created by a Western world and defined as such in contraposition to an Orient, has at least recalled the attention to the cultural nature of the definition of the West. Many books have been published in the last decades about the definition of the West and its "others" (see, for example, Federici 1995), its meaning in world history (cf. Stearns 2003), the long history of its supposed crisis or decline (Herman 1997), the changing conceptual framework in contemporary Western scenes, and even its supposed uniqueness in world history (Duchesne 2011). All of this, on one side, attests to all the problems around the definition itself of a history and a culture using a geographical concept such as the West, but on the other side also that a supposed part of the world sharing something coming from the history of European civilization and in the last centuries spread in other continents (America and Oceania) exists or is apt to be described as such, i.e. a whole sharing something. And this notwithstanding that cultural concepts change and are subject to erosion, re-evaluation, and that they sometimes also give origin to differing and contrasting meanings depending on the different observers (cf. Bonnett 2004). The list of references on the topics related to the West would be long and not useful to our book. What is apparent is that it makes sense for the sake of this discussion to accept the identification of a Western space, more or less corresponding in Muslim theory to a part of the *dar al-harb*, and more specifically the part occupied by European civilization, abruptly corresponding to Europe, America, and Oceania.

## The book

This volume is consequently compiled from contributions about the history and the present situation of the Muslim communities living outside of the abode of Islam and who inhabited or today inhabit Western countries. The essays focus on some episodes of this contact and of this particular situation which leads some Muslims outside their regions in the Muslim world, to Europe and America above all. It is thus a history of the contacts between two supposedly different realms, which reflect cultural and geographical boundaries which shift over time and are still in flux following on from the events of the last decades and also those happening now.

The volume is divided into two parts, one dedicated to historical events and one to the current situation. This does not aim to be a historical portrait, but historical cases must be brought to the reader's attention since they reflect relevant aspects of the relation between Islam and the West and bear still some significance to the situation today, and even to the current presence of Muslims in some regions. However, the chapters in Part 1 of the volume are not meant to give a simple historical description of what happened, but rather to focus on some related themes in which to insert the most important data regarding the history of Muslims in Europe and America. The contributions touch on history, but also aim to emphasize some concepts and specific concerns of the presence of Muslims in the West, in a given place and time. Though different in content, the perspective and approach in Part 2 of the volume is similar. The topics of the contributions reflect the desire to highlight single questions and themes, considered relevant to the subject as a whole, and upon which to measure a specific, national, or continental situation, but also giving some information on what is happening on the other continent. Also here, there are no historical or descriptive outlines, but a tentative attempt to deal with sensitive points of the present and also of the near future.

Before going to an introductory description of the themes identified and the main questions emerging from the individual contributions, it is necessary to underline the originality of this approach, which aims to contribute to the large literature on these topics which has appeared in recent years. No doubt, other works deal with the question of Islam inside the "Western" space, sharing the same comprehensive attitude to combining a historical perception of past episodes with the contemporary situation prompted by the new presence of immigrant Muslim communities in the West. The works edited by Dakhlia and Vincent (2011) and Dakhlia and Kaiser (2013), for instance, take this same approach, beginning with the suggestions of the present situation and trying to answer the questions of why the Muslim presence before the twentieth century has been so much neglected, and furthermore whether the terms Muslim and European can coexist. The two volumes thus give a historical outline of the situation *grosso modo* between the fifteenth and the eighteenth century in the Mediterranean Sea. As a matter of fact, not many works have tried to give a comprehensive portrait including Europe and America, but there are some examples (cf. Metcalf 1996 on Muslim spaces in Europe and America). Much more similar to the themes dealt with in this volume is the collection of essays edited by Y. Yazbek Haddad (2002) titled *Muslims in the West*; the volume includes two sections on Europe and North America, and emphasizes the question of a Muslim space in the Western societies, but discusses only contemporary cases. The anthology of articles collected by D. Westerlund and I. Svanberg under the title *Islam in the West* (2010), along with proving the need for a definition of the terms in question, that is, the transformations of Islam in Western societies and their repercussions in Islamic or predominantly Muslim countries in Asia and Africa, includes more than seventy chapters on the topic. The material, which has all been previously published, is collected together in this volume for the first time, and divided into chapters on various topics, alternate historical cases, and contemporary themes, ranging from Europe to America, though American subjects are few.

The large historical part at the beginning tries to give a comprehensive portrait of the main chapters of the Muslim presence in Europe and America; contributors to the second contemporary section have been asked to deal with specific cases, but at the same time they keep one eye open to the situation across the ocean, with the aim of giving for the first time a comprehensive portrait around a concept dealing with Muslims in Europe and America. We are perfectly aware how difficult it is to find parallel concepts and to touch comprehensively differing situations and cases, but the aim was to see the story of Muslims in Europe and America as a possible common experience, though leading to differing responses. In this regard, the contributions collected here no doubt bear some new considerations in the depth of literature on these topics.

## History: Europe

But let us come now to the concrete discussion of what emerged from the contributions that in the two parts and five sections constitute the volume as introduced above. The first section in Part 1 touches upon historical episodes of the Muslim presence in Europe. The prominence given to Europe is due to the historical connections and relations between European civilization and Islam since its emergence in the beginning of the seventh century. As a matter of fact the wave of the first conquest was the occasion which brought Muslims to Europe, and to places that today belong to European countries. There are indeed many episodes in the first centuries after the advent of Islam which attest to Muslim presence between France, the Italian coasts, and in general all the northern Mediterranean shores. Also in this regard we have plenty of studies, mostly touching specific cases and historical episodes.

However, there is no doubt that the more relevant case in history connected to the presence of Muslims in Europe is that of the Iberian Peninsula, the medieval al-Andalus of the Muslim sources. It is a history of almost a thousand years, rich in detail, questions, and also still a sensitive point in contemporary Spain. Notwithstanding the political judgment of Muslim and even Jewish presence in the Iberian Peninsula, their role in respect to the modern Spain and Portugal, and the historical reality connected to the proper myth of al-Andalus, this constitutes the main chapter of Islam in Europe. And one that, because of its relevance, fits in this conceptual framework with some difficulties, since while Spain and Portugal are part of Europe, on the other hand, classical Islamic theory considers them as *dar al-islam*. In the economy of the volume as a whole, notwithstanding all these questions, the contributions dealing with it are dedicated to two specific issues, more related to subjects of relevance in the definition of the relation between Muslim communities and a surrounding outer world. Alessandro Vanoli (Chapter 1) has delved into the question of the moving borders that followed the Muslim conquest and that determined the Arabization and Islamization of part of the Peninsula, living side by side with Christian entities in the north. The question of the borders is relevant since the presence of Muslims gave rise to a Muslim space which gained wide renown and prestige in the Islamic world. But it was at the same time a frontier place, and this double sense of belonging and precariousness, well underlined by Vanoli, constitutes a fundamental aspect of the long Islamic history in the Iberian Peninsula. Though it is not easy to draw a clear line in a history of almost a thousand years, Vanoli no doubt succeeded in showing how concepts of belonging around these moving borders shaped complex ways of coexistence and interaction, thus marking the most important experience of Islam in Europe.

After the end of the Nasrid reign of Granada there is the last chapter in the history of Islam on the Iberian Peninsula, the story of the Moriscos, the crypto-Muslims who faced restrictions and persecutions by the Catholic crown and were forced into exile in 1609. Dealing with them is thus the description of a minority living in a Christian European country facing persecution but strongly fighting for its faith and traditions. Mercedes García-Arenal (Chapter 2) takes into consideration, in particular, this cultural resistance and discusses historical testimonies on the diffusion of the written culture which was hidden and preserved at high risk in the Morisco communities. Under the evangelizing efforts of the Christian crown and the surrounding new Spanish societies, Moriscos were strongly attached to their faith traditions. Taken from a different perspective, it is indeed a story of failed assimilation according to Christians and, at the same time, of resistance and fierce adherence to traditional knowledge through their specific literature and lore according to the Muslims. What is listed and discussed is indeed the first and unique example of Muslim literature (in Arabic or Aljamiado) copied by Muslims and diffused in modern Europe before the twentieth century. García-Arenal mentions also the question of the Lead Books, an *affaire* bearing relevance also in the history of Arabic studies in Europe which led some Moriscos to move in European countries and in general prompted a better knowledge of Islam in all of Europe thanks to the Moriscos and their books and knowledge (cf. García-Arenal and Rodríguez-Mediano 2013).

Another well-known episode of Islamic presence in European territory in medieval times is the case of Sicily. It is a history of a long political and social Islamic presence and of a longer cultural influence. As maintained by Annliese Nef (Chapter 3), the problem of the Islamic historical presence in Sicily and southern Italy cannot be discussed without the complex interrelation between historical and ongoing contingences in the representations. This accompanies the generations of scholars and studies and complies with the contemporary removal of the Islamic history which represents the core of the problems in today's conceptualization of a European Islam. In this perspective the study of the passage from the two-century Muslim rule (ninth to eleventh century) to the Hauteville domination, and the use or survival of Islamic imagery both at court and in society are indeed a possible paradigmatic declination of the relation of Islam and the West, both dynamic and involving political, religious, social issues and material culture.

A further chapter on Islam in Europe relates to the eastern part of the continent and it is the long history of the Ottoman presence from which originated the present Muslim communities surviving in the Balkans. As a matter of fact, Ottomans found in Europe their first direction of expansion, and thus their presence in the Balkan lands went on in some cases for almost five hundred years. The chapter on the topic by Nathalie Clayer (Chapter 4) succeeds in giving a general portrait which brings to the fore one major question, i.e. that the Muslim communities surviving from the Ottoman past to the European presence today share a substantial removal by the European and Western consciousness. Stereotyping attitudes around the question of Islamic presence are underlined by a contribution which, on the contrary, delineates specificities and discusses in depth what took place with the birth of the Balkan states in the nineteenth century. In fact the situation of the last two centuries, between nationalisms, definition of national identities, and the "creation" of the concept of Muslim minorities, is indeed a perspective bearing much relevance to the general topic of Islam and Muslims in the West. And it gives testimony to the present situation delineating Muslim communities reflecting various trends and attitudes.

The main historical episodes connecting the Balkans, Sicily, and Spain to Islam should not obscure the fact that across the whole Mediterranean relations, communalities, and exchange of goods, men, and relationships went on with no interruption from late medieval times onwards (cf. Catlos 2014). Many recent studies have brought some new light in relation to various aspects of the relations between Muslims and Europe and the presence of Muslims in Europe in the Modern age (sixteenth to eighteenth century). This took place not only in the remains in the story of Islam in the Iberian Peninsula, such as the fate of the Moriscos, or in relation to the warfare between the two shores or in the political relations with Ottomans, but also on the northern shores of the Mediterranean Sea such as in southern Italy (see, for example, Boccadamo 2010) and thus, more or less, in Europe as a whole (cf. Valensi 2012).

It is also for this substantial historical continuity that the event of twentieth-century Muslim immigration touching all European countries can be hardly defined as a new phenomenon *per se*. The contribution by Brigitte Maréchal and Ghaliya Djelloul (Chapter 5) delineates the fact, highlighting questions of Muslim identity and representations connecting the various and heterogeneous European situations. Though it appears difficult to trace common lines among different countries, including differing communities, formed in different times, coming from various Muslim places and living under differing juridical conditions, the chapter attests first and foremost to the complex nature of the definition of Islam and "Muslim." But notwithstanding specific concerns and differences, there is a sort of European Muslim identity which emerges in the "political" and "cultural" movements.

## History: America

The history of Muslim presence in America is a different case. The discovery of America by Europeans in 1492 marks the beginning of the migration of Muslims from their countries to North, Central, and South America. No doubt other individual presences could have existed before that date, but no relevant historical data are available to ascertain this. What characterizes Islam in America is that a common base is shared from north to south in relation to the definite first manifestations of Islam. They are connected to the slave market and the capture, captivity, and transfer to America of Muslim Africans collected by merchants on the coasts of Africa, mostly in the Gulf of Guinea and coming from inland areas. The memory of all this is difficult to recover. Further, the continent experienced Islam through a further wave of migration, mostly from the Syrian region, from the second half of the nineteenth century onwards. After that, the emergence of national differences and the specific case of African American Islam attest to the fact that Islam in America is a complex phenomenon displaying difference and specificity.

The origins of Islam in North America are delineated by Kambiz GhaneaBassiri (Chapter 6), who is also the author of the most stimulating essay on Islam in America which has appeared in recent years (GhaneaBassiri 2010). In his contribution, the question of the origins of the North American Muslim presence complies with questions of evidence and memory, intersecting with the similar problems in documenting a history of black slavery. Early testimonies go back to the seventeenth century and, though there are quite a few, still bear significance for the resistance and violently repressed and erased heritage of a Muslim faith diffused among slaves. The wave of the first emigration from Arab countries from the 1880s represents a distinct and different stage of the diffusion of Islam. From this time onwards the question of Islam in the USA is related to the main issue of the construction of a changing American identity, or rather its ideal significance in the making of the nation, built on the conflation of race, religion, and progress. Islam emerges as a marginal actor in relation to the building of the nation, but still present in the early twentieth century in various forms, and then with an increasing role when African American Muslims entered into the game. Touching partially the period discussed in Chapter 6, the story of Muslims in the USA would not be complete without a specific treatment of African American Muslims. What is relevant in relation to this topic is the perspective of its author. Herbert Berg (Chapter 7) is an Islamicist and thus approaches the question also in relation to religious definition and perception, and not only in terms of its impact on the American political scene. The focus is the Nation of Islam and its evolution from its origins and through figures such as Drew Ali, then Muhammad Fard, and above all Elijah Muhammad and Malcolm X. Religious consciousness is accompanied by the actual use of Islam as a name and a reflection of peculiar beliefs. Berg describes these beliefs, thus highlighting originality and a peculiar Islamic setting for a construction of a counteracting mythology in the dynamics of a racist environment. With Malcolm X a new story starts, but the richness of the expressions of the Nation of Islam makes its history a unique case in the story of Islam.

Kathleen Moore (Chapter 8) follows up this story and deals with the second part of the twentiethth century up to today, focusing on the main question of developments, i.e. the relation between Muslim African American communities and the growing Muslim immigrant communities. This contributed to enlarging the composite character of the American Muslim presence, given by the various actors but also by evolutions and changes in the existing communities. This complex situation is then measured in relation to the perception of Muslims in American society, and through the organization of Islamic presence and its interaction in American identities and perceptions. In this regard the facts of 9/11 are central, but no doubt come in a period of growing participation in the public scene, and though it constitutes a period of difficulties and of related phenomena such as Islamophobic feelings and stereotyping attitudes, it represents a first moment of strong visibility of a religious community of relevance in the contemporary USA.

Though less known and even celebrated, the presence of Muslims in Central and South America surfaced more and more in the last century. In all these countries, though the presence of Islam dates back in individual cases to the sixteenth century, it is only in the second half of the nineteenth that it inoculated the seeds of a more relevant presence as an effect of the immigration waves from the Arab world. Mark Lindley-Highfield of Ballumbie Castle (Chapter 9) focuses on Mexico and then completes information on the other Central American countries, speaking of an increasing presence of Islam. The Mexican situation reflects the common setting of Arab Muslims coming from Syria and the presumed low percentage they represent amongst a Christian majority. Muslim presence was mostly underground until the 1970s and only after that various organization networks reflecting differing attitudes as most typical of composite Muslim lines of thought and traditions start to emerge. In Mexico, as in the other countries in Central America, the emergence of Islam challenges issues of identity and the historical connection to Spain and Catholicism. South America is instead the center of the study of Marco Gallo (Chapter 10). Argentina and Brazil are the main focus of his analysis, which delves into a complex and ancient history founded on the memory of the Muslim faith of the Moriscos who migrated and then of Muslim African slaves at least from the eighteenth century. But apart from myth and problematic historical attestations, the second half of the nineteenth century is here the period of the entry of Islam through migration from the Syrian region, attracting Arabs, the majority of whom were Christian but who still included a significant number of Muslims. The parable of Islam here is common to most countries. A first period of supposed assimilation is followed by growing visibility and by the most recent emergence of Islamic communities in all their particular various elements of visibility: cultural centers, mosques, institutions, and all that brought the need for confrontation in political and public spheres.

## Contemporary cultures: interactions

The contemporary situation of the Muslim communities in the Western world has attracted a lot of research interest in recent years. The scholarly production on the social, anthropological, and religious conditions of the various communities in the different countries and continents is consistent and growing. Though a distinction operates between Europe and America, many lines of research, though divided by different histories and conditions, share perspective, methodology, and disciplinary consciousness, applied to various cases.

A consistent number of further essays have described in recent years the situation of Muslim communities in specific places, nations, or major towns, between America and Europe, and there would be no sense in listing and discussing some of them here. Some studies do already take care to give broad descriptions according to national situations, and thus to provide the essential information from which to ground analysis (see, for example, Nielsen et al. 2011). As stated above, the aim of this part of the volume is not to give a description or a map of the Muslims in the Western world, but to suggest some possible sensitive points interrogating contemporary questions in the relation between Islam and the West. The three further sections into which this part is divided reflect the point of view of what would be expected by the confrontation of what may be defined, according to the limits and problems introduced at the beginning, as Muslims in the West. Thus, it is expected to have interactions at various levels, interactions which may cause conflict and convergence in the social scene and in religious and cultural confrontation; further, it is supposed and expected that the contemporary novelty of the Muslim presence may provide a cross-influence introducing new themes or elements in one community or tradition, such as Western themes and concerns in Muslim communities or Islamic perspectives in the West. The first question of interest is how today's Muslim presence in the West challenges and influences a supposed Western identity and, on the other hand, a supposed Muslim identity. The question of identity/identities is a debated issue in human sciences, all displaying various definitions and contrasting attitudes towards it. Luca Mavelli (Chapter 11) wonders how Western identity, a Western identity in crisis, is challenged by the Muslim presence. The perspective is to analyze this conflation around what is considered as the typical product of Western modernity – that is, secularity – in the face of the Muslim presence. The most famous aspect of this confrontation, the French *affaire du foulard*, is one example in a confrontation which more recently has shifted toward the defense of a supposed European identity different from Islamic values. The argument of Mavelli is that the sensitivity of these reactions reflects a crisis in European identity, which is the crisis of its concept of secularity. And that the theoretical bases of the complex relation between reason and faith, going back to philosophical traditions and finding major expressions such as in the thought of Immanuel Kant, are subject to inner contradictions which opened the space to the crisis of secular consciousness. This proper crisis in the values of the modern instrumental rationalization of Western identity no doubt now conflates with the problem of the integration of Muslims in Europe. The other side of the problem, i.e. the question of an Islamic identity and how this is challenged by the supposed Western values among Muslims residing in Western countries, is discussed by Adis Duderija (Chapter 12). The specific concern which he answers is whether a Western Muslim identity exists or has been emerging in the last two or three decades. Many factors indeed point to the fact that Islamic identities in Western Muslim communities are the product of a reconstruction rather than traditional transmission. The point here is the ways to realize this, implying privatization or individualization of Islamic faith and practice, given by the new condition of being a religious minority and no longer in majority Muslim countries. The chapter further discusses a few issues by which to measure a process of growing institutionalization and presence of Islam in Europe and the West, before offering a final definition and description of two different types of Western Muslim among many others: the Neo-traditionalist Salafi and the Progressive Muslim.

Many sensitive issues are connected to the confrontation between Islam and the West in the Western world. Some of them are mentioned in the above discussions on identity, and one of these is the concept of multiculturalism to which Anna Triandafyllidou's chapter is dedicated (Chapter 13). The starting point is the declared and affirmed death of multiculturalism, above all in northern Europe, and the related questions emerging in relation to the Muslim presence. The definitiveness of this statement comes from the belief that it was indeed the possible solution facing Muslim immigration until a couple of decades ago, but that the start of the new century brought about bitter disillusionment. After some data on the Muslim presence in Europe and America, Triandafyllidou outlines the evolution of the concept, from the definition of tolerance to the various theoretical definitions of the concept of multiculturalism. Another sensitive question relating to the confrontation and reaction between the two terms is the Islamophobic phenomena and reaction by some Western societies discussed by Salua Fawzi (Chapter 14). Focusing in particular on the American situation, she develops a theme which has received wide attention also in the European context, especially after the events of 9/11 (see Allen 2010). In this case the problem is the creation of an essentialized "other" and its coalescence with concepts such as terrorism, differing values and behaviors, and so on, all leading to marginalization and stereotyping attitudes from surrounding societies. Though on the feeling and conditions, above all in the last decade in the USA, there may be wide consensus, however, a proper definition of Islamophobia as a concept creates some problems and the discussion of the theoretical elaborations makes perfect sense. Some practical examples bearing on American societies further deepen into a better understanding of what Islamophobic feelings are. Marginalization and similar tendencies cannot deny the fact that some case of different ways of commonality exists. The condition of the Ismaili communities dealt with by Karim H. Karim (Chapter 15) is an example in this direction. It recalls differing settings from the old historical Muslim communities and the recent immigrant waves. The Ismaili's is a story of presence since the beginning of the twentieth century and of relations with Western countries since the colonial period. Though it represents a sort of elite and specific Islam, Karim no doubt has good reasons to explain that they have produced a unique form of Muslim modernity, well evidenced by their presence in around forty Western countries. They are engaged in various directions, such as the creation of institutions which aim to provide for the needs of their followers and the societies in which they live. As an exemplary model, in the all-positive vision of Karim, the essay follows the formation of this Ismaili engagement with the contemporary world through the twentieth century.

One other typical field of relation between religious communities is represented by conversion in one or the other direction. Patrick Bowen (Chapter 16) describes the phenomenon, attempting almost for the first time to compare European and American evidence. He underlines that there has been a marked rise in conversion to Islam by Westerners of various backgrounds in the last few decades. Cultural artifacts and the new religious space emerging in the West since the nineteenth century are the ground where interest in Islam and conversions to it arise, displaying differing background and approaches. Though a small part of Islamic communities, no doubt the role of Muslim converts in the various Western societies is destined to grow. If conversion is a sort of reaction to the contact with the "other," radicalization in the fundamentals of one's own faith is the opposite. Tahir Abbas has discussed Islamic radicalization in the West (Chapter 17), a topic he has dealt with recently in an important monograph (Abbas 2011). Following similar trends of Islamic societies, which started with the processes of re-Islamization of the 1970s, radicalization may appear, on one hand, to be both a product of the contact with the trends in the majority Muslim countries and a reaction to Western environments and lifestyles. There is in fact, as is suggested, a connection between Islamophobia and radicalization as counter and at the same time self-perpetuating reactions. Many factors are discussed and presented, with a specific reference to the British situation: external racism, the decline of masculinity, and the emergence of Salafi Islam. Social factors are also relevant when connected to the level of seclusion of the Muslim communities and their interacting with the outer world, though it is not possible to state that one condition generates an attitude.

## Contributing to the Western world

The presence of Muslims in Europe and America has brought novelty in a number of fields, from landscape and the simple visual perception to many other sectors of Western life. The phenomenon, given the numbers of Muslims, is destined to increase and produce further issues in which Muslim contributions can introduce novelty and help build the present and future of the West.

The visual landscape of the West is the first and immediate result of the Muslim presence and the one where the Muslim contribution is evident. Eric Roose (Chapter 18) discusses the presence of new Islamic architectural elements such as mosques, Muslim centers, etc. which are coloring Europe and America. After a long historical introduction describing how architectural presence reflects dynamics of physical testimonies and that copying is a typical attitude in the diffusion and evolutions of styles, Roose comes to the current situation in the West. The argument is that the building of Muslim architecture in the West challenges a tradition born in different places and conditions and leads to the creation of a pan-Islamic "Muslim" style. In this perspective the extent of non-homogeneous Islamic elements from different and distant traditions is challenged by the problem of iconographic representation in relation to the Muslim tradition and history. Along with this, other phenomena attest to the Islamic presence. Elisa Banfi (Chapter 19) has looked into the Islamic welfare system and its contribution to European and also American welfare systems, and describes this as a step towards the creation of a "Public Islam" in relation to existing similar, civil or religious, services. In this regard economic crisis gives a relevant possibility in this direction, and the case of European countries is a perfect case study in which to check the effectiveness of the Islamic welfare agencies, and how Islamic public actors have developed a relevant welfare strategy that is similar to that of Catholic/ Protestant organizations. This no doubt constitutes something new but at the same time attests to the rise of a new typology of Islamic associations begun during the 1990s in connection with exclusion from citizenship and its consequences in terms of access to national social welfare.

Amongst the expressions of Muslim life in the West, the artistic dimension begins to be a relevant factor, if not of integration, then at least of participation in the European and American scenes. Two chapters deal with the situation in North America and in Europe. Sylvia Chan-Malik (Chapter 20) covers the American scene with an inspiring analysis exploring the wide range of meaning of culture. And in this perspective the point in her contribution is to see how Islam and Muslims have contributed to the constructions of American culture, and how Muslims themselves have worked to express their Islamic identities through artistic expression. The result is a wide description of a Muslim American culture, and its interaction with its perception in American cultural scenes. In this regard the products in music are important, in blues and jazz in particular, not only in terms of artistic presence, but also for the relevance of this phenomenon in relation to political and social discussions of recent decades connected to African American community. Recent years, also with contributions from Muslim immigrants, have instead seen the emergence of a proper Muslim American culture permeating the arts in various directions, and confronting the mainstream American artistic scene with a new consciousness.

Miriam Gazzah (Chapter 21) approaches the topic from the perspective of the mixing of popular culture and religion, which is how a common popular ground realizes a better way of cross-interaction and attests to the introduction in Europe of new forms of expressiveness. This no doubt brings an original contribution on the European and American scenes and further represents a relevant fact given the diffidence and religious questions surrounding, first of all, musical expression. But there is much more: pop music, watching TV, playing games on the PC, chatting with friends online. In some ways, it clearly appears that the mosques have lost their monopoly over Islamic knowledge and interpretations, and above all over the definition of what is sacred versus the profane. As a consequence, Western Islamic popular culture, also through the specific case of Dutch Moroccan youth, appears to be something which permits a positive presence of Muslims in the European public sphere, above all in urban areas. In close connection with musical and cultural activities there are also the aspects of material culture prompted by the increasing forces of consumer capitalism. This topic has attracted the attention of some recent studies not only in Western communities but also in Muslim majority societies (Pink 2009). Johan Fischer (Chapter 22) has dealt with this by taking as a case study the situation of London and thus the new market scene introduced by the consistent Muslim community living there. As literally stated, the proliferation of Islamic markets contributes to social and cultural space-making in a city such as London. From *halal* butchers to all the other kinds of shop, visual landscapes change and add new Islamic elements. It is not easy to evaluate this social phenomenon in relation to the Muslim world. Fischer suggests that contrary to the tendency to see ethnic and religious traits reinforced in a migratory context, the opposite effect is possible, and that the effects of the reactions to 9/11 have encouraged modern Islamic markets which are global in scope.

## Contributing to Islam

A number of topics can be considered as relevant to Islamic traditions, i.e. questions emerging from the Western experience of Muslim communities living outside majority Muslim countries which interrogate Islam. One major question in this regard, and one which has already been mentioned above, is the discussion of the juridical questions related to the presence of Muslims as a minority under non-Muslim rule. This new situation, challenging the classical construction of a *dar al-islam* and *dar al-harb*, from where the Muslim should come away as soon as possible, has given origin to the *fiqh al-aqalliyyat*, the "jurisprudence of the Muslim minorities," which is discussed by Uriya Shavit and Iyad Zahalka (Chapter 23). The setting recalls the questions most typical of the juridical elaboration and the use of the *fatwa*s on Western soil, so as to contribute to solving the problems of what is defined as a unique condition. Divergences and contrasting evaluations, which are most typical in juridical debates and interpretations, no doubt surface also here, for instance in relation to the activities of the European Council for Fatwa and Research and on the prominent role of Yusuf al-Qaradawi. As rightly underlined, *fiqh al-aqalliyyat* enhances the understanding of Muslim minorities in the West as well as of contemporary jurisprudence, and can thus contribute to Islamic law as a whole.

Questions of major impact on Muslim communities in general and on those living in the West are those connected to ethical questions and to those values defined as a product of Western experience. Needless to say, the questions of the imposition of these values and the double standard in their application according to political situations are well-known phenomena. Notwithstanding this, questions such as democracy, individual rights, etc. stress Muslim Western experience. Francesca Forte (Chapter 24) deals with this, premising how pluralities and differing attitudes may prevent us from giving clear and uniform answers on the various questions. Problems of authority and representation intersect when facing the actual globalization of some Western values, and this condition challenges Muslim communities in the West. The theoretical problem here is no doubt the relation with theology and tradition, hence the debate on the universalism of ethical values, with some differences between European and American discussions. According to these premises the topics of major discussions on the Islamic agenda are no doubt human rights and their ascribed universalism, also in connection to sensitive gender issues. This is realized by analyzing the assumptions and positions of some Muslim intellectuals with respect to the possibility of integrating so-called Western values within the

Islamic framework. The gender issue, given its relevance and centrality in contemporary Muslim debates, and in particular so-called Islamic feminism, is the topic dealt with by Juliane Hammer (Chapter 25). It is an analysis of the American Muslim women scholars at the intersection of the American academy and American Muslim communities, to provide insights in critical thought. The first part is thus a historical portrait leading from Elijah Muhammad and Malcolm X, Ismail al-Faruqi, Seyyed Hossein Nasr, Fazlur Rahman, and many others, to Amina Wadud and Asma Barlas, and other major figures in contemporary debates. The second part is a long discussion of intellectual lives and cultural elaborations between reform and individual testimony in light of criticism and problems connected to being Muslim in the USA and being feminist in Muslim communities. In this regard, the fact that in cultural elaboration and confrontation Muslim women scholars and their ideas also challenge the authority of male Muslim scholars has much relevance, thus introducing a new competition around religious leadership and power.

Gian Maria Piccinelli (Chapter 26) has discussed a different question in which confrontation and mutual exchange are growing more and more, with interchanges and interconnectivities destined to further expand in the near future. Islamic banking and financial systems made their appearance some years ago now, and contact with Western realities challenges old assumptions and traditional attitudes. This is no doubt the result of a general continuing growth of Islamic banking assets in the global markets and of new answers in searching for an Islamic economy based upon a more attentive reading of the prohibition of usury (riba). This implies the elaboration of a different capital and labor association in different economic activities which bears some significance also in relation to the West since all this challenges it ethically. Great Britain, France, and the USA are the case studies for analyzing in detail some of these developments, while the Islamic capital market reflects similar attitudes in financial activities. One completely different question in relation to Islam in the West is the production of Islamic knowledge in Western Muslim communities. Stefano Allievi (Chapter 27), who has also edited a significant volume on this topic (van Bruinissen and Allievi 2011), discusses this, underlining how Islam in Western countries has very different characteristics from that in countries where Islam is the majority religion. Most relevant in this regard is that cultural production that comes from Muslim countries implicitly refers to situations where Islam is hegemonic and in power. This bears many consequences for Western Muslim communities, which are more heterogeneous and display easier mixing of ideas and personal experiences. This no doubt has an influence on the production of Islamic knowledge and prompts the production of originality, or at least novelties, mainly about the question of how to be a Muslim.

Finally, among the connection and shared communality in the religious sphere an important novelty prompted by Islamic presence in the Western world is to be connected to the large space which various and different forms of religiosity have gained in the last decades. Francesco Alfonso Leccese (Chapter 28) in this regard has discussed the question from the perspective of the contacts and common themes between so-called postmodern phenomena and Sufism. The expression "melting pot" well reflects the exchange and interrelationship, and the result is given by new religious forms that contribute to Western societies and also to Islamic religious discourse according to Western attitudes and novelty in the religious realm. Though this is a recent phenomenon, no doubt the fascination with Sufi knowledge and tradition goes back to well-known figures such as René Guénon or Frithjof Schuon and others, who really contributed to the birth of a Western Sufism in the second half of the twentieth century. This played a substantial role in relation to early New Age manifestations and found its specific forms in recent decades.

Roberto Tottoli

## Conclusion

Other topics could have been dealt with in the second part and no doubt also some more specific chapters might have focused on minor episodes of the Muslim presence in Europe. I think that the contributions succeed in giving a comprehensive portrait dealing with both the American and European situations. I am grateful to all the authors who accepted this approach and the challenge to try to produce reflection and analysis on the Muslim Western communities between Europe and America. I also thank all of them because they accepted suggestions and discussions on various points with the aim of completing the volume as it is now.

There are also a number of people I would like to mention and thank. Routledge staff immediately accepted this proposal and helped from the beginning of the editorial work. Joe Whiting, first of all, was always sympathetic to the process as a whole and also waited patiently during the time it took to collect the almost thirty contributions. Kathryn Rylance took care of many things which I cannot list in detail here, but was fundamental in all the phases of the work. The editorial staff also did excellent work, especially in relation to making all the contributions consistent and in revising, when necessary, the English style of some of us. Last but not least, I mention two colleagues. Armando Salvatore was very helpful in the conception of the volume and I benefited greatly from discussions with him. He also suggested some of the contributors who appear in the volume. Alessandro Vanoli, apart from his own contribution, helped me in the revision of some of the contributions on American Muslims and I am indebted to him for his generosity.

## Bibliography

Abbas, T. (2011) *Islamic Radicalism and Multicultural Politics: The British Experience*, London and New York: Routledge.

Abou El Fadl, K. (1994), "Islamic Law and Muslim Minorities: The Juristic Discourse on Muslim Minorities from the Second/Eighth to the Eleventh/Seventeenth Centuries," *Islamic Law and Societies* 1: 141–87.

Allen, C. (2010) *Islamophobia*, Farnham and Burlington: Ashgate.

AlSayyad, N. and Castells, M. (2002) *Muslim Europe or Euro-Islam: Politics, Culture, and Citizenship in the Age of Globalization*, Lanham, MD: Lexington Books.

Boccadamo, G. (2010) *Napoli e l'Islam. Storie di Musulmani, schiavi e rinnegati in età moderna*, Napoli: D'Auria.

Bonnett, A. (2004) *The Idea of the West: Culture, Politics, and History*, Basingstoke: Palgrave Macmillan.

Calasso, G. (2010) "Alla ricerca di *Dār al-islām*. Una ricognizione nei testi di giuristi e tradizionisti, lessicografi, geografi e viaggiatori," *Rivista degli studi orientali* 83: 271–96.

Catlos, B. (2014) *Muslims of Medieval Latin Christendom, c. 1050–1614*. Cambridge: Cambridge University Press.

Clayer, N. (2003) *Religion et nation chez les albanais XIXe–XXe siècles*, Istanbul: ISIS.

Dakhlia, J. and Kaiser, W. (eds.) (2013) *Les Musulmans dans l'histoire de l'Europe*, vol. 2: *Passages et contacts en Méditerranée*, Paris: Albin Michel.

Dakhlia, J. and Vincent B. (eds.) (2011) *Les Musulmans dans l'histoire de l'Europe*, vol. 1: *Une Intégration invisible*, Paris: Albin Michel.

Daniel, N. (1960) *Islam and the West: The Making of an Image*, Edinburgh: Edinburgh University Press.

Dassetto, F. (1994) *L'Islam in Europa*, Torino: Fondazione Giovanni Agnelli.

Duchesne, R. (2011) *The Uniqueness of Western Civilization*, Leiden and Boston: Brill.

Farrar, M., Robinson, S., Valli, Y., and Wetherly, P. (eds.) (2012) *Islam in the West: Key Issues in Multiculturalism*, London: Palgrave.

Federici, S. (ed.) (1995) *Enduring Western Civilization: The Construction of the Concept of Western Civilization and its "Others"*, Westport, CT: Praeger.

García-Arenal, M. and Rodríguez-Mediano, F. (2013) *The Orient in Spain: Converted Muslims, the Forged Lead Books of Granada, and the Rise of Orientalism*, translated by C. López-Morillas, Leiden and Boston: Brill.

GhaneaBassiri, K. (2010) *Islam in America*, Cambridge: Cambridge University Press.

Haddad, Y.Y. (ed.) (2002) *Muslims in the West: From Sojourners to Citizens*, Oxford and New York: Oxford University Press.

Haneda, M. (2007), "Modern Europe and the Creation of the 'Islamic World'," *International Journal of Asian Studies* 4: 201–20.

Herman, A. (1997) *The Idea of Decline in Western History*, New York: Free Press.

Lewis, B. (1993) *Islam and the West*, New York: Oxford University Press.

Malik, M. (ed.) (2010) *Anti-Muslim Prejudice: Past and Present*, London and New York: Routledge.

Mavelli, L. (2012) *Europe's Encounter with Islam: The Secular and the Postsecular*, London and New York: Routledge.

Metcalf, B.D. (ed.) (1996) *Making Muslim Space in North America and Europe*, Berkeley: University of California.

Miquel, A. (1967–88) *La géographie du monde musulman jusqu'au milieu de 11e siècle*, 4 vols., Paris, La Haye, and New York: Mouton.

Nielsen, J.S., Akgönül, S., Alibašic, A., Goddard, H., and Maréchal, B. (eds.) (2011) *Yearbook of Muslims in Europe*, vol. 3, Leiden and Boston: Brill.

Pink, J. (ed.) (2009) *Muslim Societies in the Age of Mass Consumption: Politics, Culture and Identity Between the Local and the Global*, Cambridge: Cambridge Scholars Publishing.

Said, E.W. (1978) *Orientalism*, New York: Vintage Books.

Stearns, P.N. (2003) *Western Civilization in World History*, New York: Routledge.

Valensi, L. (2012) *Ces Etrangers familiers. Musulmans en Europe (XVIe-XVIIIe siècles)*, Paris: Payot.

Van Bruinissen, M. and Allievi, S. (eds.) (2011) *Producing Islamic Knowledge: Transmission and Dissemination in Western Europe*, London and New York: Routledge.

Westerlund, D. and Svanberg, I. (eds.) (2010) *Islam in the West*, 4 vols., London and New York: Routledge.

# Part 1
# History

# Part 1.1
# European paradigms

# The borders of Muslim Spain

*Alessandro Vanoli*

## Al-Andalus: an Islamic space and its relationship with the "West"

The conquest started one day in the summer of 710, but few people in Spain realized it: only a few Arabic sources tell us about the first boats from North Africa that in July arrived on the southern coast of the Iberian Peninsula. It is more evident in the sources what happened one year later, in the late spring of 711, when the governor of Ifriqiya, Musa ibn Nusayr, decided that a military effort on a wider scale would be possible: the troops led by Tariq, governor of Tangeri, reached the point that would take his name: mountain of Tariq, in Arabic *jabal Tariq*, Gibraltar; soon came the moment of the clash with Roderico, the last king of the Visigoths, and in October of the same year the fall of Cordova that opened the way to the north. This is the very well-known starting point of a long history: the history of the farthest Occidental region of the Islamic world, that will take the Arabic name of al-Andalus; the history of the most Occidental frontier with Christian territories.

It is hard to say where the Muslims exactly stopped their advance but it is sufficiently true to say that, after a period of raids in the north of the Pyrenees, the Western borders of Islam would place themselves in the south of the line shaped by the towns of Lugo, Astorga, León, Amaya, la Bureba, and Alava (García de Cortázar et al. 1985: 53) that is immediately to the south of the long chain of mountains that, starting from Asturias, runs as far as the Mediterranean Sea. It is also hard to say if this territorial achievement corresponded to a clear military *limes*: this is actually a complex problem that intimately touches the interpretation of the so-called *Reconquista*, because it touches the interpretation of these physical borders and above all the interpretation (and the religious and cultural "identity") of the populations that lived there (Manzano Moreno 2006: 240–1). In any case, in the south of the Atlantic mountain chains, the Iberian Peninsula became a province (*kura*, pl. *kuwar*) of the vast empire of the Caliphate of Damascus. And, starting from these very first years, the Christian "West" became a fundamental point of reference for these Arabs and Berbers that probably leaned on the intellectual and social traditions of the conquered people: Visigoths, Christian clergy or Jews.

In a certain sense, also in the new name that the Muslims gave to the conquered part of the Iberian Peninsula, al-Andalus, we can find the trace of this strong relationship with the "West." As we know, nowadays the etymology is disputed. At least three specific hypotheses have been proposed by Western scholarship, all three presuming that the name al-Andalus arose after the Roman period: from *Vandalicia*, that is, "land of the Vandals" (this thesis has been proposed by Reinhard Dozy, Christian Friedrich Seybold and Évariste Lévi-Provençal); from the Goth term *landahlauts*, that is, "lot lands" (Halm 1989); and even from the Arabic adaptation of the name Atlantis or Atlantic (Vallvé 1983). But none of these hypotheses are supported by conclusive historical evidence.

In any case, al-Andalus, an emirate under Umayyad guidance, became a prosperous and powerful Islamic space in the Iberian world. At the same time, the first small Christian political spaces were developing at the north of the Peninsula: the first two centers were in a land that had been bypassed by Islamic forces: the mountain kingdom of Asturias and, soon after, the kingdom of Navarre. New geographic and cultural frontiers were defined and in the following centuries they saw continuous changes. The inheritors of the Omayyad caliphs were proclaimed emirs of al-Andalus (756), and in 912, under 'Abd al-Rahman III, they took the title of Caliphs, inaugurating what will be remembered as the most splendid period in the history of al-Andalus.

## A new society

Therefore, a large part of Spain became Muslim, even if it is not easy to say something certain about the process of the Islamization of the Peninsula; that is, about the numbers and the pace of conversion of the natives. Some indicators, such as the construction of mosques, the proliferation of Muslim cemeteries and textual evidence, furnished by the so-called "biographic dictionaries" (*tabaqat*), show a phenomenon that appears fast enough (Fierro and Marín 1998); a process of conversion that would be increased with the increase of mutual contacts and that became evident in the Caliphal period. In any case what is certain is that, beyond the strictly religious aspect, the Islamic conquest determined, step by step, a new social and cultural space, a process of Arabization that gradually produced a space of cultural unity given by the Islamic religion and the Arabic language – a space connected to a wider world: a social, political, and economic network that extended all over the South Mediterranean and, from there, as far as the Orient.

These Islamized urban spaces of al-Andalus determined not only a class of merchants, artisans, and smallholders, but also a class of experts in religion, *ulama* and *faqih* (it is well known how difficult it is to distinguish between these two categories: Benaboud 1984), that strongly contributed to making the legal and religious culture of al-Andalus conform to the Malikite school of law (Calero Secall 2001).

The complexity of this Arabized space was given not only by the internal distinctions between Arabs and Berbers, or among the many social groups: the upper classes, soldiers, lawyers, merchants, peasants, or even slaves. This Arabization also involved the members of other religions, Christians and Jews, that continued to profess their religion also under Islamic power. Indeed, for Islamic law, people belonging to another monotheistic religion may enjoy an engagement pact of protection, the *dhimma*, by which the Muslims undertake to safeguard the life and property of the non-Muslim in question, called *dhimmi*. This treaty provides them with all duties deriving from it, in particular the payment of a tribute, a fixed poll-tax called *jizya*. These *dhimmi*s of al-Andalus, both Mozarabs (as the *dhimmi* Christians will be known in the Latin world) and Sefardies (as the Jews from Spain called themselves), contributed to the cultural and economic growth of this Iberian Arabic space, maintaining their own relationships with the Christan world, in Spain and in the rest of Europe, and with the Jewish Mediterranean network.

From another point of view, due to this Arabization, al-Andalus absorbed the Islamic culture developed in the Oriental lands, developing a high esteem of local literary and scientific production. As has been observed (Vernet 1968; Fierro 2011: 37), the Andalusians began to feel a sense of superiority not only over the Christians (for instance in the field of medicine) but also over the Islamic people of the Oriental lands. A sense of superiority confirmed also by the Byzantine embassies: the presence of the powerful and rich Oriental Romans was a confirmation of the Imperial level reached by al-Andalus.

Andalusian Muslims felt themselves to be an indissoluble part of the "land of Islam" (*dar al-islam*), with which they shared religion, culture, and language. People who went from al-Andalus to the East returned with new knowledge and new books, and with an enhanced feeling of being part of a single religious and cultural community. But al-Andalus was located at the periphery of the Islamic world. And as a land of frontier, it is perhaps possible to perceive in its formation a sense of insecurity, the sense of living on an island surrounded by the sea and by Christians. Maybe it was this condition of "land of frontier" that facilitated trade with the West, and determined its relations with the Islamic world.

## Al-Andalus as a frontier

Al-Andalus as a frontier could be described from different points of view: from a geographical standpoint, but also from a social and a cultural perspective.

Starting from the space, in the Arabic sources the idea of al-Andalus as a frontier is present in many different terms. In the geographical texts, for instance, it is evident how al-Andalus is perceived so close to the Christian territories, called (among other names) "land of polytheism" (*balad al-shirk*) or "land of war" (*balad al-harb*). As the traveler al-Muqaddasi will remember, "the inhabitants of al-Andalus, as the Sicilians, practice the *ghazwa* and are always in *jihad* and in departure for the battle" (al-Muqaddasi 1906: 103). All these kinds of ideas were strictly connected with a particular concept of frontier. Indeed, for all the Arabic sources, the northern frontiers of al-Andalus were technically defined as *thaghr*. With this term the Arabic meant a zone of passage, an opening to pass through; so, from a geographical and political point of view, those particular territories of the Islamic world that are in contact with a non-Muslim space (that is, lands outside the *umma*, the community of believers). These are territories to which the jurists assigned a specific definition: they are "hostile areas"; in a word, territories of the *jihad* (Chalmeta 1991).

To be more precise al-Andalus, taken as a whole, was not a *thaghr*: indeed the Andalusians (perhaps starting only from the Caliphal period: Manzano Moreno 1991: 48–50) used this concept to designate the northern territories close to the Christian reigns. Basically, the Arabic sources distinguished between a farther frontier and a closer one, *al-thaghr al-aqsa* and *al-thaghr al-adna*. But some contemporary Arabic authors proposed a more complex division for al-Andalus, using terms as *al-thaghr al-sharqi*, "East frontier," *al-thaghr al-gharbi*, "West frontier," and *al-thaghr al-jawfi*, "northern frontier," and so on: terms that were used during the Caliphal period and that reflected a perception of the territory closely related to the administration of power (the frontiers are indeed "closer" or "distant" always starting from a focal point, that is, the city of Cordoba, the siege of the Caliph).

However, more than geographical definitions, the frontiers of al-Andalus (the northern regions of al-Andalus, I mean) were shaped by specific social and political forms. Here it is impossible to analyze the complex dynastic history of these liminal spaces. It is a story, in fact, that begins in the early days of the conquest and that has its place in the chronicles mainly owing to the continuous rebellions against the central power. Starting from the ninth century, in these frontiers we record the exponential increase of indigenous lineages: groups that almost always had relationships of *wala'* (that is, the relationships between client and patron) with Arab families. Among these lineages of the frontiers were the Banu 'Amrus, the Banu Shabrit, the Banu Rashid, and the most famous Banu Qasi, whose domain is attested in the area of contact with the Basques, and that reached the control of the large centers of Huesca and Saragossa. Some of them were from indigenous families, of Gothic or Roman origins, that converted to Islam at the beginning of the conquest; others had Arabic or Berber origins (Sénac 2000a). What is more important for our problem is the fact that these muwallad families of the region also established alliances with their Christian neighbors throughout the eighth, ninth, and tenth centuries (for instance, the Banu 'Amrus addressed themselves to the Emperor Charlemagne to affirm their power at the beginning of the ninth century: Sénac, 1999: 349–54). But not only this. A few decades later, Muhammad al-Tawil married Domna Sanzia, the daughter of the Aragonese Count, Aznar Galindez II, and she gave him four sons and a daughter, Domna Velazquita. And we also know that Furtun b. Muhammad allied with King Sancho Garcés of Pamplona after a marriage, and that he fought at his side against 'Abd al-Rahman III during the Mitonia campaign of 918. These families headed societies between two worlds; however, as has been shown (Acién Almansa 1997; Sénac 2000a), they actively participated in the Islamization of their regions (not by chance, the Banu Qasi's decline in power corresponds with the end of 'Umar b. Hafsun's revolt in Andalusia; the Umayyad efforts to reclaim these lands in the tenth century were part of the larger "reconquest" movement led by the caliph 'Abd al-Rahman III in the 930s).

Historians usually refer to these people of the frontier as warriors. This is true in a certain sense; but far from being only the place of a secular clash between Islam and Christianity, and also far from being a structured defensive system (Manzano Moreno 1999: 387), the *thaghr al-Andalus* was obviously a territory of war, with special administrative specificities (for instance, the men of the frontier enjoyed a tax regime which was the lowest in the Muslim territory), but it was also and above all a place with an extraordinary fragmentation and a great capacity of adaptation to local necessities and to historical modifications. This situation was strongly related to an increasing political autonomy, which permitted the people of these border countries, the *ahl al-thaghr*, to define social structures relatively similar to those that appeared in the same period in the Christian context. In these frontiers many Muslims experienced direct, if not sometimes daily, contact with local Christian territories. We know almost nothing about them, about their everyday lives and their habits, and also the archeological data is often contradictory.

The experience of a Muslim life in a Christian land came later, when the fortune of al-Andalus changed. Also this was a long history: the collapse of the Caliphate occurred in the first decades of the eleventh century. These were the years of the *fitna*, the civil war that led to the end of the Umayyad government (1031); and, after, to the years of fragmentation of al-Andalus into a group of small weak Islamic kingdoms, known by the Iberian historiography as *reinos de taifa*. It was the same period in which, in the north, the Christian reign faced a new period of prosperity. The Iberian Middle Ages didn't know the word "*reconquista*" (which is an invention of the nineteenth century), but the pressure of the Christian armies was rising, contributing to transforming the political ideology of the northern Iberian kings.

In 1085 Toledo, the ancient capital of the Visigoth reign, and for centuries one of the greatest towns in al-Andalus, fell into the hands of Alfonso VI. This conquest would be followed by other wars and other Islamic dynasties fighting for the control of the Iberian space: first the Almoravids and then the Almohads. For a number of Muslim people, this period was the beginning of a completely new life in a non-Muslim territory.

## Mudejars: geography and periodization of the Muslims in Christian Spain

In the second half of the eleventh century, with the beginning of the Christian military advance, more and more Muslims started to live as minorities in the newly conquered territories. They are usually defined by historians as Mudejars, a term derived from the Arabic *mudajjan*, "dominated" (and its synonym *ahl al-dajn*, "people who stay") and used by the Iberian Muslims in a negative sense. Not by chance, this word was first used, at least during the centuries of the Middle Ages, by Muslims, while its Castilian adaptation, *mudéjar*, came into use among Christians above all from the fifteenth century (Ladero Quesada 2004: 105).

It is a very complex and articulated history, in which the experiences of the Mudejars changed depending on the period, the geography, the different politics, and the cultural context. The most ancient Islamic presence in the Iberian Christian territories is related to the conquests at the end of the eleventh century: they are attested in Aragon, Castile y León, and Portugal, even if the historiographic problem of depopulation and population of the Duero valley is not cleared up and it is still difficult to say anything certain about the hypothetical presence of Muslims in the northern regions of Spain (Echevarría Arsuaga 2001–2: 34). In the reign of Castile, a point of no return was certainly the surrender of Toledo, in 1085. But also in this case it is difficult to document this history: for the fifteenth century, the archivistic sources certify the presence of Mudejars in approximately seventy centers of the Crown of Castile (it has been calculated that of a total of around four million inhabitants, around 20,000 to 25,000 were Muslims: 35–40 percent in the north of the Central System, 20–30 per cent in Castile la Nueva and in Extremadura; 10 per cent in Andalusia and around 20 per cent in Murcia). We know that they came mainly from the south, becoming part of towns such as Valladolid, Ávila, Arévalo, Palencia, Burgos, or Segovia (García-Arenal 1995: 26–35); but we know very little about the time and the modalities of their displacement: in many *fueros* (the new civic laws) there are no references to any Muslim presence; so it is possible to suppose that in a number of Castilian cities the Muslims arrived long after the conquests, as was the case, for instance, in Ávila (Tapia Sánchez 1991: 49–50).

This kind of doubt has been expressed also for Toledo (Molénat 1997: 27–41), even if an Arabic source such as Ibn Bassam (twelfth century) testifies to the arrival of Muslim people before 1085.

The conquest of Andalusia and the valley of the Guadalquivir, between 1224 and 1264, produced important changes in the geography of the Mudejars. The terms of surrender permitted many Muslims to live in rural zones. This lasted until a great rebellion, between 1264 and 1265, that convinced Alfonso X to change his policy towards this minority, when he decided to expel the Mudejars, deporting them to the cities of the north (but also in this case we know very little about this dramatic process). From that moment on, the few Islamic groups in Andalusia would be concentrated above all in cities such as Seville and Cordoba.

The situation in Navarra and in the territories of the Crown of Aragon was different. The starting point in Aragon was the conquest of Huesca in 1096; then came the time of Alfonso I, el Batallador, and his conquests of many cities in the Ebro valley, among them Saragossa (1118). From this period the Muslim population in the Aragonese territory appears to be concentrated in the fertile valleys of the Isuela, Flumen, and Cinca rivers, in the actual provinces of Huesca, Queiles, Huecha, Ebro, Jalón, Aguas Vivas, Jiloca, and Saragossa; with numerous localities having a Mudejar population only, and others a mixed population.

Some authors estimated that the number of Mudejars in the Ebro valley in the thirteenth century had to be around 100,000; this could be a reasonable estimate, but it is nothing more than a hypothesis (Hillgarth 1976–8, I: 30; Catlos 2004: 119).

In Catalonia, the Mudejar demography is different, this presence being weaker than in other regions of the Crown of Aragon. Also here, this situation is difficult to analyze due to lack of data. For instance, we know almost nothing about towns such as Tortosa and Lérida, but by the end of the fifteenth century historians have calculated that the Mudejar presence could have been around 1 percent of the population (Mutgé Vives 1992; Biarnes Biarnes 1972).

The situation in Valencia was different. The city was conquered in the thirteenth century by Jaime I (1232–45): a great number of Muslims stayed there and in its territory (perhaps 1,000 people inside the city; that is, no more than 3 percent of the population). The submission of the rebel al-Azraq, at the beginning of the rein of Pedro III (1276), put an end to other Islamic revolts and marked a moment of progressive aristocratic control on the *aljamas*, the Mudejar social groups, in the Ebro valley.

## Juridical and social conditions of the Mudejars

The legal basis that regulated Muslim life in the Christian territories was at first the terms of surrender and the royal law, which basically guaranteed the Mudejars their personal freedom, the practice of their religion and their laws, as well as their occupations.

However, these conditions were costly. In Castile, for instance, the *Cortes de Alcalá* in 1348 limited the access of the Mudejars to landholding and to activities related to public administration, the court, medicine, and feeding. The *Cortes* also forbade them to be treasurers and coroners, to make contracts and practice usury.

In Navarra, Aragon, and Valencia the situation was quite different, but it is almost impossible to generalize. From the Aragonese point of view, it has been underlined (Ledesma Rubio 1994b) that, to the south of the Ebro river, the repopulation process had a juridical pragmatic attitude. For instance, the Fuero of Alcalá de Selva, one of the first ones, equalized the Muslims with the rest of the *pobladores*: "cristianos, moros y judíos un fuero y una costumbre tengan": "Christians, Moors and Jews must have one law and one custom." The same was true in La Cañada de Benatanduz and in Aliaga. But it is also true that this initial equality was the fruit of those first few years after the conquest, in which it was necessary to attract settlers, regardless of their professed religion, but over time, in the thirteenth century, when power was consolidated, there were important modifications for the Aragonese Mudejars, even if the official protection of the king was always maintained. It is also true that the Mudejars were often viewed with hostility and suspicion: in the *fuero* of frontiers such as Calatayud, Daroca, Alcalá de la Selva, Cañada de Benatanduz, and Aliaga, where references to the acquisition of Muslim captives were frequent, but also in the *fueros* of Teruel and Albarracín, that attested to a climate of violence with murders, rapes, abductions, the ban on selling weapons to the Moors, or the forced conversion of the Mudejars to Christianity and so on (as, for example, in the case of Aliaga: Ledesma Rubio 1991). These examples show a context relatively far from the most peaceful coexistence attested to in the central regions of Aragon, where it is confirmed, for instance, that it was essential to have a great number of Muslim peasants to maintain the agricultural economy of these regions.

Scholars agree that there was no common taxation for all the Mudejars, because situations changed according to different aristocratic power or to the specific civic jurisdiction. As usual, sources are insufficient to define the Mudejar taxation in particular and its transformation over time. In general, Muslims were obliged to accept the protection of the king by the payment of special taxes. In Castile, this was named *pecha* or *cabeza de pecho*: an amount that every Islamic group (but also every Jewish group) had to pay in return for the acknowledgment of royal protection. Another similar tax always in Castile was the *servicio y medio servicio*, a kind of extraordinary payment that was introduced in 1388, and became an annual tax in the second half of the fifteenth century, under the Catholic kings. Something similar was the ordinary *peyta* in Aragon and Navarra, also called *alfarda* in Valencia. But this kind of taxation was more complex: first, as there were sometimes great differences between taxation in towns and in the country (where other taxes on animals or agricultural production were imposed); second, because different taxation between Muslims and Christians was not always the expression of a social separation, and in the Late Iberian Middle Age there were a lot of cases of common civic resistance to the imposition of new taxes (Catlos 2007: 48–5). This last point introduces a series of questions, first about the social nature of the Islamic groups in Christian territories, and second about the relationship between different religious and cultural groups.

## *Aljamas*: the Islamic communities

The most important Mudejar unities formed communities called *aljamas* (the same term also used for Jewish communities). The study of these institutions poses some difficulties, due above all to the absence of internal documentation and to the inaccuracy of the demographic data for the Middle Ages. But the studies devoted to specific *aljamas* are continually increasing in number. Usually, the absence of leaders in Mudejar communities has been highlighted (leaders who would have left the cities immediately after the conquest to emigrate to Granada or to the Maghreb), but this generalization is not so certain. Indeed, if it is true that between the eleventh and twelfth centuries there was an emigration of political and social leaders, this reaction to the Christian conquest was not uniform, and many important people decided to stay in their places of origin (Marín 1995; Molénat 2001). This difference is also the reflection of an inner debate inside Islam: between some jurists who recommended emigration (owing to the impossibility of living in the Christian territories according to Islamic law) and others who recognized the possibility of staying. Moreover, the same concept of "leaders" or an "elite" is difficult to define. It seems that the Islamic minorities made (or were obliged to make) the structure of their leaders conform to the model of the Catholic Spanish elite. Indeed the political elite was made up of Muslims who surrounded the king and his court, such as the *alcalde mayor de las aljamas* in the Castilian reign, or the *alcadí* in Tudela-Navarra and the *alamín* in Aragon. The urban oligarchy was formed by merchants, usually in strict contact with the other *aljamas* all over the Iberian Peninsula. Finally there was also an elite of knowledge, formed by *alfaquíes* and *ulemas*, responsible for preserving the Islamic religion and the Arabic language as a vehicle of sacred expression among the Mudejars (actually, the structure was more complex; for example, the Castilian sources also mention an *almohadar* and a *muecín* responsible for convoking the assembly: Villanueva Zubizarreta 2010: 352).

Something similar is attested to in the Aragonese sources: also there, the *aljama* was the institutional representation of a collective fact and the key to the preservation of Islamic identity. Its functioning was granted by the Crown, even if it is not so easy to determine how these *aljamas* were autonomous. It's difficult to imagine that these institutions were really independent from the king, owing to the growing interference of Christian functionaries in their activities or because, at the beginning of every new kingdom, the *aljamas* had to spur the king to confirm their privileges (Hinojosa Montalvo 2009).

Also, regarding the Aragonese *aljamas* at the end of the Middle Ages, we know about the presence of elites with different offices, but we also know that they varied notably depending on the different places and the political and economic importance of every *aljama*. The basic authority was the *cadi*, with juridical, civil, and penal competences, basing his judgment on the "sunna e xara," that is, Islamic law. He was usually also responsible for the collection and administration of taxes, for some business, for weddings, etc. These figures were related to Christian power in many ways. We know, for instance, that at Tortosa in 1263 Abubaquer Avinahole was appointed *cadi* by Ramón Moncada and at Lérida, on May 17, 1263, Muça de Marrochs received the office of *alamín* and *cadí* directly from King Jaime I (Mutgé Vives 1992: 197–8, doc. no. 6). So, as we have seen, an inevitable phenomenon that also occurred in the Jewish *aljamas* was the influence of Christian institutions on the government of the mosque: Christian public officials sometimes acted as *alcaide* to the Muslims, and in the royal *aljamas* the bailiff (*baiulus*) was responsible for administration, whose mission was to collect the rents paid by Mudejars and to resolve some juridical problems inside the Mudejar community.

Despite the frequent absence of an intellectual elite, and despite the limitations imposed by the new Christian government, the Mudejars retained their religious Muslim practices, following them usually with discretion and without public events. It is said that good knowledge of the Islamic religion was increasingly threatened by the almost general loss of the Arabic language. But the textual evidence tells of a more complex situation. Indeed, until the end of the sixteenth century, inside the Islamic communities of Castile and Aragon texts were produced in the Arabic language, but a literary Islamic communication in the local Romance languages was also developing. This requires some consideration.

First, the case of the affirmation of Islamic literature in a non-Arabic language (in this case Castilian) is not exceptional (even today with English). Second, inside this production we must distinguish among Islamic literature written in Arabic (with Arabic or Latin characters), the Islamic literature written in a Romance language using the Latin alphabet, and Islamic literature written in a Romance language using the Arabic alphabet; this last one is the so-called *aljamiado*, that would be used in a massive form, above all by the Moriscos after the conquest of Granada.

Among the first texts of the Islamic Castilian literature (perhaps) there is the well-known *Poema de Yúsuf*, possibly from the thirteenth century (some authors have proposed postponing the dating to the fifteenth or the sixteenth century: Casassas Canals 2009). For other authors, also the *Leyes de moros* can be dated to the same period (considered for a long time an anonymous juridical treaty, it has been shown that it is a partial version of the juridical treaty *al-Tafri* of Ibn al-Jallab: Abboud-Haggar 1997). We must also add works such as the *Poema en alabanza del Profeta Mahoma* and the *Aljutba de Pascua de Ramadán* to this short list (both in the thirteenth and fourteenth centuries).

A special mention must be made of the work of Isa Gebir, mufti of the *aljama* of Segovia in the second half of the fifteenth century: for his Castilian version of the Qur'an, written at the request of the theologian Juán de Segovia, and his *Breviario Sunní*, composed in 1462, that had great importance in Christian Spain. Indeed this book suffered a strong transformation at the hands of the Christian authorities, and the detailed description of the Islamic religious practices became an official part of the arsenal used by the Inquisition against the crypto-Muslims, both in Spain and in the New World.

## The social life of Mudejars: what about the "convivencia"?

The *aljamas*, as institutions, were projected in a space and in a complex society. It is usually said that the Mudejars lived in specific spaces of the city called *morerias*; this is true for certain periods but not in general. Until the fifteenth century the Mudejars in Castile lived among the rest of the population: there were some attempts at segregation (the *Cortes* of Jerez in 1268 or the *Concilio* of Palencia in 1388), but only in the *ordenanzas* by Catalina de Lancaster, in 1412, and later in the *Cortes* of Toledo in 1480, did this kind of enclosure become concrete in many cities of the reign. Moreover, there's a longstanding discussion among historians about whether this reclusion was only something imposed by the sovereigns, or also something desired by the Mudejars.

In almost all the urban spaces of Castile and Aragon, for centuries we find the presence of Muslims living in the different quarters of the city, with commercial activities carried out by Muslims all over the urban space and the presence of mosques in spaces nominally "Christian." And when there were specific Muslim quarters, they were marked by a new mosque, baths, and commercial activities frequented by Christians too. In Castile, the *morerías* created after 1480 (in a strict relationship with the war of Granada) were more isolated spaces; in some cases outside the city walls. This was, for instance, what happened to the Mudejars of Ávila and Valladolid: the sources inform us about the existence of an *almají*, or house of prayer, and "other houses" for weddings or for the *alfaquí* and other places used by the community of the Mudejars (Moratinos García and Villanueva Zubizarreta 1999–2002). Not far from the urban space, usually outside the walls and near the gates, were the cemeteries, the *maqbar*s. Through recent archeological discoveries, we know that the Mudejars maintained Islamic funerary rituals: the corpse was buried wrapped in a shroud, on the right side, the feet to the east and the head to the west, while the face was turned towards the southeast, that is, towards the city of Mecca (Ruiz de Marco et al. 1993).

Similar *morerías*, similar Islamic spaces inside and around the urban context, are also attested to in Aragon and in Catalonia, sometimes defined by walls and gates. But in some cases, as in Huesca, the Mudejars lived inside the wall but not in a precise quarter. In other cases, more definite spaces are attested to but not so enclosed, such as in the Catalan Lérida (Mutgé Vives 1999: 101–11).

Recent studies have shown that Mudejar society was not close. In spite of the prohibitions of commerce among the Peninsula kingdoms and the restriction imposed on the Mudejars, their elites managed to maintain relationships and true networks with the other peninsular Islamic communities and with the rest of the *dar al-islam* too. This happened, for instance, in Valencia, where strong activity by some Mudejar families is attested to. This is the case of the Xupió, the Ripoll, and the Belvís, true "Lords of Moors," "señores de Moros" (Ruzafa García 2000); or the Castilian Albarromoní, who did business on both sides of the frontier between Castile and Aragon.

But the analysis of Mudejar society is a difficult issue that often has been omitted or has produced easy generalizations. One of the reasons for this is the lack of Islamic sources, which has determined the massive recourse to Christian sources, with the obvious simplifications and distortions. Indeed, this society has usually been perceived as homogeneous, without large internal differences, and with a majority of the population composed of humble peasants or artisans. On the contrary, the most recent studies show a complex society that experienced strong changes during the centuries. There were urban elites that often maintained their previous familiar structures and that developed complex relationships with Christian power; there were artisans, intellectuals, slaves, etc. In addition, as we have seen, there were also strong ties with the other Iberian Islamic communities and, in general, with the other parts of the *umma*, the community of believers.

Certainly, it is true that agriculture remained the main occupation of the Muslim population in most of the peninsular kingdoms during the centuries after the Christian conquest. In Aragon this was strongly determined by the preceding system of irrigation and distribution of water during the Muslim period (and it is interesting to observe that the common use of these systems of irrigation forced an important interaction between Christians and Muslims). It is also true that in the urban *morerías* we may register many different artisan activities such as pottery, wood and metalwork (boilermakers, knifemakers, etc.), weaving wool, linen and silk, and dyers, shoe-makers, or the manufacture of soap (this last one being a very typical profession of the Mudejars in numerous territories of the Crown of Aragon, such as Valencia, Xàtiva, or Elche). There were also Mudejars who worked as merchants, both in the inner Muslim context and with Christians outside the frontiers of Aragon and Catalonia. Other Mudejars served the Christian court, sometimes also as translators or interpreters. And it was just in the urban context and in the *morerias* that the contacts between Christians and Muslims were more frequent; and this was due not only to the market but also to the working environment.

The problem of the interethnic relationships in the medieval Iberian Peninsula is an impor-tant topic in contemporary historiography. The analysis of the relationships among these dif-ferent groups and their communication needs has produced studies about, among others, commerce, mixed marriages, the common use of the water, and even war, which in the end can be considered a terrible but very frequent form of communication. The positions of scholars seem ingenuous who in this long period of intercultural relationships see only a moment of relatively peaceful coexistence among Christians, Jews, and Muslims: a period of intellectual and artisanal exchanges, translations or common mystical experiences, in a context of (anachronistic) "tolerance." To avoid the risk of an overly irenic perception, the contemporary historiographic use of the term *convivencia* is useful, utilized to indicate the quotidian practice of the cultural and social relationships among different groups (Vanoli 2006; Bensoussan 2007; Jaspert 2011).

In this sense, the Mudejars were a normal part of the urban landscape even if the authorities continued to be worried by the contacts, above all by the physical and spiritual ones. Maybe the Christians accepted the Mudejars better than the Jews: apart from the very well-known negative connotation, as "infidels" the Muslims were often perceived as good workers, above all in the territories of Aragon and Catalonia. In everyday life we have much evidence of good relation-ships between Christians and Muslims. But these good relationships do not exclude moments of difficulty and social tension; including an increase, after the thirteenth century, of pressure for conversions, due also to the great influence of the Mendicant Orders (it is difficult to say how many Muslims decided to convert to the Christian religion; but there must have been many of them, above all in Valencia). Moreover, these "good relationships" do not exclude the exis-tence of a series of measures addressed to recall Christian superiority (e.g. men had to have a long beard and women had to wear the "*aldifara*," a kind of tunic imposed also on Jews) and to avoid any kind of promiscuity and religious contamination between Christians and Muslims (e. g. the prohibition of mixed marriage or of any sexual relationship between members of the two religions). To respect Christianity, they were obliged not to work publicly on Sundays, to show reverence for processions in the streets, kneeling on their way, not to use blasphemy, and not to go into Christian churches during liturgical acts.

But all these aspects were not always respected, both in everyday life (for instance, there were some Mudejar musicians during the processions of Corpus Christi) and at the highest cultural level. In this last sense, the intellectual relationships between Mudejars and Christians had per-haps already begun at the end of the eleventh century. When Alfonso VI conquered Toledo (1085) he entered a rich city, populated by Muslims and Jews. In that city the cultural memory of the Islamic presence remained strong for some time. That's why a scholar such as Gerard of Cremona (d. 1188), went to Toledo, on the trail of ancient books and classic culture. There he lived, devoting the rest of his life to the Latin translation of Arabic works of science and phil-osophy. Also thanks to him, Toledo became the center of intense translation activity. Perhaps it is incorrect to define it as a "school," and it should be emphasized that recent studies have identified a number of Spanish centers of translation. Regardless of this, however, there is no doubt that the work of these groups led to impressive results. The method of Gerardo stood out, producing texts perhaps not impeccable from a philological point of view, but often significant for their literalness and, in general, for their effort of reflection on the original Arabic vocabulary. Moreover, the literalness is not to be taken for granted: the most frequent method used by the translators from Arabic texts, presumably, was the simultaneous translation, word by word, sentence by sentence, from Arabic to vernacular and from vernacular to Latin. At least two people participated in this operation: a Mozarab or a Jew and a Christian expert in Latin. This group translated ancient Greek works such as Ptolemy's *Almagest*, but also contributed to the knowledge of Arabic medicine, with the translation of books such as al-Razi's *Introduction to Medicine* or Ibn Sina/Avicenna's *Canon*. This tradition continued for a long time: from Latin authors, such as Dominicus Gundissalinus (the translator of al-Farabi's *Division of Sciences* and Avicenna's *De Anima*) and Marco from Toledo, who translated Galinus and other Arabic medicines such as Hunayn ibn Hishaq; to Michael Scot, who at the beginning of the thirteenth century was in Toledo to translate the zoological treatises of Aristotle.

But this high level of intellectual exchange was the history of an elite. The political changes at the end of the Middle Ages showed another reality.

## The kingdom of Granada and the end of al-Andalus

In the second half of the fifteenth century, the Nasrid kingdom of Granada was caught between the Cordillera Bética in the north and the Mediterranean Sea in the south. This last strip of Muslim Spain, which stretched towards Africa, included the cities of Malaga, Almeria, and of course the capital Granada in the mountains of the Sierra Nevada.

The Nasrid had founded, *de facto*, the dynasty with the entry into the city of Muhammad ibn Yusuf ibn Nasr (1237), but the Emirate of Granada was born as a result of the Christian conquest of the valley of the Guadalquivir in the days of Fernando III. Indeed, this Christian king recognized Granada as a vassal kingdom of Castile in 1246, integrating it into its political sphere. This temporary situation was then prolonged indefinitely: many Muslims fleeing from other parts of Spain decided to take refuge there, while in North Africa the Moroccan dynasty of the Merenides decided to support the emirate. The protection of this little political space was assured not only by its geographical position, but also by the political security derived from the passivity of the kings of Aragon and by the maritime cooperation of Genoa, which left a good deal of diplomatic activity to the Muslims.

In other terms, Granada was strongly involved in the policy of the Christian spaces that surrounded it. In this sense, from the beginning of the fifteenth century this little piece of al-Andalus was increasingly involved in Castilian court intrigues and this led to an explosion of inner tensions, producing a complex plot of conspiracies, vengeances, and political murders.

Regardless of these political troubles, however, the ephemeral existence of Granada was magnificent in many ways. Throughout the fourteenth century, the Nasrid capital was one of the most populous cities in Europe, and, moreover, in the following century the population increased, as the city continued to welcome Muslim refugees: sources attested to the presence of about 200,000 people; more likely there were about 50,000, in any case an enormous number for the period.

But that little Muslim world was coming to an end: worn out by infighting, bereft of any true support from the North African Muslims, increasingly threatened by the ambitions of the Christian sovereigns. In 1453 there came some news that was perceived by the king of Castile, Henry IV, as related to the Iberian situation: to the east, across the Mediterranean, Constantinople fell into the hands of the Turks. The idea of the Crusade reappeared in Europe and in Spain, and the king of Castile decided to go back to the conquests. Between 1455 and 1457,

31

six military incursions were launched against the Moorish kingdom, carried out by mighty forces but without significant results. In any case, the climate was evidently favorable to war, and when Isabella of Castile and Ferdinand of Aragon came to the throne, the capture of Granada became inevitable.

The attack took place in 1482: each year, or nearly every year, the territory was worn away, stronghold after stronghold. It was a long war of sieges, carried out by soldiers partly recruited in Castile and Andalusia, in part mercenaries, but a large part were also volunteers coming from all over Europe. In 1488, the city of Granada was almost all that remained in the hands of the Muslims. In 1490 the army encamped near the city, a siege operation of such magnitude as to require the building of a new town, Santa Fe. On January 2, 1492, Granada surrendered and the Catholic kings entered the city. Boabdil, the last emir of Spain, offered the keys of the Alhambra to Ferdinand, while the vessels of the Spanish monarchs were shut up in the towers of the city. However, the history of Islam in Spain didn't end with this event. Muslims and their culture continued to be present in the next centuries, until the last expulsion of the Moriscos. The traces of this heritage strongly contributed to the construction of Spanish society and culture. And finally, also in the Islamic world, the memory of al-Andalus continued to feed ideas, culture, and dreams, and continues to this day.

## The memory of al-Andalus in the Muslim world

The end of al-Andalus soon echoed in the Muslim world. As early as 1580, the anonymous Turkish author of a work devoted to the discovery of the West Indies (*Tarih-i Hindi-i garbi*) also wrote about the loss of the last Iberian Muslim territories, remembering the noble mosque of Cordoba, adorned and decorated with the most beautiful things; unique in its beauty and perfection (Gruzinski 2008: 147).

It is also possible to find this kind of admiration of the Islamic Iberian past among later Muslim travelers, such as the Moroccan al-Ghassani (who was in Spain in the years 1690–1), al-Ghazzal (1766), and Ibn 'Uthman al-Miknasi (1779–80). Starting from the nineteenth century, in the Islamic world the interest in al-Andalus was increasingly related to the reconstruction of the past determined by the influence of Occidental policy and culture.

In the year 1863, in Istanbul, the great intellectual Ziya Paşa (1825–80) published the Turkish translation of Louis Viardot's *Essai sur l'histoire des arabes et des mores d'Espagne*, with the title of *Endelüs Tarihi*, "History of al-Andalus." This work obtained stunning success: it was reprinted in four volumes between 1886 and 1887, and it inspired a whole series of poems, plays, and stories set in al-Andalus; for instance the work of 'Abdülhak Hamid (1852–1937), *Tariq*.

This success was not limited to the Turkish coast: on every side of the Islamic Mediterranean and beyond, there was a rapid spread of Moorish nostalgia, memories of the Alhambra, and sentimental descriptions of Cordoba. Of course, also in this case Europe had a lot to do with this change of historical interest: the new Islamic intellectual elite read the Western Orientalists avidly, and they, in turn, began to be interested in Spain (one for all: think about the fundamental *Histoire des musulmans d'Espagne* of Reinhart Dozy, published for the first time in 1861).

So many Arabic authors began to observe the Iberian coast for the first time, searching out the traces of its past. It is impossible to draw up a thorough list, but there are cases and people that should be recalled. First of all, probably, the celebrated Jirji Zaydan, whose work as a novelist was inspired by Dumas and Walter Scott and who is known for his employment of historical material: "We do everything" – perhaps declared with some exaggeration – "for the historical truth to prevail over fictional appearance, in opposition to what the

Westerners do, focusing their interest mainly on the invention of a story." Zaydan wrote, among other things, a novel about the Arab conquest of the Iberian Peninsula, which was focused on the figure of the leader Tariq ibn Ziyad (*Fath al-Andalus aw Tariq ibn Ziyad*, 1965). Other authors went in the same direction: Ahmad Shawqi with *Amirat al-Andalus* (Cairo, 1932), 'Ali al-Jarim in his *Hatif min al-Andalus* (Cairo, 1979), or 'Abd al-Rahman al-Barquqi with *Hadarat al-Andalus*; names that may not be very well known but that contributed significantly to the formation of a new idea about the past of the Islamic Mediterranean world. However, this was not only a product of novelists. Many travelers in the nineteenth and the twentieth centuries saw the Spanish lands with new eyes, Muhammad Labib al-Batnuni (*Rihlat al-Andalus*, 1927), for example, or Muhammad Kurd 'Ali (*Ghabir al-Andalus wa hadiruha*, 1923), which strongly contributed to transmitting the idea of a lost Spain. This process was not only tied to the Mediterranean area. The Indian Muslims also perceived the problem in similar terms: inspired by Western studies (and therefore by Western categories), in 1870 they discovered the work of the Andalusian Ibn Rushd, the Latin Averroes. However, starting from this moment there was a plethora of new interest: there were Urdu translations of Andalusian works (e.g. Ibn 'Arabi's *Fusus al-hikam*), translations of Western studies such as the work of Meakin, *Moorish Empire* (the translation is from 1904), and the production of original works such as the biographies of the Iberian Ibn Bajja and Ibn Abi Hayyan. Beyond the scientific value of these studies, their importance was in the literary and political mythology that surrounded the memory of al-Andalus. In this sense a good example is the work of the famous poet Muhammad Iqbal (d. 1938), in which the figures of the heroes of Muslim Spain, Tariq and 'Abd al-Rahman I, become examples of the virtues of a lost world. His poetry dedicated to the great Mosque of Cordoba, *Masjid-i Qurtuba*, is famous, a tribute to Islamic art which broadens towards the admiration of the creative genius of an entire culture.

In the Islamic world, this attraction to the cultural and historical greatness of Muslim Spain was strongly related to deep psychological and political tensions. Also, it was obvious, both in the poetry and in the historiographic essays, that the Islam evoked by the memories of Spain was reflected in contemporary Islam, fought by the European colonial powers. Al-Andalus was a kind of world upside down: it was from that territory that the Muslims had given science to the West; it was in that land that the cultural and artistic developments were so superior to the miseries of medieval barbaric Europe.

Inside this complex mix of ideas, the myth of the lost Spain started to be linked to the memory of the Crusades. When, in the nineteenth and the twentieth centuries, the Arab lands adopted new political forms step by step – for instance the idea of revolution or the concept of nation – they also necessarily adopted the tools to ground and define these ideas. And among these tools there was also a complex rewriting of their history. Not by chance, in a part of the Islamic culture of that period surfaced the idea that al-Andalus had been lost due to a Crusade. This idea has been spread through literature and, more generally, the literature strongly contributed to shaping the image of the medieval al-Andalus. This process continued until this image became a cultural cornerstone of the identity of lands such as Morocco or Syria. In this sense, the poems of the Syrian Nizar Qabbani are paradigmatic. Qabbani was an intellectual celebrated mainly in Syria and in the Arabic world, but well known in Europe too; his poetry inspired by al-Andalus was read publicly in Spain in 1963, when Cordoba celebrated the millennium of the birth of Ibn Hazm with civic solemnity. In addition to Qabbani, other intellectuals, filmmakers, and writers, such as Radwa Ashour, Tariq Ali, and Mahmoud Darwish, to name but a few, have used al-Andalus "as a backdrop for works that are nostalgic and proud, looking back on a previous time during which Arab culture reigned supreme, and using al-Andalus as a way to depict and discuss contemporary events" (Elinson 2009: 2).

The constellation of ideas offered by similar intellectual and artistic creations is clear in its general sense: al-Andalus was a place of high civilization that nurtured crude medieval Christianity; but it was crushed by a Crusade, which in turn is an expression of the violent and prevaricating Christian imperialism. In this sense, al-Andalus is an integral part of this system of decoding history and interpreting reality: it is the Garden of Eden of the peaceful coexistence of the people of the Book under the protection of Islam. But this myth also works well for all the people who, regardless of religion, see in the Western world and in its cultural tensions a place of despair and the denial of many humanistic values. In this sense, in this deep relationship with the contemporary history of the Muslim people in Western lands, the adventure of the Mudejars and the tragic destiny of the Moriscos are still contemporary signs: part of a narrative and a myth that still contribute to the writing of history.

## Bibliography

Abboud-Haggar, S. (1997) "Las Leyes de Moros son el libro de al-Tafrî," *Cuadernos de Historia del Derecho* 4: 163–201.

Abou el-Fadl, K.H. (1994) "Islamic Law and Muslim Minorities," *Islamic Law and Society* 1/2: 141–87.

Acién Almansa, M. (1997) *Entre el Feudalismo y el Islam. Umar Ibn Hafsún en los historiadores, en las fuentes y en la historia*, Jaén: Ed. Universidad de Jaén.

Ahmad, A. (1962) "L'Islam d'Espagne et Inde musulmane," in *Études d'orientalisme dédiées a la mémoire de Lévi-Provençal*, Paris: Maisonneuve et Larose, vol. 2, pp. 461–70.

Al-Muqaddasi (1906) *Ahsan al-taqasīm fi ma'rifat al-aqalim*, ed. M.J. de Goeje, in "Bibliotheca Geographorum Arabicoru," III, Leiden: Brill.

Álvaro Zamora, M.I., Borrás Gualis, G., and Sarasa Sánchez, E. (2003) *Los mudéjares en Aragón*, Saragossa: Caja de Ahorros de la Inmaculada de Aragón.

Benaboud, M. (1984) "El papel público y social de los 'ulamâ en al-Andalus en el período de los taifas," *Cuadernos de Historia del Islam* 11: 7–52.

Bensoussan, D. (2007) *L'Espagne des trois religions: grandeur et décadence de la convivencia*, Paris: L'Harmattan.

Biarnes Biarnes, C. (1972) *Moros i moriscos a la Ribera de l'Ebre (710–1615)*, Barcelona: CSIC.

Boswell, J. (1977) *The Royal Treasure: Muslim Communities under the Crown of Aragon in the Fourteenth Century*, New Haven, CT and London: Yale University Press.

Bulliet, R.W. (1979) *Conversion to Islam in the Medieval Period: An Essay in Quantitative History*, Cambridge, MA: Harvard University Press.

Calero Secall, M. (2001) "El derecho islámico y su aplicación en al-Andalus (siglos XIII–XV)," in Roldán Castro, F. and Hervás Jávega, I. (eds.) *El saber en al-Andalus*, Seville: Universidad de Sevilla, III, pp. 31–44.

Camera D'Afflitto, I. (1998) *Letteratura araba contemporanea*, Roma: Carocci.

Casassas Canals, X. (2009) "La literature Islámica Castellana: siglos XIII-XVII," *Al-Andalus Magreb* 16: 89–113.

Catlos, B.A. (2004) *The Victors and the Vanquished: Christians and Muslims of Catalonia and Aragon, 1050–1300*, Cambridge: Cambridge University Press.

——(2007) "Impuestos e identidad: comunidades fiscales y confesionales en la Corona de Aragón en el siglo XIII," in *X Simposio Internacional de Mudejarismo*, Teruel: Instituto de Estudios Turolenses, pp. 481–5.

Chalmeta, P. (1991) "El concepto de tagr," in Sénac, P. (ed.) *La Marche supérieure d'al-Andalus et l'occident chrétien*, Madrid: Casa de Velázquez, pp. 15–27.

Corral Lafuente, J.L. (1999) "El proceso de represión contra los mudéjares aragoneses, Aragón en la Edad Media, XIV–XV," in *Homenaje a la profesora Carmen Orcástegui Gros*, Saragossa: Universidad de Zaragoza, Facultad de Filosofía y Letras, vol. I, pp. 341–55.

De La Granja, F. (1998) "El problema del mudejarismo en la lengua y en la literatura," *Qurtuba* 3: 183–94.

De Miguel, J.C. (1989) *La comunidad mudéjar de Madrid*, Madrid: Asociación Cultural Al-Mudayna.

Del Val Valdivieso, M.I. and Villanueva Zubizarreta, O. (eds.) (2008) *Musulmanes y Cristianos frente al Agua en las ciudades Medievales*, Santander: Universidad de Castilla—La Mancha and Universidad de Cantabria.

Diago Hernando, M. (1993) "Mudéjares castellanos en la frontera con Aragón. El caso de Ágreda," in Lorenzo Sans, E. (ed.) *Proyección histórica de España en sus tres culturas*, Valladolid: Junta de Castilla y León, I, pp. 67–72.

Echevarría Arsuaga, A.M. (2000) "Mudéjares y moriscos en el reino nazarí de Granada," in Viguera, M.J. (coord.) *Historia de España Menéndez Pidal,* Madrid: ESPASA, vol. VIII t. 4, pp. 367–440.

——(2001–2) "Los mudéjares de los reinos de Castilla y Portugal," in *Revista d'Història Medieval* 12: 31–46.

——(2004) *La minoría islámica en la Península Ibérica. Moro, sarraceno, mudéjar,* Malaga: Sarriá.

Elinson, A.W. (2009) *Looking Back at Al-Andalus: The Poetics of Loss and Nostalgia in Medieval Arabic and Hebrew Literature,* London.

Ferrer i Mallol, M.T. (1987) *Els sarraïns de la Corona catalano-aragonesa en el segle XIV. Segregació i discriminació,* Barcelona: CSIC and Institució Milà i Fontanals.

Fierro, M. (1999) "Los mawali de 'Abd al-Rahman I," *al-Qantara* 20(1): 65–97.

——(2011) *Abderramán III,* Donostia-San Sebastián: Nerea.

Fierro, M. and Marín, M. (1998) "La islamización de las ciudades andalusíes a través de sus ulemas (siglo II/VIII-comienzos del siglo IV/X)," in Cressier, P. and García Arenal, M. (eds.) *Genèse de la ville islamique en al-Andalus et au Maghreb occidental,* Madrid: Casa de Velasquez, pp. 65–97.

Fuentes Cornejo, T. (ed.) (2000) *Poesía religiosa aljamiado-morisca. Poemas en alabanza de Mahoma, de Alá y de la religión islámica. Otros textos complementarios,* Madrid: Fundación Menéndez Pidal.

García-Arenal, M. (1977) "La aljama de los moros de Cuenca en el siglo XV," *Historia. Instituciones. Documentos,* 4: 35–47.

——(1995) "El hundimiento del conllevarse: La Castile de las Tres Culturas (I). Minorias religiosas," in Aróstegui, J. (ed.) *Historia de una cultura, III. Las Castiles que no fueron,* Valladolid: Junta de Castile y León, pp. 26–35.

García de Cortázar, J.Á. et al. (1985) *Organización social del espacio en la España medieval. La Corona de Castilla en los siglos VIII a XV,* Barcelona: Ariel.

García Sanjuan, A. (ed.) (2003) *Tolerancia y convivencia étnico-religiosa en la Península Ibérica durante la Edad Media: III Jornadas de Cultura Islámica (Collectanea/Universidad de Huelva 73),* Huelva: Universidad de Huelva.

Garulo, T. (1998) "La Nostalgia de Al-Andalus: Génesis de un Tema literario," *Qurtuba* 3: 47–63.

Goodrich, T.D. (1990) *The Ottoman Turks and the New World: A Study of Tarih-i Hindi-i garbi and Sixteenth Century Ottoman America,* Wiesbaden: Otto Harrassowitz.

Granara, W. (2005) "Nostalgia, Arab Nationalism, and the Andalusian Chronotope in Evolution of the Modern Arabic Novel," *Journal of Arabic Literature* 36(1): 57–73.

Gruzinski, S. (2008) *Quelle Heure est-il là-bas?,* Paris: Seuil.

Guichard, P. (1976) *Al-Andalus: estructura antropológica de una sociedad islámica en Occidente,* Barcelona: Barral.

Halm, H. (1989) "Al-Andalus und Gothica Sors," *Die Welt des Orients* 66: 252–63.

Harvey, L.P. (1990) *Islamic Spain, 1250 to 1500,* Chicago: University of Chicago Press.

Hillgarth, J.N. (1976–8) *The Spanish Kingdoms, 1250–1516,* Oxford: Clarendon.

Hinojosa Montalvo, J. (1994) *La morería de Elche en la Edad Media,* Teruel: Centro de Estudios Mudéjares and Instituto de Estudios Turolenses.

——(2002) *Los mudéjares. La voz del Islam en la España cristiana,* Teruel: Instituto de Estudios Mudéjares.

——(2009) "Los mudéjares en Aragón y Cataluña en el reinado de Jaime I," in Sarasa, E. (ed.) *La sociedad en Aragón y Cataluña en el reinado de Jaime I (1213–1276),* Saragossa: CSIC, pp. 157–98.

Jaspert, N. (2011) "Religiöse Minderheiten auf der Iberischen Halbinsel und im Mittelmeeraum. Eine Skizze," in Herbers, K. and Jaspert, N. (eds.) *Integration – Segregation – Vertreibung. Religiöse Minderheiten und Randgruppen auf der Iberischen Halbinsel (7. bis 17. Jahrhundert),* Münster-Berlin: LIT Verlag, pp. 15–44.

Lacarra, J.M. (1981) "*Introducción al estudio de los mudéjares aragoneses,*" in *I Simposio Internacional de Mudejarismo (Teruel, 1975),* Madrid-Teruel: IET.

Ladero Quesada, M.Á. (1981) "Los mudéjares de Castile en la Baja Edad Media," in *Actas del I Simposio Internacional de Mudejarismo (Teruel 1975),* Madrid–Teruel: Instituto de Estudios Turolenses, pp. 349–90.

——(2004) "Los mudéjares de la España cristiana," in Valdeón Baruque, J. (ed.) *Cristianos, musulmanes y judíos en la España medieval,* Valladolid: Ámbito, pp. 103–24.

Ledesma Rubio, M.L. (1979) *Los mudéjares aragoneses,* Saragossa: Anubar.

——(1991) *Cartas de población del reino de Aragón en los siglos medievales,* Saragossa: IFC.

——(1994a) *Vidas mudéjares,* Saragossa: Editorial Mira.

——(1994b) "El poder real y las comunidades mudéjares en Aragón," in *XV Congreso de Historia de la Corona de Aragón,* Saragossa: Diputación General de Aragón, I, pp. 187–96.

——(1996) *Estudios sobre los mudéjares en Aragón,* Teruel: Centro de Estudios Mudéjares.

Lemay, R. (1963) "Dans l'Espagne du douzième siècle. Les traductions de l'arabe au latin," *Annales ESC* 18: 639–65.

Lewis, B. (1973) "The Cult of Spain and the Turkish Romantics," in *Islam in History: Ideas, Men and Events in the Middle East*, London: Alcove Press.

Maíllo Salgado, F. (1985) "Algunas consideraciones sobre una fatwa de al-Wansharisi," *Studia Historica* 11(2): 181–91.

Manzano Moreno, E. (1991) *La frontera de al-Andalus en epoca de los Omeyas*, Madrid: CSIC.

——(1999) *La frontera de al-Andalus en época de los Omeyas*, Madrid: Consejo Superior de Investigaciones Científicas.

——(2006) *Conquistadores, Emires y Califas*, Barcelona: Crítica.

Marín, M. (1995) "Des Migrations forcées: les 'ulama' d' Al-Andalus face la conquête chrétienne," in M. Hammam (ed.) *L'Occident musulman et l'Occident chrétien au Moyen Age*, Rabat: Faculté des Lettres et des Sciences Humaines-Rabat, pp. 43–59.

Martínez Montávez, P. (1992) *Al-Andalus, España, en la literatura árabe contemporánea*, Madrid: MAPFRE.

——(1998) *Al-Andalus y Nizar Kabbani: la Tragedia, Ilu. Revista de Ciencias de las Religiones*, vol. 1, Madrid: Universidad Complutense de Madrid, pp. 9–24.

Meakin, B. (1899) *The Moorish Empire*, London: Sannenschin & Co.

Menjot, D. (1992) "Les Mudéjars du royaume de Murcie: minorités religieuses dans l'Espagne médiévale," *Revue du Monde Musulman et de la Méditérranée* 63–4: 165–78.

Miller, K.A. (2000) "Muslim Minorities and the Obligation to Emigrate to Islamic Territory: Two Fatwas from Fifteenth Century Granada," *Islamic Law and Society* 7(2): 256–87.

Molénat, J.-P. (1983) "Les Musulmans de Tolède aux XIVe et XVe siècles," in *Les Espagnes médiévales. Aspects économiques et sociaux. Mélanges offerts a Jean Gautier-Dalché*, Nice: Annales de la Faculté des Lettres et Sciences Humaines de Nice, pp. 175–90.

——(1986) "Les Musulmans dans l'espace urbain tolédan aux XIV et XV siècles," in *Minorités et marginaux en Espagne et dans le Midi de la France (VIe–XVIIe siécles)*, Paris: CNRS, pp. 129–41.

——(1994) "L'Arabe a Tolède, du XIIe au XVIe siècle," *Al-Qantara* 15: 473–96.

——(1996) *Les Mudéjars de Tolède: occupations professionnelles et localisation dans l'espace*, Temel: ASIM VI, pp. 429–35.

——(1997) *Campagnes et Monts de Tolède du XIIe au XVe siècle*, Madrid: Casa de Velázquez.

——(1998) "Tolède à la fin du XIe siècle et au début du XIIe: le problème de l'émigration ou de la permanence des musulmans," in Laliena Corbera, C. and Utrilla Utrilla, J.F. (eds.) *De Toledo a Huesca. Sociedades medievales en transición a finales del siglo XI (1080–1100)*, Saragossa: Institución Fernando el Católico, pp. 101–11.

——(2000) "Les Sources chrétiennes sur l'histoire des 'musulmans soumis' dans la Péninsule Ibérique médiévale," in Sidarus, A. (ed.) *Fontes da História de al-Andalus e do Gharb*, Lisbon: Centro de Estudos Africanos e Asiáticos and Instituto de Investigação Científica e Tropical, pp. 159–73.

——(2001) "Le Problème de la permanence des musulmans dans les territoires conquis par les chrétiens, du point de vue de la loi islamique," *Arabica* 48(3): 392–400.

Moratinos García, M. and Villanueva Zubizarreta, O. (1999–2002) "Consecuencias del decreto de conversión al cristianismo del 1502 en la aljama mora de Valladolid," *Sharq al-Andalus* 17–18: 115–39.

Mutgé Vives, J. (1992) *L'aljama sarraïna de Lleida a l'Edat Mitjana. Aproximació a la seva història*, Barcelona: CSIC.

——(1999) "La aljama sarracena en la Lleida cristiana: noticias y conclusiones," in *VII Simposio Internacional de Mudejarismo (Teruel, 1996)*, Teruel: Centro de Estudios Mudéjares del Instituto de Estudios Turolenses, pp. 101–11.

Niclós, J.-V. (2001) *Tres culturas, tres religiones: convivencia y diálogo entre judíos, cristianos y musulmanes en la Península Ibérica*, Salamanca: san Esteban.

O'Callaghan, J.F. (1996) *El Rey Sabio. El reinado de Alfonso X de Castile*, Seville: Universidad de Sevilla.

Peña, S. (ed.) (2009) *Iraq y al-Andalus. Oriente en el Occidente islámico*, Almería: Fundación Ibn Tufayl.

Pérès, H. (1937) *L'Espagne par les voyageurs musulmans de 1610 à 1930*, Paris: Maisonneuve.

Ruiz de Marco, A. et al. (1993) "Las necrópolis de rito islámico en Castile y León, Numantia, Arqueología en Castile y León," *Numantia (Soria)* 4: 207–18.

Ruzafa García, M. (2000) "Élites valencianas y minorías sociales: la élite mudéjar y sus actividades (1350–1500)," *Revista d'Història Medieval* 11: 163–87.

Seco de Lucena Paredes, L. (1975) *La Granada nazarí del siglo XV*, Granada: Patronato de la Alhambra.

Sénac, P. (1999) "Note sur les premiers comtes aragonais," in *Hommage à Pierre Bonnassie. Les Sociétés méridionales à l'âge feudal (Espagne, Italie et sud de la France Xe–XIIIe siècle)*, Toulouse: Université de Toulouse-Le Mirail, pp. 349–54.

——(2000a) *The Lords of the Upper March (ashab al-thaghr): The Banu 'Amrus and Banu Shabrit of Huesca*, framespa.univ-tlse2.fr/servlet/com.univ.collaboratif.utils.LectureFichiergw?ID_FICHIER=12538059845 66&ID_FICHE=321.

——(2000b) *La Frontière et les hommes (VIIIe–XIIe siècle). Le Peuplement musulman au nord de l'Ebre et les débuts de la reconquête aragonaise*, Paris: Maisonneuve et Larose.

Shannon, J.H. (2007) "Performing Al-Andalus, Remembering Al-Andalus: Mediterranean Soundings from Mashriq to Maghrib," *Journal of American Folklore* 120: 308–44.

Tapia Sánchez, S. (1991) *La comunidad morisca de Ávila*, Salamanca: Universidad de Salamanca.

Torres Balbás, L. (1956) *Esquema demográfico de la ciudad de Granada*, Madrid: CISC.

Utrilla Utrilla, J.F. and Esco Sampériz, C. (1986) "La población mudéjar en la Hoya de Huesca (siglos XII y XIII)," in *II Simposio Internacional de Mudejarismo (Teruel, 1984)*, Teruel: Instituto de Estudios Turolenses, pp. 187–208.

Vallvé, J. (1983) "El nombre de al-Andalus," *Al-Qantara* 4: 301–55.

Van Koningsveld, P.S. (1992) "Andalusian-Arabic Manuscripts from Christian Spain: A Comparative Intercultural Approach," *Israel Oriental Studies* 12: 75–110.

Vanoli, A. (2006) *La Spagna delle tre culture. Ebrei, Cristiani e Musulmani tra storia e mito*, Roma: Viella.

Veas Arteseros, M. del C. (1993) *Mudéjares murcianos: un modelo de crisis social (siglos XIII–XV)*, Murcia: EDITUM.

Vernet, J. (1968) "Los médicos andaluse en el Libro de las generaciones de los médicos de Ibn Yulyul," *Anuario de Estudios Medievales* 5: 445–62.

Viguera, M.J. (1992) "Les Mudéjars et leurs documents écrits en arabe: minorités religieuses dans l'Espagne médiévale," in Marín, M. and Pérez, J. (eds.) *Revue du Monde Musulman et de la Méditérranée*, vol. 63–4, Aix en Provence: Presses Universitaires de Provence, pp. 155–63.

Villanueva Zubizarreta, O. (2010) "Los escenarios de la sociabilidad para los mudéjares e la cuenca del duero: la vida en las morerías y el duelo en las maqbaras," in Martín Cea, J.C. (ed.) *Convivir en la Edad Media*, Burgos: Dossoles.

Wiegers, G. (1994) *Islamic Literature in Spanish and Aljamiado*, Leiden: Brill.

Wiegers, G. and Van Koningsveld, P.S. (1996) "The Islamic Statute of the Mudejars in the Light of a New Source," *al-Qantara* 17: 19–58.

Zaydan, J. (1965) *Fath al-Andalus aw Tariq ibn Ziyad*, Cairo: Dar al-Hilal.

# 2

# The converted Muslims of Spain

## Morisco cultural resistance and engagement with Islamic knowledge (1502–1610)

*Mercedes García-Arenal*

It would be difficult to find a group of Muslims in early modern Europe of more interest to the social or cultural historian than those known as the "Moriscos," i.e. the Muslims converted to Catholicism by Royal decree who lived in Spain through the entire sixteenth century until their expulsion in 1609–14. This was a group which was subjected to strenuous evangelizing and assimilating efforts by mainstream society but which was at the same time the victim of marginalization and stigmatization and, eventually, a process of expulsion with all the features of ethnic cleansing. Most contemporary European readers will feel a sense of deep discomfort when reading about the treatment of the Moriscos, reminiscent as a process and as a cultural and political problem of much of what occurs today in reaction to the immigration of Muslims into Europe.

### Different groups, different options. How Muslim were the Moriscos?

The Moriscos were to a certain extent the product of colonization, especially in Valencia and Granada. Rather than constituting one unified mass, the Moriscos should be seen as a number of subgroups with widely varying beliefs and behavior. After compulsory conversion, one group remained resistant and sought to preserve and observe its original Islamic religion. A second Morisco group clung to Islamic vestiges as a form of cultural identity rather than as a dogmatic set of religious beliefs, many of them because of sheer ignorance of Islamic law. The Islamic sense of belonging of such individuals was linked to the notion of participation in a "community of emotion" which identified with the Muslim world. Both of these groups were inevitably given to dissimulation and secretiveness as well as doubt and the gradual erosion of belief. Finally, at the other end of the range, there were the fully assimilated and Christianized Moriscos, who certainly existed, though they left less of an imprint in the contemporary documents. The extent to which Moriscos held on to Islamic beliefs and culture depended on specific conditions in the kingdoms in which they lived and the length of time since the Christian conquest of the region, as well as demographic particularities such as the number and density of the Morisco population in relation to the Christian population.

The current depth of interest in the Moriscos can be gauged by the amount of historiography devoted to them, especially as a result of the recent 500th anniversary of the Expulsion of 1609, which saw a series of conferences, books, and fresh approaches, as well as the presentation of much new evidence (García-Arenal 2009a: 888–920; Amelang 2011). Some of this work has discussed the issue of Morisco identity, i.e. to what extent they were Muslims and whether the accusation launched at them by their contemporaries that they were impossible to assimilate is a stereotype or whether there were in fact large numbers of assimilated Moriscos, or at least Moriscos among whom there was a notable hybridization of cultures and religions. At the same time, there has been a resulting interest in the nature of Islam among the Moriscos, in how possible it was for Moriscos to possess knowledge of Islamic religion and the Arabic language once their religious elites were lost and it was forbidden to own books written in Arabic. In this article I intend to concentrate on precisely these issues, i.e. on what the Islamic culture of the Moriscos was like, on the knowledge, sources, and books to which they had access, on the question of which books they copied and translated in some parts of the Iberian Peninsula as their command of Arabic began to elude them. To this end I will make use of Inquisition material and literature produced by the Moriscos themselves. I propose to show the originality of the Morisco experience and an ability to uphold and transmit, as well as create, Islamic knowledge in a manner which reveals a close interconnection with contemporary Christian Hispanic culture as well as a polemical engagement with it.

## Political events and legal dispositions concerning Moriscos

I will begin by outlining briefly who the Moriscos were and the circumstances in which their experience in the Iberian Peninsula took place. During the Middle Ages, part of peninsular territory had been under Islamic political control and had later experienced a long, slow, and uneven process of Christian conquest which contemporaries perceived in terms of the "loss and recovery of Spain." The so-called "*Reconquista*" was followed at the beginning of the early modern period by a powerful movement towards conversion and expulsion with Messianic overtones. On the one hand this movement stressed the need for integration and homogenization, but on the other it argued for expulsion and purification. It was legitimized by a providentialist interpretation of the past of Spain as a "nation" forged during the struggle against Islam.

The sequence of events regarding the Moriscos was as follows: in the early years of the sixteenth century, the Catholic monarchs, who had expelled all Jews from Spain in 1492 – the same year in which they completed their conquest of the Islamic kingdom of Granada – decreed the compulsory conversion to Christianity of all Muslims living in the territories of the Crown of Castile. This decree of conversion of the Castilian Muslims, dated 1502, was extended in 1526 to cover the territories of Aragon and Valencia. The decree brought an end to the legal existence of Muslims in the Christian territories of Iberia, where they had been living under the name of Mudejars throughout the entire medieval period. Thus the long century (until the Expulsion of 1609–14) of what is known as the "Morisco problem," "Morisco" being the name by which the forced converts were known, began.

From 1502 onwards, Islam was forbidden and therefore deprived of all legal or administrative support. Its institutions were dissolved, its religious elites converted or exiled, its mosques closed, its books destroyed. Circumcision ceased to be practiced except in Valencia and, to a lesser extent, in Aragon. The Arabic language also disappeared everywhere except in Valencia – even in Granada, the switch to Castilian Spanish was virtually complete by the 1560s. Accompanied by the decrees of conversion, a series of measures was promulgated which aimed to eliminate the cultural differentiators of the new Christians, such as their music and dress, the way they cut their hair or their use of *hammams*, and, most specially, the use of Arabic. Measures were also implemented which kept them in a position of social inferiority, such as a ban on possessing arms or slaves. From the Christian point of view, the Morisco problem was further heightened throughout the sixteenth century by the problem of the corsairs of North Africa, who frequently attacked and inspired fear in the coastal towns of south and eastern Spain. These attacks meant that Spaniards of the period rarely made a distinction between their conflict with foreign Islam and their relations with Islam within the Peninsula; the struggle was also related to the confrontation with the Ottoman Empire. The Moriscos found themselves under constant observation and were suspected of conspiring with neighboring Muslim countries in the planning of armed revolts, which did, in fact, take place. The most important of these was the Granadan revolt which led to what is known as the War of the Alpujarras (1568–70). This was an uprising which it was difficult for the Christians to suppress and which eventually amounted to a second Christian conquest of the kingdom of Granada. It was a war carried out with extraordinary ferocity on both sides, leaving fear of the Morisco indelibly imprinted on the Christian mind. It ended with the deportation of Granadan Moriscos to Castile in 1570–1, and it erased any chance of integration or acceptance of inhabitants of Muslim origin in mainstream Christian society.

## A Muslim European culture

Hispanized or Christianized Moriscos have left very little trace in the records, and this makes it easy to form a distorted image of the "unassimilable Morisco" who remained a staunch Muslim in spite of all the measures adopted by the Christian authorities. Reality was undoubtedly much more complex, as can be deduced from accounts of the difficulties faced by those who were expelled when they tried to integrate into the Islamic societies of North Africa. But this is not the only evidence available: notarial documents from Granada, especially wills, reveal the large number of Moriscos who asked for masses to be said for them after their deaths or who belonged to Catholic religious brotherhoods, took part in processions, left money for the restoration of their parish church, etc. Resistance was not only religious but rather cultural and social, and was fed by rejection of a mainstream society which discriminated against the Moriscos and marginalized them. At the same time, in order to go unnoticed the Moriscos had to adopt the language, ways, and customs of that same society, meaning that they internalized, albeit unconsciously, an entire Catholic cultural world. Probably the clearest sign of this process of hybridization is the literature in *aljamía*: a literature written in the Spanish vernacular but using the Arabic alphabet in which religious terms and concepts were generally expressed in Arabic, as were entire quotations from the Qur'an. *Aljamía* also borrowed syntactic, stylistic, lexical, and semantic structures from Arabic. It was a special language, the Islamic variant of Spanish. Literature in *aljamía* was of a didactic nature, mainly dealing in religious and legal themes, and sought to transmit and preserve among the Moriscos the groundings of Islamic law and belief, as well as stories about Islamic heroes, epic narratives on the beginnings of Islam, stories of the prophets, etc. It was, in other words, what might be described as "sacred history." Together with such themes, we also find in it popular medicine and magic, prophesies, moral sayings, punishments, and itineraries (i.e. instructions for fleeing from Spain). The literature also contains narratives, theater, and poetry from contemporary Hispanic literature which the Moriscos clearly knew and enjoyed, just as they knew and used Catholic devotional works. The use of Christian sources is obvious, for example, in what are probably the most important two works of Morisco literature: first, the *Tafsira* or "Treatise" by the author known as "El Mancebo de Arévalo," an account of a journey in search of knowledge and science which the author conducts throughout different Spanish Morisco communities in the years immediately after the decrees of conversion. This *aljamiado* text was written in the early sixteenth century, and is a Muslim text with interwoven Christian threads of both a devotional and literary nature. Experts on El Mancebo's text have demonstrated his use of Thomas à Kempis's *Imitatio Christi* and literary texts such as *La Celestina* by Fernando de Rojas (Narváez Córdoba 2003). The Morisco text contains echoes of the Catholic principles of the *devotio moderna* together with the words of Petrarch, which Rojas translates and makes his own and which are in turn a quotation from Heraclitus. Second, a century later, an anonymous Morisco who had already been expelled from the Peninsula was to write, in Spanish and using Latin script, a text in Tunis entitled *Tratado de los dos caminos* ("Treatise of the two paths"), an account of the two paths along which men either lose themselves or accede to salvation. This book includes memorized texts from Lope de Vega, Góngora, and Quevedo, and makes reference to Spanish painting and theater of the period, as well as using and quoting from the usual works by Gazzali, Qadi Iyad, and Ahmad Zarruq. These two works, so far removed from each other in time and space, both contain a spiritual itinerary and a compendium of knowledge which they seek to transmit to those who come after and who will inevitably belong to an entirely new world. In short, *aljamiado* literature is a literature written by Moriscos for Moriscos. It is a "secret literature" (Galmés de Fuentes et al. 2005). The Moriscos were indeed a complex Islamic group, open to the transmission and translation of religious ideas, images, and emotions from the Christian milieu within which they lived. Subjected to the pressure of intense polemic, they could not help but define themselves through their confrontation and interaction with the world around them.

The Moriscos also wrote in Arabic. By far the most interesting example of this is the forgery known as the Lead Books of the Sacromonte, produced in Granada in the late sixteenth century. They were a series of texts written in Arabic on circular sheets of lead, in a supposedly ancient slanting Arabic script without diacritics or vowels, similar to the kind of writing used in talismans and magical writings. These works claimed to be a text from Christian antiquity, a gospel dictated in Arabic by the Virgin Mary to a group of Arab disciples who traveled with Saint James to Spain, where they founded the city of Granada and were martyred. This is a case of an allegedly Christian text constructed from Islamic sources: no references are made in it to any of the aspects of Christianity deemed unacceptable to Islam, such as the divine nature of Christ, the Holy Trinity, worship of images, or oral confession. The stories from the life of Jesus which it contains are taken from the life of Muhammad, and its vocabulary and spirituality are clearly Islamic. The forgery was carried out by Moriscos who had targeted two groups of potential readers. The first group was the Christian Church and civil authorities, to whom they wished to prove that Arabic was a Christian language, or that it could be one, and that there was therefore no reason to ban its use. It also sought to persuade this group of readers that the first Christians in Granada had been Arabs and that the Moriscos were therefore fully fledged Granadans and not aliens who had to be expelled. But the text could also be read from a Morisco point of view as a text of religious polemic directed against Christianity, as well as a way of upholding an eschatological dissimulation (that is to say, until the End of All Time, seen as very close) which spoke of a Christianity that had been cleansed and made admissible to secret followers of Islam. The text of the Lead Books showed a profound knowledge of the boxes that had to be ticked in order to guarantee it the success which it certainly enjoyed among the Christian authorities of Granada and the Spanish population in general. It provided "proof" of Saint James's journey to Spain, it spoke of the Immaculate Conception of Mary, and it offered up relics ensuring the sacred origin of Granada. The books were tremendously successful and continued to be considered genuine even after they were anathematized by the Vatican in 1682, a century after their first "discovery" (García-Arenal and Rodríguez Mediano 2010).

It was in an attempt to discover which Islamic texts the late sixteenth-century Granadan Moriscos who created the Lead Books may have been able to use that I first started to examine Inquisition material making reference to Islamic writings, especially books, and such material will be the subject of the main part of my essay. However, I would like first to outline briefly the nature of Inquisition proceedings against Moriscos.

## Inquisition and the erasure of memory

From the 1530s on, the Moriscos were subjected to persecution by the Inquisition as apostates, and were accused of *mahometizar* (lit. "Muhammadizing"). The Inquisition persecuted Moriscos suspected of engaging or shown to have engaged in Islamic activity, and catalogued in great detail the religious practices, prayers, beliefs, knowledge, and intentions of the Moriscos it brought to trial. Because of these trial records we know that a significant part of the Morisco population continued to observe Islamic practices (including some which were as difficult to carry out, given the circumstances, as the pilgrimage to Mecca) within a family and communal structure which in the areas where there were dense populations of Moriscos remained very closely knit.

The Inquisitors were especially keen to track down and persecute those known as *alfaquíes* (Arabic *faqih*), i.e. those with knowledge of the Law, who were accused of being "dogmatizers" who taught and spread Islamic principles or encouraged Moriscos to cling to Islamic beliefs and practices. This was considered the worst crime of all. However, the *alfaquíes* managed to hold on in the well-knit communities of Aragon and Valencia, and their presence was essential not only because of their role in imparting religious teachings but because they were mediators in conflicts and interpretations of the Law or in the arrangement of rituals. They were entrusted, for example, with the task of signaling the start of the month of Ramadan and, during that month, the moment at which "the star was seen" and fasting could be ended. The Moriscos took advantage of their employment in small-scale hawking from village to village or in the transport of merchandise to consult *alfaquíes* in the areas where they happened to find themselves.

The Inquisitors were also especially vigilant when it came to observing the activities of midwives and matrons or the older women who prepared brides or washed the chrism of Morisco children brought back to the community after being baptized. These women were in charge of the ceremony of the *fadas*, by which a child was given a Muslim name, a ceremony very frequently recorded in Inquisition trial proceedings. They were also responsible for teaching children prayers and rites as well as hygienic and feeding customs, a process which started at an age when the child was deemed to be wise enough not to talk about it outside the family home. These older women were therefore, together with the *alfaquíes*, the greatest "dogmatizers" and those who went from house to house upholding cultural habits in a private world perceived by Christians as a threat, like all forms of difference. The fields of humor, food, language, and sex form part of the "polemical confrontation" (to borrow Cardaillac's term) between Moriscos and Old Christians. Sex, and the obsession with how prolific the Moriscos were said to be given that they did not even refrain from "incestuous" marriages between cousins, also came to be seen as an alleged Morisco weapon for infiltrating and destroying Christian society. Such notions were linked to stereotypes of sexual incontinence which anti-Islamic religious polemic delighted in underlining in the biography of the Prophet Muhammad himself.

When the Cortes Valencianas banned the use of spoken and written Arabic in 1564 and Philip II followed suit through a 1567 decree which applied to the territories of the Crown of Castile, the Inquisition launched itself into a campaign directed against all traces of the Arabic language, written or spoken, which were unfailingly identified with the practice of Islam. Inquisition proceedings contain extremely detailed information on the language and its written forms, whether in trial records or reports on visits and confiscations. Books were found as a consequence of denunciations made against those who owned them, by embargo during raids of homes made specifically for that purpose, or accidentally during the course of a search for other things forbidden to the Moriscos, such as weapons. The Inquisition discussed within the bosom of its own institution the question of the status which should be granted to the Arabic books it constantly confiscated.[1] In practice, possession of a text written in the Arabic alphabet or the mere use of the spoken language led inexorably to a conviction for heresy. Identification of the language with the religion was unswerving and knew no exceptions (García-Arenal 2009b: 495–528).

## Inquisition and Arabic writings

Proof of the eagerness with which the Inquisition sought out and confiscated Arabic texts can be found in the records of every tribunal of the Holy Office, although such records have come down to us unevenly. For example, complete trial records only exist for Saragossa, Toledo, Cuenca, and Valencia (and not all those which were initiated), whereas from Granada or Llerena only the *relaciones de causa*, i.e. lists of summarized cases, have survived. It is therefore impossible to draw a complete and all-inclusive picture. However, the material which we do possess makes it possible to sketch out the following summary. The possession of books written in Arabic was, in Valencia, the accusation which most frequently brought Moriscos before the Inquisition (Halperin Dongui 1980: 115–64). In Saragossa, some 900 Inquisition records of trials of Aragonese Moriscos have survived, dated between 1568 and 1609: 409 of these Moriscos were accused of owning books written in Arabic (Fournel-Guérin 1979: 243–5). Inquisition records show that in Aragon there existed a veritable hive of bookselling activity, which involved the sale, above all, of copies of the Qur'an throughout the last third of the sixteenth century. There were also a number of Qur'anic schools, such as the one which was found to exist in Calanda in 1580 or another in Almonacid de la Sierra. During Inquisition interrogations, Moriscos mentioned schools where as many as fifty young men gathered to learn from a master the rudiments of the Arabic language and Islamic law, and there was also a network of contacts with *alfaquíes* from Valencia and Aragon who provided consultation services and books (Carrasco 1993: 192). It should be noted that the possession of books was not, however, necessarily indicative of knowledge of Arabic, as we will see on p. 47 (Vincent 2006b: 105–17). This was the case in Castile, where there was a clear general decline of both spoken and written Arabic from as early as the first quarter of the sixteenth century, and where Moriscos relied greatly on the communities of Granada and Valencia to obtain sacred books, translations, or instructions on ritual. After the arrival of the Granadan Moriscos who had been deported in 1570, the picture altered and there was a certain revival in knowledge of the language and in the ownership of books and writings, i.e. of Islamic culture in general. References to such items appear with great frequency in Inquisition trial records of the tribunal of Toledo, to which I will refer on pp. 50–1. In Extremadura, pockets of Arabic speakers held on throughout the sixteenth century in places like Hornachos. In 1540, the *alcaide* of the Holy Office of the Inquisition of Llerena made a request for more personnel to manage and supervise the Inquisition's jails because "the Morisco prisoners know Arabic and if we do not watch them very carefully they can talk to each other."[2]

However, except in Valencia, Inquisition material does not always allow us to distinguish between the possession of books or writings and knowledge of the language; nor does it allow us to arrive at reliable estimates of the degree of Arabic literacy in the different communities. An extra difficulty derives from the use of the terms *aljamía/aljamiado* by the Inquisition (and by some contemporary records) to denote either a Morisco who knew Castilian or a piece of Morisco writing which was written in Castilian using the Latin alphabet. For example, when the Inquisition recorded that in 1542 it had confiscated from Lope de Hinestrosa, a Morisco from Daimiel, a "book of polemic written in *aljamía*," this refers to a book written in, and probably translated into, Spanish.[3] Not a single reference has yet been found in Inquisition records to writings in what we now term *aljamía*, i.e. texts written in the Romance language but using Arabic script. This is because everything that was written using Arabic characters was assumed to be in the Arabic language – it must be remembered that the Inquisition only had employees who were familiar with Arabic in Valencia and Granada (regions where *aljamía* did not exist), and that the items confiscated in Aragon or Castile were not catalogued or studied until much later, generally by individuals who were not familiar with the Morisco milieu and who probably just ignored all those writings which they did not understand. In the sixteenth century the Inquisition's informers and interpreters were often also Moriscos, who limited themselves to following instructions and tried to determine which of the confiscated books were religious. The tag most often used was that of "alcoranes y libros de la secta de Mahoma" ("Qur'ans and books of the sect of Muhammad"). They did not trouble themselves by going any further or providing titles or information about content, since this was not required of them by the Inquisition. Despite this, the information provided by Inquisition records does shed light on some trials connected with Morisco *aljamiado* literature and its features. Let us examine one example which I find particularly interesting because it is related to the affair of the Lead Books of the Sacromonte. It was among these books that Marcus Dobelius, one of the translators who traveled to Spain from Rome to examine them, found reasons to argue that the texts were Islamic.

## Libraries and collections of books

In 1631, some twenty years after the Expulsion of the Moriscos, commissioners from the Toledo Tribunal of the Inquisition visited the territories under their jurisdiction. One of the places they visited was the town of Pastrana in La Alcarría, where they were informed that on two previous occasions "a large number" of books in Arabic had been found in houses left behind by expelled Moriscos. The Holy Office of Toledo made an official request for information concerning these findings in Pastrana (García-Arenal and Rodríguez Mediano 2010). The local archdeacon made a sworn statement to the effect that a cache of books had been found some sixteen years earlier (in about 1615) and another one nine years earlier, in 1622, in houses in the district known as Albaicín, which had been mainly occupied by Moriscos from Granada: "books in the Arabic tongue bound and with a bundle of sheaves of blue and red damask and borders of gold, he does not remember how many there were, in a house which the Moriscos left and which was close by the kitchen garden of the friars of San Francisco." The books were found in a cellar, inside bags containing sprigs of lavender (to protect them from the damp), and among them there were also books in Spanish. Another Inquisition document from 1622 confirms this story, stating that the Duke of Pastrana had told the Inquisitor General of the finding of the books, and that he had sent him "six sacks" of them. From the accounts declared by the cartwright who transported them and who charged a price for them based upon their weight, we know that these six sacks of books weighed 28 *arrobas* (approximately 325 kilos), which would seem to indicate a very considerable number of volumes. In highlighting this finding in Pastrana, which proves that books in Arabic were read in Castile right up to the period of the Expulsion, I wish also to show how inextricably interwoven *aljamiado* literature was with the works in Arabic which were acquired, saved, and copied by Arabic-speaking Muslims (both Mudejars and Moriscos) in the Iberian Peninsula and to insist that literature in *aljamía* was basically literature translated from Arabic. The fact that such translation took place raises issues concerning the knowledge of Arabic among the Castilian and Aragonese Morisco populations – for example, who chose the texts to be translated and who translated and codified them? These are questions to which I will return on p. 48.

Pastrana was a town in which many Granadan Moriscos had settled. Inquisition evidence allows us to see that the use of Arabic was maintained there up to the period of the Expulsion and even afterwards, for an indeterminate number of Moriscos stayed on in Pastrana to manage some of the tasks involved in the town's silk production industry. The same Inquisition visit of

1631 in which statements were made about the findings of books also produced a statement claiming that there were fifteen houses in Pastrana belonging to Moriscos who had not been expelled. The Inquisition emissary wrote that he had no wish to investigate this claim unless he was told to do so.[4] The Morisco problem was over and it was perhaps for that reason that part of the cache of books was preserved and could be studied.

## The survival of Arabic language

The books were examined by Marcus Dobelius, a Middle Eastern Christian who traveled to Spain from Rome, where he had been teaching Arabic at La Sapienza. Dobelius had been sent to Spain to translate the apocryphal texts of the Lead Books of the Sacromonte produced by Granadan Moriscos in the late sixteenth century (Rodríguez Mediano and García-Arenal 2006: 297–334). Dobelius recorded that he picked out the best items from among those he catalogued for the Holy Office, but that he, Dobelius, paid particular attention to the books which helped him to understand the context and Morisco sources of the Lead Books of the Sacromonte on which he was working. He wrote that among them were books on "philosophy, geometry, medicine, grammar and different vocabularies." Dobelius speaks of books in both Arabic and Castilian Spanish, but makes no reference to texts in *aljamía*. The books of the Pastrana collection which he mentions in most detail are Arabic books like the *Kitab al-shifa'* by the al-Qadi 'Iyad or the *Kitab al-anwar* by al-Bakri, which he drew upon to show that the stories of Jesus's life included in the Lead Books were in fact stories about the Prophet Muhammad. The books of "necromancy, spells and superstitions" which deal with seals (*sigilos*), the planets "where the seal of the Moon is written hexagonally, as by the author of the Lead Sheets," also enabled him to identify the formal provenance of the circle-shaped Lead Books and their writing system and signs. The sources included a *Kitab al-asrar*, or "Book of Secrets." Judging by Dobelius's description of the manuscript, this was an Arabic book which was exactly the same as an *aljamiado* version found in Ocaña and which was published and studied by Joaquina Albarracín Navarro and Juan Martínez Ruiz in 1987 under the title *Misceláneo de Salomón* (Albarracín Navarro and Martínez Ruiz 1987). This book was not very different from another *aljamiado* title recently published as the *Libro de los dichos maravillosos* by Ana Labarta.

For his study of the Lead Books, Dobelius made particular use of the *Qisas al-anbiya'*, or books of "Stories of the prophets," by al-Tha'labi and by Ibn Wathima which had appeared in Pastrana, with which he collated the story of Solomon's Seal exactly as it features in the Lead Books. He was able to show that this was the legendary Islamic story of Solomon and his signet ring, the object which allowed him to rule over demons and which gave him esoteric knowledge (Roisse 2006: 141–71). Also to be found in the Pastrana cache was an *Apología contra la ley de los cristianos* and a Spanish translation of the well-known *fatwa* of the man known as the "mufti of Oran," authorizing Moriscos to live on in the Iberian Peninsula hiding their beliefs and ritual practices without losing their status as Muslims, in addition to a series of legal treatises. The books of Pastrana thus included titles found in other collections of Morisco volumes, such as the collection of Arabic and *aljamiado* books which appeared in Almonacid de la Sierra.[5] Like that of Pastrana, this included works on magic and divination such as the previously mentioned *Libro de dichos maravillosos* and, in particular, a copy in Arabic of the *Qisas al-anbiya'* by Ibn Wathima and several other *aljamiado* texts also belonging to the genre of stories of the prophets, which had been very common in al-Andalus. The books from the Pastrana Morisco collection used by Marcus Dobelius (a collection which is now lost or is at least no longer a collection as such, although it was probably the source of some items held in the Vatican Library) are clearly of the same kind as those unearthed in other similar findings, i.e. in other caches of books hidden by Moriscos, except that in the case of Pastrana the collection seems to have been considerably richer and broader than in other places. It is also one of the few lots of books found in Castile (together with that of Ocaña) to include the aforementioned *Misceláneo de Salomón*. All of these books were probably brought, written, or, as it was then expressed, "*trasladados*" (lit. translated, i.e. copied) and preserved by Granadan Moriscos deported after the War of the Alpujarras of 1570. Let us take as an example other collections of Granadan books, such as those confiscated from Pedro de Mendoza, *capitán* of the Moriscos of Güéjar, in 1570, as is stated in proceedings brought against the Moriscos of Valdeinfierno. The books were taken to the Holy Office of Granada, where they were translated. Most of them contained "the law and sect of the Moors and what they must believe and perform according to the sect and law of the Moors and in the opinion of Muhammad" (Barrios Aguilera 2009: 144ff.). However, they also contained books of magic which dealt with "dreams and sneezing and other superstitious things." Another book found among the belongings of the Morisco leader contained "*nóminas* ('lists') which the Moors perform to bring about certain effects, in which they invoke and speak words with Muhammad; and the first of them is called the list of the messenger of God, with which they say that Muhammad cured all passions and illnesses; the others are for entering upon wars and talking to kings without fear. In all of them they name Muhammad and deny the Holy Trinity." Or there were the books of al-Jayyar, an *alfaquí* from Cútar (Malaga), who had a small collection of three manuscripts of legal and personal papers as well as poems of a prophetic nature, sermons and hadiths, and – inevitably – a manuscript on magic. Or the collection of books held by the Granadan Inquisition which was catalogued by its Arabic interpreter, Francisco López Tamarid (Ron de la Bastida 1958: 210–13).

There is also a resemblance to a collection of eighteen books which appeared in Muel (Aragon) and which the Inquisition attempted to confiscate. These books were catalogued by the Maronite Miguel Casiri, according to records in the Biblioteca Nacional de España.[6] Casiri, who also compiled the catalogue of Arabic books held at the Library of El Escorial, pointed out in his report and catalogue list of 1763 that some of the volumes from Muel were written in a Castilian Spanish "altered and corrupted by Arabic characters with such artifice that one who did not know the secret thereof would believe it to be another unknown language": Casiri is the first non-Morisco of whom we have record that he understood what *aljamía* was about. This collection included, as well as books on "civil and canon law," a dictionary and a grammar, a treatise on physics by Averroes, a work by al-Ghazzali, and another "*Libro de las Luces*" or *Kitab al-anwar* like the one found in Pastrana. This last book was extremely popular among the Moriscos, as can be seen from the existence of several *aljamiado* versions still preserved today, and which come from findings in Ricla, Uclés, and Urrea de Jalón (Lugo de Acevedo 2008). The work was even rewritten in verse form by an Aragonese Morisco, Mohamad Rabadán, and widely distributed in this form (Lasarte 1991: 73–270; Corriente 1990). The *Libro de las luces* is a thoroughly detailed study of the genealogy of the Prophet Muhammad, with the glorious deeds of the Prophet and all his descendants related in a legendary manner. It was a holy lineage which brought the Muslims closer to their Creator than any other people and invoked a series of glorious deeds which spoke of a triumphal past. The widespread popularity of the *Libro de las luces* is also attested to by Inquisition records, which link its success to its emphasis on past Muslim victories, described as "our glorious past deeds" (García-Arenal 1978: 87; Fournel-Guérin 1979: 251).

What did the Inquisition do with all these confiscated books? In many cases, they were burned or were stored in places where they suffered deterioration (or were lost). Such places included the prisons of the Holy Office. Ana Labarta records the curious and significant anecdote of the Morisco prisoners Jaime Alturi and Salvador Zuncar, from whom their prison *alcaide* had taken a Qur'an which they had hidden under a pillow. Zuncar declared that he had picked up the Qur'an after being taken prisoner "from a corner where there are many books lying around," and as they were "rotting away in the room they passed some of the time reading from the said book" (Labarta 1980: 125). On a few occasions, though not many, confiscated books were preserved or sold and went on to form part of collections in Spanish and foreign libraries. However, the proportion of books "saved" must have been very low if we consider the extent of ownership and circulation of books attested to in Inquisition records.

Such findings were made in the territories of the Crown of Castile and in Aragon. But *alja-miado* literature must also be understood within the framework of events in Valencia, an area where Arabic was spoken right up until the time of the Expulsion and where *aljamía* was never used. Valencia was, for those living in the territories close to it, a place from which books were supplied, a place of learning where scholars were trained and sought out. Valencia was, like Granada before the War of the Alpujarras, an access route to learning of the written language and to works of grammar. There were workshops where manuscripts were copied, with some centers such as Paterna especially active in this regard; unlike Aragon, the area was Arabic-speaking and in contact with North Africa. Inquisition records of the Castilian tribunals, especially those of Cuenca and Toledo, provide evidence of contacts with Valencia, where Moriscos traveled to learn the written language, to fetch Arabic books, and to receive religious instruction and liturgical guidance.

A fascinating recent book (Barceló and Labarta 2009) containing surviving documents and manuscripts concerning the Moriscos of Valencia from the Middle Ages until the Expulsion reveals a surprising thematic continuity between the items used by the Arabic-speaking Muslims of Valencia and those in the collections of Aragonese books, whether in Arabic or in *aljamía*. First, there were books on the sources of Islamic law: the Valencians had basic and important works of *fiqh* such as the *al-Muwatta'* of Malik and the commentaries of Ibn al-Jawzi and Ibn Muzayn, the *Risala* of Ibn Abi Zayd al-Qayrawani, with the commentaries by al-Jilani and Ibn al-Fajjar, the *Mukhtasar* by Jalil, and the *Mudawwana* by Sahnun. These works all deal with the subject of the doctrinal sources of Islamic law, both Sunni and *shari'a*, although works of applied law also circulated. This is important because it forces us to re-evaluate the traditional notion of the "deteriorated Islam" of the Moriscos. The proliferation and circulation of copies of the Qur'an throughout the kingdom of Valencia is extraordinarily significant. To quote the words of an individual arrested by the Inquisition in 1584: "he has read another Qur'an belonging to Sangarrén, an inhabitant of Segorbe … and another Qur'an belonging to Miguel Marrán – a prisoner – he has read many times, when he and the daughter and all of them lent it to him over the balcony … and he has also read the Qur'an in other places, wherever he went, asking for it from those who had it for it is everywhere," to which the accused added that "some know how to read and others do not, but the good Moor is proud to have it at home; and it used to be only the *alfaquíes* who had them all together but now they can be found in many homes because they are sold cheaply" (Barceló and Labarta 2009: 57). Contacts with North Africa through relatives who had fled the Peninsula made it easier for the Valencians to acquire books. In 1608, one Gaspar Rahech was convicted as an *alfaquí*, because

> he usually carried with him the book of the Qur'an to read out the sect of Muhammad; and he had in his home a mosque for the teaching of it, where many Morisco men and women would go to learn; and twelve *alfaquines* came together and agreed that they lacked a book called Hizbalbac, which was a large book containing in detail all of the sect of Muhammad and it could not be found in these kingdoms but in Algeria, and they decided to send one of the older *alfaquines* for it.

> *(Barceló and Labarta 2009: 63)*

It is striking that the book which the *alfaquíes* felt they needed should be the *Hizb al-bahir* by al-Shadili, one of the most renowned mystical thinkers in Islam, after whom one of the most important mystical brotherhoods in Western Islam was named.

Science was another important field in the culture of the Islamic community of Valencia, with medicine seen as particularly important. Works on medical themes seized by the Valencian Inquisition are second only to those on religion, and the activities of physicians, healers, and surgeons also feature significantly.

Among the documents published by Barceló and Labarta there are a large number which make reference to a series of activities relating closely to science and remedies, and which were known at the time by names such as witchcraft, spells, charms, talismans, treasure-hunting, divination, and so on. Such writings are also related to prophesies, interpretations of dreams, and horoscopes. We now tend to use the term "magic" to cover all such activities, but the Inquisition catalogued them under the title of "superstitions," a label also used by nineteenth-century scholars. All such themes play a prominent role in *aljamiado* literature, as can be seen in the recent book by the *aljamía* specialist Luce López-Baralt (López-Baralt 2009). Such interests show that Morisco Islam was very close to that of the contemporary Maghreb, where the cult of the families descended from the Prophet was highly important. Such a cult derived from and at the same time encouraged extraordinary worship of the figure of Muhammad, the perfect and inimitable example, and the deeds and victorious battles of the Prophet and his followers acquired a special significance for the defeated Moriscos. This was a set of beliefs in which magic, esotericism, and mystical brotherhoods caused worship of the Prophet Muhammad to overlap with that of the figure of Solomon, a hero versed in magical powers and a superhuman figure in the popular mind who must have served as a great consolation to the Moriscos.

## Circulation of books and processes of translation

These Valencian findings show that *aljamiado* literature was a fully Islamic literature mainly derived from translations from Arabic, as was claimed as long ago as 1958 by L.P. Harvey and as has been confirmed in more recent work by Barceló and Labarta, Wiegers and others. The thematic coincidences between the two literatures, the systematic matching of their titles, is just one more proof of this idea. There is, however, one aspect of *aljamiado* literature which sets it apart, and that is of course its use of Romance (vernacular Spanish), a language common to Christians and Moriscos. For the latter, the conceptual contents and values embedded in words and idiomatic formulations must have conditioned their thought structures and produced at least a partial or unconscious acceptance of the Christian and Hispanic culture in which they were immersed. Mere use of the language would have forced the person speaking or writing it to establish a tacit dialogue with the culture which he or she rejected, or at least defended himself or herself from. López-Baralt claims that some of the original Arabic texts were transformed when expressed in *aljamiado* and became proselytizing texts and even works of polemic precisely because of this inevitable process of dialogue and participation in that which was being rejected.

If most *aljamiado* texts were translations from Arabic, who made these translations? Clearly, it must have been the *alfaquíes*. The perfection of a technique for translating Arabic into *aljamiado*, the existence of a system of standardized transliteration, and a community of use of religious terminology imply at the very least a series of contacts and agreements among *alfaquíes*, the "guardians of Islam."[7] It also implies that decisions were made concerning what it was necessary or advisable to translate from Arabic (in this context, we must remember Yça de Guebir and his Romance translation of the Qur'an). In the Morisco period these *alfaquíes* were no longer *fuqaha'* in the classical sense of the term but men with a grounding in reading and writing who had access to legal and religious works, and who could therefore read out passages from the Qur'an to an illiterate audience. Morisco populations were mainly rural and, like their Christian contemporaries, a high percentage of them were illiterate. Statements made to the Inquisition tribunals of Castile provide ample proof of this action of reading aloud texts which were translated at the same time as they were read out. One example is provided by Juan de Hinestrosa, of Daimiel (Miller 2008). He is said to have met other Moriscos "in a certain gathering-place where they read aloud a Moorish book written in the Arabic language containing prayers of the Moors … and the person who read it out explained in Spanish what was written in Arabic in the said book." Or, as another witness declared, many persons of quality gathered and met in his home:

> new Christians who were Moors and descendants of those he knew well and thus gathered together the said Lope de Hinestrosa and another person read out to them from a book of the Qur'an and from other books of the sect of Muhammad which were written in the script of the Moors, all of which was done with the doors of his home locked and even with a guard on the door so that no-one but those people they desired could enter … the person who read aloud then explained the text in the Castilian language.

Or there is the case of Brianda Suarez, tried in Toledo in 1546–7, who participated in meetings of the same kind as those just described:

> Persons descended from generations of Moors gathered to read a book or quire written in the Castilian language which contained Moorish prayers and other things and the said Brianda and the other persons heard it with attention and devotion because they were believers in the sect of Muhammad and had the intention of Moors and read in the said book or quire a kind of story of how a knight from Axen came asking after Moorish things and their old prophets and the said book or quire also contained Moorish prayers written in Arabic and translated into Castilian, especially the prayer of alhandu and coluha and in the said gathering the said Brianda and other Morisco persons spoke of how the law of the Moors was a good law.

The *alfaquíes* were thus teachers and transmitters of various forms of knowledge to relatives, friends, or neighbors, and their knowledge and wisdom were recognized and acknowledged. In this way a veritable semi-clandestine plot of cultural transmission took shape in the mid-sixteenth century which can be traced through the Inquisition records. As it was put during the trial of Salama ibn 'Ali, an *alfaquí* from Yátova in Valencia, in 1578, the defendant, wanting "the sect of Muhammad to spread and grow, has studied and read Arabic books for many years, and has two panniers full of them so that as an *alfaquí* he may teach new Christians" (Barceló and Labarta 2009: Doc. 98). Contacts with Valencia are frequently mentioned in the Castilian tribunals: for example in the records for Álvaro de Córdoba, a Morisco from Granada who was tried in Toledo between 1589 and 1592 because he "had had in his possession some books of the sect of Muhammad in which there were lists and prayers from the Qur'an and he had read aloud from them in the presence of others of his caste." Moriscos from Toledo are guilty of bringing Arabic books from Valencia.[8] They also received translated Islamic writings from this region. I will cite some examples from the tribunal of Toledo: in the trial records of one Juan de Sosa there is a letter sent by a Morisco from Valencia which related miracles performed by Muhammad and explained the hours at which the five daily prayers had to be said. The letter was written in Castilian Spanish and many copies of it were made for circulation among the new Christians of Arévalo.[9] Or there is the case of Antonio Casado, who had a book in which "on one side the prayer was written in Moorish and on the other it was written and translated into Romance, and in such a way were all the prayers in the said book laid out." These Castilian Moriscos, who had no real knowledge of the language, were assailed by doubts about whether to pray in Arabic or in Spanish. In the trial of Juan de Sosa, the accused said that he had asked if it was better for the new Christians who met him in Toledo to pray in Arabic or in Castilian Spanish (although he, apparently, spoke Arabic) and he was given the answer

> that they ought not to pray in Arabic but in Spanish because praying in Arabic, as they did not understand what they were saying they could have no devotion in what they were praying and they would be thinking of other things, and the said Juan de Sosa asked what prayers they should say and was told that they should praise the Lord as well as they could and the said Juan de Sosa, with the belief that he has had and continues to have as a Moor, has always said and continues to say his Moorish prayers in Arabic.

This statement is complemented by another made by Jerónimo de Rojas, who said that the Christians were deceived by their priests and councils, who used Latin which was understood by no one. In any event, the translation process ("*traslado*," as it is expressed in the records) was a constant one. This is confirmed by the same trial of Jerónimo de Rojas, from Toledo, who had told another new Christian that he would like to know whether

> in Toledo he would find very wise men who would sell him books translated into Castilian in such a way that he understood them all very well, and asking if they would be clearly written he was told that it depended on the money available for it, and that there are very learned and wise men who correct them and these men will give him to understand all that the other has written.

He even mentions one Gaspar de Soria, "who was able to give him very good books from his sect translated into Spanish."

This trial of Jerónimo de Rojas reveals the respect and care with which *alfaquíes* and "learned persons" were sought out and treated both in Valencia and Granada. Rojas had found "news of a great *alfaquí* that there is in Málaga or in a little place close to it whose name is García and who knows a lot about the law and has large books." And another witness at the same trial said that "Rojas had been given the news that a great *alfaquí* had been condemned to row in the galleys and was attempting with the assistance of the merchants (Moriscos of Toledo) to raise 500 ducados, for he could not be ransomed for less."

There was, then, a constant need for translation. But the references we find in the Castilian trials are to translation into Castilian Spanish and using Castilian Spanish script. The Inquisition may simply have believed all writings in the Arabic alphabet to be written in Arabic. In any event, very few *aljamiado* books from Castile have survived.

There is also frequent evidence in the Inquisition records of the possession of copies of the Qur'an, which were always deeply prized by their owners, for whom they had an added emotional value: they touched them, kissed them, kept them very close to their persons or in their clothing, very often under the mattress, and they were deeply upset when these books were confiscated from them. Such was the case of Francisco de la Guerra, a Morisco from Osuna, who was found in possession of a Qur'an and tried to recover it by bribing an Inquisition official, whom he also sought to persuade not to file a report on the finding.[10]

Another inhabitant of Osuna, Alonso de Madrid, had a book in Arabic taken from him, and was deeply troubled by the confiscation. Inquisition experts later decided it was the "Qur'an of Muhammad."[11] There were also many cases among women, most of whom were illiterate. One example is provided by Catalina Mandarán.[12] A neighbor saw her

> leaving her home in an errand carrying a bundle beneath her shawl. And going after her [he saw that] she reached out with her hand to pass the bundle on to another Morisco woman. And not being able to do so, she hid it under her skirts. And taking it from her with great force and in the face of great resistance he saw that it was a book written in Arabic.

Or there was the case of Ángela Magón, an inhabitant of Elda,[13] who

> had placed in her bed, beneath the mattress, a little book like a book of hours and she tried to hide it and keep it from sight, and then they took it from her and saw that it was written in Arabic … and because she cried and protested so much they gave it back to her and then the priests came and took it from her and having found out that the said book contained prayers taken from the Qur'an of Muhammad she was taken prisoner.

All of this goes to prove that the language, especially in its written form, acquired a talismanic force and that the revealed written Word was seen by Moriscos as their best protection. A very large number of trial records make reference to the possession by Moriscos of papers or small fragments written in Arabic and containing *cédulas* ("sheets") or *nóminas* ("lists"), often described by their Arabic name *hirz* ("amulet") in trials. These were amulets or talismans containing a verse from the Qur'an together with magical tables, signs, or symbols which had various protective, preventive, or curative properties. They were generally wrapped in a small piece of waxed cloth like a scapulary and kept close to the body, under the arm, or sewn into the skirts of women. Ana Labarta carried out a study of the important collection of amulets gathered for the trials of Valencian Moriscos, but references to them abound in the records of the Inquisition tribunals of every region (Labarta 1980). Moriscos, and especially Morisco women, put up tremendous resistance whenever Inquisition officials tried to prise such amulets from them. For example, there was the woman called Beatriz Zahori who was found to be carrying a piece of writing in her clothing and who defended herself vigorously from attempts to take it from her, although she later alleged "that she was not defending the piece of paper but was angry with the man because he put his hands on her breasts, and being an unmarried woman she took this as an affront." When she was eventually deprived of the text "she became overwhelmed with grief and crying." In almost every case of the finding and confiscation of an amulet, the owner wept, fainted, struggled, and fought, showing signs of extreme pain and consternation. This was especially true of women.

The woman in this case, as in many others, was illiterate. The function of the written word was not dependent on its being read and understood but was related to the power which the believer assigned to that writing. In other words, the word did not necessarily form part of an act of communication but took on a magical or talismanic character, and was used as such. This magical function of writing was not independent of the work of the *alfaquíes*, who were generally the makers of such talismans. Thus, in Arévalo, Francisco Hernández was said to have given a Morisco woman a whole series of Arabic books in his possession with instructions to keep them safely for him, at a time when Inquisition officials were about to seize them from him. Francisco Hernández had once argued with another Morisco about fasting regimes, and "he said that he had the book of the Qur'an at home and that he was learning to be an *alfaquí* in his home town and that he knew more about that law in his sleep than Agustin when waking." We do not know what his home town was, but when Francisco left the Inquisition jail

> he went to Arévalo to ask the converts for help in paying the fine imposed upon him by this holy office and they assisted him with what they could and the said Francisco gave certain *cédulas* in Arabic to many of the converts of Arévalo. The accused says he does not remember the name of these *cédulas* in Arabic ... they are good for fevers and other illnesses which people have.[14]

The information provided by Inquisition material sheds a very precise light on the need for translation and on the issue of who carried out such tasks. Above all, it tells us something about the talismanic value of writing in Arabic for the Moriscos. It is also worth noting that in the cultural milieu memory was important and had tremendous prestige, to the extent that different authorities claimed to be (or were said to be) wise because of the books they had memorized, not because of the books they owned.

To summarize, we are faced with the production of copies of books and the process of translation occurring in the heart of communities conditioned by a lack of intellectual elites, by a difficulty in the circulation of knowledge. What we also see is that knowledge nevertheless survived and works circulated up until the time of the Expulsion, and that these works were very much the same as those which were used in the contemporary Maghreb. This survival of the maintenance and transmission of knowledge was merged with the immersion in the Castilian language of the Moriscos, with their knowledge of and participation in Christian culture even in some of its religious manifestations such as processions, burials, and Christmas plays. It is the conjunction of all these elements which makes Morisco Islam such a singular and profoundly interesting phenomenon.

As one last illustration, let us consider a brief anecdote taken from a treatise of religious polemic against Islam: in 1519 (i.e. before the 1526 decree of conversion), Martín de Figuerola, a priest who was preaching to convince the Muslims of Valencia and Aragon to abandon Islam, wrote a treatise entitled *Confutación del Alcoran* in which he reported a story he claimed to have heard from the Muslim *qadi* of Cocentaina (Valencia). The latter had told him that in marriage contracts between local Muslims it was customary for women to demand that their husbands take them to the capital city of Valencia for the springtime festivities of Corpus Christi and those of the Virgin Mary in August. Or another one, which includes, as in all Iberian polemical arenas, *conversos* or new converts from Judaism: in the market of Saragossa, on a Sunday in September 1487, a group of women and men were watching a play (*entremés*). The actors, Moors (Mudejars – the date is previous to conversion), were representing the biblical story of the golden calf. A *conversa* present in the public watching the play exclaimed: "and the Christians let this happen! They let the Moors express contempt for the religion of Moses" (Gutwirth 1996: 273).

This small yet fascinating anecdote points to the existence in sixteenth-century Iberia of a strong polemical milieu which did not impede the existence of transversal currents common to different religious groups, areas of local religiosity in which different religions overlapped, and fuzzy or hybrid sorts of religiosity which indicate the blurring of clear ascriptions, categories, and borders (García-Arenal 2012). These processes remain insufficiently explored and they make the study of the Moriscos a subject of great and multifaceted interest. It is this process which makes Moriscos so relevant for the study of other Muslim groups in Europe and in the West. The case of Moriscos provides the possibility of observing the tension between joint movements of assimilation and resistance, of integration and marginalization, both at the intersection and in the interstices in which Moriscos lived. Especially, I think, it gives evidence of how well-defined and generalizing categories (such as "Muslims") do not let us see the wide variety included in the groups so labeled or the differences which are included in a single term which can no longer be accepted at face value but is in need of differentiation by historians.

## Notes

1  Archivo Histórico Nacional (from now on AHN), Inquisición, Libro 1239. 411–16.
2  AHN, Inquisición, Libro 574. f.75/96v.
3  AHN, Inquisición, Leg. 3205.2.
4  AHN, Inquisición, Leg. 3105, 1, abril de 1631.
5  Preserved in the Library of the Centro de Humanidades del CSIC in Madrid (as part of the collection known as "Manuscritos de la Junta" because it belonged to the Junta para Ampliación de Estudios before the CSIC, its administrative heir). A catalogue of it has been made by F. Ribera, as well as a digitized version of the whole collection.
6  I am grateful to Fernando Rodríguez Mediano, who is working on these records in the Biblioteca Nacional de España, for allowing me to consult his notes.
7  Fournel-Guérin (1979).
8  AHN, Inquisición Toledo, Leg. 192.3.
9  AHN, Inquisición Toledo, Leg. 197.6.
10  AHN, Inquisición, Leg. 2075.14.
11  AHN, Inquisición, Leg. 2075.15
12  AHN, Inquisición, Libro 938, f.263r.
13  AHN, Inquisición, Leg. 2022.9
14  AHN, Inquisición Toledo, Leg. 192.15.

## Bibliography

Albarracín Navarro, J. and Martínez Ruiz, J. (1987) *Medicina, farmacopea y magia en el "Misceláneo de Salomón" (Texto árabe, traducción, glosas aljamiadas, estudio y glosario)*, Granada: Universidad.

Amelang, J. (2011) *Historias paralelas. Judeoconversos y moriscos en la España Moderna*, Madrid: Akal.

Barceló, C. and Labarta, A. (2009) *Archivos moriscos. Textos árabes de la minoría islámica valenciana.1401–1608*, Valencia: Universidad.

Barrios Aguilera, M. (2009) *La suerte de los vencidos. Estudios y reflexiones sobre "la cuestión morisca,"* Granada: Universidad y legado Andalusí.

Barrios Aguilera, M. and García-Arenal, M. (eds.) (2006) *Los Plomos del Sacromonte. Invención y tesoro*, Valencia, Granada, and Saragossa: Universidad.

Benítez Sánchez-Blanco, R. (2001) *Heróicas decisiones. La Monarquía Católica y los moriscos valencianos*, Valencia: Institució Alfons el Magnànim.

Cardaillac, L. (1977) *Morisques et chrétiens, un affrontement polémique (1492–1640)*, Paris: Klienseck.

Carrasco, R. (1993) "Le Refus d'assimilation des morisques: aspects politiques et culturels d'après les sources inquisitoriales," in Cardaillac, L. (ed.) *Les Morisques et leur temps*, Paris: Edisud, pp. 169–216.

Corriente, F. (1990) *Relatos píos y profanos del manuscrito aljamiado de Urrea de Jalón*, Prólogo de Ma. Jesús Viguera, Saragossa: Fundación Fernando el Católico.

Fonseca, G. (2003) *Relación y ejercicio espiritual sacado y declarado por el Mancebo de Arévalo en nuestra lengua castellana*, Madrid: Fundación Menéndez Pidal.

Fournel-Guérin, J. (1979) "Le Livre et la civilisation écrite dans la communauté morisque aragonaise (1540–1620)," *Mélanges de la Casa de Velazquez* 15: 243–5.

Galmés de Fuentes, A., Villaverde Amieva, J.C., and López-Baralt, L. (2005) *Tratado de los dos caminos, por un morisco refugiado en Túnez (Ms. S2 de la Colección Gayangos, Biblioteca de la Real Academia de la Historia)*, Instituto Universitario Seminario Menéndez Pidal (Universidad Complutense de Madrid), Seminario de Estudios Árabo-Románicos, Universidad de Oviedo.

García-Arenal, M. (1978) *Inquisición y moriscos. Los procesos del Tribunal de Cuenca*, Madrid: Siglo XXI.

——(2009a) "Religious Dissent and Minorities: The Morisco Age," *Journal of Modern History* 81(4): 888–920.

———(2009b) "The Religious Identity of the Arabic Language and the Affair of the Lead Books of the Sacromonte of Granada," *Arabica* 56(6): 495–528.

———(2012) "A Catholic Muslim Prophet: Agustín de Ribera, the Boy 'Who Saw Angels'," *Common Knowledge* 18(2): 267–91.

García-Arenal, M. and Rodríguez Mediano, F. (2010) *Un Oriente español: los moriscos y el Sacromonte en tiempos de Contrarreforma*, Madrid: Marcial Pons.

———(2013) *The Orient in Spain: Converted Muslims, the Forged Lead Books of Granada and the Beginnings of Orientalism*, Leiden: Brill.

Gutwirth, E. (1996) "Gender, History and the Judeo-Christian Polemic," in Limor, O. and Stroumsa, G. *Contra Iudaeos. Ancient and Medieval Polemics between Christian and Jews*, Tübingen: JCB Mohr, pp. 257–78.

Halperin Dongui, T. (1980) *Un conflicto nacional, moriscos y cristianos viejos en Valencia*, Valencia: Instituciò Alfons el Magnanim.

Harvey, L.P. (1992) *Muslims in Spain, 1500 to 1614*, Chicago: University of Chicago Press.

Labarta, A. (1980) "Inventario de los documentos árabes contenidos en procesos inquisitoriales contra moriscos valencianos conservados en el Archivo Histórico Nacional de Madrid (legajos 548–56)," *Al-Qantara* 1: 115–64.

Lasarte, J.A. (1991) *Poemas de Mohamad Rabadán. Canto de las lunas. Día del juicio. Discurso de la luz. Los nombres de Dios*, Saragossa: Universidad.

López-Baralt, L. (2009) *La literatura secreta de los últimos musulmanes de España*, Madrid: Trotta.

Lugo de Acevedo, M.L. (ed.) (2008) *El Libro de las luces. Leyenda aljamiada sobre la genealogía de Mahoma*, Madrid: Sial Ediciones.

Miller, K. (2008) *Guardians of Islam: Religious Authority and Muslim Communities of Late Medieval Spain*, New York: Columbia University Press.

Narváez Córdoba, M.T. (2003) *Tratado (Tafsira) del Mancebo de Arévalo*, Madrid: Trotta.

Rodríguez Mediano, F. and García-Arenal, M. (2006) "De Diego de Urrea a Marcos Dobelio, intérpretes y traductores de los Plomos," in Barrios, M. and García-Arenal, M. (eds.) *Los Plomos del Sacromonte. Invención y tesoro*, Valencia and Granada: Universidad, pp. 297–334.

Roisse, Ph. (2006) "*La Historia del sello de Salomón*. Estudio, edición crítica y traducción comparada," in Barrios, M. and García-Arenal, M. (eds.) *Los Plomos del Sacromonte: Invención y tesoro*, Valencia and Granada: Universidad, pp. 141–71.

Ron de la Bastida, R. (1958) "Manuscritos árabes en la Inquisición granadina (1582)," *Al-Andalus* 23: 210–13.

Vincent, B. (2006a) *El río morisco*, Valencia: Universidad.

———(2006b) "Reflexión documentada sobre el uso del árabe y de las lenguas románicas en la España de los moriscos (ss. XVI–XVII)," in *El río morisco*, Valencia: Universidad, pp. 105–17.

# 3

# Muslims and Islam[1] in Sicily from the mid-eleventh to the end of the twelfth century

## Contemporary perceptions and today's interpretations

*Annliese Nef*

There is a tendency in the Mediterranean countries of Europe to forget or to ignore, more often than not, the Islamic past of a noticeable part of the region. This is true for Spain and al-Andalus, but even more for Sicily,[2] Malta, or the southern Italian mainland (as we are reminded by Marazzi 2007; Metcalfe 2009 is still focused on Sicily), let alone when it comes to the important Muslim presence in medieval Europe which has been recently underlined and is increasingly being investigated (Dakhlia and Vincent 2011; Dakhlia and Kaiser 2013). Fortunately, these conceptions are slowly changing, but in a certain way, and paradoxically, for Italy the precursory researches were made on what has been usually called "Norman Sicily," an expression justly criticized (Metcalfe 2002: 289; 2003: 24–5), rather than on the previous period of its history. Even more, the interest of the Sicilian political authorities in this "Islamic" past and its promotion have been focused predominantly on eleventh- to twelfth-century Sicily rather than on ninth- to eleventh-century Islamic Sicily.

Since Michele Amari (1806–89), who gave birth to the first scientific and systematic approach to the history of what he called "the Muslims of Sicily" from the ninth to the thirteenth century (Nef 2010a), and until the recent evolution we just recalled, the main historiographical current has presented the Hautevilles' period predominantly as one of insertion in the European context for Sicily. For a long time, the history of medieval Sicily has thus seemed to begin with the twelfth century, while the high Middle Ages have long been forgotten (Nef and Prigent 2006). Nonetheless, since the 1990s a few researchers, among them Adalgisa De Simone, Jeremy Johns, and Alex Metcalfe, have drawn attention from distinct points of view to what has been considered the Islamic dimension of the Hautevilles' elaboration (De Simone 1996, 1999a, 1999b; Johns 2002; Metcalfe 2003). This evolution was the first manifestation of a renewed interest in the "Islamic" dimension of Sicily's medieval history.

We will tackle two questions here: What do we know about the evolution of the Sicilian Arab Muslim population during the eleventh and twelfth centuries? And how were the elements of this period which are today considered Islamic, or even Muslim, perceived by the Hautevilles' contemporaries? What makes this question difficult is that Sicily experienced Islamic domination immediately before the period examined here. At the heart of the debate have thus often been, in one way or another, the possible continuities between the two epochs. We will suggest that this is not the most effective way to approach eleventh- and twelfth-century Sicily from a methodological point of view.

## Sicily in the mid-eleventh century: needing original solutions

In order to understand better what is at stake, it is necessary to describe the Sicilian situation when the Hautevilles first set foot on the island. We will thus see what problems they faced and the limits which informed the solutions they promoted. Let us insist, in these liminary lines, on the fact that "the Hautevilles" here refers to the milieu that elaborated the eleventh- to twelfth-century State in Sicily rather than to the members of the dynasty, who could not have done much on their own.

In the 1040s, the Kalbid emirate which administered the island in the name of the Fatimids, an Ismaili Shi'i dynasty, imploded and gave birth to autonomous political entities centered around the main Sicilian cities (Palermo, Syracuse, Catania, Agrigento, Mazara) which have been compared to the contemporary Andalusian *tayfas* (the small political entities born after the end of the Umayyad caliphate of Cordoba). The tensions between these Sicilian units were recurrent. One of these episodes incited Ibn al-Thumna to seek help against his adversaries on the continent, where groups of mercenaries of Norman origin had established an earldom, whose capital was Mileto. His choice suggests that contacts between the two banks of the Messina straits were maintained all through the Islamic period and even later, in spite of the emergence of a Norman authority in Calabria.

Once on the Sicilian side, and after the death of Ibn al-Thumna, Robert Guiscard and Roger, two brothers and members of the Hauteville family, began to conquer the island, sustained in their enterprise by the pope, though from a distance. This conquest was not an easy task: it required their efforts from 1061–2 to 1092. It thus took the shape of a slow takeover. Moreover, since before the Islamic conquest the island had been a Byzantine province between the sixth and the middle of the ninth century, the idea of a *Reconquista* was absent in the enterprise led by the Hautevilles. Even if the papacy could see in this intervention the opportunity to get back the lands it owned and which were confiscated by Constantinople in the mid-eighth century, the pope was on too bad terms with the Normans to really nourish this dream (Loud 2002). As for contemporary texts describing the conquest, they contain almost no allusion to holy war (Bresc 2003) and present themselves rather as the celebration of an elected people: the Normans (Nef 2011: 53–61).

In order to apprehend better what happened in twelfth-century Sicily, it has to be remembered that the historical insular context was at this time characterized by a unique conjunction, which would then become a little more familiar in Europe and in the Levant. It was the first time a Latin, very minority, group of conquerors took control of a majority Muslim population. Whereas the presence of the Muslims who evolved in medieval Europe was as a minority and temporary, that of non-Muslims in the *dar al-islam* (the regions administered by governments which defined themselves as Muslim) was stable and as the majority for several centuries. Thus, unlike the Muslims did for the *ahl al-dhimma* – the non-Muslims whose presence was accepted in the Islamic world, mainly Christians, Jews, and Zoroastrians, although they were subjected to an inferior juridical status and were taxed more heavily than the Muslims – and even if the elaboration of this status did take some time in the Islamic world, the Christians of the Latin world, although they accepted a Muslim presence, temporary more often than not, did not give a specific juridical status to the Muslims in Europe before the Sicilian experiment. The problem was indeed not a simple one since the Christians considered islam a heresy, but in contrast to Judaism, which had preceded Christianity, did not interpret it as a witness of the Old Alliance.

The difficulty was all the more true as the Normans were themselves considered good Christians neither by the inhabitants of south Italy who had to put up with their exactions nor by the papacy they did not obey. Their refusal to participate in the First Crusade could not but reinforce this general suspicion. Moreover, the Hautevilles themselves were considered *parvenus*, adventurers, and certainly not future kings (Houben 2002: 11–12).

In this context, the specificities and obstacles we just evoked are easily explained, although they do not induce in a mechanical way *one* solution, which is why the Hautevilles had to be inventive in order to benefit as much as possible from Sicily's prosperity and strategic position in the Mediterranean.

## Taxes and law: a reinterpretation of the Islamic State by the Hautevilles

The solution they imagined was indeed original: rather than developing a feudal monarchy and the seigneurialization of the Sicilian countryside, they chose to develop a fiscal state. Contrary to what might be thought, and as Jeremy Johns has shown (Johns 2002), this policy was neither conceived nor realized as the prolongation of an anterior system. The preceding administration had been shaken by the disappearance of the Kalbid emirate and a thirty-year conquest. Thus, the Hautevilles were inspired by contemporary systems, predominantly that of the Fatimids. In a nutshell: if the fiscal state the Hautevilles promoted was certainly based on conceptions and practices shared by both Byzantium and Islam, they acted more as restorers and reformers than as conservatives. Although the general philosophy of the fiscal state had been present during the Islamic period in Sicily, the continuities exist in the view of today's observers rather than in twelfth-century practices.

In this construction, the role of George of Antioch, a native of Antioch and a long-time official in the Ifriqiyan revenue system, who was Roger II's main adviser from the 1120s until his death in 1151, was probably important, although not exclusively so. It is underlined even by Arabic sources, and in particular al-Maqrizi, who, in his fifteenth-century biography of George writes that he was in charge of the offices (*dawāwīn*) of Sicily and "amassed the revenues and organized the foundations of the kingdom" (al-Maqrizi 1991: 18–20; for an English version, see Johns 2002: 80–2, esp. 81 and 82; De Simone 1999a, 2009). George's good knowledge of the Ifriqiyan taxation (unlike the historians, who unfortunately know very little about it in the twelfth century because of lack of documentation) probably explains his role. At this point, let us underline that the main individuals who knew Arabic and introduced or maintained Islamic administrative elements at court never had a Sicilian origin during the twelfth century, and that they were all Christians (or rather they were expected to be so and considered as such), either because they had converted or because they had never been Muslim. Moreover, a significant number of them were slaves and eunuchs. The promotion of newcomers to very high positions, even slaves, is a common Islamic (and Byzantine) practice of government. It clearly inspired the Hautevilles.

The principles of the Islamic fiscal system were in some way reversed, the Jews and the Muslims paying a poll-tax which underlined their inferiority, called *jizya*, and a land tax. As for the status of the Christians who already lived on the island when the Hautevilles conquered it, it is not very clear. Without entering into detail, the Arab Muslim population, among whom some Christians are documented in the region south of Palermo, was divided into three statuses, according to their link with the land they cultivated (Nef 2011: 481–516). This supposed an administration which issued a list of taxpayers and maintained the limits of the fiscal units. These specific tasks, assumed by the *diwan al-ma'mur* (the "prosperous (royal) office") and the *diwan al-tahqiq al-ma'mur* (the "prosperous (royal) office of verification"), which were in charge of investigations, gave birth to documentation in Arabic or, more often, bilingual Arabic–Greek. Such articulation supposed the coexistence of a local administration and of local elites able to play the role of intermediaries with taxpayers and, most probably, the existence of local archives.

As for the Latin barons, they were the beneficiaries of what appear to be fiscal concessions more than land concessions, a practice more akin to that of the Islamic *iqṭā'*, or fiscal concession, than to the Latin fief. They were thus in a situation of dependency on an administration which used a language they, at least as far as the first generation of conquerors (or of Latin immigrants who arrived after the conquest) is concerned, could not understand. If there were other reasons which led the Latin aristocrats to denounce what they considered to be a monarchy that did not make enough room for Latin magnates in the king's entourage, it is clear that they saw as positive neither this way of limiting seigneurial realities nor the distance imposed by the Hautevilles and their state apparatus between them and the center of power. This is all the more true as the aristocracies of conquests or frontiers are often more egalitarian than others, their cohesion being reinforced by the idea of a "common enemy" (Bonnassie 2000: 579 about Catalonia): the distance imposed by the Hautevilles was thus even less easily accepted.

Following the same logic, the Hautevilles, as did the Islamic State, let each group, be it Jewish, Christian, or Muslim, administer itself according to its law, as far as civil matters were concerned. This aspect is documented by surviving Arabic Palermitan notarial documents, written according to the Malikite school of law. Palermitan Muslim judges (*qadi*) thus appear during the whole of the twelfth century (Nef 2011: 322–3; Johns 2002: 88–90).

The situation in the rural areas is little known, although the society reflected by the fiscal lists appears diverse. The role and the exact definition of the *quwwad* (pl. of *qa'id*, "chief," "military officer"), who were part of the local elites, are, for example, not completely clear. They played the role of *boni homines* and they were consulted for their expert knowledge of the tax districts (Bresc 1989; Nef 2011: 463ff.). In this sphere, as in others, if the general inspiration is more Islamic or Byzantine than Latin, it should be kept in mind that the vocabulary which is used (in order to designate the categories of taxpayers, the administrative institutions and functions, etc.), at the very least, is a field of invention. This inventiveness is also to be found in the court sphere, which has attracted most interest and analysis as it is better documented.

## The inventive construction of a monarchy

We should immediately underline that we know (part of) what happened at court, in the royal palace, while the rest of the society is much less documented, an imbalance which leads to a focus of studies on the former. This limit should not suggest reading what we are going to outline as a kind of communication trick orchestrated by the Hautevilles (cf. Johns 2002: 284ff.). The fact that it was limited to court life makes it no less significant and it should be interpreted with care. It was a costly edifice and it did not help the Hautevilles' integration in the Latin European horizon, to say the least. It was thus a conscious choice to build this system, which does not mean, of course, that all the parameters that led to this decision were totally clear for the groups in charge of the royal government over the decades.

Twelfth-century Sicily has often been presented as a space where a synthesis took place between what is usually described as three "civilizations" (for a necessary criticism of this notion, see Dufal 2009), Latin, Greek, and Islamic, a synthesis whose symbol is supposed to be the royal court. Such an interpretation gives the historical approach a miss. One bias should in fact be avoided: the "philological" approach which consists in attributing to each element of the Hautevilles' construction a cultural identity, an "origin," in a kind of ethnicizing way. There are at least three reasons to avoid such an approach: (1) what is exemplified by Sicily is the existence of a *koiné* relating the caliphal, Byzantine and Latin courts; (2) the introduction of an element in a context which is not the original one modifies its meaning and function, above all when, as it has been underlined, it is not deprived of appropriation, adaptation, and/or innovation; (3) just as they did not think in terms of continuities, contemporaries seldom conceived the elements composing court life in this "philological" way, as we will see on pp. 65–6.

I will of course here concentrate on elements which are identified *nowadays* as "Islamic" in Sicilian court life and its frame (palace, *sollacia*, etc.) in order to try and understand how they were conceived and used, as far as this can be reconstituted. It is only after this effort to reconstruct their conceptual context that I will come back to the question of their interpretation by twelfth-century contemporaries and by today's historians.

The use of the Arabic language in order to exalt the Hautevilles, either in poems (De Simone 1999b; Nef 2008; 2011: 178–90), in monumental inscriptions (De Luca 2002; Nef 2011: 178–90), or in royal titles (Johns 2002; Nef 2011: 94–116), is well known and has been studied recently. What is interesting is that all three spheres combine Arabic language with Islamic, but not expressly Muslim, references and Christian assertions. The royal titles thus mix Islamic uses and terms, although potentially non-Muslim (*malik*, i.e. "king," rather than *imam* or *khalifa*, which were used to designate the caliphs), with the exaltation of the protection of God (although the name "Allah" is quite ecumenical in Arabic) or mention of the sovereign's fight for Christianity. As for the poems, and in a lesser way the monumental epigraphs, they used images which had become part of the Islamic language of power but were not Muslim, such as references to Sasanid palaces, evocations of King David, etc., as well as Muslim references which had lost part of their primary meaning.

The context of use of the monumental inscriptions is also important: the Arabic epigraphs of the Palermitan Cappella Palatina (Brenk 2010) can certainly not be analyzed as if they decorated a Muslim building (Nef 2011: 145), or even a suburban palace built for the Hautevilles' leisure. Let us remember that Arabic inscriptions decorated numerous Palermitan churches in the twelfth century (Nef 2011: 157–61). Everything suggests, in this specific context, the development of a Christian Arabic expression which coincides with the promotion of an Arab Christian milieu related to the court and in particular with the Palatine chapel, but not only this. Although we cannot be very precise on this point, sufficient evidence seems to be the existence of an inventory of Christian liturgical books written in Arabic and kept in the treasury of the Cappella Palatina (Nef 2011: 217–21), as well as the proximity of some Arab Christians to the latter (Bresc and Nef 1996: 154). Besides its real extension, what remains little known is the composition of this milieu: part was probably converted, another part came from outside (George of Antioch, the de Indulciis), yet another belonged to families which had remained Christian during the period of Islamic domination, all were linguistically Arabicized and culturally Islamicized. We know that they were recognized as a group until the fourteenth century (Mandalà and Moscone 2009: 189–90). What is interesting is that among them there were Christians relating to a church whose liturgy was in Greek (as George of Antioch), but also others for whom it was in Latin (the origin of the de Indulciis is identified with al-Andalus; and the books whose titles are transliterated in Arabic in the abovementioned list were in Latin). Moreover, these groups were close to some of the eunuchs and to Latin individuals who had learned Arabic and were part of the eunuchs' party and defenders of the Hautevilles' elaboration and ideology. A good example is Matthew of Aiello, who came from the mainland and was for over thirty years one of the most powerful men in the government (Mandalà and Moscone 2009: 204–11). He was a good enough Arabicist to be entrusted with the re-elaboration of the archives of the central offices of the kingdom, which had burned down in a Palermitan rebellion in 1161. Another one, although much less documented, is Grisandus, known by the quadrilingual tombstone (Arabic, Judeo-Arabic, Greek, and Latin) by which he celebrated the memory of his dead mother in 1149. It has been shown that what is exalted in all four alphabets by Grisandus, who defines himself as the priest of the king, is Christianity and conversion to it (Johns 2006: 519–23). These remarks clearly underline that convergences were as much political as they were cultural, just like the tensions we will detail on pp. 62–5.

Another important instrument of legitimization was coinage, for coins are one of the most largely diffused support for an expression of political authority. Its evolution has been described in various publications (Travaini 1995). It is obvious that some parameters, such as trust in money, also determined the choices made in this matter. Nonetheless, the perpetuation of the two Islamic currencies (the golden *tari* and the silver *kharruba*, to which a copper *follis* was added) in twelfth-century Sicily, a decision which is clearly linked with fiscal choices, and the presence of Arabic legends on coins until the end of the dynasty cannot be explained only by a trust problem. Little by little, Christian symbols and inscriptions made their appearance on the coins, but they were never exclusive of Islamic ones.

Life at court and the practices of power are also fundamental within the sphere of domination. Here again, establishing whether such and such a practice was inspired by Byzantium or by the Islamic courts is not an easy task, but this might not be the main point. The royal ceremonial and clothing could have been inspired by both: public appearances by the king were veiled and rare (al-Maqrizi 1991: 20; Johns 2002: 82); he used what were interpreted by the Arab Muslim authors as Islamic elements – such as an umbrella or clothes qualified "as Islamic" (al-Maqrizi 1991: 20; Johns 2002: 82) and which carried inscriptions in Arabic (Johns 2006) – and was revered through *proskynesis* (Nef 2011: 122–4), which designates different types of prostration. The production of textiles in the royal palace factory, an equivalent of the Islamic *ṭiraz*, and of the Byzantine *ergasterion*, and moreover of textiles bearing Arabic inscriptions, is not a Latin practice.

The presence of eunuchs at the Sicilian court is another distinctive characteristic underlined by twelfth-century authors. This widely diffused medieval practice was absent from the Latin courts. Eunuchs, supposedly figures of submission, since they were slaves and deprived of family, not only often exercised high-level functions and were close to the king, but, in Sicily as elsewhere (De La Puente 2003; Nef 2011: 340–2), they were the heads of properties and dependants. They were known in the city of Palermo, where they were able to mobilize combatants.

All this quite complex elaboration raises a question: Who were its recipients? A large part of the elements we have listed here were not known only by a few courtiers. Beyond coins, a lot of them were known by the Palermitans, just as the eunuchs were, but they were also seen outside of the capital when the king traveled in Sicily or to the mainland. Obviously, this is not to say that this construction was intended to be seen by all, and even very material facts (inscriptions located at the top of a monument, etc.) demonstrate it. This is not specific to twelfth-century Sicily and has been analyzed by historians and art historians. It does not prevent us from trying to determine the virtual recipients of this construction, or rather, the ambitions the Hautevilles expressed by means of these instruments. This is all the more important as, from the end of the eleventh century, parallel contexts had given birth to other political elaborations in the Iberian Peninsula and in the Levant. The meaning of the Hautevilles' choices thus has to be interrogated.

## An imperial and Mediterranean horizon

The figure of the eunuch introduces us to the imperial dimension of the Hautevilles' construction. Coming from outside, carrying political references common to the greatest part of the contemporary Mediterranean, and in particular to the imperial entities (Byzantium, the Fatimids, and the Abbasides) which displayed their power in it, the eunuch is considered antithetic to Latin conceptions of kingship for he is the product of a modification of "human nature" contrary to God's will and a slave, but nonetheless exercises very important functions. The Latin conquerors of Sicily could, and sometimes did, perceive them as a limit for their own role and as an abuse of power on the king's part. We saw, besides, that Muslims of Sicilian origin are not attested to at the court. These elements suggest that part of the political language used by the Hautevilles, and thus of its recipients, has to be understood and looked for in a wider context. All of the instruments of legitimization we detailed above can, in the same way, although with different connotations, be read as having recipients not only within the realm but also outside it, embassies and temporary visitors who might describe it to others, just as the Hautevilles' envoys were the bearers of this elaboration abroad. Other elements, besides its sources of inspiration and audience, can be added in order to reinforce this interpretation, which gives the Hautevilles' enterprise an imperial dimension.

First of all, the Hautevilles developed a strategy and a policy of expansion in the Mediterranean which is worth analyzing. Sicily's position, which made it a lock between the Occidental and the Oriental basins of the Mediterranean, and the window Puglia opened on the Adriatic Sea explain part of their choice to lead a "straits strategy" which aimed to control both sides of each strait bordering their domain (Strait of Otranto, Strait of Messina, and Strait of Sicily) and the islands close to their territories (Malta, Pantelleria, and Corfu) (Bresc 2002). This military motivation and the will to limit piracy could perhaps explain their expansion in Ifriqiya, in central Maghreb and Libya (Bresc 1998; Nef 2011: 590–2, 607–9, 619–20) through the control of coastal *emporia* as well as the conquest of Jerba and Pantelleria. They justify less the Hautevilles' distrust towards the Crusades or their interest in Byzantium and in Egypt parallel to the Fatimids' twilight (Nef 2011: 619–20). And they explain even less the construction which is that of the Ifriqiyan *emporia*: their population was paying the *jizya* just as the Muslims of Sicily did; their governors benefited from the Sicilian kings' delegation and received from them a diploma of investiture and robes of ceremony, as in the *dar al-islam*. Moreover, Ifriqiyan coinage referring to the Hautevilles' authority is attested. This hierarchization of entities and integration of groups through specific juridical statuses has been defined as typical of the imperial conceptions (Burbank and Cooper 2010: 8; Nef 2013).

Above all, simple strategic considerations do not explain the intensity of the relations between Sicily and Ifriqiya all through the twelfth century and other dimensions of the Hautevilles' policy such as their patronage of written production in Arabic, texts that only a number of their court and a very small number of the Arabic-speakers of Sicily were able to access. The welcoming of Arab Muslims in Sicily was constant: just as the Hammudids in the eleventh century (a family the geographer al-Idrisi belonged to), who converted in part (Johns 2002: 235ff.; Nef 2010b), and George of Antioch had been, the Hammudids were refugees in the island in the middle of the twelfth century (Nef 2011: 168–9), and numerous Muslim authors were also temporary hosts to the Hautevilles. This is the case for al-Idrisi, whose exact relations with Sicily are still an object of debate (Nef 2010b); but also for Ibn Qalaqis, an Egyptian poet who visited Sicily in 1168–9 and sung to William II an Arabic *qasida* (De Simone 1996; Nef 2008); for Ibn Jubayr, who was welcomed after the ship which took him back to al-Andalus from a pilgrimage to Mecca sank at Messina in 1185 (Dejugnat 2010); and for Ibn Zafar (Nef 2011: 207–10).

All of these authors integrated Sicily and their kings in a literary Islamic horizon: through geography, an imperial discipline, which was conceived for the first time in a long time on the scale of the entire oikoumene by al-Idrisi (1999: introduction); through a *rihla*, a literary genre born in the Western part of the Islamic world in the thirteenth century and which consists in the relation of a pilgrimage to Mecca, in which Ibn Jubayr redefined the position of Sicily in relation to a world of Islam which was slowly diminishing before the eyes of the Arab Muslim writers, above all when they were Andalusians (Dejugnat 2010); through laudatory poetry, in which Ibn Qalaqis gave the language of power an Arabic expression; while Ibn Zafar illustrated, through his mirror for princes, another genre yet, which takes into account the past and universal history in order to define what good government should be in Islam.

This interpretation of the Hautevilles' elaboration does not pretend to assert that it operated a consensual synthesis or to deny that tensions existed at court and in the realm about its opportunity, but it questions the analyses which have been made of such tensions until now.

## Tensions and diverging interpretations

In a quite Manichean way, two interpretations of the fate of Muslims and of Islamic culture in twelfth-century Sicily have been proposed. The first emerged during the period of decolonization in the second half of the twentieth century. It presented Sicily as an example of a non-crusading kingdom which had promoted a harmonious synthesis between cultures and languages (Giunta and Rizzitano 1967). The second, more recent, one has to be understood in the context of the growing international and national tensions around Islam which began in the 1990s in Europe and in the United States of America. It describes the Hautevilles' policy as one of exclusion and violence exerted against the insular Muslims that Frederick II would have achieved with their deportation towards Lucera (Johns 1992; Maurici 1995), and "Islamic" court life and Arabic administrative production as having a very limited real impact (Johns 2002: 284–300). Far from denying this apparently ambiguous historical reality, we think that the imperial dimension of the Hautevilles' ambitions is a key to its understanding. The recipients of this construction are not only, and probably not in the first place, the Muslims of Sicily. Moreover, the tensions which manifested themselves in the kingdom have to be interpreted less as tensions between religious groups than as tensions around the exercise of power and around the definition of the very nature of royal power in twelfth-century Sicily. Thus, it might be useful to come back to the phases of this elaboration and to the manifestations of the tensions which accompanied them in order to analyze them more closely.

As far as the theme we are treating is concerned, a first important date is 1112. It is the year in which Count Roger came of age after the regency of his mother Adelasia. It was also marked by a change of capital in Sicily, Messina being abandoned in favor of Palermo. Motivated in part by a baronial revolt against the countess's government, which is little documented, this decision was probably also motivated by the idea of using a city which was one of the important capitals of the Mediterranean and was considered as such not only by Islamic geographers but also by Latin chroniclers. Thus, the chronicle of Alexander of Telese, which ends in 1136, describes the magnates advising Roger II to become king with the following arguments:

[The councilors] added that the center and capital of the kingdom should have been Palermo, which, formerly, in the past, they said, had had kings who had ruled over the province [of Sicily], and which, subsequently, after many years, through an impenetrable divine plan, had remained without a king until that date.

*(Alexander Telesinus 1991: 23)*

What is certain is that the political center of the kingdom shifted towards the Islamic world, strengthening the Hautevilles' links with Islamic political practices.

The second important date is 1130, the year Roger became king of Sicily. It is at the same time a point of arrival and a point of departure in what appears to be a re-Arabization of the administration and the documents it produced and as a promotion of Islamic political references, among others. This way of introducing a distance between the king and his subjects was perceived by contemporaries. The period beginning in 1130 (up to the death of Roger II in 1154) is also that of the reinforcement of links with Ifriqiya and with the Fatimids.

Nonetheless, the period is not devoid of tensions: George of Antioch seems to have been a promoter of this reorientation at the expense of another adviser of the king, more closely linked with Byzantium, Christodoulos, who was imprisoned in the 1120s (Nef 2011: 587–8). Another moment of tension during the same period is the execution of the eunuch and chief of the fleet, Philip of Mahdiyya, who was burned in public for apostasy in 1153. Although earlier sources insist on the religious dimension of this condemnation, Roger II being attributed a kind of Christian fervor as he gets nearer to death (Metcalfe 2002: 305–7), it has been justly suggested that it could be understood in relation to Islamic conceptions (Bougard 2013: 42–4)[3] since fire is the punishment reserved for apostasy in Islam. Moreover, this happened during the month of Ramadan, a choice which is meaningful. Here again, Islamic is not equivalent to Muslim for the supporters of Roger II.

William I's reign is particularly dense in political confrontations. The main source for this period is the Pseudo-Falcandus's chronicle (Loud and Wiedemann 1998), which describes the Sicilian events between 1154 and 1169. All specialists consider the anonymous author to be a Latin, born in northern Europe and who lived for a long period in Sicily before leaving it. During the reign of William I and the beginning of the regency of his widow, Margaret of Navarra (whose origin cannot be forgotten in the context of the Iberian Peninsula's *Reconquista*), the criticisms of the Hautevilles' choices, some of which were abandoned, are better documented. The Italian mainland and Sicily's Latin barons manifested their opposition to a power which, they thought, did not leave them enough room. This opposition did not take the form of a simple anti-Muslim movement. It was at first a movement against the new chief minister of the kingdom, Maio of Bari, then it led to the abandonment of Ifriqiya (1160) (Loud and Wiedemann 1998: 78–81), and, only afterwards, to the murder of Maio and to massacres of Muslims (1161) in Palermo and around Piazza (Loud and Wiedemann 1998: 121–2), where a royal army, formed in part of Muslims, was sent to subdue the Latin rebels, thus generating fights between Christians and Muslims within the army (Loud and Wiedemann 1998: 124). Piazza was a Lombard (northern Italian) settlement and the hatred between Muslims and Lombards engendered by these events is said to have persisted. All the same, Palermo's murders are said to have provoked revenge trials organized by the eunuch Martin, who was in charge of watching the city and the palace of Palermo (Loud and Wiedemann 1998: 130–1). He was helped in this enterprise of revenge by a Latin, Robert of Calatabiano, who was in charge of the Sea's Castle, which contained a prison (Loud and Wiedemann 1998: 135–6).

After the death of William I in 1166, a new period began. The aristocracy seems to have thought that it could take the opportunity of the regency to reinforce its power. The arrival in

Sicily in 1167 of Stephen of Perche, brother of the Queen Margaret, who designated him as chancellor, appeared as an opportunity to see judged the eunuchs and those who were accused of abuses against the Christians (Robert of Calatabiano, among others). Some measures were taken in this direction but they were limited and appear above all as a communication policy.

This is not to say that tensions disappeared altogether. The eunuch Peter, who benefited from a posthumous emancipation by the king, was promoted by the queen and at the same time fiercely criticized and suspected of treason and apostasy; he thus fled to Ifriqiya (Loud and Wiedemann 1998: 146–8). Here again, though, the problem is more political than religious, as the details reveal. An important element seems to be the ascension of a "nobility of State," to paraphrase Pierre Bourdieu, accessible to individuals of low birth to the detriment of the inherited nobility. For example, Matthew of Aiello, who, as we have seen, was on the eunuchs' side and a promoter of the Hautevilles' program, was criticized by the aristocracy from this point of view (Loud and Wiedemann 1998: 134). Peter, all the same, not being a slave anymore, became an example of an aristocracy born exclusively of service to the king. That the denunciations of this political party by its opponents should have sometimes taken the form of accusations of apostasy or of Islamicization is quite banal. Nonetheless, even once Peter left, he was still defended by some Latins: thus, Richard of Molise defied in single contest whoever would accuse Peter of having betrayed the king of Sicily in 1160 in front of Mahdiyya and justified his flight by the pressure exerted upon him.

One last argument which has to be commented upon is the recurring idea which is expressed in various sources, that the royal palace's servants, officially converted, remained in reality Muslims. First of all, and without taking a position on the reality of this situation (for more arguments in favor of it, see Johns 2002: 251–3), it should be remembered that this assertion is not frequent. Moreover, it can be found in two different contexts: a Latin, critical, one (Loud and Wiedemann 1998: 78) and an Islamic, positive, one (Ibn Jubayr, in Johns 2002: 212–15).

In the first case, the first occurrence coincides with the loss of Mahdiyya and the second with the accusations against Robert of Calatabiano. In 1160, the chronicler known as the Pseudo-Falcandus, although he criticizes the eunuch Peter's failed military intervention, does not accuse him expressly of treason and attributes the political responsibility of Mahdiyya's abandonment to Admiral Maio (Loud and Wiedemann 1998: 78–81; Johns 2002: 223 is wrong on this specific point). Nonetheless, on this occasion he specifies that, like all the eunuchs, Peter remained Muslim at heart.

In 1167, when Stephen of Perche became chancellor, numerous accusations were expressed against Christians who had converted to Islam in secret, in particular against Robert of Calatabiano, who had been an instrument of the royal repression after the rebellion of 1161. He is accused of ill treating specifically the Christians, favoring, for example, the rape of Christian virgins by Muslims (Loud and Wiedemann 1998: 166–8), a topic accusation,[4] but to which the pope Alexander III seems to have given some credit since he wrote to the chancellor in order to ask him what he had done to punish these crimes (Loud and Wiedemann 1998: 166, n.184). The passage in the Pseudo-Falcandus's chronicle is very interesting because it clearly exposes how the case of Robert of Calatabiano, who seems to have been pitiless but also crystallized fantasies, is used and manipulated by all the court's factions in their own interest. As for the queen, she ends up protecting Robert. He is judged, imprisoned in the Sea's Castle because he cannot pay his debts, and dies there.

Interestingly enough, the problem here is more the idea of Muslim proselytism and of the dissimulation of reality than the fact of being Muslim *per se*, but the loyalty to the king (or to the queen) of the eunuchs and of the individuals suspected to have converted in secret is not questioned. We thus understand better the intervention of the pope, who tries to remind his interlocutor of the hierarchy of priorities from his point of view: religion, and not politics, should be the first preoccupation of the chancellor. Moreover, if the magnates were hostile to Robert of Calatabiano, they were also to accuse Stephen of Perche of being a stranger and of concentrating too much power (Loud and Wiedemann 1998: 169). Once again, the religious interpretation is not sufficient to explain tensions at court.

As for the degradation of the Muslim peasants' situation, which is documented at least in a part of Sicily, it is not necessarily linked with these events. Indeed, the evolution towards seigneurialization supported by beneficiaries of fiscal concessions is certainly not a specificity of twelfth-century Sicily. That the Hautevilles were favorable to Christianity and Christians to the detriment of Muslims or Islam is not contradictory with the integration of Islamic elements in their innovative system. One might be interested by taxes, feed imperial ambitions, and be nonetheless deeply Christian. That they might in precise circumstances give priority to the stability of government over questions of faith is not contradictory with their attachment to Christianity either. In this field, the historian should avoid oversimplifying. Another way of looking at this question is to check how Muslim, or even Islamic, the elements listed above were considered to be by contemporaries.

## Reading twelfth-century testimonies

The interpretation sustained here, according to which the main reason for the recurring tensions in twelfth-century Sicily was not the opposition between the distinct religious, cultural, or even linguistic groups which were present on the island, but rather political competition around the exercise of power and the royal ideology,[5] seems to be supported by the testimony of contemporaries. They not only give evidence on political events but reflect the fact that what we qualify today in retrospect as "Islamic," "Muslim," "Arab," or "Arabic," with little distinction, was not qualified as such, or as anything whose "otherness" would have needed to be underlined in the twelfth century.

On this question, we can imagine, even if we do not associate a political position with each of them, that the perception of the authors, informed and shaped by their personal history and by their social background at the time when they wrote, differed. We will thus see what were the positions of an Arab Muslim close to the Hautevilles, and above all who spent much time in the island, what were those of an Arab Muslim who was passing through, of a Latin who came from outside, and of a Greek-speaking Christian native of the island.

Let us begin with the "insiders." On the one hand is al-Idrisi, author of the geography described as "Roger's Book." His description of Sicily (after 1158) is quite interesting. The author mentions the Christianity of his patron at the beginning of the *opus*, but the description of the island could be that of an Islamic region. Roger I and II are introduced and their conquest of Sicily is sung, but with no allusion to their religious creed. What is more, no church is mentioned in the whole text if we exclude Catania's Benedictine monastery because it shelters the elephant symbolizing the city. Palermo's cathedral is evoked as "Friday's mosque or rather the building which had this function in the past and which turned to be what it was before" (al-Idrisi 1999: 308; 1989: 591)! If the Islamic past and domination are often evoked, the contemporary ones are never qualified. Moreover, the maritime and commercial relations between several Sicilian localities and the *dar al-islam* are expressly alluded to, such as in the case of Trabia, Messina, Sciacca (from Tripoli and Ifriqiya), Marsala (al-Idrisi 1999: 309, 312, 318–19; 1989: 592, 595, 600–1), without taking into account the various allusions to merchants coming from all horizons which characterized many of the maritime ports. Everything thus works here as if the Hautevilles prolonged the life of a past Sicily (Marsala destroyed and restored by Roger I being the only exception) which is nonetheless not qualified as either Muslim or Islamic.

On the other hand, there is Philagete of Cerami, a Sicilian author of Christian homilies and other religious texts. Invited to pronounce a sermon in Palermo's Cappella Palatina, he describes the chapel. This text written in Greek has been preserved (Lavagnini 1990). What is interesting is that no element is qualified as Islamic or Oriental, or even considered as surprising, not even the ceiling, on which books have been written by modern historians.

As for the "outsiders," a first author is Latin, although his exact identity is not known. The Pseudo-Falcandus is considered to be the author of a chronicle already evoked and of a *Letter to the Treasurer of the Church of Palermo* written after 1189 (Loud and Wiedemann 1998: 252–63). His *Letter* cries over the disappearance of the Hautevilles' Sicily threatened by Henri VI's "*furor teutonicus*" after the death of William II, who left no heir, since the emperor had married Roger II's daughter, who was born after Roger's death. Two of the *Letter*'s aspects are related to the question tackled here. First, it contains a description of Palermo, presented as the symbol of the Hautevilles' elaboration, which never qualifies any element as Islamic or Muslim (toponyms excepted, such as the "Sarracens' forum"), even if the Palatine chapel, the palace, the palatine workshops, and all the fruits introduced during the Islamic domination are exalted and detailed (Loud and Wiedemann 1998: 258–62).

Second, the author attributes the predictable defeat of the population by Henri VI to its divisions and explicitly to the oppression the Christians imposed on the Sarracens, an oppression which prevented the population from joining together (Loud and Wiedemann 1998: 255). But, if read carefully, it is clear that the absentee of the text is Tancred of Lecce, who was linked to the Hautevilles' family, although his birth was illegitimate, and opposed Henri VI. The author does not seem to think he would be the king of unity he is hoping for. The reason for this silence is linked with the evocation of the Sarracens' oppression. Indeed, Tancred of Lecce was among the perpetrators of the massacres of Muslims in 1161. It is thus not a general position which is expressed by the anonymous author but a way to remind the well-informed reader of the impossibility of Tancred's reign and a call to designate a third man, whose name is not suggested (Nef forthcoming).

If we follow the reading of Sicily's history, using Pseudo-Falcandus's key, the Muslims of Sicily rebelled against the government which emerged after William II's death, because it was made up of individuals they identified, with some reason, as hostile to the Hautevilles' program.

Another outsider is Ibn Jubayr, an Arab Muslim from al-Andalus. His description is opposed to al-Idrisi's. The beginning of the text is indeed characterized by a kind of wonder in the face of the seemingly Islamic way of governing and court life. Nonetheless, the tone changes pro-gressively and the text can be seen as a platonic unveiling of Sicilian reality. His travel from East (Messina) to West (Trapani) shows the author that the Muslims' situation on the island is not to be envied and is marked by oppression. Here again, one should not forget that every text is drawn by a demonstration and a strategy which a reading limited to the pages dealing with Sicily cannot make explicit. It has been shown that Ibn Jubayr is describing a journey towards the sources of Islam (Damascus and Baghdad) in an attempt to ward off the mortal threat al-Andalus is facing. On this journey, it is clear that Sicily cannot be an example but, on the contrary, the symbol of what has to be avoided.

Of course, one might think that all these texts cannot be read as a neutral expression about Sicily, that the first two defend the Hautevilles' conceptions, while the last two express a hostile position for distinct motivations. This should certainly be kept in mind. Nonetheless, one should not forget that in reality all these texts converge: what we classify as "Islamic elements" are Islamic, and above all Muslim, neither for insiders nor for outsiders, even those who at first believed, or rhetorically pretended to believe, the contrary. All of them underline wonder, the extraordinary, but they do not qualify it in a "philological way."

This should also make us very careful about the speed with which changes happen in societies, rather than to suppose, often constructed, *a posteriori* continuities. What might have appeared as strange, other, foreign to the first conquerors was not so for the regional population, and soon was not so either for the descendants of the conquerors.

## Conclusions

It appears difficult to deny an Islamic dimension to the Hautevilles' Sicily at the end of this quick overview, but what it means exactly has to be given greater thought. Islam in twelfth-century Sicily is only partially Muslim, and described as such by contemporaries with precise aims. The Sicilian example does thus invite us to rethink the categories we use. Considering the interpretation of the actors and of contemporaries is important in this process, but we should also interrogate our own questioning and categories.

Questioning the "authenticity" of the Arabic and Islamic dimension of this royal elaboration in this context, as has sometimes been done, is quite problematic, as is the notion of authenticity itself. The constant social evolution and permanent reinterpretation of the social reality cannot be the object of a value judgment by historians and other social scientists. What we exposed can be interpreted in two different ways. Either this dimension cannot be qualified as Islamic because it is quite a surprising construction mixing references borrowed from the Islamic culture and Christianity, or it is a peculiar expression of Islamic culture in a specific context. This last option can be difficult to accept for fundamentalists, be they religious or culturalist, for it contrasts with an essential definition of Islam, but it should not be difficult for historians and social scientists.

This Islamic dimension was not seen as a problem, and often not even perceived as such, in the twelfth century for it was seen as a part of Sicilian reality. Its cultural realizations were extolled and its religious dimension was manipulated politically by the opponents of the Hautevilles, although the sovereigns themselves certainly did not exalt Muslim religion.

## Notes

1 We distinguish here by the use of distinct terms what is religious (islam, Muslim) in today's categories and what is more largely part of Islamic societies and can be other than Muslim (Islam, with a capital "i," Islamic); the expression "Arab Muslim" will here qualify individuals or groups which may be Arabic speakers or not, Muslim or not, but part of an Islamic society, that is, whose government defines itself as a part of the *dar al-islam*. We have no space here to underline how central these questions of definition are (Nef 2011).

2 Islamic Sicily was forgotten for a long time. From the end of the nineteenth century to the 1980s and 1990s, the two main works were: Amari 1991; Talbi 1966 from the point of view of Ifriqiya. A few sectors have known occasional but constant renewal: art history; philology; numismatics. This has changed in the last decade and the historical (and archeological) study of Islamic Sicily is flourishing today.

3 In this article F. Bougard, whom I thank for this communication, contemplates this possibility but ends by rejecting it in favor of an interpretation emphasizing renewed concepts linked with Roman Law, punishment by fire having disappeared during the High Middle Ages in the Latin world. He confirmed to me orally, though, that a systematic study he is preparing on this subject will leave more space for the Islamic dimension of the re-emergence of punishment by fire in contexts where it is plausible, such as Spain and Sicily.

4 Limiting the investigation to the Pseudo-Falcandus, beyond Robert of Calatabiano, two men are accused of rapes and/or prostitution of virtuous women: Maio (Loud and Wiedemann 1998: 76) and the *strategos* Richard in Messina (Loud and Wiedemann 1998: 83); both were killed. The three

characters gave birth to a strong hatred in the population, and the same accusation is made against all three, although two were Christians.

5 Another dimension of the question is socio-economic and has to do with the degradation of the peasants' situation, which, though partially and indirectly, is documented. We leave this aspect aside here for there are very few testimonies about the rural evolution.

## Bibliography

Alexander Telesinus (1991) *Alexandri Telesini Abbatis ystoria Rogerii regis Sicilie Calabrie atque Apulie*, ed. Ludovica De Nava, comm. Dione Clementi, Rome: Istituto storico italiano per il Medio Evo.

Amari, M. (1991) *Storia dei Musulmani di Sicilia*, re-edition C.A. Nallino, Catania 1933–9; re-edition with same pagination Catania: Ed. Dafni.

Bonnassie, P. (2000) "Sur la Genèse de la féodalité catalane: nouvelles approches," in *Il feudalesimo nell'alto medioevo*, vol. I, Spoleto: Centro italiano di studi sull'Alto Medioevo, pp. 569–606.

Bougard, F. (2013) "Le feu de la justice et le feu de l'épreuve, IVe–XIIe siècle," in *Il fuoco nell'alto Medioevo (Atti delle Settimane di Studio del Centro Italiano di studi sull'alto Medioevo)*, Spoleto, Centro Italiano di studi sull'alto Medioevo di Spoleto, 2013, pp. 389–432.

Brenk, B. (ed.) (2010) *La Cappella Palatina a Palermo*, Rimini: Panini.

Bresc, H. (1989) "De l'État de minorité à l'État de résistance: le cas de la Sicile normande," in Balard. M. (ed.) *État et colonisation au Moyen Âge et à la Renaissance*, Lyon: La Manufacture, pp. 331–47.

——(1998) "Le Royaume normand d'Afrique et l'archevêché de Mahdiyya," in Balard, M. and Ducellier, A. (eds.) *Le Partage du monde. Échanges et colonisation dans la Méditerranée médiévale*, Paris: Publications de la Sorbonne, pp. 264–83.

——(2002) "Du Ribât au presidio, les enjeux et les contrôles des Détroits siciliens," in Villari, R. and Bono, S. (eds.) *Controllo degli Stretti e insediamenti militari nel Mediterraneo*, Rome: Laterza, pp. 97–127.

——(2003) "Les Historiens de la Croisade. Guerre sainte, justice et paix," *Mélanges de l'École française de Rome-Moyen Âge* 115(2): 727–53.

Bresc, H. and Nef, A. (1996) "Les Mozarabes de Sicile (1100–1300)," in Cuozzo, E. and Martin, J.-M. (ed.) *Cavalieri alla conquista del Sud – Studi sull'Italia normanna in memoria di Léon-Robert Ménager*, Bari: Laterza, pp. 134–56.

Burbank, J. and Cooper, F. (2010) *Empires in World History: Power and the Politics of Difference*, Princeton and Oxford: Princeton University Press.

Dakhlia, J. and Kaiser, W. (2013) *Les Musulmans dans l'histoire de l'Europe. II. Passages et contacts en Méditerranée*, Paris: Albin Michel.

Dakhlia, J. and Vincent, B. (2011) *Les Musulmans dans l'histoire de l'Europe. I. Une intégration invisible*, Paris: Albin Michel.

De La Puente, C. (2003) "Sin linaje, sin alcurnia, sin hogar: eunucos en al-Andalus en época omeya," in De La Puente, C. (ed.) *Identitades marginales*, Madrid: CSIC, pp. 147–94.

De Luca, M.A. (2002) "L'uso della lingua araba nelle iscrizioni edili e nelle monete normanne," in La Duca, R. (ed.) *Storia di Palermo. III. Dai Normanni ai Vespri*, Palermo: L'Epos, pp. 241–62.

De Simone, A. (1996) *Splendori e misteri di Sicilia in un'opera di Ibn Qalāqis*, translation of *Al-Zahr al-bāsim wa-l-'arf al-nāsim fi madīḥ al-ajall Abī-l-Qāsim*, Soveria Mannelli: Rubettino.

——(1999a) "Il Mezzogiorno normanno-svevo visto dall'Islam africano," in *Il Mezzogiorno normanno-svevo visto dall'Europa e dal mondo mediterraneo (XIII giornate normanno-sveve, Bari, 21–24 oct. 1997)*, Bari: Dedalo, pp. 261–93.

——(1999b) *Nella Sicilia «araba» tra storia e filologia*, Palermo: Tipolitografia Luxograph.

——(2009) "Note sui titoli arabi di Giorgio di Antiochia," in Re, M. and Rognoni, C. (ed.) *Byzantino-Sicula V. Giorgio di Antiochia: l'arte della politica in Sicilia nel XII secolo tra Bisanzio e l'Islam. Atti del Convegno Internazionale (Palermo, 19–20 aprile)*, Palermo: Istituto Siciliano di Studi Bizantini e Neoellenici, pp. 284–308.

Dejugnat, Y. (2010) "Voyage au centre du monde. Logiques narratives et cohérence du projet dans la *Rihla* d'Ibn Jubayr," in Bresc, H. and Tixier du Mesnil, E. (eds.) *Géographes et voyageurs au Moyen Âge*, Nanterre: Presses universitaires de Paris Ouest, pp. 163–202.

Dufal, B. (2009) "Faire et Défaire l'Histoire des civilisations," in Büttgen, P., De Libera, A., Rashed, M., and Rosier-Catach, I. (eds.) *Les Grecs, les Arabes et nous. Enquête sur l'islamophobie savante*, Paris: Fayard, pp. 317–58.

Giunta, F. and Rizzitano, U. (1967) *Terra senza crociata*, Palermo: Flaccovio.

Houben, H. (2002) *Roger II of Sicily: A Ruler between East and West*, Cambridge: Cambridge University Press.

al-Idrisi (1989) *Kitāb nuzhat al-mushtaq fi ikhriraq al-afaq (Opus geograficum)*, Rome, 1970–6; reed. Beyrouth: 'Alam al-kutub.

——(1999) *La Première géographie de l'Occident*, ed. and translated by H. Bresc and A. Nef, Paris: Aubier.

Johns, J. (1992) "Monreale Survey. L'insediamento umano nell'alto Belice dall'età paleolitica al 1250 d. C.," *Giornate internazionali di Studi sull'area elima. Atti*, vol. I, Pisa-Gibellina: Scuola Normale Superiore di Pisa and CESDAE, pp. 407–21.

——(2002) *Arabic Administration in Norman Sicily: The Royal Dīwān*, Cambridge: Cambridge University Press.

——(2006) "Iscrizioni funerarie VIII.7," in Andaloro, M. (ed.) *Nobiles Officinae. Perle, filigrane e trame di seta dal Palazzo Reale di Palermo. I. Catalogo*, Catania: Giuseppe Maimone editore, pp. 519–23.

Lavagnini, B. (1990) "Profilo di Filagato da Cerami con traduzione della Omelia XXVII pronunziata dal pulpito della Cappella Palatina in Palermo," *Bollettino della Badia greca di Grottaferrata* 44: 231–5.

Loud, G. (2002) "The Papacy and the Rulers of Southern Italy, 1058–1198," in Loud, G.A. and Metcalfe, A. (eds.) *The Society of Norman Italy*, Leiden, Boston and Cologne: Brill, pp. 151–84.

Loud, G. and Wiedemann, T. (trans.) (1998) *The History of the Tyrants of Sicily by "Hugo Falcandus" 1154–1169*, Manchester and New York: Manchester University Press.

Mandalà, G. and Moscone, M. (2009) "Tra Latini, Greci e 'Arabici': ricerche su scrittura e cultura a Palermo tra XII e XIII secolo," *Segno e testo* 7: 143–238.

al-Maqrizi (1991) *Kitab al-Muqaffa*, ed. M. Yalaoui, Beyrouth: *Dar al-gharb al-islami*.

Marazzi, F. (2007) "*Ita ut facta videatur Neapolis Panormus vel Africa*. Geopolitica della presenza islamica nei domini di Napoli, Gaeta, Salerno e Benevento nel IX secolo," *Schede Medievali* 45: 159–202.

Maurici, F. (1995) *Breve storia degli Arabi di Sicilia*, Palermo: Flaccovio.

Metcalfe, A. (2002) "The Muslims of Sicily under Christian Rule," in Loud, G.A. and Metcalfe, A. (eds.) *The Society of Norman Italy*, Leiden, Boston and Cologne: Brill, pp. 289–318.

——(2003) *Muslims and Christians in Norman Sicily: Arabic Speakers and the End of Islam*, London: Routledge.

——(2009) *The Muslims of Medieval Italy*, Edinburgh: Edinburgh University Press.

Nef, A. (2008) "Un poème d'Ibn Qalāqis à la gloire de Guillaume II," in Grévin, B., Nef, A., and Tixier, E. (eds.) *Chrétiens, juifs et musulmans dans la Méditerranée médiévale – Études en hommage à Henri Bresc*, Paris: De Boccard, pp. 33–44.

——(2010a) "Michele Amari ou l'histoire inventée de la Sicile islamique: réflexions sur la *Storia dei Musulmani di Sicilia*," in Grévin, B. (ed.) *Maghreb-Italie, des passeurs médiévaux à l'orientalisme moderne (XIIIe–milieu XIXe siècle)*, Rome: École française de Rome, pp. 285–306.

——(2010b) "Al-Idrīsī: un complément d'enquête biographique," in Bresc, H. and Tixier du Mesnil, E. (eds.) *Géographes et voyageurs au Moyen Âge*, Nanterre: Presses universitaires de Paris Ouest, pp. 53–66.

——(2011) *Conquérir et gouverner la Sicile islamique aux XIe et XIIe siècles*, Rome: École française de Rome.

——(2013) "Imaginaire impérial, empire et œcuménisme religieux: quelques réflexions depuis la Sicile des Hauteville," *Cahiers de Recherches Médiévales et Humanistes* 24: 227–49.

——(forthcoming) "La *Lettre à Pierre trésorier de l'église de Palerme* ou de l'art de choisir ses ennemis," in Planas, N. (ed.) *La figure de l'ennemi*.

Nef, A. and Prigent, V. (2006) "Per una nuova storia dell'alto medioevo siciliano," *Storica* XII: 9–64.

Talbi, M. (1966) *L'Émirat aghlabide 184–296/800–909. Histoire politique*, Paris: Librairie d'Amérique et d'Orient Maisonneuve et Larose.

Travaini, L. (1995) *La monetazione nell'Italia normanna*, Rome: Istituto storico italiano per il Medio Evo.

# 4

# The Muslims in southeastern Europe

## From Ottoman subjects to European citizens

*Nathalie Clayer*

When one speaks about Islam in Europe, one generally has in mind the presence of Muslims migrants in Western Europe or the ancient past of al-Andalus. One refers rarely to the long-lasting presence of Muslims in the southeastern part of the continent since the fourteenth century and the beginning of the Ottoman conquest of the region. Yet, today three Balkan states have a (relative or absolute) Muslim majority: Albania (with 1,950,000, that is, 70 percent of the total population), Bosnia-Herzegovina (1,800,000, 45 percent), and Kosovo, which proclaimed its independence in 2008 (1,600,000, 90 percent). There are also sizeable groups of Muslims in Macedonia (700,000, 30 percent), Bulgaria (900,000, 12 percent), and Montenegro (100,000, 16 percent), and less sizeable but significant groups in Greece (450,000, 4 percent), Serbia (250,000, 4 percent), Slovenia (50,000, 2.5 percent), Croatia (60,000, 1.5 percent), and Romania (70,000, 0.3 percent), all these figures being only estimates.

It is true that Europe is often conceived as Western Europe, another factor in the "invisibility" of these other European Muslims being the fact that they were for half a century behind the Iron Curtain – except those in Greece and those who joined the ranks of the "*Gastarbeiter*." More generally, southeastern Europe, labeled as the Balkans since the nineteenth century, has always been considered by (West) Europeans as the "Other within," or as an intermediary space between the "West" and the "East" (Todorova 1997; Allcock 2000; Neuburger 2004). Of course, here, we are facing the issue of the always subjective definition of Europe, as an artifact. There are debates on the rightness of considering "southeastern Europe" separately from Anatolia, with which political boundaries have existed only for the last hundred years (Vezenkov 2009). In any event, when the existence of the Balkan Muslims is taken into account in the Muslim landscape of Europe, it is often as disappearing Muslim islands or as an example of Muslims claiming a "European Islam," that is to say a non-fundamentalist, non-fanatic Islam, or a Sufi Islam, very different from the Arab and even the Turkish Islam, or, on the contrary, as fundamentalists threatening the Balkan and European order and values. The first type of allegation is only partly true, because it is bound to the idea of Balkan Muslims always undergoing events and suffering since the end of the Ottoman rule. They seem not to act themselves. The second type of discourse is quite essentialist, and does not help us understand the complexity of Muslim societies and Islam in this part of Europe.

Indeed, the political, social, and religious dynamics which have shaped the history of the Muslims in the Balkans from the fourteenth century up to the present are quite diverse according to time and space. To understand the main dynamics, however, it is necessary to consider first the establishment of Islam and Islamic rule in the region, and the (non-)specificities of Balkan Muslims within the Ottoman realm. Then we will analyze the mechanisms of transformation which accompanied the end of Ottoman rule during the long nineteenth century. In the twentieth century, three ruptures affected the Balkan Muslims and their non-Muslim fellow countrymen alike: World War I and the end of the Ottoman, Russian, and Austro-Hungarian Empires, which had a direct influence on the region; World War II and the establishment of socialist regimes (except in Greece); and the end of these socialist rules in 1989–90, followed by the enlargement of the European Union. These ruptures did not hinder continuities, as we shall see, but they are significant enough to help us understand the main evolutions of Muslim populations and Islam in the region in the last hundred years.

## The establishment of Ottoman rule and of Islam in southeastern Europe

The presence of Islam in the Balkans is mainly due to the Ottoman conquest of the region. Some Balkan Muslims insist on an Islamic presence before the Turks in order to disconnect "Islam" from "Turk" (or "Ottoman"). Contacts have existed indeed between the *dar al-islam* (Islamic countries) and the Balkans through commerce and travel (see, for example, the Arab geographer al-Idrisi and the travel of the famous Arab travelogue Ibn Battuta). Some groups of Muslims have also lived in different regions of the Peninsula since the tenth century, such as the Turkomans settled in the mid-thirteenth century by the Byzantine emperor in Dobruja in order to protect the frontier, but who later went back to Anatolia. Nevertheless, an enduring presence of Muslims in the region began only with the passage of the Ottomans from Anatolia to the Balkan Peninsula around the mid-fourteenth century, one hundred years before the fall of Constantinople, at a time when the Byzantine Empire was already considerably weakened by regional powers.

The Ottoman conquest of a large part of southeastern Europe is a long and complex process which, especially in the first phase, was the result not only of military campaigns launched in the name of the Holy War (*gaza*) or military raids made by the *akıncı* (frontier warriors), but also of alliances with local Christian landlords. With time, and despite losses and rebellions against it, the Ottoman dynasty affirmed its power, from the Aegean Sea and the Black Sea in the east, to the Ionian Sea and the Adriatic in the west, and from the south of the Peninsula to the Hungarian lands. Ottoman troops even besieged Vienna twice, in 1529 and 1683, but in vain. Moreover, the second siege was the starting point of a "Christian reconquest" of different parts of the Peninsula: the Ottoman parts of Hungary and Croatia, notably; parts of Serbia and Bosnia, but for a very short time; Morea also, this southern extremity of the Peninsula being placed again under the Ottoman rule between 1715 and 1821.

The remaining European territories of the Ottoman Empire were, however, slowly, not in a linear way, considerably weakened during the long nineteenth century, that is to say from the end of the eighteenth century till the Balkan Wars (1912–13), when only eastern Thrace around Edirne remained in Ottoman hands. Different interrelated factors have played a role in this evolution: the imperialist policies of Russia, France, England, and later on of the Habsburg Empire and Italy; the balance of power in the Ottoman provinces and its evolution following a series of military, fiscal, and administrative reforms; the autonomization of territories, a phenomenon which was only partly the result of the development of the nascent Balkan nationalisms. Therefore new states appeared on the regional scene, putting large Balkan territories under new non-Islamic sovereignties. Greece, with a limited territory, was officially recognized as an independent state in 1831 and later acquired new lands to the north. An embryonic Montenegro had already had a kind of self-government, with the help of Russia, since the end of the eighteenth century, but became officially independent only in 1878. The Pashalik of Belgrade gained autonomy in 1815, and, as the principality of Serbia, was recognized in 1830 as a vassal state. Its independence was also recognized in 1878, with a larger territory. As for the Romanian provinces, Moldavia and Wallachia, from 1829 they were put under joint Russian and Ottoman authority, before gaining independence in 1878. The Congress of Berlin in 1878 created also an autonomous Bulgarian state, enlarged in 1885 by the annexation of Eastern Rumelia, and declared independent in 1908, when Austria-Hungary annexed Bosnia-Herzegovina. The political map of southeastern Europe changed again following the Balkan Wars (1912–13) with the recognition of independence of an Albanian principality under the guarantee of the Great Powers. However, this time, the new entity was to be the first European political entity with a Muslim majority.

With these heterogeneous phases of territorial expansion and decline, the different regions of the Balkan Peninsula remained for various periods of time under Ottoman rule. While Thrace, Bulgaria, Macedonia, Kosovo, and parts of Albania were part of the Empire for more than 500 years (sometimes even almost 550 years), Hungary remained Ottoman for 150 years. But, above all, the form of integration into the Ottoman realm has varied from one region to another, the more remote zones often being governed indirectly. As for the classical period (sixteenth to eighteenth centuries), for example, Gilles Veinstein (1989) has defined three circles. The most outlying of these circles was composed of the Ottoman possessions north of the Danube (Moldavia, Wallachia, Transylvania, Hungary), the integration of which, defined by relations of protection, tribute, or administration of military defense areas, remained limited. In these provinces there were no or few Muslims. The second circle was formed by the territories that were in the border areas with Venice and Austria (Bosnia, Montenegro, Serbia, Albania, and Greece). They were more integrated into the Empire through the implementation of the *timars* system (temporary distribution of lands by the sultan to the military chiefs for their service in the army). But in many cases they benefited from special regimes (notably concerning taxes). The presence of Islam in this second circle was generally greater than in the first, due to conversions to Islam. Finally, the first circle was formed by the regions closest to the Ottoman capital (Bulgaria, Thrace, Macedonia, Thessaly, Dobruja), where central government control was the longest standing and the most direct – even if some areas enjoyed considerable autonomy within this ensemble. Muslim populations, especially Turkish-speaking Muslim populations, were more numerous in this first circle.

The Ottoman imperial system relied very strongly on adaptation to local features. However, beyond recognition of the authority of the Ottoman sultan, integration generally constituted the implementation of Ottoman military and fiscal institutions, based on the *timars* system and on a complex set of special taxes or exemption of taxes against services. Governors, as well as *qadis* judging in the *shari'a* courts, were in charge of respect for the Sultan orders, the *kanun* (Sultanic Laws), and Islamic law (local laws were also taken into account). *Qadis* belonged to the religious hierarchy which was progressively established, also made up of *muftis* (Islamic legal authorities who give a formal legal opinion in answer to an inquiry by a private individual or judge) and *müderris* (professors in madrasas). Ottoman subjects were divided into the "*asker*," people exempted from taxes (the military and religious hierarchies), and the "*reaya*," people paying taxes, be they Muslims or Christians. As for religious relations, according to the *dhimma* pact, if they had accepted the authority of the sultan the Christians were to pay a special tax (the *jiziye*), but were free to profess their religion.

Another aspect of the Islamicization of the Peninsula was the establishment of a Muslim presence beyond the ranks of the Ottoman military and religious administrations. Indeed, directly or indirectly the Ottoman power favored the installation of groups of Muslim populations, particularly in the first phase of the conquest and in the eastern part of the Peninsula. Beside these settlement policies, which were also sometimes exile policies, Islamicization was also due to conversions to Islam of local people. This process is vividly debated to this day, because it is linked to the issue of autochthony and legitimacy of the Balkan Muslims. In fact, it is difficult to know precisely how and why people individually or collectively became Muslims, because the sources generally remain silent on this topic. At the beginning of the establishment of the Ottoman powers, only landlords converted, in order to be integrated into the system and to keep their lands (at the very beginning they were not obliged to). Then the rhythm and scale of conversions changed. It was first a mainly urban phenomenon. From the end of the sixteenth century, however, it began to touch also rural areas. In some areas, such as Kosovo and Northern Albania, conversions occurred till the end of Ottoman rule. The process was particularly strong on the western fringe of the Peninsula, in Bosnia-Herzegovina, in Albania, while on the eastern fringe and in the central part, migrations contributed more to the formation of local Muslim groups of population.

Be they descendants of Muslim settlers or of converts, what were the specificities of Muslims and their Islam in "European Turkey" compared to Muslims and Islam in the rest of the Ottoman Empire? As in Anatolia and in the Arab provinces, they were members of the dominant stratum of the society, while the Christians and other non-Muslims were not. They could aspire to social mobility within the Empire's institutions. Istanbul was for many the political, economic, religious, and intellectual center. The religious networks they belonged to, whether Sufi or not, very often had their center in the Ottoman capital, sometimes in Anatolia, more rarely in the Arab provinces. Islam in the Balkans was extremely diverse, with the development of a wide range of trends: from the more "heterodox" (such as the Kızılbashs and the Bektashis) to the more "orthodox." However, in contrast to Anatolia and the Arab provinces, European Turkey was a place were Muslims remained less numerous than non-Muslims. Just before the Balkan Wars, Ottoman statistics found 51 percent of Muslims in the remaining territories in Europe, at a time when the proportion of Muslims was much higher than before, because of migration; however, the figure is very doubtful. Nevertheless, contacts with Christians – which existed also in the rest of the Empire – and with Europe due to geographical proximity, were greater in the Balkans. Another specificity was the diversity of vernacular languages the Muslims spoke, beside their use of Arabic, Turkish, and Persian as written languages: Turkish, Albanian, Slavic languages, Romani languages, Greek. Above all, their political and social environment changed considerably with the important Ottoman territorial withdrawal which began at the end of the eighteenth century and the formation of non-Muslim sovereignties in the region.[1]

## Balkan Muslims between the new Balkan states and the Ottoman Empire

The creation of the Balkan states changed radically the situation of Muslims living in southeastern Europe. For many of them, until the Congress of Berlin of 1878, the conflicts, the rebellions, and the emancipation of Balkan territories from the Ottoman authority led to death, exile, or very difficult life conditions. Very few international acts guarantied their rights. The result was that only a few Muslims remained under the rule of these first non-Muslim powers in

Montenegro, Serbia, and Greece. Those who survived preferred to flee to the Ottoman Empire, as *muhacir* (following the model of the Prophet's flight from Mecca to Medina), doing as other Muslim refugees from the lands conquered by Russia in Crimea and Caucasus had. This, with other factors – such as the urbanization of Christians, the *Tanzimat* reforms decided by the Ottoman authorities, the greater presence of Western European powers in the Ottoman economic sphere – provoked important changes in the demographic and political balance between Muslims and Christians, not only in the new entities, but also in the Ottoman territories.

However, with the Berlin Congress, which established the independence of Serbia, Montenegro, and Romania, and the creation of a Bulgarian autonomous Principality, things changed considerably. Despite the massacres and the forced departures which occurred during the conflicts that broke out between 1875 and 1878, large groups of Muslims henceforth stayed in the new territories gained by these countries, and in the province of Bosnia-Herzegovina occupied by Austria-Hungary. The main reason was that rights were officially given to Muslims – as well as to Christians in the Ottoman Empire – by the treaties which followed the Congress. In Bosnia-Herzegovina, some local '*ulama*' even issued *fatwas* stating that the province remained part of the *dar al-islam* and therefore there was no reason for Muslims to emigrate to the Ottoman Empire (a theme that will be taken up by the reformist Egyptian Rashid Rida in 1909, certifying that the Muslims of Bosnia-Herzegovina are not obliged to emigrate if they can perform their religious duties without hindrance).

This desire of the Great Powers to guarantee the rights of what were not yet called "minorities" was important for the maintenance of Muslim populations in the new Balkan states. Furthermore, in all these new Balkan countries, laws were passed which concerned Muslims; decisions and actions were taken at the national level regarding their political and civil rights, their property and religious institutions, their schools and the *shari'a* courts, creating specific conditions in each state. But these actions were often driven by "nationalizing," "de-Ottomanizing," and "civilizing" projects, which might violate international terms. In particular, their application depended on the willingness and constraints of different types of actors at different levels (national, regional, local): hence the obvious differences with the legal order, politically, economically, and in religious matters; hence the difficulties daily faced by Muslims, and so the departure of many of them.

As for the religious sphere, in particular, there was a tendency of state authorities to control religious hierarchies (which they also did with Christian hierarchies) and to weaken their links with the Ottoman Empire. This was generally accompanied by control of the income of the *waqf* properties, and the appointment and payment by the state of the highest religious officials, previously paid by the Ottoman state. In the case of Bulgaria and Bosnia-Herzegovina, where the new authorities tried to create *de facto* independent religious institutions from Istanbul, tensions appeared. Especially in Bosnia-Herzegovina, Muslim notables formed a movement for religious autonomy.

Indeed, even in Bosnia-Herzegovina, during this period the Muslims of southeastern Europe who came under non-Muslim sovereignty were still tied to the Ottoman Empire, and the efforts of non-Muslim authorities to cut them off from Istanbul were partly in vain. In fact, if the "pan-Islamism" of Abdülhamid was largely a fantasy of the Great Powers, the sultan did inaugurate a policy *vis-à-vis* Muslims from outside, and especially *vis-à-vis* Muslims of the lost territories. For François Georgeon (2003), the Caliphate, which was an important institution for Abdülhamid, was also an ideological response to the territorial decline of the Empire. This was a mirror-image of the Great Powers' and the Balkan states' policies towards the Christians of the Empire. More generally, many actions were taken by the Ottoman authorities to link the

Muslims of the Balkan states to ideological and cultural developments that were taking place in the Empire. Beyond the spiritual and political ties that still bound them to the *Şeyhülislam* and the sultan-caliph, other unofficial channels enabled the Muslims of the Balkan countries to maintain relations with the Empire. First, networks were created because of migration. On the other hand, the press that developed in and outside the Empire helped to create a public space beyond the Ottoman borders and to circulate information.

How were the Balkan Muslims seen and how did they see themselves in this changing space and these transforming societies where reforms and state building processes were at work? Before the Berlin Congress, an image of the Balkan Muslims as having a Christian origin, converted by force or by interests, and to be (re-)converted to Christianity developed in the Western and Balkan literature. Some Christian nation-builders nevertheless conceived of the integration of the Muslims speaking their language in their nation, without envisioning their conversion. Among the Balkan Muslim elite, the Ottomanism of the Young Ottomans, synonymous with patriotism, constitutionalism, and exaltation of Islamic values, met with a favorable response. Patriotism, however, meant, both at the level of the Empire and locally, introducing local specificities, especially among the Bosnians and the Albanians. A part of these elites came also to be influenced by a nascent Turkism inspired by European research on the Turks. Concerning the Albanians, the development of Albanianism among the Albanian-speaking Christians affected by Hellenism (in southern Italy and then in the Balkans) led to the spread of this idea among a few young Muslims also concerned by Hellenism and by the issue of reforms in the Empire.

After the Berlin Congress, the Muslims of southeastern Europe, like their Christian neighbors, were facing more directly the development of Balkan nationalisms which were more concretely implemented through state policies inspired by a desire to join the "concert of civilized nations" and to "de-Ottomanize" their national space, as well as through the activity – violent or not – of nationalist and irredentist groups. Balkan Muslims also faced the sultan's policy of building an Ottomanism strongly tinged with Islam, and, directly or indirectly, the consequences of the policies of the Great Powers. This context favored a gradual politicization of identities among the Muslims, a population still overwhelmingly rural and illiterate. But this was a fairly hesitant, non-linear, and heterogeneous process, which often knew peaks in periods of violence, the latter favoring the polarization of identities. This politicization developed in two main registers – national and religious – the two often intermingling. However, the national register was still relatively little used by the Muslims of southeastern Europe and, paradoxically, in the Ottoman Empire it was more important.

Indeed, among Muslims of the Ottoman Empire, many intellectual and political currents developed concurrently and combined: Ottomanism, Islamism (sometimes in a version of pan-Islamism), and Turkism (also in a pan-Turkist version). But in the European part of the Empire, including in the capital, Albanianism was also spreading, in close connection with the question of the fate of Ottoman Balkan territories. Among Muslims in Bulgaria and Romania, who maintained close relations with the Empire, the politicization of identities was also stimulated by resentment of mistreatment and by failure to respect the rights of Muslims, but also by the ongoing process of nation building. This was often bound to a reformist spirit, especially for a younger educated generation, emerging from the 1890s on, who were challenging the authority of the traditional elites (including the religious elite). In Bosnia-Herzegovina, the Bosnian Muslim elite was hesitating between Serbian and Croatian nationalism, and a Bosnism, promoted by the Austro-Hungarian authorities around the Bogomils thesis (the thesis of the heretical Christian origin of the Muslims and of the immediate conversion to Islam at the beginning of the Ottoman period of this heretical group).

However, the decade of wars that began with the Balkan Wars (1912–1913), went on with World War I, and ended with the Greek–Turkish war (1919–22) changed considerably the balance of power in southeastern Europe.

## The interwar period and the building of Muslim "minorities"

The successive fall of the Russian, Austro-Hungarian, and Ottoman Empires represented a major turn in world history. In southeastern Europe the consequences were also very important. Beyond the trauma of wars and forced displacements, a new political order was established in the aftermath of the Great War. During the Peace Conference which was held in the French capital, a new political map was drawn up by the various treaties signed in 1919 and 1920. The Kingdom of Serbs, Croats, and Slovenes, whose existence was proclaimed on December 1, 1918, was recognized. Moreover, the borders of the Albanian state established in 1913 were confirmed, while the Greek and Romanian territories were expanded considerably at the expense of the Ottoman Empire and Bulgaria. At the end of the Greco-Turkish war, the Treaty of Lausanne (1923) sanctioned the loss of territories that Greece had conquered in Asia Minor and on the European side, leaving to Turkey Istanbul and eastern Thrace.

Outside of the Albanian state, which included a majority of Muslims, the Muslim populations remained minority groups in the Balkan states. From a politico-social point of view, these groups (though to a lesser extent in Bosnia-Herzegovina) were affected by two major processes: emigration – as in earlier periods – and minority constructions. Indeed, Muslims were becoming "minorities," as this new concept took shape with the treaties of 1919 and the creation of the League of Nations. The two processes were closely related to the legal status granted to Muslims and the gap between this legal status and daily realities. They also depended strongly on agrarian reforms, especially since the latter were often conceived according to national lines. Even if we can see continuities with the previous period, the policy of the nationalization of society that guided interwar leaders – including politicians in Turkey – enhanced their migration policies in relation to the Muslims. After 1923, the exchange of populations – despite how traumatic it was – remained a solution to address what was perceived as a security issue. In the late 1930s conventions were concluded between Turkey and two Balkan countries for the emigration of "Turks" to Turkey: Romania in 1936 and Yugoslavia in 1938. However, emigration was a far more complex phenomenon, because policies as they were realized were the result of a complex relationship between various local actors, including Muslims.

The links with Turkey had also changed. The abolition of the Ottoman Caliphate and of the charge of the *Şeyhülislam* in 1924 changed the situation considerably. The new Turkish Directorate of Religious Affairs now depended directly on the Turkish Prime Minister and was no longer supposed to have authority over Muslims outside Turkey. However, in the case of Romania, Bulgaria, and Greece especially, the debates and controversies that emerged during the interwar period have often been interpreted as an opposition between "Kemalists" and "old Turks," that is to say between supporters and opponents of reforms carried out by Mustafa Kemal in Turkey (adoption of the Latin alphabet, education reform, dress reform – abolition of the veil for women, wearing of hats for men – abolition of the *shari'a* courts and adoption of the Civil Code, etc.). It has also been considered that the "Kemalists" were supported or even encouraged by Turkey, and the "Old Turks" by local governments eager to cut ties with Turkey.

It is true that there were contacts between the Balkan Muslims and the new Turkish Republic. Turkey was, under certain conditions, interested in the migration of Muslims from the Balkans. Thrace was the target of Turkish irredentism. The Turkish government and diplomacy tended to support the adoption of reforms similar to the Kemalist reforms by Muslims in Romania, Greece, and Bulgaria, particularly. But the action of the Kemalist authorities was primarily guided by the desire to eliminate the development of any opposition that could spread from Bulgaria to Turkey, for example (Boyar and Fleet 2008). It is also true that opponents of the Kemalist regime (the famous "hundred and fifty" people expelled by Mustafa Kemal, members of the Ottoman dynasty, and others) were to be found in some Balkan countries, where they sometimes held important positions in Islamic religious institutions or in the press, because the local authorities, on the other hand, did use Balkan Islam against the development of a Turkish nationalism. This was particularly the case in Bulgaria and Greece, where the presence of Muslims in border regions rendered these authorities very sensitive to the issue.

However, this vision of an opposition between "Kemalists" and "Old Turks," or "reformists" and "conservatives" in the case of Bosnia-Herzegovina, downplays the importance of local issues, local competition for power, and the integration of Muslim actors in the local and national arenas. Religious and secular reformisms, nationalism, and conservatism had their own historicities in these areas and were forged through transnational circulations that were not necessarily the result of state policies. In general, if the issues of internal reforms were addressed with multiple positions in the debates, they were inextricably linked to the questions of the political and civic integration of Muslims (or their elites) in the states of the region, based on existing social and political relations. In Yugoslavia, where the Turkish-speaking Muslims were a minority in the southern provinces and were absent in Bosnia-Herzegovina, the situation was different. But, in the same way, the issues of internal reforms were inextricably linked to questions concerning the political and civic integration of Muslims (or their elites), based on existing social and political relations. In Bosnia and Herzegovina, it was often translated by a choice between the different national options (Yugoslavism, Serbism, or Croatism), while, in the 1930s, some Muslims of the younger generation were attracted by Communism (like many other young people – Muslims or not – in other regions of the Peninsula).

The case of Albania is, of course, special because of its Muslim majority (69 percent of the million people recorded in 1930). However, from its creation the Albanian state had no official religion, neither Islam nor any other religion. After World War I, this principle was reaffirmed, while the liberty of every cult was guaranteed. It is interesting to note that the two countries of the region having a Muslim majority – Albania and Turkey – always put a strong emphasis on their supposed secularity ("*afetarizmi*" in the case of Albania, "*laiklik*" in the case of Turkey), which was also an emphasis on their Western or European character (which the countries with a Christian Orthodox majority did not do). But, in contrast to Turkey, neither the political opposition nor the construction of the nation and citizenship was mainly expressed in terms of opposition between "reformists" and "conservatives" or "reactionaries." Of course, Zog (who became king in 1928) launched a package of reforms, including reform of Islam (Islamic religious institutions were reformed in 1929, the *shari'a* courts were abolished in 1929, the veil was banned in 1937), but the main opposition to its power was not perceived as religious opposition. Rather, it was denounced as Bolshevik, and Muslim reformist circles were rather close to power. To prevent future generations from being attracted to Communism and to strengthen their loyalty to the king, in 1937 the latter even ordered the reintroduction of religion classes at school. Then in 1938 he married a (non-Muslim) Hungarian countess, but he reinforced the image of his dynasty by building mosques, such as the new mosque in the port of Durrës, which bore his name.

From a more specifically religious perspective, the interwar years saw major changes related to local circumstances, but also to transformations in the Islamic world. The treaties of 1919 reaffirmed, in the various Balkan countries, the rights of Muslim minorities in terms of education, exercise, and religious administration. In most cases, the context of nationalization and modernization was also driving nationalization and institutionalization of Islamic religious institutions, and there was a kind of beginning of nationalization of Islam (especially with the use of vernacular languages and the foundation of local reformed schools for the education of Muslim clerics). Nevertheless, two interesting phenomena are to be noted here.

During the interwar years, the networks of Balkan Islam were also redefined at the international and transnational level. Indeed, the closure of the *madrasa*s and of the dervish lodges (*tekke*s) in Turkey led to the reorientation of the training and scholarly networks, mainly towards Cairo in Egypt, where young Balkan Muslims went to study. But some Balkan Muslims also had connections with the Islamic transnational network of the Lahori Ahmadiyya. This proselytizing network, founded by Muhammad Ali in the late nineteenth century in British India, gave birth to two groups: the Lahoris and the Qadiyanis, both very active groups of missionaries. As for the Lahoris, they were preaching the compatibility of Islam and modernity and wishing to contribute to rebuilding the image that Muslims had of themselves. During the interwar period they were present in Berlin and London, where they were managing mosques and publishing journals. From the end of the 1920s they had an important impact on some leading religious Muslim leaders in Albania, both directly and throughout Turkey (translation of their production, sending students to Lahore), but also in Bosnia-Herzegovina (use of the Qur'an commentary of Muhammad Ali for the commentary elaborated by two local '*ulama*', connections with Muslim in Prague through the Berlin mosque).

Some Balkan Muslims were also connected to other transnational networks which were established between Europe and the Muslim world, such as, for example, the network of Shakib Arslan, the Arab activist who published in Geneva the famous newspaper *La Nation arabe*. When he organized the European Muslim Congress in 1935, Muslims from the Balkans were present, except from Albania, because the Albanian government did not recognize the Congress. Yet Shakib Arslan's new notion of "European Islam," or rather "Islam in Europe," was also developing in Albania, where Muslims' religious leaders tried to reform Islam to make the country an acceptable European state with a Muslim majority.

## Secularization and nationalization under socialist rule

The outcome of World War II in southeastern Europe was dramatic because of huge human losses. Politically, it was also fraught with consequences since socialist regimes were established by the Partisan movements and/or the Russian army in all the countries of the Peninsula, except in Greece. There the Civil War lasted till 1949 and was won by the monarchical forces, helped by Great Britain and the USA. At that time, Yugoslavia had already broken with the Soviet Union (1948) and taken a special path within the Eastern Bloc. In 1962, it was a founding member of the Non-Aligned Movement. At the internal level, its leaders opted for the decentralization of political structures. The socialist regimes' policies led to significant political, but also social, transformations. Changes were important, for example, in the fields of economy (collectivization, industrialization), of education, of transport (electrification, means of communication), and at the social level (consumption, rural exodus, demographic transitions, emancipation of women).

Concerning religion, the socialist regimes adopted from the beginning anti-religious policies similar to Stalinist policies: confiscation of property, purging and control of hierarchies, campaigns in favor of atheism. However, contrasting changes occurred in the 1960s. While in Yugoslavia there was liberalization, in Romania and Bulgaria the religious policies remained the same, and in Albania there was a hardening of policy with the ban of religious practices in 1967 (and the inscription of atheism in the Constitution in 1976). These policies, as well as social transformations, produced an important secularization of Balkan societies. Even in Greece, where there were no such anti-religious policies, the secularization that Western Europe experienced was also experienced there.

As for the Muslims, these policies resulted in the abolition of the *shari'a* courts, as had already happened in interwar Albania, but also in the nationalization of the *waqf* properties, the closing of religious schools, as well as in the banning of the veil. In Greece, where the clauses of the Treaty of Lausanne remained valid, religious institutions and practices were not abolished or constrained in an authoritarian way, as in the rest of the Peninsula. However, the Greek authorities succeeded in suppressing some *mufti* positions outside Thrace and restricting the competences of the local Muslim institutions (*cemaat*), obliging the Muslims to create their own organization for the management of religious life.

Among Muslims, policies of collectivization and imposition of schooling for girls were difficult to accept. This and the general situation led many of them again to migrate to Turkey. Migration waves were particularly strong in the 1950s from Bulgaria (150,000 people) and Yugoslavia (200,000 people). From these two countries, they went on, accompanying flows also from Greece and Romania. However, from the 1960s on, from Yugoslavia and Greece, Muslims migrated to Western Europe and to America as well, just like their non-Muslim fellow countrymen. This significant shift is proof of the integration of Muslims as citizens in Balkan countries. This integration was facilitated by the disappearance of former elites and the emergence of new elites linked to the Communist parties and produced by social transformations (teachers, doctors, engineers). These new secular elites played a key role in the crystallization of national identities, a prominent phenomenon of the period.

During the socialist period, the Balkan state apparatuses introduced new principles to manage the national question. But these principles varied from one country to another and sometimes over time too. For example, a Turkish national identity was promoted in Bulgaria and Greece in the 1950s, while it was repressed in the 1970s and 1980s, and a Muslim nation was recognized in Yugoslavia only in 1968. This is also because the Muslims were not passive objects of state policies: through their elites, they participated in the assertion of new national identifications, or opposed the policies of assimilation or marginalization. Moreover, national identifications were henceforth largely shared outside the elite circles. From this point of view, the Balkan Muslim populations were also expressing their citizenship.

In the Yugoslav federation, where the Soviet system of nations and national minorities was implemented, the recognition of a "Muslim nation" (or nation of the "Muslims") by the League of the Communists of Bosnia and Herzegovina in 1968 is to be seen in the context of the use of national identities by republican and provincial elites who wanted to legitimize their own project at the expense of a common Yugoslav project. This recognition led to tensions and ambiguities, because of the name which had a religious connotation, regarding its scope (in 1971 it was finally recognized for the whole Yugoslav territory) and the guarantor institutions (political or religious). The recognition was also used by some Bosnian Muslim intellectuals who expressed their desire to have their own cultural institutions, which provoked a hostile reaction of Croats and Serbs. In the southern part of the federation Albanians were recognized as a national minority and, from the end of the 1960s, they really enjoyed greater political and cultural rights. Nevertheless, in a context of economical stagnation, Albanian demonstrations broke out in Kosovo in 1968 and in 1981, around the claim for the transformation of the autonomous province of Serbia into a republic. From 1981, the socialist authorities of Kosovo and Macedonia fought everything they suspected of being "Albanian nationalism," and paradoxically contributed to increasing it.

In Bulgaria there was no such federal system, but, with the establishment of the new regime, a Turkish nation was recognized. From the mid-1950s, however, the authorities feared a "Turkish nationalism" which was also appealing to the Pomaks (Slavic-speaking Muslims). In 1956 Bulgarian political leaders returned to a definition of Bulgaria as a homogeneous nation-state (the new Bulgarian Constitution of 1971 no longer mentioned the existence of national minorities). As a consequence, Turkish schools were closed down, and from the beginning of the 1960s campaigns of forced assimilation of the Pomaks and Gypsies were launched, with the imposition of Bulgarian names and a fight against "backward" religious and cultural traditions. In December 1984 the authorities decided to extend these policies to the Turkish population and launched the famous campaign called the "revival process." With the support of the police and army, the names of some 800,000 Turks were changed and their religious and cultural practices were prohibited. The Turkish language was also banished from the public sphere. This policy provoked strong resistance, with several dozen deaths and hundreds of people imprisoned. In the second half of the 1980s, clandestine organizations were formed, and Turkish intellectuals joined the nascent Bulgarian dissident movement. The "revival process" led paradoxically to the crystallization of a Turkish national sentiment and the politicization of Turkish elites.

During this period, the networks of Islam in the Balkans and the connections with the Islamic world were considerably weakened, mainly in the first two decades and particularly in Albania, where religion was banned and international connections cut. The Islamic networks were also transformed because of the monopoly the official hierarchy was given over the religious sphere (Sufi orders were even banned in Bosnia-Herzegovina). However, the monopoly was not complete. In Bosnia-Herzegovina notably the pan-Islamist network of the Young Muslims (*Mladi Muslimani*), formed in 1941, re-emerged in the 1960s and was to play a central role in the political and religious reconfigurations of the 1980s and 1990s. Moreover, the contacts formed with the Arab world from the 1960s onwards, through the exchange of students from Yugoslavia and Greece – who went to al-Azhar and other Islamic universities – and from Arab countries, were a factor in the spread of new Islamic trends in the Balkan realm, such as Neo-Salafism. This happened in the 1980s, when religion became increasingly present in the public sphere, in a context of growing political and social tensions.

## Muslims as political actors and citizens in the turmoil of the post-socialist era

Perestroika and the fall of the Berlin Wall contributed to an increase in tensions and to the fall of socialist regimes in the Balkans. In Yugoslavia it led to the dissolution of the federation and to a succession of bloody wars in Croatia (1991), Bosnia-Herzegovina (1992–5), Kosovo (1998–9), and Macedonia (2001). Among the dramatic events that went with these changes in the region were the massive exodus of the Turks from Bulgaria in 1989 and the civil war which broke out in Albania in 1997. More generally, social and economic hardship and migration became the fate of many Balkan people.

In the new political context, which put the region in a new position *vis-à-vis* NATO and the European Union (Romania and Bulgaria became members in 2007) but also enabled the introduction of multiparty systems, a significant evolution occurred for the Balkan Muslims: their political organization. Indeed, while Muslims had had their own political party only in Bosnia-Herzegovina during the first three decades of the twentieth century, at the beginning of the 1990s they emerged everywhere as an independent political factor. Stimulated by the strengthening of their national identification, they founded their own political parties, except in

Albania and Greece. In Albania, the political structure is independent of religious belonging, while in Greece Muslim mobilization remained at the religious level. Elsewhere, however, the new political parties are led by secular elites and religion does not play a central role, except in Bosnia-Herzegovina. There Alija Izetbegović and the "Young Muslims," with their pan-Islamist ideology, succeeded in creating the Stranka Demokratske Akcije (SDA; Party of Democratic Action) and in being at the center of the local political scene. This new phenomenon, which is synonymous with full citizen status for the Muslims, is reinforced in the case of Bosnia-Herzegovina and Kosovo by the fact that in these two new sovereign entities Muslims are henceforth in a numerical majority position.

If Islam is not at the center of the political restructuring among the Balkan Muslims, the political evolutions led to a complex redefining of the relationship between Islam and national identity. In Bosnia-Herzegovina, during the war, there was a re-Islamization of national identity. Among the other groups of Muslims, ties between Islam and national identity also became closer. Within the Albanian space, debates broke out on this issue. In Kosovo and Macedonia, Muslim belonging is used to bind Turks, Roma, and Slavic-speaking Muslims to the Albanians. In Albania, the new political leader Berisha made the country a member of the Organization of the Islamic Conference. However, Islam did not supersede national identifications. Pan-Muslim mobilizations, for example, remained marginal, even during the conflict. In Bosnia-Herzegovina, despite the key role of the SDA, the re-Islamization of national identity, and the use of Islam as an ideology of substitution after the fall of Communism in war time, the SDA is more a nationalist party and lost its position on the political scene after the conflict. Besides, the party itself had decided in 1993 to rename the "Muslim nation" the "Bosniak nation," in order to underline its sovereignty and to increase its international legitimacy.

This partial and complex re-Islamization of national identities is also partly due to a clear increase in the activities and in the visibility of Islamic religious institutions. Indeed, with the fall of the socialist regimes the liberty of religion was re-established; the official Islamic religious hierarchies could reorganize themselves – often with the help of diasporas and foreign Muslim networks (be they state sponsored, NGOs, or other proselytizing groups) – and recover some of their property. However, the new situation led to the end of the monopoly these official hierarchies had over the religious scene. New Muslim actors – foreign as well as local – began to act independently. Even within the official institutions tensions and conflicts appeared. In particular, young people influenced by Neo-Salafism (after their return from Islamic universities or their contact with Neo-Salafist groups in the Balkans) began to oppose, from within or from outside, the older generation leading the official institutions. Among them, we should distinguish two different trends: the jihadists (mainly foreign *mujahidin* who came to fight in Bosnia-Herzegovina or to take refuge in the Balkans, and who were violently anti-Western and sometimes involved in terrorist acts); and the Pietists (primarily students returning from the Muslim world, who are more concerned with the re-Islamization of morals). Sufi networks also developed within the Balkan realm, as well as the neo-Brotherhood movements coming from Turkey. In general, it is interesting to notice that after 9/11 cooperation with Turkish Islamic actors was favored over contacts with actors coming from Arab countries. The network of Fethullah Gülen, very active in the educational field and already present in the Balkans in the 1990s, experienced a significant diffusion in the region in the first decade of the twenty-first century. This also provoked debates about the feature of Balkan Islam, but also the role of Balkan Muslims in the shaping of a "European Islam." Thus, in 2005, Mustafa Cerić, chief of the Bosnian '*ulama*', published a "declaration of the European Muslims," in which he condemns terrorism, but which is in line with some claims of the Muslim Brotherhood in Western Europe.

Despite the increased visibility of Islam in the public sphere, through the activities and declarations of these religious actors and the building of new mosques, *madrasa*s, etc., the post-socialist era is mainly characterized for the Balkan Muslim population by the long-lasting effects of socialist secularization and by individualization of the faith. Regular religious practice remains exceptional. Even in Bosnia-Herzegovina, the attacks made during the war by the SDA and the Islamic official institutions against mixed marriages, consumption of alcohol, and the celebration of Christmas and New Year faced strong resistance within the population and have been abandoned. Moreover, as elsewhere in the world, the faith and the way of believing is increasingly individualized. Among the more popular religious works among Balkan Muslims are books referring to personal concerns (Islam and the family, Islam and sexuality, Islam and health). So, the more perceptible Neo-Salafism should be seen as one form of religiosity among others in a much diversified religious landscape where conversions to Christianity also represent a possible choice (as is particularly the case among the Albanians in Albania or in the diaspora in Greece and Italy).

## Conclusions

The political trajectories of the Balkan Muslims since the territorial losses of the Ottoman Empire during the long nineteenth century reflect a complex and difficult passage to a non-Islamic sovereignty. Often driven directly or indirectly to migration, the Balkan Muslims have experienced very diverse situations, related to their socio-economic status, to the state they were living in, and to the period. Their place in the Balkan states follows two conflicting tendencies: rejection, which experienced its peak with the ethnic cleansing during the wars of the end of the twentieth century, and the integration made possible in different ways (granted rights, "minoritization" policies or citizenship). This place was and is not only shaped by state policies, but also by socio-political changes that also affected their fellow non-Muslim countrymen, and by their own agency. By the way, at the beginning of the twenty-first century three of the Balkan political entities have henceforth a Muslim majority (absolute or relative).

As for religious aspects, Balkan Islam cannot be reduced either to a Sufi or to a fundamentalist component. There has always been in the region a diversity of Islamic currents, and their evolutions have always been tied to evolutions in the Islamic world, first at the Ottoman level, and then, already since the interwar period, at a more globalized level (even to a lesser extent during the socialist period). Beyond the evolutions of Islam, Balkan Muslims, as European citizens, experienced and are experiencing also more general changes.

## Note

1 This chapter is largely inspired by the following book: Xavier Bougarel and Nathalie Clayer (2013) *Les Musulmans de l'Europe du sud-est (XIXe–XXe siècles)*, Paris: Karthala, where details are to be found.

## Bibliography

Adanir, F. and Faroqhi, S. (eds.) (2002) *The Ottomans and the Balkans: A Discussion of Historiography*, Leiden, Boston, and Köln: Brill.

Akan Ellis, B. (2003) *Shadow Genealogies: Memory and Identity among Urban Muslims in Macedonia*, Boulder, CO: East European Monographs.

Allcock, J.B. (2000) "Constructing the Balkans," in Allcock, J.B. and Young, A. (eds.) *Black Lambs and Grey Falcons: Women Travelling in the Balkans*, New York: Berghahn Books, pp. 217–40.

Basha, A. (2011) *Rrugëtimi i fesë islame në Shqipëri (1912–1967)*, Tirana.

Bougarel, X. (ed.) (2007) "Balkan Muslims and Islam in Europe," *Südosteuropa* LV(4).

Bougarel, X. and Clayer, N. (eds.) (2001) *Le Nouvel Islam balkanique. Les musulmans, acteurs du post-communisme (1990–2000)*, Paris: Maisonneuve & Larose.

——(2013) *Les Musulmans de l'Europe du sud-est (XIXe–XXe siècles)*, Paris: Karthala.

Bougarel, X. and Iseni, B. (2007) "Islam et politique dans les Balkans occidentaux," *Politorbis* 43: 3–71.

Boyar, E. and Fleet, K. (2008) "A Dangerous Axis: The 'Bulgarian Müftü', the Turkish Opposition and the Ankara Government, 1928–36," *Middle Eastern Studies* 44(5): 775–89.

Bringa, T. (1995) *Being Muslim the Bosnian Way: Identity and Community in a Central Bosnian Village*, Princeton: Princeton University Press.

Clayer, N. (1994) *Mystiques, Etat et société. Les Halvetis dans l'aire balkanique de la fin du XVe siècle à nos jours*, Leiden, New York, and Köln: Brill.

——(2007) *Aux Origines du nationalisme albanais*, Paris: Karthala.

——(2011) "Muslim Brotherhood Networks in South-Eastern Europe," in *European History Online (EGO)*, Mainz: Institute of European History (IEG), www.ieg-ego.eu/clayern-2011-en.

Clayer, N. and Germain, E. (eds.) (2008) *Islam in Interwar Europe*, London: Hurst.

Cossuto, G. (2001) *Storia dei Turchi di Dobrugia*, Istanbul: Isis.

Dogo, M. and Franzinetti, G. (eds.) (2002) *Disrupting and Reshaping: Early Stages of nation-Building in the Balkans*, Ravenna: Longo Editore.

Duijzings, G. (2000) *Religion and the Politics of Identity in Kosovo*, London: Hurst.

Gaborieau, M. and Popovic A. (eds.) (2001) "Islam et politique dans le monde (ex-)communiste," *Archives de sciences sociales des religions* XLVI(115) (July–September), Paris: EHESS.

Gangloff, S. (ed.) (2005) *La Perception de l'héritage ottoman dans les Balkans*, Paris: L'Harmattan.

Gelez, Ph. (2009) *Safvet-beg Bašagić (1870–1934): aux racines intellectuelles de la pensée nationale chez les musulmans de Bosnie-Herzégovine*, Athens: Ecole française d'Athènes.

Georgeon, F. (2003) *Abdülhamid II. Le sultan calife*, Paris: Fayard.

Ghodsee, K. (2010) *Muslim Lives in Eastern Europe: Gender, Ethnicity and the Transformation of Islam in Postsocialist Bulgaria*, Princeton: Princeton University Press.

Giomi, F. (2011) "Fra genere, classe, confessione e nazione. 'Questione femminile musulmana' e associazionismo in Bosnia e Erzegovina (1903–41)," thesis, University of Bologna-EHESS.

Grandits, H. (2008) *Herrschaft und Loyalität in der spätosmanischen Gesellschaft. Das Beispiel der mulitkonfessionellen Herzegowina*, Vienna: Böhlau.

Grandits, H., Clayer, N., and Pichler, R. (eds.) (2011) *Conflicting Loyalties in the Balkans: The Great Powers, the Ottoman Empire, and Nation-Building*, London: I.B. Tauris.

Grivaud, G. and Popovic, A. (eds.) (2011) *Les Conversions à l'islam en Asie mineure et dans les Balkans aux époques seldjoukide et ottomane*, Athens: Ecole française d'Athènes.

Gruev, M. and Kalionski A. (2008) *Văzroditelniat proces: Mjusjulmanskite obštnosti i komunističeskiat režim*, Sofia: Siela.

Hatiboğlu, I. (2006) "*Inshai* Interpretation of Islamic Sciences in Transition to a Multicultural Environment in Bulgaria during the First Half of the 20th Century: The Case of Yusuf Ziyaeddin Ezheri," *Proceedings of the Second International Symposium on Islamic Civilization in the Balkans*, Istanbul: Ircica, pp. 135–48.

Hersant, J. (2009) "Souveraineté et gouvernementalité: la rivalité gréco-turque en Thrace occidentale," *Critique internationale* 45(4): 141–62.

Höpken, W. (1996) "Flucht vor dem Kreuz? Muslimische Emigration aus Südosteuropa nach dem Ende der osmanischen Herrschaft (19./20.) Jahrhundert," *Comparativ* VI(1): 1–24.

Hrabak, B. (2003) *Džemijet. Organizacija muslimana Makedonije, Kosova, Metohije i Sandžaka 1919–1928*, Beograd.

Hysi, Sh. (2006) *Muslimanizmi në Shqipëri në periudhën 1945–1950*, Tirana: Mësonjëtorja.

Immig, N. (2009) "The 'new' Muslim Minorities in Greece: Between Emigration and Political Participation, 1881–86," *Journal of Muslim Minority Affairs* 29(4) (December): 511–22.

"Islam in the Balkans" (1994) *Journal of Islamic Studies* 5(2).

"Islam in the Balkans" (1997) *Islamic Studies* XXXVI(2–3) (summer–autumn): 137–581.

Janjetović, Z. (2005) *Deca careva, pastorčad kraljeva. Nacionalne manjine u Jugoslaviji 1918–1941*, Beograd: INIS.

Karateke, H.T. and Reinkowski, M. (eds.) (2005) *Legitimizing the Order: The Ottoman Rhetoric of State Power*, Leiden and Boston: Brill.

Karčić F. (1999) *The Bosniaks and the Challenge of Modernity*, Sarajevo: El-Kalem.

Karić, E. (2004) *Prilozi za povijest islamskog mišljenja u Bosni i Hercegovini XX. stoljeća*, Sarajevo: El-Kalem.

Kretsi, G. (2003) "From Landholding to Landlessness: The Relationship between the Property and Legal Status of the Cham Muslim Albanians," *JGKS* 5: 125–38.

Krstić, T. (2011) *Contested Conversions to Islam*, Stanford: Stanford University Press.

Kurz, M. (ed.) (2005) "Islam am Balkan," *Wiener Zeitschrift zur Geschichte der Neuzeit* V(2): 3–130.

Lory, B. (1985) "Le Sort *de l'héritage ottoman en Bulgarie. L'exemple de villes bulgares, 1878–1900*, Istanbul: Isis.

Mančeva, M. (2003) *State–Minority Relations and the Education of Turks and Pomaks in Inter-war Bulgaria, 1918–44*, Ph.D. thesis, Central European University, Budapest.

Mazower, M. (2000) *The Balkans: From the End of Byzantium to the Present Day*, London: Phoenix.

Memić, M. (1984) *Velika medresa i njeni učenici u revolucionarnom pokretu*, Skopje.

Mentzel, P. (ed.) (2000) "Muslim Minorities in the Balkans," *Nationalities Papers* XXVIII(1) (March): 7–204.

Methodieva, M.B. (2010) *Reform, Politics and Culture among the Muslims in Bulgaria, 1878–1908*, Ph.D. thesis, Princeton University.

Methodieva, M. and Somel S.A. (2004) "Keeping the Bonds: The Ottoman and Muslim Education in Autonomous Bulgaria, 1878–1908," *Turcica* 36: 141–64.

Mirkova, A. (2009) "Citizenship Formation in Bulgaria: Protected Minority or National Citizens?," *Journal of Muslim Minority Affairs* 29(4) (December 2009): 469–82.

Neuburger, M. (2004) *The Orient Within. Muslim Minorities and the Negotiation of Nationhood in Modern Bulgaria*, Ithaca and London: Cornell University Press.

Niblock, T., Nonnenman, G., and Szajkowski, B. (eds.) (1996) *Muslim Communities in the New Europe*, Berkshire: Ithaca Press.

Okey, R. (2007) *Taming Balkan Nationalism: The Habsburg "Civilizing Mission" in Bosnia, 1878–1914*, Oxford: Oxford University Press.

Öktem, K. (ed.) (2010) *After the Wahhabi Mirage: Islam, Politics and International Networks in the Balkans*, Oxford: European Studies Center, www.balkanmuslims.com.

Omerika, A. (2012) *Islam in Bosnien-Herzegowina und die Netzwerke der Jungmuslime 1918–1991*, Wiesbaden: Harrassowitz.

Paić-Vukić, T. (2007) *Svijet Mustafe Muhibbija, saraejvskoga kadije*, Zagreb: Srendja Europa.

Pezo, E. (2009) "'Re-Conquering' Space: Yugoslav Migration Policies and the Emigration of Non-Slavic Muslims to Turkey (1918–41)," in Brunnbauer, U. (ed.) *Transnational Societies, Transterritorial Politics: Migrations in the (Post-)Yugoslav Region 19th–21st Century*, Munich: Oldenbourg, pp. 73–94.

Popovic, A. (1986) *L'Islam balkanique*, Berlin and Wiesbaden: Harrassowitz.

——(1994a) *Cultures musulmanes balkaniques*, Istanbul: Isis.

——(1994b) *Les Derviches balkaniques hier et aujourd'hui*, Istanbul: Isis.

——(1994c) *Les Musulmans des Balkans à l'époque post-ottomane. Histoire et politique*, Istanbul: Isis.

Poulton, H. and Taji-Farouki, S. (eds.) (1997) *Muslim Identity and the Balkan State*, London: Hurst.

Sorabji, C. (1989) *Muslim Identity and Islamic Faith in Sarajevo*, Ph.D. thesis, Cambridge University.

Todorova, M. (1996) "The Ottoman Legacy in the Balkans," in Brown, C.L. (ed.) *Imperial Legacy: The Ottoman Imprint on the Balkans and the Middle East*, New York: Columbia University Press, pp. 45–77.

——(1997) Imagining the Balkans, New York: Oxford University Press.

Toumarkine, A. (1995) *Les Migrations des populations musulmanes balkaniques en Anatolie (1876–1913)*, Istanbul: Isis.

Tsitselikis, K. (2012) *Old and New Islam in Greece: From Historical Minorities to Immigrant Newcomers*, Leiden: Brill.

Ülker, E. (2007) "Assimilation of the Muslim communities in the first decade of the Turkish Republic (1923–34)," *European Journal of Turkish Studies* [Online], ejts.revues.org/822.

——(2008) "Assimilation, Security and Geographical Nationalization in Interwar Turkey: The Settlement Law of 1934," *European Journal of Turkish Studies* [Online], ejts.revues.org/2123.

Veinstein, G. (1989) "Les Provinces balkaniques (1606–1774)," in Mantran, R. (ed.) *Histoire de l'Empire ottoman*, Paris: Fayard, pp. 265–340.

Vezenkov, A. (2009) "History against Geography: Should We Always Think of the Balkans as Part of Europe," www.kakanien.ac.at/beitr/balkans/AVezenkov1/.

Voss, Ch. and Telbizova-Sack, J. (eds.) (2010) *Islam und Muslime in (Südost)Europa im Kontekst von Transformation und EU-Erweiterung*, Munich: Otto Sagner.

Zürcher, E.J. (2004) *Turkey: A Modern History*, London and New York: I.B. Tauris.

# 5

# Muslims in Western Europe in the late twentieth century

## Emergence and transformations in "Muslim" revindications and collective mobilization efforts

*Ghaliya Djelloul and Brigitte Maréchal*

## Introduction

In the wake of the pioneering work of Felice Dassetto and Jorgen Nielsen published in the early 1980s, the number of research projects dealing with European Islam is ever on the increase. Although this subject has received little generally focused treatment, certain logics of action do emerge in the literature available, addressing the subject of the collective mobilization efforts of Muslims (whether they are religious or religiously inspired). Indeed, the dynamics of the implantation and consolidation of the presence of Muslims in Europe are primarily approached from three perspectives: either in terms of the specific features of the national context of each of the various European countries[1] or based on the activities of one or the other Islamic current – Sufi, missionary, political, etc. – among others transnational, testifying to ideological sensitivities and specific models of action, or based on mobilization efforts within a relatively well-defined sphere of activity, such as political representation, interreligious dialogue or *halal* business.[2]

All sphere of activities taken together, here we present a panorama of the major lines of influence of European Muslims' militant involvements, even if our anchoring in the Belgian context might quite likely appear determinative in our considerations. To start with, we shall provide some background, particularly the distribution and specific features of Muslim populations in Western Europe in connection with a periodization of the processes of emergence and anchoring of these individuals and/or communities. We shall then present their types of mobilization and revindications. Finally, we shall develop axes of interpretation with a view to understanding the possible particularities of these militant engagements in Europe, before concluding with the transformations all that represents and implies, not only for Muslim communities, but also, in a broader scope, for European societies.

## The emergences and trajectories of "Muslim" communities

The presence of "Muslims" in Europe results from three distinct settlement processes. The earliest (seventh to eighth century) dates back to the arrival of Muslim armies in southern Europe (Spain and Sicily), from where they were subsequently driven back. The second took place in Eastern Europe, in the Balkans region and Central Europe. It was bound up in the Ottoman Empire's military expansion from the fifteenth century on and ended in the early twentieth century with that empire's gradual disintegration. The last process of implantation began in the 1960s; it manifests the specific characteristics any new dynamic involves.

At the geographical level, this implantation is broader than in the past not only from a quantitative point of view but also because it has gradually extended throughout European space (from southern Italy to the north of the Scandinavian countries, from Scotland to Berlin). Moreover, unlike a good part of the earlier encounters, this one is peaceful and largely composed of working-class members issuing from the four corners of the Islamic world. Their distribution throughout European territory re-establishes older, imperial or colonial connections: those who come from the Maghreb countries are predominantly implanted along the countries of the European Atlantic coastline, from Spain to the Netherlands, as well as in Italy and to a lesser extent in Germany. Those coming from the Indian peninsula and Pakistan initially established themselves in the United Kingdom. Today, these populations circulate and are present in other European countries too. Those coming from sub-Saharan Africa (especially West Africa) are established in France, Spain, and Italy. Others, arriving from Turkey, settled in Germany, Austria, as well as in France (particularly in Alsace), Belgium, the Netherlands, Sweden, Norway, and Finland. Subsequently, others have been arriving more recently from Kosovo, Bosnia, Chechnya, Afghanistan, Iran, and elsewhere (Dassetto 1996; Nielsen et al. 2009).

### An unequal and growing implantation in European countries

Quantifying the "Muslim" presence raises many questions of definition (Dassetto 1996; Jeldtoft 2009; Spielhaus 2011). Among others: on what bases can one measure religious affiliation in the absence of reliable censuses on the subject? How is one to account for the diversity of identities and affiliations which, linked to the multiple positions that are possible with regard to Islam (spiritual, normative, cultural, civilizational, and political postures, *inter alia*), themselves lead to commitments with very variable intensities? And beyond the efforts to take them into account through typologies, are these categories mutually exclusive or do they frequently overlap? The difficulties involved in making subjective affiliations intelligible lead us to place the term "Muslim" in quotation marks and insist that it is above all a matter of people directly or indirectly originating from mainly Muslim countries, while remaining aware that it is important to consider the presence of converts to Islam, who are often actively involved in religious matters. Moreover, on the basis of the rare data existing, we can say that in Western European countries roughly 30 percent of people of Muslim origin actively express their religious identity in an explicit and visible manner – participation in Friday prayers, wearing headscarves, etc. – whereas only 10 percent of them engage in some form of collective militant mobilization efforts, whether they do so regularly or only occasionally.

To provide ourselves with points of reference, however imperfect they might be, we provide the figures here of the number of people of "attributed" Muslim origin (Table 5.1), i.e. affiliated to Islam on the basis of ethno-national criteria, according to their origin in one of the five following cultural geographical areas (the Maghreb and other Arab countries, Turkey, the

*Table 5.1* Number of people of "attributed" Muslim origin

| Country | Muslim population in 2000/1 (Maréchal 2002) | % of total population | Muslim pop. in 2009/10 (Nielsen et al. 2011) | % of total population |
|---|---|---|---|---|
| Austria | 300,000 | 4 | 500,000 | 6 |
| Belgium | 370,000 | 3.7 | 450,000 | 4 |
| Denmark | 150,000 | 2.8 | 216,880 | 4 |
| Finland | 20,000 | 0.39 | 50,000–60,000 | 1 |
| France | 4,000,000 | 6.6 | 5,300,000 | 7 |
| Germany | 3,400,000 | 3.2 | 3,800,000–4,300,000 | 4.6–5.25 |
| Greece | 370,000 | 3–3.5 | 350,000 (in 2008) | 3.1 |
| Ireland | 19,147 (in 2002) | 0.5 | 49,204 | 1 |
| Italy | 700,000 | 1.2 | 1,420,000 | 2.4 |
| Netherlands | 695,600 | 4.6 | 857,000 | 5 |
| Norway | 56,468 | 1.3 | 150,000 | 3 |
| Portugal | 30,000–38,000 | 0.3 | 38,000–40,000 | 0.4 |
| Spain | 300,000–400,000 | 0.75–0.1 | 1,320,000 | 2.85 |
| Sweden | 250,000–300,000 | 2.8–3.3 | 350,000–400,000 | 3.8–4.4 |
| Switzerland | 310,000 | 4 | 400,000 | 5.2 |
| United Kingdom | 1,400,000 | 2.5 | 2,870,000 | 4.6 |

Indian peninsula, Africa, and the Balkans), adding the number of converts. For a correct grasp of the growth in figures between 1999 and 2009, we should note particularly that the estimates become appreciably more precise when self-identification surveys are introduced, as in the Netherlands in 2006.

These populations have grown rather quickly in most countries. On average, they accounted for 3.5 percent of the total European population in 2001, and then 5.5 percent in 2010, but strong disparities exist between countries: the spread ranges between 7 percent in France and 0.4 percent in Portugal. Additionally, the implantations are mainly urban, given that Muslims sometimes make up a non-negligible part of that population, which is, moreover, often concentrated in certain zones (such as the old central districts or the interstices and peripheries of cities): thus populations are over 15 percent Muslim in certain cities like Birmingham, Marseilles, Brussels, Berlin, and Utrecht. As for demographic projections, they show the possibility of higher rates in the future even if it is not certain that this tendency will continue given the fact of a progressive rapprochement in behavior as regards birth rates (Westoff and Frejka 2007).

## A continual succession of migratory waves and the anchoring process: from Islam in exile to established Islam

Assuming that mass dynamics are especially dependent on the variable attractiveness of contexts, the last wave of implantation of "Muslim" populations into Western Europe evolved over the course of four phases (Dassetto 1996). The first among them was the fruit of a more or less voluntarist policy favoring the immigration of mainly male workers with the aim of supporting the European economic boom, particularly after the signing of labor agreements between states. This began in the 1960s in most of the countries of the center and north of Western Europe (the United Kingdom, Netherlands, Belgium, Switzerland, Austria, Norway, Denmark, and Sweden) and in the southern States (Spain, Portugal, Italy, and Greece) from the 1980s on.

There were some exceptions to this for specific historical reasons: France, for example, witnessed the installation of "Muslims" from the 1920s on because of its colonies and protectorate in North Africa. Ireland has welcomed a large number of "Muslim" students since the 1950s, but only experienced a more massive surge and diversification in the profiles of this "Muslim" immigration during the economic boom of the 1990s. Lastly, Finland saw a first community of "Muslims," Tatars and Kazakhs, settling from 1830 on, at the time of its annexation by the Russian Empire. Their descendants have been officially organized as a community since 1923 and were only joined by other "Muslims" in the 1990s thanks to policies admitting refugees.

Despite the border closings decreed by the traditional countries of immigration (Germany, the Netherlands, Belgium, and France) after the first oil crisis in 1973, a sizeable influx of "Muslim" immigration went on unabated, becoming more diversified: it especially increased in connection with family reunifications. Barely arrived, all of these populations rapidly found themselves confronted with the worsening economic crisis, unemployment, and an atmosphere of hostility.

During the 1980s a third phase witnessed the installation of new waves of immigrants in southern Europe, and in northern Europe particularly by means of marriage. Among these immigrants were now to be found students and political refugees, young, educated, and from urban environments, whereas the first waves of migration had been primarily made up of illiterate people from rural environments.

Since the late 1980s we have also seen a relative resumption of clandestine immigration and asylum requests from persons coming from the Balkans, Central Asia, and Africa. Additionally, many activists and Islamist movement leaders, above all issuing from the Machrek and the Maghreb, took refuge in European capitals, as in the case of London, reputed for the pragmatic British reception, in conjunction with their foreign policy interests. Thanks to the growing number of naturalizations, an increased number of these people circulate within European spaces – without mentioning the emergence of a new category of Muslims who are starting to count from a numerical point of view: that of native Europeans converted to Islam and who frequent, among others, the second or even the third generations of people originating from Muslim countries.

## Religion's complex and changing role: between piety, militancy, and hedonism

The arrival of four great waves of "Muslim" populations has fostered various inclinations involving the propensities and modalities of mobilization efforts, religious among others. Their variety quite likely depends on multiple economic, juridical, and socio-cultural factors, as well as on the length of the European stay (which affects integration and even the degree of facility in the host society), the religious offers available, and the types of leadership, as well as the respective weight of each generation and gendered social group (the most recent immigration remains male in the majority, composed of single men, but the influence of the presence of women, in connection with family reunifications, is increasingly making itself felt). These elements affect not only social, political, and cultural practices in general, but also the formulation of expectations with regard to religion, in terms of European contexts as well as contexts involving national origin, or even the dynamics of world Islam.

Indeed, until the mid-1970s, the offer and demand of Islam remained relatively weak and other frames of reference took precedence: tribal and/or regional affiliation, nationality of origin – and this much more so when it is supported by a strong nationalism – as well as culture, understood as an ensemble of habits and ways of acting (Dassetto 1996, 2000). But the migratory project evolved in connection with children who grew up alongside an Islamic revival – promoted by certain currents – notably missionary, such as the Jama'at at-Tabligh, and political, such as the Muslim Brotherhood and the *Jama'at-i-Islami* – in Muslim countries; the latter was exported and found itself progressively valorized from the mid-1980s on, before being extended by other dynamics, such as the Salafists in the 1990s. These religious mobilization efforts seek to produce a strong identity, thought to be able to consolidate the Muslim community and favor socially integrating young generations in particular (Césari 1998). In addition to issues of a specifically religious nature (related to the valorization of rites, beliefs, affiliations, etc.), it nonetheless leads to identity constructions of an "ethnic"[3] type, which arouse and then consolidate political issues (representation before local and national authorities and ethnic voting), economic issues (*halal* consumption), and cultural issues (among others, the valorization by some of Islamic law juxtaposing positive law, by questions introduced concerning conceptions of secularity, private–public spaces, etc., notably based on promoting the wearing of headscarves).

The decades of the 1990s and 2000s thus became the theater of more contrastive dynamics, so much more so in that Sufi movements also sought to assert themselves further. And the arrival, by marriage, of (future) Muslim leaders who import concerns and visions anchored in the countries of origin (of Muslim majority) and the return of youths of the second generation of immigrants after having followed studies in Islamic sciences in Muslim countries (in the absence of valid education being provided in Europe) allowed "peripheral" networks to be interconnected (Allievi and Nielsen 2003). European Islam is thus reworked by the dynamics of world Islam, which is no longer (just) imported but indeed henceforth conveyed by actors of European descent. In parallel, on the Muslim world scale, the European experience represents a first, since, in a stable way, Muslims are experiencing the universality of the *umma* beginning with the confrontation of very varied ways of being Muslim in a pluralistic context where Islam is no longer transplanted (Dassetto and Bastenier 1984) but henceforth implanted.

The phases retraced here describe a process in countries in the center or northern part of Western Europe which have experienced the same temporality of mass immigration. In countries where the surge came later, we find "selected" or illegal immigrant workers providing low-cost labor, as well as students, refugees, and people who arrived via family reunifications (Nielsen et al. 2009). Their presence in Europe being more recent, one finds fewer generational cohorts there. However, since the 1990s that presence has been marked by an international context at once more strained with the Muslim world and more globalized, i.e. animated by a permanent flow of information and people (Allievi and Nielsen 2003); the Muslim populations there have been more rapidly made visible and more directly engaged on the collective scene (Nielsen et al. 2009; Allievi 2009).

## *Juridical recognition, institutionalizing the Islamic reality, and the role of context*

One basic contextual element involves the concrete recognition the Islamic religion enjoys in a state. Depending on the pre-existent national juridical structures, the processes for the official recognition of Islam usually date back to the 1970s and 1980s and are more or less linked to the Muslims eventually appointing one or more representative authorities, which has seemed hard to achieve for people who do not have a legitimate model of religious structure at their disposal. Yet this process has just as readily taken place in countries where recognition is guaranteed by a universalist system (France, Sweden, and the Netherlands) as in those which have established a system of conditional recognition (like Belgium, Spain, and Austria). The countries where the institutionalization of Islam has not yet advanced find themselves in this situation either because they have not yet completed a recognition procedure (Switzerland, Germany, Italy, and

Luxembourg) or because one church is recognized as particularly dominant there (Portugal, the United Kingdom, and Denmark), which does not, however, mean that those states have done nothing as regards recognition: because of their sizeable Muslim populations, Germany and the United Kingdom have, for example, set up processes for consultations with high-ranking state authorities (Nielsen et al. 2009, 2010, 2011, 2012).

Generally speaking, we agree with jurist S. Ferrari that Islam and Muslims find their place in European states on the basis of respect both for the principles of religious liberty (since exercising civil and political rights is independent of religious beliefs) and for the autonomy of religious organizations (non-interference in their doctrines and internal organization). After fifty years' presence in Europe, cooperation between states and Muslim communities is being achieved; Islam is gradually being placed in a position of equality in relation to other religions even if certain juridical and social difficulties remain: among other cases, when certain European values are questioned, as in the examples of male–female equality, human dignity, and democratic citizenship, etc. (Ferrari 2007).

Yet, like every other community, the social construction of Muslim communities clearly extends beyond juridical structures. It results from a dialectical relationship between the group's available resources and its social environment. However, aside from reactions *vis-à-vis* a limited number of events with global repercussions, like the Danish caricatures of the Prophet (Klausen 2009), most Muslim mobilization efforts involve national and/or local political issues which thus depend on the structures of political, juridical, and cultural opportunities. In this context, Césari and McLoughlin (2005) propose observing interactions between Muslim groups and segments of Western societies in order to ascertain transformations in political specificities (secularism, nationalism, multiculturalism … ) resulting from the establishment of new relationships between religion(s) and cultures.

Along these same lines, Amiraux and Jonker (2006) remind us that public visibility is related to the opportunities offered by a context and a specific institutional landscape wherein processes constructing the imaginaries and reciprocal representations intervene too. Hence they consider the "politics of visibility" to be a co-construction, i.e. a performance on a public stage where everyone has the opportunity of considering "alterity," and physically meeting one another. If religion finds its place on the public scene in terms of these reciprocal social stagings, it is interesting to observe that attempts at transplantation of revindications or forms of mobilization between different national contexts have proven more or less successful, as witnessed by the experiment carried out in Belgium by Sharia4Belgium, based on mobilization efforts similar to those of the Sharia4UK group (Dassetto 2012).

Concretely, the main issues addressed relate to the recognition of religious institutions (among others, in relation to state authorities), the possibility (or not) of organizing religion courses in public schools, the exercise of chaplaincy in prisons, hospitals and the armed forces, in mentioning the (in)direct financing of religious activities and/or institutions, such as faculties in state universities, and, finally, recognition of the civil effects of religious marriage. We also find supplementary requests in certain countries (where the installation is older), such as recognition of Islamic holidays and the availability of dishes which respect food interdictions in state institutions, or requests for the possibility of legally organizing ritual slaughters, perhaps more or less co-organized by public authorities, etc. It might also involve agreeing to women wearing headscarves on their identity card, having a channel with privileged access to national media – following the example of other recognized religions – or, in rare cases, the possibility of officially recognizing religious decisions adopted in conflict regulation, particularly with regard to family law, via the mediation taking place on an intra-community level (Foblets 2003).

Yet, aside from this long enumeration, an exhaustive comparative study of *reasons for commitment* within Muslim populations in the United Kingdom, the Netherlands, France, and Switzerland (Koopmans et al. 2005: 146–79) underlines the discrepancy between the extensive space given over to community revindications in the literature on multicultural citizenship and reality. Moreover, analysis of the influence of the political and institutional context on the emergence of such revindications shows here that the countries which maintain the migrants politically and culturally at the furthest distance from the host society are those wherein one finds the fewest, or no, community revindications. That leads us to believe that a minimum of reception is needed for the immigrant populations and their descendants to feel politically strong and autonomous enough to formulate requests for "special treatment."

Moreover, comparison of three national approaches to Islam shows each one's limits (Koopmans et al. 2005: 146–79). In the Netherlands, the fact of easily granting collective rights leads to a process of communitarian withdrawal following increasing demands which have merely reinforced an "amongst ourselves," which becomes disaffiliated from the rest of the population, without counting the fact that this "communitarian" policy stimulates strong intra-community competition. In the United Kingdom, where religious revindications are the most substantial and controversial, encouragement of political participation as a religious "community" leads to a proliferation of unresolved conflicts. And finally, in France pressures to assimilate tend to distance the migrant groups from identification with the political process, constraining them to make an increasingly polarized choice between a strictly privatized or politicized Islam.

We can thus conclude from this that the multicultural or pillar models (the UK, the Netherlands) support mobilization efforts of an "offensive" type, because the context they put in place presupposes socially active and organized communities. On the other hand, since the assimilationist or differentialist models (France, Austria) take a dim view of particular group revindications, mobilization efforts based on religious factors are carried out in a "defensive" mode.

### The symbolic construction of Islam in the imaginaries and in European social spaces: some reactions to Islam envisaged as a figure of social disdain

The historical process of making Islam visible in Western Europe remains unfinished (Martiniello et al. 2007). After a period of silent and forgotten presence during the first decade of implantation, characterized by a weak Islamic demand on the immigrant populations' behalf, coupled with the autochthonous populations' lack of interest in the newcomers, Muslim populations gradually became aware of the less and less transitory, and then definitive, character of their installation. That stabilization went hand in hand with the desire to set up infrastructure, particularly places of religious socialization for the younger generation. Experienced as familiar and reassuring places in unknown territories, mosque building, as well as associative engagement, met the needs of adult Muslims in creating places of exchange and solidarity in crisis contexts, among others, following the 1974 oil crisis. However, this domestic demand on the part of immigrant populations went hand in hand with an "Islamic revival" in the abovementioned Muslim countries, eventually sustaining many political-religious logics.

From the 1980s onward, the increasingly visible presence of Islam drew upon the decline of certain urban spaces: mosques were established in abandoned stores or warehouses, 1950s vintage workshops, cafés and cinemas having closed their doors, etc. Around them, the "ethno-Islamic" districts formed, made up of stores (among which were Islamic *halal* butcher shops), bookstores, cafés, etc. imbued with an ever stronger presence of the corporeal signs of "Muslimness" (Dassetto 1999). That presence causes a growing uneasiness in public opinion, all the more likely to lead to the development of an anti-immigrant racism when those populations gradually come to be associated, or are even confused, with the dramatic and incessant events of the Middle East. After the Iranian Revolution, new fears subsequently developed concerning the presence of Islam in European territory, beginning with the Rushdie affair and the events concerning "Islamic headscarves" in Creil, France, in 1989. The absence of leaders and spokespeople able to formulate an audible discourse on the issues involved and provide European societies with reassuring answers resulted in Muslims withdrawing into their own, lively communitarian life. At the same time, the mosques, but perhaps to an even greater degree the associative fabric, thenceforth became the incrementally more structured anchoring point of a movement fostering the local re-Islamization of populations; particularly with young males and females finding a strong identity instrument in Islam, to appropriate for themselves, and/or as a foundation on the moral level.

Two major events, the fall of the Soviet bloc in 1991 and the September 11, 2001 attacks in turn further marked ways of perceiving Muslims in European societies, who were in effect gradually going to incarnate the face of the Other, or rather, a step further, the face of a "disturbing strangeness."[4] On the one hand, the first ratified a radical expansion of liberalism as a dominant political and philosophical principle in Europe, affecting how the elites considered social cohesion. Consequently, the centrality of individual freedom and civil rights in "traditional" liberal thought ran up against the equally increasing demand for a recognition of rights specific to ethnic or religious communities, especially when certain rules were perceived as contradicting the basic principles of liberalism (Nonneman et al. 1996), such as the right of people to self-determination in their own lives, whereas these very people testify to a form of submission to constraints which are at least apparently imposed by some particular group. If states retain control over the political orientations they intend to privilege, the demand for certain (collective) rights for minorities nonetheless challenges the limitations of human rights (Kymlicka 1995); all the more so in that the European Court of Human Rights (ECHR) regularly adopts new orientations in the area of respect for religious liberty, following the appeals introduced, especially since the early 1990s, by certain Muslims, among others, calling for observation of their fundamental rights, considered to have been violated by national states.[5]

The second factor further affecting European societies' relationships with Islam and Muslims throughout the last decade relates to the events of September 11, 2001. The perception of Islam as a diffuse and internal threat reached its paroxysm at that moment and the media reacted in supporting the collective memory. Thereupon George W. Bush declared "The War on Terror," completely transforming American and British political agendas around a double strategy aimed at prevention and launching a struggle against Islamic extremism, yet while maintaining privileged relationships with Muslim organizations who were already initially engaged, in Great Britain in any case, in a veritable "faith relation industry" aimed at encouraging social cohesion (McLoughlin 2005). But opinions became polarized and, subsequently, radicalized.

On the one hand, Samuel Huntington's thesis (1996) describing a "clash of civilizations" had far reaching influence on public opinion and affected public policies, followed by a long list of "affairs," from the Van Gogh assassination (in 2004) to international tensions created by the propagation of the Danish caricatures of the Prophet (in 2005), from the attacks in Madrid and London in March 2004 and July 2005 to various amalgams related to forced marriages and the emergence of *shari'a* courts, etc. If what was above all fostered in European societies was a certain mistrust, strains were sometimes exacerbated to the point of engendering Islamophobic feelings and/or attitudes towards Islam and Muslims, who were seen as representing the antithesis of Europe and its values. On the other hand, many personalities came forward to address these imaginaries, fed by a culturalist approach to the reality of Islam, considered an exceptionalism, thus explaining its refusal to be assimilated, unlike previous (intra-European) migrations. These figures testified to the internal pluralism of Muslim communities in their identities, their affiliations, and their practices: they pointed out the complexity of identity constructions and the development of sentiments of loyalty to the host country (Seddon et al. 2003), and called for the construction of a veritable spirit of "living together." Within Muslim communities, too, where religion is more or less serenely increasingly thought of as passing into the order of private affairs, certain voices have arisen denouncing past laxity in dealing with radical Islamist currents at the intra-community level.

## The specificities of Muslim mobilization efforts and revindications in Europe

Having outlined the multiple social contexts of European Islam in the twentieth century, let us turn to the ongoing mobilization efforts and revindications being made in the name of religion so as to provide a progress report on their evolution. Indeed, along with the national social, political, cultural, and economic contexts, they undergo transformation once the temporary implantation of the Muslims is converted into a permanent installation and communities more or less withdrawn into themselves come to include young people involved at the intra-community level and/or on the extra-community public scene: besides the fact of trying to have their needs met, the latter seek to express their singularities therein or to symbolically defend Islam or the Muslims, or even to bear witness to a certain exemplarity on the level of values in European societies. But then who are the actors in these Islamic mobilization efforts and what dynamics guide their engagements among the multitude of forms existing? To grasp the long and complex history of the construction of European Islam, we propose the following typology, distinguishing intra-communitarian organizational dynamics from political activities and symbolic mobilization efforts.[6] This presents the advantage of showing the basic tendencies, although it hardly brings national specificities to light.

### Mobilization efforts to meet intra-community needs above all

From a historical point of view, local community investment has been European Muslims' privileged reason for mobilization and remains so today. This involves multiple venues and manners of engagement, which implies, besides the ability to collect private or even public funds, organizing themselves to open and animate places of worship with the possibility of setting up courses in Arabic and/or initiation into, or even advanced study of, religion. Under the auspices of these places of worship – which generally remain very strongly divided along the ethnic-national lines of the countries of origin and Islamic organizations professing adherence to various tendencies[7] – and then, gradually, independently of them, commitment to religious transmission increased from the late 1970s on, once the need for socializing children in Islam appeared.

Thus, besides the courses proposed in mosques, a few dozen Muslim primary schools were also rather rapidly created from the 1980s on in countries like Great Britain, Denmark, Sweden, and the Netherlands, while the phenomenon has remained quite marginal in other European countries, among other reasons because the teaching of Islamic religion courses has in places been gradually inserted into pre-existing school networks, as in the cases of Spain, Austria, Finland, certain German *Länder* (federal states), and Belgium, where no fewer than 700 professors are financed by the state (Maréchal et al. 2003; Nielsen et al. 2011).

With regard to higher education levels, they only began to be a subject of concern in the 1990s, with, for example, the Muslim College in London, or the European Institute of Social

Sciences in France, or the Islamic University of Rotterdam in the Netherlands all proposing degree programs for becoming an imam and/or teaching the Islamic religion. Existing institutes of higher education are usually the result of private initiatives and, with exceptions, their official, or even unofficial, recognition by the state structures of European countries remains rather weak. To meet increased educational needs, new programs have nonetheless begun to be set up in universities financed by certain states, as in Germany, where the universities of Erlangen-Nuremberg and Osnabrück have just begun organizing programs for professors of the Islamic religion (Nielsen et al. 2012).

Besides the organization of worship and teaching, which thus represents *the* primordial and ongoing investment for Muslim communities, if only to continue to improve the practical conditions for the exercise of worship or consolidate offers of instruction in Islam, local-level involvement concerns other important needs too. We especially have in mind developing networks for the supply of *halal* meat, via more or less informal channels or based on the creation of Islamic butcheries.[8] But this also involves the establishment of associations organizing pilgrimages to Mecca or setting up networks of solidarity for repatriating the bodies of the deceased to their countries of origin, prior to the subsequent consideration of creating specific burial areas through the recognition of Muslim plots in cemeteries.[9]

In these domains, the task of many, we notice a relative predominance of first generation men, especially with regard to the management of mosques; the young hardly compete with them there, except that young people's intervention is sometimes required, for instance when a better knowledge of the external context is required, among other things for the collection of public funds (Allievi 2009). In the meantime, since the mid-1990s these youths' investment has thus concentrated on founding new associations with varied socio-cultural goals, which do not enter into competition with the places of worship but rather aim to supplement and/or diversify the offers of service proposed by the elders (Dassetto 1996): organizing talks, setting up or following school or extracurricular activities, investment in humanitarian activities or cultural events centered on awareness of Islam, etc. These domains of activity are quite often mobilized just as much by young women as men, even if mixed associations remain proportionally rare, and subsequently we see that many places of worship try to take over some of these efforts, placing them under the auspices of the mosque, if only by making their buildings available. In the last decade, it is nonetheless interesting to notice the extent to which more and more women are committing themselves to teaching, among other areas, whether it be in public or private schools, as well as in the associative sector (Ben Mohamed 2006).

Within the context of a major diversification of actors, let us finally note the progressive visibility and recognition of minority Islamic tendencies: in a report concerning the conflicts surrounding the construction of mosques in Europe, for example, the extent to which authorities can play a deciding role or influence intra-Islamic competition by means of granting (or refusing) building permits for places of worship has been shown (Allievi 2009).

## Contrastive mobilization efforts at the political level

Early on, any possible political mobilization efforts by Muslims who arrived in Europe, when they came to light, were primarily directed towards their countries of origin. Some of them reaffirmed their "nationalitarian" anchoring (Frégosi 2009) in their society of origin, or even loyalty to its regime. On the other hand, for a minority, certain currents of which are known as "Islamist," the issue revolves around contesting the regimes in power in the name of Islam, which is that much more easily accomplished by having acquired student or political refugee status in Europe, enabling them to invest in creating social change in Muslim countries, also noting that, when measured by the passing decades, their deployment in European space sometimes represents a factor of internal transformation of their own ideas and ways of acting (Maréchal 2008).

These two opposing dynamics have each seen an upsurge in the past decade. On the one hand, since the mid-2000s, states like Morocco and Turkey have shown the extent to which they are willing to invest or reinvest in the Muslim populations in Europe, in propagating their own conceptions of Islam under the cover of managing to struggle against the radical offshoots which have led to attacks in Europe as well as on their own soil, while they remain quantitatively few in number, and research processes of de-radicalization (Coolsaet 2011). In addition, the onset of the Arab spring has engendered strong mobilization efforts within European Islamist ranks – and not just to support the political changes already in progress (Brandon and Pantucci 2012). However, many have already benefited from the Arab spring to return to their countries of origin. Yet maintaining contact with European Muslim populations remains important, since while preserving the nationality of their country of origin, they benefit from European political rights. While these dynamics may lead to some passing fads or even commitments, including among the young, the latter nevertheless prefer to invest their efforts locally, in developing an "associative fabric independent of chancelleries and national federations" (Frégosi 2009), or sometimes even investing in humanitarian causes, paid or voluntary, which require both local and transnational mobilization efforts (Krafess 2005).[10]

These young Muslims generally tend to withdraw from forms of strong organizational affiliation and instead prefer to participate in one-shot mobilization efforts. For that matter, the influence of the means of communication (internet, social networks), coupled with these youths' preference for timely forms of engagement over the organizational, probably goes a long way towards explaining the influence Salafist discourses exert on these youths' religious terrains, concentrating as they do on questions of personal or family morals and normative precepts in the light of the prophet's exemplarity (Dassetto 2011).

As regards Muslim investment in European national, political, and institutional scenes in their own right, as voters and then as candidates, it began in a second phase, with the migrant individuals obtaining the nationality of the countries concerned, depending on whether that possibility is favored, or not, by the specific rules of each country. Some countries, following the example of the Scandinavian countries, among others, have also authorized the possibility of participating in local elections, the only condition being the ability to prove a relatively long stay in the country concerned (Allievi, in Maréchal et al. 2003; Nielsen et al. 2012). All levels taken together, let us note from the outset that Muslims' political mobilization efforts are usually concretized within and to the advantage of traditional political parties, given that, if the religious dimension of elected Muslim officials has usually hardly produced spectacular effects in this domain, that dimension may sometimes appear to be more clearly affirmed than in the early 2000s. Yet this religious dimension seldom results in the founding of Muslim parties, strictly speaking. Admittedly, certain initiatives have particularly stood out, among others the Noor party in 1999, which became the Islam Party in Belgium in 2012, Suomen Islamilainen Puolue (the Finnish Islamic Party) in 2007 (Nielsen et al. 2011), the Islam4UK party, finally banned in Great Britain in 2010 (Nielsen et al. 2012); but these initiatives have only obtained 1 percent at best of the total vote in the various districts concerned, which hardly confers any more than a token weight on them, inversely proportional to the media din they have generated.

All these developments should not hide the fact that the political mobilizing of Muslims was not all that self-evident at the start because, for certain minority milieux more or less influenced by political Islam, it was only in the early 1990s that clear declarations began circulating which dissociated the acquisition of a new nationality of a European country from a form of disloyalty towards the Islamic *umma*, one which saw Europe beyond the simple classical geopolitical dichotomy between a "land of Islam" and a "land of war," describing it, among other things, as a "land of ease"; This gradual transformation of the paradigm, fostering promotion of the possible compatibility of citizenship and "Muslimness," remains contested from a religious viewpoint within certain minority milieux among Muslims who are devoted to Salafism, who remain in the background or even distrust these institutional policies.[11] Hence, in these areas, sharing a common reference to Islam can function as a lever in mobilizing one or more networks and stimulating the constitution of an ethnic and/or religious vote (Zibouh 2010; Nielsen 2013), but it can just as readily favor an *identity* policy (a defensive reaction to being stigmatized) as a (proactive) politics of Muslim citizenship, like that developed by certain young urban elites, concerned for the common good (Pędziwiatr 2010). This ongoing development of civic consciousness implies actively supporting projects of European states as well as stressing the duties shared by all citizens, independently of their origins and religious references. In this context, struggles against economic and social discrimination come in a variety of forms of engagement, denunciation, protest, and resistance, etc., but they also affirm an attachment to the common values of equality and democratic progress, and so on.

In countries where the implantation is the oldest, we witness the development of forms of religious engagement in other extra-community spaces, notably on the social and juridical level, supporting appeals for such things as recognition of cultural-religious specificities like wearing headscarves in schools or workplaces, the regulation of sanitary arrangements on occasions of festivals of sacrifice, the possibility of recognizing places for prayer in businesses. Their revindication of "normalization" of the Islamic religion relates to several areas: that of state institutions (schools, administrations, sanitary regulations, national medias … ), private law, labor law, etc. It bears witness to a desire for *incorporation*, for integration into the workings of institutions, as seen in the investment made in order to present the Muslim religion to states, whether this has been in England, France, Belgium, or Sweden, and some time ago in the Netherlands. Indeed, the advantages the welfare state can offer are not negligible, whether it be in the area of taxation, obtaining building permits for places of worship or subsidized land, or the recognition and even education and employment of chaplains.

Although we find mobilization efforts for community representation on several decision-making levels (local, national, and European, coupled with the development of certain lobbies, among which are the Federation of Islamic Organizations in Europe), their forms and their range of interest are largely dependent on the political and institutional structure of each state (Nonneman et al. 1996: 17), which often determines the shape of dialogue with Muslim representatives, and even the development of a representative body (composition and functioning). Hence, this power of recognition that the state has exerts a major influence on the internal, associative dynamic of the communities. The state thus plays the regulatory role in a highly competitive field between various Islamic movements and organizations, sometimes favoring the fragmention of initiatives or, on the contrary, their centralization under umbrella associations (Allievi 2009; Nielsen et al. 2009, 2010, 2011, 2012).

In Germany, the Ministry of the Interior set up the Deutsche Islam Konferenz, in 2006, an equal representation assembly composed of fifteen representatives of the state and fifteen others from Muslim communities. The ministry chose them from among the country's principal Muslim organizations and from various sectors of civil society, which did not fail to elicit sharp polemics, among both Muslims and their non-Muslim compatriots (Nielsen et al. 2012). In the Netherlands and in Belgium, state control is not as direct but the indirect influence remains important. If Muslim communities have benefited from the historical pillar system for assuming a certain degree of self-organization, the breach has also been capitalized on by foreign states

(Morocco, Turkey), where the majority of the migrants of this confession come from, in maintaining their influence. If in Belgium the Executive of Muslims of Belgium functions, despite sharp tensions due to external interference (Nielsen et al. 2012), in the Netherlands this situation has ruined attempts at federating the representative organizations. To this day they are split between these two communities of national origin, although they take an equal part in consultations organized by the Dutch state. Other associations have denounced the influence of foreign countries and the monopoly of organizations whose members are severely lacking in generational and gendered variety (Nielsen et al. 2012).

Muslim communities' difficulties in organizing amongst themselves are also felt on the level of the official media channels, which consequently often remain inaccessible to them; on the other hand, their investment in the world of media appears to be ever on the increase and diversified, beginning with the mobilization of young Muslims in what were initially marginal media channels (the plethora of blogs, internet sites, etc.): this seeks to give a voice to those *without a voice* and/or to broadcast material with content sensitive to the concerns of Muslims living in a pluralistic context (following the example of oumma.com, Radical Middle Way, Generation M, etc.).

## Growing mobilization efforts on the cultural and symbolic levels

All of these mobilization efforts contribute to the construction of an – at times essentialized – "European Muslim identity," which in a great many cases has predominated over other factors of belonging and identity.

This identity is certainly the clearest result of the Muslim Brothers' influence in Europe, building networks, promoting the global character of Islam (Maréchal 2008), and encouraging specifically Islamic *and* European cultural events like the Le Bourget fair, in France, which commemorated its thirtieth year in 2013, as well as pro-headscarf discourses from the late 1980s on, and creating the European Council for Fatwa and Research in 1997, issuing laws for specific minorities. Beyond their attempt to develop an Islamic thought suited to its context, the intellectual means nonetheless remain very limited by the classical framework of Muslim thought, making it hard for really reformist ideas to take hold.

Meanwhile, new ways of being Muslim are making their presence felt and in fact represent the last field of engagement: integration by means of cultural and economic production. Constructing this "self," which resides in a relationship of symbolic recognition, requires a mobilization involving various forms of artistic expression, such as mosque architecture (Roose 2009), fashion, and music – including rap (El Asri 2014). It is characterized by a diversity of values and modes of expression in asserting a cultural identity, all conforming to the surrounding society's codes, aware that information technologies have undoubtedly speeded up the ethnicization process here via semi-communitarian channels which boost networking with the rest of the (Muslim) world as well as (generational, sexual, etc.) mixing.

It is also marked by the appearance of a niche market enjoying exceptional potential: the "*halal*" market, i.e. "conforming to Islamic law." Initially restricted to meat, this label has been extended to many goods and services (food, drink, clothing, tourism … ) (Bergeaud-Blackler 2005). From here on in it also involves the consumption of Islamic symbols, an ethnic marketing strategy, creating the accessories materializing and presenting an Islamic lifestyle (Haenni 2005; Boubekeur 2005; Pink 2009). In finance, for example, this goal of conformity implies the impossibility of Muslims using most of the financing and investment products available on the market because most of them are based on the payment or collection of interest rates. But this market arouses envy and the United Kingdom is far and away the first European money market for the development of Islamic finance (Sor 2012).

"Muslimness" also resides in the expression of symbolic struggles for the recognition of marginal identities, for example Muslim homosexuals or feminists, among others, via investment in internet networks (Ali 2012; Djelloul 2013). They form part of European societies, all the while incarnating a militant posture which is opposed to the system: whether that system be patriarchal, economic, or one stigmatizing the religious affiliation of these (mostly marginalized) populations. Considering the role of the gender dimension in the construction of reciprocal imaginaries, the extent of women's engagement is the greatest of these symbolic revindications (Guénif Souilamas and Macé 2004). For some, the latter symbolizes a "civilizational" frontier, a marker of the incompatibility of Islam with "Western" values; for others, a rampart of protection of Muslim specificity and social gender identities, nonetheless threatened on all sides by social evolution. We need only recall the innumerable affairs of headscarves, niqabs, and burqas, to realize the symbolically very strong impact of this in most European countries; more so in that the media attention paid to it in fact amplifies the ethnicizing effect of the construction of an alterity. For their part, the (young) girls struggling to wear headscarves in places where it is objected to describe this choice as personal, concerned with such things as their freedom of expression, of conscience, to have freedom of decision over their own bodies. Thus, for them, this clothing choice symbolizes emancipation from social pressures and a feminist appropriation of their own bodies (Boubekeur 2004).

Lastly, mobilization efforts linked to events of global scale, interpreted as touching on the integrity of Islam (the Rushdie affair, prohibition of the veil in France in 2004, the caricatures affair, the Ratisbonne speech, prohibition of total covering in Belgium in 2011, and so on), refer to more or less exacerbated religious sensitivities or to politicized actors. For the groups on the attack, most often by legal means, against media hostility towards Islam (like "Vigilance Musulmane" in Belgium) or against various basic discriminations (e.g. at work, at school, racist) defense of the integrity of Islam plays a "social face" role in Goffman's sense (Goffman 1967). The creation of these groups is thus often caused by specific events and their efforts converge towards the recognition of Islam as a fully fledged religion in European space. These mobilization efforts have perhaps become greater in number today, as, under the weight of the moral panic surrounding Islam since September 11, 2001, the defensive reactions of "Islam" have increased. They especially relate to youth (the educated but not exclusively, involved or not in networks, etc.) because it is essential to them to put an end to aberrations and change mentalities, statuses, and even ways of being in European societies with a view towards a stronger co-inclusion (De Changy et al. 2007).

It seems to us that this bears witness to a surpassing of strictly material concerns, favoring instead immaterial considerations together with a certain acculturation *vis-à-vis* dominant currents and a certain ease with the host society's paradigms (surfing on consumerism while investing in the economic domain, whereas that materialism appears far removed from spirituality; surfing on the wave called Islamophobia to denounce the society's incoherencies, etc.). The subjacent issue at stake is always recognition (Honneth 2002; Caillé 2007), with the first recipients of these actions being henceforth the *Others*, i.e. the societies called *host*, although these mobilization efforts also play a role in developing the community's consciousness of its status and weight. At the same time, other mobilization efforts, like interreligious dialogue, now seem unattractive to young people. That is probably due to the emphasis placed on strengthening identity constructions.

These efforts seem paradoxical in that what they are revindicating is just as much the fully fledged recognition of a collective specificity as a status as "Muslims" led to anchor themselves in the European landscape. And what's more, isn't the expression of these specific needs more readily sayable once it is recognized from the outset (Césari and McLoughlin 2005)?

Might we not speak of a process of "indigenization of Islam" whereby a factor of ethnicizing, identity construction in the collective development of social structures is crystallizing around this motive for engagement (Sunier 2009)? We might then postulate that the more collective specificity is recognized from the outset, the more it generates demands for differentiation, alongside the development of loyalty at the heart of efforts made for recognition.

## Axes of interpretation

Studying the Muslim discourses most disseminated within Muslim communities, among others inspired by literalistic, political, and missionary currents, shows the extent to which individual and collective engagement remains a fundamental concept: propagating the message, the *da'wa*, remains a promoted value, even if it is sometimes done more discreetly and is increasingly likely to take various forms, among others based on exemplary behavior, as promoted by the Fethullah Gülen movement, which has known a significant development. Yet, not only do the forms of engagement vary in terms of the manners of identification and affiliation with Islam (given that a large majority of Muslims are reserved about their religious practices), this palette becomes even more colorful given the pluralization of individual experiences in connection with globalization, the increase in possibilities for contact with intra-Muslim sensitivities other than those transmitted by parents, as well as other philosophical and religious cultures and traditions, etc. Between the Salafists (whose religious vision determines not only the principles of their individual ethics but their performative aspects as well, to the detriment of other approaches to understanding reality, which are set aside) and many Sufi groups, potentially more open to the wealth of the Other and concerned about living-together, as a factor of mobilization, Islam can just as readily be a motive for distantiation/detachment from the political scene or, on the contrary, can motivate engagement. Moreover, the terrain for religiously based mobilization efforts is changing at the intersection of two processes: the discovery of an ever-increasing internal plurality ever more openly expressed in its difference; and new extensions in Muslim visibility where the forms of expression leave the strictly religious and cultural sphere, instead investing efforts in various social spheres (artistic, economic, cultural, and political). How are we to understand this evolution and diversification in forms of religious mobilization in a European space scrutinizing contemporary theories describing a growing distance and bursting of engagement (Ion 1997)? What is bringing about a paradigmatic change in Muslim mobilization efforts?

### The constitution of a European intra-Islamic field and its integration into global (Muslim) space

The first hypothesis we reach is that of the (ongoing) constitution of an intra-Islamic field, in Pierre Bourdieu's sense (Bourdieu 1971). We offer as evidence the increase in types of Muslim mobilization efforts mentioned above, expansion in the spheres invested in, accompanied by an increasing competition between Muslim movements, while at the same time some (not that many) revindications of specificities may also appear as a safety valve in managing to *find oneself* – over and above a major acculturation process. The increasing room that expressing religiosity takes up in the public domain is transformed by the media and social networks into a space for collective elaboration of the social codes of an Islamic lifestyle, based on a process of social distinction (Bourdieu 1979). Economic issues structure this space in part, as shown by the power struggles for *halal* certification – generating substantial financial dividends – the passion for Islamic marketing, Islamic fashion, etc. Thus this hypothesis does not signal withdrawal but indeed a redefinition and extension of the community beginning with the religious domain. The mobilization efforts we have observed in the past two decades mark a certain emancipation from worries related to their countries of origin and entry into the national and international political and cultural scenes, seeking visibility and a recognition of their citizenship as "Muslims."

## Three major lines of tensions

### De- vs. recommunitarization

Some of the social dynamics affecting Muslim populations are the same as those encountered by other European populations. The exhaustion of the mobilizing ideologies, beginning with the importance attached to individualism and hedonism (versus a philosophy of effort and sacrifice, etc.), has led to a secularization of individual religious practices and influenced the forms the mobilization efforts and engagements through which European Muslims make their specificity exist. More concretely, these collective dynamics bear witness to a certain political apathy (little investment in democracy or human rights) except for contesting perceived injustices or incoherencies in European systems. We thus find, on the one hand, a way out of a strictly communitarian frame of reference, to the benefit of an increased attention to the social regulations of the surrounding society and its ways of thinking, and, on the other hand, an overfocusing on the religious domain, inspired by speeches conveyed – often unconsciously – by the predominant movements, such as the Salafist branch or the Muslim Brothers, resulting in a propensity to react in the face of a kind of social disdain, or even to valorize Islam at all costs. This paradox leads us to the hypothesis of a "recommunitarization," founded on the symbolic struggle for recognition of the identities, rights, and dignity of "Muslims" and the affirmation of an aspiration to a moral dimension in the society in promoting the values of Islam. This recommunitarization produces revindications reflecting a will to integrate and make their specific contribution to the national and European community visible.

### Making belief private vs. visible

Another contradictory dynamic at work in the European intra-Islamic field is the process of belief privatization (Fadil 2008), contemporaneous with its further affirmation in extra-community public spaces. In effect, evolutions in Muslim forms of religiosity in non-Muslim societies are influenced by the fact that Islam no longer enjoys external support there (such as law inspired by Islamic principles or social pressure), as is the case in societies of origin. So we may consider that the religiosity practiced involves an individualization of practices and choices, a characteristic of European societies (Roy 2002). However, paradoxically, the history of these mobilization efforts surrounding the religious object has, on the contrary, shown us a process of the forms of religiosity becoming increasingly visible, notably its extension through multiple forms involving daily practices, and conferring on them a much greater symbolic significance than "classical" Islamist engagement would have (Mandaville 2011).

### Domestication vs. transnationalization

The Europeanization of Muslim identity, or its "domestication" (Sunier 2009), goes hand in hand with an intensification of the religious frame of reference among these populations. Indeed, the re-elaboration of the social codes and symbolic systems of Islam in the various

European contexts results in a *visibility* as well as a *readability* of the symbolic border founding the community (Poutignat and Streiff-Fénart 1995).

These evolutions are also connected to the Muslim world, and interpenetrate one another in "mutual feedbacks" (Allievi and Nielsen 2003). The historical Islamist movements are transformed and translate their goals into "European" terms (Reetz 2009; Schulze 2009), integrating European Muslims into the scene of global intra-Islamic competition (such as with the emergence of *global leaders* like Yusuf al-Qaradawi) (Caeiro 2009; Skovgaard-Petersen and Gräf 2009). These elements lead us to supplement our hypothesis of the constitution of an intra-Islamic European field with that of a transformation of Islamic loyalties: no longer just national to the country of origin, but also Islamic (towards the *umma*), in being the basis of a hybrid loyalty, on the level of European and global Islam (e.g. debates on Muslim British soldiers being allowed to fight in Afghanistan) (Birt 2006).

## Conclusion

Europe forms part of the Muslim world today and European Muslims have become fully fledged actors in their societies and in transforming the Muslim world (cf. the British monthly review *Q-News* or, further, the role of the European Council for Fatwa and Research, whose views may serve as a reference for other zones in the world where Islam is the minority religion, etc.). Here we have retraced the implantation process, the Muslim populations' coming to awareness of their installation, subsequent extra-community revindication, and the construction of a European Muslim collective identity project. All of these investments have created the dynamics of an intra-European Muslim field marking its specificity/drawing its borders with both the Muslim world and non-Muslim European societies.

In attempting to reflect on the specificities of Muslims as related to the ongoing national struggles/debates, we may refer to a relatively recent emergence – aside from struggles against stigmatization and, above all, intra-community concerns. We might underline the pioneer role of a figure like Tariq Ramadan, inviting Muslims to become involved in both the development of their own community and the national society. But in the last few years, energetic new forces with more or less antagonistic aims have shown their desire to change a society where contradictory positions, in particular on freedom of expression, are likely to be a major stumbling block in the way of mobilization efforts to come. In fact, while some Muslims want to limit freedom of expression, particularly when they judge that comments attack the sacred, they are just as vehement in not wanting be limited in their identity expressions (cf. headscarves, etc). In the final analysis, these mobilization efforts necessitate an evolution in European thought as well as Muslim thought, while recalling that societal identities and projects are always collective constructions whose evolution is the job of everybody.

## Notes

1 Besides the monographs which only deal with one country, see comparative works, such as Gerholm and Lithman (1988), Nonneman et al. (1996), Shadid and van Koningsveld (1991, 1995, 1996), Vertovec and Peach (1997), Hunter (2002), Rath et al. (2001).

2 See, among others, Maréchal et al. (2003), who, based on information expressly collected about each of the various countries of the enlarged Europe, have constructed a structured synthesis involving the fields of actions Muslims are engaged in. Since 2009, the *Yearbook of Muslims in Europe*, edited by Nielsen et al., has offered an overview, this time by country, of ongoing transformations, in paying particular attention to topics like the Muslims' relationships to states, the construction of mosques and the development of teaching programs or of varied publications on Islam, the opening of Muslim plots

in cemeteries, Muslim chaplaincy, among other places in prisons, the availability of *halal* food, the organization of religious festivities, investment in interreligious relations and in public debates. These domains are the object of larger or smaller mobilization efforts depending on the contexts, which evolve with time.

3 For an exhaustive panorama of the existing literature on ethnicity, see Poutignat and Streiff-Fénart, who propose the following definition of it: "variable and never ending processes through which the actors identify themselves and are identified by others on the basis of an Us/Them dichotomization established on the basis of supposed cultural traits derived from a common origin and placed in relief in social interactions" (Poutignat and Streiff-Fénart 1999: 144).

4 An expression taken from an essay of the same name by Sigmund Freud, appearing in 1919, evoking the idea of something not belonging to the house and which yet remains there.

5 See notably the list of ECHR decisions concerning Islam established by Prof. Louis-Léon Christians, www.uclouvain.be/260898.html (accessed March 21, 2013), which cites two further reference articles on this subject (Garay 2005; Danchin 2011).

6 Two helpful articles on the forms of Muslim collective mobilization efforts have already been written by Frégosi (2009, 2012), distinguishing religious, socio-political, and identity mobilization efforts. Quite marked by the French context and anchored in a political science gaze that accentuates aspects of political organization, these very stimulating texts go so far as to include radical secular mobilizations. For our part, we only deal with mobilization efforts established in the name of Islam here, including cultural ones which include but also go beyond mobilization efforts of an identity sort.

7 For a panorama of intra-Islamic currents, see Pew Forum on Religion and Public Life (2010). Based on the reality in Brussels, see Dassetto (2011).

8 According to a study carried out by the Institut français du Proche-Orient (IFPO), 59 percent of Muslims buy *halal* meat, while a study by the French Ministry of Agriculture reports that economists calculate the tons of meat necessary for the four million Muslims in France at 250,000–300,000 tons (Bergeaud-Blackler 2005).

9 Whereas most cemeteries in the United Kingdom reserve plots for Muslims, in France there are three Muslim cemeteries and 70 plots placed at the disposal of Muslims in Paris or in cities like Montpellier and Marseille (Nielsen et al. 2010).

10 Aside from occasional actions resulting from obligation, in order to accomplish the *zakat* (the annual alms intended for the poorest) required of all Muslims, forms of structured activity carried out in unison with NGOs like Islamic Relief and Muslim Hands have also existed since the 1980s. Among the causes they are committed to we find a desire to respond to the social and humanitarian needs of civil populations in majority Muslim countries at war (Palestine, Iraq, Syria, etc.), but not exclusively, taking, for example, recent mobilization efforts to help the persecuted Muslim Rohingyas populations in Burma.

11 For a contemporary, engaged theological argument on these questions, see, for example, Ramoussi (2012).

# Bibliography

Ahmad, W.I.U. and Sardar, Z. (2012) *Muslims in Britain: Making Social and Political Space*, New York: Routledge.

Ali, Z. (2012) *Féminismes islamiques*, Paris: La Fabrique.

Allievi, S. (2009) *Conflicts over Mosques in Europe: Policy Issues and Trends*, NEF Initiative on Religion and Democracy in Europe, London: Alliance Publishing Trust.

Allievi, S. and Nielsen, J.S. (eds.) (2003) *Muslim Networks and Transnational Communities in and across Europe*, Leiden: Brill.

Amghar, S., Boubeker, A., and Emerson, M. (eds.) (2007) *European Islam: Challenges for Public Policy and Society*, Brussels: Centre for European Policy Studies.

Amiraux, V. and Jonker, G. (eds.) (2006) *Politics of Visibility: Young Muslims in European Public Spaces*, Bielefeld: Transcript Verlag.

Ben Mohamed, N. (2006) *Femmes d'origine étrangère dans l'espace public: dirigeantes d'associations et élues politiques à Bruxelles*, Louvain-la-Neuve: Académia-Bruylant.

Bergeaud-Blackler, F. (2005) "De la Viande halal à l'halal food. Comment le halal s'est développé en France?," *Revue européenne des migrations internationales* 21(3): 125–47.

Birt, Y. (2006) "Between Nation and Umma: Muslim Loyalty in a Globalizing World," *Islam21* 40: 6–11.

Boubekeur, A. (2004) *Le Voile de la mariée, voile et projet matrimonial en France*, Paris: l'Harmattan.

——(2005) "L'Islam est-il soluble dans le Mecca Cola? Marché de la culture islamique et nouveaux supports de religiosité en Occident," *Maghreb-Machrek* 183: 45–66.

Bourdieu, P. (1971) "Genèse et structure du champ religieux," *Revue française de sociologie* 12: 295–334.

——(1979) *La Distinction. Critique sociale du jugement*, Paris: Les Editions de Minuit.

Brandon, J. and Pantucci, R. (2012) "UK Islamists and the Arab Uprisings," *Current Trends in Islamist Ideology* 13, www.currenttrends.org/research/detail/uk-islamists-and-the-arab-uprisings (accessed February 1, 2013).

Caeiro, A. (2009) "Public Religion, Yusuf al-Qaradawi, and the Integration of Muslims in Europe: Minority Fiqh in the Arab World and in the West," in Mandaville, P. (ed.) *Transnational Islam: Identities, Networks and Movements*, Washington: Pew Forum, unpublished paper.

Caillé, A. (ed.) (2007) *La Quête de reconnaissance. Nouveau phénomène social total*, Paris: La Découverte/ MAUSS.

Césari, J. (1998) *Musulmans et Républicains: Les Jeunes, l'islam et la France*, Paris: Editions Complexe.

Césari, J. and McLoughlin, S. (eds.) (2005) *European Muslims and the Secular State*, Farnham: Ashgate.

Coolsaet, R. (ed.) (2011) *Jihadi Terrorism and the Radicalisation Challenge: European and American Experiences*, 2nd ed., Farnham and Burlington: Ashgate.

Dakhlia, J. and Vincent, B. (2011) *Les Musulmans dans l'histoire de l'Europe: I. Une intégration invisible*, Paris: Albin Michel.

Danchin, P.G. (2011) "Islam in the Secular Nomos of the European Court of Human Rights," *Virginia Journal of International Law* 32: 643–747.

Dassetto, F. (1988) *Le Tabligh en Belgique. Diffuser l'Islam sur les traces du Prophète*, Sybydi Papers no. 2, Brussels and Louvain-la-Neuve: Academia.

——(1990) "Visibilisation de l'Islam dans l'espace public," in Bastenier, A. and Dassetto, F. (eds.) *Immigrations et nouveaux pluralismes: une confrontation de sociétés*, Brussels: De Boeck.

——(1996) *La Construction de l'islam européen. Approche socio-anthropologique*, Paris: L'Harmattan.

——(1999) "Leaders and Leaderships in Islam and Transplanted Islam in Europe," in Helander, E. (ed.) *Religion and Social Transitions*, Helsinki: Department of Practical Theology.

——(ed.) (2000) *Paroles d'islam. Individus, sociétés et discours dans l'islam européen contemporain. Islamic Words: Individuals, Societies and Discourse in Contemporary European Islam*, Paris: Maisonneuve & Larose.

——(2011) *L'Iris et le croissant: Bruxelles et l'Islam au défi de la co-inclusion*, Louvain-la-Neuve: Presses universitaires de Louvain.

——(2012) "Sharia4 … all, éléments d'analyse et de réflexion à propos d'un groupe extrémiste," *Papers Online du Centre Interdisciplinaire d'Etudes de l'Islam dans le Monde Contemporain*, www.uclouvain.be/cps/ ucl/doc/epl-corta/documents/Sharia4all.pdf (accessed February 1, 2013).

Dassetto, F. and Bastenier, A. (1984) *L'Islam transplanté. Vie et organisation des minorités musulmanes de Belgique*, Antwerp and Brussels: EPO.

——(1991) *Europa: nuova frontiera dell'Islam*, rev. ed., Rome: Edizioni Lavoro.

Dassetto, F., Ferrari, S., and Maréchal, B. (2007) *Islam in the European Union: What's at Stake in the Future?*, Report for the European Parliament – Directorate-General for Internal Policies of the Union, Brussels: European Parliament.

De Changy, J., Dassetto, F., and Maréchal, B. (2007) *Relations et co-inclusion: Islam en Belgique*, Paris: L'Harmattan.

Djelloul, G. (2013) *Parcours de féministes musulmanes belges, de l'engagement dans l'islam aux droits des femmes?*, Louvain-la-Neuve: Académia-Bruylant.

El Asri, F. (2014) *Rythmes et voix d'islam. Enquête auprès d'artistes musulmans européens*, Louvain-la-Neuve: Presses universitaires de Louvain.

Fadil, N. (2008) *Submitting to God, Submitting to the Self: Secular and Religious Trajectories of Second Generation Maghrebi in Belgium*, Leuven: Lirias KU Leuven.

Ferrari, S. (2007) "Juridical Profiles and Political Management of Muslims' Presence in Europe," in Dassetto, F., Ferrari, S., and Maréchal, B. *Islam in the European Union: What's at Stake in the Future?*, Report for the European Parliament – Directorate-General for Internal Policies of the Union, Brussels: European Parliament.

Foblets, M.-Cl. (2003) "Muslim Family Laws before the Courts in Europe: A Conditional Recognition," in Maréchal, B., Allievi, S., Dassetto, F., and Nielsen, J. (eds.) *Muslims in the Enlarged Europe: Religion and Society*, Leiden: Brill.

Frégosi, F. (2009) "Formes de mobilisation collective des musulmans en France et en Europe," *Revue internationale de politique comparée*, De Boeck University, 1(16): 41–61.

——(2012) "Muslim Collective Mobilisations in Contemporary Europe: New Issues and New Types of Involvement," in *Conference of the Yearbook of Muslims in Europe*, Vienna, June 4–6, unpublished paper.

Garay, A. (2005) "L'Islam et l'ordre public européen vus par la CEDH," *Revue belge de droit international* 82(1): 117–55.

Gerholm, T. and Lithman, Y.G. (eds.) (1988) *The New Islamic Presence in Western Europe*, London: Mansell.

Goffman, E. (1967) *Interaction Ritual: Essays on Face-to-Face Behavior*, New York: Random House.

Guénif-Souilamas, N. and Macé, E. (2004) *Les Féministes et le garçon arabe*, La Tour d'Aigues: Editions de l'Aube.

Haenni, P. (2005) *L'Islam de marché. L'Autre révolution conservatrice*, Paris: Seuil.

——(2009) "The Economic Politics of Muslim Consumption," in Pink, J. (ed.) *Muslim Societies in the Age of Mass Consumption: Politics, Culture and Identity between the Local and the Global*, Newcastle: Cambridge Scholars Publishing.

Honneth, A. (2002) *La Lutte pour la reconnaissance*, Paris: Cerf.

Hunter, S. (ed.) (2002) *Islam, Europe's Second Religion: The New Social, Cultural, and Political Landscape*, Westport, CT: Praeger.

Ion, J. (1997) *La Fin des militants?*, Paris: Les Editions de l'Atelier.

Jeldtoft, N. (2009) "Defining Muslims," in Nielsen, J.S., Akgönül, S., Alibašić, A., Maréchal, B., and Moe, C. (eds.) *Yearbook of Muslims in Europe*, vol. I, Leiden and Boston: Brill, pp. 9–14.

Klausen, J. (2009) *The Cartoons that Shook the World*, New Haven, CT: Yale University Press.

Koopmans, R., Statham, P., Giugni, M., and Passy, F. (2005) *Contested Citizenship: Immigration and Cultural Diversity in Europe*, Minneapolis: University of Minnesota Press.

Krafess, J. (2005) "L'Influence de la religion musulmane dans l'aide humanitaire," *Revue internationale de la Croix-Rouge* 87: 123–8.

Kymlicka, W. (1995) *Multicultural Citizenship: A Liberal Theory of Minority Rights*, Oxford: Oxford University Press.

Lewis, P. (2007) *Young, British and Muslim*, London: Continuum.

McLoughlin, S. (2005) "The State, New Muslim Leaderships and Islam as a Resource for Engagement in Britain," in Cesari, J. and McLoughlin, S. (eds.) *European Muslims and the Secular State*, Farnham: Ashgate.

Malik, J. and Hinnells, J. (eds.) (2006) *Sufism in the West*, London and New York: Routledge.

Mandaville, P. (2011) "Transnational Muslim Solidarities and Everyday Life," *Nation and Nationalisms (Journal of the Association for the Study of Ethnicity and Nationalism)* 17(1): 7–24.

Maréchal, B. (ed.) (2002) *L'Islam et les musulmans dans l'Europe élargie: radioscopie – A Guidebook on Islam and Muslims in the Wide Contemporary Europe*, Louvain-la-Neuve: Académia-Bruylant.

——(2008) *The Muslim Brothers in Europe: Roots and Discourses*, Leiden: Brill.

——(2012) "The European Muslim Brothers' Quest to Become a Social (Cultural) Movement," in Meijer, R. and Bakker, E. (eds.) *The Muslim Brotherhood in Europe*, London: Columbia University Press/ Hurst.

Maréchal, B., Allievi, S., Dassetto, F., and Nielsen, J. (2003) *Muslims in the Enlarged Europe: Religion and Society*, Leiden: Brill.

Martiniello, M., Réa, A., and Dassetto, F. (eds.) (2007) *La Belgique face aux nouvelles migrations: menace ou chance?*, coll. Intellection, no. 4, Louvain-la-Neuve: Academia-Bruylant.

Masud, K. (ed.) (2000) *Travellers in Faith: Studies of the Tablighi Jama'at as a Transnational Movement for Faith Renewal*, Leiden: Brill.

Meijer, R. (2009) *Global Salafism: Islam's New Religious Movement*, London: Hurst.

Meijer, R. and Bakker, E. (eds.) (2012) *The Muslim Brotherhood in Europe*, London: Columbia University Press/Hurst.

Nielsen, J.S. (1992) *Muslims in Western Europe*, Edinburgh: Edinburgh University Press.

——(1999) *Towards a European Islam*, London: Macmillan Press.

——(ed.) (2013) *Muslim Political Participation in Europe*, Edinburgh: Edinburgh University Press.

Nielsen, J.S., Akgönül, S., Alibašić, A., Maréchal, B., and Moe, C. (eds.) (2009) *Yearbook of Muslims in Europe*, vol. 1, Leiden and Boston: Brill.

——(2010) *Yearbook of Muslims in Europe*, vol. 2, Leiden and Boston: Brill.

Nielsen, J.S., Akgönül, S., Alibašić, A., Goddard, H., and Maréchal, B. (eds.) (2011) *Yearbook of Muslims in Europe*, vol. 3, Leiden and Boston: Brill.

Nielsen, J.S., Akgönül, S., Alibašić, A., and Racius, E. (eds.) (2012) *Yearbook of Muslims in Europe*, vol. 4, Leiden and Boston: Brill.

Nonneman, G., Niblock, T., and Szajkowski, B. (eds.) (1996) *Muslim Communities in the New Europe*, New York: Ithaca Press.

Pędziwiatr, K. (2010) *The New Muslim Elites in European Cities*, Saarbrücken: VDM Verlag.

Pew Forum on Religion and Public Life (2010) *Muslim Networks and Movements in Western Europe*, Washington: Pew Research Center.

Pink, J. (ed.) (2009) *Muslim Societies in the Age of Mass Consumption: Politics, Culture and Identity between the Local and the Global*, Newcastle: Cambridge Scholars Publishing.

Poutignat, P. and Streiff-Fénart, J. (1999) *Théories de l'ethnicité*, Paris: Presses universitaires de France.

Ramoussi, M. (2012) *La Citoyenneté – Clef d'une contribution civilisationnelle des musulmans d'Europe*, La Courneuve: Bayane Editions.

Rath, J., Penninx, R., Groenendijk, K., and Meyer, A. (2001) *Western Europe and Its Islam*, Leiden, Boston, and Cologne: Brill.

Reetz, D. (2009) "The Piety of Modernity: The Tablighi Jama'at in Europe," in Mandaville, P. (ed.) *Transnational Islam: Identities, Networks and Movement*, Washington: Pew Forum, unpublished paper.

Roose, E. (2009) *The Architectural Representation of Islam: Muslim-Commissioned Mosque Design in the Netherlands*, Amsterdam: Amsterdam University Press.

Roy, O. (2002) *L'Islam mondialisé*, Paris: Seuil.

Schulze, R. (2009) "Da'wah from Saudi Arabia: Transnationalism in the Context of Muslim World League," in Mandaville, P. (ed.) *Transnational Islam: Identities, Networks, and Movements in Public Life*, Washington: Pew Forum, unpublished paper.

Seddon, M.S., Hussain, D., and Malik, N. (eds.) (2003) *British Muslims: Loyalty and Belonging*, proceedings of a seminar held on May 8, 2002, Markfield: The Islamic Foundation & the Citizen Organizing Foundation.

Shadid, W.A.R. and van Koningsveld, P.S. (eds.) (1991) *The Integration of Islam and Hinduism in Western Europe*, Kampen, Netherlands: Kok Pharos.

——(1995) *Religious Freedom and the Position of Islam in Western Europe*, Kampen, Netherlands: Kok Pharos.

——(1996) *Muslims in the Margin: Political Responses to the Presence of Islam in Western Europe*, Kampen, Netherlands: Kok Pharos.

Skovgaard-Petersen, J. and Gräf, B. (eds.) (2009) *Global Mufti: The Phenomenon of Yusuf al-Qaradawi*, London: Hurst.

Sor, K. (2012) "De l'Economie à la finance islamique: itinéraire de l'ajustement d'un produit identitaire à la globalisation libérale," *Religioscope: Etudes et analyses* 25, religion.info/pdf/2012_04_Sor.pdf (accessed February 1, 2013).

Spielhaus, R. (2011) "Measuring the Muslim: About Statistical Obsessions, Categorisations and the Quantification of Religion," in Nielsen, J.S., Akgönül, S., Alibašić, A., Goddard, H., and Maréchal, B. (eds.) *Yearbook of Muslims in Europe*, vol. 3, Leiden and Boston: Brill, pp. 695–715.

Sunier, T. (2009) *Beyond the Domestication of Islam: A Reflection on Research on Islam in European Societies*, inaugural address (November 27), Amsterdam: VU University Amsterdam.

Welzbacher, C. (2008) *Euro Islam Architecture: New Mosques in the West*, Amsterdam: SUN.

Vertovec, S. and Peach, C. (eds.) (1997) *Islam in Europe: The Politics of Religion and Community*, New York: St. Martin's Press.

Vertovec, S. and Rogers, A. (eds.) (1998) *Muslim European Youth: Reproducing Ethnicity, Religion, Culture*, London: Ashgate.

Westoff, C. and Frejka, T. (2007) "Religiousness and Fertility among European Muslims," *Population and Development Review* 33 (December): 785–809.

Zibouh, F. (2010) *La Participation politique des élus d'origine maghrébine*, Louvain-la-Neuve: Academia-Bruylant.

# Part 1.2

# Muslims in the Americas

# 6

# Islam in America

## The beginnings

*Kambiz GhaneaBassiri*

On a recent research trip to an East Coast mosque, a mosque employee who was interested in my research asked me, "Where do you begin your history of Islam in America?" I have been a professional student of religion long enough to know that when people casually ask me a question about my work they are not so much interested in my expert opinion as they are politely looking for an opening to share their own thoughts and convictions.

"I begin with the early European exploration and settlement of the Americas. Where do you think the history of Islam in America should begin?"

"Ah, you see … most people begin with slavery," he retorted, "but there were Muslims who came here long before that." He went on to explain that there were seamen as early as the ninth century who traveled westward from Muslim Iberia and West Africa, and they recorded their journeys, describing lands and peoples similar to those found in the Americas. Muslim scholars, he insisted, are uncovering archeological evidence of these voyages in South America today. "It's important to talk about these things," he advised me. "People talk about us as though we are recent transports here, and they need to know that that's not the case."

These claims are based on dubious readings of ancient Muslim geographies found in some popular histories of Muslims in America (Dirks 2006: 28–38). They tell us more about some American Muslims' desire to establish their own American foundation myth than about the activities of ancient Muslim sailors. Nonetheless, they are important reminders of the social and political stakes of narrating the early history of Islam in America for American Muslims, who, since the attacks of 9/11, have come under suspicion and feel like outsiders.

While there is no conclusive evidence to suggest a pre-Columbus Muslim presence in the Americas, the history of Islam in America begins in the context of early modern imperial and commercial rivalries and encounters that shaped the Atlantic world. Given the enormous impact the European discovery of the Americas had on the modern era, it is easy to forget that during the fifteenth and sixteenth centuries European empires navigated along the coast of Africa and across the Atlantic in order to establish new trade routes that would circumvent the routes that went through Muslim-controlled territories in West Asia and North Africa. As Europeans conquered and colonized the Americas, an Atlantic world emerged, triangulating Africa, Europe, and the Americas through mercantile relations and imperial networks. Muslims from North and

West Africa were active participants in this triangle, and some of them ended up in America as slaves.

The extant evidence of the earliest history of Islam in America is scant. We mainly possess scattered information about the lives of individuals whose extraordinary lives or circumstances attracted the attention of Euro-American contemporaries. Some of these individuals were not identified specifically as Muslims but came from Muslim-majority territories. One of the earliest mentions of a person who came to America from a Muslim-majority region is Estevanico de Dorantes, "a black Arab originally from Azamor," Morocco (Cabeza de Vaca 1906: 144). Estevanico's life is the stuff of legends. He, along with his master, Andrés Dorantes, were on Pamfilo de Narváez's 1527 expedition from Spain to the northern Gulf Coast, which ended in a shipwreck. They crisscrossed the Gulf Coast for about six years, occasionally as lost wanderers but usually as captives among the natives. During this time, Estevanico often acted as a medicine man and at times served as an intermediary between the Spanish and the Native Americans. Later, the Spanish viceroy in Mexico, Antonio de Mendoza, ·purchased Estevanico from Dorantes, and appointed him to act as a scout and guide on a new expedition to the northern frontier of Mexico, where he was reportedly killed in 1539 by the natives of the Pueblo of Háwikuh (GhaneaBassiri 2010: 10–12).

In 1630, Anthony Jansen van Salee, also known as Anthony Jansen van Vaes and Anthony "the Turk," immigrated to New Amsterdam as a colonist of the Dutch West India Company. "Turk" was a derogatory term for Muslims at the time, and "van Salee" and "van Vaes" signified that Anthony was "from Salé" or "from Fez," Morocco. He was later joined by a possible brother or half-brother, who was also referred to by contemporaries as "the Turk" and "the Mulatto." Anthony was in all likelihood the son of Jan Jansz van Haarlem, a Dutch privateer in the Mediterranean who was captured in 1618 by North African Muslims and found privateering with the "Moors" more profitable than with the Dutch. He "turned Turk" and became Admiral Murat Reis in the fleet of Moulay Zaydan in Salé. In 1676, Anthony settled as a farmer and, at times, real estate entrepreneur in territories that eventually formed New York City (GhaneaBassiri 2010: 9–12). While there is no known record of Anthony's religious identity, one of his descendants, in the late nineteenth century, discovered family heirlooms that included a copy of the Qur'an and a copper teapot that he believed belonged to Anthony (McClain 1932: 71).

Further evidence of the possible presence of Muslims in seventeenth-century America was found in 1991. During the archeological exploration of the African Burial Ground in Lower Manhattan, some graves were uncovered that suggest some early African arrivals in America may have been buried according to Islamic customs (Mack and Blakey 2004: 13). As inconclusive as this evidence is in identifying the earliest history of Islam in America, it nonetheless reminds us that this history begins in the triangular relations between Europe, Africa, and the Americas that shaped the founding of America.

It is not until the eighteenth and nineteenth centuries that we encounter solid evidence of the presence of Muslims in America. Scholars of the African diaspora estimate that "tens of thousands" of African Muslims were brought to the territories that eventually formed the United States (Gomez 2005: 166; Austin 1997: 22). The heyday of this forced migration coincided with the *jihad*s of the late eighteenth and early nineteenth centuries in West Africa. These wars were led by Muslim reformers who dramatically increased the presence of Islam in West Africa and sought to purify West African Islam from native practices that they considered superstitious and heretical. These *jihad*s resulted in the establishment of a number of Muslim states in sub-Saharan Africa, the best known of which is the Sokoto Caliphate founded by the Fulbe scholar-warrior 'Usman dan Fodio.

Non-Muslims taken as captives during these wars were often sold into slavery, and, as Michael Gomez has argued, it seems that these *jihad*s were "responsible for nearly all of the captives coming from the interior" of West Africa. The African trade in humans, of course, did not commence with the transatlantic slave trade or with the West African *jihad*s of this era. Slave routes traversed the Sahara, the Mediterranean Sea, and the Indian Ocean for hundreds of years, reaching markets in North Africa, the Middle East, and the Indian Ocean, respectively. The transatlantic slave trade, however, altered the nature of the slave market, making it, by the time of the West African *jihad*s, an engine of the continent's economy. As a consequence, West African Muslim states established in this period depended heavily on the transatlantic slave trade and sought to monopolize slave exports (Lovejoy 2000). These *jihad*s, as Gomez has observed, were not "one long, uninterrupted Muslim march to victory. Non-Muslim populations fought back," and their war captives were often sold into the transatlantic slave market (Gomez 1994: 680).

We know very little about how Islam was practiced by enslaved African Muslims because slave owners were not interested in the native religions of their human property. The few African Muslim slaves who left us a historical record did so because they drew the attention of white Americans as a result of their ability to read and write Arabic.[1] Memories of some Muslim slaves on the Georgia Sea Islands were also preserved in interviews conducted with descendents of enslaved African Muslims in the 1930s (Georgia Writers' Project 1972 [1940]). Collectively this evidence shows that Islamic beliefs and practices were, on the one hand, a means of self-identification by which Muslims were distinguished and, on the other, a means by which Muslim slaves made sense of their new experiences and encounters and formed new individual and communal relations in antebellum America.

An example of how Islamic beliefs and practices distinguished Muslims from others could be found in the life of Job Ben Solomon (anglicized from Hyuba Boon Salumena in Fula or Ayyub bin Sulayman in Arabic), who was enslaved in Maryland from 1730 to 1733 and later emancipated and transported to England, where he became an agent of the Royal African Company in order to help promote English trade in gold and gum Arabic in the interior of Africa. While in Maryland, Job was known to "often leave the Cattle, and withdraw into the Woods to pray" (Bluett 1744: 19–20). In England, he at first refused to sit to have his portrait painted because of Islamic sensibilities toward the portrayal of human images as a potential form of idolatry. He only consented to the portrait once he was told that it was a means of remembering him (Bluett 1744: 50–1).

Georgia Writers' Project's interviews with the grandchildren of Muslim slaves also reveal that Islamic practices set Muslims apart in their environments. Katie Brown, for example, recalled:

> Magret an uh daughtu Cotto use tuh say dat Belali an he wife Phoebe pray on duh bead. Dey wuz bery phticluh bout duh time dey pray and dy bery regluh bout duh hour. Wen du sun come up, wen it straight obuh head an wen it set, das duh time dey pray. Dey bow tuh duh sun an hab lill mat tuh kneel on. Duh bead is on a long string. Belali he pul bead an he say, "Belami, Hakabara, Mahamadu." Phoebe she say, "Ameen, Ameen."
>
> *(Georgia Writers' Project 1972 [1940]: 154)*

Muslim slaves were also distinguished by their abstinence from alcohol and pork products. The Georgian plantation owner James Hamilton Couper described his head slave driver, Salih Bilali, as a "strict Mahometan; [who] abstains from spirituous liquors, and keeps the various fasts, particularly that of the Rhamadan" (Austin 1984: 321). Charles Willson Peale, who painted a portrait of Yarrow Mamout, recalled in his memoirs that "acquaintances of [Yarrow Mamout]

111

often banter him about eating Bacon and drinking Whiskey – but Yarrow says 'it is no good to eat Hog – & drink whiskey is very bad'" (Austin 1984: 70).

While Islamic beliefs and practices, in some cases, set Muslims apart from other slaves, Islamic beliefs and practices were not simple transplants from Africa nor did they survive unaffected by African Muslims' new circumstances. A close examination of the writings and practices of African Muslim slaves shows that the polyvalence of Islamic beliefs and practices allowed enslaved African Muslims to bridge racial, ethnic, and religious differences without eradicating them. By way of example, on December 29, 1828, Condy Raquet, a former US *chargé d'affaires* in Brazil, met 'Abdul Rahman in Philadelphia and asked him to inscribe the Lord's Prayer in Arabic. 'Abdul Rahman instead wrote down the first chapter of the Qur'an – *al-Fatiha* (Austin 1984: 190). This act could be interpreted as subversive or as a subtle form of resistance, however, Rahman was a man who had consented to help spread Christianity to Africa in exchange for the repatriation of his family and who had married a Christian woman whom he reportedly accompanied to church (Austin 1984: 187, 168). A more likely interpretation, however, is that in the poly-religious context of slave life in antebellum America, *al-Fatiha* was functionally polysemous for 'Abdul Rahman. *Al-Fatiha*, like the Lord's Prayer, is a scriptural prayer memorized for ritual citation in daily prayer. By writing down *al-Fatiha* when asked to inscribe the Lord's Prayer, 'Abdul Rahman was writing the Lord's Prayer that he knew and in the process founding common ground with Christianity and ascribing a new sphere of meaning to both *al-Fatiha* and the Lord's Prayer.

Another African Muslim slave, 'Umar ibn Said, who was viewed by his contemporaries as a convert to Christianity, likewise understood *al-Fatiha* to be interchangeable with the Lord's Prayer. In his autobiography, he wrote (in broken Arabic):

> At first, [as a] Muhammad[an]. When praying, [I] said: "Praise belongs to God the Lord of the worlds … [the rest of *al-Fatiha*]." Yet now, when praying, the saying of our Lord Jesus the Messiah: "Our Father, who art in heaven … [the rest of the Lord's Prayer]."
>
> *(Said 2011 [1831]: 74)*

By presenting these prayers as interchangeable, 'Umar did not syncretize Islam and Christianity; rather, he established a poly-religious common ground that maintained the distinctness of each religion while at the same time allowing him to step in and out of both. He apparently sought common ground with Christianity within his own Islamic worldview. In his autobiography, while acknowledging that he and his master's family, the Owens, were brought up with different scriptures, he asked, "God, our Lord, our Creator, and our Ruler, the Restorer of our state … open my heart to the Gospels, to the path of guidance." He followed this with a phrase from the Qur'an, "Praise belongs to God, the Lord of the Worlds" (Qur'an 1:2, 6:45, 40:65), and then went on to quote the Gospels, "Because the Law (*shar*') was made for Moses and grace (*al-ni'ma*) and truth (*al-haqq*) were for Jesus the Messiah" (John 1:17; Said 2011 [1831]: 72, 74). In this passage, 'Umar simultaneously stepped in and out of both the Qur'an and the Gospels by appealing to a conception of God shared by Muslims and Christians as the Creator, Lord, and Ruler of all of existence. Tellingly, he cited a verse from the Gospel of John that would not offend Muslim religious beliefs, ignoring both preceding and proceeding verses that describe Jesus as the Son of God or as the Word made flesh. While clearly aware of the differences between Islam and Christianity, 'Umar's focus on their commonality allowed him to enter into a communal relation of sorts with the Owens.

Another use of Islamic practices in forming communal relations with non-Muslims was found in the plantations of Georgia, where interviewees of the Georgia Writers' Project remember their ancestors making "funny flat cakes," which they called *saraka* or *sadaqa* (a form of voluntary alms in Islam) and distributed to the kids on special occasions. The interviews do not explain the intent behind the distribution of *sadaqa* cakes, but they clearly had a communal dimension to them. That *sadaqa* was given to children demonstrates a use of Islamic practice to forge new communal relations with the next generation, with whom African Muslims did not have clear kinship or tribal ties. The fact that their grandchildren, many years later, recalled *sadaqa* as a "flat cake" and did not associate it with Islam suggests that African Muslims' use of this practice was not intended necessarily to create an Islamic community but rather to sanction Islamically the existing community in which they participated (Georgia Writers' Project 1972 [1940]: 137, 155, 173).

Islamic practices were distinctive but nonetheless a feature of everyday life among African Muslims in antebellum America. Muslims adapted their practices to their new context, and used Islam to participate in a poly-religious and multi-ethnic community. The extant evidence, however, suggests that they never formed communal institutions and practices that could ensure the continuity of Islam among their descendents. Their demise thus marked the end of an era in the history of Islam in America.

The next wave of Muslims, estimated at around 60,000 (GhaneaBassiri 2010: 135–50), arrived voluntarily in the United States between the 1880s and 1910s from Eastern Europe, South Asia, and the Middle East. They arrived at a time of great changes in American society stemming from the emancipation of slaves, increased immigration, industrialization, and urbanization. These changes called for a rethinking of American identity as they altered not only the social and religious landscape of America but also its economic and political power structures. In the antebellum period, Anglo-American Protestants had not felt a necessity to assert their pre-eminence in society. Their cultural, political, and economic dominance was palpable in all aspects of American life. After the Civil War, however, not only was there more ethnic, racial, and religious diversity in the country but there were also new classes of elites emerging from these varying communities in urban centers throughout the United States. Industrial capitalism allowed for the emergence of a *nouveau riche*, cosmopolitan class. This new post-Civil War era was characterized not by poly-religious practices, but by religious competition over the cultural authority to define America's national identity and to lay claim to its economic, industrial, and scientific advancements.

During this time cultural authenticity was sought by conflating industrial development, commercial capitalism, Enlightenment ideals, the white race, and Protestant Christianity to argue for the superiority of Anglo-American, liberal Protestantism. I refer to this in shorthand as the conflation of race, religion, and progress with a caveat; race, religion, and progress were not seen as separate entities that could be conflated with one another at this time. It is only in hindsight that we see them as discrete categories that were conflated together to define what it meant to be American. In the late nineteenth century, this conflation reached a triumphant pitch under the influence of social evolutionary ideas developed around the works of Herbert Spencer and Charles Darwin.[2] The Congregationalist minister Josiah Strong, for example, cited Spencer in his bestseller *Our Country*, arguing that the mixing of the Aryan races in America "will produce a more powerful type of man than has hitherto existed. … [T]he Americans may reasonably look forward to a time when they will have produced a civilization grander than any the world has known" (Strong 1885: 172). Strong went on to associate America's successes with divine providence and liberal Christian ideals of liberty and individual rights. He wrote:

> It was the fire of liberty burning in the Saxon heart that flamed up against the absolutism of the Pope. … This mighty Anglo-Saxon race, though comprising only one-fifteenth part of

mankind, now rules more than one-third of the earth's surface, and more than one-fourth of its people. ... Does it not look as if God were not only preparing in our Anglo-Saxon civilization the die with which to stamp the peoples of the earth, but as if he were also massing behind that die the mighty power with which to press it? ... The physical changes accompanied by mental, which are taking place in the people of the United States are apparently to adapt men to the demands of a higher civilization.

*(Strong 1885: 159–61)*

Strong's Anglo-Saxon vision of America struck a chord with popular nativist opposition to the increased ethnic, racial, and religious diversification of the United States at this time. As historian William Hutchison observed, "Neither he nor most of his readers felt any doubt about just who it was that *our* [in *Our Country*] referred to" (Hutchison 2004: 139).

The conflation of race, religion, and progress was not only popularized in the late nineteenth century by noted elites, it was also extravagantly performed at world fairs, the most important of which was the 1893 World's Columbian Exposition in Chicago. The perceived relation between race, religion, and progress was unmistakable in the Columbian Exposition's spatial ordering of Chicago's Midway. The Teutonic and Celtic races represented by German and Irish villages were situated closest to the appropriately named White City. In the middle were the "semi-civilized" worlds of the Muslims and other West and East Asians. At the opposite end of the White City were the "savage races" of Africa and Native Americans. The didactic message of the fair's evolutionary ordering of space and time was not lost on contemporaries. "What an opportunity," wrote the *Chicago Tribune*, "was here afforded to the scientific mind to descend the spiral of evolution, tracing humanity in its highest phases down almost to its animalistic origin" (November 1, 1893: 9).

A number of congresses were held at the Exposition to discuss varying aspects of human progress. One of these, titled World's Parliament of Religions, brought representatives of varying religions to Chicago to discuss the contributions of "world religions" to advancements in the modern world. This Parliament aimed for followers of different religions to be heard in their own voice, but there is no doubt that the expectation was that when Americans heard these differing voices, their superior opinion of their own faith would be reinforced. The chair of the Parliament, John Henry Barrows, stated in his introductory remarks that "the members of this Congress meet, as men, on a common ground of perfect equality. ... But no attempt is here made to treat all religions as of equal merit." He further asserted that the very fact that the Parliament was planned and realized by American Protestant Christians, who possess the ability, the foresight, and the religion "fitted to the needs of all men," shows the superiority of their faith:

Christendom may proudly hold up this Congress of the Faiths as a torch of truth and of love which may prove the morning star of the twentieth century. ... Justice Ameer Ali, of Calcutta, ... has expressed the opinion that only in this Western republic would such a congress as this have been undertaken and achieved.

*(Seager 1993: 24–5)*

Even though the Parliament intended to put all of humanity on equal footing, Barrows and others believed that once white, Protestant Americans spoke about their faith and its contribution to human progress – as evidenced by the industrial, scientific, and aesthetic wonders on display at the White City – they would convince others of the superiority of their religion.

The conflation of race, religion, and progress, which underpinned the articulation of a white, Protestant American national identity at this time, significantly affected the history of Islam in America through governmental efforts to exclude non-whites and non-Protestants from the America body politic. Such efforts included not only Jim Crow laws but also restrictive immigration and citizenship laws. In 1882, Congress passed the Chinese Exclusion Act, which suspended Chinese immigration for ten years and barred Chinese immigrants from becoming naturalized. This act was renewed and remained effective until 1943. In 1917, Congress instituted a literacy test for all new immigrants and established the Asiatic Barred Zone. Since by this time elementary education had become common in northern and Western Europe and since East Asians were barred from entry into the United States, the literacy test was intended primarily to restrict immigration from predominantly non-Protestant parts of Europe and secondarily from Western Asia and Africa. Finally, the Immigration Act of 1924 established quotas that favored northern and Western European countries: "The annual quota of any nationality shall be two percentum of the number of foreign-born individuals of such nationality resident in continental United States as determined by the US Census of 1890, but the minimum quota of any nationality shall be 100." This restriction heavily favored immigrants from Germany and Great Britain, with a quota of 51,227 and 34,004, respectively. All countries with a significant Muslim population outside of the 1917 Asiatic Barred Zone were given the minimum quota of 100 persons.

Muslims' entry into the United States was further restricted by the Immigration Act of 1891, which added "polygamists; or persons who admit their belief in the practice of polygamy" to the inadmissible classes. Between 1909 and 1917, 73 out of 2,457 Indians were barred from entry into the United States on account of their religion permitting polygamy (Das 1923: 13). In 1920, the Indian missionary of the Ahmadiyya Movement in Islam, Muhammad Sadiq, was detained for seven weeks because he adhered to a religion that allowed polygamy. He successfully argued for his release by explaining that while Islam permitted polygamy, it did not command it, and since Islam obligates its adherent to obey the laws of the land where they reside, Muslims in America were forbidden from having multiple wives (Sadiq 1921).

The ideal of America as a white, Protestant nation at this time was also evident in naturalization procedures. The Naturalization Act of 1790 granted citizenship only "to aliens being free white persons." Congress amended this law in 1870 to give citizenship "to aliens of African nativity and to persons of African descent." The ambiguities surrounding the racial status of Turks, Indians, and Levantine Arabs resulted in challenges to their eligibility for citizenship. Levantine and South Asian immigrants responded to these challenges by trying to insert themselves into the matrix of race, religion, and progress that shaped America's national identity. They argued in courts that they too are "white" or members of the Caucasian race. Levantine Arabs further asserted that if they were denied citizenship, Jesus Christ, who was born in their homeland, would have to be considered non-white. In 1915, the Fourth Circuit Court of Appeals ruled that Levantine Arabs were indeed "white," but this did not settle the citizenship status of non-Levantine Muslim immigrants with darker skin tones. In 1923, the US Supreme Court unanimously denied citizenship to Bhagat Singh Thind, a World War I veteran from Punjab, India. In 1942, a Michigan District Court denied citizenship to Ahmed Hassan from Yemen. The court argued that Arab Muslims were of sufficiently different culture that they could not be considered "white" within the meaning of the Naturalization Act of 1790 (*In re Ahmed Hassan*, 48 F. Supp. 843). The issue was raised again as late as 1944, when a Massachusetts District Court upheld the citizenship of Mohamed Mohriez from Yemen (*Ex parte Mohriez*, 54 F. Supp. 941). The Massachusetts court, reflecting the national mood at the time of America's entry into World War II, argued that exclusionary immigration policies contradicted

America's liberal democratic principles. In light of the racist atrocities the Nazis committed in the name of racial superiority, the conflation of whiteness, Protestantism, and progress as a predominant means of defining American national identity became much less defensible.

The conflation of whiteness, Protestantism, and progress in American national identity, which manifested in terms of restrictive immigration and citizenship laws, hampered the presence of Muslims in the United States, but ironically it also opened doors for distinctive American manifestations of Islam, particularly among spiritual seekers and African Americans. The strong association made between religion, race, and material progress turned some Americans who saw themselves both as rational and spiritual to look to the "East" in search of "scientific" forms of spirituality and metaphysics. Chief among these was the Theosophical Society, which sought to assimilate science and "Eastern" religions into a new "Western" religious discourse (von Stuckard 2005: 122–32). Theosophists, thus, served as intermediaries between liberal Protestants and the "East," providing intellectual means and social networks through which the imagined religious other could be embodied. Indeed, the sole spokesperson for Islam at the World's Parliament of Religions in 1893, Mohammed Alexander Russell Webb, was a Theosophist and an American diplomat who converted to Islam around 1888 and, with the support of some Indian merchants, went on to found the American Islamic Propaganda in New York City in 1892.

Webb was a spiritual seeker in the sense that he believed in an immortal soul and spiritual existence but was disillusioned by the notion of salvation through the church. He recalled that in his youth he enjoyed the "sermons preached by God Himself through the murmuring brooks, the gorgeous flowers and the joyous birds" more than "abstruse discourses of the minister" (Webb 1892: 24). He encountered Islam primarily in Sufi writings, from which he concluded that Islam instantiated a "rational" and "universal" religion (Webb 1893: 26–7). In his missionary newspaper, *Moslem World*, he addressed himself to "progressive people in nearly all large American cities" and admonished them that "the time has now arrived for the spread of the true faith from the Eastern to the Western Hemisphere. [Islam's] adoption as the universal religion seems only a question of comparatively short time" (May 12, 1893). Webb disassociated his "spiritual" understanding of Islam from its "exoteric" dimensions, which he rationalized as laws that could be shown to be "thoroughly applicable to all the needs of humanity" rather than as divine commands. He focused on "the spirit that prevailed among the Moslems of the higher [spiritual] class" and on an unnamed "spiritual truth" taught by Muhammad that "every man who knows anything of the spiritual side of religion ought to know" (reproduced in Seager 1993: 275–6).

Webb's mission misjudged the depth of anti-Muslim sentiment in the United States. His appeal to Islam was ridiculed in newspapers as a "fad for those curiously constructed beings who are always chasing after new and strange doctrines" (*Chicago Daily Tribune*, December 25, 1892). Some in the audience of the World's Parliament of Religions hissed at his speech. "Cries of 'Shame' greeted him when he spoke of polygamy," reported the *Chicago Daily Tribune*, "but there was enthusiastic approval when he said that the Mussulman daily offers his prayers to the same God that the Christian adores" (September 21, 1893).

The Sufi Order of the West, founded by Inayat Khan, is another example of how the material success of the United States in the early twentieth century paved a way for "Eastern" religions to enter into the middle and upper classes as repositories of "old-world" spirituality in the modern world. Inayat Khan came to the United States with his brother and cousin in 1910 as Indian musicians. They performed in varying circles, including among spiritual seekers involved with the Vedanta Society. Inayat Khan eventually formed the Sufi Order of the West and fashioned himself as a bridge between a spiritual, mystical "East" and a materialist, rational "West." In a redacted autobiography, he recalled that he "found among the people [Americans] love for [spiritual] knowledge, search for truth, and tendency to unity," but he also lamented that "commercialism" and the "reign of materialism" in "the West" made working for a "spiritual Cause ... like traveling in a hilly land, not like sailing in the sea, which is smooth and level" (Khan et al. 1979: 84, 112).

While propagating his spiritual teachings, Khan found both his skin color and his Islamic heritage an impediment. In 1923, he was detained on Ellis Island because "the quota of Indians was completed for that month." One of his white disciples had to intercede on his behalf to free him (Khan et al. 1979: 106). He described his confrontation with the conflation of race, religion, and progress in America thus:

> There is still to be found in America a prejudice against colour which is particularly shown to the Negroes. ... They think Negroes are too backward in evolution to associate with. ... An ordinary man in America confuses an Indian with brown skin with the Negro. Even if he does not think that he is a Negro, still he is accustomed to look with contempt at a dark skin, in spite of the many most unclean, ignorant and illmannered (*sic*) specimens of white people who are to be found there on the spot. ... The prejudice against Islam that exists in the West was another difficulty for me. Many think Sufism to be a mystical side of Islam, and the thought was supported by the encyclopedias, which speak of Sufism as having sprung from Islam, and they were confirmed in this by knowing that I am Moslem (*sic*) by birth. Naturally I could not tell them that it is a Universal Message of the time, for every man is not ready to understand this.
>
> *(Khan et al. 1979: 87–8, 113)*

Inayat Khan sought to transcend his race and the stigma of Islam by deliberately framing his teachings in the context of a metaphysical discourse on "universal religion" in which Islam became the accidental religion of his birth. In one of his earliest biographies published by the Theosophical Publishing Society, he was said to have outgrown the legalism of his Islamic heritage and discovered the "inner truth" of existence through esoteric Sufism (Khan 1914: 7–15).

While Inayat Khan and Webb looked to "the East" for the spiritual antidote to "Western" materialism and found their efforts impeded by the stigma associated with race and Islam, others looked to Islam as a means for African Americans to turn the table on white, Christian America through a conflation of Islam, the black race, and progress. The Ahmadiyya Movement and its first missionary, Muhammad Sadiq, who arrived in the United States in 1920, made an influential articulation of this conflation. The Ahmadiyya touted Islam as "the only religion for the uplift of humanity in both the Eastern and Western worlds" (*Moslem Sunrise* (1924) 3(1): 20). However, when Sadiq was introduced to the United Negro Improvement Association through Muhammad Duse, an Egyptian author and pan-Africanist, he found among African Americans some of his most ardent followers (GhaneaBassiri 2010: 206–7). By 1923, the Ahmadiyya mission was in large part directed at African Americans:

> My Dear American Negro ... the Christian profiteers brought you out of your native lands of Africa and in Christianizing you made you forsake the religion and language of your forefathers – which were Islam and Arabic. You have experienced Christianity for so many years and it has proved to be no good. It is a failure. Christianity cannot bring real brotherhood to the nations. Now leave it alone. And join Islam, the real faith of Universal Brotherhood which at once does away with all distinctions of race, color and creed.
>
> (Moslem Sunrise *(1923) 2: 263, cited in Turner 2003: 129)*

117

Sadiq's message resonated among African Americans. Some, such as Wali Akram, who founded the First Cleveland Mosque, eventually broke away from the Ahmadiyya Movement, which deviated from the beliefs of the majority of Muslims by acknowledging its founder, Mirza Ghulam Ahmad (1835–1908), as a prophet and the awaited Mahdi or Messiah, and centralized religious authority within his spiritual lineage in South Asia.

Alongside the Ahmadiyya mission in the 1920s and 1930s, new religious movements emerged that used Islamic beliefs, rites, and symbols to define a black Muslim national identity through which African Americans could participate in America's prosperity. Chief among these groups were the Moorish Science Temple and the Nation of Islam, both of which saw a lack of national unity as an impediment to the progress of African Americans and propagated Islam as a religion that not only ensured the salvation of humanity but provided a discipline and a structure through which African Americans could shed the social stigma of their color and unite to advance economically as a community. In a society where race, religion, and progress were conflated, Noble Drew Ali, the founder of one of these pioneering movements known as the Moorish Science Temple, linked racial and religious identity to an "American Moorish" identity, arguing that a positive national identity was requisite of African Americans' progress in America. "The object of our Organization," he wrote, "is to help the great program of uplifting fallen humanity and teach those things necessary to make our members better citizens" (Ali 1928: 12). These "things" could be summed up as American middle-class values of honest hard work, sobriety, dedication to family and community, and entrepreneurship. "A beggar people," Noble Drew Ali taught, "cannot develop the highest in them, nor can they attain to a genuine enjoyment of the spiritualities of life" (Ali 1928: 13–14).

The founder of the Nation of Islam, Wallace D. Fard (also known as Master Fard Muhammad),[3] similarly conflated race, religion, and progress by teaching that African Americans were a godly race descended from the tribe of Shabazz. They had been stolen from the Holy City of Mecca about four centuries ago by whites. Fard's mission was to restore blacks to their original religion, language, and culture through Islam and in doing so restore them to their original divine nature. Like Noble Drew Ali, he sought to instill discipline and middle-class values in his followers in order to uplift them in American society. He preached obedience to God's will, sobriety, and abstinence from alcohol and pig products. These ills, he taught, were part of the "tricknology" used by Caucasian devils to enslave blacks and keep them illiterate, economically destitute, and ignorant of their true selves (Beynon 1938).

Both Noble Drew Ali and Master Fard Muhammad were prophetic figures who, like prophets in general, sought to universalize their particular experiences through religion. Through an eclectic mixing of healing practices, nationalism, entrepreneurialism, prophecy, and Islamic symbols and rites they sought to universalize African American experiences in order to reconfigure the conflation of race, religion, and progress to free blacks from the social stigma of their skin color. Prophecy was crucial in this process because, unlike white Protestants, Noble Drew Ali and Master Fard Muhammad could not point to military, scientific, and industrial achievements to celebrate African American civilization or progress. Their conflation of blackness, Islam, and progress rested on a prophetic argument for their divinely endowed potential for "civilizational" progress. Not only did their appropriation of Islamic symbols, myths, and practices lend divine authority to their prophetic claims, but Islam also provided a non-Christian, non-white context in which their prophetic teachings became sensible as an African American religion.

In addition to Muslim missionary efforts and the formation of prophetic African American religious movements, the first half of the twentieth century also saw the building of Islamic communities and institutions by immigrant Muslims from Eastern Europe, the Middle East, and

South Asia. These immigrants generally came to labor in factories or farms. Many took up peddling (Naff 1985). They generally identified with co-ethnics rather than co-religionists because of social and political prejudices against Muslims. Anecdotal evidence suggests that many Muslims changed their names to more Christian-sounding names to ward off any unfavorable attention at points of entry. A. Joseph Howar, a successful businessman in Washington, DC, came to New York in 1903. In 1975, he told a reporter, "My true name is Mohammed Asa Abu-Howah. But people I met on the boat told me I'd better change my name. They said it labeled me as a Muslim, and no immigrant officer would allow a Muslim to enter the United States. ... I made my American name A. Joseph Howar. That's how I was naturalized in 1908" (Harsham 1975: 14–15).

A lack of recognition of their religious identity, however, did not stop Muslim immigrants in this period from practicing their religion to the best of their abilities, and as their numbers increased and their finances improved, they also began building institutions and organizations to address their varying religious and social needs. As early Muslim immigrants aged and died in the absence of their family members, a pressing concern for early Muslim immigrants was the provision of Islamic burials. In 1918, for example, Turkish and Albanian Muslims in Biddeford, Maine got together to purchase a burial plot in Biddeford's Woodlawn Cemetery for their co-religionists who had died from the Spanish Flu (Rost-Banik 2004). Syrian and Turkish Muslims in Cleveland, Ohio founded the Association of Islamic Union of Cleveland in 1918 "to foster social relations and solidarity among the Moslems" and to purchase a burial plot in Highland Park Cemetery (Grabowski 2005; Dannin 2002: 98). And long before South Asian Muslims built their mosque in Sacramento in 1947, they formed the Moslem Association of America in 1919 in large part to establish proper burial grounds in central California for their deceased co-religionists (Das 1923: 89; Leonard 1992: 83).

In 1907, Eastern European Muslims founded the American Mohammedan Society in Brooklyn, New York (Ferris 1994: 211). Contemporaries in 1920 regarded it as "the only real mosque" in New York City (Aijian 1920, 40), and it maintained this reputation until the late 1930s. Between the world wars, mosques were build in such diverse places as Michigan City, Indiana; Cedar Rapids, Iowa; Ross, North Dakota; Highland Park, Michigan; Chicago, Illinois; and Cleveland, Ohio (GhaneaBassiri 2010: 183–9). The practice of Islam within these institutions was often improvisational and adapted to local circumstances. The variety of social, religious, and political activities in which Muslims engaged can be gleaned from the activities of a remarkable Sudanese immigrant and missionary named Satti Majid, who appointed himself "Sheikh of Islam in America."[4] In 1920, Satti initiated the Detroit chapter of the Kizilay, or the Red Crescent, and purchased plots for Muslim burials at Roselawn Cemetery. In 1928, he registered the Society of Africans in America with the Commonwealth of Pennsylvania. Other organizations attributed to him include the Islamic Benevolent African Society and the African Moslem Welfare Society of America (Abu Shouk et al. 1997: 189–191). In a 1935 interview with *al-Balagh* newspaper in Cairo, Satti explained that the impetus for organizing Muslims in America was a call for subscriptions from subjects of the Ottoman Empire to bolster its navy:

> We organized the first meeting for this in order to collect donations. ... When I saw the number of Muslims, I realized that religious duty necessitates undertaking what God has obliged us to do by way of prescribed prayers, the fast of Ramadan, and the pilgrimage to the sacred House of God. ... We established a society by the name of Islamic Benevolence Society in Detroit, Michigan, and our first act was to build a mosque there next to Henry Ford, the giant of the automobile industry. Then we organized another society in this city

by the name of Islamic Union, and all of these societies worked together to spread the message of Islam under my leadership. We continued to work as such until 1914 when the war started and the organizations assisted with the aid of those who had been afflicted in the Ottoman State.

*(August 14, 1935, reproduced in Aḥmad 2005: 117–22)*

By 1919, Satti had clearly come to see himself as the pastoral representative of Muslims in America. In a letter he wrote to the French Embassy in that year on behalf of 300 Syrian Muslims who wished to repatriate to Syria but could not afford to do so, Satti identified himself as "the imam and sheikh of Muslims, who speaks on behalf, and is a missionary of the religion of Islam in this country of freedom, the United States" (Aḥmad 2005: 134–5). In a 1921 letter to the British Consulate General on behalf of Yemeni sailors who had served the British during World War I and were desolate and jobless in New York City, Satti introduced himself as "the leader of Muslims in the state of New York" (Aḥmad 2005: 137). Satti also proselytized among African American Muslims and was particularly offended by the teachings of Noble Drew Ali. He left the United States in 1929 to attain a *fatwa* from al-Azhar against him and have himself recognized as the official missionary of al-Azhar in the United States. Scholars at al-Azhar granted him the *fatwa* but deemed him unqualified to lead a mission. Unable to garner funds for his return, he kept up communication with some of his followers in America but eventually returned to the Sudan.

The diverse activities of Satti Majid along with the various institutions Muslims built in this period attest to how African Americans and West Asian and North African immigrants participated in building America in their own vision despite social prejudices and legal restrictions. The history of Islam in America at the turn of the twentieth century, just like the history of Islam in colonial and antebellum America, thus calls attention to the relations formed between peoples of diverse regions and backgrounds that shaped local communities in America despite exclusionary laws and visions of America as a white, Protestant nation. The story of the beginnings of Islam in America is, at its heart, a story of how forces of homogeneity as well as diversity have shaped America and American Islam.

## Notes

I would like to thank Katie Lantz for her assistance in preparing this chapter.
1 For a discussion of the historical importance of Arabic in antebellum America, see Alryyes (2011).
2 It should be noted that Darwin himself disavowed any relation between his biological findings and social evolutionary theories espoused by Spencer.
3 The identity of the founder of the Nation of Islam is shrouded in mystery. For some varying theories of his origins, see Gomez (2005: 277–8).
4 My account of Satti Majid's activities are based on Abu Shouk et al. (1997), Abusharaf (2002: 17–32), and Aḥmad (2005).

## Bibliography

Abu Shouk, A., Ahmed, I., Hunwick, J.O., and O'Fahey, R.S. (1997) "A Sudanese Missionary to the United States: Sātti Mājid, 'Shaykh al-Islam in North America,' and His Encounter with Noble Drew Ali, Prophet of the Moorish Science Temple Movement," *Sudanic Africa* 8: 137–91.

Abusharaf, R.M. (2002) *Wanderings: Sudanese Migrants and Exiles in North America*, Ithaca, NY: Cornell University Press.

Aḥmad, 'A.H.M. (2005) *Satti Majid: al-da'iyya al-islami al-sudani bi-Amrika, 1904–1929*, Khartoum: Manshurat al-Khartum 'Asimat al-Thaqafa al-'Arabiyya.

Aijian, M.M. (1920) "Mohammedans in the United States," *Moslem World* 10: 30–5.

Ali, D.N. (1928) *Moorish Literature*, n.p., in The Moorish Science Temple of America Collection, New York Public Library's Schomburg Center for Research in Black Culture.

Alryyes, A. (2011) "Introduction: 'Arabic Work,' Islam, and American Literature," in Alryyes, A. (ed. and trans.) *A Muslim American Slave: The Life of Omar ibn Said*, Madison: University of Wisconsin Press, pp. 3–46.

Austin, A. (1984) *African Muslims in Antebellum America: A Sourcebook*, New York: Garland Publishing.

——(1997) *African Muslims in Antebellum America: Transatlantic Stories and Spiritual Struggles*, New York: Routledge.

Beynon, E.D. (1938) "The Voodoo Cult among Negro Migrants in Detroit," *American Journal of Sociology* 43: 894–907.

Bluett, T. (1744) *Some Memoirs of the Life of Job, the Son of Solomon, the High Priest of Boonda in Africa*, London: Printed for Richard Ford.

Cabeza de Vaca, A.N. (1906) *Relación de los Naufragios y Comentarios de Alvar Núñez Cabeza de Vaca*, vol. I. Madrid: Libreía General de Victoriano Suárez.

Dannin, R. (2002) *Black Pilgrimage to Islam*, New York: Oxford University Press.

Das, R.K. (1923) *Hindustani Workers on the Pacific Coast*, Berlin: Walter de Gruyter.

Dirks, J.F. (2006) *Muslims in American History: A Forgotten Legacy*, Beltsville, MD: Amana Publications.

Ferris, M. (1994) "To 'Achieve the Pleasure of Allah': Immigrant Muslim Communities in New York City 1893–1991," in Haddad, Y.Y. and Smith, J.I. (eds.) *Muslim Communities in North America*, Albany, NY: SUNY Press.

Georgia Writers' Project – Savannah Unit (1972 [1940]) *Drums and Shadows: Survival Studies among the Georgia Coastal Negroes*, ed. Mary Granger, New York: Anchor Books/Doubleday.

GhaneaBassiri, K. (2010) *A History of Islam in America: From the New World to the New World Order*, New York: Cambridge University Press.

Gomez, M.A. (1994) "Muslims in Early America," *Journal of Southern History* 60: 671–710.

——(2005) *Black Crescent: The Experience and Legacy of African Muslims in the Americas*, Cambridge: Cambridge University Press.

Grabowski, J.J. (2005) "Turks in Cleveland," in *The Encyclopedia of Cleveland History*, ech.case.edu/ech-cgi/article.pl?id=TIC (accessed November 8, 2012).

Harsham, P. (1975) "One Arab's Immigration," *Saudi Aramco World* 26: 14–15.

Hutchison, W.R. (2004) *Religious Pluralism in America: The Contentious History of a Founding Ideal*, New Haven, CT: Yale University Press.

Khan, I. (1914) *Sufi Message of Spiritual Liberty*, London: The Theosophical Publishing Society.

Khan, I. et al. (1979) *Biography of Pir-O-Murshid Inayat Khan*, Madras: East–West Publications.

Leonard, K.I. (1992) *Making Ethnic Choices: California's Punjabi Mexican Americans*, Philadelphia: Temple University Press.

Lovejoy, P.E. (2000) *Transformations in Slavery: A History of Slavery in Africa*, 2nd ed., Cambridge: Cambridge University Press.

McClain, E.L. (1932) *The Washington Ancestry and Records of the McClain, Johnson, and Forty Other Colonial American Families*, vol. 3, Greenfield, OH: Privately Printed.

Mack, M.E. and Blakey, M.L. (2004) "The New York African Burial Ground Report: Past Biases, Current Dilemmas, and Future Research Opportunities," *Historical Archaeology* 38: 10–17.

Naff, A. (1985) *Becoming American: The Early Arab Immigrant Experience*, Carbondale: Southern Illinois University Press.

Rost-Banik, C. (2004) *Woodlawn Cemetery – Muslim Burial Ground*, Cambridge: The Pluralism Project, www.pluralism.org/research/profiles/display.php?profile=73366 (accessed November 8, 2012).

Sadiq, M. (1921) "No Polygamy," *Moslem Sunrise* 1: 9.

Said, O. ibn. (2011 [1831]) "The Life of Omar Ibn Said, Written by Himself," in Alryyes, A. (ed. and trans.) *A Muslim American Slave: The Life of Omar ibn Said*, Madison: University of Wisconsin Press, pp. 48–79.

Seager, R.H. (1993) *The Dawn of Religious Pluralism: Voices from the World's Parliament of Religions, 1893*, La Salle, IL: Open Court Publishing.

Strong, J. (1885) *Our Country: Its Possible Future and Its Present Crisis*, New York: The Baker and Taylor Co.

Turner, R.B. (2003) *Islam in the African-American Experience*, 2nd ed., Bloomington: Indiana University Press.

von Stuckard, K. (2005) *Western Esotericism: A Brief History of Secret Knowledge*, London: Equinox.

Webb, M.A.R. (1892) *Three Lectures of Mohammed Alexander Russell Webb*, Madras: Hasan Ali, Lawrence Asylum Press.

——(1893) *Islam in America: A Brief Statement of Mohammedanism and an Outline of the American Islamic Propaganda*, New York: Oriental Publishing.

# 7

# Black Muslims

*Herbert Berg*

The term "Black Muslim" would seem to encompass all African American Muslims and African Muslims. It is, however, a term that is largely reserved for African Americans in the Nation of Islam (NOI), a movement founded in the early 1930s by the enigmatic Wali Fard Muhammad and led for almost four decades by his Messenger and successor, the Honorable Elijah Muhammad. Where one begins the story of Black Muslims often reflects one's views about the orthodoxy of the NOI. If one begins the tale with Estavan, a Moroccan Muslim slave who arrived in Florida with a Spanish fleet in 1527, or with the approximately 15 percent of Africans who were Muslims brought to North America as slaves, then the NOI is a reappropriation of a lost Islamic heritage. It may be heretical and on the margins, but it stands inside the *umma*. If one begins with the history of Fard Muhammad, or, worse, with Wallace D. Ford, then the NOI is a scam and a brazen usurpation of a Muslim façade with a racist agenda that preyed on African American's ignorance of Islam; its use of the words "Islam" and "Muslim," or even its inclusion in a volume such as this, is anathema. Where one ends the story of Black Muslims also reflects one's view about the NOI. To end the story with Louis Farrakhan is usually to highlight the unreformed differences between the NOI and other older or more traditional forms of Islam. If one instead ends with Malcolm X or Warith Deen Muhammad, the son and successor of Elijah Muhammad, then one likely sees the NOI as a necessary, but temporary, stepping-stone towards Sunni orthodoxy.

Since another chapter in this volume discusses African Muslim slaves (Chapter 6), this one will begin with the immediate precursor to the NOI, the Moorish Science Temple (MST) founded by Noble Drew Ali, and end with both Warith Deen Muhammed and Louis Farrakhan. The latter two represent the inherent but conflicting forces in the NOI as initiated by Fard Muhammad and promulgated by Elijah Muhammad. These conflicting forces are also evident in the at times acrimonious interactions of Elijah Muhammad with other Muslims. As Black Muslims and foreign Muslims became increasingly aware of each other, initial acceptance turned to suspicion and then to hostility. Rapprochement became possible only when Black Muslims opted to become Muslims who were black.

## What's in a name? The first Black Muslims in America

African Muslim slaves were not merely Muslims living as a minority in a non-Muslim community. They lived in a society that actively sought to erase their cultures, languages, and names. Their original diverse cultural identities were reduced to "Negro slave." With a few notable exceptions, it was not long before their religion, Islam, was eliminated. Some vestiges may have remained, such as an association of Islam with Africa, but the scripture, the prayers, and the rituals were forgotten. When the first Ahmadi missionary came to the United States, what few African Americans he converted had been Christians.

The dominance of Christianity among African Americans in the early twentieth century also helps explain the peculiar formulation of Islam created by Noble Drew Ali. Timothy Drew was a descendent of slaves and born in 1886 in North Carolina. Later legends claim that he passed a test in the Temple of Cheops in Egypt and so became Sharif Abdul Ali, or Noble Drew Ali. In response to a dream instructing him to found a religion "for the uplifting of fallen mankind," especially the "lost-found nation of American blacks," he founded the Canaanite Temple in Newark, New Jersey in 1913. After a dispute within the movement, Drew Ali moved to Chicago and restarted the movement, with several name changes, settling on the Moorish Science Temple of America, Inc. in 1928. A year earlier he had published his *The Holy Koran of the Moorish Science Temple of America*, commonly known as the *Circle Seven Koran*.

Drew Ali saw African Americans as the descendants of Canaanites, Moabites, and the later Moors. Although originally "Asiatics," they populated Africa and, as Moors, were said to have ruled Asia and Europe. Asiatics were said to include all of the original inhabitants of the Americas and India. In other words, it encompassed all but white Europeans and their descendants. For Drew Ali, the original, natural, and only suitable religion for Asiatics was Islam, whereas Christianity was the religion best suited for whites. It is precisely because they had not "honored their mother and father," that is, by forgetting their true religion, that African Americans suffered slavery. A return to Islam would bring freedom, equality, justice, and love.

Drew Ali called his religion Islam, his followers "Moslems," and his scripture the Koran. But this is where close parallels with other forms of Islam end. The Circle Seven Koran draws most of its material directly from Levi H. Dowling's *The Aquarian Gospel of Jesus the Christ* (1908) and Sri Ramatherio's 1925 edition of *Unto Thee I Grant*. Apart from selecting the chapters from this book, replacing "God" with "Allah," and editing out the former's references to a blond, blue-eyed Jesus, Drew Ali added only four chapters of those materials. Thus half the book is about Jesus, whereas Muhammad is mentioned only twice, once as the "founder of the uniting of Islam" and once as he who "fulfilled the works of Jesus of Nazareth" (Ali 1927: 57).

Drew Ali's purpose was not to reintroduce Islam – at least not in any recognizable form – but to capitalize on Islam's reputation as a non-European religion with a rich history. He benefited from Islam's association with "the East" and Africa and its apparent longstanding hostility to white Christianity. The name and its symbolism mattered. In that sense, the terms "Koran" and "Moslems" mattered in the same way that the fezzes, turbans, sashes, and names such as Bey and El mattered. Drew Ali was forging a new identity, separate from that of white Christianity, based on an idealized and imagined past.

Drew Ali may have had as many as 10,000 followers, but with this success also came turmoil. When a rival was murdered in 1929, Drew Ali was arrested, released on bond, but died very shortly thereafter under suspicious circumstances. His movement survives in various forms to the present, but it was soon eclipsed by a new movement born in the cities of the North, to which millions of rural Southern blacks had so recently migrated. His significance lies in having reintroduced the terminology of Islam, such as Moslem and Koran, to African Americans and in formulating a racialist Islam.

## The Islam of Black Muslims

The Nation of Islam was a movement begun in 1930s Detroit by the mysterious Wali Fard Muhammad. He disappeared in 1934, and his movement of 5,000–8,000 followers fractured. One of his prominent ministers, Elijah Muhammad, fled Detroit and then Chicago not long after the disappearance because of rivals. But he continued to proselytize and founded Temple No. 4 in Washington, DC. There his movement came under Federal Bureau of Investigation (FBI) scrutiny and he was arrested and convicted of draft dodging in 1942, even though he was then 44 years old. By the time of his release in 1946, his rivals had disappeared and he then led the NOI until his death in 1975.

In many ways the movement was recognizably more Islamic than the MST. The members called themselves Muslims, worshipped Allah, and used the Qur'an – not their own Koran as Drew Ali had. The Prophet Muhammad was revered, the Judgment Day was central, and prayer and fasting were practiced. The consumption of alcohol and pork was also prohibited. But each of these beliefs and practices also highlights differences with other Muslims. They also demonstrate that every aspect of the Black Islam was understood in light of a mythology that seems to go back to Fard Muhammad himself and highlights the experience and interaction of blacks and whites in Western society.

According to this mythology, humanity's origins do not lie with Adam and Eve. Rather, they represent only the most recent and evil development in human history. Fard Muhammad (as narrated by Elijah Muhammad) taught that the earth was some 66 trillion years old, and its current form resulted from Allah seeking to destroy humanity after failing to unite it. The tribe of Shabazz, however, survived the destructive blast that separated the moon from the earth, and settled in Mecca and the Nile valley. Thus all ancient civilization is black and Muslim. The white race, however, was only created 6,600 years ago by the evil Mr. Yakub after he became embittered towards his own people. He began a selective breeding program on the island of Patmos using his black followers and thus created an increasingly lighter people. The net result was a blond, blue-eyed, naked, evil white race. Thus original humanity was black, with white people having lost the original color. That is to say, they are the "colored" people. They are the sinful Adam and Eve created in "our image" (that is, the image of black humanity) and out of "black mud" (Genesis 1:26 and Qur'an 15:28). Six thousand years ago, these newly created people returned to their ancestors' Mecca, but they were soon exiled to Europe by blacks, and there they remained living in caves despite the attempts by Moses to reform them. Jesus, too, failed. Muhammad's success delayed their evil for almost a millennium. But then this race burst out of Europe, conquered the Americas, stole the land, and enslaved Africans. Whites robbed blacks of their religion and their names, forcing them to worship a god who looked like the same white devils who had enslaved them.

But Allah had not forgotten this Lost Nation of Islam in the Wilderness of North America. He came to Detroit to find them and return them to their original religion: Islam. Spiritual, mental, physical, social, and economic freedom from the white devil was only possible by returning to that religion. Christianity, they were taught, was "one of the most perfect black-slave-making religions on our planet" (Muhammad 1992: 70). It makes blacks worship a false, white god and turn the other cheek in the face of oppression, waiting for the next life for justice. Islam, by contrast, offers freedom, justice, and equality now, under the leadership of the true god, Allah, in the person of Wali Fard Muhammad. Soon, Allah will destroy the evil white race. Only the independent and separated Black Muslims will escape this destruction of the United States and Europe. For that reason, it was "far more important to teach the separation of Blacks and Whites in America than prayer" (Muhammad 1992: 204).

Allah is, therefore, understood quite differently than in most other forms of Islam. Muhammad should not be confused with the notion of incarnation in the Christian or Druze senses. Nor is Allah anything other than human:

> They are spooky minded and believe that Allah (God) is some immaterial something ... The ignorant belief of the Orthodox Muslims, that Allah (God) is Some Formless Something and yet He Has An Interest in our affairs, can be condemned in no limit of time. I would not give two cents for that kind of God, in which they believe.
>
> *(Muhammad 1969: 20–1)*

In addition, there had been earlier Allahs, such as the one who split the moon from the earth, but with Fard Muhammad there is monotheism. He is the Allah of the age. Although powerful enough to destroy the earth and knowing humanity's secrets, his purpose was to suffer persecution for three and half years in order to bring Islam to his lost nation. After resurrecting this nation, he continued to guide it via his successor, Elijah Muhammad.

Elijah Muhammad employed the titles Apostle of Allah and Messenger of Allah for himself – after all, he had received personal instruction from Allah himself. Muhammad's role is largely restricted to having constrained the expansion of the white race's evil for almost a millennium. Elijah Muhammad tended to read Qur'anic passages usually thought to be about Muhammad to be prophecies about himself. For example, the prayer of Abraham is about Elijah Muhammad, as is the prophet sent to a people to whom no warner has been sent (Qur'an 32:3 and 2:127–9). Similarly, every reference to Satan in the Qur'an and the Bible was read by Elijah Muhammad as reference to the white race, who had been "grafted" by Mr. Yakub. Elijah Muhammad not only used the Qur'an as scripture, but in so doing made it scripture among his followers who had never read it or perhaps even heard of it before:

> The book that the so-called American Negroes (The Tribe of Shabazz) should own and read, the book that the slave masters have but have not represented it to their slaves, is a book that will heal their sin-sick souls that were made sick and sorrowful by the slave masters. This book will open their blinded eyes and open their deaf ears. It will purify them. The name of this book, which makes a distinction between the God of righteous and the God of evil, is: Glorious Holy Quran Sharrieff. It is indeed the Book of Guidance, of Light and Truth, and of Wisdom and Judgment. But the average one should first be taught how to respect such a book, how to understand it, and how to teach it. ... This book, the Holy Quran Sharrieff, is not from a prophet but direct from Allah to Muhammad (may peace and the blessings of Allah be upon him!) not by an angel but from the mouth of Allah (God) ... to get a real Holy Qur'an one should know the Arabic language in which it is written.
>
> *(Muhammad 1957: 50–1)*

But the "how to understand it" was not through the traditional *'ulum al-Qur'an* or the classical collections of *tafsirs*, both of which he was unaware, but in light of his overarching racial mythology. The Bible, on the other hand, was a poisonous book that should be read with caution. "The Bible means good if you can rightly understand it. My interpretation of it is given to me from the Lord of the Worlds" (Muhammad 1992: 88). The truth in the Bible resided in the symbolic history of the races within it, and in the prophecies for the imminent end times. Of particular significance were the Creation stories in Genesis, which for Elijah Muhammad related the birth of the white race, the Gospels, which prophesied Fard

Muhammad, and the Book of Revelation, said to have been written by Mr. Yakub himself and which prophesies the destruction of his white race. These prophecies had remained hidden, like those in the Qur'an, and could only be unlocked by Elijah Muhammad because of Fard Muhammad's guidance. This approach allowed him to employ the scripture with which the majority of his followers were most familiar, the Bible, and the scripture other Muslims would assume they understood better, the Qur'an, in ways that made them entirely dependent on him for their interpretation.

For Elijah Muhammad, the other most important prophecies contained in the Bible and the Qur'an are those of the end times. They, too, form part of the racial mythology and have been completely misinterpreted by both Christians and Muslims. The Last Day does not consist of the end of the world, a bodily resurrection, and one's appearance before Allah to be judged and then assigned to the Garden or the Fire. Humanity is already in the end times, Heaven and Hell describe the contemporary racial situation, and the resurrection describes a mental transformation. The purpose of Fard Muhammad's coming was to resurrect the "mentally dead so-called Negroes," permitting them to free themselves from the devil's rule and influence – that is, Hell – and achieve freedom, justice, and equality – that is, Heaven. The de-spiritualization of the afterlife (which is not in fact an "after" life) parallels that of Allah by Elijah Muhammad.

The racial mythology was also fully integrated into the practices of the NOI. These practices remained recognizably Islamic, and prominently included the traditional pillars of Islam: the *shahada*, *salat*, *zakat*, *sawm*, and, to a lesser extent, *hajj*. But each was again understood in light of his racial mythology. For example, the *shahada* appears in Arabic in Elijah Muhammad's booklet *the Supreme Wisdom*, but is contextualized thus:

> The Muslim begins his prayer by declaring that ALLAH IS THE GREATEST and that he bears witness that there is "No God but ALLAH," and that none deserves to be served (worshipped) but Him. He further declares that Muhammad is his Last Apostle (an Apostle whom Allah would raise from the lost and found people of the seed of Abraham in the Days of Judgment).
>
> *(Muhammad 1957: 45–6)*

That is to say, Allah is Fard Muhammad and Elijah Muhammad is the Apostle. Prayers were in English, not Arabic, and showers were recommended, not the standard ablutions. Communal services were not on Friday at noon, but Sunday afternoon, and modeled on Christian services. Similarly, followers gave money, but this was modeled on Christian tithing more than *zakat*. Elijah Muhammad advocated fasting, not during the month of Ramadan in commemoration of the initial revelation of the Qur'an to Muhammad, but in December to focus his followers' on Fard Muhammad instead of on Christmas. In the 1970s, however, he began to encourage his followers to fast during Ramadan. Members of the NOI were also encouraged to fast at least three days each month. Their fasts were twenty-four hours long, starting at five o'clock in the morning. Elijah Muhammad performed the '*umra*, but never the *hajj*. Nor did he strongly encourage his followers to do so. In his own writings, Elijah Muhammad did not speak of Mecca as the site of the Ka'ba or as the location of the *hajj*. He described it as "the only holy spot on our planet – the Holy City of Mecca" (Muhammad 1957: 45). Its significance was not as the birthplace of Muhammad, but as that of Allah, Fard Muhammad, and as the ancient capital of the Tribe of Shabazz. All of these differences from other older forms of Islam caused grave concerns, even outrage, among other Muslims (see pp. 132–3).

Equally problematic were political, economic, and social concerns of Black Muslims that non-NOI Muslims would not normally associate with Islam. Edward Curtis IV has argued politics and religion were wedded in the NOI (Curtis 2006: 2); and, as I have argued elsewhere, viewing Islam as a religion fundamentally devoid of these concerns does not reflect the history of Muslims, essentializes Islam in distorting ways, and makes the scholar an advocate of a normative Islam (Berg 2009). It also reflects a Protestant understanding of religion that focuses on the interior experience. Nor are such "exterior" concerns foreign to other, older formulations of Islam. Elijah Muhammad demanded separation of the races, not merely segregation, and went so far as to demand several states in the continental USA for blacks. They needed their own nation, not only as reparations for slavery, but because he believed that "We are the original owners of the earth and will take it and rule it again. This is the time" (Muhammad 1992: 233). Barring that, the segregation offered by white Southerners was preferable to the integration demanded by the Civil Rights Movement. He encouraged and exemplified black businesses that were independent of whites. African Americans were to pool their resources to establish their own stores, farms, banks, etc. "Observe the operations of the white man. He is successful. He makes no excuse for his failures. He works hard in a collective manner. You do the same" (Muhammad 1992: 174). And he encouraged the men of the NOI to protect their women: ensuring they dressed modestly, avoided going to bars, and, most importantly, did not intermarry with whites.

Elijah Muhammad's economic, political, and social agendas were in many ways radical when compared to the Civil Rights Movement. They were clearly at odds with other formulations of Islam. His Islam teaches justice, freedom, and equality, and so these economic, political, and social reforms are just as much part of Islam as prayer. It was an Islam that would free African Americans from the religious, social, economic, and political corruption of whites and prepare them for the coming Fall of America. But in many ways the agendas were also conservative: economically capitalist, politically separatist, and socially patriarchal. The experience and interaction with Western society, with Western society understood to be white society, was to be avoided. But in the end, it was modeled almost exclusively on that society, not other Muslim societies.

## The lost-found Nation of Islam in the Wilderness of North America

Elijah Muhammad credited all of these teachings to Fard Muhammad. How one speaks of this founder of the NOI often reflects one's attitude towards its Islamic legitimacy. If the story begins with the convicted felon Wallace Dodd Ford, the man outsiders, including the FBI, claim was the founder, Fard Muhammad, the implication is that the whole movement was founded by a conman who veiled his racist tenets with an Islamic façade. To begin the story with Fard Muhammad's appearance in Detroit in 1930 buys into the NOI's own mythology. A further complication to this story is the sources. In the 1940s the FBI began to take serious notice of this movement, and particularly one of his followers, Elijah Muhammad, who claimed to be Fard Muhammad's rightful successor. By this time, Elijah Muhammad had already begun to teach that Fard Muhammad was Allah in person. Fard Muhammad seems to have not made that claim. Some of the splits in the movement after Fard Muhammad's disappearance in 1934 stem from a rejection of this elevation to godhood. Thus, with the exception of one sociological article about the NOI (Beynon 1937–8: 894–907), most of the information about this early period largely comes from hostile FBI sources or hagiographic NOI sources.

Wali Fard Muhammad, also known as Master F.D. Muhammad, began preaching in the streets of Detroit in 1929 or 1930. He claimed to have been born in Mecca to the tribe of the Quraysh in 1877. As Elijah Muhammad would later tell the story, Fard Muhammad's father had prepared his son to come to America to find the members of the lost tribe of Shabazz who had been stolen and enslaved by the evil white race centuries earlier and to return them to their original religion of Islam. He began his ministry as a silk peddler and used this as an opportunity to preach to his customers. Soon he needed to rent buildings for his meetings. So popular were they that 700–800 people would turn up in halls that could hold only half that number.

In his three-and-half-year ministry, Fard Muhammad converted thousands of people to his Allah Temple of Islam, later renamed the NOI, including Elijah Poole. The latter had been born in Georgia in 1897. He was the child of poor sharecroppers, and his father was a lay Baptist minister. Extreme poverty and Southern racism drew him north in 1923 in search of a better life for his family. As many African Americans of the Great Migration discovered, racism was not absent in the North. And when the Great Depression struck, they were the first to lose their jobs. Elijah Poole's own despair drove him to alcohol, and some reports suggest that Fard Muhammad's movement saved him from alcoholism. After joining, he soon became one of its ministers. Fard Muhammad personally trained him, gave him new names, first Elijah Karriem and later Elijah Muhammad. As Temple No. 1 in Detroit grew, they together established Temple No. 2 in Chicago.

In May of 1933, the Detroit police arrested Fard Muhammad in connection with a murder by one of his followers. The police report listed his ancestry as "Arabian," his race as "Caucasian," and his profession as "minister." A later FBI report states that the official police report included that "[Wallace] Dodd [Ford] admitted that his teachings were 'strictly a racket' and he was 'getting all the money out of it he could'" (FBI file 100–43165). He was not charged with a crime, but was ordered to leave Detroit, and so he departed for Chicago. There he was arrested again and visited by Elijah Muhammad. In 1934 he disappeared. In the 1963 article that accused Fard Muhammad of being Wallace Ford, Ford's estranged wife, Hazel, claimed that he had returned to Los Angeles in 1934. Ford stayed for two weeks, visited his son, and then left by ship for New Zealand to visit relatives. Elijah Muhammad, on the other hand, stated that he received his last letter from Fard Muhammad in March 1934 from Mexico.

The FBI reported that the fingerprints of Fard Muhammad taken by the Detroit police were the same of those of Wallace D. Ford, a criminal arrested in 1918, 1926, and 1927 in Los Angeles, and who had been imprisoned after the latter arrest in San Quentin for bootlegging and possession of narcotics. The later investigations have suggested a Polynesian, Jamaican, Arab, Indian, or Turkish origin, though he claimed to have been born in 1891 to Hawaiian parents then living in Portland, Oregon. The FBI favored reports claiming a birth in New Zealand to a British father and Polynesian mother. Scholars suggest that after his release from prison in 1929 he made his way to Chicago, where he might have had contact with Ahmadi Muslims, Marcus Garvey's United Negro Improvement Association, and/or Drew Ali's MST. From there he made his way to Detroit.

Was Wali Fard Muhammad really Wallace Dodd Ford? Yes, unless another plausible candidate is found and evidence of an FBI conspiracy is produced. A more important question is the origin of his knowledge of Islam. Given the limited time he could have spent within the MST and the nature of its teachings, it could hardly be the sole source. Another equally interesting question is why Islam was so adaptable to the racial situation of some African Americans. Sherman Jackson suggests that Islam was particularly suitable for black religious protest against white supremacy and anti-black racism. Islam was, of course, associated with Africa. It also had a reputation for opposition to these Europeans, a claim to an independent non–white civilization, a simple theology (at least compared with trinitarianism), a conservative social ethic, a retributive justice from the Qur'an, a lack of an ecclesiastical hierarchy (in Sunni Islam), and, perhaps most importantly, white Americans hated and feared Islam (Jackson 2005: 44). In the cultural rhetoric of white America, Islam had since the seventeenth century been idealized as the antithesis of an America imagined to be democratic, Christian, and virtuous (Marr 2006). Equally important was the general ignorance of Islam among African Americans. This allowed first Drew Ali to extract authoritative terminology from Islam, and later Fard Muhammad and Elijah Muhammad to reformulate the common elements in Islam so as to blend with their racial mythology.

The powerful pull of this formulation of Islam can be seen in the story of Elijah Poole, who experienced the worst of white racism in the South and even witnessed lynchings. His early experiences in the North did not dispose him to think any differently of whites. There he had witnessed white policemen shooting a black man in the street with no consequences. His experiences made him particularly susceptible to the powerful message of Fard Muhammad. Once introduced to the movement, he soon became an ardent follower of Fard Muhammad, even believing him to be the one named Jesus whom the Bible said would return at the end times (Sahib 1951: 91). Soon Elijah Poole was given permission to preach and received personal instruction from Fard Muhammad. Fard Muhammad used the title Master, but the renamed Elijah Muhammad was the first to refer to him as a prophet and later as Allah. After Fard Muhammad's mysterious disappearance, the latter became a point of contention. One rival sought to displace Fard Muhammad and therefore belittled him, but Elijah Muhammad emphasized the godhood of Fard Muhammad. In any case, he was forced to leave Detroit after being arrested for keeping children out of the public school system in favor of the NOI's University of Islam. He left for Chicago, but the minister he left in charge of Detroit formed his own group and in Chicago his own brother helped lead Temple No. 2 against him. He fled and began traveling to the cities on the northeast coast, settling in Washington, where, in addition to establishing another temple, he is said to have gone to the Library of Congress to read a list of 104 books Fard Muhammad is said to have given him. It was his preaching against black participation in a "white war" which brought him to the attention of the FBI in 1941.

After his arrest, conviction, and imprisonment for draft dodging in 1942, Elijah Muhammad emerged in 1946 with his rivals gone and his remaining few followers deeply committed to him. In prison, he experienced firsthand how no political, social, or religious organizations were seeking to help or reform African American prisoners. He decided to give this group his attention. Many of them had suffered the most under white racism and were the most in need of his transformative message, as evidenced by the conversion a few years later of Malcolm X. From Malcolm X's release in 1952 to his departure from the NOI 1963, by which time he had risen to the rank of National Minister, the NOI went from having approximately 10 temples to having over 50. He also established the NOI's own newspaper, *Muhammad Speaks*. His rapid rise within the organization and his media prominence fostered jealousy among the older leadership of the NOI, including Elijah Muhammad. This jealousy led to the rupture between the two men as much as Malcolm X's awareness of Elijah Muhammad's infidelities and his act of disobedience by commenting on President Kennedy's assassination. Malcolm X soon moved to a more Sunni understanding of Islam, as had two of Elijah Muhammad's sons, Wallace and Akbar (see pp. 131–2). Elijah Muhammad weathered all this turmoil of the mid-1960s well. His movement survived, particularly with the help of his new protégé, Louis X (later Louis Farrakhan). However, Elijah Muhammad had had health problems since the early 1960s, initially just bronchial asthma and later also diabetes, leading to power struggles within the NOI by the early 1970s.

The NOI was a wealthy and powerful organization. It had seventy-six temples throughout the cities of the United States and many of them ran Universities of Islam. Membership rolls were kept secret, but there were as many as 100,000 members. Supermarkets, bakeries, restaurants, a fish-importing business, and 15,000 acres of farmland added up to an empire worth $45 million. On January 29, 1975, Elijah Muhammad was checked into the hospital. While there, he suffered congestive heart failure and died on February 25, 1975. The next day, at the annual Saviour Day's rally, it was his son Wallace D. Muhammad who prevailed and was proclaimed the new Supreme Minister. Almost immediately he began the process of transforming his father's NOI into a far more Sunni-like Muslim movement.

## The Nation of Islam and other Muslims

Even if non-NOI Muslims did not consider Elijah Muhammad and his followers to be Muslim, there is no doubt that NOI Muslims did. The relationship and interaction between the NOI and other Muslims is quite complex, and Elijah Muhammad's reaction to them depends very much on the origin of these other Muslims. If they were former members of the NOI, Elijah Muhammad saw them as hypocrites. Other American Muslims, whether immigrants or African American converts, were seen as rivals to be insulted. The most interesting relationship was with foreign Muslim critics, for that relationship evolved significantly between 1959 and 1975. For over forty years he steadfastly believed that Allah himself had appointed him to be his Messenger. The only other authority he seemed to recognize, the Bible and the Qur'an, simply confirmed for him everything he had been taught by Allah about Islam, including the racial mythology. However, it is precisely his primary claim of authority – the commission from Allah as Fard Muhammad – that all of these non-NOI Muslims found so objectionable.

Muslims within the NOI were expected to give absolute obedience to Elijah Muhammad as the Messenger of Allah and to his appointed representatives. Those who challenged his authority on doctrinal issues were expelled and, if they did not recant, labeled as "hypocrites." His use of this term highlights two interesting aspects of the NOI: the growing influence of Qur'anic terminology and Elijah Muhammad's tendency to identify the passages in the Qur'an as being uniquely applicable to contemporary situations. When he first used the word in print, he used it to describe white Christians' treatment of their black co-religionists. But with the turmoil of the mid-1960s, he began to employ it for those who broke with his authority. He retroactively applied it to his brother, who had challenged him after the disappearance of Fard Muhammad. It was then applied most forcefully against Malcolm X, who was described as the "chief hypocrite" and "the number one hypocrite of all time." Elijah Muhammad cited passages from the Qur'an repeatedly for years afterward about the dangers of hypocrites and the need for absolute obedience. Even errant sons did not escape this charge. Wallace Muhammad had had doubts about his father's teachings for many years, especially when he began reading the Qur'an for himself. He gradually moved towards a more Sunni understanding of Islam – what he described as the "Islam of the Qur'an." Since it was he who had confirmed to Malcolm X that the rumors about his father's infidelities were true and since he had objected to the corruption of some NOI officials, it is not clear whether his excommunication was due simply to his heretical beliefs. Akbar Muhammad, another son, was a hypocrite for purely doctrinal reasons, however. He had been sent to study at al-Azhar in Cairo and thus had the most firsthand experience of Sunni Islam within the NOI. When he returned in 1964, it provoked this condemnation in *Muhammad Speaks*:

> On Sunday, November 26, 1964, at Muhammad's Temple No. 7 in New York City, a speech was made by Akbar Muhammad containing statements and views which were not in keeping with the teachings and principles of the Honorable Elijah Muhammad, the Messenger of Allah. It has therefore been decreed by the Messenger that Akbar Muhammad is no longer to be regarded as a follower of his father in what Allah has revealed to his

father in the person of Master W. F. Muhammad. Akbar is now classified as a hypocrite by his father and by all those who follow him.

*("Decree Akbar Muhammad" 1965: 9)*

Hypocrites had but one option: to submit themselves humbly to Elijah Muhammad's authority or be expelled. Malcolm X and Akbar Muhammad left the NOI; Wallace Muhammad recanted, but it was he who was able to transform the NOI (see pp. 134–5). Passages in the Qur'an were often interpreted as prophecies about the rebellions that Elijah Muhammad faced. Even sympathizing with hypocrites was a form of rebellion. He warned: "God is very hard on those who disobey His Messenger. He warns in his Holy Qur'an not to quarrel and dispute or raise our voices above the Messenger's voice. Strict respect and honor is demanded for His Messengers" (Muhammad 1992: 260).

Elijah Muhammad could not expel those not part of the NOI, such as leaders of rival Muslim movements, whether African American or immigrant. Elijah Muhammad almost never addressed their critiques, opting to respond only with *ad hominem*. Talib Ahmad Dawud, for example, was the African American leader of an organization called the Muslim Brotherhood USA. In the late 1950s he condemned the assertion that Allah appeared in the person of Fard Muhammad, the depiction of race as central to the teachings of Islam, the denial of a bodily resurrection, and the use of improper prayers. Dawud also employed *ad hominem*, claiming that Fard Muhammad was a Turkish white man who was once a Nazi agent, and that Elijah Muhammad was not a Muslim, but an ex-convict and teacher of racial hatred. Elijah Muhammad retorted:

> Talib Ahmad Dawud and his TV blues-singing Miss Dakota Staton (who the paper says is Mrs. Alijah Rabia Dawud in private life) and whom the world can hear her filthy blues and love songs and see her immodestly dressed, were successful last week in getting a chance to breathe their venomous poison against me and my followers in this paper and in the local Chicago paper, *The Crusader*. Mr. Dawud is from the West Indies (Antigua) and was born a British subject. He was known by the name Rannie (sounds like a devil's name). He is jealous of the progress with which Allah (to whom praises are due) is blessing me and my followers, and this jealousy is about to run Mr. Dawud insane. (*The Crusader* erroneously called him an Imam.) Mr. Dawud and Miss Staton should have been ashamed to try to make fun of me and my followers while publicly serving the devil in the theatrical world. I do not allow my followers to visit such, nor do I allow my wife and the believing women who follow me to go before the public partly dressed. If they would, never would I claim them to be mine any more.
>
> *(Muhammad 1959: 14)*

Elijah Muhammad responded in the same manner to Jamil Daib, a Palestinian Arab who was once the principal of Elijah Muhammad's University of Islam in Chicago and who criticized the use of different books, prayers, and fasts. These attacks continued from various groups periodically throughout the 1960s and early 1970s, and Elijah Muhammad's responses were consistent. When an Ahmadi Muslim criticized him, *Muhammad Speaks* claimed that the Ahmadi movement originated in British India and was financed by Christians to help pacify Muslims who were revolting against British rule. The charge that the movement had tailored a translation of the Qur'an "to meet the needs and objectives of the foreign occupier" (Baghdadi 1972: 2) is ironic given his own use of an Ahmadi translation of the Qur'an. In any case, he may have relied so heavily on personal attacks because these Muslim critics had centuries of traditional Islamic doctrine on their side. In many cases they knew the Qur'an better than he. His usual trump card, his unique access to Allah, held no value with these opponents.

Initially, foreign Muslims, whom Elijah Muhammad himself referred to as "Orthodox Muslims" or "Eastern Muslims," were more problematic. He saw the NOI a part of the larger Muslim world. This larger Muslim world was united, at peace, rich, and black (in the sense of all colors except white). Members of the NOI would be "welcomed with sincere and open arms and recognized by his light-skinned or copper-colored Arab brother" (Muhammad 1957: 37). Elijah Muhammad's personal experience during his 'umra likely disabused him of his rather naive assumptions of unity and wealth of other Muslims. But the obvious religious differences were dismissed as merely due to different circumstances:

> My brothers in the East were never subjected to conditions of slavery and systematic brainwashing by the slavemasters for as long a period of time as my people here were subjected. I cannot, therefore, blame them if they differ with me in certain interpretations of the Message of Islam. In fact, I do not even *expect* them to understand some of the things I say unto my people here.
>
> *(Muhammad 1957: 4)*

If his travels made him disillusioned with these copper-colored brothers, it also reinforced the beliefs for which these other Muslims viewed him with suspicion (Clegg 1997: 144). For his part, Elijah Muhammad at first continued to minimize the differences, believing that the Eastern Muslims would come around to his point of view. Moreover, since he so clearly saw that the Qur'an confirmed his beliefs, he was certain that the learned Muslims were well aware that he was correct. Their greater facility with Arabic and the centuries of scholarship on the Qur'an were irrelevant: "I am sent from Allah and not from the Secretary General of the Muslim League. There is no Muslim in Arabia that has authority to stop me from delivering this message that I have been assigned to by Allah. ... I am not taking orders from them, I am taking orders from Allah (God) himself" (Muhammad 1963: 3–4).

By the mid-1960s Elijah Muhammad had become far more cognizant of the danger that "Orthodox Islam" posed because of his sons Akbar and Wallace, and because of his former protégé Malcolm X. Orthodox Muslims were not, in fact, coming around to his point of view. Rather, they were becoming increasingly hostile as they became more familiar with the NOI. He began to accuse them of not understanding the Qur'an (Muhammad 1992: 187) and being "spooky minded" in their conception of Allah. By the 1970s, he became more hostile and began criticizing "old world" Muslims for following an "old Islam led by Whites" and claiming that they were no better than white Christians. And from there, it was an easy step to calling them "white": "We have a New Islam coming up. The Old Islam was led by white people, white Muslims, but this one will not be. This Islam will be established and led by Black Muslims only" ("Allah's Last Messenger ... " 1972: 3–4). Their Islam differed little from Christianity: "The Christians and most old world Muslims are alike: not having a true knowledge of the Supreme One, referred to as Allah, and God makes most people believe that God is something other than a man" (Muhammad 1974: 61). "Copper-colored" Orthodox Muslims of the East had become *white* Muslims, with all the evil that comes with that pejorative adjective. When Elijah Muhammad was forced to choose between his Islam and Muslim unity, he chose the former.

## The race myth vs. the *umma*

Elijah Muhammad's tense relationship with other Muslims seems to suggest that he and his Black Muslims were gradually moving away from them. But the examples of Wallace

Muhammad, Akbar Muhammad, Malcolm X, and many others demonstrate that there was always a tension within the NOI: one force that pulled people to the powerful racial message within Islam as formulated by Fard Muhammad and Elijah Muhammad, and one that pushed people towards conceptions of Islam that were much closer to that of Muslims outside the NOI. While Elijah Muhammad lived, those competing forces were kept in check, unless one left the NOI.

Wallace Muhammad remained within his father's movement, even though he had been repeatedly expelled for his heretical beliefs. On Saviour's Day, February 26, 1975, just one day after his father's death, Wallace Muhammad became the new Supreme Minister of the NOI. More than a decade earlier, he had told Malcolm X that "the only possible solution for the Nation of Islam would be its accepting and projecting a better understanding of Orthodox Islam" (X with Haley 1973 [1964]: 339) or what he often called the Islam of the Qur'an. As the new leader, he rapidly pushed for Black Muslims to become just Muslims. The nationality of his followers was changed from the tribe of Shabazz to Bilalians, since Bilal was an African slave in Mecca who converted to Islam in the time of Muhammad. Of course, this identification with a Companion of Muhammad was also unusual, and was later dropped. The NOI became the Community of al-Islam in the West, then the American Muslim Mission, and later the Mosque Cares, whose leadership consisted of a council or *shura*. He preferred the title "Imam" and even changed his own name to Warith Deen Mohammed. His father was spoken of as "Master," not Apostle or Messenger, and whites were no longer devils – though many had a devilish, racist mindset. Fard Muhammad was not Allah, but merely a "wise man." Warith Deen Mohammed, rather implausibly, suggested that Fard Muhammad had secretly planned to bring African Americans to Orthodox Islam. But when he found them in 1930, they were unfamiliar with the Qur'an and did not recognize its authority. The NOI was his "strategy, a temporary strategy, a temporary language environment, to hold uneducated Blacks … long enough to come into an independent mind … and then later study the Qur'an" (Mohammed 2002). Once their minds were freed from the bondage created by slavery and racism, they would come to see that the racial mythology he had created contained the seeds of its own destruction. And then, they would be ready for the Islam of the Qur'an. Warith Deen Muhammad even believed that his father died a Sunni Muslim, having privately rejected his own teaching that Fard Muhammad was Allah.

The other force within the NOI was conservative, believing that the essence of Islamic teachings and practices was those about race. It pushed members to cling to the unique racial teachings that were part of Fard Muhammad's and Elijah Muhammad's formulation of Islam. Without them, all Black Muslims would end up doing is trading a white Christian model for an Arab Muslim one. In other words, it is the "Black" in Black Islam that is essential. Louis Farrakhan, originally Louis Eugene Wolcott and then Louis X, led this conservative movement. Although he was Elijah Muhammad's right hand man, filling the vacuum left by Malcolm X, he lost the power struggle to succeed Elijah Muhammad. He only pledged to support his rival Warith Deen Mohammed reluctantly and in a restricted manner. In 1977, dismayed by the massive reforms, he re-established the NOI with its original teachings. Louis Farrakhan was a far more charismatic speaker than Warith Deen Mohammed, far more controversial, and far more ambitious, and so he has received far more media attention. His NOI's dispute with the Jewish community over Jewish involvement in the slave trade and his Million Man March in 1996 made him a household name in the United States. But this does not indicate that he was more influential than Warith Deen Mohammed among African Americans. In the last decade and a half, even Louis Farrakhan has made tentative steps to bring his NOI closer to Sunni Islam.

In stark contrast to Louis Farrakhan and his NOI, by the time of Warith Deen Mohammed's death in 2008, he and the Muslims in his organization were accepted by Muslims worldwide. They became part of the Islamic Society of North America (ISNA), on whose Majlis ashShura he served. He was also appointed to the World Supreme Council of Mosques, a body within the Muslim World League. The ISNA obituary stated:

> Warith's father, Hon. Elijah Muhammad, was the leader of the Nation of Islam from 1934 to 1975, an organization that preaches a form of Black nationalism. Elijah Muhammad died on February 26, 1975. After his father's death in 1975, Warith Deen Mohammed was accepted by followers of the Nation of Islam as their leader. With his new understanding, based on his lifelong study of the Qur'an and the life of Prophet Muhammad, he brought about many reforms, which brought the followers of the Nation of Islam closer to mainstream Islam and away from Black nationalism.
>
> *("Imam Warith Deen Mohammed ... " 2009)*

As this obituary highlights, there remains a consistent effort to separate the father's movement from the son's. But it would be wrong to assume that the transformation of the NOI would have gone so smoothly had it not harnessed forces that were already present among Black Muslims *because* of Elijah Muhammad. Elijah Muhammad's use of the Qur'an to justify his own teachings "elevated the status of traditional Sunni Islamic discourse, especially its sacred texts, within African-American Islamic thought" (Curtis 2006: 18–19). Employing the Qur'an in this fashion for so many decades created an authority for the Qur'an, which had already begun to hand the advantage to his non-NOI Muslim opponents, whose facility with the Qur'an so outweighed his own. And it was the Qur'an and his opponents' interpretation of it that drove a wedge between him and his own sons, Akbar Muhammad and Warith Deen Mohammed.

The story of Black Muslims in the United States beginning with Drew Ali is one of the most unique in the history of Islam. Islam was redeployed in such a way as to create a new identity for African Americans, but that identity was one which other Muslims could not recognize as similar (enough) to their own. Despite what the detractors of Black Muslims may have thought, Islam and the Qur'an were essential to that new identity. Elijah Muhammad had invested all authority in himself as the Messenger of Allah who taught a new Islam and who interpreted the Qur'an in light of it. In so doing, he almost single-handedly did something no other person calling him- or herself a Muslim had been able to do: More effectively than the millions of Muslim immigrants to the United States, he brought millions of Americans to Islam and made Islam part of the American religious landscape. But once he died, the authority of Islam and the Qur'an that he had worked forty years to create in African Americans was no longer subservient to his own charismatic authority. Warith Deen Mohammed did not have the desire for the absolute authority that his father had wielded. He deferred to the authority of the Qur'an, and in so doing handed over doctrinal matters to an orthodox Sunni formulation of Islam – "the Islam of the Qur'an."

## Bibliography

Ali, N.D. (1927) *The Holy Koran of the Moorish Science Temple of America*, hermetic.com/moorish/7koran. html.

"Allah's Last Messenger Answers Questions You Have Always Wanted to Ask! Muhammad Meets the Press!" (1972) *Muhammad Speaks* (February 4): 3–4.

Baghdadi, A. (1972) "Who's behind the Splinter Group? Messenger's Attackers Exposed," *Muhammad Speaks* (May 5): 2.

Berg, H. (2009) *Elijah Muhammad and Islam*, New York: New York University Press.

Beynon, E.D. (1937–8) "The Voodoo Cult among Negro Migrants in Detroit," *The American Journal of Sociology* 43 (July–May): 894–907.

Clegg, C.A., III (1997) *An Original Man: The Life and Times of Elijah Muhammad*, New York: St. Martin's Press.

Curtis, E.E., IV (2006) *Black Muslim Religion in the Nation of Islam, 1960–1975*, Chapel Hill: University of North Carolina Press.

"Decree Akbar Muhammad" (1965) *Muhammad Speaks* (January 1): 9.

Dowling, L.H. (1930 [1908]) *The Aquarian Gospel of Jesus the Christ: The Philosophical and Practical Basis of the Religion of the Aquarian Age of the World and of the Church Universal, Transcribed from the Book of God's Remembrances, Known as the Akashic Records*, London: L.N. Fowler.

"Imam Warith Deen Mohammed, Passed Away on September 9, 2009," (2009) ISNA: Islamic Society of North America, www.isna.net/articles/News/IMAM-WARITH-DEEN-MOHAMMED-PASSED-AWAY-ON-SEPTEMBER-09-2008.aspx (accessed June 1, 2012).

Jackson, S.A. (2005) *Islam and the Blackamerican: Looking Toward the Third Resurrection*, Oxford: Oxford University Press.

Marr, T. (2006) *The Cultural Roots of American Islamicism*, New York: Cambridge University Press.

Muhammad, E. (1957) *The Supreme Wisdom: The Solution to the So-Called Negroes' Problem*, Newport News, VA: The National Newport News and Commentator.

——(1959) "Mr. Muhammad Speaks," *Pittsburgh Courier* (August 15): 14.

——(1963) "Mr. Muhammad Answers Critics: Authority from Allah, None Other," *Muhammad Speaks* (August 2): 3–4.

——(1969) "Black Man of U.S.A. and Africa," *Muhammad Speaks* (October 17): 20–1.

——(1974) *Our Saviour Has Arrived*, Chicago: Muhammad's Temple of Islam No. 2.

——(1992 [1965]) *Message to the Blackman in America*, Newport News, VA: United Brothers Communications Systems.

Mohammed, W.D. (2002) *Address to the University of North Carolina at Wilmington*, February 2.

Ramatherio, S. (1925) *Unto Thee I Grant*, San Francisco: Oriental Literature Syndicate.

Sahib, H.A. (1951) *The Nation of Islam*, M.A. thesis, University of Chicago.

X, Malcolm, with Haley, A. (1973 [1964]) *The Autobiography of Malcolm X*, New York: Ballantine Books.

# 8

# American Muslim associational life from 1950 to the present

*Kathleen Moore*

## Introduction

There has been a great deal of scholarship in recent years on the role of religious organizations in American public life (e.g. Layman 2001; Wald et al. 2005; Cleary and Hertzke 2006; Sager 2010). Much of this scholarly interest arises from a concern for the relationship between religion and government. Religion has always played a central role in American public life, yet in recent times this role has demonstrated the potential to expand precipitously as faith-based groups, coalitions, and leaders from a range of perspectives have elicited debate about the proper understanding of religion's place in contemporary society. A previous consensus around a secularizing, if somewhat Judeo-Christian, view of American public life, in which individuals and society may be cognizant of religion but the polity may not be, has broken down in recent decades to be replaced by a debate about the significance for the relationship between religion and government of the ever-increasing diversification of religious faith in America. New religions are on the rise; older religious movements once reviled, such as Mormonism, have gained legitimacy; and, since the latter half of the twentieth century, through new immigration patterns, a greater variety of faith traditions have arrived on America's shores. Further, the "nones" – those who identify with no particular religious affiliation – are on the rise, constituting one-fifth of the American public and fully one-third of those under the age of thirty.[1] Can Americans rethink their identity as a nation in a way that reflects this new stage of diversification? Will this change the way Americans think about the balance between "church" and "state"?

Religion is an organizing framework not to be overlooked when it comes to citizen participation in public life. Today there is a growing awareness of the power of religion and how it influences politics, for better or worse. Those who theorize about political theology (e.g. Kahn 2012; Critchley 2012) hold that in order to make sense of the political we must make recourse to such religious concepts as faith, the sacred, and ritual. Even basic questions about the boundary between the political and the religious, and whether politics is conceivable today without religion, can turn on strongly partisan terms and strain public debates. The crux of the matter is: can politics become effective at shaping, motivating, and mobilizing people without some dimension that is religious, without "some sort of appeal to transcendence" (Critchley

2012: 24) or an immanent frame which can be a powerful tool for persuasion? Some argue that a motivational deficit typifies modern political life, and religious institutions are poised to fill it (Habermas et al. 2010). Churches mobilize and educate for civic engagement; they have the potential to increase congregants' levels of civic skills, political efficacy, and political knowledge depending "on the frequency of church attendance and the denomination one attends" (Verba et al. 1995: 89, also cited in Jamal 2005: 522). Several studies show how religious institutions mobilize people to take political action, becoming directly involved in political processes. Recently, Catholic activists tried to influence lawmakers in Washington, DC, on such hot-button issues as immigration and health care, in the name of religion. By the same token, politicians sometimes use religion to shore up their own election bids. Political endorsements from the pulpit are on the rise, as candidates for public office – particularly those on the con-servative right – receive an increasing number of endorsements from religious leaders in spite of tax regulations prohibiting endorsements of candidates but not ballot issues (see Johnson 2012). This trend has led to a more explicitly political consciousness on the part of many religious believers, as well as to a more established place for religious organizations among Washington lobbyists.

In this context, relatively little attention has been given to the organizational efforts of American Muslims, although they have become increasingly politically important. Few have studied American Muslim organizations as such (see, however, Jamal 2005; Bagby 2012a, 2012b; Leonard 2013), so this has been an area based on (sometimes polemical) speculation rather than reliable data. Although they make up a remarkably small percentage of the overall population, the way Muslims are viewed by the general public is vitally important, and the level of attention paid to American Muslims belies their modest number. Muslims and Islam increasingly have become the target of suspicion and fear since the 1979 Iranian Revolution and American hostage crisis, but emphatically so since 9/11. The mainstream political environment by the second decade of the twenty-first century is greatly influenced by anti-Islamic populism. The stigma afforded Islam is borne out in public opinion polls that indicate that Americans are fairly evenly divided about whether Islam is consistent with American values and way of life (Abu Dhabi Gallup Center 2011; Public Religion Research Institute 2011). Looking further into the surveys' findings, we can see that most Republicans, Americans who identify with the Tea Party movement, senior citizens, and those who most trust Fox News agree that Islam is at odds with American values and way of life, and most Democrats, Independents, Americans under the age of thirty, and those who most trust CNN or public television do not share that assessment (Harbin 2013). Such partisan differences over American values now divide the nation very sharply and have pushed Americans to opposite corners even on issues (e.g. Muslim presence in the United States) that were less charged little more than a decade ago. Further, in discursive arenas ranging from talk radio and cable news networks to congressional hearings, public figures continue to discredit American Muslim organizations as "hard core" and not "authentically" American, while they also openly question: Can Muslims be loyal citizens of the United States?

Particular stress points might further exacerbate this even divide. For instance, in the 2010 controversy regarding a Muslim community center in midtown Manhattan (dubbed the Park51 controversy) and a series of attacks on mosques and mosque building projects through-out the country, the American public was also evenly divided and demonstrated a definite ambivalence toward the continued presence of Muslim institutions in American society. The cover of *Time Magazine* asked the trenchant question in August 2010: "Is America Islamophobic?" The 2010 midterm elections produced a handful of ballot initiatives across the country to "ban the *shari'a*," which called into question the loyalty of American Muslims. In

March 2011, New York congressman Peter King, the powerful chair of the US Congress's Committee on Homeland Security, led a congressional inquiry into the radicalization of American Muslims, asking the rhetorical question whether there are "too many mosques" in America. Other political leaders, such as the 2012 GOP (Grand Old Party) presidential candidate Mitt Romney, suggested wire-tapping American mosques as a measure to prevent future terrorist attacks (Jamal and Albana 2013: 107), and it was recently disclosed that the New York City Police Department has secretly designated entire mosques within its jurisdiction as terrorist organizations, thus allowing the police to use informants to record sermons, spy on imams, and open investigations on anyone who attends prayer services even without any specific evidence of criminal wrongdoing.[2]

These instances grow out of a deeply embedded and prevalent worry that there is an abiding association between Islam and extremism. A concern often heard is that mosques and Islamic centers serve as recruiting grounds for homegrown terrorists. This bromide is common even though instances of American Muslim terrorism are relatively rare, and in most cases the perpetrators had come to the attention of law enforcement because of American Muslims' self-policing against radicalization within their own community organizations (Kurzman et al. 2011: 471–2; Schanzer et al. 2010). Some argue that American Muslim community building has been a significant factor in the prevention of radicalization, and "almost all observers agree that Muslim-Americans have stepped up community-building in all forms over the past two decades" in order to strengthen American Islam and to serve community goals, including not only the protection of civil liberties but also deepening Muslims' faith and spreading Islam's message to non-Muslims (Kurzman et al. 2011: 478).

While the political environment of the twenty-first century has been largely negative, there are also positive engagements with Islam. Perhaps the most powerful statement of support for Islam and Muslims in the United States came in the form of President Barack Obama's 2009 speech delivered in Cairo. The president began this speech by offering:

> I have come here to seek a new beginning between the United States and Muslims around the world, one based upon mutual interest and mutual respect; and one based upon the truth that America and Islam are not exclusive, and need not be in competition. Instead, they overlap, and share common principles – principles of justice and progress, tolerance and the dignity of all human beings.
>
> *(Barack Obama, quoted in Hammer and Safi 2013: 7)*

He also remarked, "faith should bring us together, [a]nd that is why we are forging service projects in America to bring together Christians, Muslims, and Jews," promising to turn dialogue into good works.[3]

In this chapter, I begin with a brief demographic profile of Muslims in the United States. Then I provide an overview of the recent history of American Muslim associational life in the larger context of civic voluntarism and American organizations from the latter half of the twentieth century to the present. While it is clearly impossible to do justice to the details of this history in such a brief essay, it is important to lay the foundations for exploring the possibility that patterns can be discerned, and that these patterns may indicate something about an ongoing set of dynamics that constrain voluntary groups in the American setting. While 9/11 has made it more difficult to be Muslim in the United States in various ways, it has also catalyzed Muslim associational life. According to a poll released by the Council on American–Islamic Relations (CAIR) in 2003, in the wake of 9/11 almost half of all American Muslims reported that they had increased their social, political, interfaith, and public relations activities (cited in Jamal and

Albana 2013: 106). American Muslims have mobilized *qua Muslims* to favor greater visibility in public life in the post-9/11 era, but the roots of this mobilization reach well back into the twentieth century. To what extent are the processes of institutional growth and representation of collective interests giving way to a critical engagement with public norms of fairness and democracy? The core argument of this chapter is that the hardening of public attitudes toward Islam and Muslims is propelling major American Muslim organizations into major transformational change.

## Demographic profile

The Muslim population of the United States remains relatively small. The community's size, estimated between two and ten million, remains a matter of some dispute. Leaders of American Muslim advocacy groups generally have given estimates at the upper end of this range, citing higher levels of Muslim immigration since the 1960s and increased conversion and birth rates as contributing factors (Senzai 2012: 12). At the low end of this range are estimates provided by national surveys such as the Pew Research Center (Pew Forum on Religion and Public Life 2011; estimate of 2.75 million) and the National Opinion Research Center (Smith 2001). Even with its relatively small size – less than 1 percent of the overall population – one should keep in mind that the Muslim community continues to grow at a faster pace than other religious communities in the United States.

The majority of American Muslims today are post-1965 immigrants or their children. The Pew Research Center indicates that nearly two-thirds of Muslims in the United States (63 percent) are first- or second-generation immigrants, many of whom come from the Middle East, North Africa, and South Asia. About one-third trace their heritage to the Arab world or Iran. Currently about one in six Muslims (16 percent) in the United States have arrived from South Asia. Similarly, African Americans, some of whom are converts and some of whom are descendants of African Americans who converted during the early twentieth-century growth of American Islam, comprise another 20–30 percent of the Muslim population. Aside from these three largest groups – Middle Eastern, South Asian, and African American – there are many smaller groups of European and sub-Saharan African immigrant Muslims, and a growing number of converts who are Latino, white, or other ethnicities. Moreover, while remaining an exceedingly small proportion of the overall population, Muslims in the United States have grown dramatically in visibility and in number in recent decades. According to Pew, an astonishing 40 percent of American Muslims have arrived since 2000, while only 12 percent came to the USA before 1979 (Pew Forum on Religion and Public Life 2011).

The same study also shows that Muslims generally are far more integrated into American society than are their counterparts in Western Europe; whether they are foreign born or not, approximately 70 percent of American Muslims are US citizens. American Muslims' income and education levels are similar to those of the general public. While American Muslims are mostly middle class and are as likely as anyone else in the United States to hold a college degree (between 26 and 28 percent), in Britain, France, Spain, and Germany the average annual incomes of the Muslim populations fall far below the average incomes of non-Muslims.

While much of the current population of Muslims in the United States came to America as voluntary immigrants or are second-generation American Muslims, a considerable portion are the result of what are called indigenous forms of Islam, which developed from the early twentieth century within the African American community. A renaissance of pan-African movements at the turn of the century, World War I and the age of prosperity immediately following the war, and the Great Migration by thousands of African Americans from the rural South to the industrialized North between 1915 and 1930, cultivated an atmosphere in which people rejected the "negro" label in favor of reconstructing the self through a new ethnic or religious identity. Out of this period there arose numerous Black Jewish groups, and the two most notable African American Islamic movements of the first half of the twentieth century, the Moorish Science Temple of America (MSTA) and the Nation of Islam (NOI), with a black nationalist agenda (Knight 2013: 88–9). As "American Islam's most influential conversion movement" (Knight 2013: 92), the NOI produced America's most widely recognized conversion narrative found in any faith tradition, Malcolm X's autobiography (as told to Alex Haley), and constructed an organizational network and belief system that have withstood the trials of time over the many decades since its creation, albeit in a much changed form. Reoriented after the death of its founder in 1975, the NOI under the direction of Warith Deen (W.D.) Muhammad underwent several changes which resulted in the founding of a non-profit organization and ministry called the Mosque Cares. Islamic schools were pioneered by the NOI from the 1930s as Sister Clara Muhammad Schools (formerly University of Islam schools) as alternatives to the inferior and racially segregated public schools available in America's inner cities in the mid-twentieth century. Under W.D. Muhammad's leadership, these schools maintained their high academic standards and emphasis on black pride, but replaced the NOI theology classes with Sunni thought and theology. This triggered a reaction from the Rev. Louis Farrakhan, the rival leader who remained faithful to the original teachings of the NOI, and he re-established the University of Islam K-12 schools in inner cities across the country in 1989 to compete with the Sister Clara Muhammad schools, offering religious instruction in the original theology of the NOI (Grewal and Coolidge 2013: 250).

After 1965, when Muslim immigrants began to arrive in larger numbers, many times to fill professional and technical jobs, many bypassed the inner cities, where African American converts and other minorities lived, in favor of suburban life. Thus mosques were built to serve local communities and were residentially segregated, with inner city mosques serving largely an African American constituency and suburban mosques by and large serving immigrant populations. At the same time, racial differences have also been reflected in sectarian differences and other kinds of orientation toward religious practices. Since the late nineteenth century Sufism has attracted white Americans, and Marcia Hermansen has argued that since the 1960s Sufism has appealed to "young, middle class, Americans [who] located the cause of racism, the Vietnam War, and the evils of technocracy in a spiritual sickness that the establishment religions in America had not only failed to solve but had fostered" (quoted in Abdullah 2013: 73). Similarly, by the close of the twentieth century African American Muslims had gravitated toward Sunni Islam – and there are Black Sunni movements with distinctive beliefs in black pride, such as Darul Islam and the Islamic Party of North America – though a small number of African Americans have followed Shi'i Islam, especially since the 1979 Iranian Revolution.

## Associational life

There are two main approaches to the public significance of religion. A large branch of political science literature is devoted to how people organize for political action, and within this branch we find an offshoot which highlights the role of religious institutions – churches, synagogues, mosques, and other houses of worship – in fostering civic and political engagement. Though religious institutions were neither designed for nor intended to organize for political activity, several studies have highlighted the myriad ways in which they have equipped their constituents for action (Wald et al. 2005: 121; Chappell 2004; Putnam 2001: 35; Greenberg 2000; Verba et al. 1995). These institutions develop skills important for civic participation and political advocacy in both clergy and laypersons. Participation beyond simply attending services inevitably leads to the development of both leadership and civic skills. Verba et al. discover that religion can be a powerful resource that promotes and encourages political participation, at times enabling some racial and ethnic minorities to overcome deficits in education and wealth. Asserting the importance of the church in the polity rests on claims that locally based institutions play an essential role in linking people to the political process, by building social capital – the networks, norms, and trust that enable individuals to act together to pursue common objectives – and by functioning as a part of broader networks, which mobilize people into civic engagement by providing participatory information and resources (Greenberg 2000: 377–8). In short, this line of reasoning posits that houses of worship channel civic engagement and result in a stronger polity.

Another type of study, though, suggests that the linkage between religious institutions and political strength is highly contingent and should not be presumed. With respect to Muslims in the United States, Amaney Jamal (2005) shows us that mosque participation is not necessarily linked to broader forms of political activity across all Muslim subgroups.[4] She finds that frequent attendance at mosque is highly associated with membership in civic groups for both Arab and South Asian Muslims in the United States. However, only in the case of Arab Muslims is frequent mosque attendance associated with greater political activity. Moreover, for African American Muslims, mosque participation relates neither to greater civic involvement nor to political activity. In short, Jamal finds that high levels of religious activity link to higher levels of involvement in civic life – being a member of an organization that helps the poor, the sick, the elderly, or the homeless, or a neighborhood or community group – for American Muslims of Arab and South Asian descent, but has no effect on African American Muslim civic involvement or political activity. Thus the mosque may serve as a site for the acquisition of civic skills for some, but there is little evidence to suggest that the mosque mobilizes political engagement across the board. Three important factors – culture/identity, resource mobilization, and political opportunity structure – have been under-studied, particularly with respect to mosque communities in the USA.

Studies such as Jamal's raise important questions about religiously based political action. It is clear that while traditional houses of worship such as mosques were not created for political mobilization, they can perform important, though limited, functions in channeling political action. While these institutions were created primarily to offer religious services, formalize and maintain religious doctrines and rituals, transmit the religion from one generation to the next, provide religious leadership for their congregants, and train clergy and develop their leadership skills, it is also equally unmistakable that the resources needed for political mobilization overlap considerably with the resources necessary to perform these religious tasks. Many of the questions concerning religious expression in public life could be better addressed if we kept in mind the fact that for many Americans the pathways to political action are mediated through structures (often religious institutions) that help to cultivate communal identities in culturally and contextually specific ways. To put it another way, to appreciate this contingent development of associational life we need to understand motive, means, and opportunity: "the motives that draw religious groups into political action, the means that enable the religious to participate effectively, and the opportunities that facilitate their entry into the political system" (Wald et al. 2005: 124).

When we think about Muslim American associational life, by the second half of the twentieth century three kinds of institutions became evident: mosques and Islamic centers; a range of non-profit associations providing public service, charity, and educational products; and advocacy groups. Each of these will be taken in turn as we consider motive, means, and opportunity for civic engagement and political activity of Muslims in the United States.

## Motives that draw different Muslim groups into political action

Appreciating the importance of Muslim organizations in civic engagement and political activity in the latter half of the twentieth century requires a look at the bigger picture. At mid-century, Americans in general launched more nationally visible voluntary associations than ever before. Roughly half of all voluntary associations in 1950 were business associations, yet these lost their proportional share over the years, as they shrank to 40 percent in 1960 and less than 18 percent by 1990 (Skocpol 2004: 4). The field of associational life diversified, and Americans of both genders and all educational levels were likely to join and hold office in voluntary associations, often claiming one or more memberships in church-related associations, civic-political groups, and fraternal lodges, becoming by the 1960s eager participants in fellowship associations that emphasized and expressed solidarity among citizens (Skocpol 2004). While business associations shrank as a portion of the total field of voluntary groups, expanding categories consisted of public benefit organizations and non-profits that aim to further specific value-laden under-standings of the public good, such as environmental groups, family values groups, anti-poverty groups, veterans' groups, and associations dealing with the interests of women, racial minorities, and so on. As sociologist Theda Skocpol puts it, "the balance of organized voice in US public affairs shifted markedly in the late twentieth century, as many new kinds of associations came to be heard, speaking for more causes and constituencies than ever before" (Skocpol 2004: 5).

At the same time the trend was toward more professionally managed associations, away from the popularly rooted and restrictive membership model of organizations. This key social change accompanied the civic shift in favor of civil rights and the new attitudes and practices about race and gender. At roughly the same time, a bubble of legislation appeared – which peaked in the 1960s and 1970s – which constituted an "age of improvement," in which the federal gov-ernment attempted to influence new realms of American social and economic life, ranging from women's and minority rights to environmental and social security policies. The appearance of nationally oriented civic associations closely tracked the expansion of federal legislative activism, especially in areas of federal rights and social regulation. So, for instance, new rights advocacy organizations sprang into being *after*, rather than before, the Civil Rights Act of 1964, and the establishment over the next few years of federal agencies to enforce and monitor compliance with civil rights legislation (Skocpol 2004).

It is within this atmosphere and this evolution of federated networks of civic associations that Muslim organizations grew in the second half of the twentieth century. What motivated Muslims to organize and join in the professionally managed groups? Throughout much of the twentieth century, associational life revolved around the mosque or Islamic center, the house of worship for Muslim Americans. Many who had immigrated to the United States or had con-verted to Islam during the early decades of the century showed little overt interest in partici-pating in civic life beyond ad hoc volunteering at the local level. Aside from a small but significant number of foreign missionaries and Black Muslim movements, few Muslims thought about establishing Islam at the national level prior to World War II. Instead, Islamic practices either were private and individualistic or were limited to one's immediate community (GhaneaBassiri 2010: 178).

The unique historical context that helps explain the course that American Muslim life took – why Muslims began to form national-level organizations – accounts for adaptations of religious resources and ideals to prevailing institutional arrangements. At the inauguration of the Islamic Center in Washington, DC, in 1957, when President Dwight D. Eisenhower spoke of a global context in which religion formed the foundation for a geopolitical bond among allies, his speech was remarkably prescient of President Obama's "new beginnings" speech in Cairo. Even though the debates about political changes and dangers at mid-twentieth century concentrated on the threat posed by global communism rather than global terrorism, Eisenhower's assertions of what matters bear a strong resemblance to Obama's narrative of shared principles and institutional arrangements co-constituted by commitments to values like freedom and respect. Eisenhower spoke of the relationship between the United States and the Islamic world:

> This fruitful relationship between peoples, going back into history, becomes more important each year. Today, thousands of Americans, both private individuals and government officials, live and work – and grow in understanding – among the peoples of Islam. At the same time, in our country, many from the Muslim lands – students, businessmen, and representatives of states – are enjoying the benefits of experience among the people of the United States. From these many personal contacts, here and abroad, I firmly believe there will come a broader understanding and a deeper respect for the worth of all men; and a stronger resolution to work together for the good of mankind … Under the American Constitution, this Center, this place of worship, is as welcome as could be any similar edifice of any religion. Americans would fight with all their strength for your right to have your own church and worship according to your own conscience. Without this, we would be something else than what we are.[5]

Yet while Eisenhower's comments might have indicated there was room for Islam to grow in the United States, it was still viewed as something foreign and new, and recognition of the presence of Muslims in the United States proceeded at a slow pace. From 1948 to 1965, the number of students from Muslim countries in the United States increased fivefold (GhaneaBassiri 2010: 264). Those who belonged to Islamist movements who fled in fear of persecution from secular, nationalist regimes that came to power after independence and viewed Islamist organizations as a political threat had a significant impact on the development of national Muslim organizations in the United States in the early 1960s. The Muslim Student Association of the United States and Canada (MSA) was founded in 1963 at the University of Illinois at Urbana-Champaign, and in the next two decades became the most successful Muslim organization founded by immigrants (GhaneaBassiri 2010: 265). The early MSA functioned for the most part as a membership organization, financed by its membership dues ($2 per year in the 1960s), personal donations, the sales of books, and modest funds from Muslim countries such as Kuwait and Pakistan (GhaneaBassiri 2010). Its membership was primarily male foreign students, with a women's committee formed in 1966. Its first center of operations was established in 1973 in al-Amin Mosque in Gary, Indiana. Later it built its present headquarters in Plainfield, Indiana. According to MSA documents, in its early years the organization sought to establish local chapters so the Muslim students might maintain their religious commitments while living in a non-Muslim society. Through its commitment to viewing Islam as a complete way of life, the MSA has seen the US organizational context as a "melting pot" experiment in which Muslims from around the world can transcend their racial, ethnic, and cultural differences to become what one scholar has called the "normative *homo islamicus* subject[s]" (GhaneaBassiri 2010: 268). While this normative vision has not been realized, and local chapters maintain a high degree of autonomy from the national leadership, other related organizations have sprouted up around the MSA. In the 1970s, Arab students created the Muslim Arab Youth Association (MAYA), and Malaysians the Malaysian Islamic Study Group (MISG). Also in the 1970s, some Iranian, Shi'i students began the Muslim Student Association – Persian Speaking Group, and some South Asian students started the Islamic Circle of North America (ICNA) (GhaneaBassiri 2010: 269).

In 1981, the Islamic Society of North America (ISNA) was formed to provide an umbrella over a greater range of activities than the MSA could provide given its specific focus on student life. ISNA oversees the interests of campus organizations (MSA), professional associations, service and youth groups, committees on legal matters, charities, interfaith relations, outreach, public relations, and so on. The maturing of the organizational model for Muslim activism was demonstrated in the letter to all members of the MSA announcing the creation of the new umbrella organization of ISNA:

> There is no longer any doubt, if there ever was, that Islam has come to North America to stay for good, insha'Allah [God willing]. Islamic presence here must, therefore pervade all spheres of a Muslim's life in this societal environment and must exert a positive influence on the non-Muslim segments of this society. To do so, Islamic work must continually grow and come to grips with new challenges and opportunities. This requires evolution and adaptation of the organizational structure of Islamic organizations so that they may provide the right type of leadership to an increasingly sophisticated and comprehensive socioeconomic order among Muslims in North America … Muslims in North America are truly at the cross-roads. The most sincere and persistent effort of every Muslim is needed to forestall fragmentation and forge a united and enlightened front of Muslims to serve the Cause of Allah.
>
> *(MSA letter, quoted in GhaneaBassiri 2010: 312)*

The 1970s and 1980s witnessed a significant growth in the number of mosques and Islamic centers built in the United States, some constructed with funding from foreign countries, but the majority the result of local fundraising efforts by Muslims. Most were built to serve a single ethnic or national origin congregation. National organizations such as the Federation of Islamic Associations, established in 1953, "understood well the local nature of American Muslim community building" (GhaneaBassiri 2010: 274) and did not impose themselves on mosque building projects. However, national organizations maintain an interest in fostering a unified strength, and so continue to offer instructional materials and financial assistance to local groups wishing to organize around a specific project.

In a related move, ethnically defined civil rights organizations were founded in the early 1980s that sought to monitor the enforcement of civil rights laws. For instance, the American-Arab Anti-Discrimination Committee (ADC) was created in 1980 to defend the civil rights of Arab Americans. Defining itself largely as a secular ethnicity, the organization expanded to include specifically the defense against anti–Muslim bigotry in the early 1990s. Similar organizations, such as South Asian Americans Leading Together (SAALT), founded in 2000, focus on community education and advocacy, and include but are not limited to bias incidents against Muslims. These organizations are not specifically defined as Muslim but include Muslims among their membership.

A primary though not the only motivation for associational life in the United States was the promotion of a particular understanding of Islam that was greatly influenced by the Islamist movements of mid-twentieth-century liberation movements in much of the Muslim world. The emergence of the Muslim Student Association set the tone for itself and several subsequent organizations that took a "top-down" approach to create a national leadership structure while stimulating the growth of local chapters.

Muslims in the United States responded to the international role the United States grew into after World War II to become a much more significant world power abroad and to change immigration laws in such a manner as to open the doors to more diverse immigration at home.

Muslims formed associations led, albeit loosely, by a national leadership whose members often were politicized by the nationalist and Islamist movements in their home countries as well as the growing significance of the United States' involvement in the affairs of Muslim countries. Sometimes these organizations were funded at least in part by Muslim countries, but they also diversified as they matured.

## The means that enable the organization of group interests into political form

Religious individuals and groups, like non-religious individuals and groups, have a right to participate in the debate on all issues that are important to political and civic life. As the Supreme Court of the United States said in 1970: "Adherents of particular faiths and individual churches frequently take strong positions on public issues ... Of course, churches as much as secular bodies and private citizens have that right."[6] For example, religious leaders and organizations often take positions on legislative bills and they sometimes boycott certain corporations or launch media campaigns about public issues. So when faith-based advocacy organizations began to appear in the public sphere to set the agenda for government, coalitions formed to advance the cause of defining social values and of challenging them.

In the field of interest group politics, religious activism and advocacy are constantly evolving. Early groups included the United Methodist Church, which established its Washington, DC, office in 1916 to promote the prohibition of alcohol, and the National Catholic Welfare Conference, established in 1919. The Peace Churches (e.g. the Brethren, the Quakers) became registered lobbyists by the 1940s to protect conscientious objector status, and by the middle of the twentieth century Jewish and Baptist organizations joined the scene to litigate church–state issues. Since the 1950s the number of religious lobbyists has expanded substantially, and in 2011 the Pew Forum on Religion and Public Life released a study that identified more than 200 national religious organizations engaging in public policy advocacy.

This increased the opportunity for Muslim activism in the field of interest group politics. In 1986, the Islamic Center of Southern California started the Muslim Political Action Committee, which within two years changed its name to the Muslim Public Affairs Committee (MPAC) and became one of the leading Muslim American advocacy organizations in the United States. Also in the late 1980s, political science professor Agha Saeed established a political coalition in northern California, initially called the American Muslim Alliance (AMA), aimed at mobilizing the Muslim vote, and continued to organize two more similar organizations, the American Muslim Political Coordinating Committee (AMPCC) and the American Muslim Task Force (AMT), which combined to become the American Muslim Taskforce on Civil Rights and Elections. The twin objectives of participating in a meaningful way in democratic elections and successfully fighting prejudice against Muslims became a motivating factor in the creation of organizations from the 1980s onward, with goals ranging from the improvement of curriculum in public education to make sure it is accurate and unbiased, to monitoring public media to correct distortions and misinformation. The Council on American–Islamic Relations (CAIR), founded in 1995, regularly monitors hate crimes and other forms of discrimination against American Muslims.

New media technologies and models of association building have also propelled the new, professionalized advocacy organization. At one time, organizations needed to rely on campaigns to gain mass membership at the local level in order to build networks that could sustain them and wield national influence. Organizations used to pressure lawmakers by mobilizing members and newspapers across legislative districts. However, today advocacy groups can start an association using membership support but then rely on computer-based systems and the internet to develop a constituency and donor relations so that they can rely less on membership dues for their budgets. This new approach means that today's associations need to keep their profiles constantly in the public eye, especially in major metropolitan centers, where politicians and advocacy spokespersons appear endlessly on talk shows, social media feeds, and blogs. This not only enhances the association's reputation but also keeps contributions flowing in from constituents. No longer do association leaders think in terms of creating a federated network of volunteer staff members. Instead, when a new issue arises, they open a national office and build an association (as well as national projects) from the center (Skocpol 2004: 10). This allows associations to concentrate on efficient management while keeping close to federal government and national media. Several American Muslim organizations embrace the tools of new media to reach their members. Social networking is common. Web destinations such as YouTube are filled with content from American Muslim advocacy organizations. The internet and other new technologies have made it easier for these organizations to reach a younger generation of Muslims and are now a permanent feature.

This also results in a cadre of national advocacy organizations that are detached from the other kind of collective institution, the local mosque or Islamic center. In fact, a significant challenge to political mobilization is that a majority of American Muslims do not feel that a national Muslim association represents their views. According to the Gallup Center for Muslim Studies, when asked which of a list of national Muslim American organizations represented their interests, 55 percent of Muslim men and 42 percent of Muslim women said that none do (Abu Dhabi Gallup Center 2011: 25) (Table 8.1).

## The opportunities that facilitate their entry into the political system

Opportunities to enter into the public sphere have expanded in the era of civil rights in obvious ways. Advocacy organizations have multiplied, in particular when it comes to the outlawing of discrimination and the rise of identity politics. Also, increasing American Muslim participation in electoral politics has led to the creation of organizations that are above the local mosque level to promote and defend American Muslim political interests. As Table 8.2 shows, according to the 2011 study by the Pew Forum on Religion and Public Life most Muslim advocacy organizations in Washington, DC, arrived there after the 1990s.

However, less visible yet more common routes to civic engagement have led American Muslims to join humanitarian or charitable organizations providing service, charity, and

*Table 8.1* No national American Muslim organization represents a large portion of the community

| Organization cited | % Muslim men | % Muslim women |
| --- | --- | --- |
| Council on American–Islamic Relations (CAIR) | 12 | 11 |
| Islamic Society of North America (ISNA) | 4 | 7 |
| Muslim Public Affairs Council (MPAC) | 6 | 1 |
| Muslim American Society (MAS) | 0 | 2 |
| Imam Warith Deen Muhammad group | 3 | 1 |
| Islamic Circle of North America (ICNA) | 2 | 0 |
| Other | 6 | 20 |
| None | 55 | 42 |

Surveys conducted via Gallup Nightly Poll from January 1, 2008 to April 9, 2011.
Source: Abu Dhabi Gallup Center (2011: 25)

*Table 8.2* Advocacy organizations listed by Pew Forum on Religion and Public Life (updated May 15, 2012)

| Name (arranged alphabetically) | DC arrival date |
| --- | --- |
| Ahmadiyya Movement in Islam, USA | 1948 |
| American Islamic Congress | 2006 |
| Center for Islamic Pluralism | 2005 |
| Center for the Study of Islam and Democracy | 1999 |
| Council on American–Islamic Relations (CAIR) | 1994 |
| Free Muslims Coalition | 2004 |
| International Quranic Center | 2007 |
| International Uyghur Human Rights and Democracy Foundation | 2005 |
| ISNA, Office for Interfaith and Community Alliance | 2006 |
| Karamah: Muslim Women Lawyers for Human Rights | 1993 |
| Kashmiri American Council | 1990 |
| Minaret of Freedom Institute | 1993 |
| Muslim American Society | 1993 |
| Muslim Public Affairs Council (MPAC) | 1997 |
| National Committee of Women for a Democratic Iran | 1990 |
| Uyghur American Association | 2004 |
| World Organization for Resource Development & Education | 2000 |

Source: Compiled from data from online directory at Pew Forum on Religion and Public Life (2011).

educational products, beginning in the 1990s but accelerating in the twenty-first century. Many Muslim organizations at local and state levels provide social services, including financial assistance for education, referrals for domestic violence solutions, and shelter services for the homeless. Several organizations are hybrids, performing some advocacy work while also providing a range of services. Still others are national service or civic organizations, such as the Muslim Boy Scouts and the Muslim Girl Scouts, or those formed for a specific segment of the American Muslim population, such as the Latino American Dawah Organization, founded in New York City in 1997 for Spanish-speaking converts, or the Muslim Alliance in North America (MANA), with its focus on African American Sunni Muslims and other American-born Muslims.

After 9/11 the pronounced appearance of Muslim women in the American public sphere was a noticeable change in American Muslim associational life. Impelled by increased surveillance and indictment of some American Muslim charities and organizations, as well as the special registration program, men began to keep a lower profile, thus creating the opportunity for women to move into the vanguard and assume more responsibility for administering important Islamic institutions. Women began to write op-ed pieces and became media professionals, pursued careers in human and civil rights, and established advocacy groups to fight for civil rights. For the first time in its history, in 2001 the ISNA elected a woman, Ingrid Mattson, to serve as vice president, and later president (2006–10) of the organization, bringing a woman into the top ranks of the national leadership. However, in the world of American Muslim advocacy and activist organizations generally, the organizational structure is gendered. While American Muslim women are among the most highly educated women (second only to Jewish women) and are as likely as American Muslim men to hold a professional job (Gallup International 2009: 56), surprisingly few women have served as top executives of national American Muslim organizations. Exceptions to this rule include Dr. Ingrid Mattson and Dr. Azizah al-Hibri, founding

*Table 8.3* Non-profit organizations by and for American Muslim women

| Name | Date founded |
| --- | --- |
| The Sisters' Wing of the Islamic Circle of North America (ICNA) | 1978 |
| International League of Muslim Women | 1984 |
| Muslim Women United (Richmond, VA) | 1989 |
| Muslim Women's League | 1992 |
| Women in Islam | 1992 |
| Rahima Foundation | 1993 |
| Karamah: Muslim Women Lawyers for Human Rights | 1993 |
| Peaceful Families Project | 2000 |
| Muslim Women Resource Center (Illinois) | 2001 |
| Muslim Advocates | 2005 |
| Women's Islamic Initiative in Spirituality and Equality (WISE) | 2006 |

executive director of Karamah: Muslim Women Lawyers for Human Rights, and Ferhana Khera, the founding executive director of Muslim Advocates, two American Muslim civil rights organizations staffed almost entirely by women. Muslim women in the United States, though, are actively engaged in political activism and civic affairs, and have gained entry in particular in post-9/11 engagements. For instance, the Muslim Women's Resource Center, started in 2001 by Suma Quraishi, and the American Muslim Women's Association (Arizona) provide services. The Muslim Women's League and the Women's Islamic Initiative in Spirituality and Equality (WISE) provide an arena to discuss the interpretation of scripture and tradition, to confront prejudice, and to raise awareness. There are too many organizations to list here, but Table 8.3 lists a selection of non-profit organizations that have been founded by and for American Muslim women.

Many activists and community leaders paved the way for these new kinds of interventions by Muslims in the American public sphere in the twenty-first century. The formulation and negotiation of the space for Muslim associational life, as it exists in the second decade of this century, began to take shape as early as the 1970s and 1980s, coinciding with the growth of federal policy and civic monitoring of equal rights guarantees and philosophies in the United States. These movements followed the religious advocacy movements of the early twentieth century in which certain Protestant, Catholic, and Jewish organizations were formed at the national level, detached from the congregational levels, to pursue policy goals and protect religious institutional interests (e.g. religious liberty, prohibition, etc.). In the world of interest group politics, religious lobbying gained momentum in the 1950s and 1960s just as new legislation guaranteed civil rights to African Americans and allowed greater Asian immigration to the United States. The impact of these combined trends changed the game plan in terms of the public significance of religion, in a nation that once considered itself to be a Protestant nation.

Recent agenda-setting works have emphasized the need to create a comprehensive history and a stronger infusion of social sciences theory into the rapidly developing subfield of Islam in America (e.g. Curtis 2009; Hammer and Safi 2013). This essay hopes to pose questions for research about the salience of religion in the development of Muslim associational life in the United States. What are the motives for belonging to associations defined by faith? Do these associations foster connections or alliances with other non-Muslim associations? Do these groups facilitate political action, and by what means? What conditions provide opportunities for associational growth and political strength?

At the end of the twentieth century, American Muslim associational life had advanced to the point where institutions, networks, and civic and professional organizations with social, economic, and political as well as religious power were well established. American Muslims may have every reason to feel marginalized in the post-9/11 environment, but their inclusion in public life has become undeniable. What follows is a short list of some of the major organizations of American Muslims.

## Major American Muslim Organizations (alphabetically listed)

- *American Muslim Alliance (AMA)* (www.amaweb.org) provides information about elections and voting. The goal of this organization is to organize and mobilize American Muslims as a voting block in local, state, and national elections, and to get qualified American Muslims to run for public office at every level. Established in 1994.
- *Council for the Advancement of Muslim Professionals (CAMP)* (www.camp-online.org) is a face-to-face networking organization for mid- to senior-level Muslim professionals in the United States with chapters in five major cities. The objective is to broaden community and philanthropic efforts. Founded in 1994.
- *Council on American–Islamic Relations (CAIR)* (www.cair.com) is considered by many to be the leading advocate for justice and mutual understanding, and aims to educate the American public about Islam, to challenge defamatory representations about Islam and Muslims, to protect the civil liberties of American Muslims, and to lobby on behalf of American Muslim interests. CAIR emerged when certain pundits were bringing to public attention the problem of militant Islam. Founded in 1994.
- *Islamic Circle of North America (ICNA)* (www.icna.org) was initially predominantly a South Asian Muslim organization that concentrated on the personal spiritual development of its membership, and was an offshoot of the Pakistani Jamaat-i Islami Party. Since the 1980s it has diversified its membership, adding outreach and social justice, charity, and Islamic savings and investment to its mission. Established in 1971.
- *Islamic Relief USA* (www.irusa.org/) is a relief organization with five regional offices in the United States that educates the public about its disaster assistance operations around the world. It holds seminars, banquets, concerts, and other events to raise awareness and raise funds for domestic and international relief efforts. Established in 1993.
- *Islamic Society of North America (ISNA)* (www.isna.net), founded in 1983 as an outgrowth of the Muslim Student Association (established 1963), functions as a broad-based organization that holds annual conventions. It is an umbrella organization representing over 2,000 mosques and Islamic centers in the United States and Canada. The ISNA has long been a service organization that has periodically taken a position on policy. More recently, in the past decade it has established a lobbying arm in Washington, DC, which it calls ISNA, Office of Interfaith and Community Alliances. The Fiqh Council of North America, an affiliate of ISNA, is a prominent network of religious scholars from the United States and Canada which offers Islamic legal advice on the application of religious principles. The Muslim Youth of North America (MYNA) is also sponsored by ISNA and plays an important role in staging conferences and events with an Islamic focus. Divided into four regions covering Canada and the eastern, central, and western United States, MYNA provides occasions for young people to talk about issues of common concern and to develop leadership skills.
- *Muslim Public Affairs Council (MPAC)* (www.mpac.org) is considered the leading civil rights advocacy organization that aims to inform and shape public opinion regarding issues of importance to the nation. It offers internships for young leaders to encourage careers in

public service and media, and works with law enforcement agencies to insure the protection of Muslim Americans' civil liberties. This organization has an affiliate, the Muslim Women's League, which promotes women's rights. Established in 1988.

- *Muslim Urban Professionals (Muppies)* (www.muppies.org/) supports the advancement of Muslim leaders in private, public, and non-profit sectors, and is built on the foundation of both professional success and community engagement. It provides social networking and mentorship opportunities as well as civic engagement with broader society. Established in 2007.
- *National Association of Muslim Lawyers (NAML)*, with its sister organization *Muslim Advocates*, is a national legal advocacy and educational organization that promotes the protection of freedom, justice, and equality regardless of faith. It uses the tools of legal advocacy, policy engagement, and education to meet its aims. In its mission statement this organization states that it endorses the founding principles of American constitutionalism, and believes that these principles can be fulfilled without compromising the nation's security. Muslim Advocates (www.muslimadvocates.org) has established itself as a networking agent among the nation's leading lawyers, community and mosque leaders, government officials, the media, and allies in the human rights and national security fields. In addition to its advocacy efforts, Muslim Advocates has provided technical assistance to Muslim charities to help them be in legal compliance. NAML was established in 2000 and Muslim Advocates founded in 2005.

## Notes

1 According to an October 2012 survey by the Pew Research Center's Forum on Religion and Public Life, many of the country's unaffiliated are religious or spiritual in some way. Two-thirds say they believe in God, and think that religious institutions benefit society by strengthening community bonds and helping the poor. See Pew Forum on Religion and Public Life (2012).
2 nation.time.com/2013/08/28/nypd-designates-mosques-as-terrorism-organizations/
3 See text at "Remarks by the President on a New Beginning," White House Office of the Press Secretary, June 4, 2009, accessed on March 30, 2013, at www.whitehouse.gov/the_press_office/ Remarks-by-the-President-at-Cairo-University-6-04-09.
4 Political activity in Jamal's study excludes voting because 70 percent of her data set were foreign born and thus not eligible to vote in elections. She defines political activity by asking four questions: Have you ever called or written the media or a politician on a given issue, or have you signed a petition? Have you ever attended a rally in support of a cause? Have you ever given a contribution or volunteered your time or services in support of a political candidate? Would you consider yourself an active member of a political party? (Jamal 2005: 528).
5 "Eisenhower's 1957 Speech at Islamic Center of Washington," last accessed Sept 10, 2013, at iipdigital. usembassy.gov/st/english/texttrans/2007/06/20070626154822lnkais0.6946985.html#axzz2f5eOIe00.
6 *Walz v Tax Commission*, 397 U.S. 664, 670 (1970).

## Bibliography

Abdullah, Z. (2013) "American Muslims in the Contemporary World: 1965 to the Present," in Hammer, J. and Safi, O. (eds.) *The Cambridge Companion to American Islam*, New York: Cambridge University Press, pp. 65–82.

Abu Dhabi Gallup Center (2011) "Muslim Americans: Faith, Freedom and Future: Examining US Muslims' Political, Social, and Spiritual Engagement 10 Years after September 11," www.gallup.com/poll/ 148916/muslim-americans-faith-freedom-future.aspx (accessed January 8, 2012).

Bagby, I. (2012a) "The American Mosque 2011: Activities, Administration, and Vitality of the American Mosque – Report Number 2," www.hartfordinstitute.org/The-American-Mosque-Report-2.pdf (accessed October 15, 2012).

——(2012b) "The American Mosque 2011: Basic Characteristics of the American Mosque and Attitudes of Mosque Leaders – Report Number 1," faithcommunitiestoday.org/sites/faithcommunitiestoday.org/files/The%20American%20Mosque%202011%20web.pdf (accessed October 15, 2012).

Chappell, D.L. (2004) *A Stone of Hope: Prophetic Religion and the Death of Jim Crow*, Chapel Hill, NC: University of North Carolina Press.

Cleary, E. and Hertzke, A.D. (2006) *Representing God at the State House: Religion and Politics in the American States*, Lanham, MD: Rowman & Littlefield Publishers.

Critchley, S. (2012) *The Faith of the Faithless: Experiments in Political Theology*, London: Verso.

Curtis, E.E., IV (2009) *Muslims in America: A Short History*, New York and Oxford: Oxford University Press.

Gallup International (2009) "Muslim Americans: A National Portait," www.gallup.com/strategicconsulting/153572/REPORT-Muslim-Americans-National-Portrait.aspx (accessed October 12, 2012).

GhaneaBassiri, K. (2010) *A History of Islam in America: From the New World to the New World Order*, New York: Cambridge University Press.

Greenberg, A. (2000) "The Church and Revitalization of Politics and Community," *Political Science Quarterly* 115(3): 377–394.

Grewal, Z.A. and Coolidge, R.D. (2013) "Islamic Education in the United States: Debates, Practices, and Institutions," in Hammer, J. and Safi, O. (eds.) *The Cambridge Companion to American Islam*, New York: Cambridge University Press, pp. 246–65.

Habermas, J. et al. (2010) *An Awareness of What is Missing: Faith and Reason in a Post-Secular Age*, translated by Ciaran Cronin, Cambridge: Polity.

Hammer, J. and Safi, O. (eds.) (2013) *The Cambridge Companion to American Islam*, New York: Cambridge University Press.

Harbin, J.P. (2013) "PRRI: Americans Nearly Evenly Divided on Whether Islam at Odds with American Values," editorial on IslamiCommentary, islamicommentary.org/2013/03/prri-americans-nearly-evenly-divided-on-whether-islam-at-odds-with-american-values/ (accessed June 6, 2013).

Jamal, A. (2005) "The Political Participation and Engagement of Muslim Americans Mosque Involvement and Group Consciousness," *American Politics Research* 33(4): 521–44.

Jamal, A. and Albana, L. (2013) "Demographics, Political Participation, and Representation," in Hammer, J. and Safi, O. (eds.) *The Cambridge Companion to American Islam*, New York: Cambridge University Press, pp. 98–118.

Johnson, M.A. (2012) "Pulpit Politics: Pastors Endorse Candidates, Thumbing Nose at the IRS," *NBC News*, usnews.nbcnews.com/_news/2012/11/04/14703656-pulpit-politics-pastors-endorse-candidates-thumbing-noses-at-the-irs?lite (accessed August 24, 2013).

Kahn, P. (2012) *Political Theology: Four New Chapters on the Concept of Sovereignty*, New York: Columbia University Press.

Knight, M.M. (2013) "Converts and Conversions," in Hammer, J. and Safi, O. (eds.) *The Cambridge Companion to American Islam*, New York: Cambridge University Press, pp. 83–97.

Kurzman, C., Schanzer, D., and Moosa, E. (2011) "Muslim American Terrorism since 9/11: Why So Rare?," *The Muslim World* 101(3): 464–83.

Layman, G. (2001) *The Great Divide: Religious and Cultural Conflict in American Party Politics*, New York: Columbia University Press.

Leonard, K. (2013) "Organizing Communities: Institutions, Networks, Groups," in Hammer, J. and Safi, O. (eds.) *The Cambridge Companion to American Islam*, New York: Cambridge University Press, pp. 170–89.

Pew Forum on Religion and Public Life (2010) "Muslim Networks and Movements in Western Europe," pewforum.org/Muslim/Muslim-Networks-and-Movements-in-Western-Europe.aspx (accessed January 24, 2011).

——(2011) "Lobbying for the Faithful: Religious Advocacy Groups in Washington, D.C.," www.pewforum.org/lobbying-religious-advocacy-groups-in-washington-dc.aspx (accessed December 9, 2011).

——(2012) "Nones on the Rise: One-in-Five Adults Have No Religious Affiliation," www.pewforum.org/Unaffiliated/nones-on-the-rise.aspx (accessed March 17, 2013).

Public Religion Research Institute (2011) "What It Means to Be American: Attitudes Toward Increasing Diversity in America: Ten Years after 9/11," publicreligion.org/research/2011/09/what-it-means-to-be-american/ (accessed March 17, 2013).

Putnam, R. (2001) *Democracies in Flux: the Evolution of Social Capital in Contemporary Society*, New York: Oxford University Press.

Sager, R. (2010) *Faith, Politics, and Power: The Politics of Faith-Based Institutions*, New York: Oxford University Press.

Schanzer, D., Kurzman, C., and Moosa, E. (2010) "Anti-Terror Lessons of Muslim American Communities," Report of the Triangle Center on Terrorism and Homeland Security, tcths.sanford.duke.edu/documents/Anti-TerrorLessonsfinal.pdf (accessed January 11, 2012).

Senzai, F. (2012) "Engaging American Muslims: Political Trends and Attitudes," www.ispu.org/pdfs/ISPU_Report_Political_Participation.pdf (accessed September 17, 2013).

Skocpol, T. (2004) "APSA Presidential Address: Voice and Inequality: The Transformation of American Civic Democracy," *Perspectives on Politics* 2(1): 3–20.

Smith, T.W. (2001) "Estimating the Muslim Population in the United States," the American Jewish Committee, www.ajc.org/site/apps/nl/content3.asp?c=ijITI2PHKoG&b=843637&ct=1044159 (accessed September 17, 2013).

Verba, S., Schlotzman, K.L., and Brady, H.E. (1995) *Voice and Equality: Civic Voluntarism in American Politics*, Cambridge, MA: Harvard University Press.

Wald, K.D., Silverman, A.L., and Fridy, K.S. (2005) "Making Sense of Religion in Political Life," *American Review of Political Science* 8: 121–43.

# 9

# Islam in Mexico and Central America

*Mark Lindley-Highfield of Ballumbie Castle*

The twenty-first century is witnessing interesting demographic changes in the religious make-up of Mexico and Central America. The gradual transformation of the religious composition of the states, together with an increase in the elasticity to religious identity, has resulted in a dynamic culture in which religious identity has become more malleable and individuals have found new forms of expression for their faith. The increasing presence of Islam in the region is a marker of, and contributor towards, this changing environment.

The earliest record of a presumed Muslim presence in Central America dates back to the arrival of Africans from the Mandinka, or Malinke, tribe in Panama in 1552 (Westerlund and Svanberg 1999). The five centuries in the interim period lead us to the contemporary situation where Latin Americans are choosing to adopt Islam as their religion in the present day. A feel for how these transformations have come about can be gained by looking at Mexico as a detailed case study. This reveals how Latin America has benefited from immigration and how Islam has enabled people to explore their spirituality, with marginalized peoples finding a voice within the religion.

## Mexico

At the time of the conquest of Mexico under Hernán Cortés, a translator was required for the Spaniards to communicate with the country's indigenous inhabitants. Thankfully for Cortés, two Spanish crew members, who came to the New World on a voyage of discovery, survived their ship being wrecked some years earlier and found their way to land, where they integrated into the local community, intermarrying and learning to speak in the native tongue. They became the gatekeepers to the Spanish dominion of this territory. According to the year 2010 census of the Instituto Nacional de Estadística Geografía e Informática (INEGI), the percentage of Mexicans aged five years or over who are declared as speaking an indigenous language now stands at slightly less than 7 percent (INEGI 2011a). The same census reveals that a little less than 83 percent of the population identify themselves as Roman Catholic at present (INEGI 2011b), such has been the impact of Cortés stumbling upon two Spaniards who were washed up by the sea.

Present-day Mexico is a country of extremes. Mexico City is now home to the richest man in the world, Carlos Slim Helú (Forbes.com 2012), with an estimated family wealth of US$69 billion, but Chiapas, Mexico's southeasternmost state, has had "no telephones or electricity at all in most of the rural areas" (Froehling 1997: 291). The country's most Catholic state, Guanajuato, with its well-respected university, established by the Jesuits in 1732, has marginally less than 94 percent of its population claiming a Roman Catholic religious identity. Mexico's least Catholic state, however, with the smallest number of people identifying themselves as Roman Catholic, is Chiapas, where (at 58 percent) this is a little over half of its population (INEGI 2011b). Often identified as a Roman Catholic nation, Mexico is beginning to increase in its religious pluralism.

Anthropologist Peter Cahn (2003: 64–5) tells us that religious freedom in Mexico was established under the 1857 Constitution, after which, in 1870, Benito Juárez suggested that the introduction of Protestantism might help to bring the indigenous peoples of Mexico under federal control. Accordingly, under the presidency of Lerdo, missionaries from the United States were welcomed in 1872. This is clearly a contributory factor to the heteropraxy that can be found in Mexico today.

Mexico is a large oil producer with substantial reserves. Nearly one-third of the government's revenue comes from this sector and it is one of the United States' major suppliers (BBC 2005a). Mexico's oil reserves are one of the contributory reasons for Chiapas having been called "a rich land and poor people" (Benjamin 1989). Despite their ongoing and co-dependent trade relationships, the *entente* between Mexico and the United States has not always been *cordiale*. The USA's annexation of Texas, and then California, between 1845 and 1846, helped lead to the United States–Mexican war of 1846, in which Mexico was heavily overpowered by its much more developed, and heavily populated, neighbor (Zoraida Vázquez 2000). In more recent history, on the issue of the war in Iraq, for example, Mexico, together with Chile, held the view that the evidence of Iraq's weapons of mass destruction was inconclusive and recommended the continuation of weapons inspections rather than the use of force. This position led former President George W. Bush to refuse to take the Mexican president's phone calls and a rejection of the reopening of discussions regarding positive US immigration reform (Valenzuela 2005). Many Mexican families are dependent on revenues earned in the United States, with migratory work being a norm. A few years ago, however, the USA reviewed the transient nature of the US–Mexican border as not only a problem of illegal immigration, but also a security issue. In May 2005, former President George W. Bush instituted a new law permitting the building of a security fence along parts of the border and rendered it illegal for temporary migrant workers to drive in the USA without having a special permit (BBC 2005b). The profile of this issue has been heightened by Republicans' claims that "poor security on the Mexican border could be used by terrorist groups to move their members into the US" (BBC 2005b). It is under these circumstances that religious conversions to Islam are taking place.

## The arrival of Islam in Mexico

The circumstances of the arrival of Islam in Mexico are left to speculation since there is no firm documentation to confirm when the first Muslims came. The broader literature on the relationship between the slave trade and the wider Americas suggests that the first Muslims in the New World were brought over from Africa under slavery. Sylviane Diouf (1998) estimates that out of around 15 million Africans taken to the Americas, about 2.25–3 million were Muslim.

There is also the possibility that Muslims traveled over with the *conquistadores* or as a result of the Spanish conquest of Muslim Spain. In 711 CE Umayyad Muslims conquered the Kingdom of the Visigoths, an area comprising the majority of present-day Spain, and by 1200 CE 80 percent of Iberia's population was Muslim (Segal 2001). As Henry Charles Lea (1901) has pointed out, following the accomplishment of the *Reconquista*, on the Christian conquest of Granada in 1492 CE Iberian Muslims had the option to convert to Christianity or face expulsion. Some religious leaders, such as Fray Jayme Bleda, remained suspicious that the Muslim converts to Christianity were awaiting the aid of Moors and Turks in order to recapture the peninsula, and called for the annihilation of the Muslims of Spain as a consequence (Lea 1901). Such threats could have caused true Muslims to hide their identities and to pretend to be Christian in order to avoid massacre or expulsion. Seth Kunin (2001: 42) documents that Crypto-Jews in New Mexico claim descent from "the Jews forced to convert to Catholicism in Spain between 1390 and 1492," showing how the threat of forced conversion has led to the occultation of religious identity and migration.

The notion that Islam may have been present in Mexico for as long as Catholicism has received widespread support from the Muslim community. A historical novel set in the sixteenth century, *Un hereje y un musulmán* by Pascual Almazán (1962 [1870]), which has a Muslim as one of its chief characters, is often cited as proof of Islam's age-old presence in the country. This text is quoted regularly as though it were a primary source, even though it was written much later, in the nineteenth century.

It is not until the nineteenth century that we have any firm evidence regarding Muslim migration to Mexico, although even this does not permit us to build a comprehensive picture. Teresa Alfaro Velcamp (2002) rightly comments that post-revolutionary perceptions of ethnicity in Mexico have discouraged any focus on immigrants since they do not fit neatly into the tripartite model of a society composed of Spaniards, indigenous Mexicans, and the hybrid *mestizo*. More recent academic work has moved on to consider migration from the Middle Eastern region, with scholars such as Martha Díaz de Kuri and Lourdes Macluf (1995), Roberto Marín Guzmán (1997), Luz María Martínez Montiel (1992), Jorge Nacif Mina (1995), and Carmen Mercedes Páez Oropeza (1984) having examined migration from the Lebanon, and with Doris Musalem Rahal (1997), María Elena Ota Mishima (1997), and Zidane Zeraoui (1997) having moved on to consider Palestinian and Arab immigration more broadly. Alfaro Velcamp's (2007) new work is the most thorough study of Muslim immigration to Mexico to date.

Mexico's openness to immigration stems from the Immigration and Naturalization Law of 1886, created under Porfiro Díaz, which automatically naturalized property owners. While immigrants suffered some torment, and in some cases murderous violence, from the nationalism evoked during the Mexican Revolution of 1910, it was not until 1922 that immigration law was tightened and immigration fees raised dramatically for "Chinese and Negroes" (Wood 1922, quoted in Alfaro Velcamp 2002: 282). This situation barely changed until World War II had passed, when the government realized that a certain amount of immigration would be beneficial to national development.

There is something of a consensus that the majority of Mexico's first Muslims came as immigrants from the Greater Syria area of the Ottoman Empire, as of the late nineteenth century. Alfaro Velcamp (2002) observes that of 8,240 Arab immigrants coming to Mexico between 1878 and 1951, 343 were Muslim, constituting a little over 4 percent. Over half of these are documented as having arrived during the five-year period from 1922 to 1927. Increased immigration in the second half of the last century saw the population rise and this increase in immigration has been complemented by a number of conversions to the religion.

Abdullah (Gregory) Weston, brother of Omar Weston, the founder of the Islamic Cultural Center of Mexico (el Centro Cultural Islamico de México, or CCIM), a Sunni organization also known as the Muslim Center de México (MCM), explains that a man called Yasin Ramirez is thought to have been Islam's first Mexican convert:

As far as I know he was the first community in Mexico. He was a convert, he was about fifty years old in 1990, and he had been a Muslim for ten years. He was a bit of a Sufi. And he used to teach here; he used to have a small mosque here, in Mexico City, and there was a committee of about ten people.

Abdullah, a Sunni Muslim with empathy for Shi'i Islam, explained how he ceased to worship with this group when he discovered it to consist of "Qadiyanis," or Ahmadiyya people, who he saw as unorthodox Muslims for not accepting Mohammad as the Seal of the Prophets, and expressed his remorse that Yasin "died in unorthodox Islam."

It is thought that the Murabitun Sufis came to carry out missionary work in Mexico in the mid-1990s, which is about the same time that the Centro Cultural Islamico de México was founded, in 1994, which is dedicated to calling native Mexicans to Sunni Islam. Since this time, proselytism has been active.

## Mexico's Muslim population

In 1986 Mohamed Ali Kettani estimated that there were approximately 15,000 Muslims in Mexico (Kettani 1986). The *World Christian Encyclopaedia* upped this estimate to 39,000 in the year 2000, based on the calculations of Mohammad Bin Abdullah Noor (Barrett 1982). Some figures as high as 318,608 have been bandied about (Wikipedia 2007); however, there are no known sources to substantiate such a high level, albeit Mexico's vast population would not seem to prohibit such a statistic, at about 0.3 percent of the total population, yet the census from the year 2000 clearly counters this claim. In 2005, the government released more detailed statistics on the religious composition of Mexico based on data from the year 2000 census and population studies. This revealed that there were 1,421 Muslims recorded as living in Mexico at this time (INEGI 2005). This figure more than doubled over the ten-year period to 2010, with there now being 3,760 Muslims in the country according to official statistics (INEGI 2011b). While these statistics stem from a reliable source, we cannot be entirely certain about how dependable they are, since people may have reasons for wishing to hide their religious identity, they may not participate in these official data-gathering exercises, relations who report such data may not acknowledge their family members' religious conversion, and the population is not static due to the regular inward and outward flow of migrants; these factors all make the official figures questionable. It was reported that there had been over 500 conversions to Islam in Mexico City for one religious community alone by 2003 (MCM 2003), and the Pew Forum on Religion and Public Life (2009) calculated that there were approximately 110,000 Muslims in Mexico in 2009, although issued a warning on the reliability of the data.

## Divergent communities

In 2002 Teresa Alfaro Velcamp carried out a cursory study of the Mexican Muslim population in English. Recent writings by Mexican researchers have complimented these findings (Ismu Kusumo 2004; Sanchez García 2004). The Muslim community is composed of a mixture of immigrants, descendants of immigrants, diplomats, and converts, although these groupings are not entirely discrete, with some individuals falling into more than one of these categories. There are Sufi and Sunni communities present in Mexico City, a group of Shi'i immigrants from Lebanon in Torreón, an active Shi'i community in the northern state of Chihuahua, some small Sunni Muslim groups in Zacatecas and Monterrey, and some Muslim medical students in

Guadalajara. There are also converts to Islam in Chiapas, Aguas Calientes, Morelia, Morelos, Puebla, and Veracruz, where small communities exist.

Mexico City shows some of the religious diversity to Islam that we might expect from a capital. Natascha Garvin (2005) comments on the presence of Nur Ashki Jerrahi Sufis, informing us that they are said to mix feminism with New Age mysticism in a relatively unorthodox form of Islam. Alfaro Velcamp (2002) points to the presence of Baha'i practitioners, and also "Qadiyanis." She also describes her attendance at a gathering of the Halveti-Jerrahi Order of Dervishes, in Colonia Roma, and states that the twenty to thirty people present were mainly women of European appearance, commenting:

> The service began at around eight in the evening and lasted until midnight, with breaks to eat and smoke cigarettes. The group differed from [a Sunni organization] not only in its predominantly female constituency but in what seemed to be its much more tolerant interpretation of Islam. As was expected, its prayer service had a more mystical feel than the Sunni service I attended, which was more structured and formal.
>
> *(Alfaro Velcamp 2002: 288)*

The Halveti-Jerrahi Order of Dervishes describe themselves as a traditional Sufi Muslim order and are international in scope, with branches in Western and central Europe, Latin America, and the United States (Jerrahi.org 2005).

Back in 2002, the Iranian Embassy coordinated meetings and events for Shi'i Muslims and diplomats in Mexico City. Now they refer worshippers to an educational center and prayer hall in Polanco that is not exclusively Shi'i (el Centro Educativo de la Comunidad Musulmana, CECM). They have held occasional conferences on Islam and have sponsored annual book fairs. The employees of the embassies of a number of Muslim countries often work with CCIM, which actively propagates the Muslim message and now operates a missionary program called "DawAmigo."

CCIM is slowly building a mosque in Mexico City and has an educational and recreational center in Tequesquitengo in the state of Morelos. The latter site has a resourceful library, a mosque area, living accommodation, hotel accommodation for raising capital, and a swimming pool. CCIM no longer rents the house from the Saudi Arabian Embassy as it was doing at the time of Alfaro Velcamp's (2002) study, but most Muslims attending the CCIM's prayer services are still male and the services are quite structured and formal. More recently, they opened a *da'wa* office in Coyoácan in Mexico City, near to the National University, UNAM, where they discuss Islam, hand out promotional literature, observe the five daily prayers, and sell goods imported from Muslim countries. This office has large ground-floor display windows facing out onto a main road very close to the Miguel Angel Quevedo metro station, and it attracts a number of curious passersby with its Arab curios and its posters about the religion.

The CCIM has ten key objectives: to facilitate prayer; to educate about Islam; to teach Arabic; to nurture Muslim children; to organize social events; to provide scholarships to Islamic universities; to translate and publish works on Islam; to disseminate Muslim literature from elsewhere in the world; to establish *musalla*s (prayer halls); and to fundraise. A number of community members have been to study at Medina in Saudi Arabia or at al-Azhar University in Egypt. Public education about Islam has taken a number of forms, including handing out leaflets to passersby; making speeches on the metro; praying in public spaces; operating shops; "flashing" prominent signs at media-concentrated events; and traveling to other cities to speak about Islam. Since Alfaro Velcamp (2002) wrote, the building of Dar es Salaam, its educational and recreational center next to Lake Tequesquitengo in Morelos, has been completed and CCIM has helped to establish *musalla*s in Guadalajara and Chiapas, in addition to Mexico City. They have also certified establishments preparing *halal* (permitted) food, which raised funds for a number of early *da'wa* (missionary) projects. They presently produce a journal on Islam in Spanish (*islamentuidioma*), have a comprehensive website with a chat room facility, and coordinate a discussion list on yahoo.com.mx. The group attracts converts from all over the Mexican nation via the internet, in addition to those who approach them, or whom they approach, in person. Its director, Omar (Mark) Weston, a former junior waterskiing champion, was born in the UK in 1968 and was raised in Mexico, having converted to Islam at the central mosque in Orlando, Florida in 1988.

Omitted from Alfaro Velcamp's original study are the Salafi center, run by a convert named Mohammad Abdullah Ruíz, and the educational center and prayer hall in the district of Polanco (the CECM). Only a handful of converts belong to the Salafi group, and the majority of the city's Sunni Muslims (of whichever affiliation) attend Friday prayers at the prayer hall in Polanco. This educational center admits to being primarily Sunni when asked, although it is visited by Muslims of varying traditions within the faith. Often there are thirty to eighty people in attendance. Men and women are segregated, the men praying on the first floor while the women congregate to the rear of the building downstairs. The *khutbah* (or sermon) is delivered in Arabic and then Spanish. There are washing facilities for *wudu'* (ritual ablutions) and there is a kitchen area, where a meal is prepared for all those in attendance at Friday prayers. There are some deep divisions between the leaders of these competing communities, many of whom have worked together at some point in the past, usually in fundraising, from which their competition principally stems (Lindley-Highfield 2008).

All three of the CCIM, the educational center in Polanco, and the Salafi center operate on a national scale, seeking to represent Islam in Mexico. They compete in terms of attracting converts to Islam in addition to their sourcing of financial support for the Muslim community from abroad. CCIM has had historical ties with Saudi Arabia and more recently has benefited from assistance from Muslims in Britain and Kuwait. The CECM educational center in Polanco is connected most strongly with Syria and Pakistan. The Salafi center is thought to be funded independently, although indubitably has Saudi connections.

Outside of Mexico City, where there is the largest concentration of Muslims, the second most substantial communities may be found in Torreón and Chiapas. More recent waves of immigration have come from Syria and the Lebanon, and there is now a strong group of Shi'i Muslims in Torreón, in northern Mexico, from these parts. Those from the first generation of these immigrants have retained a large amount of Lebanese culture and of their Islamic faith. They tend to know Arabic and are thus able to read the Qur'an. Most have managed to marry endogamously, and some even to patrilineal parallel cousins. The second generation, however, have intermarried more widely with Catholic Mexicans and, even though their spouses are unlikely to practice their faith, a Muslim marital setting has been the norm. Many are unable to read Arabic and thus approach the Qur'an in translation. Dietary prescriptions are followed by almost all, although Arabic food in particular is, in some cases, eaten only occasionally. With regard to worship, some of the group choose to pray privately at home, whereas others attend Torreón's Shi'i mosque, Suraya, which was constructed in 1989 as a memorial to the daughter of a wealthy merchant family who was killed tragically in a car accident. These Shi'i Muslims "do not appear to be actively reaching out" in so far as proselytism is concerned and produce literature for their community's sole use (Alfaro Velcamp 2002). Alfaro Velcamp (2002) asserts that this group cannot be considered *fanaticos*, or fundamentalists, considering their intermarriage into Mexican society and wider integration into the community.

In addition to those Chiapanec converts affiliated with the Centro Cultural Islamico de México, there is a Sufi group in Chiapas which belongs to the worldwide Murabitun movement (Garvin 2005). Marco Klahr (2002) reveals that a Spanish missionary, named Mohammad Nafia, came to Mexico not long after the *Zapatista* uprising of 1994 and tried, without much success, to convert EZLN members (a revolutionary group). It was thought that these revolutionaries, who fight for the rights of indigenous peoples, might relate well to the ethos of this particular brand of Islam, yet the dialogue was inconclusive. He did, however, have success with the leader of a Protestant organization who – together with his followers – had been driven out of his home in San Juan Chamula in Chiapas because of his Protestant conversion. The subsequent conversion of this group to Islam laid the foundations of what is now said to be a community of some 200 members, made up of a mixture of Tzotzil and Tzeltal Maya Indians, "*mestizos,*" other Latin Americans, and Spanish immigrants (Garvin 2005). The group now lives in a self-contained commune in the impoverished outskirts of San Cristobal de las Casas, and they have their own Islamic "school" and kindergarten, and skills workshops where they can learn carpentry and tailoring. Although it is mentioned that there are women and children within this community, its precise gender composition remains unconfirmed. Garvin (2005) has suggested that the people of Chiapas are the most open to other religions, since official statistics reveal it to be Mexico's most religiously plural state, yet stories such as that of the Protestant who was run out of his home leave this "openness" in question. Some of this religious plurality may come from religious mobility, however, where people chop and change religion, which could lead to fluctuating community populations.

The Murabitun movement has members in Africa, Australia, Europe, Southeast and Central Asia, and the United States, having originally been set up in the UK by a Scotsman, Ian Dallas, who is now known as Shaykh Abd al-Qadir as-Sufi al-Murabit. The group belongs to the Darqawi order, sympathetic to Sunni Islam, which was established in Morocco in the late eighteenth century and stresses the relationship between Islam and the cultural heritage of the West. Garvin (2005) relays that the group has been associated with Nazism and Islamic fundamentalism and that they are prone to target heavily politicized areas such as Chiapas. She also repeats the allegations that Mohammad Nafia has been imprisoned in the past for Islamist activities and that weapons were offered to Zapatistas on the condition that they converted to Murabitun Islam (Garvin 2005). While the strength of the source for the linking of the Murabitun movement to Nazism appears tenuous (a disgruntled former member of the group), the group's *shaykh is* publicly critical of Western hegemony, positivist science, and capitalism, as Garvin suggests. Garvin (2005) echoes heavy criticisms of the radicalism of this group's leader; however, the views of Murabitun Sufis may be broader than the particular depiction Garvin propagates.

## Perceptions of Islam within Mexico

Teresa Alfaro Velcamp (2002: 278) labels the "*turco*" stereotype as "perhaps [Mexican Muslims'] biggest challenge." Based upon an article by Ignacio Klich and Jeffrey Lesser (1996) and witnessed in the *telenovela*, or soap opera, *El privilegio de amar* on TV Azteca, which ran from September 1998 to February 1999, Alfaro Velcamp discerns that this stereotype "is associated with Muslims throughout Latin America." She explains:

> In a recent episode of a popular Mexican *telenovela* (soap opera), for example, the heroine whispers to her friends, "The Turk is cheap." The Arab merchant has a large hooked nose and sports a comical bushy moustache with the ends twisted up. While this character is not

particularly important to the storyline, he does make an appearance, with his stereotypical features, trying to swindle these Mexican women.

*(Alfaro Velcamp 2002: 278)*

Alfaro Velcamp describes this stereotype as "inextricably linked to the issue of Muslim identity" (Alfaro Velcamp 2002: 279). More recently, many contemporary Mexicans do not make this connection, which is perhaps more of an indication of how radically the perception of Muslims has changed in Mexico rather than any statement as to the invalidity of the particular association at this earlier date. Since Alfaro Velcamp's article was written (although before it was published), the colossal event of the destruction of the Twin Towers in New York has taken place, 9/11, which has totally transformed the general associations with Muslim identity. Following on from this, a number of derogatory news headlines have been published about the presence of Muslims in Mexico; for example: "Radical Islamic Groups Present in Mexico" (Jimenez Caliz 2003) and "Chiapas: Islamism and Family Breakdown" (Yahoo! Noticias 2004). In 2005 Gaspar Morquecho published an article in the National University, UNAM's newspaper on "Gender Equality in Speech, Traditional Servitude in Reality," in which he characterized the Murabitun Sufi group in Chiapas through its "authoritarianism, fidelity, subordination, violence, obedience, growth and splits, revolt, disobedience" (Morquecho 2005). The article reached some notional balance by painting the local Sunni community, to which some of the Sufis had "defected," in a more positive light.

In the environs of the Muslim community at their educational and recreational center in Tequesquitengo, the local community's perception of the Muslims can be ascertained by the nickname attributed to the property: "the Taliban's house" (*la casa de los Talibanes*). This "negative" depiction of Muslims is echoed by a primary school teacher who had converted to Islam, who states that the biggest stereotype with which he has been confronted is the association with "terrorism and Bin Laden."

H.G. Reza (2005), writing in the *Los Angeles Times*, quotes Marta Khadija Ramirez, who encountered Islam at a British school: "Islam was unknown in Mexico then. It wasn't easy for my family to accept my decision." Because Mexico's Muslim community is small, it has to struggle to communicate exactly what Islam is about, where perceptions of what it is to be a Muslim are created more forcefully via television and the media. It is clear that there has been a shift in the news-driven perception of Muslims in Mexico since the attacks on the World Trade Center, which is partially fueled, both positively and negatively, by Mexico's proximity to the United States. Clearly, Muslim identity in Mexico is not perceived apolitically.

## Perceptions of Islam in Mexico from the outside

The advent of Islam in Mexico has received the greatest attention in the media of the United States, far beyond the scholarly attention it has received, which has led to the transmission of the news on a global scale. A version of a US news article has, for example, been reproduced in the German newspaper *Der Spiegel* (Glüsing 2005). A brief survey of some of the articles communicates how the phenomenon has been received.

An Associated Press (2002) report entitled "Official Says Mexico Will Expel Some Islamic Missionaries" admitted that the action "was apparently based on the alleged violation of immigration laws, not terrorism concerns," yet repeated a Mexican commentator's remarks that "Authorities began investigating the group, which is linked to the Morocco-based Murabitun World Movement, following the Sept. 11 terrorist attacks." Jan McGirk (2002) wrote, in the *San Antonio Current*, "Radical Islam takes root in Chiapas" beginning "In a volatile corner of southern Mexico ... ." Susana Hayward and Janet Schwartz (2003) described the phenomenon as a "battle for converts." Such language, focusing on issues of conflict, reinforces an association of Muslims with violence. In its extreme, such an association can reinforce extreme right-wing prejudices, as responses to a *Houston Chronicle* article, entitled "Islam Taking Root in Southern Mexico," posted to FreeRepublic.com demonstrate. The following is an example of one of the posts:

> Make no mistake, Islam is attempting a full blown invasion of North America. Apparently they see south america is our "soft underbelly" and the abject poverty and misery of these people as fertile breeding ground for their propaganda, false promises and anti-America hate.
>
> *(FreeRepublic.com 2007)*

Interestingly, as Derek Copold (2001) has pointed out critically, some writers have used Mexico as an analogy for Palestine in comparing how America would act if it were attacked by Mexicans as a mode of justifying the Israeli position. Copold quotes Russell Smith: "if Mexican militants were lobbing shells across the border and sent suicide bombers to discos in Los Angeles, the US would immediately act." Copold finds a similar comparison drawn by Jonah Goldberg:

> A Mexican suicide bomber walked into a pizza restaurant in a Santa Fe, N.M. mall this morning, killing at least 15 people, mostly children. Up to a hundred others were wounded ... Militia in Tijuana, Mexico, fired rocket grenades into downtown San Diego, killing 20, wounding 50 and, once again, snarling morning traffic.
>
> *(Copold 2001)*

These jocular attempts to authenticate the Israeli position do little to dampen any fears that the presence of "radical" Muslims in Mexico would be detrimental to the US–Mexico border issue. These particular slants on the issue tend to dominate the output of the media in the American Southwest, where the readership is in closer proximity to the border.

In contrast to this negative focus, North America's Hispanic Muslim groups have responded to the advent of Islam in Mexico very positively. Michelle al-Nasr (2002) writes of "a monotheistic revolution," celebrating that "people are embracing Islam by the thousands jettisoning the Catholicism imposed upon their ancestors in Spain." In Shamim A. Siddiqi's *The Dawah Program*, a guide for Muslims who are to carry out missionary activity, he points to the Hispanic people's receptivity to Islam:

> It has been noted through Dawah efforts in this community that very often [Spanish-speaking people] are found akin to Islam. They express less indifference to Islam and the Da'ee [the individual carrying out missionary work] in comparison with other Christian communities. It is easy to talk with them with reference to their Spanish origin and its past Islamic culture, the evidences of which are still very much visible in Spain a country they fondly relate to. Many of them, I have found, are in search of literature on Islam in the Spanish language. Many a time when they saw the Qur'an in Spanish in our hands or on display on the table at marketplaces, they rushed to it with reverence. Some of them held it with tears in their eyes. In view of this, Spanish-speaking people should be given special attention by the Islamic Movement in the American perspective.
>
> *(Siddiqi 1993: 95)*

This special attention is increasingly present in Mexico.

The broader Muslim world has acknowledged the potential for Islam in Mexico and also the economic needs of the Mexican people. As a consequence, Muslim individuals and organizations have supported Muslim missionary activities in Mexico morally, logistically, and financially. For example, the University of Cambridge's Muslim Community Services group hosted Omar Weston, Director of CCIM, on November 15, 2003 for a lecture and video presentation on Islam in Mexico to promote CCIM's work and to raise funds for the Mexican Muslim community. These changes taking place in Mexico need to be understood in the context of broader transformations occurring around the world, with which the Mexican situation is inextricably linked.

## Islam in Mexico in relation to the wider global situation

Alfaro Velcamp (2002) acknowledges the identification of Mexican Muslims with the wider Islamic world and insightfully notes the arrival of a more pan-American Muslim consciousness. A foundation for this is present in the historical ties between Latin America and Muslim Spain. Hisham Aidi (2003) points to an affinity that has existed between the Latin American states and the Arab region:

> Throughout the past century, particularly during the Cold War, Latin American leaders from Cuba's Fidel Castro to Argentina's Juan Peron would express support for Arab political causes, and call for Arab–Latin solidarity in the face of imperial domination, often highlighting cultural links to the Arab world through Moorish Spain. Castro, in particular, made a philosophy of pan-Arab pan-Africanism central to his regime's ideology and policy initiatives. In his famous 1959 speech on race, the *jefe maximo* underlined Cuba's African and Moorish origins. "We all have lighter or darker skin. Lighter skin implies descent from Spaniards who themselves were colonized by the Moors that came from Africa. Those who are more or less dark-skinned came directly from Africa. Moreover, nobody can consider himself as being of pure, much less superior, race."
>
> *(Aidi 2003)*

Venezuela's Hugo Chavez also called on his people to "return to their Arab roots" in an attempt to gather up support from Venezuela's *mestizo* and black majority to act against the white Bush administration's alleged support for a coup against him (Aidi 2003). Such statements attest to cross-cultural commonalities, which add to a favorable perception of Islam for some people in Latin America.

A number of the factors attracting Muslim immigrants to Mexico, and that also draw native Mexicans into contact with Islam, are the hallmarks of secularization: industrialization, urbanization, rationalization, bureaucratization, and societalization (Wilson 1966). While globalization and the presence of Islam in Mexico facilitate the growth of the religion in this region, as Bowman et al. (2001: 73) narrate, "Wilson sees the increasing number of new faiths as part of the secularisation process." In such circumstances, we might enquire if the advent of religious pluralism in Mexico will begin to affect the social significance of religion in Mexicans' everyday lives.

With Islam's historic connection with Spain and its alternative perspective to a white-Western-dominated discourse, the divergent Muslim communities of Mexico call for our attention, while a new chapter of Mexico's history is unraveled. It is clear that a Muslim identity carries a number of strong symbolic associations with other factors in Mexican society and there is clearly a politics to these.

## Belize

Nunez (2010) looks to the 1920s and 1930s for the arrival of Muslims in Belize, citing the example of Arab males who came to the then British Honduras for trade purposes and who married local British Honduran Christian women. It was a condition of marriage at that time that the offspring of the union received a Christian education, so these settlers were integrated into the Christian-majority culture of the country. Nevertheless, Muslim names persisted in families where there was later no known Muslim relative as a consequence, leaving Islamic cultural markers within Belizean society.

After this initial migration, Islam in Belize grew particularly during the late twentieth century through the popularity of the teachings of Elijah Mohammad of the Nation of Islam. Visits from prominent Muslims such as Elijah Mohammad's son, Wallace Deen Mohammad, and the boxer Mohammad Ali encouraged the adoption of the faith. The independence movement of the 1960s and 1970s saw a rise in black nationalism through organizations such as the United Black Association for Development, and the Nation of Islam gained prominence in the country owing to an identification with the teachings and experience of the Nation's prominent members, such as Malcolm X. The Nation was led in Belize by Charles Eagan, who adopted the name Charles X after encountering the teachings of the Nation of Islam whilst in prison in the USA. Initially, the government was suspicious of the Muslim group's activities, to the extent that one of their meetings was disbanded in 1962; however, the government later eased its position, allowing Wallace Deen Mohammad's visit of 1978, in which same year an organization called the Islamic Mission of Belize came into being and received official governmental recognition.

Islam in Belize matched to some degree the trajectory of the Nation of Islam, so when the Nation returned to core Islamic beliefs, such as the equality of the races (having previously seen whites as inferior in terms of their perceived inherent evil under Elijah Mohammad), the Muslims of Belize moved on to more orthodox Islamic positions. The Islamic Mission has a pan-Islamic focus, seeing the *umma*, or Muslim people, as a single community and avoiding the age-old divisions between different factions of the faith, such as can exist between Sunni and Shi'i Islam.

During the 1970s the country's first private Islamic schools were founded. In 1979, the first of these was assessed as entitled to governmental aid (Nunez 2010), providing an elementary education in addition to supporting their spiritual needs. Pupils do not need to be Muslims to attend despite the Islamic character of the school.

Muslims from Belize visited the embassies of a number of Middle Eastern countries in Mexico City in the 1980s with the intention of creating trade links between Belize and the countries. In response to this contact, the Iranian Embassy granted financial aid to help the group to secure part of a 350 acre site leased from the government by the Mission in the Jannahville area of Belize City to provide a Muslim quarter in which they could combine homes, occupations, and education in a self-sufficient community. Other aid came in the form of security fencing for the community's school. Islam now has an observable presence in the country. It is said that the community owes its public awareness in Belize to the women of the community, who openly embrace Islamic dress.

## Costa Rica

The Muslims of Costa Rica are composed of both religious converts, most of whom are from Costa Rica and some of whom are from Colombia, and people who have emigrated from Palestine, the Lebanon, Egypt, Libya, Iran, Iraq, Morocco, Algeria, Syria, India, and Pakistan, although numbers remain small. In an interview of 2008, Dr. Abdulfatah Sasa Mahmoud, president of the Centro Islámico de Costa Rica, estimated that there were approximately 500 Muslims in the country (Leff 2008). Dr. Mahmoud describes Costa Rica as a hospitable environment for Muslims, with their having been no objections to their establishment of a place of worship for the community (Leff 2008), although Espinoza (2006) reports on misconceptions and negative stereotypes in the community principally down to media representations.

While some Costa Ricans have chosen to adopt Islam in their own country, some female Costa Rican immigrants have adopted the tradition in the USA too. Yvonne Haddad (cited in Martin 2008) explains that while Islam may restrict the liberty of converts more than their previous religion did, it brings them greater respect than they otherwise enjoyed, with Islamic values matching their Latin American ideals better, such as the status of a woman as wife and mother.

In addition to the Centro Islámico de Costa Rica, in the country's capital, San José, there is an organization known as the Centro Cultural Musulmán de Costa Rica, which also has its own place of worship, and a Tablighi Jama'at missionary group called al-Markaz in Desampardos, which actively promotes Islam, particularly amongst those who would benefit from a reformed lifestyle. Other Muslims reside in the Alajuela city region.

## El Salvador

While there is possible evidence that there was a Muslim in El Salvador as early as 1619 through the identification of someone as a Moor in inquisitor proceedings (Escalante and Daura Molina 2001), Marín Guzmán (2000) attributes the arrival of Islam in El Salvador to migration from the Lebanon, Syria, and Palestine in the early 1900s; however, the most prominent members of El Salvadorian society are Christian rather than Muslim immigrants, and the presence of Islam is thought to be sparse since there has not been much promotion of the faith in the country to date. There is, however, a Shi'i group operating the Fátimah Az-Zahra center, which has been circulating an Islamic magazine and offering the country's sole Muslim library over the past eight years. The Pew Forum on Religion and Public Life (2009) gives an estimated population of 2,000 Muslims in El Salvador in 2009.

The first Muslim community to establish a place of worship was the Sunni Centro Islámico Árabe Salvadoreño, which was established in San Salvador in 1994. Members of this organization make public appearances to dispel inaccurate portrayals of Islam and to try to increase popular awareness. A third mosque was founded in the capital in 2007.

## Guatemala

Like other Central American countries, Guatemala has also had its flow of immigrants from Palestine. The community is active and offers classes on Islam to interested parties. Their mosque, Mezquita Al Dawah Islámica, is not the sole place of worship for Muslims in the country; there is also an Ahmadiyya Muslim group, who believe that, although Mohammad was the last prophet to receive the divine laws, other prophets have followed and will follow him; a position which some Muslims consider to be unorthodox. The Guatemalan Muslim population was estimated to be approximately 1,000 in 2009 (Pew Forum on Religion and Public Life 2009).

## Honduras

The Pew Forum on Religion and Public Life (2009) identifies the Muslim population of Honduras as being about 11,000 in 2009. Arab immigration to Honduras is thought to have commenced at the tail end of the nineteenth century and to have carried on ever since. While the minority of these immigrants have been Muslims, the proportion of Arab immigrants to Honduras is higher than anywhere else in Central America, and numerically, rather than proportionately, the population size is significant. Two principal Islamic religious centers exist, the Centro Islámico de Honduras in San Pedro Sula and the Comunidad Islámica de Honduras in Cortés.

## Nicaragua

Differing strands of the Muslim faith compete in representing their interests in Nicaragua. This was seen in 2007 when the Sunni leader of the Islamic Cultural Center in Managua was ousted, to be replaced by a Shi'i figurehead, as the balance of Shi'i Muslims increased in the center (Embassy of the United States Managua Nicaragua 2007). Most of Nicaragua's Shi'i immigration hails from Iran, and this community has established the Centro Cultural Islámico Nicaragüense as an outreach organization to help to draw people to Islam.

In terms of overall immigration, however, a greater number of Muslims have come from Palestine, beginning in the late nineteenth and early twentieth centuries. The Pew Forum on Religion and Public Life (2009) places the estimated Muslim population of Nicaragua at 1,000 Muslims in 2009, which is slightly less than the US government's approximation of 1,200–1,500 people in 2007. The principal place of worship and cultural center is the Asociación Cultural Nicaragüense-Islámica. The Islamic Cultural Center, Managua, offers a substantial mosque, which accommodates Muslims from the differing sections of the faith.

## Panama

The Pew Forum on Religion and Public Life (2009) estimates that the number of Muslims in Panama stood at 24,000 in 2009. At 0.7 percent of the country's population, this is perhaps the highest proportion of Muslims in a Central American country, albeit the reliability of all the statistics is questionable. Immigrants to Panama came from India, Pakistan, and the Lebanon, amongst other places, particularly during the twentieth century. Despite this more recent influx, Westerlund and Svanberg (1999) attribute to Panama the earliest arrival of Muslims to the Central American region, in 1552. Conversions, or reversions as they are referred to in Islam, occurred in the late twentieth century, particularly during the 1970s, when the ideas of the Nation of Islam gained prominence in the country.

Community groups for Muslims have existed in Panama for a longer period than in the rest of Central America. The Indo-Pakistani Muslim Society, of Sunni persuasion, later known as the Panama Muslim Mission, was established at the close of the 1920s. In the present day, there are now four places of worship in Panama that Muslims can attend.

As the history of colonial Mexico began with a shipwreck, so does the narrative of the advent of Islam in Panama. The Mandinka, or Malinke, were an African tribe who were thought to practice Islam. Hundreds of their number were transported from West Africa to the Americas by Spanish colonialists with the intention that they would work in their copper mines. They were shipwrecked and almost 500 of their number swam for the shore, arriving in Panama. The Mandinka sought someone to represent them in the face of their slavery and nominated a man called Bayano. Bayano led a revolt of the Mandinka, which ultimately saw him exiled to Spain for the remainder of his life. It is suggested that the alleged early presence of Islam in Panama died with him. The Muslim community of Panama in the present day points to this narrative as an indication that Islam is part of Panama's past and that some Panamanians are possibly descended from Muslims themselves, which is an argument that may be employed when someone approaches the faith.

## Conclusion

The origins of Islam in Latin America are at least partially lost in the mists of time; however, myths perpetuate about the antiquity of the religion's presence in the region. The connection with Moorish Spain and the Spanish colonization of the Americas contribute to the perception that Islam may have been in the context for as long as Catholicism has been. More recent waves of immigration are more clearly documented and illustrate how religious diversity has developed through the movement of peoples to the New World. The presence of Islam in Mexico and Central America has provided the people of the region with an opportunity to explore their spirituality further and, for some, it has presented a response to marginalization and an opportunity to respond.

Although Mexico is officially a secular state, Roman Catholicism is heavily intertwined with its lived culture. Through the diversification that the presence of other religious traditions brings, religious pluralism has grown in the country, seemingly symbolizing a movement to a more rationalized approach to religion whereby the individual has the agency to adopt the religion that best fits. In this context, Islam fits well, and it seems that the position of the marginalized is respected within this religious tradition to the extent that the religion acts as a liberating force, on an ideological level at the very least.

The development of Islam in the Latin American region has only recently captured the attention and scrutiny of scholars and there is room for much work to be done to shed further light on this engaging environment of religious change.

## Note

I am grateful to the UK's Economic and Social Research Council for providing the funding that facilitated this research. In addition to a review of the literature, this work is based on a prolonged period of anthropological research spent living with the Muslim community in Mexico over a thirteen-month period from 2006 to 2007.

## Bibliography

Aidi, H. (2003) "Let Us Be Moors: Islam, Race and 'Connected Histories'," *Middle East Report* 229: 42–53.
al-Nasr, M. (2002) "Mexico Discovers Islam: A New Generation of Muslims Is Introducing Islam to Mexicans," Islam Awareness, www.hispanicmuslims.com/articles/other/mexico.html (accessed May 28, 2005).
Alfaro Velcamp, T. (2002) "Mexican Muslims in the Twentieth Century: Challenging Stereotypes and Negotiating Space," in Haddad, Y.Y. (ed.) *Muslims in the West: From Sejourners to Citizens*, Oxford: Oxford University Press, pp. 278–309.
——(2007) *So Far from Allah, So Close to Mexico: Middle Eastern Immigrants in Modern Mexico*, Austin: University of Texas Press.
Almazán, P. (1962 [1870]) *Un hereje y un musulman*, Porrúa: Colección de Escritores Mexicanos.
Associated Press (2002) "Official Says Mexico Will Expel Some Islamic Missionaries," New Jersey AP News, June 16, www.islamawareness.net/LatinAmerica/official.html (accessed July 23, 2012).
Barrett, D. (ed.) (1982) *The World Christian Encyclopedia: A Comparative Survey of Churches and Religions in the Modern World*, New York: Oxford University Press.
BBC (British Broadcasting Corporation) (2005a) "Country profile: Mexico," June 2, news.bbc.co.uk/1/hi/world/americas/country_profiles/1205074.stm (accessed August 7, 2005).
——(2005b) "New US Migration Laws Vex Mexico," May 13, news.bbc.co.uk/1/hi/world/americas/4544699.stm (accessed August 7, 2005).

Benjamin, T. (1989) *A Rich Land, a Poor People: Politics and Society in Modern Chiapas*, Albuquerque: University of New Mexico Press.

Bowman, M., Herbert, D., and Mumm, S. (2001) *AD317: Religion Today: Tradition, Modernity & Change: Course Conclusion*, Milton Keynes: Open University.

Cahn, P.S. (2003) *All Religions Are Good in Tzintzuntzan: Evangelicals in Catholic Mexico*, Austin: University of Texas Press.

Copold, D. (2001) "Palestinians Are Not Mexicans and Israel Is Not America," *Houston Review*, August 19.

Díaz de Kuri, M. and Macluf, L. (1995) *De Líbano a México: Crónica de un pueblo emigrante*, Mexico: Gráfica, Creatividad y Diseño.

Diouf, S. (1998) *Servants of Allah: African Muslims Enslaved in the Americas*, New York: New York University Press.

Embassy of the United States Managua Nicaragua (2007) "International Religious Freedom – Nicaragua 2007," nicaragua.usembassy.gov/religious_2007.html (accessed July 4, 2012).

Escalante, P. and Daura Molina, A.R. (2001) *Sobre Moros y Cristianos, y otros Arabismos en El Salvador*, San Salvador: Embajada de España en El Salvador y Agencia Española de Cooperación Internacional.

Espinoza, A. (2006) "La nuestra es una religión de paz," *Al Día*, October 1, www.aldia.cr/ad_ee/2006/octubre/01/nacionales844191.html (accessed June 7, 2011).

Forbes.com (2012) "The World's Billionaires," Forbes.com, www.forbes.com/billionaires/ (accessed August 1, 2012).

FreeRepublic.com (2007) "Islam Is Taking Root in Southern Mexico: 300 Evangelical Christians Have Converted to Islam," FreeRepublic.com, www.freerepublic.com/focus/news/705170/posts (accessed January 20, 2008).

Froehling, O. (1997) "The Cyberspace 'War of Ink and Internet' in Chiapas, Mexico," *Geographical Review* 87(2): 291–307.

Garvin, N. (2005) "Conversion and Conflict: Muslims in Mexico," *ISIM (International Institute for the Study of Islam in the Modern World) Review* 15(2): 18–19.

Glüsing, J. (2005) "Islam Is Gaining a Foothold in Chiapas," *Der Spiegel*, May 28, www.spiegel.de/international/spiegel/0,1518,358223,00.html (accessed November 3, 2005).

Hayward, S. and Schwartz, J. (2003) "In Chiapas, Missionaries Battle for Converts," Knight Ridder Washington Bureau, June 24, www.gomaya.com/glyph/archives/000592.html (accessed June 12, 2012).

INEGI (Instituto Nacional de Estadística Geografía e Informática) (2005) "La diversidad religiosa en México," Mexico: INEGI, www.inegi.org.mx/prod_serv/contenidos/espanol/bvinegi/productos/integracion/sociodemografico/religion/div_rel.pdf (accessed July 4, 2012).

——(2011a) "Censo de Población y Vivienda 2010: Estados Unidos Mexicanos," Mexico: INEGI, www3.inegi.org.mx/sistemas/mexicocifras/default.aspx?src=487 (accessed July 4, 2012).

——(2011b) "Panorama de las Religions en México 2010," Mexico: INEGI, www.inegi.org.mx/prod_serv/contenidos/espanol/bvinegi/productos/censos/poblacion/2010/panora_religion/religiones_2010.pdf (accessed July 4, 2012).

Ismu Kusumo, F. (2004) "El Islam en el México contemporáneo," unpublished dissertation, Mexico City: ENAH–INAH.

Jerrahi.org (Halverti-Jerrahi Order of Dervishes) (2005) "Who We Are," Jerrahi.org, web.archive.org/web/20010801174458/http://www.jerrahi.org/about.htm (accessed June 12, 2012).

Jimenez Caliz, E. (2003) "Grupos radicales islamicos, presentes en Mexico," *Milenio*, www.milenio.com/nota.asp?idc=117089 (accessed April 10, 2004).

Kettani, M.A. (1986) *Muslim Minorities in the World Today*, London: Mansell.

Klahr, M.L. (2002) "¿El Islam en Chiapas?: El EZLN y el Movimiento Mundial Murabitun," *Revista Academica para el Estudio de las Religiones* 4: 79–91.

Klich, I. and Lesser, J. (1996) "Introduction: 'Turco' Immigrants in Latin America," *The Americas* 53(1): 1–14.

Kunin, S.D. (2001) "Juggling Identities among the Crypto-Jews of the American Southwest," *Religion* 31(1): 41–61.

Lea, H.C. (1901) *The Moriscos of Spain: Their Conversion and Expulsion*, Philadelphia: Lea Bros.

Leff, A. (2008) "Ramadan off to Quiet Start in Costa Rica," The Tico Times Online, www.ticotimes.net/Current-Edition/News-Briefs/Ramadan-off-to-quiet-start-in-Costa-Rica_Tuesday-September-09-2008 (accessed June 24, 2012).

Lindley-Highfield, M. (2008) "'Muslimization,' Mission and Modernity in Morelos: The Problem of a Combined Hotel and Prayer Hall for the Muslims of Mexico," *Tourism, Culture & Communication* 8(2): 85–96.

McGirk, J. (2002) "Radical Islam Takes Root in Chiapas," *San Antonio Current*, March 10, sacurrent.com/special/story.asp?id=56097 (accessed January 21, 2005).

Marín Guzmán, R. (1997) "Los inmigrantes árabes en México en los siglos XIX y XX: Un studio de historia social," in Kabchi, R. (ed.) *El mundo arabe y América Latina*, Madrid: UNESCO.

——(2000) *A Century of Palestinian Immigration into Central America: A Study of Their Economic and Cultural Contributions*, San José, Costa Rica: Universidad de Costa Rica.

Martin, R. (2008) "Latinas Choosing Islam over Catholicism," NPR News, Washington, www.npr.org/templates/story/story.php?storyId=6133579 (accessed July 4, 2012).

Martínez Montiel, L.M. (1992) "The Lebanese Community in Mexico: Its Meaning, Importance, and the History of Its Communities," in Hourani, A. and Shehadi, N. (eds.) *The Lebanese in the World: A Century of Emigration*, London: Centre for Lebanese Studies and I.B. Taurus.

MCM (Muslim Center de México) (2003) "Presence of Islam in Mexico," mexicoislam.org, web.archive.org/web/20051027222911/http://mexicoislam.org/islaminmexico.php.

Morquecho, G. (2005) "Chamulas islámicas: igualdad genérica en el discurso, servidumbre tradicional en los hechos," La Journada en linea, www.jornada.unam.mx/2005/jul05/050704/informacion/83_chamulasislam.htm (accessed August 6, 2005).

Nacif Mina, J. (1995) *Crónicas de un inmigrante libanes en México: charlas de Jorge Nacif Elias*, Mexico: J. Nacif Mina en colaboración con el Instituto Cultural Mexicano Libanés.

Nunez, A. (2010) *History of the Muslims in Belize*, Bloomington, IN: AuthorHouse.

Ota Mishima, M.E. (1997) "Introducción a la historia de las migraciones asiáticas a México, siglos XIX y XX," in Ota Mishima, M.E. (ed.) *Destino México: Un estudio de las migraciones asiáticas a México, siglos XIX y XX*, Mexico City: El Colegio de México.

Páez Oropeza, C.M. (1984) *Los Libaneses en México: Asimilación de un grupo étnico*, Mexico City: INAH.

Pew Forum on Religion and Public Life (2009) "Mapping the Global Muslim Population: A Report on the Size and Distribution of the World's Muslim Population," Pew Research Center, October, www.pewforum.org/newassets/images/reports/muslimpopulation/muslimpopulation.pdf (accessed November 26, 2010).

Rahal, D.M. (1997) "La migración palestina a México," in Ota Mishima, M.E. (ed.) *Destino México: Un estudio de las migraciones asiáticas a México, siglos XiX y XX*, Mexico City: El Colegio de México.

Reza, H.G. (2005) "Embracing Islam, Praying for Acceptance," *Los Angeles Times*, October 29, articles.latimes.com/2005/oct/29/local/me-beliefs29 (accessed November 3, 2009).

Sanchez García, J.L. (2004) "El influjo y el singlar de los conversos mexicanos disidentes de cultos cristianos en la yamma de la Ciudad de México en la postrimería sigloventina y el primer trienio del siglo novel," unpublished dissertation, Mexico City: ENAH–INAH.

Segal, R. (2001) *Islam's Black Slaves: The Other Black Diaspora*, New York: Farrar Straus & Giroux.

Siddiqi, S.A. (1993) *The Dawah Program Towards Establishing "The Kingdom of Allah,"* New York: Forum for Islamic Work.

Valenzuela, A. (2005) "The United States and Latin America: The Road Ahead," *LASA (Latin American Studies Association) Forum* 35(4): 9–10.

Westerlund, D. and Svanberg, I. (eds.) (1999) *Islam Outside the Arab World*, London: Palgrave Macmillan.

Wikipedia (2007) "Islam in Mexico," Wikipedia, en.wikipedia.org/w/index.php?title=Islam_in_Mexico&oldid=169097937 (accessed December 7, 2007).

Wilson, B.R. (1966) *Religion in Secular Society*, London: C.A. Watts.

Wood, J. (1922) Letter from John Wood, Veracruz, Mexico, to Secretary of State, US National Archives, College Park, MD, US State Department Records, Record Group 59 (1910–29), October 11.

Yahoo! Noticias (2004) "Chiapas: Islamismo y desintegracion familiar," Yahoo! Noticias, web.archive.org/web/20040528090110/http://mx.news.yahoo.com/040406/26/16lmv.html (accessed July 28, 2012).

Zeraoui, Z. (1997) "Los arabes en México: el perfil de la migración," in Ota Mishima, M.E. (ed.) *Destino México: Un estudio de las migraciones asiáticas a México, siglos XIX y XX*, Mexico City: El Colegio de México.

Zoraida Vázquez, J. (2000) "War and Peace with the United States," translated by M.M. Brescia, in Meyer, M.C. and Beezley, W.H. (eds.) *The Oxford History of Mexico*, Oxford: Oxford University Press, pp. 339–69.

# 10

# Muslims in South America

## History, presence, and visibility of a religious minority in a Christian context

*Marco Gallo*

The study of Muslims and Islamic presence in Latin America has been for a long time unsystematic if not completely neglected, but in these last years a renewed interest is appearing. This is due to various different reasons but, above all, to the growing public presence of Islam not only on a global scale, but also in Latin America. It is obviously difficult, if not impossible, to summarize this history and this presence; not only because Latin America is not a homogeneous region, but also because this new Islamic presence has produced a lot of different reactions and discourses: politics, religious institutions, universities, the media, and the internet above all are producing an impressive amount of data and new sources. These sources may have been analyzed on an urban, regional, or national level but still require a complete analysis. Furthermore, much of this data is coming from Islamic groups, and is often limited to an apologetic approach. This is also strongly related to the historical problem of the first Islamic presence in Latin America.

## The first presence of Muslims in South America

Every narrative about beginnings swings between myth and history. The problem of the first Islamic presence in the New World is no different. In recent times many theories have been produced to demonstrate a pre-Colombian Islamic presence in the Americas; but, to be honest, they are essentially pseudoscientific theories that would backdate the discovery of America to the Phoenicians or to the Muslims of the first Caliphal period, often only as a result of ingenuous readings of written sources or archeological data (Taboada 2010). A different and more complex question is whether it is possible to speak about the physical presence of Muslims in the New World in the very first times after the conquest, that is, before the arrival of Muslims among the black slaves in the eighteenth and nineteenth centuries. The few scholars who have dealt with this problem agree in emphasizing the limited numbers but diverge considerably with regards to the interpretation of the collected data. It is certain that the *moriscos* that appeared before the Inquisition in the New World during the sixteenth century were few in number, and it is not easy to identify them, also because the few references to the "sect of Muhammad" in the New World are often inserted within speeches concerning certain religious relativism or generically Protestant ideas. In the Americas, in other words, the newly converted Christian who practiced his original religion secretly appears to have been uncommon. Even if it seems reasonable to admit that numbers were relatively modest and even insignificant (Taboada 2004b: 115–32), this does not make those individual cases less interesting. A famous case is that of Estevanico, a Moorish slave who survived the shipwreck of 1527 en route to Florida. His unusual history has offered a compelling subject both to the historians of the age of the conquest and to those who study the invention of tradition; while Estevanico has been celebrated by generations of Africans and African Americans as the first man of color to reach American soil, others have begun to explore his Muslim faith with a certain degree of fantasy (Vanoli 2010).

Setting aside these first and episodic cases, there is much substance to the hypothesis of a colonial Islam, brought by the African slaves, even if Islamic communities don't seem to have existed in a truly organized sense in the colonial period. An exception to this is the Brazilian groups of African origin called generally Malês, a word derived from the dialect Yoruba *imalé* (i.e. Muslim, natives of Mali). These Muslim slaves had a strong capacity for organization that manifested in different rebellions. The most famous of these incidents, known as the rebellion of Mali, occurred in 1835 in San Salvador de Bahia (Kent 1970). Perhaps only in Brazil do we have some trace of a surviving Islamic community attested to by an Arabic traveler around 1865 (Quiring-Zoche 1995: 115–24). And we may add to these traces the mysterious amulets with Arabic texts discovered in Bolivia and dating back to the nineteenth century (Cerezo Ponte 2005: 339–358).

This research and the growing possibilities given by the archeological approach could offer new data about the first Islamic presence in Latin America, but it seems sufficiently true that, in any case, we are speaking about marginal phenomena. Also after independence, Islam in Latin America was perceived as something absolutely remote. The true big change began in the second half of the nineteenth century, when Latin America moved from the post-independence consolidation phase to begin its integration in the world economy. The independent republics moved to strengthen the use of two elements in their economies, land and labor (Skidmore and Smith 2005: 40), and to provide labor the Latin American elites in several countries hoped for immigration above all from Europe. But this immigration process also dragged people from other lands: Indian Muslims passed through the English Caribbean and arrived in Panama; some Bengalis were in Venezuela and in Colombia, in the valley of the Rio Cauca (Navarrete 1997: 75–91). Small numbers at first, but by around 1870 a new impressive wave of immigrants from the Ottoman empire changed the situation again. They were mostly from Lebanon and they were above all Christians, but not exclusively. With the Maronites and the Orthodox Christians, Jews and Muslims arrived from the Ottoman territories.

In this first context, it is not always easy to recognize Muslims; the different numbers of them assumed by historians are strongly determined by the kind of sources used or by their interpretation. For example, the registers of some ports, such as Buenos Aires or Santiago de Chile, clearly testified the number of Muslim immigrants, and sometimes these numbers could be verified with the national census or the archival data of the Ottoman Empire. So, for example, in Chile the census of 1895 recorded 79 Turkish citizens, 58 of whom were indicated as "Mohammedan," who lived in different towns of the Chilean territory. Later on, in the census of 1907, the number of Muslims had risen to 1,498, all of them foreigners, thus representing 0.04 percent of the population. Sometimes we know only the place of origin, and in this case it is often difficult to distinguish among Christians, Jews, and Muslims. Moreover, sometimes we may find the case of immigrants that decided to hide their identity using a Christian name or declaring a different religious affiliation.

Some scholars indicate the presence of more than 1,500,000 Muslims in South American countries (taking into account that the Arab migration to these lands consisted of a Christian majority, and a percentage must have been Muslim). However, it is more probable that this figure is to be halved and that there were no more than 700,000 Muslims. In this regard, it is very difficult to get definite numbers, given the lack of archival sources, so that it is not easy to estimate the presence of Muslims accurately. We can thus say that at the end of the nineteenth century and until the mid-twentieth century the Muslim community in different countries of South America, whatever its total number, was rather scattered and unorganized: there were very few, and poor, Islamic centers and very few organized groups and religious activities (sometimes, as in Colombia, we have records of reunions for Ramadan). In other words, from many points of view, in these first decades of immigration Islamic identity was something perceptible merely as residual, and exactly thus was it still perceived by scholars in the second half of the twentieth century (Reichert 1965: 194; Delval 1992: 267). It has been observed (Taboada 2010) that, curiously, during this first period the greatest vitality was present in minority confessions in the *dar al-islam*: for example Shi'ism in Argentina or the Baha'is in Chile, Panama, and Ecuador.

It is difficult to suggest a unique attitude of Latin American governments towards "Arabs" and "Turks" (terms used at the time with a racial connotation and without religious implications). Even if Islam was not so evident, the significant presence of "Arabs" or "Turks" sometimes produced strong reactions in Latin American society and in governments. In general the new states favored immigration from Europe; an example of promoting the entrance of particular social groups through specific policies was the immigrants from Central Europe in Chile (Agar and Rebolledo 1997). Often "Arabs" were viewed as "second-class" people. In some countries the arrival of certain races of immigrants, such as Arabs or Chinese, was considered a danger due to the risk of interracial marriage, adding a racist argument that this could even produce physiological deformations. This happened, for example, in Argentina, where Institutions and the media spoke about this immigration as something dangerous for the Nation, because "Turks" were conceived as "biologically" inclined to "parasitical activities" (Noufouri 2009: 128). But, setting aside these negative perceptions, in general immigration policy in Latin America permitted easy entrance to the ethnic groups coming from the Ottoman Empire. In Brazil, for example, an explicit change in Brazilian immigration policy contributed to the flux of immigrants from Syria and Lebanon who (in contrast to other groups of immigrants who sought employment as farmers in the coffee plantations) directed themselves to the biggest cities to find work above all as merchants. São Paulo, in particular, was and still is the most important place for the Islamic presence in Brazil.

## The twentieth century: the social emergence of the Islamic groups

At the end of the nineteenth and in the first two decades of the twentieth century, Latin America faced the most relevant immigration from the Ottoman territories. Recent studies (Akmir 2009) calculate in these terms the Arabic demographic impact in Latin America around the year 1926: Brazil 162,000 Arabs; Venezuela 3,282; Colombia 3,767; Ecuador 1,060; Chile (in 1930) 6,703; Argentina (in 1914) 64,369.

But, given these data, it is not always easy to identify any Islamic identity or attitude among these men and women from the actual regions of Syria, Lebanon, or Palestine. This phenomenon could be determined by different reasons: perhaps by a certain "inquisitorial" attitude of the local church or Creole society; but more by the difficulty of practicing Islam in a non-Muslim land in a context of complete cultural isolation, taking into consideration the presence of women in the Islamic community in that first wave. Moreover, in that isolated context, these first immigrants tended to organize themselves in groups defined more by their common language than any religious identity; that's why "Arabs" in their early associations mixed amicably together as Christians, Jews, and Muslims (Klich 1995: 109–43). It is also possible to observe the effects of this trend in the changing of names: generally new generations did not impose Islamic names and sometimes changed their original names (Jozami 1996: 67–85). Confirming a widespread rule, the less educated immigrants tended to quickly lose their cultural distinctiveness and not transmit it to their children.

This also happened in the case of Islamic traditions; however, there were still enough signals of activity during the first half of the twentieth century. It is difficult to ascertain the knowledge and use of the Arabic language among immigrants during that period, but in any case it is true that throughout these decades there was important production and circulation of Arabic texts (books, journals, magazines) in Brazil and in Argentina. The first newspaper in Arabic appeared in São Paulo in 1895, and by 1914 there were fourteen Arabic-language newspapers, an output that surprised even the immigrants (Truzzi 1992: 45). These publications initially focused on issues in the Middle East, such as the domination of Syria and Lebanon by the Turks, but over time they began to turn their attention to events within the colony in Brazil. The same impressive production is also attested to in Argentina. The first Arabic newspaper was the *Sada al-Yunub*, published in Buenos Aires by al-Juri Yuhanna Sa'id in 1899. In the same year, also in Buenos Aires, *Al-Subh* appeared. In 1908 in Cordoba Aziz Hakim published *al-Hakim*. And later were published, among others, *Assalam* (Buenos Aires, 1902) by Wadi Sam'un, *Al-Zaman* (1905), *Al-Mirsal* (1913), *Al-Shams* (1915), *Al-Ittihad al-Lubnani* (1915), *Al-Istiqlal* (1926), *Al-'Alam al-'Arabi* (1933), *Al-'Uqab* (1936), *Al-Jami'a al-Lubnaniyya* (1937), *Ahlan wa-Sahlan* (1940), *Al-Watan* (1943), and *Al-Rafiq* (1944).

This incomplete list shows the intense cultural activity that permeated the Arabic (even if, obviously, not necessary Islamic) communities in Brazil and Argentina, a presence that was particularly strong in Brazil and Argentina, but that in these years was also visible in other Latin American Lands. So, for example, there were also publications in Chile: the first was *Al-Mursid*, published in Santiago by al-Khuri Bulus al-Khuri in 1912, followed by *al-'Awatif* and *Al-Munir* in 1916, *Al-Sabiba* in 1918, *Al-Watan* in 1920, and *Al-Islah* in 1930 (Amo 2006). But also in Cuba (the first was *Al-Irtiqa' al-Suri* in 1914), in Mexico (the first was *Al-Siham* in 1905), but also in Uruguay and Venezuela (for a more complete description of the Latin American Arabic publications, see Amo 2001).

Moreover, during that period the first forms of Islamic associations appeared. So, for example, in Brazil in 1929 Muslims organized the Sociedade Beneficente Musulmana to care for the Muslim peoples of São Paulo. This society, in addition to the contributions of the Syrian-Lebanese immigrants, raised money from the governments of Arab Muslim countries in the Middle East (Pitts 2006: 58). In the same sense, in Chile the Sociedad Unión Musulmana was founded on September 25, 1926, and the following year a society for Islamic mutual aid and charity (Centro de Cultura y Beneficencia Islámico) was also established. In Argentina, on November 15, 1931, Muslims founded their first religious institution. The main objective was to organize the Muslim community living in that region. Its original name was Asociación Pan Islamismo. Among the objectives of the institution were humanitarian principles based on charity, loyalty and fairness among all Muslims, following the principles of the Qur'an. In 1940 it was renamed Asociación Islámica de Previsión Social ("Islamic Association of Social Security") and later on, with the efforts and cooperation of Syrian and Lebanese immigrants who had settled in the country, and with the desire to maintain their religious and cultural traditions, it purchased some land in a central area of the town. Thus, in 1957, the General Assembly decided to change the name again to the final Centro Islámico ("Islamic Center"). At the same time other Islamic groups in Argentina founded their own association; for example, in 1931 the Asociación Unión Alauita ("Association Alawite Union"), in 1936 the Asociación Islámica Alauita de Beneficiencia ("Islamic Alawite Association of Charity"), and in 1943 the Asociación Pan Alauita Islámica ("Pan-Islamic Alawite Association") (Akmir 2009: 88–9).

A new wave of immigrants from Islamic lands arrived after World War II. This was both as a result of the new economic prosperity of some Latin American regions (above all Brazil, Argentina, Venezuela, and Colombia) and the political and economic crises in the countries of origin. Certain influxes occurred from Palestine in 1948 and 1967 and Lebanon in 1975, at the beginning of the Civil War, but also, in the 1970s and 1980s, from African countries (Senegal, Nigeria, Republic of Congo). Among the nations of reception, the countries who received the most Muslim immigrants in the last decades were Brazil, Argentina, and Paraguay. For example, while there were a few Muslims among the earliest Syrian-Lebanese immigrants to Brazil, they began arriving in large numbers straight after World War II. Although reliable statistics are not available, it appears that the majority of immigrants from the Middle East to Brazil after 1945 were Muslims, usually from Lebanon, but sometimes from Palestine, Syria, or Egypt, and occasionally from other Arab states. In addition to settling in cities where Syrian-Lebanese communities already existed, Muslim Arabs established their own colonies in other areas of the country, particularly in rapidly growing cities on the Paraguayan and Bolivian borders that offered exciting commercial opportunities. As a result, the Arab communities in such cities as Foz de Iguaçu, on the Paraguayan border, and Corumbá, on the Bolivian border, are almost entirely Muslim.

Indeed it was starting from the 1980s, with a new democratic tendency, that a more active Muslim presence began to be perceived, not only in Brazil, but in several states of Latin America.

Until that period, the Islamic presence seemed to assimilate, almost completely, to Argentine society's Western characteristics. This reality, and the strength of Argentine society's prejudice *vis-à-vis* a minority hailing from a different culture, have translated into some obvious religious-cultural losses; among the latter is the loss of significant documents that would have facilitated a reconstruction of its historical development. Apart from other factors, an obvious casualty of such losses has been scientific research on Argentina's Muslims; hitherto, neither scholars nor serious laymen have focused their attention on them, the late academic author of several ethno-linguistic studies excepted (Jozami 1996: 69).

The 1980s were the years in which in Buenos Aires, in the district of Constituciòn, thanks to the money of the Argentine communities, the al-Ahmad mosque was founded (1983). These were also the years during which educational activities with the goal of maintaining the use of Arabic amongst younger generations multiplied. With this purpose, the Islamic Center in Buenos Aires inaugurated Arabic-language courses and in 1990 finally founded the Colegio Argentino Arabe Omar Bin Al Jattab ("Argentine Arab School Omar Bin Al Jattab"), which is a secular school, where classes on religion are optional. The center also started to publish the magazine *La voz del Islam*, which soon became the flag of Sunni Islam in Argentina. It can also be argued that Argentine society "discovered" the existence of Muslims for the first time, not thanks to their cultural activities, but after the election of a president of Islamic origin who had converted to Catholicism, Carlos Menem (b. 1930), whose family was Syrian (Sunni) Muslim and had settled in the northwestern Argentine province of La Rioja. The second factor that determined a new attention towards Muslims in Argentina was the deep impression given by the attacks on the Israeli Embassy in 1992 and on the Asociación Mutual Israelita Argentina (AMIA) in 1994 (Méndez 2009: 39). This second attack, in particular, was Argentina's deadliest bombing ever: it occurred in Buenos Aires on July 18, 1994, killing eighty-five people and injuring hundreds. Even if the investigations didn't produce concrete results, many allegations have been made, above all those blaming the government of Iran (the attack was linked to Hezbollah); and in general more attention was given to Islamic terrorism. Not by chance, it is above all after this period that it is possible to observe a changing attitude in public Islamic speeches in Argentina: with a new attention to underlining the good relationship between Muslims and the other internal religious communities; and stressing the solidarity between Latin American Muslims and those in other Islamic lands.

## Islam in Latin America today

It is difficult to estimate exactly how many Muslims live in Latin America today. Based on the most recent data, it is possible to say that there are around 500,000 Muslims in Argentina, of whom 60 percent are Sunni, 30 percent Shi'i, and 10 percent 'Alawi, a branch of Shi'i Islam (US Department of State 2010). In Brazil the official census says that there are more than 35,000 Muslims (2010 census) living primarily in the states of São Paulo and Paraná. In Venezuela there are more than 100,000 Muslims, concentrated mainly in Nueva Esparta State and the Caracas area (US Department of State 2007). Moreover, the statistics (Pew Research Center report 2009) say that there are around 110,000 Muslims in Mexico, 24,000 in Panama, 14,000 in Colombia, 9,000 in Cuba, 2,000 in Haiti, 2,000 in Ecuador, 2,000 in Bolivia, 1,000 in Paraguay, 1,000 in Peru, and 1,000 in Puerto Rico.

These are not the only numbers available (for a methodological discussion of the different data, see Taboada 2010), but they allow us to cautiously affirm that there has been a long-term numerical increase. This increase is confirmed by the number (certainly less quantifiable) of Islamic centers, clubs, schools, social charities, *musalla*s, mosques, and even publications and websites. All these signs, together with the increase in the number of men wearing beards or of women wearing veils, lead us to conclude that Latin American Islam has become not only larger but also more visible, alongside the other communities throughout the world.

This transformation is also determined by many other factors. In recent decades a new kind of Islamic immigration has appeared: students, academic scholars, technicians, businessmen, and also religious experts sent to America to proselytize or to establish a Sufi center. But despite this new perspective, Latin American Islam continues to be mostly Arabic: it is not only a problem of numbers, but also of traditions, customs, publishing, and cultural activities.

But this new demographic and social impact has also been related to the processes of re-islamization that affected Muslim countries and that contributed to producing a new identity in South American Muslims. In this sense, the growing interest of Islamic countries toward Latin American Muslims is a new fact. In the preceding decades only Egypt paid any attention to these distant Muslims, but today there is a strong diplomatic presence of many Islamic countries: Saudi Arabia, Iran, and, at least until 2011, Libya. Oil money and the money of Islamic banks is behind the construction of several mosques and Islamic centers that appeared in Latin America in the 1990s. Two good examples are the mosques in Caracas (1993) and Buenos Aires (2001), both strongly financed and tied by a similar architectural style: the mosque of Caracas has a minaret of more than 100 meters; the impressive mosque of Buenos Aires rises in the district of Palermo and is considered Saudi territory.

These transformations have produced a new sense of belonging: now a lot of Latin American Muslims perceive themselves not only as connected to their original nationality, but also (and sometimes above all) as part of that global *umma* that in recent years has received a great deal of attention from scholars (Roy 2006). Not by chance, in this new cultural and social context, it is also possible to detect an increasing interest in conversion activity among non-Muslims. Thus, among the new religious proposals offered by natives, Christians, and Jews, it is possible to observe a new phenomenon of conversion to Islam. This happens among Latinos in the United States, among Afro-Brazilians or Mexican, Bolivian, and Chilean natives (Taboada 2010). But it is true also that this new proselytism is not always accepted by Latin American Muslims. For example, in Brazil, among the "old" Muslims, there is widespread suspicion towards converts, and this is determined both by the perception of Islam as a patrimony of the Arabs (Montenegro and Moreira 2002) and by suspicion of forms of Islam other than orthodox and too close to New Age practices.

In any case Latin American Islam seems to be in a moment of evolution and growing exposure. But this exposure has not been produced only by internal causes or the new interest of the global Islamic economy. Sadly, the geopolitical changes of the past ten years have also strongly contributed to augmenting attention towards Muslim communities all over the world, including in Latin America. The solicitations following 9/11 and the new international conditions have pushed American Islam and Muslims towards higher visibility in everyday life and in the media. It has been well studied, for example in the case of Brazilian Muslims; it is true that, as early in the 1990s but increasingly after September 11, 2001, in towns such as São Paulo there are evident signals of a growing Islamophobic feeling. These events pushed the religious communities in Brazil (i.e. the Liga da Juventude Islâmica Beneficente in São Paulo) to react with public activities and declarations, with the intention of deconstructing the image of Islam as a religion connected to the violence (Marques 2011: 35–7).

## Distinctions and perspectives

The data presented here show us a small presence in terms of numbers, but a presence that in recent decades has been able to consolidate its identity. It is always necessary to remember an obvious statement: Islam is not uniform and among its variations are also adaptations to the host land. This is also true for Latin America.

So, for example, we have the small Muslim community in Colombia, made up mostly of Lebanese and Palestinians emigrated in recent years (since the 1970s) and settled mostly in Buenaventura, Maicao, and Bogota. Related to this community there are some associations (the Asociación Benéfica Islámica de Bogota), mosques (in 1997 the Mezquita Omar ibn al-Khattab, the second largest mosque in Latin America, was inaugurated in Maicao), and schools (the Colegio Colombo Árabe Dar El Arkam in Maicao). There is also a clear increase in the rate of the groups coming from other countries in Africa and Asia. Along with this, the return of Colombian converts to Islam from the Middle East to their own country has broadened Colombian citizens' interest in the Islamic world.

In Chile the statistics are quite different: according to the 2002 census Muslims number around 3,000, including converts to Islam, and a large number of Islamic organizations are attested to and active in the country. The construction of the first mosque in Santiago began in 1988 and the second one was built almost ten years later, in a town in northern Chile, Iquique, which accounts for the largest Pakistani community in the region. In 2006 another new mosque was inaugurated in the town of Coquimbo. This articulated topography is also the expression of the plurality of Islam in Chile: the As-Salam Mosque of Santiago is for the Sunni community, but maintains relations with Jama'at al-Tabligh, an organization of Indian origin and well diffused in the Western world. Further, next to the mosque, there is also the Centro Islamico de Chile ("Islamic Center of Chile"), which is authorized to certify *halal* food. Muslim activity in Chile is also reflected in some institutions, for example the Centro Mohammed VI para el

Diálogo de las Civilizaciones, with its mosque inaugurated in 2007, or the Centro Cultural al-Mahdi, a non-profit organization, created with the help of a group of Chilean converts to Islam. In general, though the number of Muslims is small, mostly connected to past immigrations, the presence of Islam in Chile is strengthened and enhanced by many institutions and centers which have emerged in recent decades. The small number of Muslims seems to help the cohesion between various attitudes and groups rather than reproducing the division of the Muslim world. This recent evolution of the visibility of Muslim communities is further underlined by the fact that until the 1980s there were no religious leaders or centers for praying in Chile.

The Brazilian case is completely different (Montenegro 2000, 2002). As usual, there is no certainty about statistical data, and even if the most recent census speaks of 35,000, other sources (significantly of Muslim origin) estimate a presence of 600,000 Muslims. Setting aside this kind of exaggeration, in any case the Islamic presence in Brazil is a social reality. This has also been caused by the new immigration that started around the 1970s and that determined a diffusion (helped by Saudi or Iranian money) of new mosques that were built in the regions of Paraná, São Paulo, Mato Grosso, Goiás, Distrito Federla, and Mina Gerais (the mosque of Rio de Janeiro was inaugurated only in 2007). These mosques were above all Sunni, but there was also growth in the Shi'i community in São Paulo. These were also years of new conversions; today there is still an internal debate that divides Muslims of Arab origin – usually called "brasileños" – and the new converts without Arab origins. Not by chance, among the newly converted the language of communication is Portuguese, used both in the mosque of Rio de Janeiro during the Friday sermon and in the courses offered by the Sociedade Beneficente Muçulmana Chagas (2006), while in the mosque of Pari (Salah al-Din) in São Paulo, which belongs to the Liga de Juventude Islâmica, the sermon is in Arabic (with translation in Portuguese). As in other parts of the world, for the "old" Muslims Islam is not only the sacred texts, but also a series of cultural traditions (amulets, rituals, etc.) perceived as Islamic, while for the new converts to Islam, the religion is codified above all in an emphasis on the sacred texts organized in a more abstract system. But Brazilian Islam is actually more complex than this Manichean distinction: there are African Muslims from Angola, Mozambique, Senegal, and Ghana, who in 2005 founded a mosque in São Paulo dedicated to the black muezzin Bilal al-Hasbashi (Cavalcante 2008). There is a group of converted Muslims, related to the Jama'at al-Tabligh, who in 2007 founded a *musalla* in the Paraís district of São Paulo. There are also Sufi communities, not as important as in Argentina.

Indeed, the most important Islamic presence in Latin America is in Argentina: as we have seen, the number of 500,000 Muslims is probably correct, divided among Buenos Aires (the majority: between 160,000 and 200,000 people) and other provinces such as Mendoza, Tucumán, Rosario, Cordoba, and La Rioja. There is no need to underline the plurality of associations and cultural institutions, grounded in the national past of the country. Given its numbers and its history, it is clear that Islam in Argentina is different and fragmented. There are many confessional distinctions among the Muslim communities: Sunni, Shi'i, or 'Alawi; but there are also many distinctions defined by ethnic origin or the relationship with the state. As has been stated, there is a multiplicity of myths of the origins, forms of association, speech, and modalities of construction of the public presence inside these identity constructions (Montenegro 2010: 1).

Not by chance, in the 1990s the contribution of Saudi Arabia converged in Argentina, giving birth to the new Centro Cultural Islamico Rey Fahd ("Islamic Cultural Center King Fahd"), which includes the largest mosque in Latin America in the central district of Palermo in Buenos Aires. It is an impressive 20,000 square meter building that operates also as a kindergarten, school, and housing for students. But it is significant that for the "old" Muslims in Buenos Aires the mosque of reference remains the al-Ahmad.

In another sense, from the point of view of the new forms of associations, it is significant that the Organización Islámica para América Latina has been created by Muslims of Argentina with the aim, as they stated, of "coordinat[ing] and encourag[ing] the Islamic activities and projects in Latin America" and of "encourag[ing] the relationships ... with the other Islamic communities in the World" (www.islamerica.org.ar/oipal.htm). In a similar direction there is also the experience of the Conferencia Islámica Iberoamericana, with seats in Cordoba and Bogota, constituted under the influence of Iberian converts and Latin American Muslims.

In a different sense, Latin American Islam, represented by lands such as Argentina (but also Brazil or Chile), is also the expression of a new tendency in international dialogue for the relationship among cultures and religions. Among examples of this is the Foro Tripartito Latinoamericano y Caribeño about Interreligious Cooperation organized for two years in Buenos Aires. There is the project Alianza de Civilizaciones, originally inspired by Spain and Turkey in 2005, which determined the regional seminar organized in Argentina with the title "La Mujer y la Alianza de Civilizaciones. Oportunidades y desafíos." It is necessary to underline also the Comité Interreligioso por la Paz (COMIPAZ) in the city of Cordoba, and the Instituto de Diálogo Interreligioso de Buenos Aires and Sant'Egidio Community. Moreover, recently, the encounter with Jorge Bergoglio – archbishop of Buenos Aires – in the Centro Islámico de la República Argentina (CIRA) has made Catholic–Islamic dialogue in the country official.

These new tendencies are part of a complex redefinition of Islamic discourse and activities in Latin America. This redefinition, as we have seen, is strongly related with the new cultural, economical, and social global perspective, but also has a deep regional impact. In other words, the new Muslim identities that are growing in Latin America today are deeply involved in a reconstruction of the history of their presence in these territories. Not by chance recent years have seen the first encounters about the importance of the Arabic (and Islamic) presence in the history of the Argentine Nation. In this sense an example is the international congress held in Buenos Aires in 2008 with the title "Dos siglos argentinos de interculturalidad cristiano – judeo – islámica". An example among others of a tendency that will inevitably be important in the future: the American past, in its global perspective, needs to be rewritten from the other points of view. And the American Islamic past of Islam could be one of them.

## Bibliography

Abboud, O. (2006) "Los arabes musulmanes en Argentina," *La voz del Islam, Yearbook*, pp. 96–103.

Agar, L. and Rebolledo, A. (1997) *La inmigración árabe en Chile: los caminos de la integración*, in Kabchi, R. (ed.) *El mundo árabe y América Latina*, Madrid: UNESCO/Libertarias Prodhufi, pp. 283–309.

Akmir, A. (ed.) (2009) *Los arabes en America Latina. Historia de una emigraciòn*, Madrid: Siglo XXI.

Amo, M. del (2001) "Periódicos árabes en Iberoamérica: una propuesta de recuperación y estudio," in *Infodiversidad* 3: 61–80.

——(2006) "La literatura de los poriódicos árabes de Chile," in *MEAH, Sección Árabe-Islam* 55: 3–35.

Bazan, R.G. (1966) "Muslim Immigration to Spanish America," *The Muslim World* 56: 173–87.

Bestene, J.O. (1988) "La inmigración sirio-libanesa en la Argentina. Una aproximación," *Estudios Migratorios Latinoamericanos* 9: 239–67.

——(1992) "Formas de asociacionismo entre los sirios libaneses en Buenos Aires (1990–1950)," in Devoto, F.J. and Míguez, E.J. (eds.) *Asociacionismo, trabajo e identidad étinca. Los italianos en América Latina desde una perspective comparativa*, Buenos Aires: CEMLA, CESR, IEHS.

——(1994) "Realidades y estereotipos: los 'turcos' en el teatro argentino," *Estudios Migratorios Latinoamericanos* 26: 143–63.

——(1995) "La política inmigratoria argentina y la inmigración de sirios y libaneses," *Studi Emigrazione* 118: 263–76.

Bianchi, S. (2004) *Historia de las religiones en la Argentina. La minorias religiosas*, Buenos Aires: Editorial Sudamericana.

Burdiel de las Heras (1999) *La emigración libanesa a Costa Rica*, Madrid: CantArabia.

Castellanos, D. (2010) "Islam en Colombia: entre la asimilacion y la exclusion," paper prepared for the "Islam in Latin America Workshop," April, summary at lacc.fiu.edu/research/islam-in-latin-america/working-papers/islam_in_colombia.pdf.

Cavalcante, C. Jr. (2008) *Processos de Construção e Cominicação das Identidades Negras e Africanas na Comunidade Muçulmana Sunita do Rio de Janeiro*, Niteroi: PPGA–UFF.

Cerezo Ponte, C. (2005) "Hallazgo de unos amuletos musulmanes en el interior de dos piezas de la cultura atacameña: descripción, estudio histórico, traducción y análisis químico de los mismos," *Anales de America*, 13, pp. 339–58, museodeamerica.mcu.es/pdf/anales13/capitulo14.pdf.

Chickrie, R. (1999) "Muslims in Guyana: History, Traditions, Conflict, and Change," *Journal of Muslim Minority Affairs* 19: 181–95.

Ciarla, M.A.R. (1993) "Los musulmanes en Argentina," Cordoba, February, museoroca.gov.ar/articulos/arabislamicos.pdf.

Civantos, C. (2006) *Between Argentines and Arabs: Argentine Orientalism, Arab Immigrants, and the Writing of Identity*, New York: State University of New York Press.

Delval, R. (1992) *Les Musulmanes en Amerique Latine et aux Caraibes*, Paris: L'Harmattan.

Diouf, S.A. (1998) *Servants of Allah: African Muslims Enslaved in the Americas*, New York: New York University Press.

Gallo, M. (2010a) "La presencia de los musulmanes en la Argentina," in *Congreso "Hacia el Bicentenario (2010–16)" Memoria, Identidad y Reconciliación*, Buenos Aires: Educa.

——(2010b) " Las relaciones islamico-cristianas durante el pontificado de Juan Pablo II," in Gallo, M. *Mediterraneo: Puente entre religiones y culturas. Las relaciones entre el Cristianismo, el Judaismo y el Islam*, Buenos Aires: Educa.

Hallar, M.Y. (2007) "The Muslims in Latin America," *Islam Awareness*, March 2, islamawareness.net/latinamerica/adosimpo.html.

Hauser, K. and Gil, D. (2009) *Contribuciones árabes a las identidades iberoamericanas*, Madrid: Casa Árabe–IEAM.

Hilu da Rocha Pinto, P.G. (2011) "El Islam en Brasil: elementos para una antropologia historica," *ISTOR* 45: 3–21, www.istor.cide.edu/archivos/num_45/dossier1.pdf.

Jozami, G. (1988) "Aspectos demográficos y comportamiento espacial de los migrante árabes en el NOA," *Estudios migratorios Latinoamericanos* 9: 57–90.

——(1993) "La identidad nacional de los llamados turcos en Argentina," *Temas de Asia y África* 2: 189–220.

——(1994) "Identidad religiosa e integración cultural en cristianos sirios y libaneses en Argentina, 1890–1990," *Estudios Migratorios Latinoamericanos* 26: 95–113.

——(1996) "The Manifestation of Islam in Argentina," *The Americas* 53(1): 67–85.

Kabchi, R. (ed.) (1997) *El mundo arabe y América Latina*, Madrid: Ediciones Unesco.

Kent, R.K. (1970) "African Revolt in Bahia: 24–25 January 1835," *Journal of Social History* 3: 334–56.

Klich, I. (1995) "Arabes, judios y arabes judios en la Argentina de la primera mitad del novecientos," *Estudios interdisciplinarios de America Latina y el Caribe*, 6(2): 109–43.

——(2006) *Árabes y judíos en América Latina: historia, representaciones y desafíos*, Buenos Aires: Siglo XXI.

Klich, I. and Lesser, J. (eds.) (1997) *Arab and Jewish Immigrants in Latin America: Images and Realities*, London: Routledge.

Lovejoy, P.E. (2007) *Muslim Encounters with Slavery in Brazil*, Princeton: Markus Wiener Publishers.

Marín Guzmán, R. (2000) *A Century of Palestinian Immigration Into Central America: A Study of Their Economic and Cultural Contributions*, Costa Rica: Editorial Universidad de Costa Rica.

Marques, V.L.M. (2011) "Os muçulmanos no Brasil," *Etnográfica* 15(1): 31–50.

Martínez Montiel, L.M. (ed.) (1981) *Asiatic Migrations to Latin America*, Mexico: El Colegio de México.

Méndez, N. (2009) "Las colectividades judía y árabe de Argentina y su vinculación con la política exterior argentina en el caso de los atentados contra la Embajada de Israel y la Amia (1992–2008)," *Jornadas de Relaciones Internacionales: una disciplina en costante movimiento, lasco Argentina*, October 1–13, rrii.flacso.org.ar/web/wp-content/uploads/2010/09/mendez_norberto.pdf.

Menéndez Paredes, R.D. (2007) *Los árabes en Cuba*, Havana: Ediciones Boloña.

Montenegro, S. (2000) "Dilemas Identitários do Islã no Brasil," Ph.D. dissertation, Universidade Federal do Rio de Janeiro.

——(2002) "Identidades Mulçumanas no Brasil: entre o arabismo e a islamização," *Lusotopie* 2: 59–79.

——(2004) "Telenovela et Identités Musulmanes au Brésil," *Lusotopie* 11: 243–61.

——(2010) "Musulmanes en Argentina: instituciones, identitades y membresia," Working Papers: Islam in Latin America, Latin American and Caribbean Center, School of International and Public Affairs, Florida International University, Miami.

Montenegro, S. and Moreira, M. (2002) "Brazilian Muslims: Reverting to Their Islamic Past," www.islamawareness.net/LatinAmerica/brazil.html.

Morrison, S. (2005) "'Os Turcos': The Syrian-Lebanese Community of São Paulo, Brazil," *Journal of Muslim Minority Affairs* 25(3): 424–38.

Navarrete, M.C. (1997) "El caso de los hindúes en el valle del Río Cauca, Colombia," *Tzintzun* 25: 75–91.

Noufouri, H. (2009) "Contribuciones argentinoárabes: entre el dato y la imaginación orientalista," in Hauser, K. and Gil, D. *Contribuciones árabes a las identidades iberoamericanas*, Madrid: Casa Árabe–IEAM, pp. 115–54.

Noufouri, H. et al. (1999) *Tinieblas del crisol de razas: ensayo sobre las rapresentaciones simbólicas y espaciales de la noción del otro en la Argentina*, Buenos Aires: Cálamo.

Peres Oliveira, V. (2006) "O Islõ no Brasil ou o Islõ do Brasil?," *Religiao & Sociedade* 26: 83–114.

Pew Research Center report (2009), www.pewforum.org/uploadedfiles/Topics/Demographics/Muslimpopulation.pdf.

Pinto, P.G. (2010) "Muslim Identities in Brazil: Shared Traditions and Cultural Creativity in the Making of Islamic Communities," paper prepared for the "Islam in Latin America Workshop," strategicculture.fiu.edu/LinkClick.aspx?fileticket=jDk1ZPpNivg%3D&tabid=89.

Pitts, M.B. Jr. (2006) "Forging Ethnic Identity through Faith: Religion and the Syrian-Lebanese Community in Sao Paulo," M.A. dissertation, Vanderbilt University.

Qamber, R. (2003) "Anti-Islamic Bias in Sources on Latin America: Preliminary Findings," *Islamic Studies* 42: 651–85.

Quiring-Zoche, R. (1995) "Glaubenskampf oder Machtkampf? Der Aufstand der Malé von Bahia nach einer islamischen Quelle," *Sudanic Africa* 6: 115–24.

Reichert, R. (1965) "Muslim-Minoritäten in Südamerika," in Italiander, R. (ed.) *Die Herausforderung des Islams*, Göttingen, Berlin, and Frankfurt: Musterschmidt Verlag, pp. 194–218.

Roy, O. (2006) *Globalized Islam: The Search for a New Ummah*, New York: Columbia University Press.

Skidmore, T.E. and Smith, P.H. (2005) *Modern Latin America*, Oxford: Oxford University Press.

Taboada, H. (2000) "Islam," in Balderston, D., González, M., and López, A.M. (eds.) *Encyclopedia of Contemporary Latin American and Caribbean Culture*, vol. 2, New York and London: Routledge.

——(2004a) *La sombra de l'islam en la conquista de América*, Mexico: FCE/UNAM.

——(2004b) "El Moro en las Indias," *Latinoamérica. Revista de Estudios Latinoamericanos* 39, Mexico, CCyDEL, UNAM: pp. 115–32.

——(2010) "El Islam en America Latina: del siglo XX al siglo XXI," Estudios Digital, www.revistaestudios.unc.edu.ar/articulos03/articulos/1-taboada.php.

Tasso, A. (1989) *Aventura, trabajo, poder: sirios y libaneses en Santiago del Estero (1880–1980)*, Buenos Aires: Índice.

Truzzi, O. (1992) *De mascates a doutores: Sírios e libaneses em São Paulo*, São Paulo: Editora Sumaré.

——(1997) *Patrícios: Sírios e Libaneses em São Paulo*, São Paulo: Hucitec.

US Department of State (2007) *International Religious Freedom Report*, www.state.gov/j/drl/rls/irf/2007/.

——(2010) *International Religious Freedom Report*, www.state.gov/j/drl/rls/irf/2010/c39459.htm.

Vanoli, A. (2010) "Between Absence and Presence: New Paths in the Historiography of Islam in the New World," *Journal of Medieval Iberian Studies* 2: 77–91.

Zanzucchi, M. (2007) *El Islam del que no se habla*, Buenos Aires: Ciudad Nueva.

# Part 2
# Culture

# Part 2.1
# Interactions, conflicting, converging

# 11

# Europe's identity crisis, Islam in Europe, and the crisis of European secularity

*Luca Mavelli*

## Europe's identity crisis and Islam in Europe

On November 19, 2009 the European Parliament hosted a British Council-sponsored debate entitled "Europe and Islam: Whose Identity Crisis?" As the organizers of the event observed,

> we are facing a growing mutual mistrust that leaves Europe on the verge of a dangerous rift. One of the major cultural challenges that we face today is whether we can overcome the fear that difference and diversity will weaken national and social cohesion and succeed in building a Europe that is enriched by its different cultural identities.
>
> *(British Council 2009)*

Hence, "In a continent progressively challenged by mixed identities," this challenge cannot avoid the question: "who is it with the identity crisis? Europe, or Islam, or both?" (British Council 2009). Perhaps surprisingly, this question has received limited attention. Most of the literature on Islam in Europe, in fact, has tended to focus on the identity crisis of Muslims, with a particular view on the transformation of Islam within European settings, the privatization of belief, the emergence of new forms of religious authority, and the development of a distinctively European understanding of Islam ("Euro-Islam") (Peter 2006; Cesari 2004, 2003; Al Sayyad and Castells 2002). Conversely, the crisis of European identity has been analyzed in relation to a number of domains – such as the limits and failures of the European Union and its foreign policy; the wars, violence, and nationalisms that have plagued Europe for centuries; fascism and the resurgence of extreme right-wing movements; the recent economic and financial crisis – yet hardly in relation to the "question" of Islam in Europe. However, signals that Europe's identity crisis may be linked in some important ways to a growing presence of people of Islamic faith in Europe have multiplied in recent years.

For instance, the famous *affaire du foulard* in France has been interpreted by some observers as an indication of the limits of the French model of integration and its inability "to redevelop and implement secularity as an instrument of social cohesion and as token of national, republican unity" (Salvatore 2007: 146). In a broader perspective, the numerous tensions concerning the Muslim veil in several European countries have been taken as a sign of European insecurity in the face of more embodied manifestations of religiosity (Jansen 2011; Connolly 2006; Asad 2006; Mavelli 2013), and as a failure of European models of secularity to engender and sustain forms of solidarity open to diversity (Asad 2003). Similarly, in the case of the publication across Europe of the so-called "Danish cartoons" portraying the Prophet Mohamed as a terrorist, what was for many a vigorous affirmation of Europe's secular and liberal idea of freedom of speech (Glucksmann 2006) has been considered by others a symptom of its very crisis, which ultimately resulted in the grotesque celebration of "blasphemy as a sign of civilizational identity" (Asad 2009: 21). If these two cases – the willingness to restrict the use of the Muslim veil and the decision to publish cartoons considered offensive by Muslims – could still be considered by some as manifestations of the strength of European identity rather than of its weakness, the recent indictments of multiculturalism by three major European leaders – Angela Merkel, David Cameron, and Nicholas Sarkozy – explicitly linked the crisis of European identity with Muslims in Europe.

In October 2010, German Chancellor Angela Merkel declared that multiculturalism had been a "total failure" which had contributed to widening the gap in relation to those immigrants, Muslims in particular, whose different cultural and religious traditions prevented them from fully embracing European liberal and secular values, with the effect of turning them into a threat to German identity and social cohesion (BBC 2010). "We feel tied to Christian values," Merkel remarked. "Those who don't accept them don't have a place here" (Presseurop 2010). By the time of Merkel's speech, a book published a few months earlier by a Bundesbank board member which accused the country's Muslim population of "dumbing down" German society had already sold millions of copies, and the interior minister had stated that "Islam does not belong to Germany" (Spiegel 2010; Reuters 2010). In February 2011 it was British Prime Minister David Cameron who, echoing some of Merkel's remarks, declared that the "doctrine of state multiculturalism" had "failed to provide a vision of society" and that a strong national identity should be the antidote to Islamic extremism (Cameron 2011). A few weeks later, French President Nicolas Sarkozy joined the debate by stating that multiculturalism was "a failure" which had led us to be "too concerned about the identity of the new arrivals and not enough about the identity of the country receiving them" (*Irish Times* 2011). For Sarkozy, the failure of multiculturalism was ultimately "the issue of Islam and our Muslim compatriots" (*Irish Times* 2011).

This attack on multiculturalism found a most tragic instantiation in the Utøya massacre of July 2011, when Anders Behring Breivik killed seventy-seven members of the Workers' Youth League, a political youth organization affiliated with the Norwegian Labour Party. Their guilt, according to Breivik, was to be part of the future of that social democratic elite whose championing of multiculturalism, socialism, Marxism and, feminism had allowed "millions of Muslims to colonize Europe" and turn it into a "Eurabia" (Breivik, cited in Kinnvall 2012: 271). In his manifesto, "2083: A European Declaration of Independence," which was published on the internet hours before the massacre, Breivik spoke of the need for a war in defense of "Christian Europe," yet "Not a religious war but a cultural one, to defend … Europe's 'cultural, social, identity and moral platform'" (Malik 2011). In his warped and distorted mind, however, Breivik rehearsed an argument which "finds a widespread hearing" in Europe, namely the idea that "Christianity provides the foundations of Western civilisation, and of its political ideals and ethical values, and that Christian Europe is under threat from Islam" (Malik 2011). Brought to its extreme and delirious consequences, this view armed Breivik not against the

Muslim "others" but against "his own" people who made the "cultural infection" (Kinnvall 2012) possible. This auto-immunitary reaction (Esposito 2008), however extreme and paranoid it may be, suggests that, as Slavoj Žižek (2011) remarks, "The problem is not [Muslim] foreigners," but "our own (European) identity."

If these cases lend support to Tariq Ramadan's observation that "Europe's identity crisis is revealed by the Muslims" (quoted in Laurence 2007: 134), they also raise a question which awaits further research: What is it, exactly, that is revealed by these events? In this chapter I want to explore the possibility that the crisis of European identity revealed by Muslims in Europe may be conceptualized as a crisis of European secularity. This latter crisis has been the object of the recent work of a major European philosopher, Jürgen Habermas. For Habermas, modern secular formations are increasingly unable, on the one hand, to provide a framework of public engagement and civic coexistence for increasingly pluralistic societies and, on the other, to act as a reservoir of moral resources which may counter the progressive fragmentation of values and the ensuing incapacity to engage with pressing political questions, such as social justice or euthanasia (Habermas 2007). Indeed, modern secular formations are part and parcel of that process of instrumental rationalization which has enslaved the individual in the impersonal, dehumanizing, and anomic forces of "neo-liberal modernisation and globalisation" (Barbato 2010: 549). The crisis of secularity is thus, for Habermas, the crisis of a "pure practical reason" that, "armed solely with the insights of a theory of justice," can no longer hope to offer any meaningful resistance to "a modernization spinning out of control" and to the disruptive forces of "markets and administrative powers" which "are displacing social solidarity" (Habermas 2008: 211, 111). This crisis is propelling an increasing "awareness of what is missing" in secular modernity, namely a spiritual dimension to life which may be able to infuse new values and meanings by availing itself of the moral intuitions of faith (Habermas 2011; see also Habermas 2006).

Habermas does not explicitly link the *awareness* of the crisis of European secularity with the crisis of European identity, and both of these with the growing presence of Muslims in Europe. He confines himself to saying that "The Muslims next door force the Christian citizens to face up to the practice of a rival faith. And they also give the secular citizens a keener consciousness of the phenomenon of the public presence of religion" (Habermas 2007). In order to find a more explicit recognition of these connections, we need to look at the work of one of Habermas's most important intellectual partners in his critical reassessment of secularity, namely Pope Benedict XVI. Together they co-authored *The Dialectics of Secularization*, a set of exchanges on the need to find a new balance and forms of cooperation between reason and faith (Habermas and Ratzinger 2007). In 2004, the then Cardinal Joseph Ratzinger observed that, despite the fact that Europe's identity is fundamentally Christian, "Europe, unlike America, is on a collision course with its own history" as it almost denies "its religious and moral foundations" and the public relevance of Christian values (Ratzinger 2006a: 109). Islam, on the contrary, is on the rise "because of people's conviction that Islam can provide a valid spiritual foundation to their lives. Such a foundation seems to have eluded old Europe, which, despite its enduring political and economic power, seems to be on the road to decline and fall" (Ratzinger 2006b: 65).

These remarks may surprise some readers, as they suggest a seemingly positive interpretation of Islam which conflicts with the largely negative account that Joseph Ratzinger provided in 2006 at the University of Regensburg. On that occasion the now Pope Benedict XVI stirred up much controversy by comparing the mainstream Christian understanding of God with the Islamic idea of God put forward by the eleventh-century Muslim philosopher Ibn Hazm. Whereas Christianity, the Pope suggested, is shaped by Greek philosophy and thus considers human reason as a source of immanent understanding of the good and a fundamental measure of God's will, "for Muslim teaching, God is absolutely transcendent. His will is not bound up with any of our categories, even that of rationality" (Pope Benedict XVI 2006). In this latter case, because reason and faith are separated, the believer is under the yoke of "a capricious god," who is more likely to inspire acts of "unreasonable violence" (Pope Benedict XVI 2006). According to critics and Muslims all over the world who felt outraged at his words, the pope was suggesting that, unlike Christianity, "Islam commits itself entirely to faith rather than synthesizing faith with reason," and is thus "a fanatical rather than a rational religion" (Nirenberg 2008: 8), which is ultimately inferior to Christianity (Ruether 2006) and foreign to the Judeo-Christian core of Europe. Indeed, Benedict remarked, the "inner rapprochement between Biblical faith and Greek philosophical inquiry," together with the "addition of the Roman heritage ... created Europe and remains the foundation of what can rightly be called Europe" (Pope Benedict XVI 2006).

In the remainder of this chapter I want to suggest that these two seemingly conflicting assessments of Islam – the celebration of Islamic spiritual vigor as opposed to Europe's moral decay and the indictment of the Muslim incapacity to synthesize reason and faith, which places Islam outside the Christian civilizational boundaries of Europe – are revealing of a broader tension at the heart of European secularity. This is the crisis of a secular identity that from the onset has struggled to establish itself as a self-sufficient foundation of knowledge and morality. As I shall discuss in the next section (pp. 188–93), Habermas's recent call for a secular reappropriation of the moral intuitions of faith is the last instantiation of a crisis of European secularity which emerges as a tension with René Descartes, becomes manifest with Immanuel Kant and Émile Durkheim, and is explicitly acknowledged by Max Weber. Yet, I will argue, at the very moment that this crisis is recognized it is also converted into a sign of civilizational superiority to the Other of Islam.

## The crisis of European secularity and the construction of the Muslim Other[1]

Descartes's attempt to place "the self-evidence of the subject's own existence ... at the very source of access to being" (Foucault 2005b: 14) represents a remarkable break with the medieval scholastic tradition of Thomas Aquinas. Aquinas strove towards the integration of what we would now label secular knowledge and religious faith by arguing that reason and revelation represent two different epistemological domains of knowledge which nonetheless converge to the same Truth, namely the existence of God, which is the condition of possibility of all truths. Aquinas, however, also considered that the domain of reason relies on the senses, which are ultimately fallible, and therefore, although reason and faith may in principle be different avenues to the same truth, "the human mind is incapable of grasping certain truths without the aid of special revelation" (Nash 1999: 171).

Descartes agreed that the senses are ultimately fallible, but contended that the solution lay not in integrating secular knowledge and religious faith, but in separating them and in emancipating secular knowledge from the deceptiveness of the senses. To this end, Descartes envisages the possibility of a withdrawal into the space of individual consciousness by bringing "the mind away from the senses" (Descartes 1996 [1641]: 37), because "human knowledge is founded not on the senses but on 'the clear and distinct notions that are in us'" (Patterson 2000: 80). According to Descartes,

> my mind contains within itself ... [what] enables me to know ... I now know that even bodies are perceived not by the senses ... but by the intellect alone, not through their

being touched or seen but through their being understood; and in view of this I know plainly that I can achieve an easier and more evident perception of my own mind than of anything else.

*(Descartes 1996 [1641]: 22–3)*

This approach notwithstanding, Descartes was still puzzled by the unreliability of the senses. Why are they deceptive? Is there "some malicious demon of the utmost power and cunning" who is employing "all his energies in order to deceive me" (Descartes 1996 [1641]: 15)? And, if so, how is it possible that God, with His supreme goodness, may allow such a "malicious demon" to lead me astray? According to Descartes, the answer to this question lies in the fact that "the scope of the *will* [that is, of the freedom that God gave human beings] is wider than that of the *intellect* [that is, of their capacity to know]" (Descartes 1996 [1641]: 40, emphasis mine). However, instead of confining the use of the will within the same limits of their capacity to know, human beings bring their will to bear upon questions which they do not understand. It is thus man's "misuse of the will," and not God, that deceives man. Hence, Descartes' conclusion is that, if I confine myself to "what the intellect clearly and distinctly reveals, and no further, ... it is quite impossible for me to go wrong" (Descartes 1996 [1641]: 43). The reason for this, Descartes explains, is that

> Every clear and distinct perception is undoubtedly something real and positive; and hence cannot come from nothing, but must necessarily have God for its author ... God ... is supremely perfect, and ... cannot be a deceiver on pain of contradiction ... For I shall unquestionably reach the truth, if only I give sufficient attention to all the things which I perfectly understand, and separate these from all the other cases where my apprehension is more confused and obscure.

*(Descartes 1996 [1641]: 41)*

This account contains the seeds of a paradox that is central to the genealogy of European secularity. Descartes's anthropocentric secular mode of knowledge as based on a process of emancipation from the senses, in fact, ultimately requires "a benevolent God to rout the Evil Demon and guarantee his transition from knowledge of his own perceptions to knowledge of the external world" (Patterson 2000: 73). This tension is clearly identified by Bernard Williams, who observes:

> The road that Descartes constructed ... essentially goes over a religious bridge. Taking his concern to be the foundations of scientific knowledge, these are provided by God; taking it to be the foundations of the possibility of knowledge, these too ... are to be found in God.

*(Williams 2005: 146)*

The non self-sufficiency of the secular idea of knowledge envisioned by Descartes can be observed even more clearly with Kant. According to Michel Foucault (2005b: 26), Kant further advances Descartes's secular idea of knowledge "by saying: if knowledge has limits, these limits exist entirely within the structure of the knowing subject, that is to say in precisely what makes knowledge possible." For Kant, in fact, knowledge is no longer the attempt to grasp an externally God-given order, but an interrogation of the individual rational faculties based on a process of transcendence of the senses whereby the individual joins the metaphysical domain of pure intelligible beings where all moral concepts have the status of universal principles. This secular understanding of knowledge is thus grounded in "man" rather than "God," and encompasses the separation of reason and faith. Kant, however, observes that this secular route to the universal law of morality may not be enough to ensure that the moral agent will comply with the categorical imperative, particularly when this would imply a sacrifice on her part (Kennedy 2006: 138). Kant's solution is to bring back faith into the picture as a postulate of practical reason, namely as "a theoretical proposition" which is "not demonstrable as such," but which should be considered true "insofar as it is attached inseparably to an a priori unconditionally valid practical view" (Kant 1999 [1788]: 238). Hence, Kant suggests, although the ideas of God, and of faith more generally, lie beyond the domain of proper knowledge, they nonetheless retain a practical usefulness, as they can enforce compliance with the moral law through their force of moral persuasion and threat of eternal sanction. Religion thus becomes for Kant a necessary prop for the motivational moral weakness of the secular domain.

Yet, on a closer look, Kant's reliance on religion in his construction of an independent secular domain goes beyond resorting to faith as a motivational force. As Ian Hunter observes, it is the very interrogation of the individual's rational faculties as envisaged by Kant that, to return to Williams's expression, "goes over a religious bridge." For Hunter, in fact, Kant's categorical imperative is the product of an exercise in self-transcendence which belongs to the Christian–Platonic spiritual tradition. In this tradition,

> the metaphysician activates the higher intellect he shares with God, thereby participating in the self-authenticating principles of an intellect that creates what it thinks. Doubtless it will seem odd to many that the voice of Kantian reason should sound so similar to the voice of God. But this will seem the less so the more we understand that the exercise through which Kant listens to reason is in fact a version of that through which Christian–Platonists attuned themselves to the emanations of the divine intellect.
>
> *(Hunter 2002: 923–4)*

If Hunter's reading is correct, it emerges that Kant's secular domain cannot do without religious faith as an inspirational force which may compel the individual to a moral course of action, and as a form of inquiry in which the communion with God is partially superseded by the communion with our "higher intellect" shared "with God."

Why is neither Descartes nor Kant able to articulate their secular systems of knowledge and morality without resorting to a religious dimension which involves a spiritual reliance on or close association with God? An answer to this question is provided by Durkheim, who offers a critical and sociological rendering of Kant's account. For Durkheim, we need to consider that our soul – what enables us "to communicate with God" – is not a metaphysical endowment impervious to scrutiny, but more simply a product of society (Durkheim 1973 [1914]: 159). The soul belongs to the domain of the sacred, which encompasses those "collective ideals that have fixed themselves on material objects" through a process of "communion" of "a plurality of individual consciousnesses," and that inspire in us a feeling of reverence and respect (Durkheim 1973 [1914]: 159–60). Hence, for Durkheim, religion and the idea of God are an immanent instantiation of the system of collective societal representations which contributes to providing moral guidance for the individual. If these remarks bring to the fore the historical symbiosis between morality and religion, it does not follow from them that in a secular society morality may simply be stripped out of "every supernatural element" (Durkheim 1975 [1925]: 195). The force of moral norms, Durkheim contends, is a product not just of their rational content but, more importantly, of their belonging to a sacred domain. Hence, Durkheim concludes, if

> one confines himself to withdraw from moral discipline everything that is religious without replacing it, one almost inevitably runs the danger of withdrawing at the same time all

elements that are properly moral. Under the name of rational morality, we would be left with an impoverished and colourless morality.

*(Durkheim 1975 [1925]: 196)*

However, according to Max Weber, the process feared by Durkheim of withdrawing morality from religion is more than a potential threat: it is a historical development which has long been under way in secular modernity. For Weber, this process is part of a broader dynamic of fragmentation in the value spheres of those domains – the intellectual sphere, the moral sphere, the economic sphere, the political sphere, the aesthetic sphere, and the erotic sphere – which once fell under the unifying purview of faith and now have established their own "immanent laws" (Weber 1991 [1915]: 331). With the death of God, Weber contends, our moral universe has lost its original unity and is shaken by a "polytheism of values" in which "the various spheres of the world stand in irreconcilable conflict with each other" (Weber 1991 [1919]: 147–8). In this process of compartmentalization and fragmentation, Weber (1991 [1915]: 355) suggests, science "has come forward with the claim of representing the only possible form of a reasoned view of the world." However, this is a view unable to provide guidance for the most fundamental ethical questions. For instance, while modern medicine has become a remarkably sophisticated enterprise, its capacity to answer the question as to whether "life is worth living and when" (with regard, for instance, to terminally ill patients, or patients with serious brain injury) has sharply declined; jurisprudence can help us to devise rational laws, but is unable to tell us "whether there should be law and whether one should establish just these rules"; social sciences explain phenomena, yet often leaving aside the question of whether these phenomena "are worth while" (Weber 1991 [1919]: 144–5). "The intellect," Weber remarks, "has created an aristocracy based on the possession of [a secular] rational culture and independent of all ethical qualities of man" (Weber 1991 [1915]: 355).

The crisis of secular consciousness analyzed by Weber finds probably its most powerful illustration in the modern capitalist condition. As Weber argues in *The Protestant Ethic and the Spirit of Capitalism* (2001), the underlying force behind the development of capitalism is ascetic Protestantism, and in particular Calvinism and its idea of predestination. Although this notion implies that the way one chooses to live one's life does not change what God has reserved for them in the afterlife, earthly life may still "be considered as a symptom or index of one's own state of religious grace as established by god's decree," and therefore a way "to penetrate god's design … to ascertain one's own personal destiny" (Weber 1978 [1922]: 523). Hence, should a virtuous and moral behavior be accompanied by economic and social success, this may be taken as an indication of future salvation decreed by God. For Weber, the ascetic Protestant way of life thus originates in a religious calling. However, with the process of secularization and the separation of the sphere of morality from that of the economy, the process of capitalist accumulation is no longer an instantiation of a sober ethical behavior, but an impersonal and instrumental drive towards the amassing of wealth which is devoid of any moral concern. Weber's argument, though, does not stop here.

Although the separation of value spheres and the ensuing decline of a unifying spiritual dimension are the defining feature of Europe's modernity and its crisis of secularity, Weber also invites us to consider a more "positive" reading of these processes. For the German scholar, in fact, they are part of a broader dynamic of rationalization which has turned Europe into the beacon of a "broad range of ideas and cultural forces" marked by "universal validity," such as modern historiography, jurisprudence, economy, music, and architecture (Weber 2002 [1920]: 149). According to Weber, the universal force of these ideas is a product of the "capacity and disposition" of the people of Europe "to organize their lives in a practical–rational manner"

(Weber 2002 [1920]: 160) and, on a more conceptual level, a product of "the modern Occidental search for the individual self in contrast to all others – the attempt to take the self by the forelock and pull it out of the mud, forming it into a 'personality'" (Weber 2005 [1958]: 65). This argument introduces us to a civilizational geography in which there are, on the one hand, the people of Europe, whose fragmented moral horizon may well have triggered a crisis of value and meaning but has certainly contributed to making them masters of their own destiny by making the intellectual sphere independent from the religious sphere. On the other hand, there are those non-Western subjects who live in a world not of their own making (as their economy, jurisprudence, and architecture are a product of the civilizational strength of Western/European subject) and are still trapped in the "mud" of traditional forces like religion. For Weber, the archetype of the non-Western subject is embodied by the Muslim subject.

At the heart of Weber's sociology of Islam, which has been aptly described as a sociology of absence (Zubaida 2006), is the attempt to account for the uniqueness of the West by accounting for all those elements seemingly missing in Muslim societies, such as "rational (Roman) law, the modern state, the application of science to all areas of social life, ... [and] the bureaucratization of social procedures" (Turner 1994: 39). Although these features have contributed to the crisis of European societies, they have nonetheless endowed Europe with an undisputed civilizational superiority. How does Weber explain the defectiveness of Islam? Once again, we need to go back to the question of predestination.

As was argued before, the European (Protestant) idea of predestination revolved around the uncertainty surrounding the afterlife. The secular world was thus an independent space in which the individual enjoyed the freedom to pursue an ascetic way of life as a means to worldly success which could stand as a potential sign of salvation. The Islamic idea of predestination, on the contrary, revolved around the idea that "The religious fate of the individual in the next world ... [would] be adequately secured by the individual's belief in Allah and the prophets" (Weber 1978 [1922]: 574). Hence, whereas for "the puritans governed by the Christian ethic ... belief in predestination often produced ethical rigorism, legalism and rationally planned procedures for the patterning of life," in the case of Islam it required only an uncritical acceptance of the laws of Islam, which clashed with the possibility of the emergence of the rational subject (Weber 1978 [1922]: 573). As Weber explains (1978 [1922]: 573), "In the case of the Muslim warriors of the first generation of Islam, the belief in predestination often produced a complete obliviousness to self in the interest of fulfilment of the religious commandment of a holy war for the conquest of the world." Subsequently, Weber (1978 [1922]: 574–5) contends, when Islam changed from warring religion to religion of the masses, proselytizing fervor was replaced by a fatalistic attitude of compliance with the will of God which failed to produce any meaningful form of rationalization.

It is at this juncture that Weber's argument meets that of Benedict XVI discussed in the previous section (pp. 187–8). Although the two thinkers move from completely different epistemological perspectives and normative concerns, they nonetheless converge in identifying the fragmentation of the European moral horizon as a key dimension of the crisis of European secular modernity. The loss of unity following the epistemological and ontological separation of reason and faith which has enthroned secular reason as the sole and exclusive language of the public sphere and confined faith to the private dimension is the cause of a moral decay in which an underlying unifying principle is no longer available. The separation of life into "value spheres" paves the way for the crisis of a secular domain which, unable to establish itself as a self-sufficient foundation of knowledge and morality, has become the battleground of contending moral positions. This struggle has weakened the sense of identity and moral direction of the Western/European subject.

And yet, although this crisis has its very origins in the separation of secular reason and religious faith, this separation is turned into a source of civilizational superiority precisely against an Islam that, according to Weber and Benedict XVI, this separation has not experienced. The Muslim "Other" thus turns into a projection of European anxieties; into a means of displacing the crisis onto "Them," rather than reflectively interrogating ourselves on what generates our perception of "Them" as "Others." From this perspective, the construction of Muslims in Europe as Others of European secular modernity is what makes possible the reproduction of the latter, despite its longstanding crisis. Drawing on Wendy Brown (2006: 27), it can be suggested that Muslims in Europe occupy "the position of Derridean supplement; that which conceptually undermines the binary of identity/difference or inside/outside yet is crucial to the conceit of integrity, autarky, self-sufficiency, and continuity of the dominant term," that is, Europe.

## Postsecularity: a way beyond?

> [I]f [a] philosophy of the future exists, it must be born … in consequence of meetings and impacts between Europe and non-Europe.
>
> *(Michel Foucault, quoted in Afary and Anderson 2005: 2, 87)*

As was observed in the first section of this chapter (pp. 187–8), although Habermas does not explicitly connect the crisis of European secularity with the crisis of European identity and how their awareness may have been prompted by the growing presence of Muslims in Europe, he nonetheless concedes that contemporary attempts to rethink and possibly move beyond the crisis of secularity cannot ignore "the background assumptions" which make the contemporary "discussion on 'Islam in Europe' so explosive" (Habermas 2007). Equally, they cannot ignore the fact that "Muslim immigrants cannot be integrated into Western society in defiance of their religion but only with it" (Habermas 2007). Habermas's "postsecular turn" is the attempt to address both the crisis of secularity – that is, the crisis of values of modern instrumental rationalization – and the problem of the integration of Muslims in Europe. For Habermas (2008: 131), "Religious traditions have a special power to articulate moral intuitions, especially with regard to vulnerable forms of communal life," and therefore can provide a useful corrective to the distortions of modern secular rationalization:

> This potential makes religious speech a serious candidate to transporting possible truth contents, which can then be translated from the vocabulary of a particular religious community into a generally accessible language.
>
> *(Habermas 2006: 10)*

On the other hand, Habermas (2006: 8) contends, "Given that in the liberal state only secular reasons count, citizens who adhere to a faith are obliged to establish a kind of 'balance' between their religious and their secular convictions." The problem is that "many religious citizens would not be able to undertake such an artificial division within their own minds without jeopardizing their existence as pious persons" (Habermas 2006: 8). A postsecular public sphere is thus the opportunity to establish a more pluralistic space of confrontation which may take advantage of the "world-disclosing power of religious semantics" (Habermas 2008: 217) and the "regenerative power" that it can offer for a "dwindling normative consciousness" (quoted in Harrington 2007: 544). However, Habermas (2008: 243) warns, this religious semantics cannot freely flow into the public sphere, but needs to be properly translated into a secular language, the embodiment of the universality of reason, in order to protect religious and cultural minorities and, most of all, to avoid the possibility that the "boundary between faith and knowledge" may become "porous," because "once religious motives force their way into philosophy under false pretences, reason loses its foothold and succumbs to irrational effusion."

Habermas's account has been the object of extensive assessment, often resulting in the criticism that his vision of postsecularity employs the very instrumental rationality that it would want to challenge, with the effect that he reduces religion to a tool of the reproduction and moral regeneration of a "dwindling" secular domain (Harrington 2007; Mavelli and Petito 2012; Dallmayr 2012; Cerella 2012; Pabst 2012). For the purposes of this chapter, the main limit of Habermas's account is that it fails to connect the crisis of secularity with the crisis of European identity and reduces the issue of the integration of Muslims in Europe to a question of pluralism. As this chapter has attempted to suggest, the possibility of a less confrontational encounter between Europe and Islam in Europe requires a recognition of the limits of the European secular tradition, particularly its incapacity to provide a self-sufficient base for knowledge and morality and, more broadly, a sound spiritual foundation for people's lives. It requires a recognition that the anxieties stemming from this condition may be an important component of the European crisis of identity and the object of an act of displacement which projects onto the Muslim "Other" this anxiety by turning their apparent lack of secularity – which may seem to make them unaffected by the moral decay of the West – into a marker of a civilizational inferiority characterized by irrationality, indolence, and violence.

The possibility of moving beyond this asphyxiating construction requires recognition of the fragilities and limits of Europe's secular tradition, rather than entrenchment in the dogma of secularity in order to cover up its contradictions. The point, to be sure, is not to discard secularity but to reinterpret its emancipatory and pluralistic dimensions in the light of the crisis of European identity and the challenge of Islam in Europe. If Habermas (2011: 19) is correct in suggesting that "practical reason ... no longer has sufficient strength to awaken, and to keep awake, in the minds of secular subjects, an awareness of the violations of solidarity throughout the world, an awareness of what is missing, of what cries out to heaven," then what is required is a postsecularity which may be able to articulate new forms of identities, subjectivities, and solidarities beyond the strictures of a rigid separation of the secular and the religious. The possibility of such postsecular modes of being and becoming requires a Europe which may, to use the words of Étienne Balibar (2003: 334), "use its own fragilities and indeterminacies ... as an effective mediation in the process of bringing about a new political culture, a new pattern of politics." Although these words have been used in a different context, they are nonetheless very relevant to our discussion, as they open the conceptual space to imagine postsecular Europe as a "space of translation" between different cultures. Translation, in this perspective, is no longer the Habermasian conversion of the moral intuitions of faith into the supposed universality of secular reason, but an idiom in itself, indeed "the only 'genuine idiom of Europe'" (Balibar 2003: 334). This is the possibility of an idiom which may articulate a new postsecular language of identity and solidarity across the categories of the secular and the religious, where the uncertainties of one's own identities, roots, traditions, and allegiances (including those of Muslims in Europe and in America, which have been explored at length by other contributors in this volume) may be recognized in the Other, rather than projected onto them. A hope, for sure, but also a political imagination, which may help us "to have the courage to begin anew ... to abandon every dogmatic principle" (Foucault 2005a: 185), and to conceive of the possibility of different forms of encounter between Europe and its Muslim population.

## Note

1 An extended version of the argument presented in this section (although explored from a slightly different perspective) can be found in the second chapter of my *Europe's Encounter with Islam: The Secular and the Postsecular* (Mavelli 2012).

## Bibliography

Afary, J. and Anderson, K.B. (2005) *Foucault and the Iranian Revolution: Gender and the Seductions of Islamism*, Chicago: University of Chicago Press.

Al Sayyad, N. and Castells, M. (eds.) (2002) *Muslim Europe or Euro-Islam: Politics, Culture, and Citizenship in the Age of Globalization*, Oxford: Lexington Books.

Asad, T. (2003) *Formations of the Secular: Christianity, Islam, Modernity*, Stanford: Stanford University Press.

——(2006) "Trying to Understand French Secularism," in de Vries, H. and Sullivan, L.E. (eds.) *Political Theologies: Public Religions in a Post-Secular World*, New York: Fordham University Press.

——(2009) "Free Speech, Blasphemy, and Secular Criticism," in Asad, T., Brown, W., Butler, J., and Mahmood, S. *Is Critique Secular? Blasphemy, Injury, and Free Speech*, Berkeley: University of California Press.

Balibar, É. (2003) "Europe: Vanishing Mediator," *Constellations* 10(3): 312–38.

Barbato, M. (2010) "Conceptions of the Self for Post-secular Emancipation: Towards a Pilgrim's Guide to Global Justice," *Millennium: Journal of International Studies* 39(2): 547–64.

BBC (2010) "Merkel Says German Multicultural Society Has Failed," www.bbc.co.uk/news/world-europe-11559451 (accessed July 4, 2011).

British Council (2009) "Europe and Islam: Whose Identity Crisis?," www.oursharedeurope.org/whose-identity-crisis-report-09 (accessed September 4, 2012).

Brown, W. (2006) *Regulating Aversion: Tolerance in the Age of Identity and Empire*, Princeton: Princeton University Press.

Cameron, D. (2011) "PM's Speech at Munich Security Conference," www.number10.gov.uk/news/speeches-and-transcripts/2011/02/pms-speech-at-munich-security-conference-60293 (accessed July 4, 2011).

Cerella, A. (2012) "Religion and Political Form: Carl Schmitt's Genealogy of Politics as Critique of Habermas's Post-secular Discourse," *Review of International Studies* 38(5): 975–94.

Cesari, J. (2003) "Muslim Minorities in Europe: The Silent Revolution," in Esposito, J. and Burgat, F. (eds.) *Modernizing Islam: Religion in the Public Sphere in the Middle East and Europe*, London: C. Hurst & Company.

——(2004) *When Islam and Democracy Meet: Muslims in Europe and in the United States*, New York: Palgrave Macmillan.

Connolly, W.E. (2006) "Europe: A Minor Tradition," in Scott, D. and Hirschkind, C. (eds.) *Powers of the Secular Modern: Talal Asad and His Interlocutors*, Stanford: Stanford University Press.

Dallmayr, F. (2012) "Post-Secularity and (Global) Politics: A Need for Radical Redefinition," *Review of International Studies* 38(5): 963–73.

Descartes, R. (1996 [1641]) *Meditations on First Philosophy*, translated by John Cottingham, Cambridge: Cambridge University Press.

Durkheim, E. (1973 [1914]) "The Dualism of Human Nature and Its Social Condition," in Bellah, R. (ed.) *Emile Durkheim: On Morality and Society, Selected Writings*, Chicago: University of Chicago Press.

——(1975 [1925]) "Moral Education," in Pickering, W.S.F. (ed.) *Durkheim on Religion*, London: Routledge and Kegan Paul.

Esposito, R. (2008) *Bíos: Biopolitics and Philosophy*, translated by Timothy Campbell, Minneapolis: University of Minnesota Press.

Foucault, M. (2005a) "Dialogue with Baqir Parham (Spring 1979)," in Afary, J. and Anderson, K.B. *Foucault and the Iranian Revolution: Gender and the Seductions of Islamism*, Chicago: University of Chicago Press.

——(2005b) *The Hermeneutics of the Subject: Lectures at the Collège de France 1981–1982*, New York: Picador.

Glucksmann, A. (2006) "Separating Truth and Belief," *Le Monde* Online (English translation), www.signandsight.com/features/640.html (accessed July 20, 2011).

Habermas, J. (2006) "Religion in the Public Sphere," *European Journal of Philosophy* 14(1): 1–25.

——(2007) "Notes on a Post-Secular Society," *Signandsight.com*, June 18, www.signandsight.com/features/1714.html (accessed April 17, 2012).

——(2008) *Between Naturalism and Religion: Philosophical Essays*, Cambridge: Polity Press.

——(2011) "An Awareness of What Is Missing," in Habermas, J. et al. *An Awareness of What Is Missing: Faith and Reason in a Post-secular Age*, Cambridge: Polity Press.

Habermas, J. and Ratzinger, J. (2007) *The Dialectics of Secularization: On Reason and Religion*, Cambridge: Ignatius Press.

Harrington, A. (2007) "Habermas and the 'Post-Secular Society'," *European Journal of Social Theory* 10(4): 543–60.

Hunter, I. (2002) "The Morals of Metaphysics: Kant's *Groundwork* as Intellectual *Paideia*," *Critical Inquiry* 28(4): 908–29.

*Irish Times* (2011) "Sarkozy Denounces Multiculturalism as 'A Failure'," www.irishtimes.com/newspaper/world/2011/0212/1224289636274.html (accessed July 4, 2011).

Jansen, Y. (2011) "Secularism and Religious (In-)Security: Reinterpreting the French Headscarf Debate," *Krisis: Journal for Contemporary Philosophy* 2: 2–19.

Kant, I. (1999 [1788]) "Critique of Practical Reason," in *Practical Philosophy*, translated and ed. Mary J. Gregor, Cambridge: Cambridge University Press.

Kennedy, E. (2006) *Secularism and Its Opponents from Augustine to Solzhenitsyn*, New York: Palgrave Macmillan.

Kinnvall, C. (2012) "European Trauma: Governance and the Psychological Moment," *Alternatives: Global, Local, Political* 37(3): 266–81.

Laurence, J. (2007) "The Prophet of Moderation: Tariq Ramadan's Quest to Reclaim Islam," *Foreign Affairs* 86(3): 128–34.

Malik, K. (2011) "The Last Crusade," *New Humanist* 126(6), newhumanist.org.uk/2672/the-last-crusade.

Mavelli, L. (2012) *Europe's Encounter with Islam: The Secular and the Postsecular*, Abingdon and New York: Routledge.

——(2013) "Between Normalization and Exception: The Securitization of Islam and the Construction of the Secular Subject," *Millennium: Journal of International Studies* 41(2): 159–81.

Mavelli, L. and Petito, F. (2012) "The Postsecular in International Relations: An Overview," *Review of International Studies* 38(5): 931–42.

Nash, R.H. (1999) *Life's Ultimate Questions: An Introduction to Philosophy*, Grand Rapids, MI: Zondervan.

Nirenberg, D. (2008) "Islam and the West: Two Dialectical Fantasies," *Journal of Religion in Europe* 1(1): 3–33.

Pabst, A. (2012) "The Secularism of Post-Secularity: Religion, Realism, and the Revival of Grand Theory in IR," *Review of International Studies* 38(5): 995–1017.

Patterson, S. (2000) "How Cartesian Was Descartes?," in Crane, T. and Patterson, S. (eds.) *History of the Mind–Body Problem*, London: Routledge.

Peter, F. (2006) "Individualization and Religious Authority in Western European Islam," *Islam and Christian–Muslim Relations* 17(1): 105–18.

Pope Benedict XVI (2006) "Faith, Reason and the University: Memories and Reflections," *The Holy See*, www.vatican.va/holy_father/benedict_xvi/speeches/2006/september/documents/hf_ben-xvi_spe_20060912_university-regensburg_en.html (accessed July 20, 2012).

Presseurop (2010) "Mutti Merkel Handbags Multikulti," www.presseurop.eu/en/content/article/364091-mutti-merkel-handbags-multikulti (accessed July 4, 2011).

Ratzinger, J. (2006a) "Letter to Marcello Pera," in Pera, M. and Ratzinger, J. *Without Roots: The West, Relavism, Christianity, Islam*, New York: Basic Books.

——(2006b) "The Spiritual Roots of Europe: Yesterday, Today, and Tomorrow," in Pera, M. and Ratzinger, J. *Without Roots: The West, Relavism, Christianity, Islam*, New York: Basic Books.

Reuters (2010) "Germany Holds Inflamed Debate on Islam and Migration," www.reuters.com/article/2010/10/18/us-germany-islam-debate-analysis-idUSTRE69H36U20101018 (accessed October 14, 2011).

Ruether, R.R. (2006) "What the Pope Should Have Said to the Islamic World," *Holy Land Studies: A Multidisciplinary Journal* 5(2): 127–9.

Salvatore, A. (2007) "Authority in Question: Secularity, Republicanism and 'Communitarianism' in the Emerging Euro-Islamic Public Sphere," *Theory, Culture & Society* 24(2): 135–60.

Spiegel (2010) "The Man Who Divided Germany," www.spiegel.de/international/topic/thilo_sarrazin/ (accessed July 4, 2011).

Turner, B.S. (1994) *Orientalism, Postmodernism and Globalism*, London: Routledge.

Weber, M. (1978 [1922]) *Economy and Society*, Berkeley: University of California Press.

——(1991 [1915]) "Religious Rejections of the World and Their Directions," in Gerth, H.H. and Wright Mills, C. (eds.) *From Max Weber: Essays in Sociology*, Oxford: Oxford University Press.

——(1991 [1919]) "Science as a Vocation," in Gerth, H.H. and Wright Mills, C. (eds.) *From Max Weber: Essays in Sociology*, Oxford: Oxford University Press.

——(2002 [1920]) "Prefatory Remarks," in Weber, M. *The Protestant Ethic and the Spirit of Capitalism*, ed. Stephen Kalberg, London: Routledge.

——(2005 [1958]) "Protection Against the Western Search for the Individual Self," in Stephen Kalberg (ed.) *Max Weber: Readings and Commentary on Modernity*, Oxford: Blackwell.

Weber, M., Parsons, T., and Giddens, A. (2001) *The Protestant Ethic and the Spirit of Capitalism*, London: Routledge.

Williams, B. (2005) *Descartes: The Project of Pure Enquiry*, London: Routledge.

Žižek, S. (2011) "A Vile Logic to Anders Breivik's Choice of Target," *Guardian*, August 8, www.guardian.co.uk/commentisfree/2011/aug/08/anders-behring-breivik-pim-fortuyn (accessed September 22, 2012).

Zubaida, S. (2006) "Max Weber's *The City* and the Islamic City," *Max Weber Studies* 6(1): 111–18.

# 12

# Emergence of Western Muslim identity

## Factors, agents, and discourses

*Adis Duderija*

In which sense can we talk about the emergence of a Western Muslim identity (or, more precisely, types of Western Muslim identity)[1] over the last two to three decades? Is this Western Muslim identity to be thought of in terms of mere geography? Is it an issue of politico-legal allegiance (i.e. legal status, citizenship) or intellectual and cultural affinity? Is it perhaps a question of an identity based on distinct understanding of a religious tradition? Can it be best understood in terms of subscription to certain values, principles, and the philosophical and worldview assumptions underpinning these? Alternatively, is it a question of emotional attachment and belonging? Or is this emerging Western Muslim identity a combination of some or all of the above? Put differently, would the emergence of such an identity be signaled or manifested by the sociologically observable processes of (various degrees and modes) of de-ethnicization (in case of those whose sense of "Muslimness" is strongly linked with their ethnicity), de- and or transculturalization (in particular the loss of language, customs, etc. or the adoption of Western equivalents), creolization, acceptance of civic and civil rights and responsibilities, the development of a strong sense of emotional attachment and belonging to the West, the engendering of Western-Muslim-specific literature, performing and fine arts, music, norms, or the development of Western-Muslim-specific Islamic theology, legal and ethical thought. To answer the question posed above it would, of course, be inevitable for us to deal with the issue of the very definition of what makes the West Western, and to a certain extent what makes a Muslim a Muslim. Assuming that there is something clearly identifiable as the "West"[2] and as a "Muslim," this article will examine the emergence of Western Muslim identity from the last decade of the twentieth century to the present by focusing on factors, agents, and discourses which could be identified as facilitating the emergence of a Western Muslim identity primarily defined in terms of its cultural, religio-philosophical, and socio-political dimensions. In the second half of the chapter (pp. 207–10) I describe two different types of Western Muslim identity at work here, termed Progressive Muslims and Neo-traditional Salafis. Finally, in the third section of the chapter (pp. 210–11) I ask the question of which factors can be seen as contributing towards the emergence of different types of Western Muslim identity, and in this context I highlight the important role of scriptural hermeneutics.

## Some significant factors and processes facilitating the emergence of a distinct Western Muslim identity

In order to understand the processes involved in the emergence of a distinct Western Muslim identity over the last two to three decades it is necessary to start our discussion by identifying which factors, agents, and discourses play an important part in its construction because for most Muslims residing in the West, especially those who were born there, as shall be argued on p. 201, their Muslim identity is a product of a conscious process of identity (re-)construction.

Studies which examine identity construction among Western Muslims have identified a number of factors which influence this dynamic. Among the most important ones are secularization and cultural globalization, contemporary geopolitics and the nature of international affairs, the broader socio-economic, political and legal contexts of "host societies," the diversity within the Muslim communities themselves (such as ethnicity, family, and socio-economic background, the length of immigration experience), and the context of belonging to a new immigrant minority religion (Duderija 2007). The following dimensions of Western Muslim minorities have been identified by Cesari (2007: 52) as being particularly important in the construction of their identities: the meta-discourse on Islam; the influence of dominant cultural and political frameworks; the complex interaction between religion and ethnicity; the influence of global Islam; state collusion between religion, ethnicity, and social marginality and intra-Muslim theological diversity. What concerns me here is to discuss some of the factors and processes which I consider significant in facilitating the emergence of distinct Western Muslim identity(ies).

Before I move on to discussing what I consider to be significant factors and processes which facilitate the emergence of a distinct Western Muslim identity, one important clarification is necessary; namely, when talking about the emergence of a Western Muslim identity throughout this chapter I do not assume that there only exists one such identity but use it as an umbrella term for different types of specific Western Muslim identity, all of which share certain elements which make them distinctly so. This will be made more clear in the part of the article which discusses different ways of being a Western Muslim (pp. 203–7).

### Migration and identity changes in new immigrant religious minority communities in the West

One of the significant processes which play an important role in the emergence of Western Muslim identity is their status of belonging to a new immigrant-based religious minority. The vast majority of Muslims residing in the West are of recent immigrant background (Duderija 2007). So to have a better understanding of the identity dynamics at work among Western Muslim communities, the dialectic between (im)migration and identity changes in new (im)migrant religious minority communities requires some elaboration.

The impact of (im)migration on identity dynamics among new religious minority immigrant communities has not been studied until very recently, although, for a number of economic, social, and political reasons, the size and the number of new immigrant communities belonging to a religious minority from very diverse religious backgrounds have significantly increased in the West over the last forty years, and the last twenty-five years in particular (Duderija 2007).

In this context it is important to point out that one significant factor in understanding the construction of new immigrants' religious and ethnic identities is their transplantation from forming a religious majority to having a religious minority status. This applies to the majority of the Muslim immigrants since most of them have come to the West from Muslim majority countries. This is of significance because the change in context in which new immigrant communities undergo a transition from the more homogeneous majority socio-cultural setting of their country of birth to a secular, pluralist, and minority one in the West has important identity changing implications. This point is illustrated by Ammerman's (2003: 208) assertion that the context and the requirements of a culture into which immigrants enter will inevitably influence the beliefs and practices that the immigrants were accustomed to and that were taken for granted. Why this is so can be explained by the fact that in the majority context religious community and society stand in a complementary relationship, whilst in the minority context they often stand in opposition to each other. This seems to be particularly the case for new immigrant Muslims who have come from still largely traditional cultures and societies strongly influenced by traditional Islamic beliefs, practices, norms, and values.

It is in the changing nature of the relationship between their ethnic and religious identity that the identity modifications experienced by new immigrants belonging to minority religions are most readily evident. The actual dynamic between the two loci of identity varies greatly depending upon the immigrant group in question and also with respect to the extent to which immigrants emphasize their religious or ethnic identity. One useful model which can shed light on this dynamic is a threefold typology developed by Hammond and Warner (1998: 55–66) which describes the changes in the relationship between the ethnic and religious aspects of identity among immigrants from various ethnic and religious backgrounds. One such process that takes place in some groups (e.g. Amish and Jewish communities in the USA) is described as ethnic fusion, a process through which religion becomes a foundation of ethnicity.

The Greek and Russian Orthodox and Dutch Reformed Church communities are examples of the second type of relationship, named "ethnic religion" by Hammond and Warner; this applies to those religious communities in which religion comprises one of several foundations of ethnicity. Finally, Hammond and Warner's typology includes the term "religious ethnicity," in which religious tradition is shared by other ethnicities, such as in the case of Mexican, Irish, and Italian Catholics.

There are a large number of sociological studies on religion and new immigrants which emphasize the crucial role religion plays in ethnic identity and the difficulty of delineating between the two (Duderija 2007). This is demonstrated well by the fact that at the center of classical sociological studies of immigration and religion is the notion of the centrality of religion for immigrants, especially if they belong to a minority religious group (Duderija 2007). For example, Mirdal's (2000: 39–40) assertion that "religious and ethnic identity especially play an important role for persons belonging to minority groups, often to the point that they predominate above all other aspects of identity," is indicative of this. Williams forms a similar view, maintaining that

> Immigrants are religious – by all counts more religious than they were before they left home – because religion is one of the important identity markers that help preserve individual self-awareness and cohesion in the group.
>
> *(Williams 1998: 29)*

Several other studies further reinforce this idea. Yang and Rose (2001: 269–88) argue, for example, that the "internal" and "external religious pluralism" in Western liberal democracies encourages institutional and theological transformations that energize and revitalize religions of immigrants. Alba (2005: 20–49) notices the same trend in Western European societies, where religion for immigrants becomes a key institutional site for the demarcation of native immigrant boundaries. Gilliat (1994: 26), writing in the context of examining identity changes in British Muslims, notes that the process of (im)migration can lead to "an invigoration of old traditions, and thus a strengthening of identity." Waardenburg (2003: 485) makes a similar observation by asserting that "in migrant or minority situations religion may play an important role in reaffirming and integrating identity on a communal level." Smith's (2000: 1174) study of religion and ethnicity in America indicates that in the immigrant context ethnicity is determined frequently by identification with a particular religious tradition more than any other factor, such as language or feelings of nationalism. He further maintains that traditional religious beliefs "have been decisive determinants of ethnic affiliation in America" and that the religious factor in ethnic identity is strengthened by the migration experience (Smith 2000: 1174). Gilliat (1994: 279–85) notices the same trend among British Muslims, stating that for them the crucial dimension of their ethnic identity is religious identity. Based on these findings we can rather safely conclude that for many immigrant religious minority groups the religious component of their identity, in particular, becomes highly salient.[3] What implications do the processes described above have for the second and subsequent generations of immigrants who were born/raised in the West?

The first point that needs mentioning in this context is that parent immigrants, when passing their cultural heritage on to their children, consider religion to be the key to cultural reproduction of identities (Warner and Wittner 1998: 16). Eid (2002: 25) and Waardenburg (2000: 49–69) form the view that immigrant children focus on identity strategies which move away from both the host society's and their parents' prefabricated boundaries, resulting in the Western-born generations of immigrants belonging to new immigrant religious minorities arriving at their own relationships between ethnic and religious traditions. Although most first-generation immigrants continue to cling to their distinctive ethnic identities and practices, Ebaugh and Chafez (2000: 406) maintain that the "second and subsequent generation-dominated religious institutions will likely be more pan-religious and/or more pan-ethnic in their practices, identities, and memberships." The evidence that this process is already at work in Muslim immigrant communities in the West will be argued on pp. 000–00.

## The context of belonging to a new immigrant minority religious community and the emergence of Western Muslim identity

A significant number of Western Muslims have immigrated to the West over the last two to three decades. As such, Western Muslims as a whole enjoy a status of belonging to what we refer to as a new immigrant minority religious community in the context of a liberal democracy which is committed, in theory at least, to what could broadly be termed the policies of multiculturalism. As we briefly alluded to on p. 199, this particular context of Western Muslims has important implications for how they construct their identity, especially in the relation to new, Western context-specific Muslim identity potentialities. Relevant scholarship has, for example, demonstrated that the context of having a minority religion status becomes a decisive element in the transformation of Western Muslim practices and their relationship to Islam. The status of being a new immigrant minority religious community also can (significantly) alter Islamic thought, practice, and community in the West. Let us describe these processes in more detail.

As identified by Roy (2004), for new Western Muslim immigrants tensions between four levels of identity exist, namely: identity based on geography and/or kinship; the larger ethnic or national identity based on common language and culture; Muslim identity exclusively based on religious patterns with no specific reference to language (apart from basic Qur'anic Arabic, which the majority of non-Arab Muslims do not understand) or culture; and identity based on acculturation along Western patterns. The status of belonging to a new immigrant minority religion community conforms with the last two of the four levels of identity identified above. One important reason for this is that for new immigrant Muslim communities living in the West the common defining factor is the mere reference to Islam as a religion, not Islam as a dominant socio-cultural force. This, in turn, is based on the fact that the new immigrant Muslim communities share, in their totality, no common cultural or linguistic heritage. This is particularly so for the Western-born or raised generations of Muslims (as well as Western converts to Islam – see pp. 204–5), who did not inherit a set of well-defined Islamic social and cultural values and symbols from their parents' or grandparents' generations. These Western-born/ raised Muslims of immigrant background are, thus, unable to reproduce the ethno-religious identity of their predecessors but have to construct their own, thereby re-evaluating Islam in the new socio-cultural context. This new context, therefore, engenders a potential for the emergence of specific types of Western Muslim identity.

The fact that the context of belonging to a new minority-religion-based immigrant community facilitates what I term a religion-based identity as a distinct feature of Western Muslim identities is another important aspect that needs to be taken into consideration. By religion-based identity I mean that religion becomes a primary source of identity construction for these new immigrant Muslim community members. In other words, religion assumes a master locus of identity construction at the expense of other options, such as ethnicity or race. Although religious faith has lost its institutional representative power among many Western Muslims, relevant literature suggests to us strongly, as outlined on p. 201, that it is becoming a very important source for the definition of personal and collective identity. I would like to highlight again that this "I-am-a-Muslim-first" type of identity does not, however, necessarily translate into increased religious practice and religious piety, although it often can. As we saw on pp. 200–1, the literature on new immigrant communities in general indicates that the religious component of immigrant members' identity in immigrant minority communities, especially those belonging to a religious minority as well, generally takes on added significance. Several studies specific to Muslim immigrant communities are in line with these findings (Duderija 2007). One concrete way, apart from those mentioned above, that facilitates this religion-based identity construction among Western-born Muslims in particular is their desire to affirm their identity in a different, more open and assertive manner to that of their parents. The immigration-related processes of what Roy (2004: 26–29) terms de-territorialization of identity – i.e. the decoupling of its ethnic, geographical, and religious components that apply to Western immigrant Muslims – and the context of secular, plural Western societies, alongside the experience of racism, socio-economic exclusion, and the current international political climate, also foster the development of this religion-based Western Muslim identity. The idea of a global *umma*, or Muslim global brotherhood, is another important factor in the construction of this religion-based identity among Western Muslims as it can often resonate particularly in ethnically and racially diverse Muslim congregations in the West. Indeed, based on my personal experience, the idea of a Muslim global *umma* often features in, for example, the weekly Friday sermons or other similar religious gatherings in many Western Muslim mosques and other places of worship.

The context of belonging to a new immigrant minority religion also has a bearing on what we here term the forms of Western Muslim religiosity. These different forms of Western Muslim religiosity also facilitate the emergence of a distinct Western Muslim identity because they are peculiar to the specific socio-cultural context in which Western Muslims find themselves. In order to understand this point more clearly it is helpful to explain the difference between the concepts of construction or emergence of Western Muslim identity in general and religiosity in particular as employed here. By Western Muslim identity I mean a broader dynamic which includes all the elements mentioned in the first two paragraphs of this chapter (pp. 203–4), such as culture, ethics, politics, philosophy/worldview, emotions/sense of belonging, etc. By religiosity I mean something more narrow, namely the realm of faith or one's relationship with or experience of God and how that manifests itself in a person's daily life. As shall be argued on pp. 207–10, secularization of Muslim identity and the construction of Muslim identities embedded in the premodern Islamic worldview form part of these new modes of religiosity in the West. Secularization-based religiosity manifests itself in its symbolic or non-symbolic modes (on pp. 208–9 we describe the latter as Progressive Muslim), whilst the premodern-based religiosity is apparent in its apolitical revivalist fundamentalist (here termed Neo-traditional Salafi) or more politically oriented revivalist types.

One important and perhaps the most widespread distinguishing feature of Western Muslim religiosity is the process described in the relevant literature as privatization or individualization of Islamic faith and practice (Cesari 2005: 5). It should be pointed out that due to the West's peculiar historical experience of secularization and the role of religion in the public sphere as well as in the collective memory of Westerners of established stock, especially in Western Europe, the process of individualization of faith among Western Muslims is qualitatively different from that of possible secularization-like influences experienced by those living in Muslim majority nations because of the broader socio-cultural forces that operate in the Muslim majority context which resist secularization and which are largely absent in the West.

Importantly, the process of individualization of faith among Western Muslims contributes significantly to the emergence of a Western Muslim identity in at least two ways. First, it often provides emancipation from cultural, ethnic, and often patriarchal constraints, and is therefore used to disassociate individuals from established ethno-national communities. This is especially so for young Muslim women, who, as described on p. 205, are considered the main bearers and safeguards of religio-cultural authenticity. Second, and related to the first point, individualization also contests established ethno-national communities' understanding of the religious tradition itself, thereby affecting the manner in which Islamic normativity and authority are reproduced and Islamic knowledge is transmitted (Jacobsen 2006).

In summary, the context of belonging to a new immigrant religious minority is one important factor which contributes to the emergence of a distinctly Western Muslim identity.

## Western Muslim intellectuals and the emergence of a Western Muslim identity

The discourses and thought engendered by Western Muslim intellectuals, and in some cases religious leaders, is another important factor which facilitates the emergence of a Western Muslim identity. The context of residing in Western liberal democracies where ideas can be freely developed and exchanged has been crucial in the emergence of a new class of Muslim intellectuals who, by virtue of either birth or immigration (or in some cases exile), have made the West their home. These new Western Muslim intellectuals, over the last two to three decades in particular, have made serious efforts to engender new discourses aimed at developing "authentic" interpretations of the Islamic tradition which would religiously justify and promote the social, cultural, and political integration of Western Muslims without the loss of their religious identity and, thereby, attempt to create a distinctly Western Muslim identity which is culturally Western. While there is a range of often contrasting views with respect to the method, the substance, and the ultimately desired outcomes of this religiously grounded theoretical framework, all of them share one common characteristic, namely the viability of the very concept of a Western Muslim identity. For example, the proponents of the *fiqh al-aqaliyyat* project (Islamic jurisprudence for Muslim minorities in the West),[4] both in their approach to the interpretation of the normative sources of the Islamic tradition and in their views on what it means to be a Muslim residing in the West, differ from Neo-traditional Salafi and Progressive Muslims' approaches. The most "forceful" of these proposes a creation of a Western Muslim identity as a distinctly specific religio-cultural and philosophical construct based on its own and substantially different interpretation of the Islamic tradition as manifested in the development of culturally specific Islamic ethics and jurisprudence. So, just as through history Islam was shaped by African, Asian, and South Asian cultures, the advocates of this type of Muslim identity call for a European, North American, or Australian Islam. While the success of these efforts is not assured (Al-Affendi 2009), the mere presence of these discourses is a significant factor which facilitates the emergence of a Western Muslim identity. Here the works of Tariq Ramadan, with his insistence on the possibility of a specific Euro Islam and European Muslim identity, since the 1990s have significantly contributed to the engendering of the discourse on this very topic. Ramadan has been consistently arguing, and more forcefully over time, that the context of citizenship in Western liberal democracy permits Western Muslims to be genuinely Muslim, to develop their own distinct European culture as well as Islamic ethico-religious thought (March 2011), and to be law abiding citizens. In other words, Ramadan has been a proponent of the idea that Western Muslims can remain in complete fidelity with their religious identity and practices and at the same time cultivate a distinctly Western Muslim culture, thought, and identity by developing new interpretations of their inherited religious tradition.

## Increasing institutionalization of Islam in the West

Institutionalization of Islam in the West should also be seen as a significant force which contributes to the emergence of a Western Muslim identity. Over the last two to three decades Western Muslims, ever more aware of their permanent rather than temporary status in the West, have increasingly made recourse to the policies of politics of recognition. The process of institutionalization of Islam or Muslims in the West is defined here as primarily a public method of this politics of recognition. The continued, although often controversial, building of Muslim places of worship, the mushrooming of numerous Muslim schools or weekend madrasas, the growing network of *halal* food outlets, the flourishing Western-based Islamic mass media, the increasing political representation of Muslims at various levels of government either in mainstream political parties or in so-called "Islamic" parties, their solid participation in social and cultural affairs of the broader Western society are all clear signs of the progressive institutionalization of Muslim communities in the West, and the integration of these communities and their representative institutions into the broader social and political structures of Western liberal democracies. Consequently, this process of progressive institutionalization of Islam in the West is also an important element of Western Muslim identity and is also strongly indicative of its emergence.

## Western Muslim converts

Another important agent for an emergence of a distinctly Western Muslim identity is the role, activism, and the ideas of Western Muslim converts. This is so for several reasons. First, in some ways reminiscent of the Western-born generations of Muslims of immigrant background, the Islam of Western Muslim converts does not have established ethno-cultural roots. Having been brought up in a culturally Western mentality, these Muslim converts' Muslim identity and understanding of Islam is inevitably shaped by this context and is therefore distinctly Western. Indeed, their intellectual and culture-producing contributions both within and outside their newly adopted religious community are an important locus for the emergence of a distinctly Western Muslim identity. Second, by assuming the role of cultural mediators between Western Muslims with immigrant background and non-Muslim Westerners these Western Muslim converts often facilitate the acceptance of the very idea of a Western Muslim identity in the minds of both non-Muslim Westerners as well as Western Muslims of immigrant background. Significantly, based on their physical features and Western-style dress, they also problematize the idea of an "authentic stereotypical Muslim" who does not look "Western" (i.e. non-white, non-Caucasian, wearing traditional clothes from Muslim majority cultures such as *jalabiyya* or *shalwar khamis*). Third, by their very presence they demonstrate the possibility of Muslim citizenship in the West as they themselves are, of course, its citizens. Fourth, with their frequent critiques of traditional cultural or ethnic Islam (often acting in chorus with Western-born generations of Muslims with immigrant background in this respect) they contribute to the engendering of a Western Islam and thus the emergence of a Western Muslim identity. Western converts to Islam, due to their unique positions, also significantly contribute to the above-mentioned process of institutionalization of Islam with their social know-how and through the pooling of a network of relationships (including political, institutional, and religious ones). Lastly, some of these Western Muslim converts belong to the category of Western Muslim intellectuals described above (such as Anne Sofie Roald or Hamza Yusuf), who have significantly contributed to the intellectual formulation of a Western Islam and thus to the emergence of a distinct Western Muslim identity.

## *The* hijab

The wearing of the *hijab* by Muslim women in the West is imbued with multiple meanings and symbolisms. They range from those of opposition to inherited ethnic culture and racialized discourses of exclusion, to those of political protest/defiance (usually in the form of political Islam); from a sign of moral purity to that of strong commitment to religious identity or a tool of security in unfamiliar, potentially threatening environments. Importantly, research on the role and the function of *hijab* among Western Muslim communities has increasingly demonstrated that for those Western-born young Muslim women who choose to wear it the *hijab* seems to play a decisive role in the construction of new Western Muslim identities. The *hijab*, it seems, has become an overdetermined signifier for the identity of young Western Muslim women. There is also mounting evidence from many minority communities indicating that young Western-born Muslim women are increasingly adopting a more explicitly traditional religious dress, including the *hijab*, as part of asserting their specific Western Muslim identity (Duderija 2008). The wearing of an American flag-patterned *hijab* after 9/11 by many young American Muslim women is one powerful symbol of this Western Muslim identity. It is important to highlight in this context that even the styles and forms of wearing of the *hijab* of Western Muslims are often specific to their Western context, as can be seen in Muslim women's magazines in the West, such as *Aziza*[5] or *Sisters*.[6] Indeed, these types of *hijab* often invite rebukes by conservative religious scholars, who do not consider them to be in accordance with the traditionally prescribed *hijab* rules, for example in terms of color or how adequately they cover parts of the women's body that are required to be concealed in public. As such, the presence of specific forms of *hijab*-wearing among Western Muslims can often be indicative of the emergence of a specific Western Muslim identity.

## Religious music

The last three decades have witnessed a flourishing of Western Muslim religious songs sung in European languages, including French, German, Spanish, Italian, and particularly English (sprinkled with Qur'anic and other religious phrases in Arabic). This religious music is at times expressed in the form of hip hop, clearly mirroring Western equivalents, and is not restricted to American Muslims of African descent. This interesting development, much like in the case of *hijab*, plays a very important role for many a young Western Muslim in the construction of a distinct Western Muslim identity. It does so in a number of ways. First, by being truly trans-ethnic in character, it facilitates a religious rather than ethnic-based Western Muslim identity. Second, it provides an important avenue for young Western Muslims to develop a sense of Muslim self which has the potential to make Islam more meaningful and attractive to their lives (in contrast to traditional ways of Islamic *da'wa* which, apart from some Sufi groups, largely eschew music and consider that listening to it, even if it is religious in nature, is a sin), and to at least partially bridge the often wide gap between mainstream Western values and practices and those of traditional Islam. Third, especially in the context of Western Europe, it acts as one channel through which Western Muslims are able to voice their grievances of belonging to a socio-politically and religiously marginalized and often stigmatized community. This can lead to a more politically engaged and participatory Western Muslim citizenship consciousness, which, in turn, potentially facilitates their sense of belonging in the West. Fourth, this religious music is often educational in character and is aimed at bringing up law abiding and young pious Western Muslims. The works of Muslim convert Yusuf Islam, formerly known as Cat Stevens, are particularly important in this regard. Fifth, this pious Muslim music contributes to the development of a distinctly Western Muslim cultural identity, of which it is a very important element.

## Western languages

Unlike the first Muslim immigrants to the West, subsequent generations of Muslims have no problem in communicating in the official languages of the countries in which they reside. This language proficiency is an important element in facilitating Western Muslim identity in at least two crucial ways. First, it potentially enables Western Muslims to be more intimately familiar with the dominant cultural, social, political, intellectual, and legal context of their countries of citizenship/residence, thereby enhancing their ability to meaningfully integrate into the broader public sphere and be active and participatory members of it. This, in turn, enhances the levels of acceptance of Western Muslims by the broader non-Muslim community as being genuine and contributing members of the broader society in which they live. Second, it runs counter to the stereotype of (a Muslim) immigrant who does not and/or is unwilling to learn the official language of their country of residence and as such is destined to live on the cultural, social, political, and intellectual margins of the broader community.

In the context of the discussion of the importance of language in the emergence of a Western Muslim identity the issue of discursive hegemony on Islam and Muslims written in Western-based languages is of importance as well. Today the number of both academic and non-academic forms of discourse (journals, magazines, books, newspapers, internet websites and blogs, television and radio) on Islam and Muslims in English and other major Western European languages, notably French and German, far outweighs the number in any other language, including Arabic. This is true in relation to both Muslim and non-Muslim authors of these various writings. This phenomenon is of course a reflection of the global cultural and economic dominance of Western countries worldwide, especially the United States. One clear example of this dominance of European languages on discourses on Islam and Muslims is the amount of Muslim religious terminology that is being integrated into Western languages and the speed with which this is happening. To take the example of the English language, words such as *jihad*, *hijab*, and *in sha' Allah* are no longer in need of translation and have been adopted into the language. It is my contention that this process also contributes to the emergence of a distinctly Western Muslim identity because it not only provides Western Muslims a window into acquiring knowledge of their tradition, as many are unable to read in the language of their parents (especially in the case of Arabic-, Urdu-, Bengali-, and Farsi-speaking Western Muslims, whose alphabet is not based on Latin characters), but the literature on Islam and Muslims in European languages is aimed at advocating views which are in favor of the development of a Western Muslim identity. The work of Tariq Ramadan is, again, an excellent case in point. However, it must be kept in mind that some literature in European languages, often a translation written by ultra-conservative Saudi or Saudi-supported religious scholars and those who share their views, does not advocate such principles.

## Two types of distinct contemporary Western Muslim identity

In this part of the article I discuss two very different types of distinct ways of being a Western Muslim, one which is very comfortable with the idea of such an identity and another which by and large rejects it. For reasons that are outside the scope of this chapter, we refer to the former as Progressive and the latter as Neo-traditional Salafi (for details, see Duderija 2011). Before I present a discussion of the two distinct types of Western Muslim identity I would like to outline a more elaborate typology of Muslim identities operating both in Western and in Muslim majority contexts. This is necessary for two reasons. First, it helps us appreciate the diversity and complexity of Muslim identities in general and, second, it allows us to situate more specifically and therefore define more clearly the two identities under discussion. The first point that needs to be made is that the construction of distinct Western Muslim identity, as indicated on pp. 199–204, is not homogeneous and does not presuppose sameness, either in terms of how Western Muslims relate to the inherited Muslim tradition or with respect to their understanding of what it means to belong to or be part of a Western society. As such, a distinct Western Muslim identity, the way it is defined and understood here, can mean an existence of such an identity that is based not just on its acceptance but also on a conscious rejection of its very possibility by those who possess this identity, again based on their understanding of what it actually means to be Muslim and a Westerner. Nonetheless, even those among Western Muslims who object to the very notion of a distinct Western Muslim identity, indeed, for reasons outlined on pp. 199–204, in actual fact cannot construct their identity in a contextual and spatio-temporal vacuum and their identity is, in fact, by their very physical presence in the West and by the virtue of their spatio-temporal contemporariness, already unique to it.

The typology is based on and adopted from the work of Ameli (2002) and it is particularly useful for the purposes of this chapter because it approaches the issue of identity from the perspective of the dialectic between the understanding of and the adherence to the inherited Muslim tradition and understanding and orientation towards Western culture, and was developed in the context of typologizing British Muslim identities. It is also useful because it is broadly representative of all Western Muslim identities. The eight-tiered typology consists of the following types of Western Muslim identities:

1      Traditionalist, which is characterized by social conservatism, ritual centeredness, and political indifference.

2 Islamist, characterized by their emphasis on Islamic politics and movements and the comprehensiveness of the Islamic way of life.

3 Modernist, characterized by a "combination of modernization and Islamic ideology," their desire to achieve social reformation through modernization and reformation of religious thinking in accordance with modern modes of thought.

4 Secularist, characterized by rejection of the politicization of Islam, and its traditional aspects, but, unlike the traditionalist form, with active participation in secular politics and social activity, and lack of religious observance and involvement within social institutions.

5 Nationalist, characterized by those who identify themselves primarily with the culture of the parents' homelands as an expression of patriotism.

6 Western secular, with no serious inclination towards the original culture, an inability to re-assimilate into it, and absorption of attitudes, values, and norms governing Western secular culture to the point that it is indistinguishable from "native" counterparts; and with involvement in multiplex secular social relationships with non-Muslims, and comparatively less religious orientation.

7 Hybrid, characterized by no firm orientation towards the original culture as well as not giving primacy to the new Western culture.

8 Undetermined, characterized by rejection of diverse cultures one is confronted with, confusion about religious belief, and a sense of hopelessness and rootlessness.

As will become evident, the Neo-traditional Salafi and Progressive Muslim identities share to various degrees common characteristics with the list just outlined, the former being closest to what Ameli terms "traditionalist" and the latter to "modernist" identity.

## Progressive Muslim identity

On the one hand, the processes associated with belonging to a new immigrant minority religion described on pp. 199–201 have resulted in the creation of a unique, hybrid group of second-generation Muslims. They are characterized by a "mixture of (basic) Islamic Weltanschauung, an appreciation of Western democratic institutions" and a Muslim identity that is "comfortable with fluid and plural identities" (Roy 2004: 117–49). For this type, a Muslim identity which genuinely engages with mainstream Western society and yet remains genuinely Muslim is not seen as contradictory. Mandaville notes this type of Western Muslim identity in the context of European Muslims when stating that:

> there are observant Muslims who view Western norms, popular culture, and lifestyles as mostly compatible with Islam. They do not see inherent conflict in their dual identities as Muslims and Europeans.
>
> *(Mandaville 2002: 220)*

Gilliat refers to this type of Muslim thus:

> There is an important minority of young Muslims in Britain who are not only devoted Muslims, but also fully participating in the wider society when it comes to general social life ... [T]hey appear to be confident in their religious identity, and they do not rely on outward signs of this identity to bolster their inner sense of being Muslim. As a consequence they can mix freely with non-Muslims in the wider society, without feeling

threatened, or compromising their Islam. They are perhaps the ones who most aspire to being recognised as "British Muslims."

*(Gilliat 1994: 236)*

Niebuhr (as quoted in Gilliat 1994: 249) describes them as "those who have a firm religious identity that is not threatened by active participation in the wider society. It is an identity that does not have to be 'proved' to others by outward appearances." This type of Muslim is variously described as reformist, modernist, rationalist liberal, and as enlightened rationalist (Duderija 2007). Cesari (2003: 174) points to the existence of similar reformist trends in Islam as a result of "Western freedom of expression and cultural globalisation." In this article this type of identity construction is described as a progressive religious identity. Progressive Muslims consider their religious identity to be traditionally authentic and derived from a particular interpretation of the normative sources of Islam, namely the Qur'an and *Sunna* (Duderija 2011). It should not be confused with what is usually termed symbolic religious identity, which denotes a poor and fragmented knowledge of religious norms and a low level of ritual observance but a strong identification with their religion and their religious community. The existence of this symbolic Western Muslim religious and ethnic identity is also evident in the literature (Eid 2002: 37).

## Neo-traditional Salafi identity

It is interesting to note that the same processes that have facilitated what we here termed religion-based identity, including the Progressive Muslim identity, have also been largely responsible for the emergence of puritanical religious identities among Western Muslims and the creation of what Hermansen (2003: 309; cf. Roy 2004: 232–57) terms the "culture free identity Islam." For example, Gardner's (1993: 213–35) study of the Bangladeshi community in the East End of London indicates that transnational migration processes and practices can lead to puritanism, increased religious zeal, and what she terms "orthodoxy" based on scripturalism. This particular type of religious-based identity "attempts to purify Islam of cultural influences and redefine it along purely religious lines." Eid (2002: 51) refers to this type of religious identity existent among American Muslim university students as a "nonsymbolic" or "ultra-orthodox" identity which "develops parallel alternatives to mainstream institutions and cultural systems shielded from Western influences."

According to Hermansen, many aspects of this version of Islamic identity are based on:

> A mindless and rigid rejection of "The Other" and the creation of decultured, rule-based space where one asserts Muslim "difference" based on gender segregation, romantic recreations of madrasa experiences and the most blatantly apologetic articulations of Islam … replacing spirituality with arrogance and a smug pride in one's superior manifestation of visible symbols of identity.

*(Hermansen 2003: 310)*

This type of affirmation of "pure culture-free religious identity" by alienated, marginalized, and disempowered Muslim youth is most frequently associated with global, militant Islam (Roy 2004: 232–87). The widespread "neo-fundamentalist" component of the contemporary Islamic resurgence among Western-born generations of Muslims (Roy 2004), is exhibited by engaging in what Noor (2003: 322) terms the "rhetoric of oppositional dialectics," in which the question of Islamic identity is primarily approached on the basis of "the trope of the negative Other which manifests itself in a number of forms: secularism, the West, international Jewry/Zionism, capitalism etc." Labeling it orthodox, Cesari (2003: 53–6, 95–109) identifies this type of religious identity as operating within a binary view of the world in which "Islam is the positive and the West is the negative."

## Factors responsible for the emergence of different types of Western Muslim identity

Given that there exist such different distinct types of Western Muslim identity, the immediate question that emerges is what gives rise to them? I will here briefly explore one such factor that I consider to be important in this dynamic, which relates to the question of the interpretation of the normative sources of the Islamic tradition themselves and its role in identity construction.

### The role of scriptural hermeneutics

An important element in the construction of different types of Western Muslim identity is the role of religious tradition itself, and more precisely the different ways of conceptualizing and interpreting this religious tradition. According to Ammerman (2003: 216), religious tradition forms a type of a powerful "meta-narrative," a religious narrative. A religious narrative is a narrative in which "religious actors, ideas, institutions, and experiences play a role in construction of identities." Religious narratives in fact act as the "building blocks of individual and collective religious identities" (Ammerman 2003: 216).

The construction of a religious identity is also based upon a particular understanding (or interpretation) of the religious tradition itself (i.e. its primary, normative sources). Waardenburg (2000: 49–69) and Wadud (2000: 3–21), for example, argue that in the context of Muslim immigrant descendants the normative sources and the search for true, normative Islam are particularly important. This is especially true for the Western Muslim identities described on pp. 207–9, both of which engage seriously with the normative teachings in the construction of their identity.

Furthermore, the (radical) change in the context from a homogeneous majority religion/culture to that of a heterogeneous minority religion/culture brings to the foreground and facilitates the changes in interpretation of sources of faith. To borrow Vroom's (2007: 230) term, the change in context changes the "interpretative schema" of Western Muslims, which become central to their identity dynamics. Speaking in the context of Muslims in Europe, Waardenburg (2000: 55–6) asserts that what he refers to as the normative character of Islam for Muslims is a social fact and that normative Islam based on literature on Islamic law and its theory (*usul al-fiqh*) has "obtained a new relevance for Muslims living in Western societies," that it is of "utmost importance," and that it has "practical relevance." This view is confirmed by several other empirical studies conducted, for example, by Noeckel (2002) and Boos-Nünning and Karakasoglu (2005). This is so because normative Islam, that is one based upon a particular interpretation of primary sources of the Islamic worldview, is assumed to offer Muslims a comprehensive guide, with many guarantees and benefits in terms of what they should do and believe in, in order to lead the life of a good Muslim, which becomes their primary concern.

Thus any attempt to understand the variant religious identity constructions among Western Muslims needs to take this important element into account. I term this the scriptural-hermeneutical factor in religious identity construction. This phrase refers to a particular approach to the interpretation of primary sources of the Islamic worldview, namely the Qur'an and the *Sunna*. However, as I have shown elsewhere (Duderija 2011), religious tradition and its sources are subject to various interpretations based upon certain methodological and epistemological assumptions. These hermeneutical differences, argues Wadud (2000: 3), in the case of Islamic tradition are crucial in the construction of variant religious identities.

The primary, normative sources of the Islamic religious tradition are the Qur'an and the *Sunna*. The centrality of the Qur'an and the *Sunna* in Muslim thought permeates through the entire Islamic intellectual legacy. They are uniformly recognized by Muslims as the ultimate points of reference, but whose interpretation has always been a point of contention among various Muslim religious communities. Reflecting this, Waardenburg (2003: 243–5) argues that the quest for normative Islam in the Western context is constantly reconstructed by successive generations of Muslims who appeal to a "true, normative" Islam along variant lines, so that one is faced with the dilemma of the multiplicity of normative Islams. Therefore, differences in interpretative models of the Qur'an and the *Sunna* are central when examining which type of religious identity is being constructed (Wadud 2000; also Duderija 2011) because they are open to various interpretations, at times diametrically opposed ones.

As a summary of this section let me quote Raines, who highlights the political nature of the act of interpretation of religious tradition by asserting the following:

> It [interpretation] is a contentious terrain precisely because it continues to deeply affect people in their daily lives. It is contentious because interpreting the sacred shapes how power is used in society. To interpret religious tradition is to enter a conflict and to make a choice. Our appropriation of our heritage is never neutral; it displays our intention and purpose for its use. It is taking up sides even if, or perhaps especially if it claims to do so.
>
> *(Raines 2001: 2)*

## Conclusion

This chapter identified and described various processes, agents, and factors which facilitate the emergence of Western Muslim identity. It also described two different types of contemporary Western Muslim identity and discussed one mechanism which contributes to the emergence and construction of different Western Muslim identities, namely the role of scriptural hermeneutics. We can conclude that since the last decade of the twentieth century we have witnessed strong indications of the emergence of a distinctly Western Muslim identity driven by multiple processes, discourses, and agents. What is less certain, however, is what type of Western Muslim identities will in the long term predominantly take root in the West. At the very general level, it can be asserted that this will depend upon many factors, some of which are internal to Western Muslim communities themselves, while others are external to them.

## Notes

1 See the discussion in the main text on pp. 207–10.
2 The term "the West" in this article is employed in the meaning of "Western liberal democracies," namely those in Western Europe, North America, Australia, and New Zealand.
3 This does not automatically translate into the claim that Western Muslims as a result of their immigration experience become highly religiously observant but that their sense of "Muslimness" is highlighted either by the processes internal to their "Self" or by their environment, "the Other" which influences the Self. On the Self–Other identity construction dialectic, see Duderija (2008).
4 As embodied by the scholars associated with the European Council for Fatwas and Research (www.e-cfr.org/en) based in Dublin.

5 www.azizahmagazine.com/.
6 www.sisters-magazine.com/index.php.

# Bibliography

Al-Affendi, A. (2009) "The People on the Edge: Religious Reform and the Burden of the Western Muslim Intellectual," *Harvard Middle Eastern and Islamic Review* 8: 19–50.

Alba, R. (2005) "Bright vs. Blurred Boundaries: Second Generation Assimilation and Exclusion in France, Germany, and the United States," *Ethnic and Racial Studies* 28: 20–49.

Ameli, S.R. (2002) *Globalization, Americanization and British Muslim Identity*, London: ICAS Press.

Ammerman, N.T. (2003) "Religious Identities and Religious Institutions," in Dillon, M. (ed.) *Handbook of the Sociology of Religion*, Cambridge: Cambridge University Press, pp. 207–25.

Boos-Nünning, U. and Karakasoglu, Y. (2005) *VieleWeltenLeben: zur Lebenssituation von Mädchen und jungen Frauen in der Migration*, Münster: Waxmann.

Cesari, J. (2003) "Muslim Minorities in Europe: The Silent Revolution," in Esposito, J.L. and Burgat, F. (eds.) *Modernising Islam*, London: Hurst and Company, pp. 251–71.

——(ed.) (2005) *European Muslims and the Secular State*, Aldershot: Ashgate.

——(2007) "Muslim Identities in Europe," in Al-Azmeh, A. (ed.) *Islam in Europe: Diversity, Identity, Influence*, Cambridge: Cambridge University Press, pp. 48–69.

Duderija, A. (2007) "Literature Review: Identity Construction in the Context of Being a Minority Immigrant Religion: The Case of Western-born Muslims," *Immigrants & Minorities* 25(2): 141–62.

——(2008) "Factors Determining Religious Identity Construction among Western-born Muslims: Towards a Theoretical Framework," *Journal of Muslim Minority Affairs* 28: 371–400.

——(2011) *Constructing a Religiously Ideal Believer and Woman in Islam: Neo-Traditional Salafi and Progressive Muslims Methods of Interpretation (Manahij)*, New York: Palgrave.

Ebaugh, H.R. and Chafez, J.S. (2000) *Religion and the New Immigrants: Continuities and Adaptations in Immigrant Congregation*, Oxford: Alta Mira Press.

Eid, P. (2002) "Ethnic and Religious Identity Retention among Second Generation of Arab Youths in Montreal," Ph.D. thesis, University of Toronto.

Gardner, K. (1993) "Mullahs, Migrants, Miracles: Travel and Transformation in Sylhet," *Contributions to Indian Sociology* 27: 213–35.

Gilliat, S. (1994) "Perspectives on the Religious Identity of Muslims in Britain," Ph.D. thesis, University of Wales, Lampeter.

Hammond, P.E. and Warner, K. (1998) "Religion and Ethnicity in Late-Twentieth Century America," *Annals of the American Academy of Political and Social Science* 527: 55–66.

Hermansen, M. (2003) "How to Put the Genie Back in the Bottle? 'Identity' Islam and Muslim Youth Cultures in America," in Safi, O. (ed.) *Progressive Muslims: On Justice, Gender, and Pluralism*, Oxford: Oneworld, pp. 306–18.

Jacobsen, C. (2006) "Staying on the Straight Path: Religious Identities and Practices among Young Muslims in Norway," Ph.D. thesis, University of Bergen.

Mandaville, P. (2002) "Muslims in Europe," in Hunter, S.T. (ed.) *Islam, Europe's Second Religion*, Westport, CT: Praeger Publishers, pp. 219–29.

March, A. (2011) "Law as a Vanishing Mediator in the Theological Ethics of Tariq Ramadan," *European Journal of Political Theory* 10: 177–201.

Mirdal, G.M. (2000) "The Construction of Muslim Identities in Contemporary Europe," in Dassetto, F. (ed.) *Paroles d'Islam: Individus, sociétés et discours dans l'islam européen contemporain*, Paris: Maisonneuve & Larose, pp. 35–49.

Noekel, S. (2002) "*Die Töchter der Gastarbeiter und der Islam: zur Soziologie alltagsweltischer Anerkenungspolitiken einer Fallstudie*," Bielefeld: Transcript.

Noor, F.A. (2003) "What Is the Victory of Islam? Towards a Different Understanding of the Ummah and the Political Success in the Contemporary World," in Safi, O. (ed.) *Progressive Muslims: On Justice, Gender, and Pluralism*, Oxford: Oneworld, pp. 320–32.

Raines, J.C. and Maguire, D.C. (eds.) (2001) *What Men Owe to Women?—Men's Voices from World Religions*, New York: State University of New York Press.

Roy, O. (2004) *Globalized Islam*, New York: Columbia University Press.

Smith, T.L. (2000) "Religion and Ethnicity in America," *American Historical Review* 83: 1155–85.

Vroom, H.M. (2007) "Islam's Adaptation to the West: On the Deconstruction and Reconstruction of Religion," *Scottish Journal of Theology* 60: 226–43.

Waardenburg, J. (2000) "Normative Islam in Europe," in Dassetto, F. (ed.) *Paroles d'Islam: Individus, sociétés et discours dans l'islam européen contemporain*, Paris: Maisonneuve & Larose, pp. 49–69.

——(2003) *Muslims and Others: Relations in Context*, Berlin: Walter de Gruyter.

Wadud, A. (2000) "Alternative Qur'anic Interpretation and the Status of Muslim Women," in Webb, G. (ed.) *Windows of Faith: Muslim Women Scholar-Activists in North America*, New York: Syracuse University Press, pp. 3–21.

Warner, R.S. and Wittner, J.G. (eds.) (1998) *Gatherings in Diaspora – Religious Communities and the New Immigration*, Philadelphia: Temple University Press.

Williams, R.B. (1998) *Religions of Immigrants from India and Pakistan: New Trends in American Tapestry*, Cambridge: Cambridge University Press.

Yang, F. and Rose, E.H. (2001) "Transformations in New Immigrant Religions and Their Global Implications," *American Sociological Review* 66: 269–88.

# 13

# The multicultural idea and Western Muslims

*Anna Triandafyllidou*

## Multiculturalism is "dead" but Muslims are still "a problem"

The last decade of the twentieth century had been characterized by an optimistic view that Western liberal democracies had found appropriate ways to accommodate cultural, ethnic, and religious diversity. Several European countries, like the Netherlands, Britain, and Sweden, were recognized as "champions" of multiculturalism in that they allowed for migrant and native communities to create their own institutions and maintain their cultural or religious traditions. While policy approaches and political ideologies on how to accommodate diversity differed, the overall framework of recognizing not only individual but also collective difference and making room for it was largely labeled "multiculturalism." Multiculturalism became the official motto also in Australia and Canada, which incorporated it in their very national self-definition as migrant nations. It seemed that along with the reconnection of Europe and the implosion of the Communist regimes in 1989, the 1990s were also bringing forward a new and promising perspective on reconciling the tensions that ethnic and religious diversity may create in a society and ensuring equality for all.

The start of the new century brought about bitter disillusionment. The attack on the Twin Towers in New York City, now known as 9/11, became a symbolic but also real turning point both in global geopolitics and as regards the policies for accommodating diversity. At the geopolitical level, 9/11 was the origin of the US attack and war in Afghanistan and in Iraq. The speech of the then President of the USA George W. Bush introduced new terms to refer to the Western coalition and the Muslim Other when he spoke of the alliance of "the good" against "the evil." The evil was the network of Islamic fundamentalist terrorist organizations known as Al-Qaeda. However, in common parlance, the discourse often slipped to portray all Muslims as potentially "the evil" that the West had to guard itself against.

In Europe, the 2000s were marked by increasing tensions between national majorities and marginalized Muslim communities. In some cases (such as in northern England in the summer of 2001 or in France in the winter of 2005) these conflicts included a strong socio–economic marginalization component. In other instances, as in the case of the bomb attack in Madrid in spring 2004 and in London in the summer of 2005, these events were inscribed in the wider framework of international terrorism and conflict between "the West" and "Islam." The growing suspicion towards Muslims was reinforced after the Danish cartoon crisis in 2006 following the publication of pictures of the Prophet Muhammad by a Danish newspaper. Extreme right-wing politicians such as Geert Wilders in the Netherlands, the Front National in France or the Northern League in Italy gained votes by playing on the electorate's fears of the "Muslim."

The end of the 2000s was characterized by yet another negative development: the global financial crisis. The overhauling of the global economy also soon became an acute internal European economic crisis with important political implications. Indeed the crisis has provided fruitful ground for further exacerbation of social tensions and a concrete rise in racism and xenophobia towards minorities and migrants in general, Muslims in particular. Such developments were particularly pronounced in the countries most hit by the economic crisis, notably Greece and Cyprus, but also Spain and Italy.

During the first years of the twenty-first century, politicians and academics have been intensely debating what should be done to enhance civic cohesion in European societies. One question raised by these debates is *how much* or *what kind of* cultural diversity can truly be accommodated within liberal and secular democracies. Some thinkers and politicians have advanced the claim that Muslim diversity is not of the kind that can be accommodated in European societies because their cultural traditions and religious faith are incompatible with secular democratic states. Others have argued that Muslims can be accommodated in European liberal democracies provided they adhere to a set of civic values that lie at the heart of European democratic traditions and that reflect the secular nature of society and politics in Europe. Others still have questioned the kind of secularism that underpins state institutions in Europe and have pointed to the unequal treatment of majority vs. minority, and in particular of Islam, the youngest religion in Europe, in many areas of public life.

In policy terms, the main conclusion drawn from such debates has been that multicultural policies have failed and that returning to a civic assimilation approach (emphasizing national culture and values) would be desirable. The start of the new decade (2010s) has been marked by considerable pessimism, particularly in comparison to the rise of multicultural citizenship ideals and policies in the 1990s, and general optimism regarding the accommodation of Muslim claims and needs in European societies. The global and European economic crisis makes the picture particularly gloomy; the perceived competition for scarce jobs or limited welfare resources leads to xenophobic and racist incidents against people of Asian or African origin (people with darker skin or who "look foreign"). Such incidents have dramatically increased in southern Europe during the last couple of years.

This chapter seeks to provide an overview of recent developments concerning Muslims and multiculturalism in the West today. It starts with an overview of the Muslim populations that live in Western countries, notably Europe and North America. It then proceeds with a short discussion of what multiculturalism is and what the "multiculturalism backlash" has concentrated on in recent years. The fourth section (pp. 221–5) provides an overview of the multicultural idea and how it has been interpreted and applied in different countries. The concluding section (p. 225) draws up some general remarks concerning the future of the multicultural idea as a response to Muslim claims for accommodating their cultural and religious traditions in Western countries.

## Western Muslims

Triandafyllidou (2010) classifies the Muslim populations that inhabit Europe into two broad categories: native and immigrant. Native Muslims settled on the European continent during the expansive movements of the Ottoman and Russian Empires, or are native populations that converted to Islam under Ottoman rule. Thus they are mainly found in central, Eastern, and southeastern Europe (including Albania, Bosnia, Bulgaria, Greece, the Former Yugoslav Republic of Macedonia, Romania, Serbia) and in Russia. The number of Muslims that are native to countries of the European Union at this point in time remains relatively small, given that most of the southeastern and Eastern European countries do not yet form part of the EU. There are no native Muslims in North America by contrast – they have instead followed more recent immigration routes along with other Europeans and Asians to the "new continent."

Immigrant Muslim populations in Europe include economic immigrants or asylum seekers from Turkey, the Maghreb, sub-Saharan Africa, and Asia and mainly arrived in Europe during the second half of the twentieth century as a result of postwar population movements. They have settled, in their vast majority, in the industrialized and economically developed countries of northern and Eastern Europe (including Belgium, France, Germany, the Netherlands, Sweden, and Denmark).

The offspring of these post-World War II immigrant populations are now considered native to Europe as they are second- or third-generation immigrants. We place them, however, in this second "category" of European Muslims because they did not reside in their current countries of residence when these countries emerged as nation-states. Among European Muslims of non-European origin we should include the large number of Muslims that have arrived during the last two decades and have settled in southern European countries, notably Italy, Spain, and Greece. They originate from the Maghreb, Southeast Asia, or the Middle East.

Data on religious affiliation are not consistently registered in European countries since religion is considered to be an aspect of citizens' private lives and could become grounds for discrimination. Thus in most European countries there are no reliable data on the size of Muslim populations. Table 13.1 has been compiled using the data sources available and comparing between them with a view to presenting an overview of the places of settlement of Muslims in wider Europe.[1]

European Muslims are estimated to number between 14 and 18 million (see also Aluffi Beck-Peccoz and Zincone 2004: vii). The largest Muslim population is found in France (approximately 5 million), followed by Germany (approximately 3 million), the United Kingdom (more than 2 million), Italy (between 1 and 1.5 million) and the Netherlands (approximately 1 million).

Concerning Europe, Table 13.1 suggests a native vs. migrant Muslim distribution along a rough Eastern–Western Europe axis. Native Muslims are found only in central and southeast Europe, while immigrant Muslims are concentrated in Western and northern Europe. Among EU countries, it is only in Bulgaria (1 million approx.), Greece (85,000), and Romania (70,000) that we find native Muslim minorities. And of these three countries it is only in Greece that Muslims coexist with immigrant Muslim populations. Native Muslim minorities in Bulgaria and Romania enjoy a special status of rights, public recognition, and political representation, related to and organized on the basis of their ethnic background (in Bulgaria they are Turks and to a lesser extent Pomak and Roma; in Romania they are Tatars and Turks) rather than their religion. By contrast, in Greece (see Triandafyllidou 2010b), native Muslims (of Turkish, Pomak, or Roma ethnicity) receive state recognition and special rights on the basis of their religious minority identity rather than their ethnicity.

A different case is Turkey, whose belonging to Europe and/or the EU may be seen as a contested issue. Turkey is a majority Muslim country with a total population of approx. 70 million people.

At the geographical outer border of Europe, Russia is also an interesting case. It has a large Muslim population, which is, however, geographically concentrated in a few regions. As of

*Table 13.1* Muslim populations in Europe and North America

| Country | Estimate of Muslim population (including non-citizens) | Source |
|---|---|---|
| Austria | 340,000–475,000 | Wieshaider 2004–Pew Report 2011, estimate for 2010 |
| Belgium | 320,000–638,000 | Hallet 2004–Pew Report 2011, estimate for 2010 |
| Bulgaria | 746,000 | Zhelyazkova et al. 2011 |
| Canada | 940,000 | Pew Report 2011, estimate for 2010 |
| France | 4.7–5 million | Pew Report 2011, estimate for 2010–Rohe 2004 |
| Germany | 3.8–4.3 million | Faas 2010, Pew Report 2011 (estimate for 2010: 4.1 million) |
| Greece | 525,000 | Triandafyllidou 2010, Pew Report 2011 |
| Italy | 1–1.58 million | Kosic and Triandafyllidou 2007–Pew Report 2011, estimate for 2010 |
| Netherlands | 0.9–1.1 million | Pew Report 2011, estimate for 2010–ter Wal 2007 |
| Portugal | 30,000–65,000 | Leitão 2004–Pew Report 2011, estimate for 2010 |
| Romania | 70,000 | Iordache 2004 |
| Russia | 16.4 million | Pew Report 2011 |
| Spain | 0.7–1 million | González Enríquez 2007–Pew Report 2011, estimate for 2010 |
| Sweden | 350,000–450,000 | Otterbeck 2004–Pew Report 2011, estimate for 2010 |
| Turkey | 75 million | Pew Report 2011, estimate for 2010 |
| UK | 1.6–2.9 million | Modood and Meer 2010–Pew Report 2011, estimate for 2010 |
| USA | 2.75 million | Pew Report 2011 |

Source: Author's own compilation from a variety of sources.

2009, four out of five Muslims in Russia resided in two of the seven federal districts, the Volga and Southern districts. More specifically, in 2009 they were concentrated in five traditionally Muslim homelands: Dagestan (16.3 percent of all Muslims), Bashkortostan (14.6 percent), Tatarstan (13.5 percent), Chechnya (7.4 percent), and Kabardino-Balkaria (4.7 percent). Smaller numbers of Muslims lived in three other Muslim homelands: Ingushetia (3.0 percent of all Muslims), Karachaevo-Cherkessia (1.9 percent), and Adygea (0.8 percent). Altogether, about two-thirds of all Muslims in Russia (62.3 percent) resided in one of the traditionally Muslim homelands (Pew Report 2011). In addition, it should be noted that Moscow has become a migration magnet for people from elsewhere in Russia, as well as beyond Russia. More than 600,000 Muslims reside in Moscow (3.7 percent of all Muslims in Russia) and an additional 517,000 live in the oil-rich Tyumen region (3.0 percent), which borders Kazakhstan to the south (Pew Report 2011).

Muslims in North America are mainly a migrant population. In the case of the USA they are generally rather recent arrivals to the country. More than one in four US Muslim adults arrived in the country after 2000 (Pew Report 2011). In addition, nearly two-thirds of all US Muslims (63 percent) were born abroad. About one in five (22 percent) are a third, fourth, or later generation of Americans, while 15 percent are second generation. This distribution testifies to a recently arrived population. However, they are characterized by very high rates of naturalization, as among those who arrived in the 1990s or earlier nearly all are US citizens (80 percent of those who arrived in the 1990s, 95 percent of those who arrived in the 1980s, and virtually all of earlier arrivals). Even among recent arrivals 42 percent have already been naturalized. This testifies to a well-integrated population (Pew Report 2011).

As regards countries and regions of origin, Muslims in the USA come from seventy-seven different countries but their main region of origin is the Arab countries (accounting for 41 percent of foreign-born US Muslims, or 26 percent of all Muslim Americans). Southeast Asia is the second main region of origin (for about 26 percent of all Muslim Americans and 16 percent of all US Muslim citizens), while Pakistan is the single largest country of origin, accounting for 14 percent of first-generation immigrants of Muslim religion and 9 percent of all US Muslims. Other important regions of origin for US Muslims are sub-Saharan Africa and Europe (Pew Report 2011). The same is true for Muslims in Canada, who also come from a large variety of countries, including not only war-torn countries like Somalia, Iraq, and Bosnia, but also Albania and Bangladesh. They are generally recent immigrants or refugees and come to Canada for employment and to seek a better life (Pew Report 2011).

Overall there is thus an important difference between central Eastern, east Eastern and southeastern Europe on one hand and Western/northern Europe or North America on the other, as in the former region there are large native Muslim communities, while in the latter Muslims are immigrants and relatively recent arrivals.

Actually it is perhaps the integration of migrant Muslims, and particularly in Europe, that has hit the headlines several times in the last decades and this is the topic that the rest of this chapter concentrates on, notably the main concepts used to make sense of integration, and in particular how these concepts have translated into policies in specific European countries and the challenges that Muslims have posed to such policies.

## Dealing with cultural diversity: from tolerance to multiculturalism

One of the first concepts put forward to deal with religious diversity in Europe has been the notion of tolerance. In its basic form, tolerance means to refrain from objecting to something with which one does not agree. It involves that one rejects a belief or a behavior, that one believes her/his objection to this behavior or idea is legitimate, and that one decides to tolerate this negative behavior along with its possible consequences (King 1997: 25). As King argues, tolerance is meaningful when the "tolerator" has the power to suspend an act but does not exert this power. It can also be seen as a liberty which obtains only when a response which has a genuine negative motivation (to suppress the particular behavior or action) is voluntarily suspended (King 1997).[2]

The term tolerance is generally used to refer to the principle and the virtue of being tolerant, while the term toleration refers to the actual behavior or practice that "tolerates." However, often the two are used interchangeably to describe contexts where practices or attitudes that are disapproved of are allowed to exist. It should be noted that tolerance as a principle also requires that discriminatory practices or behaviors towards those who engage in the "tolerated" practices are prohibited. In other words, it may also be seen as a prohibition of discrimination.

Historically, the development of a body of theory on the subject of toleration began in the sixteenth and seventeenth centuries, in response to the Protestant Reformation and the Wars of Religion. It started as a response to conflict among Christian denominations and the persecution of witchcraft and heresy. In the sixteenth and seventeenth century, writers such as Montaigne (Langer 2005) questioned the morality of religious persecution and offered arguments supporting toleration. In the seventeenth century the concept of toleration was taken up by English thinkers such as John Milton and was further developed in the late seventeenth century by John Locke in his *Letters Concerning Toleration* and in his *Two Treatises on Government* (Kaplan 2007; Mendus 1988). Enlightenment philosophers such as Voltaire in France and Lessing in Germany further developed the notion of religious tolerance, although these ideas did not prevent intolerance and violence in early modern Europe (Zagorin 2005). Tolerance was then understood in reference to religious diversity (the dominant religion's toleration of minority religious groups), while today the concept is applied to all forms of difference, including race, ethnicity, religion, sexuality, and gender.

Already in the Enlightenment years, a distinction was made between mere toleration (i.e. forbearance and the permission given by adherents of a dominant religion to religious minorities to exist although they are seen as mistaken and harmful) and the higher-level concept of religious liberty, which involves equality between all religions and the prohibition of discrimination among them (Zagorin 2005). Indeed, this distinction is probably the main weakness or the main strength of the concept of tolerance. Some thinkers see tolerance as primarily a practical consideration, since each society or state has to set the limits of what and whom it tolerates and what or whom it does not tolerate; tolerance then becomes important as a way to approach issues of diversity and discrimination against minorities (for further discussion, see Mendus and Edwards 1987; Mendus 1988; King 1997). Then there are others, such as Galeotti (2002), who propose an advanced concept of toleration that involves not only acceptance and recognition of diversity, but also a combating of negative stereotypes and identities surrounding minority groups.

In contrast, for many political theorists today and in political discourse in general, toleration of something or someone implies a negative view and hence a form of discrimination. Despite the more open and progressive origins of the concept, in current discourse we "tolerate" something "bad" that we do not want to suppress for various reasons, but which we do not consider legitimate. In other words, toleration today is certainly more about "not objecting" to something rather than about "embracing" it, let alone respecting it.

Political scientists who are in favor of an egalitarian, thick concept of tolerance actually usually privilege the notion of multiculturalism. Multiculturalism and the notion of multicultural citizenship (Modood et al. 2006) respond to the need for a normative and theoretical perspective for dealing with diversity. Diversity may be defined as value heterogeneity (Rawls 1993), as groups oppressed on the basis of their "difference" (Young 1990), as historic cultural communities (Taylor 1994), or as indigenous peoples and ethnicities in multi-ethnic states (Kymlicka 1995). It is generally understood that the presence of new, especially non-white, ethnic and religious groups formed by migration alongside native groups, and their quests for tolerance and recognition, are the main constituents of contemporary diversity.

There have, however, been different views on what are the normative and conceptual principles on which multiculturalism rests, and a divergent set of programs on what kind of policies multiculturalism should support. Vertovec (1998) identifies eight types, while Delanty (2003) proposes nine different varieties of multiculturalism. Indeed, what probably is characteristic of the multicultural idea is the fact that it provides for a loose framework within which different norms and different policies can fit. However, there are a number of common features that bring the different multiculturalism approaches together into a minimal common framework on what multiculturalism entails: (1) the recognition that cultural and religious diversity is a good thing that has to be preserved and to be allowed to exist in societies regardless of whether a minority is a native historical minority or a post-migration community; (2) the acknowledgment that for different cultural and religious communities to flourish there is a need to acknowledge not only individual rights and claims but also collective rights; (3) that such a recognition of group rights and claims has to respect the fundamental principles of liberalism and democracy. One might argue that multiculturalism also entails a fourth element: a preference for contextual answers to claims rather than one-size-fits-all solutions. In fact it is this very element that probably makes multiculturalism a loose normative and policy framework rather than an actual specific model of policies and practices.

As Vertovec and Wessendorf (2010: 3) point out, multiculturalism applies in several areas of public and social life, involving a variety of practices. Thus, in the area of law multiculturalism suggests the need to make exemptions to general rules in order to accommodate minority claims (e.g. allow Sikhs to wear a turban even when riding a motorcycle). In the area of language policy it suggests that multiple languages should be used to communicate essential public policy information. In the area of religion multiculturalism involves the accommodation of minority religions, permitting and even supporting the establishment of new places of worship or cemeteries. The list of practices and policies that fall within the notion of multiculturalism is long and varied. It is sufficient perhaps to say that multiculturalism tends to privilege positive answers that open up new channels and create new services in response to minority and migrant claims. It is less often the case that multiculturalism functions through prohibitions or monitoring, although this may also be the case, as, for instance, with regard to ensuring non-discrimination in broadcasting and the media.

While reviewing the full range of normative and policy approaches to multiculturalism goes beyond the scope of this chapter, it is useful to consider the main features of multiculturalism and its efforts to balance individual vs. group rights and claims in liberal democratic societies as these are expressed in the work of Tariq Modood.

Modood (2013) sees as a constitutive aspect of multiculturalism the idea that the social world is made up of individuals as well as groups, and that groups are as "real" as individuals in terms of their function in the social world. He acknowledges that there are different types of social attributes that form the basis of group identities, notably race, religion, and ethnicity, and hence that there are different types of "diversity" with which a democratic and plural society has to come to terms. Moreover, he notes that not all groups experience their group identity with the same intensity or with reference to the same realms of life. Thus, some minority groups may be more concerned with socio-economic disadvantage and prioritize education and professional advancement, while other groups may concentrate their claims and actions in the cultural and symbolic realm of recognition.

Moreover, Modood notes, members of a group may experience their group identity with varying degrees of intensity and may see it as relevant in different modes and in different realms of their lives. Indeed, while (British) Muslims are often portrayed as a monolithic block of people with a strong religious identity, Modood notes that

> For some Muslims – like most Jews in Britain today – being Muslim is a matter of community membership and heritage; for others it is a few simple precepts about self, compassion, justice and the afterlife; for some others it is a worldwide movement armed with a counter-ideology of modernity; and so on. Some Muslims are devout but apolitical; some are political but do not see their politics as being "Islamic" (indeed, may even be anti-"Islamic"). Some identify more with a nationality of origin, such as Turkish; others with the nationality of settlement and perhaps citizenship, such as French. ... So it is no more plausible to ascribe a particular politics (religious or otherwise) to all Muslims as it to all women or members of the working class.
>
> *(Modood 2013: 124)*

Having said this, Modood, nevertheless, warns against the danger of excessive recognition of individual difference that would lead us to believe that the dominant form of life is a "hybridic, multiculture, urban melange." He points out that, instead, the different types and degrees of "groupness" professed by different minorities in different contexts should alert us to the fact that a multicultural approach to accommodating diversity needs to be flexible enough to offer to each minority a mode of representation and participation in the national whole that is commensurate with its needs and wishes. This political perspective on multiculturalism, offered by Modood (2013), argues for greater recognition of and respect for minority difference, and is closely knit with socio-political realities in modern communities. In other words, while the concepts on which this approach is based remain constant – democratic liberalism, moderate secularism, and religious pluralism – its actual applications, in terms of the institutions that it will be expressed through and the practices that it will inform, remain subject to the specificities of each national context and its corresponding minorities.

In recent years multiculturalism as a concept and as a framework that guides policy-making in the field of cultural and religious diversity has come under attack. Vertovec and Wessendorf (2010: 6–9) summarize these critiques in seven main points, which I would rather summarize in four. First, multiculturalism is a single doctrine that eventually puts the state to the service of left-wing liberals and ethnic minority activities, leading eventually to the "racial, ethnic and cultural balkanisation" of society, as Melanie Phillips (2006) put it. A second critique is that multiculturalism stifles debate because it imposes too much political correctness and deals with cultural and religious diversity as if they were taboo issues. It thus denies real problems like the failure to socio-economically integrate minorities or immigrants at school or in the labor market. The third and perhaps most pervasive critique is that multiculturalism leads to parallel societies rather than providing a framework for integrating minorities and as such undermines the existence of a common set of values that keep a society together. A fourth main point is that multiculturalism supports reprehensible practices such as honor killings, female genital mutilation, or overall the oppression of women, and in addition provides a haven for Islamic terrorists precisely because it involves too much of a laissez-faire policy towards minorities.

Although, as Vertovec and Wessendorf (2010: 18) point out, the backlash against multiculturalism in public and political debates has not led to such a wholesale reorientation of migrant integration policies, it would be fair to affirm that in several European countries with relatively large Muslim immigrant populations the 2000s have been marked by several new measures that included the tightening up of naturalization provisions and the introduction of civic integration tests, not only for naturalization but also for legal immigration. In the next section I discuss briefly how five European countries have reoriented their migrant integration and naturalization policies, emphasizing how such developments were a reaction to the concern that Muslim populations are not successfully integrated and remain rather socio-economically but also culturally marginalized.

## National interpretations of the multicultural idea

### From multiculturalism to civic assimilationism: the Netherlands

The first case is the Netherlands, a country that has been considered a forerunner in multicultural policies since the 1980s but which in recent years become a champion of civic assimilationism. During the 1980s and 1990s, the Netherlands had a liberal entry and naturalization policy and also allowed migrant communities to set up their own cultural and religious institutions largely within the framework of the pillar model of Dutch society. This has changed during the last decade as there has been a widespread recognition by politicians, and to a certain extent by scholars, that Dutch multiculturalism has failed to achieve its objectives, notably to allow minorities to retain their cultures but also to ensure social cohesion and socio-economic integration of migrants in Dutch society. The perceived failure of the Dutch multiculturalism model focused on both socio-economic and cultural issues: the significantly higher percentage of people of migrant backgrounds who were dependent on welfare (compared to natives), the higher rates of school abandonment and unemployment among second-generation migrant youth, but also the perceived lack of integration of certain communities within the Dutch polity, notably the inability of people to speak Dutch and to participate in public and political life. While the debate has been generalized, the groups that it focused on in the Netherlands were Moroccans and Turks (the two largest immigrant communities in the country), which were quickly lumped together as "Muslims."

In the 2000s, the Netherlands has discontinued some emblematic multiculturalist policies such as dual citizenship programs, national-level funding for minority group organizations and activities supporting cultural difference. At the same time it has introduced some policies specifically tailored to ignore ethnic minority differences such as reallocating the small percentage of public broadcasting time dedicated to multicultural issues and ceasing to monitor the rates of labor market participation by ethnic minorities (Entzinger 2007, 2003; Van De Vijver et al. 2006). Integration courses have been introduced for all immigrants (both newcomers and earlier arrivals) and a civic integration test is held in the migrants' country of origin before they arrive in the Netherlands (ter Wal 2007; Vasta 2007; Sunier 2010). The "drastic break with multiculturalism" (Entzinger 2007: 201) made by the Dutch has been widely recorded and may be said to have kicked off the "failure of multiculturalism" debate.

## Reluctant multiculturalism: Germany

Germany is a second case of special interest as it is home to one of the largest Muslim communities in Europe. Germany was a latecomer to, if ever a follower of, multicultural policies for Muslim migrant integration. Following decades of pursuing an ethno-national citizenship, Germany has since the late 1990s undergone significant changes in its management of immigration, integration, and its conception of citizenship. Thus, and after federal policies had previously focused almost entirely on the control and return of migrants (Schönwälder 2001), in 1998 the Red–Green government characterized Germany as an "immigration country" and amended the Citizenship Law (2000) to introduce the principle of *ius soli*. These developments have been accompanied by others such as the introduction of the Immigration Law (2005), which encourages the cultivation of "integration strategies," and which in turn was followed by the invitation to migrants and civil society actors to take part in a National Integration Summit (2006). Yet the content of this "integration" has also included a nationalist imperative, whereby newcomers are expected to undertake 300–600 hours of German-language classes and lessons on German society and history (Jacobs and Rea 2007)

The key word for the last decade in the German public and policy debate on migration and cultural difference has been "integration." Integration has been conceived mainly as a socio-economic issue: integration policies have privileged the education and labor market insertion of the second generation rather than an opening up of German national identity to recognizing that it's becoming multi-ethnic and multi-religious. Indeed, in recent years the debate over a German *Leitkultur*, which seeks the promotion of a German "leading culture," has become more explicit than in its traditional conception of ethnic citizenship. Indeed, this is despite, or perhaps because of, significant movement away from the latter, at least in law (Mühe 2010).

The accommodation of Muslim demands for cultural or religious issues has been much more hesitant, and public discourses, like the "famous" Thilo Sarrazin debate, have generally stigmatized Muslims as backward, uneducated, violent, and incapable of integrating into German society. Thus, while the 2000 Citizenship Law was much more liberal, it led to a higher level of scrutiny of naturalization applications and a growing suspicion towards Muslims (Schiffauer 2006; Green, 2005). Indeed this trend culminated in the 2010 declaration by Chancellor Angela Merkel that multiculturalism has failed in Germany, even if in reality Germany had never applied any multicultural policies.

## Multiculturalism reconsidered: Britain and Sweden

Britain and Sweden are among the few European countries that have not turned away from the ideals and policies of multiculturalism. Although the British government introduced a "Life in the United Kingdom test" (a civic integration test) and civic ceremonies in an attempt to retrieve cohesion based on an inclusive understanding of Britishness, particularly in the aftermath of the July 2005 London bombings, politicians and political theorists have emphasized the importance of reorganizing or reconsidering rather than abandoning multiculturalism (Modood and Meer 2010; Modood 2013).

Meer and Modood (2011) argue that in the case of Britain the reorientation (rather than abandonment) of multiculturalism has come from the center-left, beginning with proposals to remake Britishness under the terms of "Cool Britannia" and "re-branding Britain" (Leonard 1997). Not only was this a strand within what is probably the most multiculturalist government Britain has had (1997–2001), but the ideas of rethinking and remaking Britishness in response to ethnic diversity were stimulated by ethnic minority intellectuals (Gilroy 1987; Modood 1992; CMEB 2000).

Following perhaps from the civil unrest in northern English towns in the summer of 2001, there has been a strong public debate on whether knowledge of one of the national languages (English mainly, but also Welsh or Scottish/Gaelic) should be a requirement for long-term residence and naturalization. Indeed the Nationality, Immigration and Asylum Act (2002) explicitly introduced a test (implemented in 2005) for residents seeking British citizenship. Thus, applicants should show "a sufficient knowledge of English, Welsh or Scottish Gaelic" and also "a sufficient knowledge about life in the United Kingdom" (Home Office 2002: 11). Those immigrants seeking to settle in the UK (applying for "indefinite leave to remain") equally have to pass the test, which has effectively been implemented since April 2, 2007. If applicants do not have sufficient knowledge of English, they are required to attend English for Speakers of Other Languages (ESOL) and citizenship classes. The government has, however, insisted that "it would be unfair for migrants to have to answer questions on British history that many British people would have difficulties with" (McNulty, quoted in Kiwan 2008: 69). Accordingly, the emphasis is on the experience of living in Britain rather an attempt to test Britishness in terms of scholastic knowledge.

The arrival of the Conservative Party in power (in coalition) in 2010, however, marked a new turning point in British policy, with a certain shift away from multicultural accommodation of ethnic and religious diversity. The Prime Minister David Cameron called for a more "muscular liberalism" that would leave less space for appreciating the collective needs and religious specificities of minority groups, notably Muslims. This, however, has not yet translated into concrete policy changes or, rather, remains a discourse that seems to be destined more for internal consumption than an effective new guide for policy design.

In Sweden, another stronghold of multiculturalism, the multicultural approach to cultural and religious diversity has been predicated on a strong social welfare system and a political ideology that, though secular, has allowed for Muslims to express their identities on an individual and collective level. In this sense Sweden is different from Britain, as migrants, and particularly Muslims, have been expected to integrate through strong social welfare and employment policies. This welfare framework was seen as somehow neutralizing cultural or religious diversity, which, however, could be expressed freely and could take advantage of state funding for cultural and religious associations. In recent years, however, there has been rising concern with the poor educational and labor market performance of some Muslim groups. This has led to a reconsideration of the multiculturalism and welfare model, with now a greater emphasis on individual responsibility during the integration process in the destination country (Otterbeck 2010). The shift in multicultural policies has been part, though, of a wider shift of the Swedish welfare system and civic culture towards a notion of the individual's responsibility to find employment and integrate in society at large.

## Renewed Republicanism: France

In France, the question of migrant integration has largely evolved in relation to nationality laws and citizenship acquisition. The issue became politicized in the 1980s. Right-wing parties have generally advocated a more selective approach to naturalization, especially for the second generation (applying instead of "automatically becoming" French), while left-wing political forces have generally privileged an open access to French nationality for the children of immigrants born in France. While laws on citizenship acquisition have been quite generous in France, allowing for people to acquire citizenship after five years of legal residence, the 2003 Citizenship Law added the requirement of proving sufficient knowledge about the rights and responsibilities of French citizenship. Alongside the Netherlands, the French government considered the possibility of introducing civic tests when implementing the New Reception and Integration Contract (Nouveau contrat d'accueil et d'intégration). Eventually tests were not introduced, but since 2007 newly arrived immigrants have been encouraged through this "contract" to learn French and acquire knowledge of French laws. While naturalization is not obligatory, the compulsory steps that each foreigner should take make it clear that it is a desirable outcome (Escafre-Dublet and Kastoryano 2011).

The question of migrant integration and the meaning of French citizenship (which is largely defined in civic and voluntaristic terms) have come center-stage again after the then newly elected President Nicholas Sarkozy created a Ministry of Immigration and National Identity. Among other activities, in 2009 the ministry launched a series of debates on French national identity to take place in all regions of the country. The creation of the ministry and the debates campaign attracted considerable criticism. In 2010 the Ministry of Immigration and National Identity was abolished, though the indirect questioning of naturalized French citizens' loyalty to the country and successful integration continues. Interestingly, in a speech delivered in response to violence which occurred during the summer of 2010 in Grenoble (southeast France), President Sarkozy announced the possibility of stripping offenders of their French nationality if they had been naturalized in the previous ten years.

However, the question of Muslim integration and multiculturalism in France has always been closely related to the issue of laïcité. Laïcité, defined as the principle and practice of fully separating church and state in all issues of public life, has provided the framework for the coexistence of different faiths in French society. It is embodied in the 1905 law separating church and state, and rules out any official representation of religion in public places. It also implies that religious affiliation is not considered a legitimate basis for the identification of groups. This is seen as a way to guarantee the neutrality of the state and the equal treatment of individuals on the basis of citizenship. The notion of laïcité has been increasingly discussed in connection with Islam in the past two decades.

The approach to issues pertaining to Islam in terms of *laïcité* can be traced back to the first headscarf affair, which took place in 1989 in Creil, an outer suburb of Paris, when the principal of a secondary school took the decision to exclude three girls because he considered that their Muslim headscarves were religious symbols and undermined the principle of *laïcité*. The State Council, however, ruled that the wearing of the headscarf was "not contradictory to the values of the secular and republican school" and left it to the teachers and school heads to decide whether or not pupils were using this as an instrument of proselytism and disturbance of school activities. The 1989 interpretation of *laïcité* by the State Council was later challenged and given a more restrictive twist with the establishment of the Stasi Commission in 2003 and the passing of the 2004 law forbidding the wearing of "ostentatious" religious symbols (including of course Muslim headscarves) in schools.

## Conclusion

The new century has been marked by intense debate and policy considerations as to how best to integrate Muslim immigrant populations in Western countries and in particular in Europe. While in the USA perhaps most emphasis has been put on finding out whether Muslim Americans are more or less radical in their views of Islam (Pew Report 2011), in Europe the debate has been quite intense, looking at issues of both socio-economic and cultural integration. Prominent politicians from traditional immigration countries like Britain, Germany, and the Netherlands have to a smaller or larger extent subscribed to the "multiculturalism has failed" debate. Scholars have spoken of the multiculturalism backlash, although on closer scrutiny, apart from an emphasis on civic integration tests, the shift away from multiculturalism has not been as "seismic" as Joppke (2004: 249) predicted.

However, while in northern Europe countries were caught up in concerns with jihadist terrorism and social unrest among immigrant communities, the so-called "new hosts," such as Spain, Italy, and Greece, were "left to their own devices." Struggling with their new realities as immigrant host countries, these countries have been discouraged from even acknowledging their by now *de facto* multicultural and multi-ethnic composition. The perceived failure of the Muslim migrant integration approach adopted by the "old hosts" discourages multicultural integration policies in southern Europe, and reinforces the view that immigration's economic advantages may only be reaped after immigrants become assimilated into the dominant national culture (Zapata-Barrero 2006; Triandafyllidou 2002; Ambrosini 2004). Although immigrant populations in southern Europe are not predominantly Muslim, the question of religious diversity slowly comes to the fore as these populations settle and the Muslim sectors begin expressing their particular needs and wishes (Triandafyllidou 2010; Triandafyllidou et al. 2011).

## Notes

1 Most reliable data usually use a combination of sources, including national censuses but also the so-called country of origin principle, for estimating the religion of migrants. In other words, the Muslim migrant population of $X$ country of destination is estimated by looking at the countries of origin of the migrants. If a migrant comes from $Y$ country of origin where 90 percent of the population are Muslims, it is estimated that 90 percent of the $Y$ migrant community at the $X$ destination country are Muslims. Thus if there are 100,000 immigrants from the $Y$ country in $X$ country it is estimated that 90,000 immigrants from $Y$ country living in $X$ country are Muslims. This method is adopted by the Pew reports on Muslim Americans and Muslims in the world and a number of other studies.
2 This section draws partly on arguments that I have presented already in Triandafyllidou 2010a: ch. 1, Introduction.

Anna Triandafyllidou

# Bibliography

Aluffi Beck-Peccoz, R. and Zincone, G. (eds.) (2004) *The Legal Treatment of Islamic Minorities in Europe*, Amsterdam: Peeters and FIERI.

Ambrosini, M. (2004) "Il futuro in mezzo a noi. Le seconde generazioni scaturite dall'immigrazione nella societa italiana dei prossimi anni," in Ambrosini, M. and Molina, S. (eds.) *Seconde Generazioni. Un'introduzione al futuro dell'immigrazione in Italia*, Torino: Fondazione Giovanni Agnelli, pp. 1–54.

Commission on the Future of Multi-Ethnic Britain (CMEB) (2000) *The Future of Multi-Ethnic Britain*, London: Profile Books.

Delanty, G. (2003) *Community*, London: Routledge.

Entzinger, H. (2003) "The Rise and Fall of Multiculturalism: The Case of the Netherlands," in Joppke, C. and Morawska, E. (eds.) *Toward Assimilation and Citizenship*, Basingstoke: Palgrave Macmillan, pp. 59–86.

——(2007) "The Parallel Decline of Multiculturalism and the Welfare State in the Netherlands," in Banting, K. and Kymlicka, W. (eds.) *Multiculturalism and the Welfare State*, Oxford: Oxford University Press, pp. 177–202.

Escafre-Dublet, A. and Kastoryano, R. (2011) "Tolerance in Discourses and Practices Addressing Cultural and Religious Diversity in French Schools," ACCEPT-PLURALISM, 2011/05, cadmus.eui.eu/handle/1814/19792.

Faas, D. (2010) "Muslims in Germany: From Guest Workers to Citizens?," in A. Triandafyllidou (ed.) *Muslims in 21st Century Europe: Structural and Cultural Perspectives*, London: Routledge, pp. 59–78.

Galeotti, A. (2002) *Toleration as Recognition*, Cambridge: Cambridge University Press.

Gilroy, P. (1987) *There Ain't No Black in the Union Jack: The Cultural Politics of Race and Nation*, London: Routledge.

González Enríquez, C. (2007) "Spain," in Triandafyllidou, A. and Gropas, R. (eds.) *European Immigration: A Sourcebook*, Aldershot: Ashgate, pp. 321–35.

Green, S. (2005) "Between Ideology and Pragmatism: The Politics of Dual Nationality in Germany," *International Migration Review* 39(4): 921–52.

Hallet, J. (2004) "The Status of Muslim Minority in Belgium," in Aluffi, R. and Zincone, G. (eds.) *The Legal Treatment of Islamic Minorities in Europe*, Amsterdam: Peeters, pp. 39–59.

Home Office (2002) *Secure Borders, Safe Haven: Integration with Diversity in Modern Britain*, London: HMSO.

Iordache, R.E. (2004) "The Legal Status of the Islamic Minority in Romania," in Aluffi, R. and Zincone, G. (eds.) *The Legal Treatment of Islamic Minorities in Europe*, Amsterdam: Peeters, pp. 195–213.

Jacobs, D. and Rea, A. (2007) "The End of National Models? Integration Courses and Citizenship Trajectories in Europe," *International Journal on Multicultural Societies* 9(2): pp. 264–83.

Joppke, C. (2004) "The Retreat of Multiculturalism in the Liberal State: Theory and Policy," *British Journal of Sociology* 55(2): 232–57.

Kaplan, B.J. (2007) *Divided by Faith: Religious Conflict and the Practice of Toleration in Early Modern Europe*, Cambridge, MA: Belknap Press.

Kelly, P. (2002) "Introduction: Between Culture and Equality," in Kelly, P. (ed.) *Multiculturalism Reconsidered*, Cambridge: Polity Press.

King, P. (1997) *Toleration*, London: Routledge.

Kiwan, D. (2008) "Citizenship Education at the Cross-roads: Four Models of Citizenship and Their Implications for Ethnic and Religious Diversity," Oxford Review of Education 34(1): 39–58.

Kosic, A. and Triandafyllidou, A. (2007) "Italy," in Triandafyllidou, A. and Gropas, R. (eds.) *European Immigration: A Sourcebook*, Aldershot: Ashgate, pp. 185–99.

Kymlicka, W. (1995) *Multicultural Citizenship: A Liberal Theory of Minority Rights*, Oxford: Oxford University Press.

Langer, U. (2005) *The Cambridge Companion to Montaigne*, Cambridge: Cambridge University Press.

Leitão, J. (2004) "The New Islamic Presence in Portugal: Towards a Progressive Integration," in Aluffi, R. and Zincone, G. (eds.) *The Legal Treatment of Islamic Minorities in Europe*, Amsterdam: Peeters, pp. 179–95.

Leonard, M. (1997) *Britain TM: Renewing Our Identity*, London: Demos.

Meer, N. and Modood, T. (2009) "The Multicultural State We Are In: Muslims, 'Multiculture' and the 'Civic Re-Balancing' of British Multiculturalism," *Political Studies* 57(3) (October): 473–97.

——(2011) "The Multicultural States We're In," in Triandafyllidou, A., Modood, T., and Meer, N. (eds.) *European Multiculturalisms*, London: Palgrave, pp. 61–87.

Mendus, S. (ed.) (1988) *Justifying Toleration: Conceptual and Historical Perspectives*, New York: Cambridge University Press.

Mendus, S. and Edwards, D. (eds.) (1987) *On Toleration*, Oxford: Clarendon Press.

Modood, T. (1992) *Not Easy Being British: Colour, Culture, and Citizenship*, London: Runnymede Trust/ Bentham Books.

——(2013) *Multiculturalism*, 2nd ed., Cambridge: Polity Press.

Modood, T. and Meer, N. (2010) "Britain: Contemporary Developments in Cases of Muslim–State Engagement," in Triandafyllidou, A. (ed.) *Muslims in 21st Century Europe: Structural and Cultural Perspectives*, London: Routledge, pp. 78–103.

Modood, T., Triandafyllidou, A., and Zapata-Barrero, R. (eds.) (2006) *Multiculturalism, Muslims and Citizenship: A European Approach*, London: Routledge.

Mühe, N. (2010) *Tolerance and Cultural Diversity Discourses in Germany*, ACCEPT PLURALISM Project Report, 2010/10, cadmus.eui.eu/handle/1814/19783 (accessed January 23, 2014).

Otterbeck, J. (2004) "The Legal Status of Islamic Minorities in Sweden," in Aluffi, R. and Zincone, G. (eds.) *The Legal Treatment of Islamic Minorities in Europe*, Amsterdam: Peeters, pp. 233–55.

——(2010) "Sweden: Cooperation and Conflict," in Triandafyllidou, A. (ed.) *Muslims in 21st Century Europe: Structural and Cultural Perspectives*, London: Routledge, pp. 103–21.

Pew Report (2011) *The Future of the Global Muslim Population*, January, www.pewforum.org/2011/01/27/ future-of-the-global-muslim-population-regional-europe/#1 (accessed January 23, 2014).

Phillips, M. (2006) *Londonistan: How Britain Is Creating a Terror State Within*, London: Gibson Square.

Rawls, J. (1993) *Political Liberalism*, Oxford: Oxford University Press.

Rohe, M. (2004) "The Legal Treatment of Muslims in Germany," in Aluffi, R. and Zincone, G. (eds.) *The Legal Treatment of Islamic Minorities in Europe*, Amsterdam: Peeters, pp. 83–109.

Schiffauer, W. (2006) "Enemies within the Gates: The Debate about the Citizenship of Muslims in Germany," in Modood, T., Triandafyllidou, A., and Zapata-Barrero, R. (eds.) *Multiculturalism, Muslims and Citizenship: A European Approach*, London: Routledge, pp. 94–117.

Schönwälder, K. (2001) *Einwanderung und ethnische Pluralität. Politische Entscheidungen und öffentliche Debatten in Großbritannien und der Bundesrepublik von den 1950er bis zu den 1970er Jahren*, Essen: Klartext Verlag.

Sunier, T. (2010) "Islam in the Netherlands, Dutch Islam," in Triandafyllidou, A. (ed.) *Muslims in 21st Century Europe: Structural and Cultural Perspectives*, London: Routledge, pp. 121–37.

Taylor, C. (1994) "Multiculturalism and 'The Politics of Recognition'," in Gutmann, A. (ed.) *Multiculturalism: Examining the Politics of Recognition*, Princeton: Princeton University Press.

ter Wal, J. (2007) "The Netherlands," in Triandafyllidou, A. and Gropas, R. (eds.) *European Immigration: A Sourcebook*, Ashgate: Aldershot, pp. 249–63.

Triandafyllidou, A. (2002) "Religious Diversity and Multiculturalism in Southern Europe: The Italian Mosque Debate," www.socresonline.org.uk/7/1/triandafyllidou.html.

——(2010a) *Muslims in 21st Century Europe: Structural and Cultural Perspectives*, London: Routledge.

——(2010b) "Greece: The Challenge of Native and Immigrant Muslim Populations," in Triandafyllidou, A. (ed.) *Muslims in 21st Century Europe: Structural and Cultural Perspectives*, London: Routledge, pp. 199–218.

Triandafyllidou, A., Modood, T., and Meer, N. (eds.) (2011) *European Multiculturalisms*, Edinburgh: Edinburgh University Press.

Van De Vijver, F., Schalk-Soekar, S., Arends-Tóth, J., and Breugelmans, S. (2006) "'Cracks in the Wall of Multiculturalism?' A Review of Attitudinal Studies in the Netherlands," *International Journal on Multicultural Societies* 8(1): 102–18.

Vasta, E. (2007) "From Ethnic Minorities to Ethnic Majority Policy? Multiculturalism and the Shift to Assimilationism in the Netherlands," *Ethnic and Racial Studies* 30(5): 713–41.

Vertovec, S. (1998) "Multi-Culturalisms," in Martiniello, M. (ed.) *Multicultural Policies and the State*, Utrecht: ERCOMER, pp. 25–38.

Vertovec, S. and Wessendorf, S. (2010) (eds.) *The Multiculturalism Backlash*, London: Routledge.

Wieshaider, W. (2004) "The Legal Status of the Muslim Minority in Austria," in Aluffi, R. and Zincone, G. (eds.) *The Legal Treatment of Islamic Minorities in Europe*, Amsterdam: Peeters, pp. 31–9.

Young, I.M. (1990) *Justice and the Politics of Difference*, Princeton: Princeton University Press.

Zagorin, P. (2005) *How the Idea of Religious Toleration Came to the West*, Princeton: Princeton University Press.

Zapata-Barrero, R. (2006) "The Muslim Community and Spanish Tradition: Maurophobia as a Fact, and Impartiality as a Desideratum," in Modood, T., Triandafyllidou, A., and Zapata-Barrero, R. (eds.) *Multiculturalism, Muslims and Citizenship: A European Approach*, London: Routledge, pp. 143–62.

Zhelyazkova, A., Hajdinjak, M., and Kosseva, M. (2011) "Country Profile: Bulgaria," in Triandafyllidou, A. (ed.) *Addressing Cultural, Ethnic & Religious Diversity Challenges in Europe: A Comparative Overview of 15 European Countries*, ACCEPT PLURALISM Project Report, 2011/02, pp. 89–91, cadmus.eui.eu/bitstream/handle/1814/19254/ACCEPT_PLURALISM_2011-02_WP1_ComparativeReport_rev.pdf?sequence=5 (accessed January 23, 2014).

# 14

# Social and political Islamophobia

## Stereotyping, surveillance, and silencing

*Salua Fawzi*

Much of the literature treating Islamophobia credits the infamous Runnymede Trust publication *Islamophobia: A Challenge for Us All* (Runnymede Trust 1997) with being the first to use this term in contemporary discourses. The report explains how the term Islamophobia describes the prejudice, hostility, and hatred directed towards Muslims that excludes them from mainstream political and social affairs, and proposes solutions for minimizing its effects. Since its appearance in the Runnymede report, the term Islamophobia has continued to generate a plethora of academic literature.[1] Some of this literature has attempted to determine its expediency and articulate how it is useful in describing some of the many injustices directed at Islam and Muslims, especially those living in the West.[2] Other literature suggests that "Islamophobia comes off as a nebulous and perpetually contested category" (Sayyid 2010: 2), that it "is the term plus its social histories, including contestations, in materially embedded forms" (Vakil 2010: 72), and that it possesses no widely agreed upon or accepted definition that "permits systematic comparative and causal analysis" (Bleich 2011: 1581).

Despite these valid and even cautionary insights encouraging a thorough, concrete,[3] and more transparent conceptualization of how the term is being employed and what social phenomenon it is in fact describing, politicians, academics, activists, lawyers, and ordinary citizens continue to use the term with little hesitation in a variety of polemical discourses. Thus, despite the contestable and ambiguous nature of the term "Islamophobia," one reality looms bright. Islamophobia, whether it accounts for a form of racism, a moral panic, or a deep-seated fear of a religion or individuals who practice that religion, is gravely affecting the lives of Muslims living in the West and does not appear to be subsiding in spite of outspoken critics from both within and outside of various Muslim and non-Muslim circles. It is not surprising, then, that Islamophobia, given its occupied space in political, academic, religious, and media discourses, has come to define a bitter social reality in which Islam and Muslims are considered threats to social security and welfare. However, while Islamophobia may initially target a particular religion or the followers of that religion, its ramifications extend beyond Islam and Muslims, in that its influence has demonstrated that the restriction of civil liberties is possible so long as a socio-political agenda, whether or not it is warranted or justified, has gained clout amongst a frightened and consenting population.[4]

This chapter will begin by exploring examples of Islamophobia in the United States and Europe and how Muslims have responded to the challenges imposed on them. It will then move to a discussion of American Muslim youth as well as the NYPD's counter-terrorism program, which targeted Muslims in New York and neighboring states, especially Muslim students. In doing so, it hopes to contribute to research on the experiences of Muslim American youth and highlight the negative impact that Islamophobia continues to have on the identity formation of an impressionable demographic that respectfully continues to resist and challenge the stereo-typical and discriminatory policies that are preventing it from exercising its freedom of religion and speech, in a nation that has often taken pride in offering its citizens such privileges.

## Political and social Islamophobia

According to Greg Noble (2012: 215), "Islamophobia as the intensification of a long-standing anti-Muslim prejudice amounting to a widespread hostility in the West, is a complex and dynamic phenomenon." As such, it is important to bear in mind that those who may be deemed "Islamophobes" or acts that might be considered "Islamophobic," like those Muslims they target, cannot fall into one clean and unified camp, which is a significant point to consistently bear in mind for those attempting to pinpoint the reasons, fears, and anxieties fueling such rhetoric and behavior.

One argument that has gained popularity in anti-Islamic discourses since 9/11 is whether or not Western societies should be accommodating towards Islam and Muslims. Bryan S. Turner (2011: 169) contends that "the possibilities for pluralism and tolerance have since 9/11 been severely tested and constrained by a discourse of terrorism and security" whereby an "intelligent and cosmopolitan treatment of Islamic communities in Europe and elsewhere has been halted by legal and political responses to 'terrorism'." While discourses regarding the maintenance of security are not detrimental to social order or cohesion *per se*, the more recent establishment of binaries that pin good vs. evil, non-Muslims vs. Muslim as well as us vs. them divide society and erode any potential for constructive and engaging dialogue that encourages mutual understanding and respect. The need for nurturing such potential is becoming increasingly urgent when politically driven public discourse on terrorism and national security still dominate and undermine the potential for a cohesive and pluralistic society.

As Mehdi Semati (2010: 259–61) notes, the current discourse on Islam and Muslims is "inextricably bound with the issue of terrorism, which tends to frame all other issues concerning the Middle East" and has led to the "intensification of the generic category of 'Arab-Middle Eastern Muslim' Other." This essentialized "other" takes root in a variety of popular discourses fashioning Muslims into a homogeneous, fixed, and unwavering category that is anti-modern and, more importantly, anti-Western, with little regard for the easily detectable and accessibly identifiable nuances that in fact represent Muslims from all around the world who simply do not embody this negative and dangerous depiction.

If such nuances exist, and terrorist acts initiated by Muslims only account for a small percentage of the larger Muslim population, why then does an Islamophobic sentiment still dominate popular Western discourses? According to Stephen Sheehi (2011: 131), "Islamophobia is not a political ideology in and of itself nor is it an isolated dogma just as Islam itself is not simply a political ideology." He cautions that Islamophobia is in fact something more "substantive, abstract, sustained, ingrained and prevalent," and that it derives from a "culture that deploys particular tropes, analysis, and beliefs, as facts upon which governmental policies and social practices are framed" (Sheehi 2011: 131). These Islamophobic beliefs, as Sheehi and many others have articulated, have very real consequences and deeply affect American Muslims, Arab

Americans, and people of Southwest Asia on a variety of levels (Sheehi 2011: 141). Some of these consequences include torture, kidnappings, incarcerations, executions, surveillance, entrapment, racial profiling, banning the building of mosques, Islamic schools and prayer rooms, along with more rampant hate crimes such as vandalism and hate speech. The American-Arab Anti-Discrimination Committee (ADC) and the Council on American–Islamic Relations (CAIR) have diligently recorded these incidents.[5]

Other consequences have included federal policies that have supported unwarranted arrests, searches, and seizures, the closing of charities suspected to be affiliated with terrorist organizations, interrogations, detentions, deportations, all working under the assumption that Muslims are potential enemies within the state that must be controlled and punished by the state. Thus, given the aforementioned policies, "what is most problematic about Islamophobia is its essentializing and universalizing quality, which casts both Islam itself and all Muslims as real or potential enemies in a way that, if similarly applied to Jews or Christians, would seem delusional at best, vile at worst" (Shryock 2010: 9). One of the issues at stake, then, is that Islamophobia has not proven successful in generating policies that simply target these potentially dangerous threats to society and has expanded to the "familiar pattern of racial scapegoating," where much of the stereotyping and discrimination affects those who are members of "groups crudely demarcated primarily by physical appearance" and are subsequently discriminated against in the same manner as Muslims (Love 2010: 193–4). The fact that non-Muslims are also being targeted based on physical appearance represents the racist elements of Islamophobia that do not constructively or strategically pinpoint potential threats and have instead included non-violent Muslims and non-Muslims under its questionably protective umbrella.

## The media and Islamophobia

Nathan Lean's (2012: 40) account of Islamophobia argues that the threat of Islam has been purported by a variety of individuals who "used lurid imagery, emotive language, charged stereotypes, and repetition, to exacerbate fears of a larger-than-life, ever lurking Muslim presence." Lean (2012: 184) also notes that the Islamophobia "industry" in the United States is growing, and has created and exploited fear as a means to coerce society, resulting in the perpetuation of prejudices and stereotypes that have found a niche in right-wing populism which has percolated into American and European societies, affording governments the opportunity to curtail civil liberties and constitutional rights without sufficient opposition from the general population. Frank P. Harvey (2008) similarly addresses this notion of amplified and fluid fear, in light of issues pertaining to the maintenance of homeland security, arguing that weak theories of fear can produce counterproductive policies that do not always assuage public anxieties. In the aftermath of the 9/11 attacks, this fear has manifested itself beyond the fear of Muslims and Islam but has had a reverse effect in its inspiring fear amongst Muslims in the United States, who now fear their own government.[6]

According to Louise Cainkar (2010: 182), the federal government's handling of domestic security post-9/11 via "its use of 'us and them' narratives, sweeping generalization, and dragnet actions buttressed the sentiments of hate-mongers by giving credibility to the notion that there was an identifiable terrorist phenotype and mode of dress." A brief list of these fear-mongers includes some right-wing politicians (Conason 2010), supporters of America's Tea Party movement such as Pamela Geller (Burghard and Zeskind 2010), conservative news agencies such as Fox News,[7] online bloggers, among others, who feed into the clamoring of a Muslim threat, oftentimes with questionable evidence. Furthermore, as Nasar Meer and Tariq Modood (2010: 131) note, "while Muslims are increasingly the subject of hostility and discrimination ... their status as victims of racism is frequently challenged or denied." Thus, what is problematic about the rhetoric espoused by these fear-mongers is their almost condescending ignorance of anti-Muslim prejudice as a substantial social phenomenon that needs to be addressed. This ignorance stages variant obstacles for Muslims[8] because it dismisses the need for social reforms which will afford them respect and safety.

Much of this media discrimination is apparent in various domestic debates. Such examples include the construction of Park51,[9] a proposed Islamic community center near the World Trade Center,[10] as well as debates over the eminent danger of *shari'a* (Awad 2012).[11] Ultimately, this mass media coverage, which is "central to the development of a threatening environment and hatred of Muslims and Islam" (Iqbal 2010: 95), mythologizes Islam and creates a construction of Islam as an eternally backward and dangerous global threat in need of surveillance and control. Moreover, it remains dismissive, condescending, or skeptical of the internal and longstanding debates amongst Muslim intellectuals, thinkers, and activists who continue to make a concerted effort to address Islam's relationship with modernity and the West in their writings and activist efforts.[12]

In addition, very little media coverage has been afforded to the positive achievements of Muslims throughout the world, including the efforts of activists vying for political and social reform. This is problematic given that these efforts might afford American and Western audiences the opportunity to reconsider the overarching threat of Islam and Muslims in a more informative way. Modifying the negative media coverage of Islam and Muslims is an arduous task, but, as Samer Shehata (2007: 81) notes, "If the communication traffic flows only in one direction, there is no dialogue. Muslims, both individuals and organizations, must demonstrate a concerted effort to combat radicalism." While Shehata's point should be well taken, it is also important to note that, given Arabs and Muslims do not possess the resources nor the media required for altering such widespread public opinion, "the tides of public opinion continue to operate against them" (Jamal 2009: 213). As such, it has yet to be determined whether their voices will gain resonance as a predominant or more widely accepted norm representing the larger Muslim community, especially when, in order to combat many of these stereotypes, American Muslims are faced with a complex system of relatively longstanding and negative portrayals[13] that cannot be swiftly erased by acceptably pleasing moderate, liberal, acculturated voices from within the Muslim community. These stereotypes can in fact only be diffused rigorously on the part of the media, which must own up to its responsibility in critically engaging with its depictions of Muslims and Islam in order to rectify the distance that has been created between Muslims and their peer communities, a social distance that has since 9/11 "been exacerbated, especially in places where people interpret Muslims as posing a serious cultural threat to American liberalism" (Cainkar 2010: 179).

Thus far, this chapter has described the media's role in propagating Islamophobic rhetoric. However, Islamophobic American citizens are also to be held accountable for maintaining these stereotypes by not being discerning enough to educate themselves about Islam and whether or not terrorism and violence are indeed the values the majority of Muslims in the world share. I write this because counter-Islamophobic rhetoric has become increasingly accessible and abundant since 9/11. While it would take energy and discipline to sort through these multiple narratives in order to arrive at a nuanced and more comprehensive conclusion, the fate of reform lies among all people, who, as responsible citizens, should engage with these ongoing debates in an open and constructive manner, rather than succumb to propaganda that inspires counterproductive fear, if nothing else.

In Europe, Muslims, too, find themselves compelled to contest negative stereotypes along with a slew of other xenophobic acts since 9/11, including attacks on their mosques, schools, and other centers (Awan 2010: 526). As Joceylne Cesari (2010: 9) astutely notes, the "securitization" of Islam might appease European citizens fearful of prospective terrorist attacks, but in the same vein has caused a catch-22 in that "the measures intended to prevent radicalization actually engender discontent and prompt a transformation of religious conservatism to fundamentalism."

Throughout Europe, concerns over migration have proven to have an "important impact on the success of populist and radical right parties in Western Europe" (Helbling 2012: 2). The link between Islam and discriminatory immigration policies has resulted in the constriction of immigration laws directed at migrants from Muslim majority countries, partially as a result of poor socio-economic conditions (Cesari 2010: 11). Many of these new restrictions require potential immigrants to establish their integration before becoming members of the European Union. As Ibrahim Kalin notes, Muslims who are living in the West "are asked to embrace assimilation and thus lose their identities," even though no such identity can be clearly defined or encompass all those it represents under its umbrella (Kalin 2011: 13). As such, these restrictions "demonstrate changing expectations of immigrants, who are now required to show more compatibility than ever with lifestyles of host countries" (Cesari 2010: 12), oftentimes lifestyle choices that do not necessarily reflect that country's socio-cultural majority but are in fact elements that would inevitably alarm more conservative Muslims. Thus, Muslims in Europe face an exclusionary attitude predicated upon their being situated as immigrants who must prove their assimilation even before being afforded an opportunity to organically integrate into their new host countries, an unwelcoming and unsettling obstacle for any immigrant desiring to build a new life for themselves and their families.

Ultimately, the questions surrounding Muslim integration and the anti-immigration tendencies deriving from nationalist and exclusionary sentiments can essentially be dubbed "Islamophobic" or "anti-Muslim" in that they have categorized Muslims as a potentially threatening "other." As Cesari (2010: 13) notes, "it has become acceptable to associate Muslim immigration and the potential for terrorism," which has generated the view that these Muslims are "foreign enemies." Thus, the practice of Islam remains under close monitoring in some parts of Europe. For example, in Spain, France, and the Netherlands, preaching in mosques deemed radical by these states has aroused cause for concern and has even resulted in the deportation of imams (Cesari 2010: 17). Other Islamophobic policies in Europe which infringe the civil liberties of Muslims include arbitrary legal rulings based on preconceived stereotypes about "Islamic norms"[14] in Germany and France. Islamophobic legal security measures include police surveillance and the monitoring of financial transactions in France, as well as the freezing of funds "associated with terrorism or proscribed groups" in the UK, which has resulted in the detention of foreign nationals and the deportation of others (Cesari 2010: 21).

It is important to bear in mind, though, that examples of "Islamophobia" in Europe range from country to country and reflect the respective country's political stances, and the incidents that have facilitated growing concerns of securitization in light of potential or past terrorist attacks such as the July 7 subway attacks in London. Other causes for concern include the fact that Muslims face poor economic integration in major Western European nations (Pew Research Center 2007: 19). My reason for emphasizing these specificities is to highlight that any prospective monitoring of Islamophobic tendencies in European countries should include the particular socio-economic milieu inspiring particular policies and creating certain attitudes, not as a means to justify these developments but to provide a more nuanced treatment of how they have emerged, what end they serve, and whether or not the treatment of Muslims has improved in particular states that have found ways to effectively integrate Muslims culturally and socio-economically.

## Reactions to Islamophobia

Given the foothold of Islamophobia in Western societies, it is not surprising that many American Muslims and immigrant Muslims, as previously noted, have become more out-spoken and engaged members of their communities, expressing critical views regarding both foreign and domestic policies affecting Muslims worldwide, as well as countering negative stereotypes associated with terrorism and Islam's incompatibility with Western values. In light of the 9/11 attacks and the War on Terror, this realm of belonging has been colored by a variety of actors who proclaim variant views concerning what it means to represent and belong in Western society. These debates alert us to the processes of negotiation many Muslims in the West are currently entrenched in, processes that attempt to weave together their religious identity with a sense of national belonging in spite of the fact that such efforts are not always met with success and there continues to be suspicion regarding Muslims' patriotism and loyalty to the state.

The efforts of Muslim Americans have positioned their community and Islam in a more public manner in the heat of ongoing debates regarding whether or not Muslims must adhere to a rather rigid and somewhat contestable[15] set of Western standards. As Katherine Ewing (2008: 10) points out, "although some individuals chose to downplay their identity as Muslims, many others became more self-conscious in asserting it," with their involvement in Islamic institutions in their respective Muslim communities all the while maintaining an American identity "consistent with their understanding of Islam." Jen'nan Ghazal Read (2008: 123), in her in-depth interviews with Muslim and Christian and Arab Americans, also concluded that both groups had a "universal attachment" to their American identity despite their religious affiliations because in the USA they felt they had the freedom to practice their religion.

Many individual Muslims, mosques, and organizations have remained outspoken advocates that Islam is not a terrorist religion and have condemned the 9/11 attacks. For example, the Council on American–Islamic Relations (2009: 269) reasserted that the American Muslim community has consistently condemned attacks of terrorism, and believes that those who break the law should be prosecuted but that this due process should extend to all. Many of these Muslims also resist hegemonic tendencies that present a one-dimensional and austere representa-tion of Islam that forbids certain practices (Ewing and Hoyler 2008: 96). Others are working through a process of "deculturalizing" Islam "as an attempt to purify Islam in the West of any specific cultural ties" (Joseph and Reidel 2008: 165), and instead opt for stressing the more universal values and ethics fundamental to certain Islamic beliefs. Such values might include tolerance, plurality, and gender equality.

Another site where Muslims are continuing to speak out is Muslim comedy, which appears to be a potential medium for a more successful combating of some Islamophobic stereotypes. According to Mucahit Bilici (2010: 196), Muslim ethnic comedy in the United States has "become a series of inversions played out against a background of Islamophobia" that "aims to bridge the divide that separates Muslims from the rest of American society by reaffirming both sides' common humanity." Inspired by Islamophobic behavior and thought, these Muslim comedians share their experiences and joke about the FBI, airport security, nuclear war signs, and represent their experiences from a distance and in such a manner that chips away at the walls of otherness and paints a "funny" rather than a "scary" picture of Muslims. Thus, as Bilici (2010: 207) notes, "Muslim ethnic comedy lifts, albeit temporarily, the restrictive limits on the self and abolishes the gulf that separates the Muslim minority from the American mainstream." While comedy may be limited in its ability to effectively challenge many of the broader strokes of Islamophobia voiced in mainstream American discourses, Muslim comedians who turn

Islamophobia into an advantageous medium inspire empathy for Muslims and innovatively inform outsiders of the injustices directed at Muslims by offering an alternate, less politically motivated and frightening space to consider these issues.

However, not all Muslims in the United States have welcomed such public attention and they have remained reluctant in speaking more candidly about the struggles the Muslim community is facing. As Jane Smith (2010: 32) notes, many Muslims living in post-9/11 America fear a potential government backlash for speaking out about their disagreement with US policies. In light of these fears and obstacles, Yvonne Haddad and Robert Ricks (2009: 14) argue that, while Muslims are working to "overcome these challenges and become fully empowered participants in civic and political life," it has yet to be determined to what extent these Muslims will be afforded the opportunity to define what it means to be American and in which direction their challenges will take them. Thus, it is still uncertain whether the future will be more optimistic for Muslims in the United States, who have been living within social and political parameters that continue to marginalize and exclude them despite their cooperative efforts.

In Europe, Muslims face similar issues in relation to their identity formation, forcing them to redefine their identity within the confines of a stigmatized and discriminatory view of themselves. Still though, European Muslims have not been fully paralyzed by such obstacles. As Justin Gest (2010: 228–9) notes, many European Muslims are participants in an identity formation that "does not necessarily require a religious foundation of any kind, so long as it accommodates local cultural understandings, satisfies government frameworks, or addresses their personal challenges." Similar to Muslims in the United States, these European Muslims are also working towards the establishment of a more global Muslim identity in a process that Arun Kundani (2008: 40) describes as being "more likely to lead to new forms of democratic activism than to political violence unless diverted from this course by counter-productive policies." While it is inevitable that a thin and perhaps even gray line outlines these prospective accommodations and what they may entail, it is clear that Muslims, like other citizens of Europe, are vying for a space where their concerns are valued and seriously taken into consideration.

Many of these requests reflect the issues at stake in that particular state. One such example would be the vote to ban the headscarf in public schools in France or the building of minarets in Switzerland. Ultimately, many Muslims in Europe remain flexible[16] in adapting to their respective Western societies while maintaining their Muslim identity. However, Tahir Abbas (2011: 109), in his study of the Muslim experience in the UK, points out that "If a minority community begins to adopt the cultural practices of the dominant ethnic community but is still rejected by majority society, assimilation is hardly a viable political or cultural option." Tariq Ramadan poses similar points when he discusses the London bombers responsible for the 7/7 attacks. He writes that the London bombers "had an adversarial mindset, a psychology, involving 'us' versus 'them'," and that while they were technically legally integrated into society they were not psychologically integrated and "in their perception they were polarized" (Ramadan 2012: 31). Abbas's and Ramadan's insights are crucial because they identify a key disconnect in the social integration of Muslims in the West, namely that their full integration not only involves efforts made on their behalf but requires society to meet them halfway for any mutual cooperation and integration to exist and, more importantly, persist against the slew of negative stereotypes that categorize Muslims in the West as being guilty by association.

## Youth and Islamophobia

One of the unfortunate consequences of Islamophobia is the troublesome impact it has on the integration of Muslims in the West, more specifically Muslim youth, who in the aftermath of

235

9/11 find themselves in a particularly sensitive and even compromising position. In the United States, for example, Karen Leonard (2005: 473) argues: "Although not all Muslims see their religion as their most salient characteristic, non-Muslims may make that identification," which in turn "encourages young people of Muslim ancestry to examine how their religion relates to other aspects of their identity as Americans, for people are multi-faceted beings with hybrid and flexible identities." This notion of flexibility and hybridity becomes increasingly significant when considering the identity formation of Muslim youth, who are pawns in debates over the meaning of citizenship, as well as measures and criteria for social classification.

For these Muslim youth, the increased awareness of their Muslim identities was inspired by many of the changes that occurred in their communities post-9/11, when the demonstration of anything Islamic was indeed subject to distrust and when their own sense of belonging became a politicized endeavor given that their own development was connected to a broader socio-political context (Ewing and Hoyler 2008: 80). As Sunaina Maira (2009: 14) notes, the discussion of Muslim American youth after 9/11 "is tinged with these deeper social and national anxieties about how Muslim, South Asian, and Arab Americans will position themselves in relation to the nation-state and what kinds of citizens they will become." Since 9/11, many scholars have addressed the identity construction of Muslim youth in North America and what is at stake in the negotiation process afflicting this demographic.

Katherine Ewing and Marguerite Hoyler (2008: 81), in their research on South Asian Muslim youth in the Raleigh-Durham area of North Carolina, note that these American Muslim youth, when asked about the tension between being both American and Muslim, "articulated a range of responses to the tension, including ambivalence, a questioning of the desirability of being American, a desire to meld cultures and efforts to resolve the tension by transcending national and particularistic cultural or ethnic identities." Ewing and Hoyler's research also found many of these youth felt compelled to display their Muslim identity in a more purposeful manner through participation in Muslim Student Association activities which sought to inform others about Islam (Ewing and Hoyler 2008: 84).

Selcuk R. Sirin and Michelle Fine's (2008: 1) research on Muslim American youth also discusses some of the many challenges directed towards this demographic, obstacles such as "particular psychological challenges." Notwithstanding these challenges, many of these Muslim youth did not give up on their American identity in favor of their Muslim identity, "despite the many pressures from Muslim fundamentalists and some Western intellectuals, who claim that one cannot be a good American and a good Muslim at the same time" (Sirin and Fine 2008: 2). Instead, Fine and Sirin's research found that many Muslim adolescents and young adults "carved out *hyphenated selves*," which "refers to their many identities, including their standings as Muslims and Americans, that are at once joined and separated by history, politics, geography, biography, longings and losses" (Sirin and Fine 2008: 3). Their research further found that, despite surveillance and discrimination, many of these Muslim Americans "seem to find a way to highlight their belonging to both cultures, illustrating once again that identity negotiation is not a zero-sum arrangement" (Sirin and Fine 2008: 127).

While the aforementioned literature provides examples of integration and negotiation, other Muslim youth continue to struggle with the Islamophobic sentiments surrounding them. For example, Ewing and Hoyler (2008: 85) explain that the rhetoric and policies that emerged from 9/11 "deprived" the youth they spoke to of a "sense of full cultural citizenship" and "posed challenges to adolescent Muslims' nascent political identities, even leading some to question the virtues and values of being American." Sherman Jackson (2011: 98) also notes that one of the effects of Islamophobia is the "less direct though equally potent contribution it makes via the alienation it spawns among second- and third-generation 'immigrant' Muslims," many of whom "lack the experiential groundedness in a 'back-home' culture to provide them with a livable, deeply felt sense of identity-in-difference."

Ultimately, the experiences of Muslim American youth cannot be reduced to a single template, and the degree and capacity in which these youth identify with their American and Muslim identities will inevitably be shaped by their own personal experiences and how they have internalized and found ways to fuse or resist elements of their multifaceted identities. However, the strain that Islamophobia imposes on this youth is a matter that should be taken seriously. As Mehdi Semati (2010: 270) argues, "one of the immediate perils of Islamophobia is that it could lead to the marginalization of those youths who might see themselves rejected by the society to which they belong." This rejection could lead these youth to feel "foreign, distant, and unwelcome" (Kalin 2011: 16), or they could find themselves dealing with "disillusionment, social disorder and in the worst case scenario irrational violence" (Ahmed 2007: 19).

## The NYPD's counter-terrorism program

In February of 2012, the effects of Islamophobia on Muslims and, more specifically, American Muslim youth reached a new climax when the Associated Press (AP) attained leaked documents[17] exposing that the New York City Police Department (NYPD) had been closely monitoring Muslims living in New York as well as neighboring states. In their extensive and Pulitzer Prize winning investigation,[18] the AP revealed that the NYPD had tracked, by employing undercover agents as well as informants, places of worship such as mosques within a 250 mile radius of New York, cafés, shopping centers, bookstores, as well as places of employment frequented by Muslims in an effort to obtain as much comprehensive information as they could about Muslims (AP n.d.a). The information gathered by the NYPD's Demographics Unit was then used to build databases monitoring all aspects of these innocent Muslims' lives (Goldman and Apuzzo 2012a).

While the extent of the NYPD's surveillance might have initially come as a surprise and inspired an uproar from the community, civil rights activists, and public officials, such invasive and arguably ineffective surveillance is in fact not novel to the counter-terrorism efforts created after 9/11. Hatem Bazian, in his discussion of the post-9/11 Counter-Intelligence Program, explains that the FBI, as well as other security agencies, has been involved in recruiting informants, targeting the Muslim community along with its institutions (Bazian 2012: 167). Bazian proposes that "a more direct conclusion drawn from these operations is that the FBI and Justice Department consider Muslim Americans as "incubators of terrorism that must be monitored and, if needed, infiltrated to preemptively catch them before they plan an attack" (Bazian 2012: 167). While the deterrence of future attacks is clearly necessary for maintaining public safety, these operations have unfortunately been successful in "creating a big gulf within the targeted community" (Bazian 2012: 199) due to the volunteering of information by Muslim informants. The volunteerism of these informants, who were speaking out of fear, inspired distrust and suspicion amongst members of respective Muslims communities. Consequently, Muslims who have, in the past, publicly expressed their religiosity and discussed their religious points of view more openly with their peers now fear those informants who might turn their backs on them in order to cooperate with the authorities.

According to AP reports, NYPD investigators considered local mosques to be the "center" of Muslim life. The NYPD sent undercover agents to these mosques to gather information from informants known as "mosque crawlers." These monitoring programs were built with "unprecedented help from the CIA" (Goldman and Apuzzo 2012d). These informants recorded the content of sermons such as responses to the Danish cartoon controversy ("Intelligence Division

Central Research Analysis Unit" 2006), and others were instructed to "create and capture," "where the informant would try to start a conversation about terrorism or another controversial topic, record the response elicited, and share it with the NYPD" (MACLC, CLEAR, and AALDEF 2013: 11). The NYPD also recorded the license plate numbers of those parked near the mosque and even put cameras on light poles aimed at these mosques (Goldman and Apuzzo 2012b). Deputy commissioner David Cohen, as well as other managers, claimed this information was collected in order to provide the NYPD with the ability to "take the pulse of the community" (Goldman and Apuzzo 2012b). This surveillance even extended outside of the NYPD's jurisdiction, infiltrating mosques in New Jersey and Long Island (Goldman and Apuzzo 2012a).

In an effort to protect the "homeland," however, these surveillance attempts have hindered local forms of police monitoring. By chipping away at the trust between the Arab American and Muslim communities and law enforcement officials, the NYPD has "undermined the community policing efforts," creating greater distance between themselves and Muslim institutions/leaders (Lane 2012: 707). The NYPD's efforts in New Jersey are also said to have "hindered investigations and created 'additional risks' in counterterrorism" (Henry 2012). Furthermore, the leaked NYPD efforts "have made Muslims more hesitant to reach out to law enforcement and less trusting" (Henry 2012). This hesitation has created dire effects for mosques and community organizations, which are now "unable to advocate for improved law enforcement practices within their community" (MACLC, CLEAR, and AALDEF 2013: 36). More importantly, the Demographics Unit, in its spying, eavesdropping, and monitoring, failed to generate a lead or incite a terrorism investigation (Goldman and Apuzzo 2012c).

In their counter-terrorism efforts, the NYPD also monitored approximately fifteen student-run Muslim Student Associations in the Tri-State area. The Associated Press revealed that the NYPD were tracking all activities, ranging from student-run trips to entries on websites and blogs, and recording the names of both professors and students who had not previously been accused of any wrongdoing for Police Commissioner Raymond Kelly (Hawley 2012). The justification for establishing such surveillance was the fact that twelve people who had previously been accused or convicted of charges related to terrorism had once belonged to Muslim Student Associations (The Takeaway 2012). Again, working outside of their jurisdiction, the NYPD monitored schools as far away as Yale and the University of Pennsylvania (Hawley 2012). These student groups gained the NYPD's interest because they attracted young Muslim men who could potentially be drawn into terrorist groups and the NYPD "worried about which Muslim scholars were influencing these students and feared that extracurricular activities such as paintball outings could be used as terrorist training" (Hawley 2012), for example.

In March of 2013, the American Muslim civil liberties groups such as the American Civil Liberties Coalition (MACLC), the Creating Law Enforcement Accountability and Responsibility (CLEAR) project, and the Asian American Legal Defense and Education Fund (AALDEF) released *Mapping Muslims: NYPD Spying and Its Impact on American Muslims*, a detailed report explaining the negative and "devastating" impact the NYPD's surveillance program has had on the Muslim community by silencing their voices in a variety of contexts as well as damaging their relationship with law enforcement, among others (MACLC, CLEAR, and AALDEF 2013). The report is divided into four parts and provides a background to the mapping and monitoring of American Muslims, findings that illustrate how this monitoring has affected the community, responses to the NYPD program, as well as future recommendations (MACLC, CLEAR, and AALDEF 2013: 3–6).

Salient points in the findings note that many interviewees contended that the NYPD's monitoring "disrupted and suppressed" their practice of Islam in terms of their dress code as well as the sorts of religious activities they participated in (MACLC, CLEAR, and AALDEF 2013: 12). The report found that the policing of mosques and other areas of worship no longer made these Muslims feel safe but compelled them to feel that they were placing themselves on the radar given that every mosque was now a potential "hot-spot" and that potential mosque goers might in fact be NYPD undercover agents who were reporting back their activities. The NYPD's leaked operation generated suspicions amongst these Muslim Americans and tainted the mosque, which was no longer considered a safe haven but rather a breeding ground for spying. This suspicion hindered the ability of the community to nurture its spiritual develop-ment, interact peacefully as a unified front, and prevented some mosques from operating as a "true community center" (MACLC, CLEAR, and AALDEF 2013: 15). Muslim Student Asso-ciation outreach efforts were also affected because press coverage of the NYPD's infiltration prevented those on college campuses from wanting to be associated with the association or its members (MACLC, CLEAR, and AALDEF 2013: 31).

As previously noted, a lack of trust permeated the Muslim community when they discovered the NYPD's operations. This lack of trust was not only directed at police officials but spread to inter-communal affairs, a development particularly problematic for many of these Muslims who "believed that suspicion of their Muslim peers went against their nature, their religious beliefs, or their desire to be active and supportive members of the community" (MACLC, CLEAR, and AALDEF 2013: 26). The report also found that many Muslim youth, fearing potential scrutiny, began exercising self-censorship in terms of their political speech and activism, the self-editing of religious Sunday school curricula, as well as their affiliations with student groups such as Muslim Student Associations. The report further notes that the NYPD's surveillance program "has, in fact, quelled political activism, quieted community spaces and strained interpersonal rela-tionships" (MACLC, CLEAR, and AALDEF 2013: 20). More importantly, the self-censorship evoked by this surveillance has infringed these Muslims' individual liberties such as free speech, freedom of religion, and the right to free assembly, and has bypassed the government's prohi-bition on discriminating against a group or individual based on religion (MACLC, CLEAR, and AALDEF 2013: 48).

## Conclusion

This chapter has highlighted the immense foothold that Islamophobia has in Western societies, as well as its negative impact on Muslims socially, politically, and psychologically. It has placed particular emphasis on Muslim youth in the West and their responses to Islamophobic rhetoric, given that these youth "are viewed as the next generation of citizens and who symbolize the possibility of threat to or support of the existing social order, giving youth a charged ideological significance" (Maira 2011: 112). Although much of the literature cited in this chapter illustrates an engaged and cooperative youth, in light of the NYPD's counter-terrorism operations it is clear that invasive surveillance has only exacerbated the struggles these young people are already facing and has planted seeds of fear amongst this demographic. While these negative effects might be considered collateral damage in a grander effort to ensure public welfare and safety, such objectives have been favored at the expense of respecting and protecting these Muslim youth, many of whom are American citizens, and are deserving of the same rights and privileges afforded to their non-Muslim peers. Moreover, such efforts have silenced the voices of this demographic, jeopardized the survival of communal and civic engagement, left them feeling ostracized and victimized, and have unjustly labeled them as potential suspects.

If anything can be learned from the NYPD's operations, it is that information is both a powerful resource and a powerful weapon. While obtaining information for the sake of protecting the state is necessary, the invasion of privacy, overly generalized and superficial assessments of Islam and Muslims, as well as the incitement of fear have only compromised the trust and cooperation of Muslims, who now feel betrayed and marginalized by their own law enforcement. Moreover, these operations, in conjunction with Islamophobic sentiments, may potentially alienate entire communities of innocent Muslims, especially those youth whose religiosity and allegiance to the state are placed under scrutiny. Only time will tell if these young people can break their silence through strength in their convictions and through the support of their communities, who must now work even harder to overcome their wariness and mistrust of law enforcement officials and each other.

## Notes

1 Edward Said's *Covering Islam* is another seminal text addressing what is now referred to as "Islamophobia," and many of the writers referenced in this chapter cite this work. In it, Said (1981: 4) writes: "Insofar as Islam has always been seen as belonging to the Orient, its particular fate within the general structure of Orientalism has been to be looked at first of all as if it were one monolithic thing, and then with a very special hostility and fear" and that the "negative images of Islam continue to be very much more prevalent than any others' reducing Islam to not what it 'is' ... but to what prominent sectors of a particular society take it to be" (Said 1981: 144). Said's work is thus relevant to the treatment of Islamophobia in that it highlights the "othering" of Islam in predominantly Western discourses.

2 *Thinking through Islamophobia* is one such text that posits conceptual questions regarding the validity of the term and polemical debates regarding the fixation on its validity that often miscast some of the larger issues at stake regarding this phenomenon.

3 Erik Bleich discusses how conceptualizing Islamophobia in a more concrete manner is crucial for drawing any comparisons concerning its levels over time and within specific geographic spaces, and "is also the foundation for more informed public debates and more effective policy decisions" (Bleich 2011: 1592–4).

4 An example of this would be the creation and putative implementation of the Patriot Act under the Bush administration or Operation Green Quest, when the homes and businesses of American Muslims were invaded.

5 See their websites, sun.cair.com/ and adc.org/, for more information.

6 Cainkar (2010: 183) explains that in his study, the fear of government "far outweighed any other post-9/11 fears among Arab Muslim Americans."

7 According to Lean (2012: 66), Fox News has been, "for the better part of the last decade, at the heart of the public scaremongering about Islam, and has recently become the home for a slew of right-wing activists who regularly inhabit its airwaves to distort the truth to push stereotypes about Muslims."

8 For an excerpt from Bill O'Reilly's show where he displays skepticism regarding the existence of Islamophobia, see www.youtube.com/watch?v=GwgxcAH2R6U.

9 The Park51 project did not receive negative attention when it was first revealed in December 2009, but in May of the following year, when plans were presented to the local community board, the project generated a great deal of national and international controversy with the help of an organization called SIOA (Stop Islamization of America) (Abboud 2012: 171).

10 Lean (2012: 40) writes that the prospective building of the Park51 center "reawakened the suppressed emotions of a nation deeply wounded by the tragedy" and that the opposition felt it was offensive to build a mosque so close to Ground Zero given that it was Muslims, despite their deviation from the mainstream Muslim population, that were responsible for the attacks.

11 The *shari'a* "scare" has appeared in both Canadian and American public discourses, especially in debates concerning whether or not *shari'a* should be employed in family law arbitration with respect to marriage, divorce, and inheritance.

12 See Safi (2003).

13 As previously noted, these stereotypes are represented in news coverage, but even Hollywood has played its part, according to Jack Shaheen (2003: 182), in "using Islam to justify violence" and in painting a picture that Arabs and Muslims pose a grave threat to the West.

14 See Cesari (2010: 15) for a list of such examples in German and French legal cases.

15 In qualifying Western standards as being contestable, I am alluding to the various debates on Western secularism and the public sphere which address issues of plurality, tolerance, freedom of expression, and in which capacity the aforementioned should take root as social norms. For example, in *Rethinking Secularism* (Calhoun et al. 2011), R. Scott Appleby's "Western Secularity," Charles Taylor's "Secularism, Citizenship, and the Public Sphere," and Craig Calhoun's "The Secular, Secularizations, and Secularisms" have either defined the term secularism, explaining its current appropriation and historical derivation, deconstructed and problematized terms associated with it, or illustrated its affects on the public sphere and demonstrated its influence on social, political, and, more important for the purposes of this chapter, religious concerns.

16 Cesari (2010: 17–19) notes that in focus groups in Paris, London, Amsterdam, and Berlin, respondents illustrated flexibility in their conception of rituals and practices such as prayer and the wearing of the *hijab*.

17 These leaked documents can be accessed online: www.ap.org/media-center/nypd/investigation.

18 For a comprehensive list of AP's coverage, see www.ap.org/Index/AP-In-The-News/NYPD.

## Bibliography

Abbas, T. (2011) *Islamic Radicalism and Multicultural Politics: The British Experience*, London and New York: Routledge.

Abboud, M. (2012) "Park 51," in Sardar, Z. and Yassin-Kassab, R. (eds.) *Critical Muslim 03: Fear and Loathing*, London: Hurst & Co.

Ahmed, P. (2007) "Prejudice Is Real and Exacts a Heavy Toll," in Nimer, M. (ed.) *Islamophobia and Anti-Americanism: Causes and Remedies*, Beltsville, MD: Amana Publications.

Associated Press (AP) (n.d.a) "AP's Probe into NYPD Intelligence Operations" www.ap.org/Index/AP-In-The-News/NYPD (accessed March 3, 2013).

——(n.d.b) "Highlights of AP's Pulitzer Prize-winning intelligence Operations." www.ap.org/media-center/nypd/investigation (accessed March 3, 2013).

Awad, A. (2012) "The True Story of Sharia in American Courts," June 13, *The Nation*, www.thenation.com/article/168378/true-story-sharia-american-courts (accessed April 28, 2013).

Awan, M.S. (2010) "Global Terror and the Rise of Xenophobia/Islamophobia: An Analysis of American Cultural Production since September 11," *Islamic Studies* [Electronic] 49(4) (Winter): 521–37, www.jstor.org/stable/41581122 (accessed January 31, 2013).

Bazian, H. (2012) "Muslims – Enemies of the State: The New Counter-Intelligence Program (Cointelpro)," *Islamophobia Studies Journal* [Electronic] 1(1) (Fall): 163–206, crg.berkeley.edu/sites/default/files/ISJ%20FALL2012%20Vol1%20No1%20CRG%20Copy.pdf (accessed May 6, 2013).

Bilici, M. (2010) "Muslim Ethnic Comedy: Inversions of Islamophobia," in Shryock, A. (ed.) *Islamophobia/Islamophilia: Beyond the Politics of Enemy and Friend*, Bloomington: Indiana University Press.

Bleich, E. (2011) "What Is Islamophobia and How Much Is There? Theorizing and Measuring an Emerging Comparative Concept," *American Behavioral Scientist* [Electronic] 55(12): 1581–600, abs.sagepub.com/content/55/12/1581 (accessed February 13, 2013).

Burghard, D. and Zeskind, L. (2010) "Who Is an American? Tea Parties, Nativism, and the Birthers," *Institute for Research & Education on Human Rights*, October 19, www.irehr.org/issue-areas/tea-party-nationalism/the-report/who-is-an-american-tea-parties-nativism-and-the-birthers (accessed April 24, 2013).

Cainkar, L. (2010) "American Muslims at the Dawn of the 21st Century: Hope and Pessimism in the Drive for Civic and Political Inclusion," in Cesari, J. (ed.) *Muslims in the West after 9/11: Religion, Politics, and Law*, London and New York: Routledge.

Calhoun, C.J., Juergensmeyer, M., and Van Antwerpen, J. (eds.) (2011) *Rethinking Secularism*, Oxford: Oxford University Press.

Cesari, J. (2010) "Securitization of Islam in Europe," in Cesari, J. (ed.) *Muslims in the West after 9/11: Religion, Politics, and Law*, London and New York: Routledge.

Conason, J. (2010) "Coalition of Fear: Tea Party, the Religious Right and Islamophobia," *Salon*, September 19, www.salon.com/2010/09/19/conason_values_voter/ (accessed March 24, 2013).

Council on American–Islamic Relations (2009) "Status of Muslim Civil Rights in the United States (2005)," in Curtis, E.E. (ed.) *The Columbia Sourcebook of Muslims in the United States*, New York: Columbia University Press.

Ewing, K.P. (2008) "Introduction," in Ewing, K.P. (ed.) *Being and Belonging: Muslims in the United States since 9/11*, New York: Russell Sage Foundation.

Ewing, K.P. and Hoyler, M. (2008) "Being Muslim and American: South Asian Muslim Youth and the War on Terror," in Ewing, K.P. (ed.) *Being and Belonging: Muslims in the United States since 9/11*, New York: Russell Sage Foundation.

Gest, J. (2010) *Apart: Alienated and Engaged Muslims in the West*, New York: Columbia University Press.

Goldman, A. and Apuzzo, M. (2012a) "With Cameras, Informants, NYPD Eyed Mosques," February 22, AP's Probe into NYPD Intelligence Operations, www.ap.org/Content/AP-In-The-News/2012/NYPD-built-secret-files-on-mosques-outside-NY (accessed March 3, 2013).

——(2012b) "NYPD Built Secret Files on Mosques Outside NY," February 23, AP's Probe into NYPD Intelligence Operations, www.ap.org/Content/AP-In-The-News/2012/Newark-mayor-seeks-probe-of-NYPD-Muslim-spying (accessed March 3, 2013).

——(2012c) "NYPD: Muslim Spying Led to No Leads, Terror Cases," AP's Probe into NYPD Intelligence Operations, August 21, www.ap.org/Content/AP-In-The-News/2012/NYPD-Muslim-spying-led-to-no-leads-terror-cases (accessed March 3, 2013).

——(2012d) "Informant: NYPD Paid Me to 'Bait' Muslims," October 23, AP's Probe into NYPD Intelligence Operations, www.ap.org/Content/AP-In-The-News/2012/Informant-NYPD-paid-me-to-bait-Muslims (accessed March 3, 2013).

Haddad, Y.Y. and Ricks, R.S. (2009) "Claiming Space in America's Pluralism: Muslims Enter the Political Maelstrom," in Sinno, A.H. (ed.) *Muslims in Western Politics*, Bloomington: Indiana University Press.

Harvey, F.P. (2008) *The Homeland Security Dilemma: Fear, Failure, and the Future of American Insecurity*, London and New York: Routledge.

Hawley, C. (2012) "NYPD Monitored Muslim Students All Over Northeast," AP's Probe into NYPD Intelligence Operations, February 18, www.ap.org/Content/AP-In-The-News/2012/NYPD-monitored-Muslim-students-all-over-Northeast (accessed March 3, 2013).

Helbling, M. (2012) "Islamophobia in the West," in Helbling, M. (ed.) *Islamophobia in the West: Measuring and Explaining Individual Attitudes*, London and New York: Routledge.

Henry, S. (2012) "NJ FBI: NYPD Monitoring Damaged Public Trust," March 7, AP's Probe into NYPD Intelligence Operations, www.ap.org/Content/AP-In-The-News/2012/NJ-FBI-NYPD-monitoring-damaged-public-trust (accessed March 3, 2013).

"Intelligence Division Central Analysis Research Unit" (2006) February 9, hosted.ap.org/specials/interactives/documents/nypd/nypd_cartoons.pdf (accessed January 24, 2014).

Iqbal, Z. (2010) "Islamophobia or Islamophobias: Towards Developing a Process Model," *Islamic Studies* [Electronic] 49(1) (Spring): 81–101, www.jstor.org/stable/41429246 (accessed January 31, 2013).

Jackson, S.A. (2011) "Muslims, Islam(s), and Race and American Islamophobia," in Esposito, J.L. and Kalin, I. (eds) *The Challenge of Pluralism in the 21st Century*, Oxford and New York: Oxford University Press.

Jamal, A. (2009) "The Radicalization of American Muslims," in Sinno, A.H. (ed.) *Muslims in Western Politics*, Bloomington: Indiana University Press.

Joseph, C.M. and Reidel, B. (2008) "Islamic Schools, Assimilation, and the Concept of Muslim American Character," in Ewing, K.P. (ed.) *Being and Belonging: Muslims in the United States since 9/11*, New York: Russell Sage Foundation.

Kalin, I. (2011) "The Context of Islamophobia: Islamophobia and the Limits of Multiculturalism," in Esposito, J.L. and Kalin, I. (eds.) *The Challenge of Pluralism in the 21st Century*, Oxford and New York: Oxford University Press.

Kundani, A. (2008) "Islamism and the Roots of Liberal Rage," *Race & Class* [Electronic] 50(2): 40–68, rac.sagepub.com/content/50/2/40 (accessed January 31, 2013).

Lane, E. (2012) "On Madison, Muslims, and the New York City Police Department," *Hofstra Law Review* [Electronic] 40(3): 689–718, www.hofstralawreview.org/wp-content/uploads/2013/02/40-43-Lane-Hofstra-Law-Review.pdf (accessed April 4, 2013).

Lean, N. and Esposito, J. (2012) *The Islamophobia Industry: How the Right Manufactures Fear of Muslims*, London: Pluto Press; New York: Palgrave Macmillan.

Leonard, K.I. (2005) "Introduction: Young American Muslim Identities," *The Muslim World* 95(4): 473–7, onlinelibrary.wiley.com/doi/10.1111/j.1478-1913.2005.00106.x/abstract;jsessionid=EE8D18D430FAE86871A5F6E60F04B482.f03t04 (accessed February 17, 2013).

Love, E. (2010) "Confronting Islamophobia in the United States: Framing Civil Rights Activism among Middle Eastern Americans," in Malik, M. (ed.) *Anti-Muslim Prejudice: Past and Present*, London: Routledge.

Maira, S. (2009) *Missing: Youth, Citizenship, and Empire after 9/11*, Durham, NC: Duke University Press.

——(2011) "Manifestations: Islamophobia and the War on Terror: Youth, Citizenship, and Dissent," in Esposito, J.L. and Kalin, I. (eds.) *The Challenge of Pluralism in the 21st Century*, Oxford and New York: Oxford University Press.

Meer, N. and Modood, T. (2010) "Refutation of Racism in the 'Muslim Question'," in Malik, M. (ed.) *Anti-Muslim Prejudice: Past and Present*, London: Routledge.

Monshipouri, M. (2010) "The War on Terror and Muslims in the West," in Cesari, J. (ed.) *Muslims in the West after 9/11: Religion, Politics, and Law*, London and New York: Routledge.

The Muslim American Civil Liberties Coalition (MACLC), the Creating Law Enforcement Accountability & Responsibility (CLEAR) project, and the Asian American Legal Defense and Education Fund (AALDEF) (2013) "Mapping Muslims: NYPD Spying and its impact on American Muslims," www.law.cuny.edu/academics/clinics/immigration/clear/Mapping-Muslims.pdf (accessed April 1, 2013).

Noble, G. (2012) "Where Is the Moral in Moral Panic? Islam, Evil and Moral Turbulence," in Morgan, G. and Poynting, S. (eds.) *Global Islamophobia: Muslims and Moral Panic in the West*, Burlington, VT: Ashgate.

Pew Research Center (2007) "Muslim Americans: Middle Class and Mostly Mainstream," May 22, pewresearch.org/files/old-assets/pdf/muslim-americans.pdf (accessed February 10, 2013).

Ramadan, T. (2012) "Multiculturalism: Commonality, Diversity, and Psychological Integration," in Farrar, M., Robinson, S., Valli, Y., and Wetherly, P. (eds.) *Islam in the West: Key Issues in Multiculturalism*, New York: Palgrave Macmillan.

Read, J.G. (2008) "Multiple Identities among Arab Americans: A Tale of Two Congregations" in Ewing, K.P. (ed.) *Being and Belonging: Muslims in the United States since 9/11*, New York: Russell Sage Foundation.

Runnymede Trust (1997) "Islamophobia: A Challenge for Us All," www.runnymedetrust.org/publications/17/32.html (accessed January 30, 2013).

Safi, O. (ed.) (2003) *Progressive Muslims: On Justice, Gender and Pluralism*, Oxford: Oneworld.

Said, E. (1981) *Covering Islam: How the Media and the Experts Determine How We See the Rest of the World*, New York: Pantheon Books.

Sayyid, S. (2010) "Out of the Devil's Dictionary," in Sayyid, S. and Vakil, A. (eds.) *Thinking through Islamophobia*, London: S. Hurst.

Semati, M. (2010) "Islamophobia, Culture, and Race in the Age of Empire," *Cultural Studies* 24(2) (March): 256–75, www.tandf.co.uk/journals (accessed February 20, 2013)

Shaheen, J.G. (2003) "Reel Bad Arabs: How Hollywood Vilifies a People," *Annals of the American Academy of Political and Social Sciences* [Electronic] 588, Islam: Enduring Myths and Changing Realities (July): 171–93, www.jstor.org/stable/1049860 (accessed April 20, 2013).

Sheehi, S. (2011) *Islamophobia: The Ideological Campaign against Muslims*, Atlanta, GA: Clarity Press.

Shehata, S. (2007) "Popular Media and Opinion Leaders Are to Blame," in Nimer, M. (ed.) *Islamophobia and Anti-Americanism: Causes and Remedies*, Beltsville, MD: Amana Publications.

Shryock, A. (2010) "Introduction: Islam as an object of fear and affection," in Shryock, A. (ed.) *Islamophobia/Islamophilia: Beyond the Politics of Enemy and Friend*, Bloomington: Indiana University Press.

Sirin, S.R. and Fine, M. (2008) *Muslim American Youth: Understanding Hyphenated Identities through Multiple Methods*, New York: New York University Press.

Smith, J.I. (2010) "Islam in America," in Cesari, J. (ed.) *Muslims in the West after 9/11: Religion, Politics, and Law*, London and New York: Routledge.

*The O'Reilly Factor* (2011) "Ahmed Rehab Debunks O'Reilly's Denial of Islamophobia," Fox News Channel, September 21, www.youtube.com/watch?v=GwgxcAH2R6U (accessed March 28, 2013).

The Takeaway (2012) "NYPD Monitored American Muslim Student Activities across Northeast," PRI: Public Radio International, February 24, www.pri.org/stories/politics-society/government/nypd-monitored-american-muslim-student-activities-across-northeast8627.html (accessed April 17, 2013).

Turner, B.S. (2011) *Religion and Modern Society: Citizenship, Secularization and the State*, Cambridge: Cambridge University Press.

Vakil, A. (2010) "Who's Afraid of Islamophobia?," in Sayyid, S. and Vakil, A. (eds.) *Thinking through Islamophobia*, London: S. Hurst.

# 15

# A Muslim modernity

## Ismaili engagement with Western societies

*Karim H. Karim*

Shi'i Nizari Ismaili Muslims (or "Ismailis" for short) are a branch of Islam who have engaged in a unique manner with modernity. Their hereditary leaders (imams) were prominent interlocutors with European colonialism and have been present in Western Europe since the early twentieth century. Following migration from Asia and Africa, Ismailis now have significant settlements in several parts of Europe, North America, and Australasia. This relatively small group of several millions located around the world has a form of communal (*jamati*) self-governance that has Western features of organization and whose structure is specified in a transnational "constitution." Many members of the community living in Western as well as non-Western countries have integrated modernity into their lives, while maintaining Islamic practice and identity. In producing new ways of engaging with the modern state, civil society, institutional organizations, international development, transnationalism, cosmopolitanism, citizenship, and traditional and contemporary knowledge, they have produced a unique form of Muslim modernity.

Ismaili communities are currently located in some forty countries, with the oldest ones being in Afghanistan, Pakistan, Syria, Tajikistan, India, Iran, and China. They emerged in these places from conversion activities of earlier times. However, the community has not conducted active proselytization since at least the eighteenth century. Ismaili history, which spans more than a thousand years (Daftary 2007), is closely tied to the community's hereditary leadership (*Imamat*), which claims direct lineal descent from Ali ibn Abi Talib (sixth to seventh century CE), the first Shi'i imam and the Prophet Muhammad's son-in-law. Aga Khan IV is the forty-ninth and present imam of the Nizari Ismailis. No Ismaili '*ulama*' exists; appointments to religious offices and *jamati* institutions are rotational and are made by the imam.

Engagement of the imam with matters of faith (*din*) as well as of the material world (*dunya*) is viewed as being central to his office (Aga Khan IV 2008c: 15–16). The history of the *Imamat* and its followers is punctuated by the rise of fall of Ismaili states, including the Fatimid Empire in the tenth to thirteenth century, and periods of severe persecution. The honorific title of Aga Khan was given to the forty-sixth imam by a Qajar shah in nineteenth-century Iran. Adverse political developments compelled Aga Khan I to move to India, which was then ruled by the British. Aga Khan III established himself in Europe by the mid-twentieth century and used the continent's international communications links to expand contacts with his transnational community. Aga Khan IV, who resides in France, became imam in 1957.

A primary characteristic of the Ismaili practice of Islam is the emphasis on the esoteric (*batin*) aspects of spirituality (Corbin 1993: 74–104). The religious quest of community members is to apprehend the inner significance of Islamic teachings. This involves an effort to understand the profound symbolism of the Qur'an and a quest for spiritual truth, an approach that has much in common with Sufi practice. Such an orientation to Islam differs from those adhering only to an exoteric understanding of religion. The role of the contemporary imam as the bearer of spiritual knowledge (*'ilm*) is vital in Ismaili theology and practice. In contrast to the majority Shi'i group of, whose imam is considered absent (*ghayb*), the living Ismaili imam is the primary interpreter of Islamic revelations for his followers – providing guidance according to the changing conditions of time. The community's members were often severely persecuted, occasionally to the point of genocide, because their beliefs were viewed as being heretical (Jamal 2002; Virani 2007).

The imam is not only a guide in matters of faith, but also provides worldly direction. Since *din* and *dunya* are intertwined in Islamic worldviews, it behooves the imam to be profoundly concerned with both aspects of life (Aga Khan IV 2008c: 95). Present-day Ismaili leadership has been intensely engaged in improving the socio-economic conditions of its followers and in this has conducted a longstanding dialogue with modernity. Given the community's attention to the inner aspects of spirituality, it tends not to have rigid attachments to theological formulations in the manner in which it approaches contemporary aspects of life. Ismailis seek to adhere to Islamic ethics and principles rather than dogma, which facilitates their engagement with modernity.

Over the last century, Ismaili imams have developed an infrastructure of institutions that address the needs of their followers and the societies in which they live. A number of *jamati* organizations tend to the religious, social, economic, educational, and health concerns of Ismailis. This group of institutions is transnational in scope, with the imam at its head. In addition to this communal self-governance structure, the current imam has established a group of organizations that are non-denominational, with their scope extending outside Ismaili communities and into areas such as architecture, aviation, and media. This Aga Khan Development Network (AKDN) is guided by a contemporary Islamic engagement with concepts such as development, democracy, civil society, and pluralism as articulated by its founder. In this, the Ismaili imam has emerged as a major Muslim interlocutor with Western societies on issues of modernity.

The Aga Khan intellectually and managerially leads the transformations wrought by Ismaili modernity. He has strong support from many of his followers who contribute financially and by providing their time, knowledge, and skills to the imam's vast institutional networks. However, the hierarchical organization of these structures does not appear to have provided for a formal articulation and theorization of Ismaili modernity, which is largely shaped by the *Imamat*. Nor has the community's articulation of concepts such as democracy, civil society, pluralism, and meritocracy been discussed in the context of its hereditary, male Shi'i leadership.

## Muslim modernities

The response to modernity in many Muslim societies in the last two centuries has been in accordance with dominant Western models. Tight control was established over society and land through the intense bureaucratization of the state apparatus, the construction of centralized communications and transportation networks, the homogenization of educational systems, the imposition of European legal frameworks, and state expropriation of religious endowments (*awqaf*). All this had the objective of unifying the country and strengthening the power of central government. The last two hundred years have also been characterized by waves of intellectual activity: "While some Muslim elements were calling for a rapid and wholesale embrace of Western ideas and institutional models, and others were holding to the past, rejecting any form of change, reformist '*ulama*', intellectuals and statesmen sought to chart a way between accommodating the new condition and preserving the Islamic identity of society" (Nafi 2004: 39).

The broad range of reformers had a common purpose in safeguarding Islamic distinctiveness in the face of the forceful challenge of modernization and at the same time overcoming what they saw as the debilitating layers of questionable traditional practices. Their twofold mission sought to contain "the Western challenge by creating a synthesis between modern values and systems and what they perceived as eternal Islamic values and systems and questioning the credibility, even the Islamicity, of the dominant traditional modes of religion" (Nafi 2004: 40). Espousing the notion of progress, the reformers challenged what they saw as the blind adherence of Muslim society to juristic opinions developed over previous centuries and asserted the mutability of the *shari'a*. They urged the revival of the independent reasoning (*ijtihad*) as an integral aspect of Islamic methodology.

However, despite their noteworthy efforts, these nineteenth- and early twentieth-century Muslim reformers (such as Afghani, Abduh, Rida, and Iqbal) were not able to influence the directions which Muslim majority states eventually took. While occasionally paying lip-service to reformist thought, governments mainly pursued policies of Westernization. By the late 1970s, the alienation that this approach had engendered in Muslim societies gave rise to a more dogmatic response usually termed "fundamentalism" or "Islamism." Nafi suggests that the work of reformists in breaking the dominance of the traditional '*ulama*' opened the way for Islamists, most of whom do not have theological training, to pursue their forceful challenge against the state. Their political activism would not have been made possible if the reformists had not "prepared the ground for the laymen, the modern Muslim intellectual and the Muslim professional, to speak on behalf of Islam" (Nafi 2004: 53).

Other contemporary heirs of the nineteenth- and early twentieth-century reformists include Muslim scholars trained in the contemporary humanities and social sciences. Some of them also have traditional Islamic training. Many of them live and work in Western countries, often because of the greater opportunities these settings afford for free expression. They use the tools of contemporary scholarship to examine Muslim theology, history, and sociology. Enlightenment and post-Enlightenment concepts are regularly employed when academic audiences are addressed, and also when the Muslim faithful are addressed.

Ebrahim Moosa states that whereas the reformists viewed modernity as an ally, "twenty-first-century critical Muslim scholars are much more apprehensive of its allure and offer a critique of modernity" (Moosa 2003: 118). While twentieth-century reformers supported women's rights and the study of contemporary sciences, most of them did not proceed to apply the intellectual tools of the day to scrutinize traditional Islamic sciences. Moosa says that Muslims need to move beyond apologetics that distort those aspects of history and theology which do not appear to conform to contemporary standards. He criticizes the tendency to look for corroboration of past practices:

> this desire to find justification in the past, in a text or the practice of a founder, suggests that Muslims can act confidently in the present only if the matter in question was already prefigured in the past. ... Does this mean that Muslims can engage in discourses of justice,

egalitarianism, freedom, and equality only if there is some semblance that the scripture of the Prophet or some of the learned savants (imams) of the past endorsed, hinted, or fantasized about the possibility of such discourses?

*(Moosa 2003: 122)*

Moosa states that these tendencies invalidate the actual experiences of Muslims in their efforts to construct the path to innovation, change, and adaptation. There is an increasing insistence among contemporary Muslim intellectuals, according to Tariq Ramadan, to take account of "the concrete realities of our societies" and "produce a *fiqh*, a legislation appropriate to our times" (Ramadan 2001: 324).

Ramadan, a prominent voice among Muslims in the West, has promoted the development of a "Western Islam" (Ramadan 2004). Muslim intellectuals living in North America, Europe, and Australasia are engaged seriously with Western modernity. There has been an attempt to give impetus to a movement of "Progressive Muslims" in the USA and Canada. Included in the "essential concerns of progressive Muslims," articulated by Omid Safi (2003), are: a critical review of the broad range of Islamic tradition; looking anew at Islamic scriptural teachings on social justice in the context of the contemporary world; striving for an "Islamic feminism"; and a pluralistic openness towards human sources of compassion and wisdom that goes beyond Islamic ones.

Aziz Esmail of the Institute of Ismaili Studies refers to a "pluralistic, universal point of view" that safeguards the particularity of the Muslim community and moves "from the inside to the outside" to gain an awareness of humanity's ethical and spiritual aspirations (Esmail 1996: 487). He proposes a common project among communities, particularly of the Abrahamic faiths, which would also critically assess cultural assumptions among Muslims. Esmail promotes a search that goes past these historical accretions in order to understand the core of the vision that gave expression to the principles of Islam.

Whereas the orientations of these contemporary Muslim scholars vary, they all urge a critical intellectual approach when examining Muslim traditions, a non-adversarial engagement with Western societies, and respect for both pluralist and universal values. They reject the notion of modernization that grants a privileged status to Western understandings of intellectual and material development. Instead they uphold the necessity of truly universal values and the importance of inter-faith and inter-cultural explorations of the common heritage of humanity, while continuing to realize the particular significance and contribution of the Islamic vision. In this lies the recognition of the multiple paths to modernity, not just those marked out by Western societies. Among these multiple paths, Ismailis have charted out a fairly distinct trajectory which has enabled them to integrate the contingencies of the contemporary world and to seek to play a role in the future of humanity.

## Ismaili engagements with colonialism

Ismailis in India (Khojas) had begun to experience the reorganization of their social lives under British norms before the arrival of Aga Khan I on the subcontinent in 1842. The Ismaili leader's settling in India provided for a situation in which the living imam was physically present among his Indian followers for the first time. There subsequently arose disputes over the control of community properties and the religious dues between the Aga Khan and some Khojas. Under British jurisdiction, "the state reserved all matters dealing with property within religious groups" (Shodhan 2010: 169; also see Purohit 2012). A series of court cases were launched against the imam, challenging his ownership of communal property and authority over Khojas. Orientalist understandings of Eastern religions informed the British judiciary in India. This was problematic for the Khojas since Western experts were not familiar with the religious pluralism that characterized their faith (Khan 2004). "The community was asked to answer for its own authenticity against the standard of orientalist scholarship *on* the community" (Steinberg 2011: 44). Following extensive proceedings, the cases were settled in favor of the *Imamat*. In particular, the judgment on the "Aga Khan Case" made in 1866 came to be presented as an authoritative legitimation of the imam's claims. Based on a modernist understanding of Ismaili history and faith, it became a vital element in the Aga Khans' engagement with the larger world. Even eighty-eight years later, Aga Khan III's *Memoirs* stated, "My grandfather had been confirmed in his rights and titles by a judgement of the Bombay High Court in 1866 ... [which] contains a classic fully-detailed account of the origins of Ismailism and of the beginnings of my family" (Aga Khan III 1954: 9). If the British judge had become convinced of the authenticity of the Aga Khans' Ismaili leadership, then the *Imamat* seemed to be reciprocally persuaded about the value of modern Western scholarship. This view appears to have been important in the steps that the imams took in promoting Western education in their community.

The Ismailis had a centuries-long tradition of fostering education and scholarship (Daftary 2007). However, apart from a few privileged families, most Ismailis in the nineteenth and early twentieth century were small-scale farmers, shopkeepers, and laborers with little schooling. They were often socially marginalized in the countries where they lived and were frequently persecuted for their religious beliefs. Aga Khan III was a visionary who strived to modernize his community and raise its standing in the world. He sought to emulate his Fatimid forebears, who had fostered a progressive society that was at the leading edge of human civilization in its time (Aga Khan III 1955: 48). Al Azhar University, built a thousand years ago in Cairo by a Fatimid imam, has remained a primary seat of Islamic learning. Yet, formal higher education was rare among Ismailis in the nineteenth century. The travails of history, featuring bouts of severe repression and massacres, had shattered most of the community's social institutions. Consequently, Ismaili leaders and their followers had practiced concealment (*taqiyya*) of their religious identities (Jamal 2002; Virani 2007). With the public re-emergence of the Ismaili *Imamat* in Iran in the late eighteenth century there began a gradual process of social and economic development. However, it was the moving of the *Imamat*'s seat to British India that accelerated the community's transformation into one of the most progressive Muslim groups in contemporary times.

Aga Khan III is particularly credited with this change; he is viewed as bringing about the "metamorphosis of a moribund society from the depths of degradation to its proud position in modern civilization during the course of only about half a century" (Thawerbhoy 1977: 19). His *Imamat* was the longest in Ismaili history. Inheriting the community's leadership from his father at the young age of eight in 1885, he was the imam for seventy-two years, until his death in 1957. Living in a period that saw the end of the Muslim Caliphate, two world wars, and independence of the Asian and African colonies where his followers lived, he was an international figure who was elected the first president of the All India Muslim League, was honored by governments of European and majority Muslim countries, and served as president of the League of Nations.

The imam adopted a step-by-step process of raising his socio-economically disadvantaged followers through various stages of development over several decades. He recognized that wealth creation would be vital for acquiring the personal and communal means for advancement. Hence, advice for the successful establishment and operation of businesses was an important theme in his guidance. He also advised his followers to share resources, information, and ideas. Conceptualizing the community's progress in generational terms, the imam stressed the proper care and education of young children. Among the earliest institutions to be established were clinics that provided pre- and post-natal care, as well as schools catering for the youngest in the community. Priority was also given to women's education and their social standing as early as the 1920s:

> In paving the way for Ismaili women to go to school, to receive both the quality and length of education that would make it possible for them to enter the professions and to strive for financial self-sufficiency, Aga Khan III laid the groundwork for moving the community away from its inherited cultural patriarchal mores and attitudes towards a partnership model where women worked alongside men to meet the challenges the community would face in the 20th century.
>
> *(Kassam 2011: 259)*

He also promoted these values in the larger Indian society and among Muslims worldwide. Institutions such as kindergartens, primary schools, secondary schools, libraries, and youth hostels, as well as clinics, hospitals, housing societies, and sports facilities, were built in South Asia and Africa, where the Indian Ismaili diaspora had settled and which was then also under European colonial rule. The Ismaili imam contributed significantly to Muslim causes such as the establishment of Aligarh University in India, and also supported the building of Hindu universities (Aziz 1998: 410–15). He was a founding member of the East African Muslim Welfare Society, which constructed educational institutions for indigenous Muslims in the region.

Most colonial regimes permitted the development of communal institutions that did not threaten their power. This provided the space for groups like the Ismailis to organize their religious and social affairs as well as to develop modes of self-governance. Applying a Weberian analysis, Jonah Steinberg notes that "the Ismaili central leadership engaged in a progressive process of bureaucratization, a discernible transition from 'traditional' forms to more 'modern' ones" (Steinberg 2011: 42). A structure of *jamati* councils was developed to address the needs of communities from cradle to grave. In the course of the twentieth century, Aga Khan III and Aga Khan IV established a series of regulations specifying community institutions and their governance. These rule books and constitutions were produced in the context of the *Imamat*'s interactions with Ismailis in India and Africa; later documents reflect the growing contact with other parts of the transnational community. Promulgated or appearing in 1905, 1925/1926, 1937, 1946, 1954, 1962, and 1986, they articulated the imam's authority and the nature of the institutional bodies. This provided for the structure of internal organization as well as the modality for interactions with governments and other communities (Hirji 2011). The contemporary organizational and bureaucratic forms characterizing Ismaili institutional structures have also facilitated effective engagement with states and international bodies (Karim 2014).

## Settlement in Western countries

Aga Khan III lived for extended periods in Europe in the early twentieth century and eventually settled there. Upon his death in 1957, his grandson, Karim Al-Husseini, was designated as the next imam of Ismaili Muslims. He combines attributes of both the East and the West. Claiming descent from the Prophet Muhammad and Fatimid caliphs, Aga Khan IV was born in Geneva of an English mother and an Italian grandmother, and was educated in Switzerland and at Harvard. The twenty-year-old imam inherited not only the religious leadership of a transnational Muslim community but also the responsibility for its material well-being in locations that are increasingly within Western societies.

Individual Ismailis had begun to settle in Europe in the 1930s. One of the earliest was Rahimtulla Harji Bhanji, the Zanzibar-born father of the renowned British actor Ben Kingsley (Krishna Bhanji), who went to study in England for a medical degree. However, the first official Ismaili congregational house of prayer (*jamatkhana*) in London was not established until 1951, when a significant number of community members were present in the city. Instability in post-independence Congo (Kinshasa) prompted some of its French-speaking Ismailis to migrate to Paris. The intensification of apartheid caused emigration from South Africa, as did the nationalization of private property in Tanzania. But it was the expulsion of Indians from Uganda in 1972 that prompted the largest exodus of Ismailis from Africa to Western countries. Many settled in Canada, the United States, Australia, the UK, and various other parts of Europe. Mozambique's long-running war led to the growth of the community in Portugal. These settlements in Western countries were later augmented by significant additions from other parts of Africa, India, Pakistan, and Afghanistan. Some Ismailis from Syria, Iran, and Tajikistan have also settled in Europe, North America, and Australasia.

Ismailis' acquisition of European languages and Western education in their previous countries served significant numbers of the migrants in seeking employment and in integrating into their countries of settlement. Many members of the relatively small community have been successful in the professions and in business. Some have distinguished themselves with notable achievements in various fields such as politics, public service, journalism, literature, academia, corporate business, and banking. Among them have been a mayor in Calgary, members of the provincial and federal assemblies and the senate in Canada, officials of the White House staff, a member of the British House of Lords, prominent journalists in American, Canadian, British, and Portuguese media, an author who has won multiple Canadian and Commonwealth awards, internationally acclaimed scholars in Canada, the USA, and the UK, the head of a major Canadian media corporation, and a high-profile British banker. However, a number of Ismailis in Western countries also are on the lower socio-economic rungs of society.

The *Imamat*'s guidance is to maintain adherence to Islamic beliefs and practices while integrating into the countries where they settle. As with other religious communities, Ismaili places of worship serve as key religious symbols as well as places of social gathering. Upon arriving in the places of settlement, the community makes it a priority to establish *jamatkhanas* even in cities with a small number of Ismailis. Whereas some other Muslim migrant groups have maintained a conservative attitude to Western societies, Ismailis have generally sought to develop an Islamic approach to modernity (Karim 2011a). This has assisted their settlement and institutional development in various Western countries.

Canada has the largest Western Ismaili settlement, with around 70,000–80,000 community members. In addition to several *jamatkhanas* in places of significant settlement, the Aga Khan has established Ismaili Centres (incorporating spaces for worship, education, administration, and social gatherings) in Greater Vancouver and Toronto, a Delegation of the Ismaili *Imamat* building and the Global Centre for Pluralism in Ottawa, and the Aga Khan Museum in Toronto. Even though the UK has a smaller Ismaili population of 10,000–15,000, it has become a global center for the transnational community. In addition to its prominently placed Ismaili Centre, London is also the site for the Institute of Ismaili Studies, the Aga Khan University's Institute for the Study of Muslim Civilisations, and a major Ismaili cultural institution. Lisbon has the landmark Centro Ismaili and a Delegation of the Ismaili *Imamat*, which has been accorded the status of a diplomatic mission by the Portuguese government. Other Ismaili Centres are planned in Paris and Houston. The prominent physical placement of these institutions in major Western cities is symbolic of the community's engagement with their public spheres (see Karim 2013). (Outside Western countries, there have long been high-profile Ismaili buildings in several South Asian and African cities; Ismaili Centres have been built recently in Bangladesh, Tajikistan, and the United Arab Emirates (UAE), and another is planned in Singapore.)

Most of the agencies of the transnational AKDN are based in Europe. The Aga Khan's own secretariat is located on his estate in Gouvieux, north of Paris, and several major AKDN organizations are headquartered in Geneva. A key node in the network is the Aga Khan Foundation, which was established in 1967 in Switzerland; it has affiliates in Canada, Portugal, the UK, and the USA, and branch offices in eleven Asian and African countries. AKDN institutions are non-denominational; however, there is a strong involvement of Ismailis in these agencies. The international mobility gained by members of the community has enabled them to be involved transnationally in the work of the network, and in this to have a cosmopolitan engagement with the contemporary world.

## The Aga Khan Development Network

Early in his *Imamat*, Aga Khan IV began to establish new institutions that were situated outside the communal Ismaili infrastructure. The Nation Media Group, which dates back to 1959, began as a newspaper company in colonial Kenya to give voice to African politicians, and has now expanded into an East African media conglomerate (Loughran 2010). Ismaili schools, hospitals, and financial institutions were increasingly opened up to non-Ismailis. The declared purpose, beyond tending to the needs of community members, was to contribute to the development of countries in Asia and Africa. Aga Khan III had been engaged in promoting the welfare of Muslims in India and in helping establish Muslim institutions in South Asia and Africa. His successor embarked on a course that began a broader engagement with the public sphere even in countries where his community did not have a significant presence.

In an address to the European Bank for Reconstruction and Development, Aga Khan IV said:

> When I became imam in 1957, I was faced with developing a system to meet my responsibilities in an organized, sustainable manner that was suited to the circumstances, demands and opportunities of the second half of the twentieth century. In a period of decolonization in Asia and Africa, the Cold War and its disastrous impact on developing countries, and painful progress towards a global movement for international development, it became essential that the *Imamat*'s economic and social development efforts be broadened beyond the Ismaili community to the societies in which the community lived.
>
> *(Aga Khan IV 2008c: 16)*

In order to achieve this goal, a key aspect of AKDN's strategy has been to mobilize international resources, particularly from developed states.

The network's organizational chart (Figure 15.1) identifies the agencies working in the areas of economic, social, and cultural development. (However, it is not a comprehensive representation of all of the *Imamat*'s endeavors; for instance, it does not list the Ismaili *jamati* organizational structure nor bodies such as the Institute of Ismaili Studies and the Global Centre for Pluralism.) AKDN operates in over thirty countries grouped under eight regions: Eastern Africa; Central and Western Africa; South Asia; the Middle East; Central Asia; the Far East and Southeast Asia; Europe; and North America. It employs some 80,000 people, the majority of whom are based in developing countries.

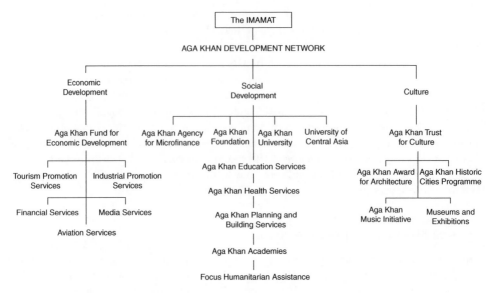

*Figure 15.1* The Aga Khan Development Network's organizational chart

The Aga Khan Foundation is the lead agency engaged in the AKDN's social development activities. It describes itself as seeking "sustainable solutions to long-term problems of poverty, hunger, illiteracy and ill-health, with special emphasis on the needs of rural communities in mountainous, coastal and other resource-poor areas" (AKDN 2007: 23; see also Kassam 2003). The Foundation's affiliates in Canada, the USA, the UK, and Portugal have cultivated relationships with Western institutional partners, which have included governmental, non-governmental, and private sector entities in North America and Europe. Another major social development initiative of the Network is post-secondary education. The international Aga Khan University, which is headquartered in Pakistan, also has campuses in Tanzania, Kenya, Uganda, and the UK. Its London-based Institute for the Study of Muslim Civilisations conducts research and offers instruction to graduate students and diplomats in various Western countries (Aga Khan University 2006: 41) and partners with institutions in the USA and Germany working on components of school curricula relating to knowledge about Islam and Muslims.

Agencies of the Aga Khan Fund for Economic Development are concerned with industrial promotion, tourism, finance, aviation, and media. This institution "works in collaboration with local and international development partners to create and operate companies that provide goods and services essential to economic development" (Aga Khan Development Network n.d.: 4). It employs 30,000 people around the world and has annual revenues "in excess of US$1.5 billion" (Aga Khan Development Network n.d.: 5). Similarly, the Aga Khan Trust for Culture has several collaborators around the world (Aga Khan Trust for Culture 2007: 37), which contribute to its efforts in running a historic cities program, an award for architecture, a music initiative, museum projects, architectural research programs, and a digital archive in various parts of the world. The Aga Khan Program in Islamic Architecture at Harvard University and the Massachusetts Institute of Technology was established to improve education, understanding, and research relating to Muslim art and architecture "in light of contemporary theoretical, historical, critical, and developmental issues" (Aga Khan Trust for Culture 2007: 26).

The AKDN is exhibiting a global transnationalism, which is simultaneously a feature of present-day global modernity and a reflection of Ismaili history. (A thousand years ago, the Ismaili proselitizing mission, the *da'wa*, and the Fatimid Empire had organized themselves transnationally.) The very barriers that European colonialism presented to national development also appear to have given impetus to and a social context for the emergence of contemporary Ismaili institutions. Similarly, contemporary regulatory restrictions in various countries, while placing administrative burdens on the AKDN, have not prevented its transnational growth. The European location of the network's head offices may have been a key factor in the success of the network's global operations – primarily due to the continent's centrality in terms of global communications connections. Furthermore, agreements with governments have enabled AKDN to emerge as a major transnational actor. For example, the accord between the Ismaili *Imamat* and the Portuguese parliament enables the *Imamat* to enter into agreements "internationally, particularly, but without restriction, within the European Union and in the Portuguese-speaking countries" (Government of Portugal 2010). As non-governmental transnational actors, the Ismaili *Imamat* and the AKDN appear to be producing contemporary innovations with respect to the relationships of institutions with states and non-state transnational organizations.

## The Aga Khan's approach to modernity

The Aga Khan's approach to modernity is characterized by the view that faith and the world are intertwined and by a pragmatism that appears to be a function of ensuring a good quality of life for his followers. He has established strong working relationships with governments and NGOs around the world. That the *Imamat* has turned to Western societies for partnership, international development assistance, and as places for resettling some members of his community is incidental to the contemporary realities – this part of the world is currently the most technologically advanced and offers hospitable milieus for Ismailis. It is not necessarily Westernization that is the goal, but a modernity that ensures possibilities for a good quality of life. The two concepts are often thought of as synonyms, but each has a distinct way of conceptualizing societal advancement. Deepak Lal offers the following view: "Whereas modernization entails a change in belief about the way the material world operates, Westernization entails a change in *cosmological* beliefs about the way that one should live" (Lal 2002).

Western societies are guided along the path of modernity by their cultural and religious heritage as well as their intellectual orientation. However, their models of modernization may not serve non-Western communities well and may cause deep conflicts with their worldviews. For example, Western secular individualism, which has provided for several social benefits in European and North American cultural contexts, poses a stark contrast to the widely held communitarian values in Asia and Africa. As a Muslim religious leader, the Aga Khan is keen to ensure that his followers and Muslims at large maintain a conscientious adherence to core Islamic principles (and to the cosmological context from which they are derived). As a champion of development in Asian and African locations, including those that have large non-Muslim populations, he wants to ensure that local values are respected.

The Ismaili leader has emerged as a public intellectual in engaging with a variety of Eastern and Western institutions on the topic of improving contemporary standards of life. His views appear to have been shaped not only through reflection but also as a consequence of the practical experience of managing a transnational development network that contends with the social, cultural, religious, infrastructural, and political problems in the various locations where it operates (Karim 2011b: 215). The Aga Khan has been dealing directly for over five decades with the operations of states and organizations as they strive to maintain ethical ideals in the face of corruption. As imam of a transnational Muslim community seeking to contribute to modernity and simultaneously maintaining its religious traditions, he also has the experience of guiding his followers to face the material conditions of life in Eastern and Western societies.

The Aga Khan describes his involvement with worldly matters of development as an intrinsic function of the *Imamat*, which is concerned with faith and the world. He presents his interaction with modernity as carried out from an Islamic basis. Speaking to a gathering of German ambassadors in Berlin, he stated that, "as a Muslim, I am a democrat not because of Greek or French thought but primarily because of principles that go back 1,400 years, directly to the death of Prophet Muhammad" (Aga Khan IV 2008c: 61). But democracy is only a means to a better life, and he underlined the importance of being cognizant of its end purposes at a university symposium in in Portugal:

> Democratic processes are presumably about sharing power, broadening the number who help shape social decisions. But that sharing, in and of itself, means little apart from the purposes for which power is finally used. To speak of end purposes, in turn, is to enter the realm of ethics. What are our ultimate goals? Whose interests do we seek to serve? How, in an increasingly cynical time, can we inspire people to a new set of aspirations, reaching beyond rampant materialism, the new relativism, self-serving individualism and resurgent tribalism? The search for justice and security, the struggle for equality of opportunity, the quest for tolerance and harmony, the pursuit of human dignity: these are moral imperatives we must work toward and think about daily.
>
> *(Aga Khan IV 2008c: 109–10)*

He refers to some of the basic needs of people in promoting not only an Islamic modernity but one that would appeal to a broader range of views, including non-religious ones.

The Ismaili imam appears to have found the language of ethics to be one with which he can communicate his views to both Muslims and non-Muslims (Karim 2014):

> When we talk about the ethical realm, when we attack corruption, we are inclined to think primarily about government and politics. I am one, however, who believes that corruption is just as acute, and perhaps even more damaging, when the ethics of the civil and private sectors deteriorate. We know from recent headlines about scoundrels from the American financial scene to the halls of European parliaments – and we can certainly do without either. But the problem extends into every area of human enterprise. When a construction company cheats on the quality of materials for a school or a bridge, when a teacher skimps on class work in order to sell his time privately, when a doctor recommends a drug because of incentives from a pharmaceutical company, when a bank loan is skewed by kickbacks, or a student paper is plagiarized from the internet – when the norms of fairness and decency are violated in any way, then the foundations of society are undermined. And the damage is felt most immediately in the most vulnerable societies, where fraud is often neither reported nor corrected, but simply accepted as an inevitable condition of life.
>
> *(Aga Khan IV 2009)*

By giving examples from aspects of life that are common across the world, he appears to articulate "a universal ethical sensibility" (Clarkson 2008: 6) that he suggests is vital as a feature of modernity. In this he allies himself with other contemporary voices that urge serious reflection upon society through the perspectives of ethics (e.g. Taylor 1991; Appiah 2005).

The Aga Khan has frequently spoken of a "cosmopolitan ethic" (Aga Khan IV 2008c: 104), which refers to engaging pluralistically in a world where one comes across people with different backgrounds, views, and values. He sees it as an approach that rises above the limitations of ecumenical and inter-faith dialogue:

> There are several forms of proselytism and, in several religions, proselytism is demanded. Therefore, it is necessary to develop the principle of a cosmopolitan ethic, which is not an ethic oriented by faith, or for a society. I speak of an ethic under which all people can live within a same society, and not of a society that reflects the ethic of solely one faith. I would call that ethic, quality of life.
>
> I have serious doubts about the ecumenical discourse, and about what it can reach, but I do not have any doubts about cosmopolitan ethics. I believe that people share the same basic worries, joys, and sadness. If we can reach a consensus in terms of cosmopolitan ethics, we will have attained something, which is very important.
>
> *(Aga Khan IV 2008b)*

He views the ability of people of various ethnicities, cultures, and religions to be able to work and live together as being vital in improving the quality of life for entire societies. A wider acceptance of pluralism is of benefit to the head of a religious community that has often been under threat from others. The Aga Khan has established, in partnership with the Canadian government, the Global Centre for Pluralism to address issues of inter-ethnic conflict around the world.

Education has become the point of confluence where he has sought to bring together the various ideas about modernity that he espouses. Speaking to the International Baccalaureate organization, he stated that

> In a world of rapid change, an agile and adaptable mind, a pragmatic and cooperative temperament, a strong ethical orientation – these are increasingly the keys to effective leadership. And I would add to this list a capacity for intellectual humility which keeps one's mind constantly open to a variety of viewpoints and which welcomes pluralistic exchange.
>
> *(Aga Khan IV 2008a)*

Pluralism, ethics, and humility are derived in this from his Islamic worldview, but they are not alien ideas to people of other backgrounds. He has sought to inculcate these values in his schools, academies, institutes, and universities located in Asian, African, and Western countries, where both the secular and religious parts of this vast educational enterprise deal with the contingencies of modernity.

## Conclusion

The Ismaili engagement with the contemporary world has produced a particular form of Muslim modernity. Whereas many of its aspects are portable to other Muslim (and even non-Muslim) contexts, some key elements are specific to the Shi'i Nizari Ismaili worldview. The discussions in many other Muslim communities are wracked with debates about the seeming incompatibility of modernity with the *shari'a*, and in some cases with the literal interpretations of the Qur'an and the Hadith (Nafi 2004). However, in the Ismaili view, engagement with modernity is integral to the Islamic concept of the intertwined nature of faith and world and is therefore unavoidable if one is to live one's life as a Muslim.

The achievements of Ismaili modernity are significant. Not only has it raised the socio-economic status of Ismaili men and women, it has had a significant impact on many of the societies in which they live. AKDN's transnational institutions have enabled the transference of wealth and skills from developed to less developed countries. The network has produced numerous innovations in international development such as village organization-based decision-making and the multi-input area development model. The Aga Khan Trust for Culture, through the intensive scholarly examination of the principles and practices of the traditions of Islamic architecture, has demonstrated the importance of rigorous intellectual reflection in order to engender a revival of Muslim material cultures. AKDN and Ismaili *jamati* institutions seek to emulate the progressive values of civil society in providing support for healthy societal development. They have also produced in Ismailis a sense of cosmopolitanism and global citizenship. The imam's leadership is vital in this endeavor. He gives guidance to his adherents on maintaining a balance between the spiritual and the material aspects of contemporary existence. However, a number of unresolved points of discussion appear to arise from this situation.

There is a seeming paradox, on the one hand, in the Ismaili imam's encouragement to value the intellect and engage in personal search and, on the other, the extensive reliance of many Ismailis on the imam's directions. The Aga Khan appears to be the primary, if not the sole, source of innovative Ismaili ideas in dealing with modernity. Whereas he conducts extensive consultations, few adherents – including those in leadership positions in *jamati* and AKDN institutions – tend to proffer independent, and even more rarely contrary, opinions. A high level of deference to the religious leader, who strives to be knowledgeable about a vast range of theoretical and technical issues, tends to provide for a largely unitary set of views. Despite the existence of a highly educated Ismaili intelligentsia and apart from some thoughtful articulations by individual authors, a contemporary school of Ismaili thought does not appear to have emerged. This is anomalous to certain earlier periods of the community's history when philosophical debates raged among Ismaili intellectuals and with other Muslim scholars on the issues of the day (e.g. Daftary 2005; Landolt et al. 2008). Most members of the community – including many institutional leaders – appear not to involve themselves in reflecting deeply upon the intersection of the Ismaili faith and the contemporary world, even though they frequently come into contact with ideas that challenge their worldview.

Issues of democracy raise some important questions in Ismaili contexts. Dominant Western views of democracy seem to be at odds with the arrangements of Ismaili institutional governance. A hereditary leadership and hierarchical organization of the *jamati* councils do not appear to manifest a democratic structure. Regarding the AKDN, a former head of graduate studies at the Institute of Ismaili Studies has critiqued its involvement in the Ismaili-populated Gorno-Badakshan region of Tajikistan as being an impediment to the development of local politics (Devji 2012). Questions have also been raised about the Network's focus on programs that do not benefit Ismailis directly in countries like Tanzania, where members of the community currently face hardships (Jiwani 2013).

There exist a significant number of historical works on the role of the Ismaili imam (and Shi'i leadership generally) in medieval contexts, but almost no theorization has been conducted of his leadership and institutions in contemporary contexts. A rigorous articulation of Shi'i Islamic concepts of governance, in relation to the unique form of Muslim modernity produced by Ismailis, would afford a necessary framework for their current discourses on ethics, pluralism, and meritocracy. This would be an important step in developing a substantive theoretical foundation providing philosophical supports for the innovative activities of the *Imamat*'s institutions in the twenty-first century.

## Bibliography

Aga Khan III (1954) *The Memoirs of Aga Khan: World Enough and Time*, London: Cassell.

——(1955) *Mowlana Hazir Imam's Talika and Messages*, Mombasa, Kenya: Shia Imami Ismailia Associations for Africa.

Aga Khan IV (2008a) "Global Education and the Developing World," the Peterson Lecture, Atlanta, Georgia, April 18, *International Baccalaureate* website, www.ibo.org/council/peterson/agakhan/index.cfm (accessed September 19, 2012).

——(2008b) "Paroquias de Portugal," interview by António Marujo and Faranaz Keshavjee, Lisbon, Portugal, July 23, *NanoWisdoms: Archiving Knowledge from the Imamat* website, www.nanowisdoms.org/nwblog/8861/ (accessed September 19, 2012).

——(2008c) *Where Hope Takes Root: Democracy and Pluralism in an Interdependent World*, Vancouver: Douglas and McIntyre.

——(2009) "Speech by His Highness the Aga Khan at the Graduation Ceremony of the University of Alberta," Edmonton, Alberta, June 9, *Aga Khan Development Network* website, www.akdn.org/Content/767 (accessed September 19, 2012).

Aga Khan Development Network (AKDN) (2007) *AKDN*, Geneva: AKDN.

——(n.d.) *Aga Khan Fund for Economic Development: An Agency of the Aga Khan Development Network*, Geneva: AKDN.

Aga Khan Trust for Culture (2007) *Aga Khan Trust for Culture: The Cultural Agency of the Aga Khan Development Network*, Geneva: AKDN.

Aga Khan University (c.2006) *The Aga Khan University: Progress Report 2006*, Karachi: Aga Khan University.

Appiah, K.A. (2005). *The Ethics of Identity*, Princeton: Princeton University Press.

Aziz, K.K. (ed.) (1998) *Aga Khan III: Selected Speeches and Writing of Sir Sultan Muhammad Shah*, vol. I, London: Kegan Paul.

Clarkson, A. (2008) "Introduction," in Aga Khan IV *Where Hope Takes Root: Democracy and Pluralism in an Interdependent World*, Vancouver: Douglas and McIntyre.

Corbin, H. (1993) *History of Islamic Philosophy*, translated by L. Sherrard, London: Kegan Paul.

Daftary, F. (2005) *Ismailis in Medieval Muslim Societies*, London: I.B. Tauris.

——(2007) *The Ismailis: Their History and Doctrines*, Cambridge: Cambridge University Press.

Devji, F. (2012) "Politics Dies in the Pamirs," *Current Intelligence*, August 24, www.currentintelligence.net/analysis/2012/8/24/politics-dies-in-the-pamirs.html (accessed September 19, 2012).

Esmail, A. (1996) "Islam and Modernity: Intellectual Horizons," in Nanji, A. (ed.) *The Muslim Almanac: A Reference Work on the History, Faith, Culture, and Peoples of Islam*, New York: Gale Research.

Government of Portugal (2010) "Agreement between the Portuguese Republic and the Ismaili Imamat," *Diário da República* 187(1), Lisbon: Government of Portugal.

Hirji, Z. (2011) "The Socio-Legal Formation of the Nizari Ismailis in East Africa, 1800-1950," in Daftary, F. (ed.) *A Modern History of the Ismailis: Continuity and Change in a Muslim Community*, London: I.B. Tauris.

Jamal, N.E. (2002) *Surviving the Mongols: Nizari Quhistani and the Continuity of the Ismaili Tradition in Persia*, London: I.B. Tauris.

Jiwani, F.N. (2013) "Welfare Production in Tanzania and Canada: The Ismaili Imamat, Ismaili Community Institutions and the Aga Khan Development Network (AKDN)," unpublished doctoral thesis, Carleton University, Ottawa, Canada.

Karim, K.H. (2011a) "At the Interstices of Tradition, Modernity and Postmodernity: Ismaili Engagements with Contemporary Canadian Society," in Daftary, F. (ed.), *A Modern History of the Ismailis: Continuity and Change in a Muslim Community*, London: I.B. Tauris.

——(2011b) "Muslim Migration, Institutional Development, and the Geographic Imagination: The Aga Khan Development Network's Transnationalism," in DeBardeleben, J. and Hurrelmann, A. (eds.) *Transnational Europe*, London: Palgrave Macmillan.

——(2013) "Pluralism, Migration, Space and Song: Ismaili Arrangements of Public and Private Spheres," in Ashley, S. (ed.) *Diverse Spaces: Examining Identity, Heritage and Community in Canadian Public Culture*, Newcastle: Cambridge Scholars Publishing.

——(2014) "Aga Khan Development Network: Shia Ismaili Islam," in Cherry, S.M. and Ebaugh, H.R. (eds.) *Global Religious Movements Across Borders*, London: Ashgate.

Kassam, T.R. (2003) "The Aga Khan Development Network: An Ethic of Sustainable Development and Social Conscience," in Foltz, R.C., Denny, F.M., and Baharuddin, A. (eds.) *Islam and Ecology*, Cambridge, MA: Centre for the Study of World Religions, Harvard Divinity School.

Kassam, Z.R. (2011) "Gender Policies of Aga Khan III and Aga Khan IV," in Daftary, F. (ed.) *A Modern History of the Ismailis: Continuity and Change in a Muslim Community*, London: I.B. Tauris.

Khair, T. (2001) "Modernism and Modernity: The Patented Fragments," *Third Text* 55: 3–13.

Khan, D.-S. (2004) *Crossing the Threshold: Understanding Religious Identities in South Asia*, London: I.B. Tauris.

Lal, D. (2002) "Modernization Versus Westernization," *Project Syndicate: A World of Ideas*, December 23, www.project-syndicate.org/commentary/modernization-versus-westernization (accessed September 19, 2012).

Landolt, H., Sheikh, S., and Kassam, K. (2008) *An Anthology of Ismaili Literature*, London: I.B. Tauris.

Loughran, G. (2010) *Birth of a Nation: The Story of a Newspaper in Kenya*, London: I.B. Tauris.

Moosa, E. (2003) "The Debts and Burdens of Critical Islam," in Safi, O. (ed.) *Progressive Muslims: On Justice, Gender, and Pluralism*, Oxford: Oneworld.

Nafi, B.M. (2004) "The Rise of Islamic Reformist Thought and Its Challenge to Traditional Islam," in Taji-Farouki, S. and Nafi, B.M. (ed.) *Islamic Thought in the Twentieth Century*, London: I.B. Tauris.

Pratt, M.L. (2002) "Modernity and Periphery: Toward a Global and Relational Analysis," in Mudimbe-Boyi, E. (ed.) *Beyond Dichotomies: Histories, Identities, Cultures, and the Challenge of Globalization*, Albany, NY: State University of New York Press.

Purohit, T. (2012) *The Aga Khan Case: Religion and Identity in Colonial India*, Cambridge, MA: Harvard University Press.

Ramadan, T. (2001) *Islam, the West and the Challenges of Modernity*, translated by S. Amghar, Leicester: The Islamic Foundation.

——(2004) *Western Muslims and the Future of Islam*, Oxford: Oxford University Press.

Safi, O. (2003) "Introduction: The Times They Are a-Changin' – A Muslim Quest for Justice, Gender Equality, and Pluralism," in Safi, O. (ed.) *Progressive Muslims: On Justice, Gender, and Pluralism*, Oxford: Oneworld.

Shodhan, A. (2010) "The Entanglement of the Ginans in the Khoja Governance," in Kassam, T.R. and Mallison, F. (eds.) *Ginans – Texts and Contexts: Essays on Ismaili Hymns from South Asia in Honour of Zawahir Moir*, New Delhi: Primus Books.

Steinberg, J. (2011) *Ismaili Modern: Globalization and Identity in a Muslim Community*, Chapel Hill: University of North Carolina Press.

Taylor, C. (1991) *The Ethics of Authenticity*, Cambridge: Cambridge University Press.

Thawerbhoy, E. (1977) "The Imam of the Socio-Economic Revolution," *Ilm* 3(2): 18–26.

Virani, S. (2007) *The Ismailis in the Middle Ages: A History of Survival, a Search for Salvation*, New York: Oxford University Press.

16

# Conversion to Islam in modern Western Europe and the United States

*Patrick D. Bowen*

## Introduction

Over the past thirty years there has been a marked rise in conversion to Islam in Western Europe and the USA. Unlike the converts one hundred years ago, today's new Muslims come from a wide variety of backgrounds and are attracted to a diverse array of Islamic beliefs and practices. A growing number of converts are also becoming leaders and spokespersons both within their local and national Islamic communities and in the public sphere. Contemporary Muslim converts, then, are a significant force shaping Islam in their regions.

Despite the diversity of today's converts, however, their understandings of Islam are often situated within discourses that frame Islam not only as the religion that exemplifies both individualistic (i.e., non-clerical) and, sometimes, rational religiosity, but also as the one that best promotes a just, tolerant, loving, and peaceful community. To understand why such themes are so prominent – particularly in times when anti-Islamic sentiment is common – their history must be considered. These discourses have roots in the modern West that extend beyond Muslim converts and are linked in many ways to what has been called the "third current" of modern Western religiosity. How this "third current" has developed over time, and the ways it has done so within different regions, has had important implications for the historical trajectory of conversion to Islam. However, over the course of the twentieth century, the "third current" became less of a distinct entity; therefore today's converts' motives and demographics – which at one time varied little – can no longer be easily characterized, even despite the fact that liberal discourses are still central for today's new Muslims.

## Historical context: the "third current" and Islam

C. McIntosh (1992: 20–1) introduced the term "third current" in an attempt to explain the new forms of religiosity that were emerging in eighteenth-century Europe. McIntosh was most concerned with the relationship of these highly diverse movements with, on the one hand, church-based orthodox Christianity and, on the other, the Enlightenment and secularism. A variety of religious movements appeared that seemed to display traits from both ends of the spectrum, particularly religions associated with mystical religiosity and Freemasonry. Also, increasingly, a number of these movements seemed to incorporate non-Christian traditions. McIntosh further observed that there was no typical political stance associated with these "third current" movements; some groups, for instance, promoted very liberal views, while others endorsed extremely conservative ones. Even more, individual movements frequently displayed seemingly contradictory positions, such as endorsing radical liberal political ideas while at the same time maintaining esoteric doctrines that were to be given only to a spiritual elite.

What the "third current" represents, then, is not the emergence of a coherent set of doctrines and institutions, but rather a cultural revolution consisting of a wide array of groups and ideas. This transmutation of Western Europe's religiosities was produced by a variety of factors: influx of wealth and widespread economic reconfigurations, scientific and philosophical developments, urbanization, the spread of literacy, modern communication and travel technologies, global immigration, the rise of Protestantism and subsequent wars of religion, changes in the relationships between the races and sexes, and Western Europe's ascent to the position of a global colonial power. The old religiosities and identities were, in the phrase of Deleuze and Guattari (1977: 33), "deterritorialized." Those with the resources and interests could now explore an almost unlimited array of religious possibilities in a globalizing world. The "third current," then, can be understood as the largely amorphous cultural space in which new types (and sometimes revived old types) as well as non-Christian types of religiosities were able to, to an extent, flourish or at least be investigated and experimented with in early modern Western Europe.

It is within this "third current" that we find early moderns who on occasion sympathized with Islam (such as Jean Bodin in the sixteenth century) and, in some rare cases, framed Islam as superior to contemporary Christianity. The authors who expressed these views were typically (though not exclusively) radical liberal Protestants living in times of religious violence who were primarily concerned with identifying a religiosity that promoted justice, religious tolerance, and peace. These writers – among which Henry Stubbe and John Toland were the most notable – were not interested in converting to Islam, but rather in holding Islam as a model towards which Christianity, and Europe, should strive (see Holt 1972; Jacob 1983). To these early apologists, Islam represented a purified religiosity (viz. Christianity) that lacked pagan attributes and idolatry, such as belief in the Trinity and the superior religious authority of clerics; had simple, clear tenets; and that promoted the individual's freedom to have and express publicly a personal relationship with God without insisting that all people should express the same beliefs. Because he thought Islam represented these ideals, John Toland in fact called for a "Mahometan Christianity."

That Islam was held up by these writers as the religion that best exemplified modern liberal ideals is very significant. Islam typically represented, in the cultural psyche, Christian Western Europe's polar opposite and greatest enemy. Islam was usually associated with violence, deception, and indulgence, and in fact was seen, because of Islamic society's encroachment on Christian majority lands, as "the most powerful instrument for the destruction of the Church" (Daniel 1962: 245). Therefore, as N. Daniel observed, "[a] society would have to be remarkably tolerant" to accept and respect a religion framed in this way (Daniel 1962: 246). By inverting the negative image of Islam, then, radical Protestants like Stubbe were effectively saying that a true commitment to religious freedom, peace, and tolerance is empty unless one is willing to stand up for it even when this means accepting the presence of one's former enemy. This position also implied that Europeans should see contemporary violent manifestations of Islam as not representative of "true" Islam.

Not surprisingly, this idea was not very popular. Europe may have been "deterritorialized" to a degree, but certain cultural dynamics remained, and religious freedom stayed limited. It would take integration within another set of "third current" movements – movements that were much more accepted in Western culture than those that simply endorsed Islam as the best religion – for this sympathetic and idealized view of Islam to be transformed into viable Islamic-identity movements.

While there has been a tendency among some scholars to see eighteenth- and nineteenth-century European interest in Islam as superficially "Orientalist," that is, as seeing Islam as an exotic, wild, and primitive Other (e.g. Rodinson 1991: 52–71), there has been a long European tradition of appreciating the so-called mystical elements of Islam. This tradition began prior to the rise of secularism, when science and religion were still commonly understood as going hand in hand, and its continued existence into the nineteenth century reflects the fact that the connection between religion and science in European minds was not suddenly severed in the eighteenth century. S. Akerman has demonstrated that Arabic (and often Islamic) texts were in fact at "the heart of" what "triggered" the "third current" movement of Rosicrucianism, which itself would provide the crucial themes and momentum for another: modern speculative Freemasonry (Akerman 1998: 238, 214). Akerman observed that Arabic astronomy (and, to an extent, geometry, optics, alchemy, and other fields) was key for the authors of the Rosicrucian and "proto-"Rosicrucian manuscripts, who saw deep millennial and "third current" significance in a number of astronomical events in the late sixteenth and early seventeenth century. In addition, in the two main Rosicrucian texts, the *Fama Fraternitatis* and the *Confessio Fraternitatis*, Christian Rosenkreutz, the Rosicrucian legend's sage-hero, is said to have traveled to gain knowledge in "Arabia" and passed it on to a fraternity that continues to exist. Rosenkreutz was likely based on the mysterious medieval figure with similar traits known as Artephius, and the story also played off Christian Europe's more general awareness of its reliance on Arabic knowledge since the twelfth century (Anonymous 2000: 4, 22; Clulee 1984: 61). It was the ideas associated with Rosicrucian as well as a the more general trend that associated Islam with esoteric wisdom and magic (Pingree 1987; Matar 1998: 87–98), given impetus from "third current" modernizing dynamics that were pushing for a reconstruction of ideological and social structures, that activated the interest in finding secret fraternities and shaped how those fraternities were understood, thus contributing to the rise of Freemasonry (which, interestingly, frequently had members who maintained an interest in Rosicrucianism) (Stevenson 1988: 100–3; McIntosh 1992).

Still, while Freemasonry flourished and increasingly incorporated non-Christian and non-Greco-Roman elements, the Islamic roots (including both the factual ones, which did not extend beyond the late sixteenth century, and the mythical ones, connected to knowledge transmitted from "Arabia") appear to have been ignored for the most part by early European speculative Masons. But by the eighteenth century, Western Europeans began exporting the Craft to Muslim majority lands, where local Muslim Masons saw the fraternity – with its discourses of math, science, esoteric knowledge (and degree systems), mysticism, religious tolerance, brotherhood, and of course its "Eastern" origins claims – as having Islamic roots that went back prior to the late sixteenth-/early seventeenth-century emergence of speculative Freemasonry in Europe. They subsequently developed Masonic genealogy myths, just as many Masons throughout Europe had done before them and would continue to after, in ways that promoted their own religious commitments and interests (Zarcone 1993).

By the nineteenth century, with the growth of the original factors that had produced the "third current," new religious movements were rapidly developing, including a number – frequently groups that resisted a strict separation between science and religion – which took an interest in "Oriental Masonry," as it was sometimes called. European Masons had long been convinced of their organization's own ancient-genealogy origins, and so, for some in the "third current," especially those already predisposed to religious discourses that promoted justice, tolerance and peace, Islamic Masonry seemed to be the true ancestor of European Masonry. This was helped by the fact that Bektashi Sufis in particular were claiming a Freemasonic identity, which would mean that those Europeans who were interested in Eastern mysticism and Spiritualism – and Masons were often among this group – would also see deep significance in Sufis (Zarcone 1993). It seems that the first waves of converts to Islam living in Western Europe (particularly Britain) and the USA were individuals involved with, directly or indirectly, "third current" movements which held that there were important mystical knowledge and/or Freemasonic roots in Islam. By the late nineteenth century, a handful of relatively influential Englishmen and North Americans had been (or claimed to have been) inducted into Islamic Masonry groups and had formed relationships with other Westerners interested in "third current" movements (Zarcone 1993: 222–7, 301–2; Geaves 2010; Bowen 2011b). These "third current"-affiliated Islam sympathizers formed the bases of the early convert communities in England and the USA, the two most prominent Western convert communities at the time.

## Conversion to Islam in Western Europe

### History

During the medieval period, Islam had, of course, many converts in southern Europe, particularly in Iberia and Sicily (Glick 1979: 33–5; Metcalfe 2003: 15–17, 32–4, 86–9). While there are rumors of *individual* converts hailing from more northern parts of Europe during the Middle Ages, we only begin hearing about relatively significant numbers of converts from the area starting in the sixteenth century. However, most of these individuals had converted while living in Muslim majority lands, and we know of almost none who returned to Europe as Muslims. The evidence suggests that in most cases early modern conversions were done either as a matter of expediency or out of attraction to the worldly benefits that a convert might acquire while living in Muslim majority lands. Sometimes captive soldiers held in Muslim lands chose to convert in an attempt to receive less harsh treatment, some found increased military or political prestige by aligning with local leaders, some conversions were undertaken primarily as a rejection of European society (this seems to have been far more common among converts from southern Europe than among those in northern Europe), and others who were living freely in these regions converted simply to improve their social standing or to avoid difficulties that Christians sometimes faced when religious antagonism was high (Matar 1998: 21–49; Allievi 1998: 51–6; Bennassar and Bennassar 1989).

In the late eighteenth century, we begin hearing isolated reports about converts in Western European lands, particularly in Great Britain and Germany; these were usually individuals who had converted while traveling in Muslim lands, but had maintained their new religious commitment after returning home (Allievi 1998: 270–1). Nevertheless, because anti-Muslim sentiment had not yet decreased significantly, there are very few examples of converts to Islam living in Western Europe prior to the late nineteenth century. The first relatively major Islamic convert movement was that led by the Englishman William H. Quilliam, who had converted while traveling in Morocco. Quilliam's understanding of Islam, notably, demonstrated the two "third current" features that were associated with the rise of Islam convert movements in the West: an interest in the Islamic roots of Masonry and a promotion of liberal religious and political values, features that were shared by many of the converts who joined his movement (Geaves 2010: 34, 62, 109, 119, 125, 322n; Köse 1996: 14–16). Even through the early twentieth century, these type of "third current" commitments – though more common than an interest in Masonry was an interest in spiritualistic religiosity – were frequently connected to Muslim convert movements, particularly those led by Sufis and the Ahmadiyyas (Bowen 2011a; 2011b: 321, 324).

By this time, however, two new dynamics were changing how Western Europeans would come to Islam. First, there seems to have been a growing acceptance – or at least presence – of "third current" religiosity. This meant that entering non-mainstream religious groups – once largely the privilege of the educated and wealthy, who had the social capital to risk – had become easier for the general public, which resulted in a slight demographic change for the converts to Islam (Zebiri 2008: 35, 36). Second, Muslim immigration to Western Europe, which had been slowly increasing for centuries, by the early twentieth century had produced a noticeable Muslim presence. Local non-Muslims were now coming in contact with Muslims on a greater scale. Social ties, particularly marriage, then became an important source of conversion, and this led to greater diversity of converts, who now sometimes came from the lower classes, which had more contact with Muslim immigrants.

Still, it seems that conversion rates were low until the 1980s, with there being no more than a few thousand Muslim converts in each Western European country. In the 1980s, however, increased conversion rates began to be noticed across Western Europe (Allievi 1998: 65–70), and today it is estimated that each Western European country has around 10,000 converts, making up, on average, 1–2 percent of each country's total Muslim population (Moreras 2002: 132; Lathion 2008: 53; Toronto 2008: 62; Zebiri 2008: 42). Because study of Muslim converts has been notoriously difficult (Allievi 1998: 62–5; Cesari 2004: 10), there is no clear explanation for the elevated rates. It seems likely, though, that two main factors have contributed to this development. First is the growing presence of Muslim immigrants in Western European countries, which, as has been explained, exposes non-Muslims to new social ties which can lead to conversion. The second factor may be related to the deep cultural transcript concerning Islam's supposed antipathy to liberal values, and the tendency for this transcript to be inverted by some who become committed to liberal values. It is in the 1980s, following a series of violent events in the Middle East that were framed in Islamic rhetoric (after several decades in which secularist discourse was dominant), that the cultural transcripts of "Islamic terrorism" and "Islamic extremism" were reinvigorated. A rise in anti-Islamic sentiment seems to have been paralleled by growing elements of sympathizers and even converts – with the latter groups frequently stressing religious tolerance and peace. The apparent spike in conversions immediately after September 11, 2001 seems to confirm this tendency (Zebiri 2008: 43).

## Traits of contemporary converts

As noted on pp. 260–2, converts in the early waves of modern Western European conversions were frequently educated and from the comfortable classes, and thus possessed the social capital to reject standard religious conventions. This seems to have remained a prominent trait among Western European Muslim converts, even if the proportion is decreasing as converts diversify for the reasons noted above. In 1996, A. Köse, in one of the first in-depth studies of modern Western converts, reported that, of his British subjects, 55 percent came from middle- or upper middle-class families, 60 percent had at least a bachelor's degree, and 20 percent had graduate degrees (Köse 1996: 80). Later studies of British converts showed roughly similar trends (see Zebiri 2008: 9, 45).

As far as religious background is concerned, Western European Muslim converts, first of all, generally share the common trait of having a weak religious upbringing, or at least never having felt very committed to the religion in which they were raised (Köse 1996: 38–9; Zebiri 2008:

44; Allievi 1998: 95; Jensen 2006: 653; Sultan 1999: 326). While this factor may be more an indication of the relatively secular cultural climate in Western Europe than of personal preference, it is notable that these converts rarely are active religious seekers prior to conversion (Zebiri 2008: 44; Köse 1996: 121).

It seems that converts also grow up relatively happy. Köse reported this as well as the fact that as children they had decent to good relationships with their fathers (Köse 1996: 32, 35), a trait also noted by A.S. Roald, who looked at Scandinavian converts (Roald 2004: 92). Nevertheless, at some point, usually during their third decade of life (Zebiri 2008: 43; Roald 2004: 109; Köse 1996: 37), the future converts often begin to feel the need to seek out a new ideology/religion, social community, or both. Köse observed that this was instigated by some sort of crisis, or at least an abnormally difficult period or event in their lives (Köse 1996: 32). Other researchers, however, have focused less on the timing of the distress and more on the issues that the future converts wanted resolved. These range from a variety of pragmatic issues to psychological, social, and spiritual ones (and these are not mutually exclusive) (see Allievi 1998: 93–145). A popular motive for looking for other sources of meaning, as reported by Zebiri (2008: 2), Roald (2004: 100), and Köse (1996: 79), is dissatisfaction with a Western, materialist culture. Other frequently cited motives are: (1) the desire for a meaning system that simultaneously allows for rational and "religious' thought (Daynes 1999: 316; Jensen 2006: 648, 654; Köse 1996: 98); (2) the desire for mystical/spiritual experiences (Daynes 1999: 316; Jensen 2006: 648, 654; Köse 1996: 98); and (3) the desire among those feeling socially and culturally uprooted for a more meaningful and cohesive community (Daynes 1999: 316–22; Wohlrab-Sahr 1999; Lakhdar et al. 2007: 13; Köse 1996: 98). The last of these three is also closely related to two other common motives: the desire for justice/fair treatment (Sultan 1999; McGinty 2006; van Nieuwkerk 2006: 7–10) and the desire for clear rules concerning morality and social interaction (Sultan 1999; McGinty 2006; Wohlrab-Sahr 1999). While conversion purely for marriage does play a role for some converts (Allievi 1998: 101–3; Roald 2004: 97; Zebiri 2008: 224; Köse 1996: 80), there have been a few scholars who have noted its decreasing importance (Lakhdar et al. 2007: 13; Jensen 2006: 644).

Many of these motives, then, revolve around two central themes: (1) Islam as a religion that is "spiritual" *and* rational, and thus is understood as a more cohesive/integrated approach to the world; and (2) that the Islamic community is one that is loving, tolerant, just, and moral. These themes are in fact closely connected to the longstanding liberal discourses described on p. 260, even despite the fact that the demographics and motives of converts appear to have changed somewhat over the last century. The reason for this continuity seems to be that modern conversion to Islam in Western Europe is deeply connected to the two longstanding socio-cultural dynamics described above: (1) the emergence of a "third current" in Western European religiosity and (2) the tendency of some people who are seeking a peaceful and tolerant yet cohesive religious society to see Islam, which is often portrayed as the opposite of this, as the religion that best exemplifies this; by inverting the typical portrayal of Islam, converts suggest that liberal religious values are worthless unless the religion, which is typically seen as the antithesis of those values, is also included in the idealized society. The psychological implications for this move are profound: It allows for those who – due to the very modernizing and globalizing forces that produced the "third current" – feel uprooted and disconnected from society and culture (i.e. "deterritorialized") to create satisfactory new roots by deeply committing themselves to modern ideals. It should be clear, however, that these ideals are often *not* framed in the rhetoric of politics, but rather as *general* social, cultural, and religious ideals.

That these dynamics are at the core of contemporary Western European conversion to Islam is reflected by a number of notable features concerning these converts. First, while there do exist among converts a wide range of understandings of Islam, and a minority even commit to particular groups – including Sufism, Salafism, and Shi'ism (Allievi 1998: 67–8; Zebiri 2008: 47–8) – there is in fact resistance among many converts to identify with any particular Islamic sectarian movement or theological stance (Jensen 2006: 653; Zebiri 2008: 47–9). This seems to reflect the primary commitment to religious tolerance and the desire for a peaceful community. Perhaps this strong commitment to liberal religious values is also what motivates so many Western European converts to become spokespersons for Islam by being active in a variety of public sphere-oriented activities, such as publishing, teaching, and lecturing (see an extensive list in Allievi 1998: 265–71). Finally, the trait of having a deep commitment to justice, tolerance, and peace – and the tendency, in order to demonstrate or justify that commitment, to hold Islam up as the religion that exemplifies these ideals – is reflected in the reported rises in conversion to Islam, which correspond with increased media attention to "Islamic terrorism" and anti-Islamic sentiment.

## Conversion to Islam in the United States

### History

The history of conversion to Islam has developed very differently in the USA than it has Western Europe. At the core of this difference is the unique role of race and racism in the USA, largely due to the longer existence of and closer experience with slavery, which produced a deep cultural and psychological dichotomization of "black" and "white." This became both a discourse and a *habitus* which still exist, to a large extent, today (Emerson 2006: 134–54). Therefore, while conversion to Islam in the USA has, as in Western Europe, been shaped by the "third current," it has been a "third current" modified by the USA's particular racial dynamics.

Early white US American sympathizers with and converts to Islam, like their European counterparts, were usually committed to liberal religious values as well as an interest in "third current" religions (Bowen 2011b). The first significant promoters of Islamic identity in the USA – Alexander Webb and A.L. Rawson – both had an interest in spiritualistic and esoteric religiosity, and Rawson in particular had ties to Islamic Masonry. The two men, in fact, for a short time aligned with each other and with Quilliam's group in England (Abd-Allah 2006; Nance 2009: 92–7; Singleton 2007: 481–2; Bowen 2011b: 323–4). The Islamic movements associated with these white US Americans, however, quickly fell apart.

These early US promoters of Islam, and white US Americans generally, were aware of Islam primarily through literature and international travel, and there does not seem to have been a strong awareness by early white Muslim converts of the significant Muslim presence among the enslaved Africans in the USA. Still, contact with enslaved African Muslims was somewhat common for white Americans. But, due to the social position of the enslaved, religious ignorance of their owners, and intentional actions to prevent slaves from perpetuating their traditional religions, Islam was often ignored, dismissed as a non-white religion, or simply not recognized when practiced. Given this association of Islam with the African American underclass, whites generally had little cultural incentive to consider converting to Islam through these local social channels, though there may have been a few exceptions (Bowen 2011b: 318).

The connection between Islam and black Americans would play an important role during the next phase of US conversion to Islam, which lasted from roughly 1900 to 1954. By the late nineteenth century, Americans were becoming increasingly aware of the fact that many Africans were converting to Islam and rejecting Christianity. Because Islam was often framed as a religion that lacked racial discrimination and thus promoted equality among all people, a few

Patrick D. Bowen

Americans, white and black (and some immigrant Muslims), began promoting the idea that African Americans should convert to Islam (e.g. Singleton 2006: 438–40; Turner 2003: 50–62). This coincided with the rise in US culture of what is known as the nadir of US race relations. In the post-Civil War USA, the termination of institutionalized slavery resulted in increased informal racism and white resentment against US blacks. As African Americans fled the rural South to Northern cities, whites there, who were encountering blacks in large numbers for the first time and had not yet fully shed traditional racist feelings, reacted with their own acts of racial intolerance. At the same time, African Americans were now coming into contact with immigrant Muslims.

Due to the influence of stories about Islam being free from racism, the growing racial tensions, and the increasing contact with immigrant Muslims, a number of African Americans – many of whom were becoming disenchanted with the black church for having withdrawn from advocating social and political reform – began converting to Islam. In the period between 1920 and 1954, there were no fewer than fifteen distinct African American majority or led Islamic movements; around fifty African American Islamic religious authorities; and hundreds – sometimes thousands – of African Americans embracing Islam in every Northern city of any significant size (Dannin 2002; McCloud 1995: 10–35). It should also be noted that, despite their diversity, almost all of the movements promoted liberal values (particularly equality and peace) and many had "third current" characteristics, including a belief in mystical experiences and Masonry (Bowen 2011a; 2011b: 324–6).

Meanwhile, it seems to have been precisely because the high level of racism, combined with white awareness of the attraction of Africans and African Americans to Islam, that was responsible for the fact that conversion of whites to Islam in the first half of the twentieth century was relatively rare. US racism had to a large extent trumped the liberal desire to invert the traditional image of Islam. Where we do have evidence of white conversions, however, it seems that these were people who displayed strong liberal tendencies and openly joined multiracial religious communities. And, while the evidence is meager, they appear to have been from the better-educated and wealthier classes.

Beginning in the mid-1950s, however, there was a dramatic transformation in the historical trajectory of US conversion to Islam. This was the result of several factors: (1) the Civil Rights Movement and the corresponding cultural wave that promoted equality, peace, and justice for all; (2) increased Muslim immigration to the USA; (3) awareness of various international anti-colonial movements; and (4) increased interest in "spiritual"/mystical religion due to the influence of the emerging New Age movement. From the mid-1950s to the late 1970s, Americans from a wide range of ethnic and social positions were being drawn to Islam, and were exploring a variety of Islamic communities and doctrines.

Despite this diversity, however, during this period the Nation of Islam (NOI), an African American Islamic sectarian movement, unquestionably became the dominant Islamic movement, and was now attracting at least tens of thousands of African American followers (Lincoln 1994: 102–3). With rhetoric highly influenced by the dichotomizing view of race that had been so prominent in the previous period, the NOI was largely responsible for the general public continuing to perceive US conversion to Islam as a "black" phenomenon. Only after its head, Elijah Muhammad, died in 1975 and his son, W.D. Mohammed, began to lead the group to be more in line with international Islam did the public perception of conversion to Islam begin to change.

Subsequently, US conversion to Islam has increasingly demonstrated tendencies similar to those in Western Europe, though, because of continued racism and the legacy of African American Islam, there is a markedly stronger emphasis on racial equality in the US context.

266

Still, the promotion of racial equality fits in easily with the other longstanding liberal discourses discussed above, and they serve to reinforce one another. This emphasis on liberal values is important as US converts increasingly take on leadership roles. In 2000, two-thirds of all US imams were African American (Bagby et al. 2001: 52) and a growing number of US converts are becoming politicians, writers, and college professors (who, notably, frequently teach and write in Islamic studies, thus shaping US students' perceptions about Islam) (e.g. Haddad 2006: 38, 42).

## Traits of contemporary converts

Because of the unique effects of race on conversion to Islam in the USA, it is difficult to make broad statements that generally apply to all US converts to Islam. Around half of all African American Muslims, for instance, primarily attend African American majority mosques, which have characteristics and demographics notably different from immigrant majority mosques, where most white and Latina/o converts are found (Bagby 2012: 12). White and Latina/o Muslims, furthermore, are more likely to join mosques in the suburbs than African American converts, who more frequently join urban mosques. The difficulty in providing general traits of US converts is further compounded by the fact that not only have there been few studies to examine these characteristics in any detail, but the studies we do have are frequently based on small sample sizes, or do not satisfactorily identify the trends in differences between converts who belong to the different Islamic communities. With these difficulties acknowledged, though, there are some general traits that have been tentatively identified.

Three major studies of US Muslims have been published since 2001 and all found that converts and their Muslim children represent around one-third of the total Muslim population (Bagby et al. 2001: 16; Pew Research Center 2007: 1, 21–2; Bagby 2012: 13). The raw numbers, however, are difficult to estimate largely because there is major disagreement about the size of the US Muslim community, which has been estimated as being anywhere from slightly over one million to over seven million. If we assume that the total US Muslim population is five million, then the convert population is around 1,650,000. All of these studies found that African Americans make up just over 60 percent of all converts (1,023,000). The most recent of the three studies noted that over the last ten years the percentage of white converts has dropped from a little under 30 percent to a little over 20 percent (363,000), while the percentage of Latina/o converts has doubled to 12 percent (198,000) (Bagby et al. 2001: 2; Pew Research Center 2007: 17–18, 22; Bagby 2012: 13). Still, when compared with findings from studies published in the early 1980s, it appears that the numbers and proportions of converts (to non-NOI communities) have increased significantly since that time for all ethnic groups (Ghayur 1981, 1984). Slightly over half of today's converts identify as Sunni, 6 percent as Shi'i, and at least 24 percent as non-specific (Pew Research Center 2007: 22). Unlike Sunni mosques, both Shi'i mosques and Sufi groups have a much higher percentage of white converts than African Americans (Hermansen 2000: 187; Bagby 2012: 17).

Only two of the large-sample studies looked at convert characteristics other than their ethnicities, locations, and percentages. However, because these two studies did not control for converts' ethnicity, they produced several findings that are, *prima facie*, not consistent with a number of other studies of US converts. However, because there is a large proportion of African American converts in both studies, it is likely that their findings are more reflective of African American convert demographics. These findings include a high proportion of male converts (68 percent) (Bagby et al. 2001: 21), a relatively young age at conversion (nearly half converting before the age of twenty-one) (Pew Research Center 2007: 22), and a high proportion of converts having been raised as Protestants (67 percent) (Pew Research Center 2007: 22). The findings in these large-sample studies are generally consistent with those for other African American convert groups (see Tinaz 2001), and differ somewhat from the observations reported in the previously mentioned studies from the 1980s, which indicated that, at least among whites, females were much more likely to convert than males (Ghayur 1981: 158; 1984: 57). In the 2001 study, African American converts also overwhelmingly displayed an interest in social justice issues; African American majority mosques were more active than immigrant mosques in community improvement programs and outreach activities to non-Muslims, including politicians, than other US mosques (Bagby et al. 2001: 41, 44). In the most recent large-sample study, however, this appears to have decreased (Bagby 2012: 20–4).

Smaller-sample studies of groups not purely composed of African Americans have tended to produce different results and look for different features. Studies in which (1) the converts' sex and ethnicity were diverse but not controlled for, (2) sex and ethnicity were not identified, (3) the converts were exclusively women, and (4) the converts were exclusively white all tended to find that converts were raised middle class, with some college education, and that at least some of the converts were professionals (Esseissah 2011: 31; Ibrahim 1995: 69–70; Robinson 2010: 60; Hedaithy 1985: 25, 34–5; Anway 2002: 6; Poston 1992: 171), though one study showed lower levels of education and employment (Bowen 2009: 46–7). Other findings about convert demographics include the tendency for conversion to take place during one's mid- to late twenties (Khan 1978: 45–6; Bowen 2009: 59; Hedaithy 1985: 25–6, 35; Ibrahim 1995: 69–70), that there is a close to equal ratio of males to females (Khan 1978: 45; Hedaithy 1985: 25; Bowen 2009: 43), and that converts generally come from a variety of Christian backgrounds, as opposed to the vast majority simply being Protestant (Khan 1978: 46; Bowen 2009: 47–9; Hedaithy 1985: 26) – though there is some disagreement over the converts' level of religiosity prior to becoming Muslim (Anway 2002: 11; Poston 1992: 165; Bowen 2009: 48; Esseissah 2011: 28–30; Robinson 2010: 63; Haddad 2006: 36).

Because the smaller-sample studies have used a variety of methodologies, it is difficult to compare their findings on motives for trends in conversion and values of converts. Still, some general themes can be tentatively identified. Islam is frequently characterized as having more clear and simple doctrines than Christianity, as being more rational/logical and as not having any intermediary between the individual and God (Khan 1978: 47; Hedaithy 1985: 28, 31; Bowen 2010: 8; Robinson 2010: 80–2; Haddad 2006: 30–1). In addition, by and large, converts were usually introduced to Islam by a Muslim acquaintance (Khan 1978: 46; Hedaithy 1985: 26; Bowen 2009: 55; Bowen 2010: 2–3, 7; Ibrahim 1995: 68–86; Robinson 2010: 76–80; Martinez-Vazquez 2010: 51–2). Among women of all ethnicities there is an emphasis on the ideal that Islam liberates and provides justice and equality for women (Robinson 2010: 82–4; Anway 2002). Among Latinas/os, there is a strong theme of equality and justice for all races (Martinez-Vazquez 2010: 92–103; Bowen 2010). While some studies reported an increase in conversion immediately after September 11, 2001, or at least a notable number of converts who became interested in Islam because of the events that day (Esseissah 2011: 1, 32–4; Bowen 2009: 42, 43; Robinson 2010: 70–6; Martinez-Vazquez 2010: 60–1), the most recent large-sample study indicates that in 2011 conversion rates were actually slightly lower than they were in 2000 (Bagby 2012: 12).

## Case study: fifteen US converts

In the summer of 2010, I interviewed fifteen Sunni Muslim converts from across the USA. Their backgrounds, experiences, and perceptions illustrate many of trends that have been presented so far.

The converts in this study represented all geographical regions in the USA equally. However, those who chose to respond were overwhelmingly non-Hispanic white (eleven in total) and female (also eleven in total). Three Latinas/os (two females and one male) and one African American female completed the sample group. A slight majority of those interviewed (eight) converted while in their twenties, five while in their forties or fifties, and only two in their late teens. While these particular demographics do not reflect the proportions reported in the major studies of Muslim converts, there are other features that are more consistent with previous research.

Fourteen of the respondents came from middle-class backgrounds, and all had at least some college education. While most of the converts had a Christian upbringing and demonstrated moderate levels of religiosity as children, there was no pattern in terms of religious denomination prior to conversion. Most shared the feature of having been raised with liberal views on race and religion despite the fact that only slightly more than half grew up having friends of multiple ethnicities and religions. At some point during or after their teen years, however, they began to make Muslim acquaintances. All but one became interested in Islam through Muslim social ties – most had been dating a Muslim, and some made Muslim friends of the same sex.

A number of these new Muslims indicated a concern with social justice issues and a desire for a peaceful society. Similarly, consistent with findings for other Western female converts, the eleven women interviewed were attracted to what they understood as Islam's superior and just treatment of women, as well as the sense that there was a strong community that would foster this treatment because this was perceived as part of the Islamic "way of life." In fact, it was repeatedly emphasized by almost all of the converts that "Islam is a way of life"; in other words, Islam was understood by them as a religion by which one's mind and actions should constantly be guided. There does not, however, appear to be a strong sense of sectarian or theological exclusivity: while almost all identified as Sunni when asked, a number of them explicitly rejected the notion that there is only one, inflexible way of life or thought for a Muslim, and that some US Muslims are too strict. Four even indicated that they "mosque-hop," regularly traveling to a variety of mosques to hear different perspectives. Finally, all indicated that they had some intellectual interests in Islam, but that their conversion was usually done because "it felt right."

## Conclusion

There are three major factors contributing to conversion to Islam in Western Europe and the USA. The first is a minor tradition in the West that dates back to the sixteenth century: the tendency of some people to define Islam as the ideal liberal religion, which, precisely because it goes against the popular tendency to see Islam as the least liberal religion, is ultimately a call for religious tolerance. This idea is particularly attractive when it is combined with mystical and/or esoteric interests. The second factor, while related to the first, differs slightly because it emphasizes the idea that Islam is uniquely free from racism, or at least better for black people than Christianity. Finally, as the Muslim population grows in Western Europe and the USA, non-Muslims there are more likely to develop relationships with Muslims. Because social ties are often crucial for religious conversion (Stark and Finke 2000: 114–38), when the potential convert desires to find a new religion there is a now greater chance that he or she will look to Islam instead of other religions.

## Bibliography

Abd-Allah, U.F. (2006) *A Muslim in Victorian America: The Life of Alexander Russell Webb*, New York: Oxford University Press.

Akerman, S. (1998) *Rose Cross over the Baltic*, Boston: Brill.

Allievi, S. (1998) *Les Convertis à l'Islam*, Paris: L'Harmattan.

Anonymous (2000) *The Rosicrucian Manifestos*, Cincinnati: Emperor Norton Books.

Anway, C. (2002) *Daughters of Another Path: Experiences of American Women Choosing Islam*, Lee's Summit, MO: Yawna Publications.

Bagby, I. (2012) *The American Mosque 2011: Basic Characteristics of the American Mosque, Attitudes of Mosque Leaders*, Washington, DC: Council on American–Islamic Relations.

Bagby, I., Perl, P.M., and Froehle, B.T. (2001) *The Mosque in America: A National Portrait*, Washington, DC: Council on American–Islamic Relations.

Bennassar, B. and Bennassar, L. (1989) *Les Chréstiens d'Allah: l'histoire extraordinaire des renégats XVI–XVII siècles*, Paris: Perrin.

Bowen, P.D. (2009) "Conversion to Islam in the United States: A Case Study in Denver, Colorado," *Inter Mountain West Journal of Religious Studies* 1: 42–64.

——(2010) "The Latino American Da'wah Organization and the 'Latina/o Muslim' Identity in the United States," *Journal of Race, Ethnicity, and Religion* 1(11): 1–23.

——(2011a) "Abdul Hamid Suleiman and the Origins of the Moorish Science Temple," *Journal of Race, Ethnicity, and Religion* 2(10): 1–54.

——(2011b) "Islam and 'Scientific Religion' in the United States before 1935," *Islam and Christian–Muslim Relations* 22: 311–28.

Cesari, J. (2004) *When Islam and Democracy Meet*, New York: Palgrave.

Clulee, N.H. (1984) "At the Crossroads of Magic and Science: John Dee's Archemastrie," in Vickers, B. (ed.) *Occult and Scientific Mentalities in the Renaissance*, New York: Cambridge University Press.

Daniel, N. (1962) *Islam and the West: The Making of an Image*, Edinburgh: Edinburgh University Press.

Dannin, R. (2002) *Black Pilgrimage to Islam*, New York: Oxford University Press.

Daynes, S. (1999) "Processus de conversion et modes d'identification a l'islam: l'exemple de la France et des Etats-Unis," *Social Compass* 46: 313–23.

Deleuze, G. and Guattari, F. (1977) *Anti-Oedipus*, translated by Robert Hurley, Mark Seem, and Helen R. Lane, New York: Viking Press.

Emerson, M. with Woo, R.M. (2006) *People of the Dream*, Princeton: Princeton University Press.

Esseissah, K. (2011) "The Increasing Conversion to Islam since 9/11: A Study of White American Muslim Converts in Northwest Ohio," unpublished thesis, Bowling Green State University.

Geaves, R. (2010) *Islam in Victorian Britain: The Life and Times of Abdullah Quilliam*, Leicester: Kube Publishing Ltd.

Ghayur, M.A. (1981) "Muslims in the United States: Settlers and Visitors," *Annals of the American Academy of Political and Social Science* 454: 150–63.

——(1984) "Ethnic Distribution of American Muslims and Selected Socio-Economic Characteristics," *Journal Institute of Muslim Minority Affairs* 5: 47–59.

Glick, T.F. (1979) *Islamic and Christian Spain in the Early Middle Ages*, Princeton: Princeton University Press.

Haddad, Y.Y. (2006) "The Quest for Submission: Reflections on the Journey of American Women Converts to Islam," in van Nieuwkerk, K. (ed.) *Women Embracing Islam*, Austin: University of Texas Press.

Hedaithy, M.I. (1985) "New Muslims in America: A Study of Religious Conversion from Christianity to Islam," unpublished thesis, Pacific Lutheran University.

Hermansen, M. (2000) "Hybrid Identity Formations in Muslim America: The Case of American Sufi Movements," *Muslim World* 90: 158–97.

Holt, P.M. (1972) *A Seventeenth-Century Defender of Islam: Henry Stubbe (1632–76) and His Book*, London: Dr. Williams's Trust.

Ibrahim, A. (1995) "Social and Cultural Experiences of Adult Conversion to Islam: Implications for Learning to Learn," unpublished dissertation, Northern Illinois University.

Jacob, J.R. (1983) *Henry Stubbe, Radical Protestant and the Early Enlightenment*, New York: Cambridge University Press.

Jensen, T.G. (2006) "Religious Authority and Autonomy Intertwined: The Case of Converts to Islam in Denmark," *Muslim World* 96: 643–57.

Khan, N.B. (1978) "The Phenomenon of Conversion," *Bulletin of Christian Institutes of Islamic Studies* 1: 45–8.

Köse, A. (1996) *Conversion to Islam: A Study of Native British Converts*, London: Kegan Paul International.

Lakhdar, M., Vinsonneau, G., Apter, M., and Mullet, E. (2007) "Conversion to Islam among French Adolescents and Adults: A Systematic Inventory of Motives," *International Journal for the Psychology of Religion* 17: 1–15.

Lathion, S. (2008) "Muslims in Switzerland: Is Citizenship Really Incompatible with Muslim Identity?," *Journal of Muslim Minority Affairs* 28: 53–60.

Lincoln, C.E. (1994) *The Black Muslims in America*, 3rd ed., Grand Rapids, MI: Wm. B. Eerdmans Publishing.

McCloud, A. (1995) *African American Islam*, New York: Routledge.

McGinty, A.M. (2006) *Becoming Muslim: Western Women's Conversion to Islam*, New York: Palgrave.

McIntosh, C. (1992) *The Rose Cross and the Age of Reason*, New York: Brill.

Martinez-Vazquez, H.A. (2010) *Latina/o y Musulman: The Construction of Latina/o Identity among Latina/o Muslims in the United States*, Eugene, OR: Pickwick Publications.

Matar, N. (1998) *Islam in Britain: 1558–1685*, Cambridge: Cambridge University Press.

Metcalfe, A. (2003) *Muslims and Christians in Norman Sicily: Arabic Speakers and the End of Islam*, London: RutledgeCurzon.

Moreras, J. (2002) "Muslims in Spain: Between the Historical Heritage and the Minority Construction," *Muslim World* 92: 129–42.

Nance, S. (2009) *How the Arabian Nights Inspired the American Dream, 1790–1935*, Chapel Hill: University of North Carolina Press.

Pew Research Center (2007) *Muslim Americans: Middle Class and Mostly Mainstream*, pewresearch.org/assets/pdf/muslim-americans.pdf (accessed August 16, 2011).

Pingree, D. (1987) "The Diffusion of Arabic Magical Texts in Western Europe," in Scarcia Amoretti, B. (ed.) *La Diffusione delle Scienze Islamiche nel Medio Evo Europeo*, Rome: Accademia Nazionale dei Lincei.

Poston, L. (1992) *Islamic Da'wah in the West*, New York: Oxford University Press.

Roald, A.S. (2004) *New Muslims in the European Context*, Leiden: Brill.

Robinson, G.M. (2010) "From Christianity to Islam, the Conversion of American Women after the September 11, 2001 Attacks," unpublished dissertation, Alliant International University–San Diego.

Rodinson, M. (1991) *Europe and the Mystique of Islam*, translation of Roger Veinus, Seattle: University of Washington Press.

Singleton, B.D. (2006) "Minarets in Dixie: Proposals to Introduce Islam in the American South," *Journal of Muslim Minority Affairs* 26: 433–44.

——(2007) "Brothers at Odds: Rival Islamic Movements in Late Nineteenth Century New York City," *Journal of Muslim Minority Affairs* 27: 473–86.

Stark, R. and Finke, R. (2000) *Acts of Faith: Explaining the Human Side of Religion*, Berkeley: University of California Press.

Stevenson, D. (1988) *The Origins of Freemasonry: Scotland's Century, 1590–1710*, New York: Cambridge University Press.

Sultan, M. (1999) "Choosing Islam: A Study of Swedish Converts," *Social Compass* 46: 325–35.

Tinaz, N. (2001) "Conversion of African Americans to Islam: A Sociological Analysis of the Nation of Islam and Associated Groups," unpublished dissertation, University of Warwick.

Toronto, J.A. (2008) "Islam *Italiano*: Prospects for Integration of Muslims in Italy's Religious Landscape," *Journal of Muslim Minority Affairs* 28: 61–82.

Turner, R.B. (2003) *Islam in the African-American Experience*, 2nd ed., Bloomington: Indiana University Press.

van Nieuwkerk, K. (2006) "Introduction: Gender and Conversion to Islam in the West," in van Nieuwkerk, K. (ed.) *Women Embracing Islam*, Austin: University of Texas Press.

Wohlrab-Sahr, M. (1999) "Conversion to Islam: Between Syncretism and Symbolic Battle," *Social Compass* 46: 351–62.

Zarcone, T. (1993) *Mystiques, philosophes et francs-maçons en Islam*, Paris: Institut français d'études anatoliennes d'Istanbul.

Zebiri, K. (2008) *British Muslim Converts*, Oxford: Oneworld.

# 17

# Muslim political radicalization in the West

*Tahir Abbas*

## Introduction

This chapter describes and explains the situation of radical Islam among young people in the Western European context, with a particular focus on the British case. The paper discusses aspects of migration, settlement, intergenerational disconnect, and problems of identity politics. It also explores the experience of Islamophobia, and the roles of foreign and domestic policy in exacerbating many of the problems that impact on anti-Muslimism and its manifestations; that is, the ways in which radicalization and Islamophobia have both internal and external discontents that are interrelated.

There are a number of issues to explore when considering the topic of migration in the context of the study of radicalization. In many instances, across Western Europe, what one is referring to is often postwar immigrant groups that have subsequently settled and adapted to parts of society, invariably in countries such as Germany, France, and England, those countries of "old Europe," and who have over the generations become citizens of their new homes. Some of these groups share the cultural characteristics of majority society, while others have not been able to adapt in the same way, largely due to issues of education, employment, and forms of residual cultural relativism. The lack of integration has led to problems that are experienced within communities but also in relation to contact with majority society, which regards these groups as the alien "other," and where such notions feed off existing racialization and exoticization as well as being a function of ongoing patterns of discrimination and prejudice. Within communities there are distinct intergenerational issues around concerns relating to identity, religion, culture, and society.

Islamophobia has many manifestations. Part of it is based on hostility to immigration. Another element is misunderstanding the idea that Muslims are monolithic, monocultural, and in many ways culturally, intellectually, and emotionally the opposite of the European self (Mavelli 2012). An association is also made with notions of terrorism and extremism, which are regarded as problems that are a function of the nature of the very religion of Islam. A great number of aspects of Islamophobia are reinforced by various media and political discourses that maintain the view that Muslims are not just a threat to forms of multiculturalism but in more recent periods a threat to the very security of the nation itself. The latter has emerged in response to the terrorism that was carried out in the 2000s in various parts of Western Europe, namely in the Netherlands, Spain, England, and more recently in Germany in 2011. Another element of Islamophobia is that it reflects a particular situation where it is related to the politics of empire, particularly in the context of US foreign policy. Islamophobia in the USA is also becoming an increasingly recognizable phenomenon that is creating alarm within certain quarters, particularly within the academy, but also among wider society in general. In many ways Islamophobia is a function of anti-Muslim and anti-racism realized in the US social fabric, especially since the events of 9/11 (Kumar 2012).

In many ways, radicalization and Islamophobia reinforce each other. There is a symbiotic relationship between the two. They effectively feed off the motivation, drive, and expectations of the other. The framework in which Islamophobia and radicalization operate is essentially political, but has local and global effects. In order to break down the cycle one needs to get to the heart of the concerns. While there is a sense of enmity between Muslims and the other, which is based on present manifestations of politics, historically there have been many positive relations between the Muslim world, Christian world, and other civilizations. However, memories are short and emotions are easily swayed. The final aspects of this paper are concerned with ways and means to determine solutions to help scholars, policy-makers, and activists in determining specific courses of positive action and change.

## Migration and settlement

It is well documented that Islam has been in Britain for over a thousand years, but the population has largely grown in the previous century (Ansari 2004), and the demographic, social, cultural, and political positions of British Muslims have developed more significantly in the postwar era (Peach 2005). In the classic Islamic period, Muslims traded with English elites and cooperated with the monarchy when expedient to all (Gilliat-Ray 2010). Queen Elizabeth I maintained positive associations with Turkish Ottomans, who played an important role in thwarting the efforts of the Spanish Armada, which came in vain to the shores of England to restore direct loyalty to the papacy (Matar 1998). The most immediately recognizable episode can be characterized as one relating to the time of the Raj. Muslims came to Britain as elites embarking on training as medics or to read law in the established higher educational institutions of the country. The experience largely catered for the needs of the privileged few, while the less fortunate could only hope for a meager income fueling the furnaces of coal-fired steamships that supported the needs of empire and war (Visram 1986).

In the postwar period, the most rapid increase in the population of British Muslims has been found, from which the subsequent generations comprise the majority of British Muslims today. Britain, short of domestic labor, was forced to encourage once-colonized citizens of the "Commonwealth" to come to the "mother country" to carry out work that few else wished for or aspired to (Institute of Race Relations 1985). Trapped in cycles of underemployment, unemployment, and low pay in general, many South Asian Muslims who came to various parts of the country during this period found themselves unable to escape from those very same locations over the generations (Simpson et al. 2009). This phenomenon remains today, over sixty years after these initial postwar booms in immigration (Phillips 2006). As a consequence of these early years of arrival and settlement, and as a result of various (limited external and internal) approaches to integration into majority society, including the important and often overlooked factor of cultural maintenance and patriarchal norms and values, it has taken many decades for Muslims to begin to act as a meaningful political and cultural voice, but one that remains far from fully formed (Anwar 2001).

The current period is one in which primary immigration from Muslim lands has all but ended. But family reunification and marriage migration from parts of South Asia adds to the growing population. In 2010, among UK–Pakistan transnational communities, there were 1.5 million journeys a year between these two countries alone, with 10,000–15,000 Pakistani wives and husbands joining their spouses in the UK every year (UK government source, personal communication, March 25, 2010). This recent period also includes those who have come to the country as "refugees and asylum seekers," and whose positions in society have been marked by various forms of state-institutionalized practices that often reduce the needy immigrant to second-class citizen in all but name.

## Exogenous and endogenous factors

In trying to understand the range of endogenous and exogenous factors that lead to the radicalization of Muslims in the West there are a number of issues to take into account. It is important to elaborate upon internal issues that affect the communities from within and then how they are affected by their positions in wider society and the role of wider society in reinforcing those concerns. These wider societal factors have national and international layers of influence. It is as if they are layers of an onion that encapsulate the individual, who rests at the center, surrounded by innumerable ongoing challenges that become deeply embedded as the status quo remains. Each of these will now be discussed in turn, with a focus on the individual, before elaborating on the different layers of the societal context. In many ways, the forces that impact on Muslims in relation to radicalization are similar to those that affect far-right groups, diverging, however, in relation to differences in religio-cultural identity politics. Therefore, many of the causes of radicalization among far-right groups have similar characteristics to those which affect Muslim groups; however, what is different is the historical migration context and the external dynamics of a global Muslim identity framework, which is sometimes negatively realized by both Muslims and non-Muslims.

### The role of external racism

Without doubt it is important to elaborate upon the context of racism in British society. In the postwar period there remains a pernicious embedded experience of racism that affects people of color in significant ways in spite of the many pieces of legislation that have been enacted, particularly since the late 1960s. This form of racism is inherited from a colonial experience, for example in relation to England in the Caribbean islands and South Asia, France in relation to the Maghreb in parts of the Middle East, Italy in relation to Libya, and a somewhat less defined relationship between Germany and Turkey (Yükleyen 2011). All of these European encounters led to the exoticization of various ethnic and religious groups, coupled with an ideological framework that led to the exploitation and the disempowerment of various groups (Back and Solomos 2000). This systematic "othering" of various groups in a historical context has found itself revealed in the contemporary period, especially in the postwar immigration phases that have characterized the movements of various ethnic groups to Western Europe. Such were the ongoing prejudices in relation to minorities, it was always felt that they would leave after the periods of employment they were engaged in terminated. This affected the ways in which they are regarded as part of society, whether as citizens of the state or more generally at the everyday level of encounter and engagement. These minorities were given the worst jobs, had limited opportunities for social mobility because of the places in which they lived and the type of employment they had, which had implications for the ways in which their children would experience their own localized forms of racialized education (Tomlinson 1980). Attending poorer schools with limited resources often stifled their ambitions as well as deliberately limiting the opportunities that they could experience, therefore reifying the notion that minorities are less ambitious or even in certain cases less intelligent (Miles and Phizacklea 1979).

What lay beneath this encounter was a deep sense of discrimination on the basis of color. This is what was characterized when minorities first came to various parts of Western Europe in the 1960s and 1970s. During the 1980s and 1990s attention shifted away from "race" towards ethnicity. It was how minorities were recognized for various cultural and religious attributes as well as their visibility in the social context. Attempts were made by various minority groups to try and bring about measures that would accept their differences in society. For example, in relation to Muslims the question of *halal* foods and Islamic places of worship were of primary concern. Since the hiking of oil prices in the mid-1970s various Western European economies had been struggling to compete. This led to deindustrialization and unemployment, which affected many young men across the Western world, in particular in relation to immigrant and minority groups, who are most susceptible to economic downturns. Given the existing patterns of unemployment and underemployment, as well as limited education and training opportunities, many minorities were simply locked out of the job market. For many it encouraged a turn to self-employment as a way in which to develop their fortunes. This occurred in parts of Western Europe, including England, Germany, and Denmark. In England the establishment of the South Asian restaurant sector led to a cultural awareness of a Muslim multicultural presence which was regarded in positive terms. Just as in the current period, when aspects of multiculturalism and its more positive dynamics are elaborated upon, there is a focus on sporting heroes from minority backgrounds, in the 1980s there was a focus on ethnic businesses, largely because of ongoing problems of deindustrialization but also because of the idea that small businesses were able to generate economic activity which would improve opportunities for all of the society (Ram et al. 2001). Part of the ethnic multicultural celebration model during this time was a function of these wider changing economic fortunes.

Therefore, it is without doubt that much of a sense of inferiority projected onto the ethnic minority other is related to a wider problem of economic downturn. The opposite is found when there are periods of economic boom. Minorities are celebrated for their differences and multiculturalism is talked about in exceedingly positive terms. Nevertheless, as a result of these economic changes, aspects of the far right in societies began to emerge as more influential figures in the political context. In Britain in the late 1970s the National Front and the Anti-Paki League were able to capture the imaginations of disaffected white working-class young men. At the same time second-generation Caribbean young men who were experiencing significant problems of over-policing, racialization, criminalization, and inner-city segregation were turning to popular music as a way to express their frustrations as well as develop a cultural form of representation (Gilroy 1991). While the Muslims in Western Europe were still visible under the banner of Asian immigrant communities, their time would come two decades later after the collapse of the Soviet Empire and the development of the clash of civilizations thesis that characterized US foreign policy, leading up to the events of 9/11 and since.

## The decline of masculinity

As a result of the changing economic fortunes of Western European economies during the 1970s and 1980s, a phenomenon known as the crisis of masculinity began to emerge. Due to these patterns of deindustrialization and the role of technology in the production process, jobs that had been guaranteed for life were no longer the norm. Moreover, men were also competing for jobs with women, particularly in the service sector economy. As the manufacture of motor vehicles and heavy engineering products shifted to Eastern Europe and the Far East, it meant that these men were no longer in a position to claim their apparent rightful ownership of a job for life. This therefore is an essential element of the problem of an attack on masculinity from without. As a result, it led to retraining and reskilling in order to find employment, and even then this employment was not guaranteed in the way it might have been in the past (Massey and Meegan 1982). This crisis of masculinity led to all sorts of inner-city conflict between various groups of differing backgrounds, Asians versus Caribbeans, Irish youth versus white fascist youth, or all youth versus the police. Many towns and cities across parts of Western Europe that were once thriving industrial zones of economic and cultural activity were suddenly reduced to ghost towns. Combined with a lack of inward investment on the part of central governments to rebuild these declining regions, this led to the ongoing exclusion, disfranchisement, and, in the case of minority groups, a systematic racialization of young men. All young men experienced problems but ethnic minority men experienced them in greater degrees (Whitehead and Barrett 2001).

Conflict between those who hold power and those who are subservient to it is a function of modern societies. This is a classic relationship between workers and bosses, proletariat and the bourgeoisie, in a system of capitalism. Various welfare state models which would attempt to provide some kind of balance in societies in order to absorb the shocks of economic decline were susceptible to moderation by various governments across Western Europe moving to the right. They began to place emphasis upon competition, individuality, and, importantly, enterprise as a way in which to generate economic success and therefore to provide the necessary contributions to the welfare tax burden. Local communities and local areas characterized by local industries were incredibly neglected by this process. The experience of minorities was even more profound given their existing experience of exclusion from society and the ways in which ongoing patterns of racism had locked these communities in the poorer parts of towns and cities across Western Europe. As a result of these shifting contours, conflict began to emerge within these inner-city groups at a far more explicit level, such that poor groups in inner-city areas were competing with each other in the most violent of ways, and yet for the crumbs of society. At the same time the discourse in relation to conflict in society focused on minorities, presented out of the center and by elite groups, placing all the attention on minorities and inner-city youth as the problems rather than the workings of society. Conservatism was rampant throughout Western European experience during the 1990s. It led to the seeds of internal conflict between poorer groups in inner-city areas that has yet to be resolved in the current period.

As Caribbean men were turning to music as a way of expressing their identity politics, Irish young men were facing the full brunt of a focus on terrorism in society that regarded the issue as one of religion and not politics. Muslim groups were largely invisible during this process. They were not regarded in any way differently to other minority groups who were also found concentrated in the inner-city areas. In the case of South Asians, they were regarded as a monolithic block in the form of Asians, and two decades previously they had all been grouped together as "colored." But by the end of the 1980s, as a result of conflicts in other parts of the world in relation to Muslim lands, namely the Iranian Revolution and its impact across the region, the Soviet invasion of Afghanistan, and the Iran–Iraq War, a form of transnational Muslim solidarity was created which defied existing notions of the decline of the nation-state. In the UK in particular, the Salman Rushdie affair captured the mood of the time. In 1989 the Berlin Wall fell. It was also the same year that the Ayatollah Khomeini died. But this was also the year in which *The Satanic Verses* was published. The emergence of the book came at a time when young men of Muslim origin were now well into the second generation and had already begun to define themselves along a spectrum of Muslim identities rather than Asian identities. This emergence of religious identity politics led to the establishment of a form of Salafism in relation to young Muslim men in the Western European context (Abbas 2011).

## The emergence of Salafi Islam

A particular issue facing British Muslims has been that of the rise and impact of a literal inter-pretation of Islam, which has emerged to create significant problems for the community from within. During the 1980s British Muslims were investing in after-school Islamic training for the second and third generation. However, many of these *madrasa*s were developed alongside certain sectarian lines, which accommodated certain groups but excluded others. The Deobandi, Jama'at-i Islami, and Tablighi groups were able to develop their Islamic educational institutions with relative ease, emerging from the mosques that local worshippers often attended, and funded through donations made by the local community. While aspirations in relation to the development of an Islamic awareness among second-generation parents were amenable, they often lacked the resources, direction, leadership, or ideological focus that would invariably be required in relation to meeting the needs, demands, and hopes of British-born Muslims. During this period, various elements from across the world, including Saudi Arabia, were using these after-school *madrasa*s as an opportunity to promulgate their particular ideological and sectarian focus, especially among institutions that were poorly resourced. Thus, a form of Salafism emerged from within the communities who were seeking to develop the Islamic awareness of the younger generations, not as a specific goal on the part of local communities but rather through the gaps that emerged in relation to resources (Jacobson 1998).

During the 1990s, because of various problems across the Muslim world and the position of the USA in relation to its foreign policy interests in the regions associated with it, namely the first Gulf War, younger Muslims, who had access to information about the events going on in these parts the world through various developments in the media, were beginning to feel a sense that perhaps Islam was and is now again the target. The events of Bosnia-Herzegovina during the mid-1990s caused further angst among European Muslims, who found refugees from those parts of the world coming to local the mosques in Western Europe and telling their harrowing stories. In effect, the first generation of present-day Western European-born Jihadis was in fact radicalized during this period (Abbas 2007a). The second generation was radicalized by the events of 9/11 and the "War on Terror" that ensued. Until the events of 9/11 and the subsequent changes to security policy, much of the literature found in local community Islamic centers or the activities of young people as they traveled abroad were not monitored by the intelligence services or the police. This changed in the light of legislation that was quickly enacted as a response to the security threat, namely the events of 9/11 in the USA and the events of 7/7 in Britain. While attempts were made to de-radicalize young Muslims through various measures to try and empower the community, the increase in the powers of various behind-the-scenes services and the ongoing problems of foreign policy, particularly in Iraq, caused further alarm among disaffected young European-born Muslims, who were still locked in the same inner-city areas as their parents and who continued to suffer as a result of low education and limited employment opportunities (Haddad 2002).

What these events across the world did to the perceptions of young Muslims was to also create a sense of the division between themselves and the generations before them (Anwar 1998). This would lead to various forms of conflict of identity, political engagement, questions on the role of women, and questions relating to integration into society which have yet to be fully resolved in the current period. These global events, as well as the responses to them by the state in the guise of various policy measures, had the deleterious effect of deepening existing fissures between the generations. Concurrently, as media and political discourses placed all the attention on Muslims as being the problem, this generated further disquiet and angst within and without. Limited opportunities to develop Islamic knowledge within the European context further led to divisions between the communities facing various forms of social isolation as well as the particular gap in relation to an Islamic awareness through the *ulama*. Susceptible to the whims of charismatic preachers, young Muslim men were easily misdirected. Limited opportunities existed for those who were serious about their Islamic education and transmission of Islamic knowledge. Classic forms of knowledge continue to be disseminated through the existing structures, but various other developments to this experience are also being found among Muslims in Europe, who are utilizing the internet, for example, and in the role of globally recognized Islamic scholars, some of whom have gained iconic status, such as Tariq Ramadan and Sheikh Hamza Yusuf. A whole host of independent Muslim satellite television channels have also had a considerable role in broadening the Islamic awareness of European Muslims. This can only be seen as a positive development in the light of ongoing persistent internal and external challenges (van Bruinessen and Allievi 2011).

## The roles of intergenerational disconnect and radical identity politics

Much before the events of 9/11, British Muslim "loyalty" to a cultural national identity was in question. The Rushdie Affair of 1989 placed the concerns of British South Asian Muslims firmly on the political and sociological map, with issues of civic engagement, multicultural philosophy, the nature and orientation of certain religio-cultural norms and values, and socio-economic exclusion and marginalization dominating rhetoric, policy, and practice throughout the 1990s (Weller 2009).

Based on a recent study carried out by the author, the aims of which were to explore and analyze the impact of the events of 7/7 from the perspectives of South Asian Muslims in a city in the West Midlands, UK, matters relating to radicalization and de-radicalization were explored (Abbas and Siddique 2012). Utilizing interview data from young men and women (aged 18–25), including university students, together with spiritual leaders, community activists, youth workers, and prominent political leaders, it was found that there were obvious differences in attitude, opinion, and perception based on differences in social class, ethnicity, and gender, but many responses in relation to the experiences of Muslims in the post-7/7 climate were universal in nature and orientation. One of the interesting findings in this study was that some young Muslims were using physical appearance as a resistance strategy against anti-Muslim rhetoric, usually expressed by young Muslim women wearing the *hijab* and men growing beards and wearing caps. Rather than heading towards a more violent ideology, these young Muslims were apparently experiencing a cultural identity shift that was more esoteric, conceivably reflecting a "softer" versus a "harder" form of radicalization. Both genders saw themselves as British, but specifically as "British Muslims." However, some expressed that they were not always made to feel British.

Questions relating to integration and their relationship with wider non-Muslim communities suggested that this was a function of local area social and economic opportunities in general. This finding, however, does not cohere with existing dominant government thinking or the persuasions of center-right think tanks, commentators, and political leaders in general (Kundnani 2008). That is, official reports have tended to suggest that there has been a problem with the Muslim integration process due to cultural divisions. Or, it is reflected in the ways in which the idea of multiculturalism, "a philosopher's tool" in relation to imagining the "good society," has received extensive criticism, for the left and the right (Kepel 2008). In reality, a lack of integration is more a function of economics and questions of social and political empowerment rather than identity, culture, or religion alone (Bhavani et al. 2005).

The negative effects of local and global events have the potential to attract young people to extremist organizations that provide succor in the face of a range of internal and external pressures. This is reasonably well documented in current commentary. However, none of the young South Asian Muslim respondents felt that organizations such as Hizb ut-Tahrir directly represent them or their views, but there was an understanding of why young people may be drawn to their messages. Some of the young Muslims argued that this was largely because they are able to provide unity in the face of racism and exclusion, together with an alternative to the traditional Muslim leadership, which is thought to be inflexible and stagnated. Aspects of the spiritual leadership within the Muslim community are said to be unyielding, unable to respond to the demands of the youth. A language and cultural barrier exists, as most imams, who often do not speak English, are unable to address how British Muslims should meet the challenges currently facing them. This, unfortunately, leads to some young people being drawn towards extremist bodies that can easily provide this support. These are just some of the many intergenerational challenges facing British Muslims in the current period. While considerable attention has been paid to questions of race, ethnicity, loyalty, belonging, and local and global identities, there remains a lack of appreciation of the nuances of the experience and the contextualization of physical space, region, and, more importantly, the impact of policy and practice which is local, national, and international, on questions of Islamophobia and radicalization.

## The limitations of domestic and foreign policy

There is no doubt whatsoever that social exclusion features prominently in the study of Muslims. Many young Muslims live in poverty, in overcrowded homes, segregated areas, declining inner-city zones, face educational underachievement, high unemployment, low graduate employment, and experience poor health (Abbas 2005). These disadvantages have significant implications for young people growing up in society as they experience limiting horizons fueling distrust, generating antagonism towards the state, and creating an acute sense of isolation. Such structural factors are endemic in any sense of alienation that young people experience. Alongside issues of economic marginalization, young Muslim men have to operate in an ever more competitive and globalized world. Essentially, they face problems of racism, discrimination, and anti-Islamic prejudice that affect a particular section of the British Muslim community. It is easy to lose sight of Muslims in parts of the Midlands and the North while focusing on urban elites and a significant politico-media class of individuals in the South of England. A cultural, intellectual, and political North–South divide adds to many of the structural problems affecting Muslim minorities.

The 9/11 attacks and the subsequent policy reactions have permeated many areas of everyday life for Muslims everywhere, and no less so in Britain. As an event, it has implications that go far beyond merely "international terrorism." In fact, these implications are linked to politics, religion, and issues of cultural differences in an effort to maintain harmonious societies and democracies in the West, which contain a significant number of Muslims (approximately 25 million in Western Europe). In the Middle East, as revealed in the aftermath of the war in Iraq, further unrest, political turmoil, and violent action and reaction are the main features of the current climate. In the near future, relations between Muslims and their Western hosts will continue to remain problematical, with discussions focusing on citizenship, civil society, multiculturalism, political representation and participation (as components of democracy), and identity, gender, intergenerational development, radicalism versus liberalism (as components of the individual).

Given that British South Asian Muslims have reached the third generation, issues of concern have shifted from cultural assimilation and social integration to religious identity and discrimination. The study of Islam and Muslims has become more vigorous, and greater emphasis is being placed on understanding the nature and orientation of British Muslims in more anthropological, sociological, theological, and political science perspectives. The first generation of South Asian Muslims kept their religious practices and expressions well within private or community spheres, but subsequent generations struggled with issues of integration and racism in the climate of the early 1960s, cultural pluralism in the 1970s, free-market economic determinism and the rolling back of the frontiers of the state in Thatcher's and Major's Britain from the early 1980s to the mid-1990s, through to the "third way" center-left politics of assimilationist New Labour. At the same time, identification with Islam is gaining strength among some members of this latest generation, both as a reaction to racist hostility as well as due to a desire to understand Islam in more precise detail.

## Intersecting Islamophobia and radicalization

Muslims experience a particularly problematic scenario in relation to how the religion of Islam and its people are depicted in various media scenarios. This is often described as a form of Islamophobia, or more simply as anti-Muslim racism. Since 9/11 these representations have become even more pernicious, as the representation of the other is routinely presented in more violent and conflictual terms. It was Edward Said's classic work *Orientalism* which first helped an understanding of how Islam and Muslims are represented. There are problems not only in relation to popular culture but also in various institutions and practices, such as the academy itself and the way in which it reproduces knowledge. It is also found among poets, journalists, novelists, and of course among politicians. There is a sharp "us" and "them" divide where a moderate Muslim is seen as a Muslim who is more acceptable in the eyes of the West. "Good Muslims are with 'us,' bad Muslims are against 'us'," which is a paraphrase of a concept first characterized by Tony Blair in the immediate aftermath of the 7/7 crisis. Power remains in the hands of the West due to the institutions that have been built over the centuries creating an inequality of wealth embedded in societies, which are demarcated as wholly separate. There is an element of chauvinism and bigotry that strikes at the heart of society. The hubris and sheer arrogance of Western powers and their approaches to the Muslim world are starkly evident. The negative representation of Islam is further enhanced by various organizations who work through clandestine measures in order to obscure an already disfigured image. While there may be a physical "war on terror" there is a war in cyberspace put forward by well-organized groups to further demonize the religion for various political and ideological ends (Ismael and Rippon 2010).

This Islamophobia has the consequence of radicalizing young Muslims, who respond to it through violent means. There is a symbiotic relationship between Islamophobia and radicalization (Abbas 2012). The cycle reproduces itself without any real attempt being made to break it by dominant hegemonic interests. Within communities the lack of representation, self-belief, and the means to generate alternative responses leads to a process without end. In Western Europe, where there are currently over 25 million settled minority Muslims, younger generations are often feeling the brunt of ongoing patterns of exclusion and marginalization. But it is crucial to understand here that another factor in the realization of the circle that is maintained around Islamophobia and radicalization is the actual multicultural contexts in which these realities are realized. A number of Western European governments have focused on the idea of providing recognition for groups in an attempt to mollify differences without necessarily working towards positive integration models. That is, ironically, though they have provided the resources to celebrate differences as a way in which to develop minority community self-confidence and belief in their roles as immigrants, minorities, and citizens, aspects of white society have regarded these actions as tokenistic or merely there to provide some kind of temporary acceptance. A sense that celebrating differences is the way in which to reassure majority society that difference is not necessarily a threat is in no way a genuine signal based on real economic and social development. A poor substitute for tackling what really has been lacking in terms of direct investment in these communities, this has created a sense of ethnicity as a vehicle for mobilizing difference when in fact it ought to be ironed out as part of appreciating minorities as equal citizens. Therefore, in many ways it is the multicultural context which in fact has fueled the cyclical process of Islamophobia stimulating radicalization, with radicalization feeding Islamophobia.

There are of course many facets of radicalization, but what is of particular interest is the nature of the relationship between it and the forces of Islamophobia. Much of the nature of the interaction process is played out within a particular function of multiculturalism itself, such that in benign forms of multiculturalism there is a sense of specific forms of identity politics emerging within the political and cultural sphere, whereas in more authoritarian forms of multiculturalism there is a greater sense of specific forms of representation, which are both political and religious. There is also the concept of integration, which suggests that there is a two-way street in relation to minorities in which minorities give a certain loyalty to the workings of the institutions of society while at the same time the state provides protections and freedoms, certainly in relation to forms of racism and discrimination. What this fails to appreciate is that France has an assimilationist notion of integration and the Netherlands works towards a culturally pluralist framework, but both countries have suffered attacks by "home-grown" radical Islamists. The problem has more to do with the intersection of the local and global in how disaffected Muslims determine their relations with others. It is also related to the perception of alienation among local and global Muslims, as much as its actual physical experience (Gest 2010). These processes have been accelerated by advances to communication technologies (Bunt 2003). The belief that the problem is Muslims is to exaggerate the debate and often return to a socio–culturalist socio–pathological argument.

As part of the migration process, Muslim minorities have brought with them various forms of Islamism, especially those from South Asia (Robinson 1988). This very same Islamism is inherited from reaction to the colonial experience, when critical Muslim thinking and progressive development were replaced with regressive and reactionary tendencies in the face of hostility from and subjugation by the "oppressor." This became a cyclical process as the British Raj attempted to moderate and mollify such tendencies, which led to further resistance among the Muslims of South Asia, some of whom felt acutely marginalized as part of the "divide and rule" policy of their English overloads. In coming to Britain in the postwar period, much of this antipathy has remained intact and even solidified in the context of disempowered experiences of life in the inner cities. Assimilation, integration, and multiculturalism in their present forms in Western Europe evolved as part of various postwar dynamics of settlement and incorporation of various ethnic minority groups. During the course of its development, it sought to provide recognition of differences, and the means through which these differences could be expressed in public and private spheres, from accommodation of religious rights of worship in the public space to acceptance of such needs as *halal* food and Islamic marriage contracts. In some senses, the development of certain forms of benign multiculturalism has given various forms of Islamist expression opportunities to remain hidden until various crises emerged, particularly from the Rushdie Affair onwards. Ineffective integration policies and aggressive foreign policies of the West have led certain Muslim groups to believe there is a "war on Islam," which is not helped by a range of ongoing negative media and political discourses. To understand the nature of extremism among various Muslim groups it is important to understand the historical and contemporary dynamics, compounded by simultaneous lack of confidence and self-esteem among Muslims, who are also then further disempowered due to the dominant corporate, military-industrial, ideological, and political concerns that enfold various groups across society (Abbas 2007b).

It is in the inner cities that most European-born Muslims remain physically concentrated (cf. Rex 1988). Invariably, neglect will remain on the part of the nation-state and the political establishment until something dramatic happens again. It is precisely where the multiculturalism model in Britain works least well. In celebrating differences and being culturally sensitive to minority interests, the notion of a universal national identity has not been sufficiently determined to permit the different ethno-cultural characteristics of ethno-religious minorities and majorities to coalesce around it. At a policy level, notions of cultural identity politics supersede those relating to the need to eliminate deep-seated socio-economic inequalities.

As a final note it is important to contrast the experience of European-born Muslims with those of their North American-born counterparts. Much of the growth of the Muslim population in the USA came about after the opening up of the immigration system in 1965. Variously highly qualified immigrant Muslim groups from various parts of the Muslim world came to America to seek higher returns on their human capital. As such, the immigration of Muslims into North America is hugely different from that of Muslims in Western Europe in the current period. American Muslims, particularly those that came after 1965, are highly qualified, highly integrated, and at the same time loyal to a state that has built its identity on the idea that hard work leads to prosperity. Therefore, the immigrant adaptation model in the USA has been hugely different from that of Muslims who came to Western Europe as part of the labor migration process at the bottom society. In relation to questions around radicalization, while Islamophobia is a growing phenomenon in the USA and various examples of it can be acutely observed in relation to all sorts of current dynamics, the question of home-grown Muslim extremism is still an untested notion, in spite of the various attempts by the US government to effectively intern Muslims of various backgrounds immediately after the events of 9/11 because of a view that many were engaged in radicalization. The latter claim is unfounded even though the draconian legislation still remains in place. Conceptually, there is a suggestion that increasing Islamophobia within the USA might encourage various forms of radicalization in the same way that it operates within the Western European context; however, the nature of North American society is quite different from that of Europe. For example, there is no colonial history in relation to its post-1965 Muslim groups, and class structure is less embedded in the workings of society.

## Conclusion

The announcement of the June 2012 University of Essex study on Britishness made headlines in practically all of the daily nationals in England (Institute for Social and Economic Research 2012). The essence of the national survey's analysis suggests that Muslims in Britain regard themselves as feeling far more British than popular sentiment would suggest. This particular finding, however, is hardly new. It is something that has been confirmed by surveys running back to the early 1990s, chiefly the Fourth Policy Studies Institute Survey. Experiencing a sense of Britishness is not the issue, nor are ideas associated with "loyalty" or national identity in general. Muslims are consumers in society, from visiting supermarkets, high street stores and fast food chains, to buying German and Japanese cars, or Tweeting, blogging, or even eBay trading. They are producers in society, from manufactures, to industrialists, to designers and innovators. British Muslims, who are variously differentiated along ethnic, class, and sectarian lines (as are other faith communities), are as integrated, certainly the younger British-born generations, as they could hope to be.

Integration is a complex topic. In brief, it is the notion that minorities accept the law of the land and contribute to and engage in the national social model as best they can. In return, the state affords protection in relation to discrimination and human rights, recognizing and respecting differences in the process. Sometimes this lack of effective integration, a focus on differences, combined with economic, social, political, and cultural pressures, creates the ingredients for radicalization. This is not just regrettable, but also deeply painful for those who regard themselves as wholly British and wholly Muslim.

Although national surveys, in this case of 40,000 people, are useful in providing an understanding of overarching patterns, there is a tendency to confirm what one knows from extensive qualitative and ethnographic research, which is being carried out in abundance in relation to Western Muslims in recent years, some of which is exceptional (Roose 2012). The other main problem is the inability to ask seriously detailed questions on all aspects of life concerning various groups of interest. This is generally due to resource constraints, and hence smaller-scale qualitative research is often able to bridge that gap. The most glaring issue remains that, while Muslims themselves feel Western and want to be Western as much as they can, Muslims do not actually feel accepted as Western. The chances are that this question is likely to reveal that minorities may aspire to all the desires of wanting to fit into society, and they almost always do, but they are not always accepted. Further details about how this integration–acceptance dichotomy is actually being played out in reality would be of real importance to our understanding of all the issues. Without it, studies such as the one produced by the University of Essex only provide at most half of the picture, if that.

The task of de-radicalization has not been easy, given the local, national, and international focus of attention since 9/11. In reality, it has been necessary to reconcile religion-based identity and citizenship, as well as individual rights and community rights, in a setting where the beliefs of others have dominated, without retreating into isolationism. In addition, European Muslims have inherited the colonial history of past relations with Europe. Combined with racism, which is endemic, this creates an atmosphere of mistrust. Moreover, the recent "war on terror," however, will wither away because it is a war that has no singular defined enemy; only a set of ideologies, falsely appropriated and actualized by the "clash of civilization" thesis. But this global picture is only part of the experience of Islam and Muslims in Western Europe. More immediate are the everyday realities (i.e. poor housing, jobs, health, and education). Once many more European Muslims have a more determined economic and social presence in society, only then will their demands, needs, and requests be met. But to be in a viable position to reach this objective, the elimination of pernicious structural and cultural racism is crucial. The nature and orientation of various forms of Western European multiculturalism are undergoing severe tests, and it will be important to observe closely how Muslims experience it over the next few years. What is apparent, however, is that 9/11 has not changed the world, but how Muslims will be regarded, considered, and treated for the foreseeable future – possibly for the remainder of the twenty-first century.

Muslims are at a crossroads in their history of immigration to and settlement in Western Europe. At the same time, one striking feature of their structural experiences is their socio-economic position. This group constitutes one of the most marginalized, alienated, isolated, discriminated against, and misunderstood groups in society (although there is a small burgeoning Muslim elite). They are negotiating a set of identities and realities that are constantly changing, and it will be important to see how they develop in the near future. As research questions continue in the areas of race, ethnicity, religion, and culture, as well as public policy concerns at the local, national, and international levels, the ongoing study of Western European Muslims and issues of radicalization and Islamophobia remain important within this contextual and analytical framework.

## Bibliography

Abbas, T. (ed.) (2005) *Muslim Britain: Communities under Pressure*, London and New York: Zed.

——(2007a) "Ethno-Religious Identities and Islamic Political Radicalism in the UK: A Case Study," *Journal of Muslim Minority Affairs* 27(3): 356–68.

——(ed.) (2007b) *Islamic Political Radicalism: A European Perspective*, Edinburgh: Edinburgh University Press.

——(2011) *Islamic Radicalism and Multicultural Politics: The British Experience*, London and New York: Routledge.

——(2012) "The Symbiotic Relationship between Islamophobia and Radicalisation," *Critical Studies on Terrorism* 5(3): 345–58.

Abbas, T. and Siddique, A. (2012) "Perceptions of the Processes of Radicalisation and De-radicalisation among British South Asian Muslims in a Post-industrial City," *Social Identities: Journal for the Study of Race, Nation and Culture* 18(1): 119–34.

Ansari, H. (2004) *The Infidel Within: The History of Muslims in Britain, 1800 to the Present*, London and New York: Hurst.

Anwar, M. (1998) *Between Cultures: Continuity and Change in the Lives of Young Asians*, London: Routledge.

——(2001) "The Participation of Ethnic Minorities in British Politics," *Journal of Ethnic and Migration Studies* 27(3): 533–49.

Back, L. and Solomos, J. (eds.) (2000) *Theories of Race and Racism: A Reader*, London and New York: Routledge.

Bhavani, R., Mirza, H.S. and Meetoo, V. (2005) *Tackling the Roots of Racism: Lessons for Success*, Bristol: The Policy Press.

Bunt, G.R. (2003) *Islam in the Digital Age: e-Jihad, Online Fatwas and Cyber Islamic Environments*, London: Pluto.

Gest, J. (2010) *Apart: Alienated and Engaged Muslims in the West*, London: Hurst.

Gilliat-Ray, S. (2010) *Muslims in Britain: An Introduction*, Cambridge: Cambridge University Press.

Gilroy, P. (1991) *"There Ain't No Black in the Union Jack": The Cultural Politics of Race and Nation*, Chicago: University of Chicago Press.

Haddad, Y.Y. (ed.) (2002) *Muslims in the West, from Sojourners to Citizens*, New York: Oxford University Press.

Institute of Race Relations (1985) *How Racism Came to Britain*, London: IRR.

Institute for Social and Economic Research (2012) *Understanding Society: Findings 2012*, Colchester: University of Essex Institute for Social and Economic Research.

Ismael, T.Y. and Rippon, A. (eds.) (2010) *Islam in the Eyes of the West: Images and Realities in an Age of Terror*, London and New York: Routledge.

Jacobson, J. (1998) *Islam in Transition, Religion and Identity among British Pakistani Youth*, London and New York: Routledge.

Kepel, G. (2008) *Beyond Terror and Martyrdom: The Future of the Middle East*, Cambridge, MA: Harvard University Press.

Kumar, D. (2012) *Islamophobia and Politics of Empire*, Chicago: Haymarket Books.

Kundnani, A. (2008) "Integrationism: The Politics of Anti-Muslim Racism," *Race and Class* 48(4): 24–44.

Massey, D.B. and Meegan, R.A. (1982) *The Anatomy of Job Loss: The How, Why, and Where of Employment Decline*, London and New York: Methuen.

Matar, N. (1998) *Islam in Britain, 1558–1685*, Cambridge: Cambridge University Press.

Mavelli, L. (2012) *Europe's Encounter with Islam: The Secular and the Postsecular*, London and New York: Routledge.

Miles, R. and Phizacklea, A. (1979) *Racism and Political Action in Britain*, London: Routledge & Kegan Paul.

Peach, C. (2005) "Britain's Muslim Population: An Overview," in Abbas, T. (ed.) *Muslim Britain: Communities under Pressure*, London and New York: Zed.

Phillips, D. (2006) "Parallel Lives? Challenging Discourses of British Muslim Self-Segregation," *Environment and Planning D* 24(1): 25–40.

Ram, R., Abbas, T., Sanghera, B., Barlow, G., and Jones, T. (2001) "Making the Link: Households and Small Business Activity in a Multi-ethnic Context," *Community, Work & Family* 4(3): 327–48.

Rex, J. (1988) *The Ghetto and the Underclass: Essays on Race and Social Policy*, Avebury: Ashgate.

Robinson, F. (1988) *Varieties of South Asian Islam*, Research Paper No. 8, Warwick: Centre for Research in Ethnic Relations, University of Warwick.

Roose, J.M. (2012) "Contesting the Future: Muslim Men as Political Actors in the Context of Australian Multiculturalism," unpublished Ph.D. thesis, Asia Institute, University of Melbourne.

Simpson, L., Purdam, K., Tajar, A., Pritchard, J., and Dorling, D. (2009) "Jobs Deficits, Neighbourhood Effects, and Ethnic Penalties: The Geography of Ethnic-Labour-Market Inequality," *Environment and Planning A* 41(4): 946–63.

Tomlinson, S. (1980) "The Educational Performance of Ethnic Minority Children," *Journal of Ethnic and Migration Studies* 8(3): 213–34.

van Bruinessen, M. and Allievi, S. (eds.) (2011) *Producing Islamic Knowledge: Transmission and Dissemination in Western Europe*, London and New York: Routledge.

Visram, R. (1986) *Ayahs, Lascars and Princes: Indians in Britain, 1700–1947*, London and New York: Pluto.

Weller, P. (2009) *A Mirror for Our Times: The Rushdie Affair and the Future of Multiculturalism*, London: Continuum.

Whitehead, S. and Barrett, F. (eds.) (2001) *The Masculinities Reader*, Cambridge: Polity.

Yükleyen, A. (2011) *Localizing Islam in Europe Turkish Islamic Communities in Germany and the Netherlands*, New York: Syracuse University Press.

# Part 2.2

## Contributing to the Western world

# 18

# Landscapes of Muslim art and architecture in the West

*Eric R. Roose*

## From Medina to Andalusia: a new look at copying in the historical dissemination of Islamic architecture

In 1989, the architectural historian Jonathan Bloom published a detailed study of the origins of the minaret in which he contested the widely held idea that Islamic architecture, since its assumedly functional beginnings in Medina, had always been automatically influenced by, or simply modeled on, the pre-Islamic architectures in the newly Muslim lands:

> They [scholars] have explained its [the minaret's] purpose as announcing the presence of Islam to non-Muslims. The common denominator of all these theories is that the minaret is always explained in terms of other cultures and scarcely ever in terms of the culture that produced it. This book attempts to correct that fault and to challenge the received view.
>
> *(Bloom 1989: 7)*

At the same time, the author shifted methodological focus from a passive process of formal–stylistic evolution to an active process of politico-religious patronage:

> Any investigation of the influence of antique Mediterranean, South Arabian, Mesopotamian, Central Asian, or Indian tower traditions on the Islamic tower is wrongly conceived, for it reverses the roles of the agent and the client. ... none of these cultures was in any position to *influence* Islam directly, because they all preceded it. Rather, Islam could only have adapted, misunderstood, copied, addressed, paraphrased, emulated, parodied, distorted, referred to, drawn on, resorted to, appropriated from, reacted to, differentiated itself from, engaged in a meditation on, responded to, or even ignored the tower traditions of the past.
>
> *(Bloom 1989: 18)*

Using an abundance of architectural and documental case studies from the rapidly expanding Muslim territories, Bloom showed how the various building elements of mosques – such as minarets – had strategically been copied from both Islamic and non-Islamic buildings by competing claimants of the Caliphate and their supporters. Their specific choices could be shown to have followed the shifting associations that came to be attached to these elements in changing contexts, and the particular selection, transformation, and removal of elements could be traced to the varying Islamic hierarchies in which the patrons positioned themselves.

Spanish Andalusia, commonly regarded as the first zone of architectural contact between Muslims and non-Muslims in the West, turned out to be no exception. Bloom treated the situation under the header "Minarets as signs of conflict in the Maghrib" (Bloom 1989: 99–124). In his opinion, for a greater intelligibility of the Islamic architecture freshly arrived in this European region, you had to stop looking at it as if it had been meant as something generally Islamic, developed with a Christian antagonist in mind. Instead, you should start with studying the architecture of the applicable Muslim competitors, for example the mosque of the Shi'i ruler al-Mahdi, the first Fatimid caliph, in his new capital Mahdiyya in North Africa. It was a close copy of the mosque of nearby Qayrawan, on a smaller scale, but the most prominent feature of the latter, the massive tower opposite the *mihrab*, had been ostentatiously replaced by a monumental portal modeled on Roman prototypes. To the Ismaili Fatimids, Bloom showed, mosque towers had become a sign of the religious power of the Abbasid usurpers and their recently deposed representatives, the Aghlabid emirs. They vehemently opposed the minaret on religious grounds, based on a produced 'Alid *hadith*, as an impious innovation. To them, the original call to prayer as requested by Muhammad had been performed, not from a tower, but by 'Ali at the entrance to Muhammad's mosque, and they had therefore chosen to transform the extant mosque type into a combination with an imperial portal, as a more genuine manifestation of Islam and their claimed leadership over it. This inevitably had its repercussions for the situation in Spain, where Umayyad descendents had also come to claim Caliphatic leadership, after Abbasid rule had been established over their former and faraway power center in Syria. Thus, although the Minaret of Cordoba had been generally attributed to be a manifestation of Islam amidst non-Islam, Bloom firmly contested this perspective. In his argument, 'Abd al-Rahman III built it, not as a symbol of Islam Triumphant towards the Christians, but as a sign of opposition to a much more threatening enemy, the Shi'i Fatimids, in the struggle for supremacy in the Maghreb. The Umayyads readily monumentalized the tower because the Fatimids had abhorred it: in their own context, its former Abbasid connotations had been lost and that had made it appropriate for the Umayyad patrons in their claim to be the authentic champions of Sunni Islam.

That the target group of such Islamic architectural transformations cannot be assumed to have been a generalized environment of non-Islamic "contemporaries" or "viewers" was shown by Bloom in a case study of the original spiral tower at the mosque of Ibn Tulun in Cairo (Bloom 1989: 125–8). Modeled, on a smaller scale, on the great mosques in Samarra, its patron had declared himself independent of Abbasid control from Samarra, while deliberately appropriating Abbasid court style. Whereas he and his courtiers had come from the originating Iraqi region, the Egyptian population never picked up on the intended architectural similarities, inventing all kinds of reasons for the estranging form and its concrete peculiarities. For example, its typifying brick piers were functionally explained as a precaution against fire or flood. Other contemporaries chose to interpret them as a manifestation of an Islam Triumphant – indeed, as an attempt to eliminate the use of columns, which had supposedly been tainted by their Christian use. And the tower's peculiar spiral form would have been the result of a discussion between the patron and his builders, who, when they had asked for instructions, were supposedly given the example of a twisted piece of paper that the disinterested governor had been toying with. The political goal was completely lost on the great majority and on critical observers, who could not have understood the reference and who could make no sense of the newly developed building other than from their own experiences, expectations, and significations. As Bloom put it, "Intention and performance were clearly at odds" (Bloom 1989: 128). However, since "no institution was able to control and channel any one particular meaning or association that a tower might acquire" (Bloom 1989: 176), such newly acquired meanings and associations always determined whether, why and how a structure, once built, might itself be transformed by a new patron in a newly commissioned Islamic building.

After his research on the intentions behind the presence or absence of building elements such as minarets, Bloom extended his argument by focusing on their particular iconographies, in an article from 1993 on the transmission of designs in early Islamic architecture (Bloom 1993). As a case study, the author took the Great Mosque of Damascus, which continued to provide a model for other buildings for at least six centuries after it was built. In this, example had been the primary means of transmission, and builders had seen either the mosque itself or one of its copies. Bloom noted that they had abstracted the principal elements of its design, and that it was not so much an exact likeness that was striven for, but rather a reference to one or several of its aspects. As the author found out, very similar processes of iconographic transformation had already been discovered half a century before, in a study of the early dissemination of European church architecture, by the architectural historian Richard Krautheimer (Bloom 1993: 28, n21). In two very influential articles, the latter empirically dismissed the contemporary formalist perspective of seeing ecclesiastical architecture as having always progressively followed a neat pattern of styles, determined by the creative genius of designers that had more recently become the ideal. Instead, the author turned attention to the continuous process in which rival Christian leaders had been using contemporary religious connotations of venerated historical prototypes by reshuffling and recombining strategic aspects of the latter, as well as of buildings with a more local importance, into wholly new and creative iconographies that served to legitimize their own claims to power versus those of contested Christian patrons. With an endless variation in politico-religious circumstances and prototypical connotations, historical examples from the Near East and from below the Alps had thus come to be transformed in the Western European context in such divergent ways that any intended connections between origins and end-results would have been recognizable only to the limited groups of allies and opponents positioning themselves in a local struggle for power. Interestingly, the verbal and visual depictions that had been used as examples for construction had themselves already consisted of such transformations (Krautheimer 1942a, 1942b). In similar vein, Bloom showed that, for instance, the Spanish Umayyad Caliph al-Hakam II, still threatened by the Ismaili Fatimid counterclaim, sent an ambassador to the Byzantine emperor requesting him to send a workman to decorate the Mosque of Cordoba with mosaics. In this, he explicitly wished to imitate the Umayyad Caliph al-Walid, who had built the Great Mosque of Damascus and decorated it with mosaics. Not only did al-Hakam identify with his Syrian forebears and wish his mosque to emulate theirs, he also wished to get his mosaics and mosaicists from the same source, which in the tenth century was believed to have been the Byzantines. This conscious recapitulation by the Spanish Umayyads of their real or imagined Umayyad past in Syria led Bloom to believe that other features of the Mosque of Cordoba had also been modeled on the mosque of Damascus. Thus, the three ribbed domes over the *maqsura*, for which no local precedent could be found, could be explained as a transformation on the basis of an enthusiastic, but inexact, description of the three domes of the Damascus mosque. As Bloom concluded, the absence of notational systems and paper in the early Islamic period would have meant that no single dynastic style of architecture could be precisely followed, while their existence in later times would have facilitated an impressive uniformity of some subsequent imperial architectural cultures, such as applied by the Ottomans and Safavids.

## In-depth case studies and thick descriptions: developing iconology in the field of Islamic architectural history

Inspired by both Bloom's and Krautheimer's iconological works, the architectural historian Finbarr B. Flood then called for a similarly comprehensive study of the phenomenon of copying in Islamic architectural history. As an example, Flood published a case study in an article in 1997 on Mamluk tombs in Cairo (Flood 1997). He showed how a whole assembly of forms, ornaments, and material media had been strategically transposed and transformed by the Qalawun sultans from the much earlier Umayyad Dome of the Rock and Damascus Mosque, instead of having been the assumed result of Byzantine influence, traveling Syrian builders, or a continuous technical application. Moreover, in their accounts of Umayyad architecture, medieval authors had singled out exactly those characteristic and celebrated features that came to be copied in the new Cairene setting. The author stressed that researchers should always study the prototypical buildings as they stood at the time when their copies were conceived and not in their later state, since relevant elements would potentially have disappeared or been changed. Even if some of the "Umayyad" features copied from the venerated prototypes had actually been added to the latter only after the Umayyad period, what mattered was that they provoked an appropriate Umayyad association. Thus, copying was indicative of a chronological eclecticism, or a perception of architecture as accretional rather than chronologically discrete. That the presence of all these features must have represented a deliberate Qalawunid revival of archaic forms became most apparent in their chronology: as suddenly as they reappeared, they disappeared again with the Qalawunid reign itself. The reason for recombining these prototypes Flood placed in the contemporary religious politics applied by the new rulers: a chronic political instability, the result both of external pressures and of internal frictions generated by the struggle for power, led to a search for symbolic legitimization that culminated in the formal re-establishment, now in Cairo, of the Caliphate. As Flood put it, "In a climate in which the issue of legitimacy was compelling, the trappings of that legitimacy were often acquired by forging (in every sense) links with the historical past and by fabricating a continuity with that past" (Flood 1997: 72). Altogether, the function of the references was to service internal Mamluk needs, and that function was inextricably linked to the perception of the prototypes, associated with supreme sanctity, with the Muslim conquest of Syria, and with aesthetic beauty. The paradisiacal or eschatological allusions in the prototypes were still contemporary associations, even if the intertextual references in Mamluk architecture were related to a contemporary interpretation of Umayyad iconography. In their new contexts, Flood concluded, these highly charged forms served equally as expressions of religiosity, if not strictly orthodox, and secular glorification.

Subsequently, an interesting attempt to combine architectural iconology with the ideal of thick description from the social sciences was made in a book on the transformation of Islamic art published in 2002 by the cultural anthropologist and art historian Yasser Tabbaa (Tabbaa 2001). He found Islamic art to be a field that still suffered from "patchy scholarship" and "thin description," permeated by essentialism and positivism instead of a focus on transformational change and dynamics (Tabbaa 2001: xi). In his perspective, transformations in Islamic art did not develop smoothly within a predetermined set of religious prescriptions, as if they were direct emanations from a central, all-encompassing dogma or system of representation. Neither were they natural developments from early or pre-Islamic art, as if everything in a certain locality automatically assumed a Persian, Turkish, or Arabic quality. Rather, their difference from what had preceded them and their selective adoption in various parts of the Islamic world strengthened the case for their specific associations and sectarian or ideological, rather than pan-Islamic, message. When studied at close range, the field of Islamic art underwent fairly abrupt transformations that were largely prompted by internal or external challenges to the central Islamic polity or system of belief. These political and theological challenges elicited visual or architectural responses and reactions that were intended to buttress the system of belief or power, to embody a new concept, and to establish its difference against the challenging force: "Art, like cultures and even religions, defines itself against its opponents, and the more intense the conflict, the sharper the self-image" (Tabbaa 2001: 7). Since interfaith conflicts had been perceived as defining moments in Islamic history, in the study of Islamic architectural history this axiom had been mainly applied to conflicts between Byzantium and the early Muslims, or between the Umayyads and Christians of Spain. Much less had been done, however, with the political upheavals and sectarian schisms that had divided Islam since early times, and the impact of these conflicts on the development of Islamic art had barely been touched upon.

Instead, Tabbaa proposed to perform in-depth case studies, for instance of the epoch of the Sunni revival in the eleventh and twelfth centuries, and to focus attention especially on the works of one patron, for instance the Syrian sovereign Nur al-Din. The author first made explicit the political and religious context of the Sunni revival, culminating in the religious politics of Nur al-Din, essentially a war of propaganda by him and the Maghrebi Almoravids against the Fatimids and other Shi'i, in support of the revived Abbasid Caliphate. Then Tabbaa moved on to a detailed analysis of the visual manifestations of that Sunni revival, to be discerned in the transformation of Qur'anic writing, public inscriptions, decorative patterns, and *muqarnas* domes and vaulting. He showed that their strategic application, at the instigation of Nur al-Din and as thus far unrecognized, was intended politically to distance the Sunni state from its Fatimid adversary while embodying some exoteric aspects of orthodox Ash'ari theology, regarding the atomistic and occasionalistic nature of the universe, against the esoteric dualism of Ismaili cosmologies. Even if this architectural manifestation of religious politics resulted in a proliferation of *muqarnas* domes and, subsequently, in what might be perceived as their "Islamization," apparently even Muslim patrons in situations such as in Andalusia, although *in abstracto* looking for ways to distinguish themselves from Christians, *in concreto* still searched for modes of expression that reflected their own particular creed and worldview (Tabbaa 2001: 130). As the author approvingly quoted the architectural historian Gülru Necipoğlu: "Rather than visual similarity, it was difference that communicated contested religiopolitical ideologies within the extensive Muslim domains, whose internal boundaries were marked by constantly shifting abstract sign systems, capable of conveying semiotic messages to insiders who were familiar with culturally determined codes of recognition" (Tabbaa 2001: 164).

## Good mosques, bad mosques: the perpetuation of formalism in the study of contemporary Islamic design

However, the very essentialism, positivism, patchy scholarship, and thin description that have recently come to be contested in studies of Islamic architectural history seem to be exempted from methodological problematization as soon as the field touches on objects created in modern times. Thus far, the architectural design of contemporary Islamic buildings has received scant analytical attention by architectural historians, leaving it to be studied mainly by architectonically trained designers, understandably upholding their assumptions on the factuality of stylistic progress and on the responsibility of the artistic creator in this process. The abrupt cession of scholarly authority on modern Islamic architecture from the iconological to the critical realm is visualized on the very last page of Bloom's book (Bloom 1989: 191). Here, the author claimed that "only in recent times has the minaret become truly pan-Islamic in its presence, as regions quite unused to mosques with towers began to adopt a neo-Ottoman or neo-Moghul hybrid as the international 'Islamic' style. With rare exceptions, present-day architects have repeated the familiar formulae of the past" (Bloom 1989: 191). In the captions of the two accompanying pictures (one an example of the multitude using an "Islamic style," and the other of one of the "rare exceptions"), as well as in a last footnote, Bloom referred his readers to a publication of the Aga Khan Award for Architecture in which the architect Ihsan Fethi had presented what may arguably be called the mother of all critical analyses of modern mosques (Fethi 1985).

Through Fethi's eyes, the architectural history of the mosque still definitely showed a continuous evolution from the supposedly austere and utilitarian house of the Prophet in Medina, to a basic number of stylistic types following the variety of cultural and ethnic characteristics within the newly conquered Muslim lands: the Arab hypostyle, the Persian cruciform, the Seljuk pillar and dome, and the Ottoman centralized dome. In his opinion, however, the arrival of modern technology and a general liberalization in architectural design had resulted in the breakdown of tradition and in a new permissiveness that was the cause of "some sound innovation" but also of "much misguided experimentation," resulting in what he saw as "stylistic transplants" and "strange hybrids" (Fethi 1985: 54). Although he found it difficult, therefore, to define the typology of modern mosque design, he saw five broad stylistic design trends emerging.

In Fethi's narrative, "Traditional/Vernacular Mosques" had distinctive regional characteristics and were essentially continuations of traditional building techniques. The majority were in rural areas and unmodernized regions of Islam. "Conservative/Conventional Mosques" largely adhered to existing regional building characteristics, using familiar and stereotyped forms, with some modern architectural materials and services. They tended to be quite modern in their structure, but conservative in the architecture and liturgical imagery. "New Classic Islamic Mosques" showed an adapted classic Islamic architectural vocabulary, especially in forms, patterns, and signs. They were essentially modern, but an attempt was made to make them fit in with the locality by the use of a traditional vocabulary and symbolism. They could not be called conservative, because they were adaptive and innovative, and they could not be called contemporary, because they clearly departed from the usual internationalist architectural idiom. In "Contemporary/Modern Mosques" a contemporary International Style vocabulary predominated in usually abstracted forms and streamlined geometry, using modern structural construction techniques, services, and materials. Consequently they did not necessarily attempt to attain a specific local identity architecturally. They were perhaps more innovative than the previous categories and some showed a remarkable degree of originality and purist simplicity. In "Eclectic/Arabian Nights Mosques" whimsical and often bizarre combinations of Islamic forms and symbols had been used. The eclectic use of symbolic elements from various regional architectural styles, such as multifarious onion domes and frilly minarets, curious arches, and excessive use of decoration, evoked Hollywood images of the Arabian nights. As such, they tended to be imaginative but often clumsy in proportion and lacking in overall discipline (Fethi 1985: 55–7).

The hundreds of badly executed and strangely hybrid mosques that Fethi saw built every year all over the Islamic world, he explained by the fact that good, experienced masons and craftsmen must have been hard to find and in any case prohibitively expensive. Some examples, in particular the Eclectic/Arabian Nights category, he found difficult to accept as serious contributions to religious architecture. He was tempted to dismiss them and to regard their proliferation as a degenerative trend in Islamic architecture if it were not for their genuinely popular appeal. But whereas he found that this manifestation might be acceptable in the design of small rural and urban *masjid*s, it could not be considered appropriate for the large-scale *jami*'s, which were architect-designed and officially sponsored and which therefore had to display a degree of dignity and gravitas. However, although the current approach to mosque design by architects all over the world seemed to favor a modern style, Fethi did recognize that the majority of mosques actually realized were in fact conservative. Thus far, few new mosques were being built in a truly contemporary style. The evidence showed a remarkable attachment to familiar and stereotyped forms, "due perhaps to the resistance of the Islamic clergy and *awqaf* to formal innovation" (Fethi 1985: 59). The author found it difficult to imagine a mosque designed in an exposed steel frame with clips and gaskets ever being acceptable to the Muslim clergy, let alone the people.

Fethi concluded that the architecture of the mosque was generally in a stagnant state. As he saw it, the resistance of the clergy to all design innovation had made most architects thus far adopt a conventional approach and the use of familiar imagery as the safest path to client satisfaction. Despite its shortcomings, Fethi found that the contemporary approach could produce bold and original results. A truly contemporary approach would have to take into account the needs and aspirations of "the people for whom the mosque was built," and the choice of technology, to be appropriate, would have to depend on "the conditions of a particular place." "It is through an honest response to such considerations rather than through a literal expression of past styles that the mosques of the future will retain their difference and remain close to the spirit of Islam" (Fethi 1985: 62).

Closely following Fethi's example, a series of publications on contemporary mosques has since come to be produced by architecture critics and architects attached to design institutes in which selective overviews of iconic objects still superseded the politico-religious penetration of newly created iconographies, and in which buildings were still formally classified into an evolution of types and styles moving towards a higher level of modernity (e.g. Salam 1990; Frishman and Khan 1994; Serageldin and Steele 1996; Holod and Khan 1997). They were expected to organically adapt to their otherwise progressing architectural environments, and the multitude of unartful pastiches that did not were largely attributed, without a foundation of empirical research, to a conservatism among "the Muslims" behind them. At the same time, the numerous variants of these quasi-historical copies on the American and European continents were firmly positioned in a generalized culture clash between Islam and non-Islam, and their perceived refusal to adapt and modernize was, again without any foundation of empirical research, blamed on the marginalized position of displaced Muslim minorities in the West – a manifestation, as it were, if not of an "Islam Triumphant," then of an "Islam Defiant," be it based on the unfortunate inheritance of colonial views of the East. The few exceptions that were perceived to have escaped such a process of "self-Orientalization" were heralded as a first glimpse of a future made possible by innovative architects. Indeed, it seems safe to conclude that in the academic field of modern Islamic architecture the empirical complexities are still believed to form part of a continuous progression, the locus of creativity is still placed in an artistic genius, and the will to understand content is still subordinated to a need to qualify form.

Thus, the architect Gulzar Haider, designer of several mosques in North America, suggested a causal relationship between the Westerner's Oriental obsession, the way in which Islamic architecture had subsequently been represented in North American movie theaters and casinos, and the kind of buildings that his Muslim patrons had carried in their minds when bringing their "mosque calendar pictures" to the drawing table. During design sessions he had sometimes felt "like a volunteer nurse in a room full of Alzheimer's patients at various stages of their condition." Consequently, in his commission for the community of the Bait ul-Islam Mosque in Toronto, which in his account quite simply wanted to "express its Islamic presence in Canada," he had creatively used the prayer rug as a conceptual inspiration and as a source of formal and decorative discipline (Haider 1996: 33, 41–2). Before he was able to do so, however, he suggested that he had confronted an overly ambitious committee, grandly imagining planting "the seeds of a Muslim town in North America on the model of the Prophet's Medina" (Haider 1990: 157). "The mosque will have to attain its rightful and self-assured place in world society, so that later generations who choose to come to North America will not be faced by a theater garbed in Moorish dress" (Haider 1996: 42).

Similarly, the librarian of the Aga Khan Program for Islamic Architecture, Omar Khalidi, found that North American mosques ranged from traditional designs wholly transplanted from Islamic lands, via reinterpretations of tradition, sometimes combined with American architecture, to entirely innovative designs. In his perspective, mosques and Islamic centers that tried to replicate the original mosques of the Islamic world lacked both the qualities and materials of traditional architecture:

> The distorted expressions of many of these buildings, their garish colours, and use of pre-fabricated industrial materials all deny the authenticity of the old monuments they aspire to imitate. Their generally crude aesthetics is also related to the low esteem in which a professional architect is held among American Muslims. Since the cost of re-creating a monumental mosque is beyond the financial means of the community, the clients will settle for a rough replica that any architect can provide simply by referring to photographs. ... The results are always imitative and unimaginative buildings passing for "authentic" Islamic architecture and they can be found in the United States from coast to coast. ... Attachment to traditional design principles is, however, by and large restricted to first-generation immigrant Muslims. Their descendants and American converts, who will eventually constitute the majority of the Muslim population, will probably tip the scales in favour of more innovative architecture.
>
> *(Khalidi 2000: 318, 322, 332)*

In the meantime, the architect Akel Ismail Kahera offered his own explanation for the American patrons' apparent love of the past:

> When building a mosque, the diaspora community ascribes emotional value to the utilization of a well-known convention or an influencing custom from the Muslim world. ... In attempting to replicate extant features from the past, the architect invariably produces a de facto facsimile whose aesthetics are severely compromised. ... In the American mosque, image is appropriated in an anachronistic manner; it is used as a display of ornament without regard to time or context. Image is essentially concerned with satisfying an emotional condition that has historical efficacy for the immigrant Muslim community. The appropriation of a familiar image vividly evokes a mental picture or an apparition that closely resembles an extant form, object, or likeness emanating from the past.
>
> *(Kahera 2000: 64–5)*

In the European diaspora, the architect Ihsan Limon also recognized three kinds of Islamic immigrants exerting their influence on mosque design. In his account, only a few had fully assimilated into the majority population, a small number had oriented itself to both the majority and their own group, and most had identified completely with their own ethnic origins and not at all with their new surroundings. However, none of their designs had used the "pure-cultural ('*in Reinkultur*') mosque types" shown in the literature on Islamic architectural history. From Limon's perspective, they generally looked like hybrid forms, consisting of European architecture mixed with building elements from the countries of origin. In his eyes, the "myth of returning" influenced mosque design in causing "culturally determined" nostalgic reactions among the first generation, expressing the need for a sense of security: "Since they have experienced discrimination, marginalization, spatial segregation etc. from the sides of politics and the majority population, ... religiosity as a defensive, compensating attitude has led to a higher demand for newly built prayer halls and has also influenced their architecture" (Limon 2000: 63–8, 125).

Similarly, and following the perspective of postcolonial criticism as propagated by the architect and Aga Khan professor Nasser Rabbat (2004), the architect Nebahat Avcioglu saw the "standstill" in both North American and European mosque design as a continuation, by Muslim minorities themselves, of Western-Orientalist modes of Islamic architectural representation, originally set up to deny productive or creative hybridity to the subject:

> a certain essentialism about these mosques continues to hold the space of Islam (or for that matter Muslim cultures) as fixed and presents it as either unchangingly distinct from the "West" or identical everywhere in the "East." Even the most recently built mosques have failed to produce an alternative representation. ... Indeed more and more purpose-built mosques in Europe and North America ... seem to strive towards a "seamless national [Muslim] identity" inspired and guided by the colonial sense that the dome and minaret were the undisputed signs, not only of Islamic cultures, but Islam itself. ... The existence of a minaret in this case is a neutral, easily manageable, generic trope, neatly tidying so many different cultures, habits, climates, and traditions.
>
> *(Avcioglu 2007: 99, 101–5)*

And finally, following Avcioglu's perspective, the architecture critic Christian Welzbacher also accused European mosque patrons of self-Orientalism:

> In so doing, Muslim immigrants confirm European clichés, taking on the "foreigner" role of their own accord. ... The dome and the minaret ... thus become visible symbols of the opposite of integration.
>
> *(Welzbacher 2008a: 43)*

> Across Europe, minarets are rising into the sky. All these buildings are the products of a traditionalist approach. They appear to reveal how much those responsible long for their home countries. In this way, the architecture of Euro-Islam becomes a symbol of the diaspora situation in which most European Muslims find themselves. They came as guest workers, live at the lower end of the social scale and have a minimal acquaintance with the language, culture and religion of their adoptive countries. This will only change with the Muslims of the third or fourth generation.
>
> *(Welzbacher 2008b: 60)*

## Islamic authority and iconographical creativity: introducing iconology in the study of modern Islamic architecture in the West

Rather than scholars from the humanities and social studies keeping falling back on such formalist tenets and critical authorities whenever they are in need of an architectural perspective in their edited volumes on Muslim space in the West (e.g. Haider 1996; Khalidi 2000; Clark 2001; Jasarevic 2009; Welzbacher 2011), I propose it is time that they themselves switched to performing in-depth case studies of modern mosques in the making. Instead of clinging to the axiomatic victimization of displaced Muslim minorities supposedly manifesting a generalized Islamic identity towards a hostile environment of non-Muslim majorities through an unfortunate emulation of Orientalist architecture, this means concentrating on the contested religious policies, strategic prototypical selections, and creative iconographical transformations of concrete Muslim patrons. The great advantage that we have over studies of historical architecture is that in contemporary cases much more documentation will have been left intact, while many patrons may be found to be still alive and available for interviews. Since this is not the right place for a full-scale design reconstruction, I will refer to two possible examples from the Dutch Muslim landscape that I recently published elsewhere in greater detail, treating some of the earliest developed plans for Muslim architecture in the Netherlands as well as some of its most recent projects. I hope to show that what may initially seem to be Orientalist and even totally dissimilar Islamic iconographies in the West would have actually been based on mutually shared prototypes that were nonetheless verbally and visually depicted in such strategically selective ways that most observers, whether Muslim or non-Muslim, would never come to recognize the resulting transformations, let alone understand them.

The first example is a comparison between alternate versions of the design for the "Universel," the Sufi temple in the dunes just South of the Dutch coastal town of Katwijk (Roose 2012a). Mentioned as an idea already in 1911, completed only in 1970, and still subjected to iconographical revisions in the following decades, it supposedly followed the precise architectural instructions of Inayat Khan (1882–1927), the renowned Chishti sage who left India with his brothers for the West in 1910. Based on a veneration of the Taj Mahal, he had verbally given some ideal temple descriptions that incorporated the Chishti notion of sacred tombs, or *dargah*s, being cosmic representations of their buried saints. The latter had reattained the Adamic or paradisiacal state of unity with god called Universal Man, and they were, in Sufi discourses, frequently pictured as sitting in meditation posture in front of their *dargah*s. Immediately after Inayat's departure for India and his untimely death there during a tomb pilgrimage in 1927, his highest initiates in the Netherlands, who were Theosophists steeped in messianic expectations of a World Teacher, steered his Taj Mahal descriptions towards a fourfold meditating Buddha. It had Inayat's bodily proportions and all sorts of religious symbols, figures, and colors, and it was to be built on the field just opposite his house in Paris where he had led a first stone ceremony himself. His brothers, however, despising the Theosophical hybridizations of what they interpreted as the essentially Islamic message of Chishti Sufism, claimed natural successorship instead and steered Inayat's descriptions back towards the mausoleal imagery of a *dargah* with a cubic substructure, an onion dome, and a paradisiacal garden around the relics of their brother. Since, in the years after the war, they blocked all of their opponents' attempts to build a meditating Buddha on the terrain in Paris, the field would eventually be lost to a public housing project. Meanwhile, they had started planning a *dargah* in the dunes of Katwijk, next to the valley where their brother was thought to have had a soul-shifting transcendental experience. It consisted of the simple cube-and-dome scheme and incorporated a number of sarcophagi for the brothers who had already died.

Inayat's son, however, had also started to claim successorship to the caliphate and as such had gained the support of the erstwhile Theosophists still opposing the brothers. He countered any attempts by the latter to remove his father's relics to Katwijk, but was countered himself by his antagonists when he later tried to have the meditating Buddha built in Paris after all, on a nearby plot. Subsequently, he versed himself in India in the Muslim Chishti fundaments of Inayatian Sufism, and started claiming legitimate leadership also from a perspective of authentic Chishti traditions. Then, after a permit was given for the construction of the sanctuary in

Katwijk, the last of the brothers died. Responding to a growing undertow of anti-Islamic feelings among their constituency, the highest leaders denied Inayat's son's Chishti claims and appointed the son of Inayat's second son, both of whom had been hosted and taught by the erstwhile Theosophists. The new patron moved the organization away from any Islamic origins back towards a message full of symbology, astrology, and numerology. Even in mid-construction, he did everything he could to change the design back from a simple *dargah* scheme to a meditating figuration, shifting the idea of the sacred garden to a mandala of paths and terraces, and removing the sarcophagi from the plans. Confronted with an already finished permit procedure, however, as for forms he managed only to remove some minor mausoleum characteristics from the design and to slightly change the dome shape towards something more like a human head. After completion, the light, mausoleum coloration of the exterior was substituted by the different shades of yellow as prescribed by the erstwhile Theosophists, and anything hinting of Islam was firmly denied. The peculiar, compromised dome shape came to be poetically explained as a heart opening itself up towards heaven, and a pedestal inside the building originally meant for the sarcophagi came to be functionally interpreted as a facility for altar stowage and winter services.

The second example is a comparison between the recently completed Taibah Mosque and Essalam Mosque, respectively in Amsterdam and Rotterdam (Roose 2012b). Both of their patrons had used the venerated Mosque of the Prophet in Medina, itself a complex accretion of building elements commissioned by a long range of competing claimants of Islamic leadership. In Amsterdam, the Surinamese South Asian patron positioned himself under the Islamic authority of the Barelvi Sufi sheikh Noorani Siddiqui from Pakistan. The latter claimed Caliphal leadership through a series of holy men represented by their tombs, starting with Muhammad himself, and resulting in a fierce theological competition with the puritanical schools, mainly Ahmadi and Wahhabi. The patron selected the substructure from the Taj Mahal, in his eyes the perfect Sufi *dargah*, and combined it with form, coloration, and materialization of the domed mausoleum-cum-minaret over the Prophet's grave in Medina. He maneuvered Muhammad's dome into the center of his new mosque and multiplied his minaret into four new corner turrets. All the while, he explicitly left out most Wahhabi-associated building elements pertaining to the modern Saudi-built complex around the Prophet's tomb from the prototypical depictions that he and other Barelvi patrons would use as an example. That even the dome and minaret of the Prophet would have been built a long time after his demise, by Mamluk usurpers, was not an issue: they merely provoked the right connotations. Then, the patron took some crucial notions from Barelvi theology and worked these into an ever more creative iconography. Windows in both the dome drum and the outer walls were shaped in the form of the silhouette of the Prophet's dome, symbolizing the *Nur* ("light") of Muhammad falling into the mosque. He also requested sun shades over the outer windows, to be modeled on the metal grille in the doors to the Prophet's grave. He attached a gilded sculpture of these doors next to the *mihrab*. Moreover, the inner dome was provided with a multitude of starry lights meant to represent the Sufi saints, channeling the Light from heaven to earth. To the back of his entrance *Iwan*, he installed marble plates in the shape of those used in the area around the Prophet's shrine, here positioned in grouted layers that were to symbolize the channeling of Gods words, by Gabriel to Muhammad in the form of the Qur'an, from the heavenly to the earthly spheres. Throughout his building, he hung posters of the Prophet's tomb, and a large banner on the mosque's inner balcony imaged venerated Sufi shrines that represented important links in the chain from Muhammad to his beloved Caliph.

In Rotterdam, by contrast, the Moroccan patron positioned himself as a follower of the Islamic Movement headed by Yusuf al-Qaradawi, the Egyptian-born sheikh associated with the

Muslim Brotherhood and propagating a pan-Islamic vision exceedingly popular among young Western Muslims. The latter were advised to return to the essence of Islam by dismissing nationalist theologies as are, for instance, embedded in the neo-Malikite fundaments of Moroccan royalty. They also had to reject the excessively held hatred of innovation by the purists, and the excessively practiced cult of the grave by the Sufis. Thus, the patron selected precisely the modern Saudi-built complex in Medina because it had supposedly incorporated all known Islamic building styles and builders: to him, it had pan-Islamic instead of Wahhabi connotations. Slowly but steadily he steered his mosque plans towards incorporating a multitude of building elements from the Medina complex, using detailed photographs and video stills and self-devised drawings in which he reshuffled, folded, and bracketed the modern Medina elevations around the municipally prescribed volume in Rotterdam. As for the central dome, in order not to provoke associations with the blasphemous cult of the grave, the patron did take the dome of the Prophet for a central roof structure, but transformed it into the non-green and modernized version that he thought abundant in the Middle East. On the inside, he prevented both Moroccan iconography and purist sobriety, instead using examples of a Middle Eastern shopping mall and the interior of the mosque in Dublin where al-Qaradawi's organization resided.

## Conclusion: avoiding pitfalls and self-dug holes in the iconological analysis of religious buildings

Logically, what is crucial in order to understand the iconography of a religious building is not so much to know how people saw and experienced it after its completion, but rather how its particular patron saw and experienced the prototypes that he selected for transformation, before his ideas ever reached the drawing table. Whether he actually visited them or not, they would have held certain connotations for him that were steered by his choices in religious politics. A consequence is that researching the meanings attributed to a religious building by its users and observers does not by definition result in any relevant facts for explaining the object's imagery. This may be hard to accept for those interested in the social life of religious buildings, used as they might be to the idea that a study of the experiences and performances in and of these objects is a *sine qua non* for making the buildings more intelligible to the outside world. From an iconological perspective, it still carries the danger of basing a thick interpretation on a thin description, since one would potentially be describing the architectural habitus of the wrong people, not those who actually made the iconographical choices. Ideally, the two perspectives would be supplemental, as long as the temptation can be withstood to explain the reason behind certain building elements *a priori* from the ways in which they were mentally or physically used after their construction. What is indeed, and by definition, interesting from an iconological perspective is when such a *post factum* attribution of meaning starts playing a role when a new building is being created in the thoughts of a new patron. After all, the meanings of the historical prototypes to the modern patrons treated above had also long superseded any possible original intent. In this way, one takes into account the phenomenon that the expanding landscape of religious buildings continuously gains new layers of meaning and thus new transformations, without losing oneself in the idea that the unlimited number of mosque visitors are all as relevant to the analysis of the Muslim architectural landscape in the modern West as its limited number of actual patrons.

However, in order to come to know how these patrons saw and experienced their selected prototypes, it is not enough to directly ask them. Since scholars and journalists, as much as the general public in the West, would have been irrelevant as a target group of a patron's chosen iconography and the political strategy behind it, the researcher will first have to extract the actual chronology of the design process from the archives of those involved: the patron himself as the initiator and coordinator of the project, the architects he hired and fired in order to turn it into an official drawing, and the municipal bodies that facilitated and restricted his ideal iconography. In fact, within modern Western discourses of minority–majority relations, the axiom that physically diverging religious buildings must manifest some sort of a communal attempt at cultural identification towards their antagonistic social surroundings has become such an accepted "fact" that any Muslim spokesman will readily call his mosque just that, no matter how many publicly unrecognized bells and whistles it carries. Only when the textual and visual depictions of the actual prototypes, collected and fabricated by the patron as examples to be incorporated, have been accessed and recovered, will a meeting be accompanied by a more fruitful and enthusiastic conversation on his particular architectural recombination and religious policy. Each of the cases treated above would have been limited to a narration, be it extensive, of only the most superficial of social, aesthetic, and functional rhetorics if it had not been for the subsequent months of plowing through archival materials, followed by return visits to key informants. Thus, a historical study is still a definite *sine qua non* for the iconological analysis of any religious building, whether age old, shining new, or even only in the planning phase.

Finally, having found out that a patron possibly reshuffled certain aspects from certain prototypical buildings, and that he did so because these selections provoked certain associations in him from a certain politico-religious perspective, perhaps the most demanding step is to accept the counter-intuitive phenomenon that both the prototypes and the end-results were not intended to be recognizable save to a limited group of insiders, leaving not only the surrounding non-Muslims but even the great majority of Muslims in the West largely in the dark. Only after the discovery that strategically selected aspects of the Taj Mahal and the Mosque of the Prophet were involved in the construction of the objects treated above, will the observer be able to, as it were, open his eyes and see these prototypes reappear in the end-results, making them more intelligible and less arbitrary. Similarly, as he was only enabled by relatively recent studies to recognize the earliest mosque architecture in Andalusia as a creative recombination of prototypical building elements for an internal Muslim market, only when his gaze is pointed in the right direction may he be expected to recognize the modern Basharat Mosque near Cordoba, the first purpose-built mosque in Spain after centuries of Christian rule, not as an "Islam Defiant" incarnate, but as a creative recombination of selected building elements from the Noor Mosque and the Minaret of the Messiah in Qadian, North India, completely obscure to critical outsiders but nonetheless of tremendous politico–religious importance to its Qadiani-Ahmadi patrons. Many Qadiani missionaries in Europe and in the non-Western parts of the world had reworked the variation of holy buildings associated with Ahmad, their founder and claimed prophet, into consistent iconographies, both in exemplary photography (retouching a picture of Ahmad's mosque as if it formed one structure with an outlying minaret) and in mosque design itself (see Roose 2009: 39–65, 322–4, and the rich photo gallery on www.alislam.org).

In similar vein, even though the architect Gulzar Haider focused attention on his use of the prayer rug as an inspiration for the Bait ul-Islam Mosque in Toronto, it is again towards its Qadiani patrons that we have to look for an explanation of the conspicuous dome and minaret obviously towering over this then-largest mosque in North America. Over time, a growing number of Ahmadi patrons shifted from merely referring to Qadian, where Ahmad's early construction had already referred to what was then known of the Prophet's mosque, to incorporating features of Medina itself as an even more authentic prototype, following the motto "Mosques will be constructed on the model of the Prophet's Mosque and make every land the land of Hejaz" (Rehmatullah 2001). The model was taken to be the building as it stood before the anti-Ahmadi patrons in Saudi Arabia extended it, with elements from its substructure, its multiple domes, and its variegated turrets visualized both in exemplary photography and, at times combined with the North Indian prototypes, in actual mosque design (Khan 1994). Recently in North America, the prototype has come to be represented, in exemplary Ahmadi photography as well as in mosque architecture, as particularly consisting of the Prophet's dome combined with its Ottoman corner minaret (Khan 2008; www.alislam.org/gallery2/v/mosques/). The latter was perhaps less adjacent to the dome than its Mamluk counterpart, but also less tainted by the inappropriate religious connotations vested in the latter by anti-Ahmadi patrons such as the Barelvi. In Canada, case examples are the Ahmadi mosques in Calgary and Toronto, where we can now better place, both historically and formally, Haider's patrons' ambition to plant "the seeds of a Muslim town in North America on the model of the Prophet's Medina." Coming full circle, even the plan for the Ismaili center in Vancouver, commissioned and co-designed by the Aga Khan, seems not to have escaped the religious politics of Muslim leaders claiming Islamic authority through architectural authenticity, particularly by building New Medinas in the newly established Muslim territories. It shared its most obvious features – especially its monumental portal and its ostentatious lack of a minaret – with the mosque of Mahdiyya, treated by Jonathan Bloom and built by Shi'i ruler al-Mahdi, great antagonist of the early Sunni caliphs and grandest among the Aga Khan's Fatimid predecessors.

A harsh conclusion would be that most of our scholarly knowledge on the formation of Islamic buildings in Europe as well as in North America has thus far been based on projections, constructed both by our sources and by ourselves. A more positive message might be that exploring a more iconological perspective on modern Islamic architecture in the West could open up a whole new, and ever-expanding, field of research for the humanities and social studies.

## Bibliography

Avcioglu, N. (2007) "Identity-as-Form: The Mosque in the West," *Cultural Analysis* 6: 91–112.

Bloom, J. (1989) *Minaret. Symbol of Islam*, Oxford: Oxford University Press.

——(1993) "On the Transmission of Designs in Early Islamic Architecture," *Muqarnas* X: 21–8.

Clark, P. (2001) "Van Fantasie naar Geloof: Islamitische Invloeden op de Openbare Ruimte in Groot Britannië," in Douwes, D. (ed.), *Naar een Europese Islam? Essays*, Amsterdam: Mets & Schilt, pp. 163–86.

Fethi, I. (1985) "The Mosque Today," in Cantacuzino, S. (ed.) *Architecture in Continuity: Building in the Islamic World Today*, New York: Aga Khan Award for Architecture/Aperture, pp. 53–62.

Flood, F.B. (1997) "Umayyad Survivals and Mamluk Revivals: Qalawund Architecture and the Great Mosque of Damascus," *Muqarnas* XIV: 57–79.

Frishman, M. and Khan, H.-U. (eds.) (1994) *The Mosque. History, Architectural Development & Regional Diversity*, London: Thames & Hudson.

Haider, G. (1990) "'Brother in Islam, Please Draw Us a Mosque.' Muslims in the West: A Personal Account," in Powell, R. (ed.) *Expressions of Islam in Buildings*, Singapore: The Aga Khan Award for Architecture, pp. 155–6.

——(1996) "Muslim Space and the Practice of Architecture. A Personal Odyssey," in Metcalf, B.D. (ed.) *Making Muslim Space in North America and Europe*, Berkeley: University of California Press, pp. 31–45.

Holod, R. and Khan, H.-U. (1997) *The Contemporary Mosque: Architects, Clients and Designs since the 1950s*, London: Thames and Hudson.

Jasarevic, A. (2009) "Anders! Das islamische Forum in Penzberg. Meine Erfahrungen als Architekt einer Moschee," in Beinhauer-Köhler, B. and Leggewie, C. (eds.) *Moscheen in Deutschland. Religiöse Heimat und gesellschaftliche Herausforderung*, Munich: Verlag C.H. Beck, pp. 99–111.

Kahera, I. (2000) *Deconstructing the American Mosque: Space, Gender and Aesthetics*, Austin: University of Texas Press.

Khalidi, O. (2000) "Approaches to Mosque Design in North America," in Haddad, Y.Y. and Esposito, J.L. (eds.) *Muslims on the Americanization Path?*, New York: Oxford University Press, pp. 317–34.

Khan, A.M. (ed.) (1994) *Mosques around the World: A Pictorial Presentation*, Ahmadiyya Muslim Association USA.

——(2008) *Mosques Around the World: A Pictorial Presentation*, Ahmadiyya Muslim Association USA,.

Kraft, S. (2002) *Islamische Sakralarchitektur in Deutschland. Eine Untersuchung ausgewählter Moschee-Neubauten*, Munster: Lit.

Krautheimer, R. (1942a) "Introduction to an 'Iconography of Mediaeval Architecture'," *Journal of the Warburg and Courtauld Institutes* 5: 1–33.

——(1942b) "The Carolingian Revival of Early Christian Architecture," *The Art Bulletin* (March): 1–38.

Limon, I.D. (2000) *Islamische Kultstätten des 20. Jahrhunderts im europäischen Raum*, dissertation, Kaiserslautern.

Rabbat, N. (2004) "Islamic Architecture as a Field of Historical Enquiry," *Architectural Design* 74(6): 18–23.

Rehmatullah, N. (2001) "Building of Mosques Worldwide: An Ahmadiyya Priority," speech delivered at Jalsa Salana USA, June, www.alislam.org/library/articles/new/building-mosques.html.

Roose, E.R. (2009) *The Architectural Representation of Islam: Muslim-Commissioned Mosque Design in the Netherlands*, Amsterdam: Amsterdam University Press.

——(2012a) "Dargah or Buddha? The Politics of Building a Sufi Sanctuary for Hazrat Inayat Khan in the West," *Journal of Sufi Studies* 1(2): 193–223.

——(2012b) "Constructing Authentic Houses of God: Religious Politics and Creative Iconographies in Dutch Mosque Design," *Material Religion* 8(3): 280–307.

Salam, H. (ed.) (1990) *Expressions of Islam in Buildings*, Singapore: Aga Khan Award for Architecture.

Serageldin, I. and Steele, J. (eds.) (1996) *Architecture of the Contemporary Mosque*, London: Academy Editions.

Tabbaa, Y. (2001) *The Transformation of Islamic Art during the Sunni Revival*, Seattle and London: University of Washington Press.

Welzbacher, C. (2008a) *Euro Islam Architecture: New Mosques in the West*, Amsterdam: SUN.

——(2008b) "The Architecture of Euro-Islam," *A10, New European Architecture* 19 (January/February): 58–60.

——(2011) "Nieuwe Moskeeën in Europa. Pleidooi voor een Euro Islam Architectuur," in Kanmaz, M. (ed.) *Nieuwe Moskeeën in Vlaanderen. Tussen Heimwee & Werkelijkheid*, Brussels: MANAvzw, pp. 29–37.

# 19

# Islamic organizations in the West

## New welfare actors in the new welfare systems in Europe

*Elisa Banfi*

## Introduction

In December 2010, the Bishop of the diocese of Milan, Dionigi Tettamanzi, sold his collection of static nativity scenes at auction to increase the resources of the diocesan fund for unemployed workers and poor families. The population hailed this event as a sign of divine providence. Contrary to popular belief, however, the Catholic fund was created in 2009 to combat the effects of the financial crisis and fill the gap created by the inability of public institutions to help the local community. Catholic organizations have also not been alone in the fight to combat the social chaos created by the global crisis. Other, less noticed actors have also organized welfare services to maintain a minimum of social cohesion in this context. For instance, although they haven't made headlines with it, local Islamic organizations have increased their distribution of daily meal vouchers and monthly family allowances, unemployment credits, and child benefits in Milan. Their services have reduced the consequences of economic instability in one of the most precarious social strata within Italian society: immigrants. Both Catholic and Islamic organizations have provided welfare services, offering real "safety valves" for immigrants, who have limited access to institutional social services.

Furthermore, Milan is not an isolated case. Beyond the Alps, other forms of Islamic welfare agencies have been developed in recent decades. For instance, in Geneva, the imam of the Bosnian community has become a source of help for Bosnian refugees over the years. Doctors, teachers, and psychologists have regularly relied on the imam's spiritual gifts in seeking to treat their Bosnian patients and students better. In addition, many other Islamic organizations have structured social activities other than religious services in an attempt to address the tragic aftermath of the war in former Yugoslavia or to ease the psychological and social burden of the emigration process.

These anecdotes briefly illustrate a new social reality that has arisen in European countries over the last two decades: increasingly, Islamic public actors have developed a relevant welfare strategy that is similar to the Catholic/Protestant one. However, this Islamic social agency is absolutely unprecedented for the simple reason that Islam is still largely an immigrant religion in

Europe. Whereas Catholic and Protestant welfare activities are the core of a historical legacy that stems from the church–state relationship, Islamic welfare initiatives are barely recognized by public authorities and seldom studied by scholars. In fact, Islamic welfare agency is commonly studied in ancient (Rijpma 2011; Arjomand 1998) and contemporary Islamic societies (Bozzo and Luizard 2011; Schultz Hafid 2010; Benthall and Bellion-Jourdan 2008; Ibrahim 2008; Clark 2004; Shatzmiller 2001), but not yet in European ones (Bäckström and Davie 2010; Bommes and Geddes 2000).

This chapter aims to describe welfare programs organized by Islamic organizations in European countries. I also simultaneously investigate three causal factors that promote such programs in Islamic organizations: (1) the migratory nature of the Islamic religious presence, (2) transnational influences, and (3) the church–state relationships across Western European countries.

First, the fact that the majority of Islamic believers are still residents (Bommes and Geddes 2000; Faist and Dörr 1997) in the studied countries has affected the welfare activity of Islamic organizations in manifold ways. As migratory regimes differ in European countries and the majority of Muslims are still immigrants, access to social welfare also varies across national contexts.

However, independently of the model of citizenship adopted, labor immigrants and their families who enter a country with a short-term permit have a limited legal position. Along with asylum seekers, refugees, and undocumented immigrants, they are prohibited from accessing many social services or benefits. In fact, neither countries that adopt the multicultural and republican model of citizenship nor countries that employ the ethno-assimilationist model grant full social benefits to labor immigrants and their families. The status of such immigrants in Western European countries is still deeply influenced by the *Gastarbeiter* model. Immigrants have to come to work, and they can stay only if they produce some added value in terms of labor productivity. Otherwise, they have to leave the country. Even though there are Muslims in Europe who are full citizens, especially in multicultural countries, the majority of Islamic immigrants continue to have a legal status that has reduced or delayed their access to social welfare systems.

In this way, Islamic organizations have had a relevant role in the lives of their members, who have scarcely benefited from public social services such as housing, unemployment benefits, and general social care. The quality and the quantity of the social services provided by Islamic organizations depend on the legal status of their members (citizens, residents, undocumented immigrants). In fact, migratory regimes create the potential for social agency for Islamic organizations, though the degree of potential varies from nation to nation. The Islamic associations that were established in the 1960s and 1970s provide religious services to the very highly educated immigrants who immigrated to Europe as students or diplomats. In the 1980s and especially in the 1990s, the same associations served a large number of labor immigrants who arrived to perform unskilled labor. For that reason, Islamic associations have reoriented their activities by restructuring their relationships with their host countries and their homeland.

At the same time, a new typology of Islamic associations began during the 1990s to provide welfare services to Islamic labor immigrants, asylum seekers, refugees, and undocumented immigrants who needed to establish themselves during that time. The emergence of the Muslim second and third generations in Europe, along with converts and Muslim European citizens, stimulated the rise of these new associations. Such organizations provide welfare services in cooperation with local associations and institutions, sometimes not only for Islamic members but also for the local poor regardless of their religious faith. They provide food for disadvantaged families and individuals, homework clubs for children, and education programs, crèches, and women's educational support centers, all intended to improve social cohesion at the local level. Overall, migratory regimes can impact the foundation and the development of Islamic associations, which offer social services to their believers based on how migratory regimes manage material and immaterial immigrant needs.

The second explanatory factor is the transnational influence of homeland Islamic reference groups, which can also influence the welfare programs of Islamic organizations in European countries. Transnational organizations such as Millî Görüş, the Nur movement, or the Muslim Brotherhood can influence economically and ontologically how different Islamic organizations implement welfare services in cities across Europe. Even though the majority of Islamic organizations are founded mainly to fulfill the spiritual demands of Muslim immigrants in Europe, they often develop parallel socio-economic activities. Furthermore, many Islamic organizations are affiliated with Islamic movements that consider welfare programs a substantial part of their religious strategy. In recent decades, many organizations have increased in strength and transformed their objectives through welfare services provided in the context of diasporas.

Last but not least, the separation of church and state is the third factor that affects how Islamic organizations produce welfare services. The quantity and quality of the welfare services provided by Islamic organizations can be influenced by the role of religious communities in the public sphere in each national context. The degree of cooperation among public institutions and religious actors in providing social services to the resident population impacts how the Islamic organizations design their welfare programs in the public space. A weak separation between governmental and religious authorities can help Islamic organizations to participate in the development of public policies as well as to provide welfare services. Islamic organizations can more easily provide welfare services in societies in which religious organizations act alongside public institutions implementing social policies. The church–state relationship partially explains the redistribution of welfare programs across various actors in state and civil society at different levels of governance. This paper focuses on these three explanatory factors in describing why the social activities of Islamic organizations vary within neighboring countries and revealing how they even adjust themselves to the local features of urban communities.

## Restructuring of public services by religious welfare actors

For centuries, each country has offered a specific welfare system (Arts and Gelissen 2002; Esping-Andersen 1990) by adopting different criteria for subsidies and redistribution as part of its national social policies (Korpi and Palme 1998; Bonoli 1997; Ferrera 1996; Leibfried 1993). Each national welfare system develops options and constraints for associations that wish to provide social services. Social policies can encourage particular sub-national cultures by helping certain associations (immigrant, religious, autochthonous, profit, or non-profit organizations) to act as agents of the welfare state (Ireland 2004). On the one hand, immigrant and/or religious associations can increase their legitimacy among members by playing relevant roles in the redistribution of welfare resources. On the other hand, public institutions can control divisions within civil society and reframe communitarian identities.

Social policies also promote various models of stratification and redistribution in civil society. Not only may social policies target subgroups within the population, but particular institutions can also aim to assist special subcategories within targeted subgroups (e.g. women, elderly individuals, young people, immigrants, nationals). However, institutions can also deprive subgroups within the population of social rights. If the welfare system distributes resources non-homogeneously, forms of "ghettoization" may destroy social cohesion. For instance, a welfare state that provides asymmetrical services to non-nationals and nationals allows these two groups to profit differently from state social benefits.

If the homogeneous redistribution of social services is intended to provide social cohesion, non-homogeneous or limited redistribution can foster decentralized and communitarian welfare systems that generate social cohesion from below. For instance, immigrants often ask for housing, schooling, and health assistance outside the institutional market for welfare provision. They are partially excluded from social citizenship by institutional policies. Consequently, they address their welfare requests to pro-minority, anti-racist, non-profit, religious, and immigrant associations.

Among these actors, religious actors are relevant because since the medieval period (Rijpma 2011; Henderson 2006) they have been invested in social welfare. In fact, religion is an important explanatory factor in the variance within the welfare state regimes in Western European countries. Recently, scholars have challenged the most traditional theory (Esping-Andersen and Van Kersbergen 1992), according to which only working-class and socialist organizations have paved the way for social democratization. The recent book *Religion, Class Coalitions and Welfare States* has accurately reviewed the corpus of theories on the contributions of religion within Western European welfare states (Van Kersbergen and Manow 2009). Van Kersbergen and Manow have showed the incompleteness of theories that represent the welfare state exclusively as an historical response to the capitalist forces that make societies disintegrate (Flora 1986) and commodify (Polanyi 1944). On the contrary, these authors have emphasized the complex and indirect role of the Christian religion in originating and fashioning the welfare states in Western European countries. They have also suggested that the church–state conflicts stemming from European national revolutions have greatly influenced the differences across the Western European welfare states (Van Kersbergen and Manow 2009).

The recent debate on the historical role of the religions in Europe in providing welfare has arisen as Christian organizations are entering a new period of social engagement in many Western countries. As social services are privatized and decentralized, the involvement of churches and other religious groups in the provision of welfare services is increasing. Moreover, the shrinking of social policies is helping to valorize religious "non-profit" organizations that provide services to citizens. However, there are still not many studies on how new residents of various religions are turning to religious organizations for welfare activities in Western societies (Beaumont and Cloke 2012). In fact, new religious actors such as Islamic organizations are facing dramatic changes within European welfare systems. Religious associations voluntarily promote social policies thanks to different forms of privatization. Their "special" workforce is becoming attractive to public institutions that have been forced by national deficits to cut social expenditure. In this way, the "subsidiarity and complementarity" of non-state actors providing social services has become the core of the new welfare programs (Powell 2007; Dahlberg 2006, 2005). Thus, public institutions are allowing religious organizations to reacquire their medieval function in financing, organizing, and providing social services.

Due to immigration, new religious organizations emerged in Europe after World War II, which has modified the religious panorama in many Western countries. As an "immigrant religion," Islam shares much of the Christian theology and social doctrine, which supports the engagement of religious organizations in social activities that benefit disadvantaged people. Equality and social justice are the core of Muhammad's revelation, and both concepts are integrated into the *arkan al-islam* through the principle of the *zakat* (Ybarra 1996). Moreover, Islam emphasizes welfare as necessary to establish an effective Islamic society (Hawting 2006). In fact, the social project of the Prophet was to redistribute and manage wealth to create cohesion within Islamic society. The redistribution of wealth is especially focused on *al-Masakin*, *al-Fuqara'*, and *al-Gharimin*, categories that are outside of the labor market, which the *zakat* enables to survive without public institutions. For centuries, redistribution through the *zakat* has provided the Islamic community with a pragmatic means of realizing the Islamic ideal of a fair society, just as Christian organizations have done in Europe.

In Europe, the *zakat* endows Islamic organizations with constant incomes that allow them to implement social services among their members, who are very often residents. In fact, European Muslims are mostly still immigrants with short- or long-term permits and limited access to welfare state services. The conflicting status of immigrants who are workers but residents creates a gap between them and other citizens in terms of access to social, political, and civil rights. In Europe, the emergence of new welfare systems is intertwined with the arrival of workers from all over the world. As in the past in Europe, the relationship between immigration and new care services appears noteworthy. As Bäckström and Davie outline,

> the transformations taking place at the start of the new millennium can be seen in some senses to mirror those that occurred some hundred years or so ago – above all in the movement of people. As industrial societies gathered pace, large sections of the European population moved rapidly from the countryside to the cities. Given the extent of these dislocations, it was hardly surprising that traditional forms of social care – those that depended on the household and the churches – no longer functioned effectively. Here, in fact, was the stimulus for new forms of social support.
>
> *(Bäckström and Davie 2010: 2)*

At the beginning of industrialization, migration and urbanization meant that religious forms of care disintegrated and fostered national, secular welfare systems. Conversely, at the beginning of this century, forms of decentralization and privatization within public social services fostered newfound involvement in welfare provision by religious agencies. In fact, the globalization of labor and recent migratory patterns have created new opportunities for capitalist forces to reorganize social services for workers or non-workers and for citizens or residents by involving religious social agencies. However, Islamic religious identity is barely associated in the public sphere with welfare services. On the contrary, Muslims are seen as "foreigners" who lack the cultural legitimacy to participate in social policies in European societies. This chapter would like to fill this gap in the available information about the Islamic contribution to welfare systems in several European countries.

## The Islamic welfare state in Europe

There are very few comparative research studies that involved data collection related to Islamic welfare agencies. For instance, the project Finding a Place for Islam in Europe: Cultural Inter-actions between Muslim Immigrants and Receiving Societies (EURISLAM),[1] funded by the Seventh Framework Programme of the European Commission, paved the way for further researchers by collecting data about the social, religious, and cultural activities of Islamic organizations in Belgium, France, Germany, the Netherlands, Switzerland, and the United Kingdom. The Institut de recherches sociales et politiques (RESOP),[2] a multidisciplinary research center within the Faculty of Economics and Social Sciences at the University of Geneva in Switzerland, has collected additional data about the welfare activities of Islamic organizations in Italy and Switzerland, especially in Geneva, Milan, Rome, and Zurich. Extending the work of these projects, in this section I analyze the cross-national variance in social engagement within different Western countries using case studies.

## Islamic welfare in London

In 2006, the Masjid and Community Affairs Committee of the Muslim Council of Britain commissioned the report *Voices from the Minarets*, which presents the results of surveys and focus groups with ninety imams who are members of the Management Committee (MC) of Mosques of the United Kingdom. The report collects quantitative and qualitative data, revealing the most typical services offered by mosques in the United Kingdom. These are counseling and family support services, supplementary education courses, and youth facilities and programs. Some mosques also provide training and development courses, adult language classes, employment services, and health and community cohesion projects. The report attests to the relevance of the welfare services offered to Muslims and non-Muslims by mosques in the United Kingdom. It shows how mosque environments can provide services to portions of the population that are difficult to reach and improve cohesion in challenging areas of cities (Maussen 2005; Lindo 1999; Joly 1995). However, the report admits that there are few mosque structures that are adequate spaces for organizing social services for women, young people, and non-Muslims and that the good examples should be imitated. The report concludes that mosques should interact more with public institutions to improve cooperation in social policies. Clearly, the Islamic associations have developed their welfare agencies differently in the public sphere in the United Kingdom. However, they have increasing visibility as agents of social cohesion, and local authorities recognize the role of such institutions by financing their services. In London, several mosques show how this partnership with public authorities can impact the functional role of religious centers. Since the 1980s, public institutions have financed the Islamic community in London to promote a large array of social policies. One relevant case is that of the North London Muslim Community Centre (NLMCC),[3] established in 1980 in Hackney. At first, this organization was financed by the Department of the Environment and Hackney Council to run youth activities. Since it was founded, the NLMCC has consistently supported projects for non-Muslim users, offering an advice center, a youth club, and a mental health project. The Department of Education funds the organization's online center, which provides free internet access and training courses. In 1999 the Department of Education refurbished the organization's original building. The advice center is one of the most popular services at the NLMCC. This program provides advice and counseling on welfare benefits, assisting users in making claims for housing benefit, council tax benefit, jobseeker's allowance, income support, employment allowance, pension credit, child benefit, working and child tax credits, social fund grants and loans. It also advises residents on general housing register applications. The advice center also provides translation and interpretation services. The Office of the Immigration Services Commissioner (OISC) has authorized the NLMCC to provide immigration advice and services through the general immigration and nationality advice program. Since 1980, the NLMCC has been providing youth and children with facilities within Hackney, one of the poorest boroughs of London. The NLMCC runs the mental health care project to help Muslims and non-Muslims who suffer from mental health problems. The center also has a mental health liaison officer who helps families to complete carer's allowance forms, visits disabled and mentally ill clients in their homes, and helps them to submit benefit applications. In addition, the Ihsan Children's Centre supports mothers and children and promotes good health for poor and vulnerable families. At the center, children and mothers can meet regularly with professionals and obtain access to health care. The center also offers pre-school respite care to foster independence and education for mothers, and is financed by the government as a part of the Sure Start initiative. Since 1984, elderly individuals have been able to participate in the old age pensioners' luncheon club in the mosques, where they can eat healthy meals and meet with professionals to discuss any health and psychological issues.

Another similar example is the East London Mosque and London Muslim Centre (ELMLMC), which is located in the London Borough of Tower Hamlets. The center implements education, health, and environmental projects with Tower Hamlets Council, the local primary care trust, the East London Communities Organisation, the Tower Hamlets Interfaith Forum, and the Metropolitan Police. The center fights anti-social behavior and drug use by providing mentoring and educational courses. The childcare services are connected with programs that promote women's participation in the cultural and social life of London. The East London Mosque also offers programs that inform Muslims and non-Muslims about different health problems and improve their access to the health services available across the territories.

The ELMLMC and the NLMCC in London show how Islamic associations and public institutions can interact to improve social policies for the most disadvantaged among the population. However, these cases show how the government interacts with and finances Islamic mosques only at the local level and in targeted "trouble spots" where the government has trouble meeting the needs of the population. On the one hand, Islamic welfare agencies are conceived of as a special local resource by public institutions. On the other hand, they are seen as occasional agencies, and the Islamic associations have had to make efforts to improve their recognition and financing in the public sphere. Public and Islamic actors have developed partnerships in providing welfare services based on short-term trends and without systematic planning. In fact, UK Islamic welfare programs are consistent with the liberal polity type described by Koenig (2005). For this author, the UK model of religious integration within the public sphere encourages a plurality of religious orientations and associated charity organizations. According to Koenig, the UK institutional structures offer the opportunity for Islamic organizations to implement religious public programs in a decentralized manner by negotiating with civil society actors at the local level.

## Islamic street welfare in France

Unlike the UK, the French state has adopted a centralized republican model that does not integrate and recognize particular religious identities in the public sphere (Koenig 2005). Consequently, French institutions do not seek out interaction with religious organizations in providing welfare services and shaping social policies. An analysis of Islamic charity in France reveals a high degree of centralization and homogeneity in the assistance provided to targeted groups that are completely isolated from state institutions.

The most important Islamic charity organizations were founded to obtain financial resources in France to implement humanitarian activities at the international level. At the national level, these activities began with the distribution of meals during Islamic festivals in the 1980s and 1990s. Especially during the last decade, French Islamic charity organizations have centralized and reorganized specific national services for the homeless and poor people, especially through meal distribution. The arrival of a large number of Islamic immigrants, refugees, asylum seekers, and undocumented individuals from Iraq, Afghanistan, Tunisia, and Libya in 2011 forced the associations to reorient their resources toward more local programs. Furthermore, the global crisis has reduced quality of life for a portion of the French population. Consequently, the Islamic charity associations also extend their services to the non-Muslim sector of society. One example of this recent trend is provided by the Islamic organization Au Coeur de la précarité (ACDLP),[4] which was founded in 2009 and has 300 volunteers who find homeless and poor people on the street and provide hot meals and psychological support. The organization also provides meals during the month of Ramadan for the homeless. These services are provided to all people independent of their religion; however, the majority of the people helped are

Muslims, immigrants, or illegal residents. The ACDLP also cooperates with the Hotel Social de Villepinte in visiting and assisting the families of refugees, offering after-school courses and food for refugee families. The organization is also engaged in cleaning activities across the most difficult neighborhoods of Paris.

Unlike the ACDLP, the Secours islamique France (SIF)[5] was founded in 1991 and was engaged mainly in humanitarian activities outside of Europe. At the beginning meal distribution for refugees and immigrants inside France was a marginal activity for this organization. However, during the last decade the association has increased its distribution of food parcels and hygiene kits among the homeless and refugees in collaboration with institutions and civil actors such as the association Restos du coeur.[6] The organization has developed a project named EPISOL in Paris that provides a network of grocery stores that provide food to low-income individuals and micro-credit offices. Since 2009, the SIF has also provided night and day residences for the homeless in the winter. At first, the association organized the distribution of meals as a seasonal activity that was not conceived of as complementary to state activities. However, during the last five years the association has transformed its offerings into regular services in cooperation with the public authorities. The SIF increasingly helps disadvantaged people to use the state health and social services in cooperation with Catholic associations. Also, the association Une Chorba pour tous,[7] which was founded in 1992, aims to improve access to public services for the most disadvantaged portion of the Parisian population. At first, the organization provided meals during Ramadan. Since 2006 it has offered daily food packages and hot meals. In addition, more recently it has organized a legal service that explains to residents and citizens how to obtain housing and social benefits from public institutions. Since 2008 it has organized regular school support courses, professional training programs, and literacy courses.

Based on the above examples, it is evident that in the last decade French associations have increased their cooperation with other civil society actors and public institutions. However, the republican model of excluding religious organizations from the public sphere still influences the patterns of the French Islamic welfare agencies. Islamic charity organizations are not integrated into the public framework for social policy. These organizations target the most excluded residents, those who are not entitled to the social rights of citizens or residents. In summary, the increase in the number of Islamic welfare agencies in France is more closely related to the worsening of conditions for urban residents than to new patterns of interaction between religious organizations and public institutions or to new subsidy programs.

## Turkish Islamic welfare programs in Germany and the Netherlands

The Islamic welfare agencies in Germany and the Netherlands provide a useful example of how transnational and national factors jointly impact the incorporation of Islamic associations into European countries. In Germany and the Netherlands, several Turkish Islamic movements include social activities as part of their religious strategy.

However, the prevailing models of citizenship and migratory regimes in the two countries impact the recognition of Islamic organizations and the social needs of immigrants differently. Consequently, the welfare services offered by Turkish Islamic organizations can vary according to the institutional environment. On the one hand, the Netherlands proposes a multicultural model of citizenship that is associated with the pillar system (Lijphart 1968). On the other hand, according to the German corporatist model only institutionalized religions can be a part of the public sphere (Koenig 2005). Furthermore, in Germany the *ius sanguinis* model of citizenship has only recently been modified. In the 1980s and 1990s, guest workers were excluded from the national welfare system via a nationality law based on an ethnic assimilationist model (Bommes and Geddes 2000). Bommes considers German Islamic organizations to have facilitated access to social resources for excluded individuals at the transnational and local levels:

> In the highly regulated German society, with its high levels of welfare provision and social services, Islamic associative networking is seen as an attempt to set up welfare services as alternatives to those offered by the German welfare state.
>
> *(Amiraux 2000: 239)*

In Germany, Turkish Islamic organizations compensate for public policy by serving residents and vulnerable citizens. For this reason, the welfare services of Millî Görüş in Germany can be seen as providing a way for the organization to play a public role even when state institutions refuse to recognize that role. In fact, the role of Millî Görüş in providing welfare services and the relevance of the association's welfare agency in Germany are proportional to the conflicting relationship between the organization and public institutions.

Conversely, in the Netherlands several Turkish Islamic movements (including the North Millî Görüş Federation) structure social activities in such a way that they are complementary to (rather than parallel to) institutional policies. For instance, Diyanet in Rotterdam owns seven mosques, only one of which is exclusively religious; the others are mainly engaged in social activism (Canatan et al. 2003). The social mosques target young people by developing after-school courses, organizing sports activities, and providing scholarships for students. On the other hand, the Gülen movement provides an array of educational services that help to improve the socio-economic integration of Turkish immigrants. In the Netherlands the Gülen movement has ten student dormitories that are a part of the National Organization of Boarding Schools (Yukleyen 2012: 214). The dormitories are part of a larger strategy that is intended to motivate second- and third-generation immigrants to achieve higher levels of education. Different research attests to the positive influence of these dormitories on student performance. For that reason, the Ministry of Education, Culture, and Science and the Rotterdam Municipality have financed some of these dormitories and their activities, as in the case of Het Centrum in Rotterdam (Yukleyen 2012: 215)

In both countries, the Islamic organizations develop similar social activities but integrate them into a different framework of state–religion interactions. In the Netherlands, the state recognizes multicultural contributions in the public sphere and encourages Islamic organizations to cooperate with public institutions in projects that foster social cohesion. In Germany, the religious welfare activities targeting residents increase the strength and the authority of Islamic organizations in proposing an alternative to state-run public services. Furthermore, in the case of Millî Görüş, the welfare agency plays a role in advocating for the recognition of religious minorities in the public sphere. The Dutch and German cases suggest that the recognition of a religious group and the national citizenship model interact in shaping the role and function of the Islamic welfare agency in European states.

## Islamic cantonal welfare in Switzerland

In Switzerland, the variety of cantons has produced twenty-six different types of integrative policy (Cattacin and Bülent 2001) and twenty-six types of relationship between secular and spiritual authorities (Marti et al. 2010). The federal constitution does not recognize any religion as the national religion. Article 72, paragraph 1 Cst. states that the relationship between religion and the state must be managed at the cantonal level.

The federal system encourages Islamic organizations to structure their social activities inside cantonal borders. Thus, the social needs of their members are connected with the model of citizenship proposed by the canton of residence. At the same time, their social programs depend on how cantonal institutions recognize the social functions of religious associations. For instance, the features of Islamic welfare agencies vary in Geneva and Zurich, two cantons that have opposing models of citizenship and separation of church and state.

In Switzerland, the first Islamic organizations were founded in the 1960s and 1970s. However, during the past two decades they have diversified their activities to cope with demographic changes in the Muslim population in Switzerland. Since the 1980s, the variety of nationalities among labor immigrants practicing Islam has greatly increased. Furthermore, family reunification among immigrants from outside Europe has enlarged the number of female members of Islamic associations. Consequently, in the last decade Islamic organizations have multiplied their social activities for young people and female members. Many cantonal networks of Islamic organizations offer social activities, including after-school courses, language courses (French and German), sports activities, economic support for members in difficult economic situations, social chaplains in hospitals, cultural mediation, and services for refugees and asylum seekers.

However, cantonal institutional structures influence the strength and the features of the social agency among Islamic associations. For instance, the canton of Geneva does not finance religious organizations based on their religious identity. However, the cantonal institutions offer economic opportunities to associations that promote civic and secular values. These policies encourage religious associations to interact with other local non-religious actors to attain recognition and visibility in the public sphere.

In Geneva, the Islamic associations founded in the 1960s and 1970s have increased their contact with non-Islamic associations to achieve common social projects. Women and youth activists play a substantial role in providing the resources necessary to implement social projects by reframing religious identity. For instance, the Islamic Center of Geneva (ICG) is one of the oldest Islamic centers in Europe. It was founded in 1961 by Said Ramadan to support Islamic intellectuals in diasporas. Recently, the ICG has increased its activities and relationships with local secular associations to support labor immigrants spiritually and materially. The ICG currently provides services to the most vulnerable immigrants in Geneva with the cooperation of local institutions such as social services and the police force. On the other side of the city, Saudi Arabia created the Islamic Cultural Foundation in 1978. This multi-service center organizes a wide range of activities. Its 1,500-person capacity makes the mosque a resource for Muslims in the city.

In both centers, many volunteers work to meet the various needs of refugees and immigrants. Furthermore, women and young people organize the most innovative activities, improving the relationship between these two centers and other civil society actors in Geneva. In addition, a new type of Islamic organization has recently emerged in the canton. The Islamic Cultural Association in Meyrin, founded in 2007, and the Association nouvel horizon, founded in 2006, focus on encouraging active citizenship among their members. Both associations have prominent female and second-generation leaders, which has improved the organizations' local strategy for interacting with other institutions and local actors. These organizations offer relevant social services such as crèches and after-school courses for Muslim and non-Muslim populations. Islamic associations of this new type, however, do not yet exist in Zurich, where the state finances the role of the churches in society and where the logic of integration is more ethno-assimilationist than in Geneva.

In Zurich, mainly mono-national (Pakistani, Albanian, Turkish, and Maghrebian) Islamic organizations offer social activities as part of their religious identity rather than because of a desire to emphasize civic engagement. The Gülen movement has encouraged school support for non-Muslim and Muslim students, especially by motivating second-generation students to continue their education. Since 1963, the Ahmadis have organized environmental activities (e.g. cleaning public parks, ecological learning) and activities that support the elderly Muslim and non-Muslim populations. The center Dzemat der islamischen Gemeinschaften Bosnians, founded in 1982, became a resource for the Bosnian community by developing social activities for children, women, and the elderly. The Albanian Muslim communities centralize their religious, social, and cultural lives around the Albanisch-islamische Gemeinschaft. This center helps families to use cultural mediation to enable successful integration by the second generation. Similar services were implemented in 2002 by the Stiftung der islamischen Jugend and in 2001 by Al Hidaya Verein, an association whose main focus is Maghrebian Muslims.

The comparison between forms of Islamic welfare in Zurich and Geneva shows how cantonal autonomy can influence Islamic welfare agencies. Cantonal institutions indirectly affect Islamic social actors by positioning differently welfare services, the separation of church and state, and immigration.

## Italy: the organizing process for Islamic immigrants

In Italy, Islamic welfare agencies have stimulated the process of self-organization among immigrants. Scholars agree that in Italy immigrants have founded associations that have helped them to survive and overcome the lack of social resources that they have faced in settling there (Mantovan 2007; Sciortino 2003). Islamic associations have improved the legal and administrative status of immigrants by asserting the right of all immigrants to housing, as well as their human rights. Islam as a supranational ideology has played a relevant role in improving immigrant self-organization. Many Islamic religious associations, such as Mouride associations, the Union of Islamic Italian Communities and Organizations (UCOII), and the Muslim Students' Union, have played a leading role in unifying several immigrant associations throughout the country. Islamic associations provide housing services, meals, and legal support for immigrants. At the same time, they also create the organizational structures for asserting the social rights of residents and illegal immigrants and for mobilizing people in the name of this cause. The most relevant example is the direct mobilization of immigrants in the late 1980s, which included squatters' movements and demonstrations for housing rights (in Rome, Milan, and Bologna). One of the first multinational organizations was created at that time. Called the United Asia Workers Association (UAWA), this organization brought together Pakistani, Bengali, and other Asian workers (Knights and King 1998). Among the UAWA leaders were many members of the Bengali associations that had founded and financed Islamic centers in Rome in the previous decade. Especially in the Pigneto, one of the poorest municipal districts in Rome, mosques founded by Bengali leaders became multi-service centers for Islamic immigrants. During the 1990s, Italian Islamic associations developed the ability to defend Islamic interests in the larger context of legal claims. Islamic immigrants have increasingly made contact with different autochthonous actors with whom they have shared several social struggles. For instance, in 1999 the Islamic centers of Turin organized a demonstration against a rule banning the wearing of headscarves in residence permit photographs. However, the demonstration eventually also addressed the social, civil, and political rights of immigrants.[8] In his speech, the imam Buriqi Boucha addressed citizenship rights, the issue of residence permit renewals for labor immigrants, and that of residence permits for illegal immigrants (Griseri 1999). Similarly, in the national immigrant demonstration in Brescia in June 2000, the Islamic contribution was crucial because many immigrant workers who requested the "regularization" of their immigration status were active in Islamic Senegalese organizations. In Bovezzo, in particular, the speeches of the *marabuts* across Mouride religious circles were instrumental in the protest (Tedeschi and Penocchio 2000).

In recent decades the Islamic associations have become more integrated within the network of local organizations such as Caritas and Catholic charity associations. These associations emphasize anti-racism and projects intended to promote integration and social cohesion. For instance, the mosque al-Huda in Centocelle jointly runs a food distribution project with local municipal institutions and Catholic associations in Rome. In Milan, the Casa della cultura islamica received a municipal official reward for social engagement in 2009. The Islamic center provides notable economic support to unemployed families; it also distributes daily meal vouchers and hot meals. In the first decade of the century, Islamic organizations became steadily aware of their political and social importance, such that in 2011 the imam of one of the oldest Islamic centers in Milan became the first immigrant candidate for municipal election.[9]

## A glance at the United States: American Islamic social programs

I will conclude this chapter by describing the recent engagement with social justice of American Muslims in the United States as the most innovative example of an Islamic articulation of the civilizing process (Salvatore 2011). American Islamic social programs in the United States are a result of structured and qualified cooperation with public institutions in the welfare field. In some ways, the US case study foreshadows future social programs by European Islamic associations.

The consequences of 9/11 reshaped Islamic welfare in the United States by producing a successful experience of cooperation between state institutions and Islamic organizations to implement a variety of public welfare programs.

At the national level, the participation of ICNA Relief in the federal program Disaster Response through Disaster Recovery[10] clearly illustrates the emergence of a new type of interaction between domestic Islamic organizations and federal, state, and local levels of government. ICNA Relief is a non-profit organization that is a branch of the Islamic Circle of North America (ICNA), a large umbrella organization of Islamic organizations in the United States. It was founded in 1993 (Curtis 2010: 289). In the aftermath of 9/11, the most relevant Islamic relief organizations in the United States, such as the Holy Land Foundation and the Global Relief Foundation, were prevented from continuing their international charity activities by the US Treasury Department (GhaneaBassiri 2010: 351).[11] These measures have led Islamic associations such as ICNA Relief to conduct their charity activities in the United States rather than at the international level. In 2005, ICNA Relief joined the American Muslim Taskforce for Disaster Relief to assist victims of hurricanes. This organization cooperates with public institutions and other volunteer organizations, such as long-term recovery committees, that assist with disasters. In fact, ICNA Relief is currently engaged in providing legal and financial assistance and information about services and benefits for the victims of Hurricane Sandy. ICNA Relief also runs health clinics for disadvantaged people, such as the Shifa Clinic.[12] Moreover, it provides telephone and online counseling for domestic violence and suicide prevention. ICNA Relief's women's shelter[13] and hunger prevention[14] programs target the entire population by systematically cooperating with local public institutions and other religious associations. At the national level, the Islamic Society of North America (ISNA), which is considered one of the largest Islamic umbrella organizations in the United States, has improved its public image by developing social programs in the United States (Curtis 2010: 298). Since the late 1990s, ISNA has created two departments for social services and community development to prevent domestic violence and to provide refugee resettlement and youth services. The consequences of

9/11 have led ISNA to increasingly focus attention on local communities and the social problems of American Muslims. This strategy has contributed to renewing organizational structures and expanding the influence of ISNA across the United States.

As international donors have decreased financing to Islamic organizations because of the fear of allegations of terrorism, Islamic organizations have increasingly based their activities on Muslim American donors. The lack of international financing has restructured the activities of the oldest Islamic organizations while paving the way for new welfare projects and new organizations that are rooted in local networks of civil society actors. The Inner-City Muslim Action Network (IMAN) is a relevant example of how "the Islamic perspective provides insights into the interplay between civilizing processes and the modes through which cultural traditions innervate a modern public sphere" (Salvatore 2011: 55). The association was founded in 1995 to connect associations and residents who were engaged in improving social cohesion in the Chicago area.[15] Afro-American Muslims and second-generation Muslims continue to be the main components of this multipurpose organization. IMAN began organizing social services by addressing various disadvantaged populations (Abdo 2006). To achieve social change, IMAN provides primary health care and support to uninsured populations on Chicago's southwest side. Its health clinic manages health emergencies as well as chronic diseases and conducts prevention activities.

IMAN uses the various migratory backgrounds of its members, especially Muslim Latinos, to promote civil rights for undocumented residents of Chicago. For instance, IMAN participated in the UCCRO[16] Arizona Human Rights Solidarity Ride to fight SB1070, a racial profiling law, in Arizona. By supporting similar initiatives across Christian and Muslim communities, IMAN aims to increase "opportunities to create broad alliances with other marginalized communities that can advance the rights of all."[17]

The association has conducted campaigns to promote voting, to oppose drugs, gangs and violence, and to support a state law to increase the number of fresh food supermarkets in poor communities.

In response to the SMART Act,[18] IMAN created drug schools as an alternative to imprisonment for drug offenders and supported job training for drug offenders that involved renovating houses in disadvantaged areas of Chicago.

INCA Relief, INSA, and IMAN develop social programs that are typical examples of the new welfare engagement of American Muslims. In a period of economic, climatic, and social crisis, institutions and civil society recognize American Muslim organizations as relevant public actors who are improving the common good across the nation.

## Conclusion

In this chapter, I analyzed several case studies of Islamic welfare programs in different European countries and in the United States. Three explanatory factors (transnational influences, church–state cleavages, and models of citizenship) interact and impact social Islamic activities differently across countries. In France and the United Kingdom, Islamic welfare programs and the relationship between Islamic organizations and public institutions are mainly influenced by the model of citizenship and migratory regimes. In Germany and the Netherlands I focused on transnational influences and migratory regimes, while in Italy and Switzerland I focused on church–state cleavages and migratory regimes. All these case studies show the emergence of the Islamic welfare presence in the public sphere across Western European countries and empirically confirm recent innovative theories.

In fact, scholars have reframed established theories on civil society by explaining the conceptual interaction between Islam and the public sphere (Salvatore 2007, 2005, 1997). In this way, "Public Islam" becomes a concept which is historically relevant and empirically fruitful. Furthermore, LeVine and Salvatore have reconciled theoretically the two concepts of "civil society and public sphere" with Islamic social agency:

> We argue that the operation performed by socioreligious movements comes close to Gramsci's notion of "good sense" [*buon senso*] as the key to mobilize politically marginalized sectors of society. Such movements thus contribute to the constitution and contestation of norms of public life by providing services to their communities and articulating social justice claims that challenge the discourse of rights that is the daily bread of secular elites. A specific combination of "resistance" and "project" identities deployed by socio-religious movements impinge on the legitimacy of both state and (more recently) NGO elites, and through them, on the allocation of resources for development, welfare and education. This process unfolds through the creation of historically novel lines of solidarity that, without being utopianly "horizontal," challenge state-centric, vertically defined, disciplinary discourses of the social.
>
> *(LeVine and Salvatore 2010: 66)*

As a result of this approach, the Islamic category of the common good (*maslaha*) has regained its relevance for the sociological and historical understanding of the Islamic presence in Europe and in Western societies in general. To conclude, in recent decades Islamic welfare programs in Europe and in the United States have indicated that Muslim communities are significantly influencing their non-Muslim surroundings by reframing concepts of social cohesion and religious social responsibility in the public sphere.

## Notes

1 www.eurislam.eu/page=site.home (accessed September 29, 2012).
2 www.unige.ch/ses/resop/index.html (accessed September 29, 2012).
3 www.nlmcc.org.uk/ (accessed September 29, 2012).
4 www.aucoeurdelaprecarite.com/ (accessed September 29, 2012).
5 www.secours-islamique.org/france.html (accessed September 29, 2012).
6 www.restosducoeur.org/content/pr%C3%A9sentation (accessed September 29, 2012).
7 chorbapourtous.wordpress.com/ (accessed September 29, 2012).
8 ricerca.repubblica.it/repubblica/archivio/repubblica/1999/10/31/la-marcia-dell-islam-torino.html.
9 www.ilfattoquotidiano.it/2011/03/02/milano-lista-multietnica-per-le-comunalishaari-la-prima-novita-da ventanni/94599/ (accessed November 15, 2012).
10 icnarelief.org/site2/ (accessed November 14, 2012).
11 The US Treasury Department charged some of these associations with terrorism. However, only the founders of the Holy Land Foundation were convicted in court by a controversial sentence.
12 shifa101.com/site/ (accessed November 15, 2012).
13 Its women's shelter program offers temporary housing for homeless women and increases their social capital by supporting them with financial and legal aid to help them reintegrate into working life.
14 The hunger prevention program targets poor families to support their basic food needs.
15 www.imancentral.org/ (accessed November 14, 2012).
16 United Congress of Community and Religious Organizations.
17 www.imancentral.org/take-action/past-actions/on-the-road-to-arizona/ (accessed November 14, 2012).
18 A bill that proposed alternative "drug schools" for non-violent drug offenders.

## Bibliography

Abdo, G. (2006) *Mecca and Main Street: Muslim Life in America after 9/11*, New York: Oxford University Press.

Elisa Banfi

Amiraux, V. (2000) "Unexpected Biographies: Deconstructing the National Welfare State," in Bommes, M. and Geddes, A. (eds.) Immigration and Welfare: Challenging the Borders of the Welfare State, London: Routledge.

Arjomand, S.A. (1998) "Philanthropy, the Law and Public Policy in the Islamic World before the Modern Era," in Ilchman, W.F., Katz, S.N., and Queen, E.L. II (eds.) Philanthropy in the World's Traditions, Bloomington: Indiana University Press.

Arts, W. and Gelissen, J. (2002) "Three Worlds of Welfare Capitalism or More? A State-of-the-Art Report," Journal of European Social Policy 12(2): 137–58.

Bäckström, A. and Davie, G. (eds.) (2010) Welfare and Religion in a European Perspective. Vol. 1: Configuring the Connections, Farnham: Ashgate.

Bäckström, A., Davie, G., and Edgardh, N. (2010) Welfare and Religion in 21st Century Europe: Configuring the Connections, Farnham: Ashgate.

Beaumont, J. and Cloke, P. (eds.) (2012) Faith-based Organizations and Exclusion in European Cities, Bristol: The Policy Press.

Benthall, J. and Bellion-Jourdan J. (2008) The Charitable Crescent: Politics of Aid in the Muslim World, London: I.B. Tauris.

Bommes, M. and Geddes, A. (eds.) (2000) Immigration and Welfare: Challenging the Borders of the Welfare State, London: Routledge.

Bonoli, G. (1997) "Classifying Welfare States: A Two-Dimension Approach," Journal of Social Policy 26(3): 351–72.

Bozzo, A. and Luizard, P.J. (eds.) (2011) Les Sociétés civiles dans le monde musulman, Paris: La Découverte.

Canatan, K., Oudijk, C.H., and Ljamai, A. (2003) De maatschappelijke rol van Rotterdamse moskeeën, Rotterdam: Centrum voor Onderzoek en Statistiek.

Cattacin, S. and Bülent, K. (2001) "Die Politik der Integration von Migrantinnen und Migranten im föderalistischen System der Schweiz," in Akgün, L. and Thränhardt, D. (eds.) Integrationspolitik in föderalistischen Systemen. Jahrbuch Migration – Yearbook Migration 2000/2001, Munster: Lit.

Clark, J.A. (2004) Islam, Charity, and Activism: Middle-class Networks and Social Welfare in Egypt, Jordan, and Yemen, Bloomington: Indiana University Press.

Curtis, E.E. (2010) Encyclopedia of Muslim-American History, New York: Facts On File.

Dahlberg, L. (2005) "Interaction between Voluntary and Statutory Social Service Provision in Sweden: A Matter of Welfare Pluralism, Substitution or Complementarity?," Social Policy and Administration 39(7): 740–63.

——(2006) "The Complementarity Norm: Service Provision by the Welfare State and Voluntary Organisations in Sweden," Health & Social Care in the Community 14(4): 302–10.

Esping-Andersen, G. (1990) The Three Worlds of Welfare Capitalism, Princeton: Princeton University Press.

Esping-Andersen, G. and Van Kersbergen, K. (1992) "Contemporary Research on Social Democracy," Annual Review of Sociology 18(1): 187–208.

Faist, T. and Dörr, S. (1997) "Institutional Conditions for the Integration of Immigrants in Welfare States: A Comparison of Germany, France, Great Britain, and the Netherlands," European Journal of Political Research 31: 401–26.

Ferrera, M. (1996) "The 'Southern Model' of Welfare in Social Europe," Journal of European Social Policy 6(1): 17–37.

Flora, P. (1986) Growth to Limits: The Western European Welfare States since World War II, Berlin and New York: Walter de Gruyter.

GhaneaBassiri, K. (2010) A History of Islam in America: From the New World to the New World Order, New York: Cambridge University Press.

Griseri, P. (1999) "I musulmani manifestano a Torino contro la questura. E non solo," Il manifesto, October 30.

Hawting, G. (ed.) (2006) The Development of Islamic Ritual, Aldershot: Ashgate.

Henderson, J. (2006) The Renaissance Hospital: Healing the Body and Healing the Soul, New Haven, CT: Yale University Press.

Ibrahim, B. (2008) "Arab Philanthropy in Transition," in Ibrahim, B. and Sherif, D. (eds.) From Charity to Social Change: Trends in Arab Philanthropy, Cairo: American University Cairo Press.

Ireland, P.R. (2004) Becoming Europe: Immigration, Integration, and the Welfare State, Pittsburgh: University of Pittsburgh Press.

Joly, D. (1995) Britannia's Crescent: Making a Place for Muslims in British Society, Aldershot: Avebury.

Knights, M. and King, R. (1998) "The Geography of Bangladeshi Migration to Rome," International Journal of Population Geography 4(4): 299–321.

Koenig, M. (2005) "Incorporating Muslim Migrants in Western Nation States: A Comparison of the United Kingdom, France, and Germany," *Journal of International Migration and Integration* 6(2): 219–34.

Korpi, W. and Palme, J. (1998) "The Paradox of Redistribution and Strategies of Equality: Welfare State Institutions, Inequality, and Poverty in the Western Countries," *American Sociological Review* 63(5): 661–87.

Leibfried, S. (1993) "Towards a European Welfare State? On Integrating Poverty Regimes in the European Community," in Jones, C. (ed.) *New Perspectives on the Welfare State in Europe*, London and New York: Routledge.

LeVine, M. and Salvatore, A. (2010) "Religious Mobilization and the Public Sphere: Reflections on Alternative Genealogies," in Shami, S. (ed.) *Publics, Politics and Participation: Locating the Public Sphere in the Middle East and North Africa*, New York: Columbia University Press/Social Science Research Council.

Lijphart, A. (1968) *The Politics of Accommodation: Pluralism and Democracy in the Netherlands*, Berkeley: University of California Press.

Lindo, F. (1999) *Heilige wijsheid in Amsterdam. Ayasofia stadsdeel De Baarsjes en de strijd om het Riva terrein*, Amsterdam: Het Spinhuis.

Manço, U. and Kanmaz, M. (2005) "From Conflict to Co-operation between Muslims and Local Authorities in a Brussels Borough: Schaerbeek," *Journal of Ethnic and Migration Studies* 31(6): 1105–23.

Mantovan, C. (2007) *Immigrazione e cittadinanza. Auto-organizzazione e partecipazione dei migranti in Italia*, Milan: Franco Angeli.

Marti, M., Kraft, M.E., and Walter, F. (2010) *Prestation, utilité et financement de communautés religieuses en Suisse*, Glaris: Rüegger.

Maussen, M. (2005) *Making Muslim Presence Meaningful: Studies on Islam and Mosques in Western Europe*, Amsterdam School for Social Science Research Working Papers series, file.setav.org/Files/Pdf/making-muslim-presence-meaningful-assr-2005.pdf.

Polanyi, K. (1944) *The Great Transformation: The Political and Economic Origins of Our Time*, New York: Farrar and Rinehart.

Powell, M. (ed.) (2007) *Understanding the Mixed Economy of Welfare*, Bristol: Policy Press.

Rijpma, A. (2011) "Estimating and Explaining Public Service Provision by Religious Organisations in the Late-Medieval Low Countries," paper presented at the Sixth Low Countries Conference, Antwerp.

Salvatore, A. (1997) *Islam and the Political Discourse of Modernity*, Reading: Ithaca Press.

——(2005) *Religion, Social Practice, and Contested Hegemonies: Reconstructing the Public Sphere in Muslim Majority Societies*, New York: Palgrave Macmillan.

——(2007) *The Public Sphere: Liberal Modernity, Catholicism, Islam*, New York: Palgrave Macmillan.

——(2011) "Eccentric Modernity? An Islamic Perspective on the Civilizing Process and the Public Sphere," *European Journal of Social Theory* 14(1): 55–69.

Schultz Hafid, M. (2010) *Emerging Trends in Social Justice Philanthropy in Egypt*, Working Paper 4, Cairo: The John D. Gerhart Center for Philanthropy & Civic Engagement.

Sciortino, R. (2003) "L'organizzazione del proletariato immigrato, in Italia," in Basso, P. and Perocco. F. (eds.) *Gli immigrati in Europa*, Milan: Franco Angeli.

Shafiur, R., Syed Tohel, A., and Shaynul, K. (2006) *Voices from the Minarets: MCB Study of UK Imams and Mosques*, London: The Muslim Council of Britain/C3ube Training and Consultancy.

Shatzmiller, M. (2001) "Islamic Institutions and Property Rights: The Case of the 'Public Good' Waqf," *Journal of the Economic and Social History of the Orient* 44(1): 44–74.

Tedeschi, M. and Penocchio, C. (2000) *I due viaggi. Storia della lotta degli immigrati bresciani*, Brescia: CGIL-Camera del Lavoro di Brescia-Grafo.

Van Kersbergen, K. and Manow, P. (eds.) (2009) *Religion, Class Coalitions, and Welfare States*, Cambridge: Cambridge University Press.

Ybarra, J.A. (1996) "The Zaqat in Muslim Society: An Analysis of Islamic Economic Policy," *Social Science Information* 35(4): 643–56.

Yukleyen, A. (2012) *Localizing Islam in Europe: Turkish Islamic Communities in Germany and the Netherlands*, New York: Syracuse University Press.

# 20

# Islam in the arts in the USA

*Sylvia Chan-Malik*

## Introduction

In his oft-cited definition of "culture" published in *Keywords*, Raymond Williams tracks the term's genealogy from the early fifteenth century onward, identifying that "culture in all its early uses was a noun of process" (Williams 1985: 87). Used to describe "the tending of something, basically crops or animals," culture's usage was eventually extended to apply to processes of human development, and by the mid-nineteenth century had begun to express its current multivalent connotations, often used in relationship with notions of civility and civilization, folk-life, and artistic work (Williams 1985). Writing in 1976, Williams explored how the word had come to be used in almost entirely metaphorical – as opposed to physical – senses. specifically as: (1) a noun describing a process of intellectual, spiritual, and aesthetic development (e.g. to become "cultured" or "enculturated"); (2) a noun indicating a particular way of life (e.g. Chinese culture, Victorian culture, New York culture); and (3) a noun denoting the "works and practices of intellectual and especially, artistic activity" (i.e. music, literature, painting and sculpture, theater and film). These varied usages of the word made culture, Williams wrote, "one of the two or three most complicated words in the English language" (Williams 1985: 87).

These multiple meanings of culture are central to this essay's focus on Islam in the arts in the United States. More precisely, I do not want simply to catalog instances of artistic creation emanating from Muslim communities and/or Islam's impact in the United States here. Rather, I seek to explore the complex "cultures" facilitated by Islam's presence in the USA, both in how Islam and Muslims have informed broader constructions of American culture, and in how Muslims themselves have worked to express their Islamic identities through artistic expressions. As per Williams's definition, critical here is the notion of *process*, specifically in thinking through how the emergence of something named "Muslim American culture" (following Williams's third definition as the works and practices of artistic activity) in the post-9/11 era has been shaped and informed by the ways in which Islam has been "enculturated" in the USA. By enculturation, I mean the ways in which Islam both as an *idea* (e.g. through cultural representations and discourses) and as a *material presence* (e.g. Muslim individuals, communities, and institutions) within the USA has found expression in American artistic milieus by Muslims and non-Muslims. Through the interactions between how Islam has been *imagined* and *lived*, I argue, emerges the process by which Islam in the arts – and Muslim American culture itself – has developed, and continues to develop, within the United States.

In order to discuss this process, this essay moves chronologically, first functioning as a brief and selective historical archive which tracks different configurations and formations of "Muslim" or "Islamic" artistic expressions in the USA from the 1600s through the late-twentieth century. As with Islam itself, these expressions are rooted in black American communities and the black experience in the USA, in which the most significant and most well-documented instances of Muslim and Islamic artistic expressions have been, and in many instances, I suggest, continue to be, found. Blackness and the creativity and labor of black people, this first section will demonstrate, are foundational to understanding Islam's cultural expressions in the USA as well as the ways Islam has been constructed in the nation's cultural imaginary. This historical centrality of blackness becomes the backdrop and central context for the second, and more extended, section of the piece (pp. 327–32), in which I move to a discussion of "Muslim American" culture, a signifier which has gained momentum in the years since 9/11. As Muslim American artists, writers, musicians, and performers gain visibility in the public sphere, the media and scholars have often characterized their emergence as a "post-9/11" phenomenon. Again returning to the notion of process, I suggest a longer historical trajectory, arguing that while 9/11 certainly spurred interest in Islam and Muslims in the USA, contemporary Muslim American cultural expressions are in fact an outgrowth of the work of black American Muslim artists and writers during the 1960s and 1970s, the contributions of immigrants from the Middle East and South Asia from the mid-1960s onward, and developing interest toward "multicultural" arts and literature in the 1980s and 1990s. Taken together, these phenomena form the backdrop for artistic expressions by Muslim American writers, musicians, actors, visual artists, and others which are rapidly gaining visibility in the post-9/11 USA. Throughout my examination and engagement with these works, I pay close attention to how issues of race, religion, and gender have figured heavily into how Islam is perceived in the USA, and how these perceptions have shaped the emergence of Muslim voices in various historical periods. In the end, I revisit how Williams's notions of process and the multiple meanings of culture are critical to understanding the continually developing discourse around Islam's presence and influence in the arts in the USA.

Before I begin, a note on terminology. I utilize the terms "Muslim," "Islamic," and "Muslim American" throughout this essay. The first two terms, "Muslim" and "Islamic," are often (mis) used interchangeably in popular and scholarly discourse. Herein, "Muslim" is used as a noun to describe individuals who identify themselves as a follower of the religion of Islam, or those who view themselves as culturally connected to a Muslim identity, whether through family, nation of origin, etc. "Muslim" is also used as an adjective referring to groups of people who identify as Muslims (e.g. the Muslim community, Muslim women, etc.). "Islamic," on the other hand, is an adjective used to denote phenomena guided or influenced by Islam's teachings and principles (e.g. Islamic art, Islamic education). Thus, I explore both "Muslim" and "Islamic" artistic expressions here, works created by individuals who self-identify as Muslim, as well as work that expresses Islamic principles. However, as I also discuss how Islam and Muslims are portrayed in mainstream American culture, I may at times cite authors and works who use the terms in different, and non-corresponding, ways, which I hope does not cause confusion. Finally, I utilize the term "Muslim American" to signify cultural and literary works created by Muslims in the USA, as well as the communities they serve, a designation directly born from a confluence out of multicultural discourse in the USA since the formal civil rights era and the political exigencies of the post-9/11 period.[1] My aim is to reveal the necessity of examining contemporary artistic expressions of Muslim Americans through a trajectory that long precedes the events of September 11, 2001, and contextualizes these works in light of historical legacies of race, gender, and religion in the USA.

## From the blues to Black Power

Islam has exerted significant influence upon the USA from the earliest days of the nation's origins. Even Christopher Columbus's "discovery" of America was shaped by Islam's influence in Spain: Columbus and his benefactress Queen Isabella were indirectly motivated to seek power due to their violent opposition to Islamic – or "Moorish" – influence in their native land. The first significant presence of Islamic practices and Muslims themselves in the USA, however, occurred with the arrival of slaves from West Africa, a presence which various historians and ethnomusicologists have argued birthed the beginnings of what is known as the first organic American art form: the blues. Of the blues' origins, Amiri Baraka writes:

> it is impossible to say exactly how old blues is – certainly no older than the presence of Negroes in the United States. It is a native American music, the product of the black man in this country; or to put it more exactly the way I have come to think about it, blues could not exist if African captives had not become American captives.
>
> *(Baraka 1999: 17)*

As Baraka infers, the blues were the cultural byproduct of the transatlantic slave trade in the USA. Though the genre did not rise to popular prominence until the early twentieth century (through artists such as W.C. Handy, Leadbelly, and Robert Johnson), the blues were undeniably rooted in the Southern plantation, its direct predecessors the work songs and field hollers sung by slaves to help them endure backbreaking labor and relentless dehumanization.

However, while the blues were born on the plantation, the music's origins lay in West Africa, where upwards of 30 percent of slaves were born. Historian Sylviane Diouf estimates that, of the roughly 400,000 African captives who were first transported to the USA, many were Sunni Muslims who came from an area known as the Sahel, a vast area in Africa "stretching from Senegal in the West to Sudan in the east" (Diouf 2009). This region, known as Senegambia, was fundamentally shaped by the contact between its natives and the Arab-Berber Islamic world since the eighth century. Islamic influences infused the local culture, in particular the region's music. Subsequently, West Africans deported through the trans-Saharan trade brought their music and rhythms (including those that had already been changed by the Arab-Islamic contact) north to the Maghreb. As Diouf writes, "There was much cross-fertilization on both sides of the desert and it is this complex heritage that West African Muslim captives brought to the United States where it found a fertile ground" (Diouf 2009). Unlike non-Muslim slave groups from coastal West Africa and Central Africa, who relied heavily on drumming and chants for their musical expression, slaves from Senegambia stood a much better chance of preserving their musical culture due to the region's traditional emphasis on string and wind instruments. Due to Southern plantation owners' fear of slave revolt and uprising, drumming and group chants were outlawed, while Sahelian slaves were able to adapt their skills to local instruments such as the fiddle or guitar, later even producing the banjo as an American incarnation of their traditional lute. As a result of the seemingly less threatening nature of their style, they were allowed to perform their music, sometimes even at slaveholder's balls, which allowed for the music's migration across the Deep South, including Mississippi, the birthplace of the blues.

Islam would resurface in the USA in the early twentieth century, as black Southern migrants flooded to Northern industrial centers such as Chicago, Detroit, New York, Philadelphia, etc. during the post-Reconstruction era. Seeking work and new opportunities, many came in contact with burgeoning discourses of Pan-Africanism, guided by the philosophies of early black nationalist thinkers such as Edward Wilmot Blyden and Marcus Garvey, who expressed a deep respect and admiration for the teachings of Islam. Pan-Africanist thought fueled interest in Islam, spurring the widespread appeal of early twentieth-century Islamic organizations such as the Moorish Science Temple (MST), the Ahmadiyyat Movement in Islam (AMI), and, most famously, the Nation of Islam (NOI). Both Pan-Africanism and Islamic organizations such as these called for the redefinition of black cultural and political identities in ways which rejected the racist and oppressive ideologies of the plantation and the Christian church. Characterized by a spirit of internationalism, a refusal of white supremacy, and acknowledgment of the creativity of black urban cultures, such Pan-Africanist and Islamically oriented ideologies were instrumental in the development of a black cultural renaissance across the North, exemplified by the Harlem Renaissance in the 1920s and 1930s. From the 1930s to the 1950s, when the genre reigned as the nation's most popular musical form, numerous prominent black jazz musicians converted to Islam, including pianist Ahmad Jamal, saxophonist Yusef Lateef, drummer Art Blakey (Abdullah Ibn Buhaina), pianist McCoy Tyner (Sulieman Saud), vocalist Dakota Staton (Aliyah Rabia), bassist Ahmed Abdul-Malik (best known for his work with Thelonious Monk), and many others.

Almost all entered the religion through the AMI, a group Richard Brent Turner has called "unquestionably one of the most significant movements in the history of Islam in the United States in the twentieth century, providing ... the *first multi-racial model* for American Islam" (Turner 1997: 110, emphasis in original). Founded by Hazrat Mirza Ghulam Ahmad (1835?–1908), a native of Qadian, Punjab, who claimed to be the Promised Messiah of Islam, the AMI was a South Asia-based missionary movement which appealed to black Americans due to its racially inclusive doctrines, ambitious internationalist scope, and notion of continuous prophecy. To these musicians, Ahmadiyya Islam was "a force which directly opposed the deterioration of the mind and body through either spiritual or physical deterrents" (Turner 1997: 139), a respite from racism, nights in smoke-filled clubs, and the perils of drugs and alcohol. At the same time, as trumpeter Dizzy Gillespie noted in his autobiography, many musicians converted to Islam merely to escape blackness; as one musician says: "Man, if you join the Muslim faith, you ain't colored no more, you'll be white. You get a new name and you won't be a nigger no more" (Gillespie 2009: 291). Thus, conversion to Islam was a "tonic" as well, providing jazz musicians spiritual protection from the harmful trappings of their profession, alongside a political safeguard from white supremacy, an identity which at times allowed them to transcend their parochial identities as "blacks" and embrace a global community of Muslims. Giving their songs titles like "Prayer to the East," "Eastern Sounds," and "Abdullah's Delight," African American Muslim musicians combined Islamic themes and messages of black protest in their recordings, while donning Islamic *kufis* and *thobes*, and incorporating Asian and Middle Eastern musical sounds and elements in their work.[2]

Yet in the blues and jazz, "Islam" had heretofore yet to be advanced within US cultural production as an *explicit* symbol of racial resistance, a positioning which would fundamentally change during the course of the politically turbulent 1960s. As film historian Donald Bogle writes, "In 1960, Negroes were quietly asking for their rights. By 1969, blacks were demanding them" (Bogle 2001: 195). Islam functioned as a major factor in this cultural and political shift, as the black militancy of the Nation of Islam captivated black America, while inspiring fear and loathing in white Americans. During this time, a distinctly Muslim American voice emerged in the literary realm, first through the publication of Alex Haley's *The Autobiography of Malcolm X* in 1965, and later through the poets, writers, and playwrights of the Black Arts Movement. Whereas the Islamic influences on the works of Muslim American blues and jazz artists were subtle, indicating their Muslim identities without actively promoting any sort of Islamic ideology or practice, the Islam of these literary expressions was bold and uncompromising, asserting the religion as integral to a black American cultural identity, which lay at the heart of the era's revolutionary zeitgeist.

*The Autobiography of Malcolm X*, written with the assistance of Alex Haley, was originally published in November 1965, and in the years since has become "the most popular autobiography of an African American in print," selling millions of copies in paperback in the USA alone (Doherty 2000: 29). At once "a political tract, a religious conversion narrative, and an underground commentary on twentieth-century American culture" (Rashid 1993: 61), the text is not only part of the American literary canon, but has become an iconographic fixture in American popular culture, in particular following director Spike Lee's film adaptation of the text in 1992. While speculation around its authorship and accuracy continues, the text is still widely viewed in the popular and US political imaginaries simultaneously as a black nationalist screed, decrying the evils of white supremacy and giving voice to the racial ideologies of the Nation of Islam (of which Malcolm was a member from 1952 to 1963), *and* as a tale of racial universalist triumph, due to Malcolm's renunciation of the NOI's racial ideologies following his pilgrimage to Mecca in 1964. Neither of these readings captures the full complexity of X's narrative, mainly due to their lack of attention to how his story reflects an African American Muslim – and thus a distinctly Muslim American – history and legacy. Beginning with Malcolm's father's participation in Marcus Garvey's Pan-Africanist Universal Negro Improvement Association (UNIA) during his childhood in Nebraska, through his move to the Northern urban industrial centers of Detroit, Philadelphia, and New York, to his membership in the Nation of Islam and subsequent conversion to the teachings of Sunni Islam, the *Autobiography* is, beyond a personal narrative, a concise mapping of Islam's historical lineage in the twentieth-century USA. The early politics of black nationalism, the racial-religious doctrines of the NOI, the move towards Sunnism, and, finally, to X's distinctly Muslim American ideological positioning through his simultaneous and passionate commitments to a black nationalist politics and an ideology of Islamic universalism at the end of his life – these components reflect the trajectory of Islam's cultural presence in America, and reveal the interplay between race and religion in this formation.

This discursive intertwining of Islam's cultural significance with the struggles for racial justice of the 1960s and 1970s was further solidified through an engagement with the poets and writers of the Black Arts Movement, founded directly following Malcolm's X's assassination on February 21, 1965. During that time, poet and writer Amiri Baraka (author of *Blues People*, 1999) established Harlem's Black Arts Repertory Theatre/School, amongst heated debates by African American intellectuals and activists concerning the split between Malcolm and the Nation of Islam, and the most viable way forward for the black revolutionary struggle. Within the Black Arts "renaissance," Islam was portrayed as a staunchly black religion, its adaptation and inclusion in the realm of black cultural struggle viewed as a means of rejecting the white man's god. Merging with popular discourses of Afrocentrism, the religion became part of a critical vocabulary of black resistance, in which cultural and political struggle were considered one and the same. Baraka himself converted to Sunni Islam in 1968 (though he later renounced the faith in 1974, citing an ideological shift to the Marxism/Leninism). Islam, Baraka would say at one point, was a holistic spiritual framework through which black people could reclaim their true connections to the Divine, and art was vehicle to achieve this contact. "As you begin to beat your way back through the symbols, getting close to what the source of Black art was," Baraka stated in a 1968 interview, "you begin to see that it comes out of Islam" (Baraka 1994: 54).

In the Black Arts Movement and beyond, however, the voices of Muslim American expression were overwhelming male. Writing of Marvin X, a central poet in the Black Arts Movement, writer Mohja Kahf characterizes X and his peers (including Baraka) as "sexist as all get out, in the way that is common for men of (their) generation and his radicalism" (Kahf 2010). Indeed, the history of Muslim American culture and literature till this point was undeniably dominated by men, and in many cases rooted in patriarchal conceptions of gender and sexuality. It is important to note, however, that this is not due to the inactivity of Muslim women in the USA in the realms of cultural and literary production, but most likely the result of what Ula Taylor has called the "crisis of archival recognition" for African American women, in which black women's stories and voices are historically devalued, and thus, she writes (citing Cheryl Harris), "overlooked, misheard, misinterpreted, misrepresented, and ultimately misappropriated" (Taylor 2008: 188). Indeed, the deeply masculinist character of the Nation of Islam and the politics of black nationalism functioned to sequester and silence the voices of black women, whom Elijah Muhammad saw as "the field to produce [the black] nation," and thus instructed black men to "control and protect … his crop" (Muhammad 1965: 58). In regards to the recounting of Muslim American women's cultural and literary histories, it is arguable that such a devaluation of women has been further compounded by debates amongst scholars of Islam concerning women's performance and artistic expression. To cite Sarah Weiss writing in regards to Muslim women and musical performance, the cultural expressions of Muslim women tend to be associated with a "relaxing of morals … when women are involved in performance, it is common to assume that they themselves are not pious" (Weiss 2007: 88). Thus, in conjunction with the ideologies of black nationalism, such an association between art and immorality served to put Muslim American women "in their place" in the home, as mothers, and as supporters of men, who were to remain cloistered, closeted, and out of the public eye.

Despite this, within the context of the Black Arts Movement, black feminist poet and writer Sonia Sanchez, who joined the Nation of Islam in 1972, created work which illuminated the intersections between black nationalism, Islam, and black, Third World, and Islamic feminist ideologies. In her poetry, Sanchez stressed the importance of black women being committed to the advancement of a strong and unified black revolutionary struggle, and, like Baraka and Marvin X, viewed Islam as a spiritual and political framework through which to engage the struggle; in other words, Sanchez's desire for black mobilization and empowerment led her to adopt Islam's religious teachings. While she ultimately left the NOI in 1975 to embrace a Pan-Africanist feminist philosophy, she wrote prolifically during her years in the organization, creating prose and poetry that placed Muslim women at the center of black revolutionary struggles, as well as in the presence of the Divine, a juxtaposition clearly revealed in a poem from the 1974 volume *A Blues Book for Black Magical Women* (1973).

## After 1965: immigration, diaspora, polyculturalism

At the moment in which such distinctive Muslim American voices, rooted in the black experience and political protest, were emerging in the 1960s, large-scale shifts in immigration policy were also taking place, namely due to the passage of the 1965 Hart–Cellar Immigration and Nationality Act, which lifted quota restrictions previously placed upon many Asian and Arab countries. As a result of Hart–Cellar, the nation witnessed a dramatic increase in the number of South Asians and Arabs living and working in the USA, a change which irrevocably changed the composition of Muslim America, and thus dramatically altered the trajectory of Muslim American identity, community, and cultural formation. Other factors also contributed to this shift from the mid-1960s through the 1970s, including (but not limited to) political turbulence in West Asia and North Africa; the steady waning of black nationalist and revolutionary political movements; the death of Elijah Muhammad in 1975 and the transition of the NOI's leadership to his son, Warith Deen Muhammad. Yet it was the aforementioned ever-growing numbers of South Asian and Arab Muslim immigrants, many of whom brought their own practices and interpretations of Islam, and eventually started their own mosques and organizations, that shifted broader understandings of Islam away from its presence in black communities. By the 1980s, the national conversation around "Islam" and "Muslims" had become almost entirely disassociated from issues of anti-racism and black political protest and was, instead, conflated with notions of Orientalized foreign threat, a development exacerbated by the 1979 Iranian hostage crisis and changing US relations with the Middle East. During these decades, certain tensions came to develop between black American and immigrant Muslims, as black Americans felt increasingly ostracized and ignored by their immigrant counterparts in the very mosques and organizations they had themselves built, as well as feeling that immigrant Muslims viewed black American practices and understandings of Islam as less authentic. Yet, as immigrants from the Islamic diaspora increasingly arrived, they also engaged, shared, and built community with black American Muslims, engendering distinctly polycultural manifestations of Islamic practice and artistic expression.

Of course, Muslims from South and West Asia had been present in the USA long before 1965.[3] However, in the realm of cultural and literary production it was not until the 1980s and 1990s – a period often called the "culture wars" in the USA, and in which "multiculturalism" emerged as a dominant rubric for understanding American identity – that writers emerging out of South Asian, West Asian, and North African Islamic diasporic traditions began to make their presence more strongly known in American literary and cultural fields. In the 1980s and 1990s, writers such as the Kashmiri American Agha Shahid Ali and Palestinian American Naomi Shihab Nye produced work infused with Islamic sensibilities that resonated forcefully within the multicultural rhetoric of those decades, while former Beat poet and white American convert to Islam Daniel Abd al-Hayy Moore drew upon his engagement with Islam's mystical Sufi tradition and his extensive travels through North Africa to produce works such as *The Ramadan Sonnets* and *Mecca–Medina Timewarp*, both published in the 1990s. It was also during this time that thirteenth-century Muslim poet and Sufi mystic Rumi became the most widely read poet in the USA, as a result of the release of translations of his writing by American poet and writer Coleman Barks. Indeed, this turn towards the "mystical" in Islam had begun in the mid- to late 1970s, as well-known rock bands such as the Doors and the Grateful Dead drew upon Islamic musical traditions and spiritual teachings in the realm of psychedelic rock, the latter releasing an album entitled *Blues for Allah* in 1975.

However, it was the rollback of civil rights gains during Ronald Reagan's presidency in the 1980s that ushered in a resurgence of black nationalist ideologies via the realm of hip hop. Rappers such as Chuck D of Public Enemy, Paris, Nas, and others touted their affiliations with black Muslim leaders such as Louis Farrakhan and expressed their respect for the teachings of Islam, while the release of Spike Lee's 1992 film biography of Malcolm X rendered the Muslim American leader a central icon of the hip hop generation. As with Islam's earlier incarnations, the religion's manifestations in the 1980s and 1990s hip-hop culture were rooted in anti-racist ideologies, both political and spiritual, yet many would argue that its portrayals were romanticized and repackaged for mass consumer consumption.

In addition, Islam's main presence in hip hop arrived through an organization that drew upon Islamic imagery but did not assert itself as a Muslim organization: the Five Percent Nation. The Five Percent was a group which preached the divinity of the Black Man, who the group's members called "Allah."[4] Even more so than the NOI, Five Percent views have been deemed heretical by mainstream Sunni Muslims, though the group has had the largest impact amongst hip hop artists themselves and the genre's terminology, symbols, and ideology. At the same time, while Five Percenters do not call themselves Muslims, preferring instead to be called Five Percenters or simply "Gods," the influence of Islam's symbols and terminology on the group is undeniable. From the late 1980s on, rappers who were members of (or affiliated) with the Five Percenters were extremely influential in the evolutions of rap music and hip hop culture, in terms of both commercial success and critical acclaim. Amongst these artists were Rakim Allah, Big Daddy Kane, Poor Righteous Teachers, Busta Rhymes, Leaders of the New School, Guru, Pete Rock, Mobb Deep, Queen Latifah, Erykah Badu, and members of the groups Wu Tang Clan and Digable Planets.

Yet despite such pockets of influence within popular and literary culture, Islam and Muslims for the most part remained largely "underground" throughout the 1980s and 1990s, as Soviet-style communism remained the nation's pre-eminent foe until the fall of the Berlin Wall in 1990, and the nation engaged in heated debates over multiculturalism and national identity during the culture wars of the 1990s. Muslim American communities, both African American and immigrant, avoided public scrutiny, as the former strived to recalibrate and restructure their communities in the wake of 1970s political struggles, and the latter developed and strengthened their own communities, as well as attempting to assimilate and weave themselves into the fabric of American society.[5] Thus, while Orientalist notions shaped by global geopolitical contexts of militarism and empire certainly engendered cultural perceptions of Islam, Muslims within the USA remained for the most part under the radar. As a result of racial, ethnic, and class differences, many Muslims in the USA often had few interactions with those outside their own local and regional communities. These types of divisions did not only pertain to Muslim communities in the USA; as Susan Koshy has written, "ethnic particularism," as she calls it, was the outcome of the shifting structure of white supremacy in an age of "multiculturalism." Indeed, "Islam" as a presence continued to develop as it always had in the USA, under the auspices of a racist and white supremacist state, in which Muslims were viewed as perennial Others. Whether black American or immigrant, Muslims American communities during this time functioned within the nation's racial calculus in ways that would directly come to bear upon how they would express themselves through art and literature following the events of September 11, 2001.

## The birth of "Muslim American" culture

Elevate Culture, formed in 2012, calls itself "a group of young professional and college students with a passion for a North American Muslim culture that is in line with the Islamic spirit and that is the voice of positive art" (www.creativemuslims.com, 2013). A registered non-profit, the organization works to raise money to "support creative project ideas in the community by providing grants, networking opportunities with mentors, showcasing work, and providing an upbeat and positive forum to discuss topics related to North American Muslim culture" (www.creativemuslims.com, 2013). A glance at their website (www.elevateculture.org) reveals over a dozen projects visitors might donate funds to if they so desire, including an indie rock record, a fashion line, a graphic design firm, and a spoken word CD. In their statement of purpose, the group states that it has a "cultural imperative" to support North American Muslim artists, inspired by their belief that "until Islam is made culturally relevant, Muslims cannot reach their full potential."

Elevate Culture's notion of the "cultural imperative" is borrowed from the work of Dr. Umar Faruq Abd-Allah, whose 2004 essay "Islam and the Cultural Imperative" has been widely circulated amongst young Muslim Americans in the post-9/11 years. In it, Abd-Allah advocates for the creation of "a sound Muslim American cultural identity," and argues that Islam's religious teaching "requires the creation of a successful indigenous Islamic culture in America and sets down sound parameters for its formation and growth" (Abd-Allah 2004: 3). Specifically, Abd-Allah chastises Islamic scholars and community leaders who have wholesale transplanted the mores and interpretations of Islam from their native lands, and labeled the arts – e.g. music, performance, theater, etc. – as *haram*, or forbidden by Islamic law. Likening Islam to a "crystal clear river," which should "reflect the bedrock (indigenous culture)" over which it flows, Abd-Allah says that, beyond the building of mosques and institutions, the primary concern of Muslims in the USA "must be the constitution of a unified self, congenial and self-assured, culturally and Islamically literate, capable not just of being a productive citizen and contributor of society but a leader of the cultural vanguard in America" (Abd-Allah 2004: 10–11).

The words of Abd-Allah, and the aims of Elevate Culture, reflect the ways in which Muslim Americans have approached, and continue to approach, the work of cultural and artistic expression in the post-9/11 era. As this essay has demonstrated thus far, Muslims have long been an active and integral part of culture-making in the USA. However, the events of September 11, 2001 thrust Islam and Muslims into a national spotlight that has not yet ceased to shine, and often in an ugly and unflattering light. Characterizing Muslims and Islam through associations with terrorism and religious fundamentalism, images of the Islamic male terrorist and the oppressed, submissive Muslim woman have flooded the US media and popular culture, reinvigorating age-old Orientalist stereotypes for the contemporary era. Yet they also draw upon racist tropes used to depict black Americans, and the state surveillance and profiling of Muslim communities closely resemble those inflicted on black Americans both historically and in the present. As such, Muslim Americans of all races, ethnicities, and national origins have been pushed to articulate and define their identities, as well as seeking out points of commonality within their communities. In light of these racializing practices, the post-9/11 cultural and literary expressions of Muslim Americans have come to reflect not only the myriad of racial, ethnic, and cultural identities and histories encompassed by their communities, but also their shared experiences as a community under attack.

Yet it is this notion of "shared experience" that has led to difficulties. As shown here, polyculturalism – the vibrant and non-essentialized contact between cultures and races – is at the heart of Islam's presence in the USA, yet the polarizing racial landscape of the USA has rendered it difficult at times for Islam to flow as the crystal clear river Abd-Allah describes above. As such, processes of Muslim American cultural and identity formation have been fraught with tension, as religious leaders, often unaware of the histories of race and power which have shaped Islam's presence in the USA, have issued opinions on the impermissibility of cultural expression. Furthermore, newer Muslim communities, also unaware of Islam's legacies in black communities, have often decried the surveillance of Muslims and US aggression in the Middle East, while ignoring the ills of racism and poverty within the United States, which disproportionately affect communities of color. On the other hand, for many black American Muslims, as well as a younger generation of non-black Muslim Americans who have grown up with the ubiquitousness of popular culture, there is an urgent desire to forge a distinctly Muslim American culture, one which expresses their religious values, critiques the War on Terror, and allies them with broader artistic and activist communities.

In creating this culture, many young people have turned to the past to draw inspiration from the traditions of political activism and social justice struggles represented by Islam's longstanding role in black American cultural politics. Thus, it is important to understand a new generation of Muslim American writers, artists, musicians, actors, etc. not as a "new" phenomenon, but one whose emergence is contextualized by the ways in which Islam has become linked with issues of social justice and political protest due to its engagements with blackness. For example, on November 7, 2001, Palestinian American poet and New York native Suheir Hammad published "First Writing Since (Poem on Crisis of Terror)" in the online poetry journal *In Motion*, in which she emphasized the presence of Arabs and Muslims in the USA and expressed her pain over the attacks:

> one more person ask me if i knew the hijackers.
> one more motherfucker ask me what navy my brother is in.
> one more person assume no arabs or muslims were killed. one more person
> assume they know me, or that i represent a people.
> or that a people represent an evil. or that evil is as simple as a
> flag and words on a page ...
> if there are any people on earth who understand how new york is
> feeling right now, they are in the west bank and the gaza strip ...

*(Hammad 2001)*

Linking the pain of New Yorkers following the attacks to that of Palestinians struggling under Israeli occupation in the West Bank, Hammad conveys the rage, grief, and ambivalence of Muslims and Arabs, particularly women, in post-9/11 America. This poem was later discovered by hip hop mogul Russell Simmons, who asked her to perform her work on his *Def Poetry Jam* series on HBO in 2002 and join the series tour, on which Hammad performed for the next two years.

As Hammad's example demonstrates, the urban cultural milieus of hip hop and the spoken word scene have been natural outlets for the post-9/11 voices of Muslim American artists. Aligning themselves with working-class, people of color, and grassroots activist communities, spoken word artists such as Hammad, Puerto Rican American Muslim convert Liza Garza, Milwaukee-based slam poet Muhibb Dyer, Bay Area poets and rappers Amir Suliman and Baraka Blue, Atlanta-based Ms. Latifah, and many others utilized their work to critique the War on Terror, the conditions of urban America, and racial, gender, and class inequality, all the while speaking to the evolving realities of being Muslim in the post-9/11 USA. Like Amiri Baraka, Marvin X, and Sonia Sanchez before them, these poets and artists attempted to merge their artistic and political visions, emphasizing Islam's focus on justice, racial egalitarianism, and the importance of charity and good works. In the realm of hip hop, artists also advanced such principles, such as Washington, DC-based rappers Native Deen, and a number of artists who have emerged from or been associated with Bay Area hip-hop collective Remarkable Current, including its founder, DJ and producer Anas Canon (also known as belikeMuhammad), rappers and vocalists Tyson Amir and Kumasi, and Puerto Rican Muslim American duo Mujahideen Team, or M-Team, featuring brothers Hamza and Suliman Perez (a.k.a. Doc Zhivago). In addition, more well-known hip-hop artists such as Mos Def, Ali Shaheed Muhammad Q-Tip, Lupe Fiasco, Brother Ali, and Busta Rhymes have publicly proclaimed their identities as Muslims. In 2012, Mos Def officially changed his name to Yasiin Bey, and he has long been extremely critical of government policies in the War on Terror. In 2013, he participated in a four-minute film made by the human rights organization Reprieve and director Asif Kapadia which featured Bey undergoing the procedure of force-feeding endured by inmates at Guantanamo Bay prison camp, who were at the time engaged in a hunger strike. Female rappers such as Mis Undastood and the UK's Poetic Pilgrimage have also been prominent in the Muslim hip-hop scene in the USA, though the longstanding marginalization of women continues to affect gender diversity. And while hip hop boasts the largest number of Muslim American artists, Indonesia-based singer Yuna plays her acoustic indie rock to large audiences, while country singer Kareem Salama and classically trained soprano Sumaiyya Ali are gaining fans both within the USA and beyond.

Links between Islam and black culture and identity have also been explored in literature and film. Novels such as Murad Kalam's *Night Journey* (2004), nonfiction works like Michael Muhammad Knight's *Blue-Eyed Devil*, the documentaries *New Muslim Cool* (dir. Jennifer Maytorena Taylor) and *Deen Tight* (dir. Mustafa Davis), and feature films *Bilal's Stand* (dir. Sultan Sharieff) and *Mooz-lum* (dir. Qasim Bashir) explore the complexities of Muslim American life for young men of color, and the intersections between black and Muslim American cultures. Cultural works have also explored other trajectories of political protest and rebellion; Knight's first novel, *The Taqwacores*, a fictional account of an Islamic punk rock scene in the USA published in 2004, spawned a real Islamic punk movement, which was the subject of an award-winning 2009 documentary titled *Taqwacore: The Birth of Punk Islam*. Black American Muslim women have also carved a niche in the publishing industry, crafting a new genre called "urban Islamic fiction." Titles such as Umm Jawayriyah's *The Size of a Mustard Seed*, Nadirah Angail's *What We Learned along the Way*, and Jatasha Sharif's *Khadijah's Life in Motion* offer fictional narratives featuring female black American Muslim protagonists navigating both their religious communities and urban landscapes, while Elle Muslimah's *The Real Muslim Wives of Philly* claims to provide "a rare view into the thoughts, family life, and intriguing practices such as plural marriage."

Since the 1970s, however, distinctive Muslim American identities have also developed and evolved out of "immigrant" Muslim communities across the country. Numerous first- and second-generation Muslims of South Asian, West Asian, and North African origin have come forward to tell their stories in the post-9/11 era, mainly in the literary realm. Many of the novels, short stories, poetry, and plays have much in common with Asian and Arab American immigrant literatures, exploring themes of generational conflict, cultural divisions, and the difficulties of assimilation. Novels such as Afghani American Khaled Hosseini's *The Kite Runner* (2004), Samina Ali's *Madras on Rainy Days* (2004), Mohja Kahf's *The Girl in the Tangerine Scarf*, Ali Yunis's *The Night Counter* (2010), Ayad Akhtar's *American Dervish* (2012), and Jennifer Zobair's *Painted Hands* (2013) offer Muslim American perspectives beyond the urban contexts detailed above, providing a glimpse into the ways Asian and Arab American Muslims in the USA have created lives in places like Bloomington, IN, Fremont, CA, and immigrant ethnic enclaves in the metropolitan centers of Milwaukee, New York, and Philadelphia. Other texts, such as H.M. Naqvi's *Homeboy* and Mohsin Hamid's *The Reluctant Fundamentalist* (which was made into a feature film directed by Mira Nair in 2013), explore the effects of state profiling and surveillance practices, detailing the lives of young "immigrant" Muslim men, in this case both Pakistani, who must endure their labeling and interpellation as "terrorists" in various ways. On the stage, Pakistani American playwright Wajahat Ali's *The Domestic Crusaders*; the *Hijabi Monologues* project – a series of monologues exploring the realities of Muslim women who wear the *hijab*, or headscarf; and Rohina Malik's one-woman show *Unveiled* have garnered large audiences and critical acclaim. Beyond stereotypical media images as terrorists and fanatics, Muslims have also begun to appear on mainstream American television: NBC's situation comedy *Outsourced*, set in a call center in India, debuted in 2010 and features a number of

Muslim characters and actors, while comedian and media pundit Jon Stewart's popular satirical program *The Daily Show* regularly features commentary from actor and comedian Aasif Mandvi, a Muslim American of Indian descent. In Canada, a prime time situation comedy, *Little Mosque on the Prairie*, ran from 2009 to 2012, and documented the quirky and comedic stories of a Muslim community in the fictional prairie town of Mercy, Saskatchewan.

Beyond the arenas of literature, music, and film, a Muslim American cultural ethos is also developing in the fields of fashion and art, as clothing retailers such as Shukr ("thankfulness" in Arabic) and Artizara offer modest, urban-inspired, and decidedly fashion-forward Islamic garments, while artists such as Australian-based Peter Gould merges vibrant and sleek graphics with Islamic visuals. Muslim American comedy is also on the rise; prominent comedian Dave Chappelle, who converted to Islam in 1998, began publicly discussing his faith in 2005, while a 2008 documentary, *Allah Made Me Funny*, follows Muslim American comedians Azhar Usman, Preacher Moss, and Mo Amer, who are, respectively, Indian American, African American, and Palestinian American. In 2013, comedian Dean Obeidallah appeared in television station Comedy Central's special *Axis of Evil*, as well as releasing a film detailing the lives of Muslim and Arab stand-up comedians entitled *The Muslims are Coming*.

A number of cities have emerged as centers of Muslim American cultural production, in particular Chicago, New York, Philadelphia, Dearborn, MI, and the San Francisco Bay Area. Two organizations, the Bay Area's Ta'leef Collective and Chicago's Inner-City Muslim Action Network (IMAN), have emerged as leading voices in, to return to the mission statement of Elevate Culture, making Islam "culturally relevant," and both connect their work to the history of Islam in the USA, specifically in relation to black America. Founded by Rami Nashashibi, IMAN "uses religion, art, and culture" to fight for social justice, and since 1997 has put on the largest Muslim cultural festival in the country, called "Takin' It to the Streets," which the organization describes as "a Muslim-led festival where artistic expression, spirituality, and urban creativity inspire social change." Featuring hip hop and spoken word artists, the event is one among many IMAN presents throughout the year, in which they draw upon the activist spirit of Islam in America while working within the urban and polycultural milieus in which Islam has long grown and thrived. In the Bay Area, the Ta'leef Collective identifies itself as an organization which "serves seekers actively interested in Islam and converts to the faith, assisting them in realizing a sustainable conversion to and practice of Islam, and a healthy, gradual integration into our greater Muslim community." While culture is not explicitly discussed in its mission statement, the group has used film, photography, and social media as integral components of its work. Filmmaker Mustafa Davis, the director of the documentary *Deen Tight*, mentioned above, is an integral part of Ta'leef and employs his skills as a filmmaker and photographer to showcase the diversity and richness of Muslim American communities, as well as calling upon Muslims themselves to express themselves through art.

Most of the artistic expressions described in the second section of this essay might be characterized as part of the "first wave" of Muslim American art and literature in the post-9/11 era, representing the ways in which a community under siege has responded to its predicament through creative expression. Yet, as this essay has shown, Islam has long been a presence within the USA, both in terms of Muslim communities themselves and as a distinctive register of art and culture. Forged at the intersections of race and religion, Islam in the arts in the USA is heterogeneous, diverse, and ever changing. Indeed, with the continued growth and development of groups such as Elevate Culture, IMAN, the Ta'leef Collective, and various others, one again sees how the notion of process comes to bear upon how Islam's meanings have shifted and evolved in recent decades. While many of the young writers, musicians, and artists discussed above have used their work to protest racist and Orientalist interpellations of themselves and their communities, as newer and younger artists emerge one sees new sets of issues arising around how to enact the "cultural imperative" Abd-Allah speaks of on p. 328. Perhaps one of the most exciting developments in this evolution is the focus on issues of gender and sexuality within Muslim America, as Muslim American women take up Islamic feminism within a US context and challenge the polarizing binaries that have characterized their representations. In addition, queer Muslim communities have increasingly gained visibility; in 2007, New York-based director Parvez Sharma released the documentary *Jihad for Love*, featuring queer Muslims in Islamic countries, while the fluidity of gender and sexuality figure prominently in many works by first-time Muslim authors, such as Bushra Rehman's *Corona* and the anthology *Love Insh'Allah: The Secret Love Lives of American Muslim Women*. As all these works demonstrate, "Islam" will continue to function as an intersectional and hybridized process of racial, class, gender, political, and religious formation in American artistic expressions, one that simultaneously reflects and challenges the multivalent histories that have characterized the rich, vibrant, and creative presence of Islam in the USA.

## Notes

1 Within the US Muslim community itself, the question of how to self-identity has been debated, with many arguing that whereas racial and ethnic identifiers (e.g. "African American," "Asian American," etc.) are aptly used as qualifiers for "American-ness," a religious identity, such as Muslim, should function as the primary term, with American being used as the qualifying adjective. While I understand the importance of these distinctions, I suggest "Muslim American" is a more inclusive term that allows for the flexibility and fluidity of Muslim identities in the United States, as some of the artists and writers I discuss herein may not strongly self-identify as Muslim in terms of their religious and cultural practices.
2 This encounter between jazz and Islam reverberated beyond the lives of converts themselves. For example, saxophonist John Coltrane's *A Love Supreme*, recorded in 1964 and often called the greatest jazz album of all time, was deeply shaped by Coltrane's exposure to Ahmadiyya Islam through pianist Tyner, his wife Naima, and a drummer named Nasseridine, who played with Coltrane in Philadelphia in the 1950s and 1960s. In the album's liner notes Coltrane writes, "Now and again through the unerring and merciful hand of God, I do perceive his ... OMNIPOTENCE ... HE IS GRACIOUS AND MERCIFUL." These words directly echo the opening lines of every chapter in the Qur'an: *Bismillah al-Rahman al-Rahim*: "In the name of Allah, the gracious, the merciful."
3 Some of these histories have been well documented, such as those of Bengali Muslim seamen in Harlem in the 1930s, Indian Muslim farm laborers on the West Coast, and Arab immigrants mainly from Syria and Lebanon in the Northwest and Midwest. For further reading, see GhaneaBassiri (2010), Gualtieri (2009), Haddad (1991), Smith (1999), Takaki (1998).
4 The basic premise of the organization is that 85 percent of people are without knowledge, 10 percent are bloodsuckers of the poor who have knowledge and power but use it to abuse the 85 percent, and 5 percent are the poor righteous teachers who preach the divinity of the black man who is God manifest and will save the 85 percent from destruction.
5 As stated above, following the death of the Honorable Elijah Muhammad in 1975, the Nation of Islam came under the leadership of Muhammad's son, Warith Deen, who transitioned the organization towards the teachings of Sunni Islam and eventually renamed the group the American Society of Muslims. Another group, led by Muhammad disciple Louis Farrakhan, maintained the group's racial separatist beliefs.

## Bibliography

Abd-Allah, U.F. (2004) "Islam and the Cultural Imperative," www.nawawi.org/wp-content/uploads/2013/01/Article3.pdf.
Baraka, A. (1994) *Conversations with Amiri Baraka*, Jackson, MS: University Press of Mississippi.
——(1999) *Blues People*, New York: Harper Perennial.

Bogle, D. (2001 [1973]) *Toms, Coons, Mulattoes, Mammies, and Bucks: An Interpretive History of Blacks in American Films*, 4th ed., New York: Continuum.

Diouf, S. (2009) "African Muslims and American Blues," *Muslim Voices: Arts and Ideas*, muslimvoicesfestival.org/resources/african-muslims-and-american-blues (accessed April 25, 2013).

Doherty, T. (2000) "Malcolm X: In Print, on Screen," *Biography* 23(1): 29–48.

GhaneaBassiri, K. (2010) *A History of Islam in America*, Cambridge: Cambridge University Press, 2010.

Gillespie, D. (2009 [1979]) *To Be, Or Not … to Bop*, Minneapolis: University of Minnesota Press.

Gualtieri, S.M.A. (2009) *Between Arab and White: Race and Ethnicity in the Early Syrian American Diaspora*, Berkeley: University of California Press.

Haddad, Y.Y. (ed.) (1991) *The Muslims of America*, New York: Oxford University Press.

Hammad, S. (2001) "First Writing Since," *In Motion Magazine*, November 7.

Kahf, M. (2010) "Marvin X and Muslim American Literature," blackbirdpressnews.blogspot.com/2011/08/marvin-x-ad-muslim-american-literature.html (accessed February 12, 2014).

——(n.d.) "Review of Marvin X's Love and War," blackbirdpressnews.blogspot.com/2013/05/marvin-x-replies-to-honorable-elijah.html (accessed August 15, 2013).

Muhammad, E. (1965) *Message to the Blackman*, Chicago: Elijah Muhammad Books.

Rashid, S. (1993) "The Islamic Aspects of the Legacy of Malcolm X," *American Journal of Islamic Social Sciences* 10(1): 60–71.

Sanchez, S. (1973) *A Blues Book for Black Magical Women*, Detroit: Broadside Press.

Smith, J.I. (1999) *Islam in America*, Columbia Contemporary American Religion Series, New York: Columbia University Press.

Takaki, R. (1998) *Strangers from a Different Shore: A History of Asian Americans*, updated and revised ed., Boston: Little, Brown and Company.

Taylor, U. (2008) "Women in the Documents: Thoughts on Uncovering the Personal, Political, and Professional," *Journal of Women's History* 20(1): 187–96.

Turner, R.B. (1997) *Islam in the African American Experience*, Bloomington: Indiana University Press.

Weiss, S. (2007) "Arts. World Music," in Suad, J. (ed.) *Encyclopedia of Women and Islamic Cultures*, Leiden: Brill.

Williams, R. (1985) *Keywords: A Vocabulary of Culture and Society*, Oxford: Oxford University Press

# 21

# European Muslim youth and popular culture

## At the crossroads of fun and faith[1]

*Miriam Gazzah*

## Introduction

The religious is relocating itself within present-day European society. The religious is increasingly found in "unexpected" places: a Christian music festival, a Muslim dating event, a dance party in celebration of the end of Ramadan, and so on. Ever since the 1990s, the mingling of religion and popular culture has attracted quite some scholarly attention, ranging through sociologists, political scientists, anthropologists, historians, and academics from the field of cultural and media studies (see Lynch 2007: 1–4; van Nieuwkerk 2011).

Fun and faith; for some this may sound like a contradiction in terms. Reality shows otherwise. Devout believers have always been looking for ethically legitimate forms of leisure. According to Mahan, "Religion and culture have always been overlapping categories and religion's interactions with the economical and cultural system of its day have always troubled and intrigued observers" (Mahan 2007: 48). So, what else is new?

In the case of European Muslim youth, the mixing of popular culture and religious choices appears to head in new directions. Their choice of lifestyle features new preferences, new products, new consumption patterns that differ greatly from their parents and are quite different from their non-Muslim peers. Among them are new fashionable trends in veiling, the consumption of *halal* commodities ranging from shampoo to food, downloading ringtones voicing a *sura* from the Qur'an, decorating bedrooms with Qur'anic calligraphy stickers, drinking Mecca Cola, and so on. The creating and shaping of Muslim subjectivities of European Muslim youth occur not only along the lines of Islamic practices and rituals such as praying, fasting, and going to Mecca on pilgrimage, but also along the lines of other, new popular culture repertoires. It is clear that popular culture and its Islamized manifestations, in whatever shape or form, have become more and more important in the identity formation processes of Muslims today.

The surfacing of consumer goods like *halal* (fast) food, Islamic fashion, and Islamic (pop) music is considered to be a form of commodification that is driven by economical motives, on the one hand (supply), and by the desire of consumers – i.e. Muslims – to construct new, modern, individualized forms of Muslimness (demand), on the other hand. Islamization of consumer goods and cultural and artistic productions should not merely be seen in light of a de-politicized search for individual self-fulfillment in an age of mass – and consumer – culture. The dynamics going on behind the scenes of these new cultural productions reveal a great concern with the making of "pious subjects" and the project revolving around "an ethical production and consumption of culture and arts" (Jouili 2012: 402–3).

In the article "Hyper-Islamism," Nabil Echchaibi links the trend of Islamization of cultural life and consumer goods to a strand of born-again Muslims (reverts) who strive for a meaningful, but individually motivated merging of modernity and their Muslimness in a rapidly changing and globalizing world. Echchaibi calls it "new Islamic revivalism" by born-again Muslims (Echchaibi 2008: 200–1, taken from Roy).

The combination of Islam and fun may seem unlikely (van Nieuwkerk 2011; Bayat 2007, 2010; Otterbeck 2008). Popular culture, especially performing arts, such as music and dance, has always raised controversy throughout Islamic history. The sensitive relationship between Islam and music, for instance, originates from the emotional effect music is deemed to have on the listener and its potential to corrupt moral behavior and instigate haram[2] activities. In these discourses, there is often fear of transgression of sexual mores and norms. Popular culture – especially music, movies, and performance arts like dance and theater – evokes images of haram behavior. And these associations dominate many of the discourses and debates on popular culture in many Muslim circles – in the Islamic world and its diasporas (cf. van Nieuwkerk 1995, 2008, 2011; Baig 2008: 255; Gazzah 2008: 141–88). What in the Western world might be considered youthful (innocent) fun (watching the newest video of some pop artist, or having a dance party with friends) could be considered a problematic activity within a Muslim household. Nonetheless, this does not keep young Muslims from having fun, of course. In fact, there is a growing supply of Islamized cultural productions, seemingly circumventing this haram–halal dichotomy.

What is accepted as "Islamic" in the context of production and consumption of popular culture prompts debates. This implies a "new thinking about Islam" (Pond 2006: 2; Gökarıksel and McLarney 2010: 1–2; van Nieuwkerk 2011) and it is increasingly taking place outside of traditional realms and expected contexts. These forces of consumer capitalism and Islamized popular culture have raised new questions about authority and power. The mosque, or any other established space of Islamic authority for that matter, has lost its monopoly over Islamic knowledge and interpretations. New interlocutors, interpretations, and expressions of Islam – including new ethics and aesthetics to join them – are found in a multitude of spaces outside and beyond the scope of mosques, imams, theologians, time-honored Islamic authority figures, and other forms of institutionalized Islam. The internet, for example, is such a space where new interpretations of Islam take shape.

The consumption and production of Islamized popular culture visualize new types of Muslim presence in the public sphere in European urban areas. The emergence of these new products (and subsequent consumption or demand for them) stems from an array of recent developments. An important catalyst in this development is the rise of the Islamic revival movement (Moors 2012: 274). Due to the crisis of many nation-states and their inability to form solid and uncontested national identities, space has been created for others than the state or religious institutions to produce identities and images, for example through popular culture.

Whereas the Islamic movement has always looked critically at popular culture and the arts, Moors writes that in light of the increasing forces of consumer capitalism and globalization the Islamic revival movement has loosened its critical stance towards entertainment and consumption and is actively engaged in producing halal (licit) forms of entertainment and consumption goods. Moors connects this development also to "a broader trend of fashioning of identities through consumption, the commoditization of 'things Islamic,' and the development of an Islamic production sector, that provides the new Muslim middle classes with their own media, services and goods" (Moors 2012: 275).

Looking at the role of popular culture from a perspective of religious self-making poses the question of how to define the boundaries between secular and religious in a new light (cf. Agrama 2012; Pond 2006; Meyer 2009: xi, 21; Moors 2012: 272–9). What was once known as secular, non-religious, could turn into something religious. In light of the increasing importance of popular culture as a breeding ground for new types of Muslimness, the traditional dichotomy of the sacred versus the profane seems to become problematic when analyzing the contemporary religious practices of European Muslim youth. As a result, what can be claimed – and accepted – as religion (or not) is increasingly difficult to define. Moors (2012: 278) concludes, therefore, that it is rather useless to define certain practices, spaces, or bodies either as secular or religious since their status is permanently ambiguous and the way people engage with them is often ambivalent:

> Things do not have either a religious or a secular, nonreligious, status; rather, the ways in which forms become or cease to be religious may well shift in the course of their production, circulations, and consumption, and depends on the intentions of those engaging with them. Some items are produced to enable a religious practice, such as for instance, *halal* food, but this may also be consumed by non-Muslims. Other things, such as headscarves, only become religious items of dress when they are worn in a particular way. Things may also become more, less or differently religious depending on where they circulate.
>
> *(Moors 2012: 276)*

The mingling of popular culture (i.e. secular popular culture) and Islam must not be seen as a unidirectional sum total of something secular and something religious, but as a continuum along which categories of interpretations flow from one to the other in the course of their production, consumption, and circulation. Production and consumption of popular culture goods are subject to continuous changing interpretations and attributions.

## Youth, popular culture, and making Islamic choices

Popular culture provides people with entertainment, distraction, and "helps" modern citizens in the pursuit of diversion and amusements outside of their working or school hours. Providing people with fun is thus a key element of popular culture. Islamic fun, however, often comes with restrictions and serves other norms and morals than average, secular entertainment.

For many young people, much of their leisure time is filled up with popular culture: listening to pop music, watching TV, playing games on the PC, chatting with friends online, buying clothes, dressing up, going out, etc. The power of popular culture lies in its ability to serve as both a symbolic boundary marker and a symbolic bridge at the same time.

Making choices is what drives consumer culture and is an essential part of popular culture. However, one can only choose when one has money: having money equals the power to buy what you choose. Matthias Zick Varul has written an interesting article about how religion and consumerism intersect. Making choices in a consumer culture often means that "Even non-choices are ascribed to individuals as if they were choices" (Varul 2008: 242). It is money that makes choices possible in a consumer-driven society. "With this freedom of choice [having money], ever more trivial decisions become identity relevant because they can be read by others as indicators of what kind of person one is or aspires to be" (Varul 2008: 242). For consumers who consider themselves to be believers, making choices in a consumer culture becomes a complex dynamic:

> Decisions and choices concerning faith may still define many of the cultural choices that follow … but they are, in keeping with the culture of consumerism, subject to revision and reversion. The only choice that is not subject to revision is that of the principle of choice itself. One might argue that religious content remains the same, no matter whether it is upheld in a traditional, industrial or consumerist society. But even the most sincere believers cannot stop their faith being qualified by the index of reversibility that is attached to their choice. This places a higher burden upon them to constantly authenticate their religious choice – expressing it in specific practices of religiously conspicuous consumption – and to make their religious choice palatable within a promotional culture.
>
> *(Varul 2008: 249)*

In other words, living in a consumerist society urges people to constantly defend the religious choices attached to their consumerist and cultural choices, and vice versa. On the other hand, in order for religion to "survive" in a consumer-driven, secular, postmodern society it (religion that is, or representations of religion) increasingly needs to become more like a commodity. It has to advertise itself and promote its user value. In doing this, Christian institutions, for example, have started to promote the therapeutic value of belief, its self-empowering effect, and its benefits for building up self-confidence, and to emphasize its spiritual experience rather than its religious truth. Ramadan is also often promoted as a way to improve your mental state, as a month in which fasting symbolizes the cleansing of the soul (Varul 2008: 249–50).

The way promoters of religion make religion into something easily consumable and which fits into the performance of religious identities connects well with consumers' and believers' search for religious experience and meaning. Many contemporary believers want to have and are in need of relevant, spiritual experiences, which may for some be even more important than adhering to and preaching words from a certain sacred textbook. This trend thus incites religious institutions or campaigners to present eye-catching elements to attract consumers of religion, i.e. believers.

All in all, the trend described by Varul indicates that a shift is occurring, taking the focus of attention away from "religious content" to "religious experience" (cf. Roy 2005). Making choices in a consumerist society seems to conflict with being religious, but many young believers connect consumption and religion fluidly. Cross-referencing religious practices in certain consumption patterns results in a lifestyle that is based upon and draws inspiration from the religious field as well as from the popular culture field. Varul reasons that "it can be precisely the stress on its [Islam's] inalterability that young Muslims in the West use in order to develop a confident self vis-à-vis the non-Muslim environment." To clarify this mechanism, Varul brings up the example of *halal* food. He explains that eating *halal* food conforms to a religious obligation, but is at the same time also a "way of expressing an apparently chosen identity" (Varul 2008: 250). So, by choosing to eat *halal* food, Muslim youth express their choice for Islam. But in a non-Muslim environment, this (free) choice becomes a clear identity marker towards the outside world. Hence, commodified forms of religion or the marketization of religion serve more than only business models. They have become an intrinsic part of the processes of identity construction and performance of contemporary believers.

In the past decade many new forms of commodified religion have emerged: a wide array of artistic, cultural, and popular entertainment and consumer culture that finds inspiration in Islam has found its way to the global market. Known examples are Sami Yusuf (Pond 2006) and

Yusuf Islam and their Islamic pop music (Varul 2008: 248), Mecca Cola, Mekka Foods, the Muslim hip-hop genre (Khabeer 2011; Chan-Malik 2011), so-called "Islamic fashion" (Moors 2012), and many other cultural products from the "*halal* industry" and the "*halal* arts scene" (Jouili 2012: 402–3). It is particularly since the events of September 11, 2001 that Muslims in Europe as well as in the USA have become more involved in creating their own niches and markets, in music, fashion, food, leisure-time activities (nightlife and dating events), humor, literature, and a range of commodity goods.

## Music, popular culture, and Islam in the USA and Europe

A great deal of writings on Islam, popular culture, and music at some point deal with the link between Islam and hip hop. The birth of hip hop is often described as having taken place in the USA. Hip hop is an American music genre that from its beginnings has been associated with or linked to Islamic discourses (Khabeer 2007: 126). The anthropologist Khabeer describes how different American-bred interpretations of Islam (Nation of Islam and the Five Percent Nation) have had a considerable impact upon the development of the American hip-hop genre. In addition, more mainstream Sunni interpretations also serve as an important source of inspiration from which American rappers take symbols, images, and text and incorporate them into their works (Khabeer 2007). In sum, Islam, albeit in different shapes, interpretations, and forms, has heavily influenced (American) hip hop.

The rise of the so-called Islamic hip-hop genre in the last decade or so is another trend within the hip-hop scene. In the USA, some very famous hip-hop artists are Muslim, like Lupe Fiasco and Mos Def, but their music is not categorized as Islamic hip hop, but as mainstream, since Islam is not an explicit focus of their music (Mandaville 2009: 156). Islamic hip hop or Muslim hip hop could be categorized as a sub-genre of the hip-hop genre, whereby from a musical and a lyrical perspective the music centers on Islam. Islamic hip hop is popular in the USA and in Europe. Even though the genre has existed since the 1990s, it is mainly since the aftermath of 9/11 that the genre started growing and many young Muslims in Europe and the USA found in music a way to express their anxieties, frustrations, and opinions about being Muslim in a non-Muslim environment. Islamic hip hop also very strongly promotes a positive image of Islam, trying to counter the Islamophobic tendencies reigning in Europe and the USA.

In the UK, Mecca2Medina have been active already since 1997 and female hip-hop band Poetic Pilgrimage have been taking over European stages from around the start of the new millennium (Mandaville 2009: 156–7; Chan-Malik 2011). Many British artists in the Islamic hip-hop scene are of Afro-Caribbean descent. Famous American Islamic hip-hop acts are, for instance, Native Deen, Baraka Blue, Anas Canon. The American record company Remarkable Current, founded in 2001 by Anas Canon, even specializes in the genre (www.remarkable current.com).

The Islamic hip-hop genre challenges traditional discourses on the perceived incompatibility of music and Islam. Some artists want to remain close to Islamic rulings that state that music can only be made with a capella vocals and certain percussion instruments. Others opt for a wider interpretation of those rulings and use other instruments as well. Islamic hip hop is able to overcome ethnic and racial differences which exist among the Muslim community. Moreover, because of Islam's precarious position in the West a great deal of Islamic hip hop is easily seen as political. Preaching about the good things of Islam, supporting the Palestinians or Bosnians, speaking out against anti-Islamic politicians, and hip hop's reputation as politically conscious associate the genre with political issues as well (Chan-Malik 2011; Mandaville 2009: 157). In the USA, it is an important marker of Muslimness, blackness, and Americanness, since many of the artists and consumers of this genre are black Americans (from different ethnic backgrounds). In Europe, Islamic hip hop is particularly popular in the UK, where there is a lively scene of British Muslim artists.

Somewhat at the intersection of these two trends, lies Muslim Cool. Muslim Cool, a term coined by Khabeer (2011: 22), denotes young American Muslims for whom hip hop "is a site through which they negotiate what it means to be an American Muslim. These young American Muslims create and consume hip hop as a way to embrace, construct, and perform their religious identity" (Khabeer 2011: 20). Muslim Cool is a practice, a lifestyle, that takes a counter-position towards American immigrant Islam and white American normativity, i.e. mainstream American popular culture. The importance of Muslim Cool is that it operates at the intersection of race (blackness), music (hip hop), and religion (Islam) (Khabeer 2011: 22–7). In fact, it is a phenomenon that is about a way of thinking and being American and Muslim, and this practice leans heavily on the use of popular culture, and hip hop in particular. An important part of Muslim Cool is claiming a Muslim American identity, whereby proving some kind of Americanness is essential (Khabeer 2011: 27). In contrast to the global phenomenon of Islamic hip hop, Muslim Cool is concerned with American society and culture.

Besides hip hop, other forms of popular culture have also been attributed to this new field of Islamic popular culture. So-called Islamic pop music by artists such as Yusuf Islam, Sami Yusuf, and Maher Zain has attracted fans from all over the world. This genre, with its pop style music, video clips, and its laudatory songs about Islam, justice, humanity, unity, and world peace, has been able to transcend national, ethnic, and internal religious boundaries. Another popular culture production that has gained popularity is comedy. Allah Made Me Funny, three American Muslim comedians, have toured the world with their performances specifically targeting a Muslim audience (Herding 2012: 102). French comedian Samia and her Oriental Comic project (Herding 2012: 107) and Uma Lamo, a group of three Moroccan-German comedians are another few examples (Herding 2012: 87).

Finally, another eye-catching trend is the appearance of so-called Islamic fashion. Both in the branch of urban street wear (hip-hop style clothing) as well as in the branch of fashionable veiling and modest clothing, there have emerged new product lines specifically targeting a (young) Muslim market (Moors 2009; Mandaville 2009: 165; Herding 2012: 102–4).

All in all, these trends are popular among some young European and American Muslims. However, they also raise controversy despite the good intentions (niyya) expressed by their producers and consumers. These practices still remain far from uncontested in the Muslim community. Themes like the compatibility of music and Islam, fashion and Islam, and comedy and Islam are often heatedly debated. Islamic doctrines and discourses that suggest the un-Islamicness of these practices often point to the potential danger of corrupting morals, distraction from performing religious duties, or transgression of the boundaries of decent, ethical behavior in general. The acceptance of these new religious practices and new ways of experiencing and expressing religiosity follows a path that is full of conflicts and obstacles.

In light of all these developments in the field of popular culture, it is interesting to gain insight into the nature of the engagement of European Muslim youth with popular culture and Islam. In this chapter I take Dutch Moroccan youth and their consumption and production of popular culture as my point of departure. A leading question in this chapter is to what extent popular culture, and the entertainment industry and consumer culture in general, have become important pools from which Dutch Moroccan youth draw inspiration in fulfilling a sense of Muslimness. As indicated earlier, the combination of popular culture and religion is not a one-sided dynamic. Their intermingling and the forthcoming productions and consumption patterns of Islamized popular culture stem from multiple endeavors, such as entrepreneurship, a personal quest for piety, musical inspiration, and political engagement. In the next sections, I will present different examples of how Dutch Moroccan youth make Islam and popular culture intersect.

## Musical events

For almost all Dutch Moroccan youth Islam plays a considerable part in day-to-day life. How to dress, what music to listen to (or not to listen to music at all), what friends to have, and what TV shows to watch; upon most of these activities an Islamic discourse is projected and Islamic norms are invoked in deciding whether certain activities are *haram* or *halal*. Hence, leisure-time activities are impacted by a sense of Muslimness. Olivier Roy has indicated that for Muslim youth living in post-migration situations the *halal–haram* divide seems more significant than for Muslim youth living in Muslim majority countries (Roy 2005: 140).

The identity construction processes of second-generation Dutch Moroccan youth are a complex and ambivalent dynamic (De Koning 2009: 70; Gazzah 2008: 231–8; Mandaville 2009: 166). According to De Koning, writing about Dutch Moroccan youth, the shaping of a Muslim self is not a matter of simply following (or not) Islamic dogmas or subscribing to Islam's creed. Nor do they prefer the "traditional" and "cultural" Islam-experience of their (grand)parents as a valuable option. Rather, Dutch Moroccan youth increasingly, and in sharp contrast to their (grand)parents, create Muslimness out of a wide range of "cultural repertoires" (De Koning 2009: 64–8; Roy 2006: 129) which go beyond the boundaries of the religious field.

Many of the mainstream leisure-time activities that average Dutch youth engage in are in Muslim circles associated with *haram* behavior: nightlife (because of alcohol use, gender mixing, and late hours), fashion (too revealing or sexy, showing too much of the skin), watching MTV (obscene images and foul language). Most of the music events targeting a Dutch Moroccan audience are not Islamic by design, meaning that they are not promoted as "Islamic" in any way. But this does not mean that these events are purely secular and devoid of religion. Most of these events implement certain Islamic norms, such as the absence of alcohol (or drugs), the absence of references to sex and violence in the programming (i.e. decent acts and genres), programming parties in line with the Islamic calendar (for example on the day of *'aid al-fitr*), the implicit behavioral code regarding the interaction between men and women, sometimes segregation of the sexes, and early start and end times of events.

The Islamization of some[3] of the events taking place in the Dutch Moroccan music scene must be seen in light of the unsettledness regarding music and performance in Islam. The normative discourse among the Dutch Moroccan community considers music and performance to be incompatible with an Islamic lifestyle (Gazzah 2008: 186–7). This normative discourse has an effect on the way Dutch Moroccan musical events are organized and set up. By giving an event an Islamic touch and aligning it to certain – what are perceived to be – Islamic norms, both organization and audience try to get round negative associations, making it more acceptable and legitimate, from a religious as well as a socio-cultural point of view, to be involved in this event.

As a result, these events have become ultimate meeting places for Dutch Moroccan youth and offer them the opportunity to express and construct a Dutch Moroccanness, by means of dancing, clothing, and socializing with other young Dutch Moroccans. Islam, and how consumers and artists in the Dutch Moroccan music scene perceive it and construct Islamic experiences, impacts the way they consume and produce music and musical events (Gazzah 2008: 141–86). The emergence of the Dutch Moroccan music scene indicates how the socio-cultural and religious preferences of Dutch Moroccan youth shine through in the way they produce and consume popular culture.

The success of the Dutch Moroccan music scene depends on several factors. One important factor is providing Dutch Moroccan youth with an opportunity to listen and dance to Arab and Moroccan music – a genre that is absent in mainstream Dutch nightlife and in mainstream Dutch concert halls or pop music venues. Moreover, as already mentioned, many Dutch Moroccan youth reject regular nightlife because of its contested status, and the Dutch Moroccan music scene provides an alternative. The fact that the scene complies with certain socio-religious norms in terms of behavior and, for example, the absence of alcohol adds to its popularity. Hereby a need to spend leisure time in a *halal* environment is facilitated.

From the point of view of the producers, Islamizing events has an important commercial purpose. It is a way for organizers to erase or lessen the negative associations and ideas evoked by musical events among the Dutch Moroccan community. By implementing "Islamic" elements organizers hope to increase the Islamic legitimacy (for its audience) and to make it more acceptable for Dutch Moroccan youth (and their parents) to come (Gazzah 2008: 151), and thus to attract larger audiences.

## Producing Islamized popular culture

Ahmed (aged 39, interviewed February 20, 2012) is a Dutch Moroccan self-made entrepreneur, media expert in ethno-marketing and a socially engaged professional active as chairman in numerous non-profit and welfare organizations dealing with diversity, youth, and social participation. He was also the director of a company that produced and promoted music concerts, parties, and events targeting a Dutch Moroccan audience (its heyday was 1996–2006). His company was one of the main players in the Dutch Moroccan music scene. His events always had a specific Dutch Moroccan character. I attended many of them between 1996 and 2006. Their focus was on programming Moroccan artists, particularly Moroccan *shaabi* artists like Najat Aatabou and Senhaji (Gazzah 2008: 83–4). Ahmed's aim was always to promote Moroccan cultural and musical heritage in the Netherlands and to raise consciousness among Dutch Moroccans about their cultural inheritance. Besides, on a more general note, it was also his ambition to stimulate the participation of Dutch Moroccan youth in general in cultural and artistic activities.

The preconditions of Ahmed's concerts and events enhanced the transformation of an undefined space into a space of Dutch Moroccanness. The design of the events, the requirements and conditions created by the organizers, such as no alcohol, the choice of venue, and the implicit and unspoken gearing of the audience towards certain behavioral codes and ethics reveals how Dutch Moroccanness and Muslimness are intertwined. In explaining this, Ahmed refers to his wish to organize an event that is in his eyes in accordance with Islamic respectability: no alcohol, drugs, and to aim for a respectful, decent interaction between men and women. Thus, Ahmed organized events that had clear traces of religiosity, albeit cast in a mold of Dutch Moroccanness. Ahmed's self-proclaimed guidelines for how to organize an event are in line with this:

> The measuring stick is that our parents should be able to walk around … My parents have performed the *hajj* and they pray five times a day. They are just normal, liberal, so to speak. But we are not so liberal that we celebrate carnival in the middle of a bar carrying a tray of beer on our shoulder. That's a bit too far out of line … It's not because I am a saint. Not at all … I do not want people to be drunk at my party … Well, that is the cultural and

religious standard that I want to keep. You know, with us [Dutch Moroccans] the cultural and religious are difficult to separate, they often coincide.[4]

Ahmed's wish to remain as close as possible to family values of the Dutch Moroccan community "forces" him to implement and reject certain elements. Muslimness is hence implicitly present in Ahmed's project, since it is linked to a cultural-religious Dutch Moroccan identity. This identity, in turn, is one whose elements, as Ahmed himself says, cannot be easily separated from each other. Muslimness and Moroccanness seem deeply interconnected. Ahmed's events are not promoted in any way as religious. However, his ambitions and motives are driven by religious as well as non-religious forces.

For consumers of Ahmed's events, the religious factor may be an important stimulus to visit them – or not. My research (Gazzah 2008) has shown that the (albeit implicit) Islamization of events is in tune with many of the visitors and their desire to reside in an environment that is adjusted to their socio-cultural and religious identities. Yet for others this seemed irrelevant. This demonstrates how one and the same product, a music event in this case, may have a religious connotation for the producer, but could well be a non-religious activity for the consumer (Gazzah 2008: 157–69). Depending on how people engage with these events and their specific intentions, the meaning and status of these events can shift (Moors 2012: 275).

In sum, the Dutch Moroccan music scene is a scene that pertains to the field of popular culture and is not a phenomenon that pertains or is considered to pertain to the religion field *per se*. Yet, it *is* a space in which processes of creating Muslimness take place. The way the events in the scene are produced and consumed may be from a religious point of view or not. Yet, many of the social dynamics going on in the scene – at concerts and parties, on stage, behind the scenes, and in the online activities surrounding the scene – indicate at least the presence and impact of Muslim subjectivities.

## Popular music and Islamic inspiration: Dutch Moroccan artists' different shades of Muslimness

> Salah Edin Al7amdulilah thank Allah swt for all positivity in my life!!! love[5]

Salah Edin (b. 1980), often considered to be one of the most controversial rappers in the Netherlands ever,[6] thanks Allah in a "Tweet," a daily routine he has picked up ever since he has been "more consciously involved with Islam."[7] Salah Edin does not publicly present himself as a Muslim artist *per se*. By this I mean that, with regard to his PR, marketing, and promotion of his music and management of his public image, his Muslim identity is mostly absent.[8] Nevertheless, on his social media sites, like Twitter and Facebook, and in interviews he makes no secret of being Muslim. And the same goes for some of his lyrics where you can find clear references to Islam. The way Salah Edin manages his Muslim identity is subtle and careful. His musical and personal biography shows a constant involvement with Islam, but continuously in differing ways.

Fathi Otmani (b. 1987) is a former rapper from Amsterdam turned *nasheed*[9] singer, making music in the genre of Maher Zain and Sami Yusuf – so-called Islamic pop music. This quotation is taken from his website:

> My aim in making my music is to spread the beauty of Islam to all the people and show everyone that Islam is not a religion of terror and war that the media portrays it as. I hope that my efforts in making my music can bring at least a small amount of change in people's

perception of this beautiful Deen [religion]. May Allah help us stay steadfast on the path of this Deen and keep our hearts clean from Shaitan's darkness. Ameen.[10]

Rajae (b. 1979) has clear ideas about the audience she is targeting with her new, forthcoming album; i.e. the *umma*,[11] in whatever shape or form it comes:

Rajae's mission is to make music for the Ummah: Brown, white, black, golden, free spirits, conservatives, truth seekers, young and old.

*(www.rajae.net)*

Rajae publicly promotes herself as a (Sufi) Muslim artist/singer.[12] Her commitment to Islam has been a constant factor in her career, as well as in her personal life.

These (online) public announcements by Salah Edin, Fathi Otmani, and Rajae, all artists with Moroccan roots, immediately point to different shades of Muslimness. All have a commitment to their Muslim identity; however, management of this commitment differs. Rajae produces music for "the *ummah*," whereas Salah Edin would "never, never, never label his music 'Islamic'."[13] Rajae advocates her music as being a product for Muslim youth, while also staging herself as a Muslim artist.[14] Fathi Otmani makes Islamic pop *nasheed* songs and specifically utters his wish to improve the – what he considers to be – distorted image of Islam by means of his music.

What all three of them have in common is that they take inspiration from Islam in the production of their music. Even though their styles and genres differ greatly, their religiosity plays an important part in their artistic work. Fathi Otmani has an ambition to make music that is in line with Islamic rulings and music that also in content (lyrics) expresses an Islamic message. Rajae's music is a mix of Arab, North African, and Western musical influences, with a jazzy, pop sound. Her lyrics often implicitly or explicitly refer to her Muslim background. In a 2010 interview talking about her album *Hand of Fatima* (2010) with *Heba Magazine*[15] she states:

60% of the World's Muslim population is younger than 23. They go through life without Muslim Hollywood heroes, because they are not seen as the mainstream and because Hollywood does not seem to like happy and fashionable Muslims. I could have recorded love songs, or exotic songs with modern oriental beats, but instead I decided to take a leap of faith and create songs that represent the emotions and experiences that the current Muslim youth silently go through … The struggles of the kids of Maghreb immigrants in Europe, who face racism, loss of identity, who deal with power struggles in broken families and the cry for inclusive societies and leadership that promotes equality and peace. I also try to simplify Islamic phrases to universal phrases, to make them more understandable for non Muslims who appreciate my music from a universal point of view.

*(www.hebamagazine.com)*

Rajae strongly promotes the use of popular culture, music in her case, as a counterpart to the Islamophobic trends she perceives as reigning in Western Europe. Moreover, she considers popular culture and its producers and key figures to be also an important part of the identification processes of European Muslim youth.

Salah Edin has been concerned with the issue of Islam in Dutch society from his first album onwards. His first major hit, "Het land van" (The country of, 2005),[16] was a reaction to a hit song by Dutch rappers Lange Frans and Baas B by the same title. This latter song was a patriotic and laudatory song about the beauty of the Netherlands and its inhabitants. Salah Edin could not reconcile himself with that image of the Netherlands. He released the song "Het land van." In his version of "Het land van" Salah Edin tells his (other, darker) side of the story. Salah Edin summarizes all the nasty, painful, and hidden nuisances of the Dutch, with a strong focus on racism and Islamophobia. Against the backdrop of the aftermath of 9/11, the murder of Theo van Gogh in 2004, and the rise of right-wing, anti-Islam politician Geert Wilders, this song caught the attention of press and mainstream Dutch media. Salah Edin's commitment to Islam and Muslims in this song is mainly a religiosity that is linked to a political ambition. There are no specific references to religion in terms of propagating a certain moral code, or advocating a more Islamic lifestyle. His lyrics deal with the struggle for acceptance of Dutch Muslims, and Muslim identity (and appearance) in particular.[17]

The accompanying video[18] shows various scenes of a dark, violent, Islamophobic, and crooked Dutch society where justice and solidarity are hard to find. Salah Edin features in the foreground, starting out as an "ordinary rapper," but slowly transforming into a "terrorist with a bomb-belt under his orange Guantanamo Bay outfit"; a lookalike of Mohammed Bouyeri, the killer of Theo van Gogh (murdered November 2, 2004). The story suggests that the flaws of Dutch society, and more specifically its discrimination against foreigners, especially Muslims, have turned "an ordinary Dutch Moroccan" into a "terrorist." It consists of many other references to the political climate in the Netherlands and the way Salah Edin sees the position of Muslims in Dutch society.

These three artists find inspiration in Islam, albeit in very different ways. Salah Edin's political engagement, in combination with his own Muslim background, inspired him to write the song "Het land van." Rajae sees in her music a way to bridge cultural and religious differences. Fathi praises his religion through his music and expresses his love for Islam also to counter negativity and stereotypes about Islam. Besides voicing a counter-message to Islamophobia, these artists and their musical productions are also significant for the identification processes of Dutch Moroccan youth. By being role models, they give Dutch Moroccan youth an example of how to be creative, cool, socially and politically engaged, *and* Muslim.

## Conclusion

In this chapter I have shown how different shades of Muslimness are watered down in a range of different popular cultural productions produced and consumed by Dutch Moroccan youth. It is interesting to note that many of the ways in which popular culture is "Islamized" relate to the implementation of what are thought to be basic Islamic codes such as the consumption of certain foods and drinks (no alcohol, no pork, *halal* food), the wearing of certain dress (Islamic fashion, and in general covering yourself decently), and gearing towards certain behavioral codes focusing on modesty and decency, specifically linked to gender relations. Certain consumption and behavioral patterns are hence labeled Islamic (or *halal*).

These codes are perceived to be clear cut and revolve around the *halal–haram* dichotomy. These codes have, according to Roy, always been important guidelines for Muslims throughout history. It is a dichotomy that seems to become even more significant and more leading when Muslims live in a non-Muslim environment. In present-day Europe, a large portion of Muslims are migrants or descendants of migrants. For those people living in a non-Muslim country who are consciously making an effort to follow Islamic guidelines, the question whether something is *haram* or *halal* becomes ever more important (Roy 2005: 140).

The importance of these ethical codes lies in the fact that they are seen as congruent with Islam. Roy argues, in reporting on the emergence of a virtual *umma*, that, as a result of searching for a "pure, deculturalized" Islam, "special national trademarks, specific cultures and histories move to the background and [this] is coupled with a search for a norm that can be applied in various contexts, or rather, a norm that need not be bothered with context: this explains why the 'salafi' message is most suitable for shaping the virtual *umma*" (Roy 2003: 162). Roy thus suggests that because of the desire to disconnect culture from religion, ethical and basic norms are reified as Islamic, since these can work in any cultural or historical context. The European minority context in which European Muslims find themselves is by definition an environment (almost) devoid of "Islamic history" and with few cultural references symbolizing Islamic history or traditions. This accelerates the prominence of these ethical codes, since they are thus "easily" implicated. It is easier to conform to ethical codes, like behaving in a modest way or eating *halal* food, than to recreate and perform Islamic rituals or traditions that require the presence of an all-Islamic environment.

To emphasize ethics which can be applied in any cultural context appeals to youth living in a post-migration, minority context who are struggling to get a grip on living a life they wish to be Islamic in form and content, with at the same time due recognition to their search for and expression of youthful popular culture. These new, innovative cultural productions pay tribute to being young, creative, cool European, *and* Muslim.

The short biographies of the three artists I presented indicate a concern with Islam that predominantly relates to its minority status in Europe. The ambition to counter Islamophobic trends reigning in Europe clearly resonates in all of their works. Their focus of interest is in creating an alternative Muslim voice in popular mainstream culture. Their way of merging Islam with popular culture stems from socio-political and religious endeavors aimed at improving the image of Islam.

## Notes

1 Research for this publication has been funded by the Cultural Dynamics Programme of the Netherlands Organisation for Scientific Research (NWO). This research is part of a larger research program entitled Islamic Cultural Practices and Performances: New Youth Cultures in Europe and is subsidized by the NWO Cultural Dynamics Programme (2008–11). This research project engages with emergent forms of Islamic cultural production in Europe, in particular artistic performances, popular music, fashionable dress, and mosque design.
2 *Haram* is an Islamic concept denoting activities or things that are forbidden. *Halal* stands for permissible.
3 Note that not *all* events targeting a Dutch Moroccan audience are "Islamized."
4 Interview with Ahmed, February 21, 2012. All interview fragments are translated from Dutch into English by the author.
5 Tweet translated into English by the author (accessed January 27, 2012).
6 www.salahedinwo2.nl/bio/ (accessed March 14, 2012).
7 Personal communication, Salah Edin, November 3, 2011, Amsterdam.
8 Besides his stage name, of course; Salah Edin's real name is Abid Tounssi. He chose Salah Edin as a stage name because it is also the name of a famous general in Islamic history who reconquered Jerusalem from the Christian Crusaders around 1170. Furthermore, the literal meaning of Salah Edin is "the virtuousness of the faith."
9 *Nasheed* (pl. *anasheed*) is a religious Islamic song, often praising Allah and the prophet. *Anasheed* are often sung a capella and only use certain percussion instruments and no melodic instruments. This is thought to be in line with Islamic rulings on music.
10 Taken from fathiotmani.net/bio/ (accessed October 17, 2012).
11 *Umma* is an Islamic concept denoting the community of (Muslim) believers.
12 "In November 2011, for the third year in a row, she was the only female contemporary singer to appear on the Arts and Culture section list of the 500 most influential Muslims in the world." Taken from Rajae's website: rajae.net/about/ (accessed October 17, 2012).
13 Personal communication, Salah Edin, November 3, 2011.
14 Interview, Rajae, with *Heeba Magazine*: www.heeba.org/featured/interview-rajae-el-mouhandiz/ (accessed March 14, 2012).

15 www.hebamagazine.com.
16 Single taken from the album *Nederlands Grootste Nachtmerrie* (Holland's worst nightmare) (2007, Top Notch).
17 See www.songteksten.nl/songteksten/73928/salah-edin/het-land-van.htm for the lyrics.
18 www.youtube.com/watch?v=ZPmwoKEPIvM (accessed October 17, 2012).

# Bibliography

Agrama, H. (2012) "Reflections on Secularism, Democracy, and Politics in Egypt," *American Ethnologist* 39(1): 26–31.
Baig, K. (2008) *Slippery Stone: An Inquiry into Islam's Stance on Music*, Garden Grove, CA: Open Mind Press.
Bayat, A. (2007) "Islamism and the Politics of Fun," *Public Culture* 19(3): 433–60.
——(2010) "Introduction: Being Young and Muslim in Neo-liberal Times," in Herrera, L. and Bayat, A. (eds.) *Being Young and Muslim: New Cultural Politics in the Global South and North*, New York: Oxford University Press, pp. 3–26.
Chan-Malik, S. (2011) "Music: Hip Hop, Spoken Word and Rap: United States of America," in *Encyclopaedia of Women and Islamic Cultures*, Leiden: Brill, pp. 1–9, www.academia.edu/attachments/6832694/download_file (accessed 22 November 22, 2012).
De Koning, M. (2009) "Islam Is Islam. Punt Uit?," *Migrantenstudies* 1: 59–72.
Echchaibi, N. (2008) "Hyper Islamism: Mediating Islam from the Halal Website to the Islamic Talk Show," *Journal of Arab and Muslim Media Research* 1(3): 199–214.
Gazzah, M. (2008) *Rhythms and Rhymes of Life: Music and Identification Processes of Dutch-Moroccan Youth*, Amsterdam: Amsterdam University Press.
Gokarıksel, B. and McLarney, E.A. (2010) "Muslim Women, Consumer Capitalism, and the Islamic Culture Industry," *Journal of Middle East Women's Studies* 6(3): 1–18.
Herding, M. (2012) "Inventing the Muslim Cool: Islamic Youth Culture in Western Europe," unpublished Ph.D. thesis, University of Cambridge.
Jouili, J.S. (2012) "Halal Arts, What's in a Concept?," *Material Religion* 8(3): 402–3.
Khabeer, S.A. (2007) "Rep that Islam. The Rhyme and Reason of American Islamic Hip Hop," *The Muslim World* 97(1): 125–41.
——(2011) "Hip Hop Is Islam: Race, Self-making and Young Muslims in Chicago," Ph.D. thesis, Princeton University, ProQuest, Ann Arbor.
Lynch, G. (ed.) (2007) *Between Sacred and Profane: Researching Religion and Popular Culture*, London: I.B. Tauris.
Mahan, J. (2007) "Reflections on the Past and Future of the Study of Religion and Popular Culture," in Lynch, G. (ed.) *Between Sacred and Profane: Researching Religion and Popular Culture*, London: I.B. Tauris, pp. 47–61.
Mandaville, P. (2009) "Hip-hop, Nasheeds, and 'Cool' Sheikhs: Popular Culture and Muslim Youth in the United Kingdom," in Timmerman, C., Leman, J., Roos, H., and Segaert, B. (eds.) *In-Between Spaces: Christian and Muslim Minorities in Transition in Europe and the Middle East*, Gods, Humans and Religions vol. 18, Brussels: PIE–Peter Lang, pp. 149–69.
Meyer, B. (2009) "Introduction: From Imagined Communities to Aesthetic Formations: Religious Mediations, Sensational Forms and Styles of Binding," in Meyer, B. (ed.) *Aesthetic Formations: Media, Religion and the Senses in the Making of Communities*, Macmillan: Palgrave.
Moors, A. (2009) "Islamic Fashion in Europe: Religious Conviction, Aesthetic Style, and Creative Consumption," *Encounters* 1(1): 175–201.
——(2012) "Introduction: Special Issue: Popularizing Islam: Muslims and Materiality," *Material Religion* 8(3): 272–9.
Otterbeck, J. (2008) "Battling over the Public Sphere: Islamic Reactions to the Music of Today," in van Nieuwkerk, K. (ed.) *Creating an Islamic Cultural Sphere: Contested Notions of Art, Leisure and Entertainment, Special Issue: Contemporary Islam* 2(3): 211–29.
Pond, C. (2006) "The Appeal of Sami Yusuf and the Search for Islamic Authenticity," *Transnational Broadcasting Studies Journal* 16: 1–13, www.tbsjournal.com/Pond.html (accessed November 7, 2012).
Roy, O. (2005) *De globalisering van de Islam*, Amsterdam: Van Gennep.
——(2006) "Islam in the West or Western Islam? The Disconnect of Religion and Culture," *The Hedgehog Review* (Spring and Summer): 127–32.

Van Nieuwkerk, K. (1995) *A Trade Like Any Other: Female Singers and Dancers in Egypt*, Austin: Texas University Press.

——(1998) "Changing Images and Shifting Identities: Female Performers in Egypt," in Zuhur, S. (ed.) *Images of Enchantment. Visual and Performing Arts of the Middle East*, Cairo: American University Press Cairo, pp. 21–35.

——(2008) "Creating an Islamic Cultural Sphere: Contested Notions of Art, Leisure and Entertainment," in van Nieuwkerk, K. (ed.) *Special Issue: Contemporary Islam* 2(3): pp. 169–76.

——(2011) "Introduction: Artistic Developments in the Muslim Cultural Sphere: Ethics, Aesthetics, and the Performing Arts," in van Nieuwkerk, K. (ed.) *Muslim Rap, Halal Soaps and Revolutionary Theatre: Artistic Developments in the Muslim World*, Austin: University of Texas Press, Austin, pp. 1–24.

Varul, M.Z. (2008) "After Heroism: Religion versus Consumerism. Preliminaries for an Investigation of Protestantism and Islam under Consumer Culture," *Islam and Christian–Muslim Relations* 19(2): 237–55.

# 22

# Muslim material culture in the Western world

*Johan Fischer*

## Introduction

When I was walking down the Edgware Road in central London[1] in August 2009, the large number of "Islamic" products and services offered caught my eye. I was there in connection with a research project that explored the proliferation of *halal* ("permitted") as a global religious market, with a particular focus on the role of Malaysia and Malays in this market in London. The Islamic market so ubiquitous in the Edgware Road signifies some wider transformations that have taken place during the last decade or so, including a changing Islamic business and entrepreneurial environment in London, but also more globally, as we shall see in this chapter. Most of the shops, restaurants, cafés, money transfer agencies, kiosks, barbers, banks, and estate agencies here are run by Muslims. The growth of Muslim businesses in London reflects the wider growth of and will to invest in ethnic minority businesses in the UK (Ahmed 2008: 655).

At the same time, scholarly interest in Islamic markets is growing. For example, from an interdisciplinary perspective the edited volume *Muslim Societies in the Age of Mass Consumption* (Pink 2009) argues that, in spite of the intensifying globalization of markets and consumption, these processes have received modest scholarly attention. More specifically, this volume explores issues such as the changing spaces of consumption, branding, and the marketing of religious music as well as the consumption patterns of Muslim minority groups.

The proliferation of Islamic commodities and services on a global scale applies to what has been called the globalization of religious markets (Lee 1993) – for the sake of argument I shall call these "Islamic markets." Politicians, bureaucrats and entrepreneurs use the popular mass media to manipulate popular desires (Lee 1993: 37). More specifically, Islamic commodities and services are advertised globally as religious necessities that fulfill private desires such as piety, purity, and health – all intimately linked to the "market for identities" (Navaro-Yashin 2002: 11). Inspired by the recent work of Daniel Miller, I understand material culture to be how things work by being invisible, unremarked upon, familiar, and taken for granted: "such a perspective seems properly described as material culture since it implies that much of what makes us what we are exists ... as an exterior environment that habituates and prompts us" (Miller 2009: 50–1).

This chapter explores contemporary Muslim material culture, paying particular attention to London. It examines different types of commodities ("paraphernalia," clothes, and *halal*) and "Islamic" services (delivered by Islamic organizations, "ethnic" consultancy companies, and banks), arguing that emerging Islamic markets raise a number of broader questions pertaining to the relationship between Muslim identities, shopping, and recognition.

More recent literature on migration shopping explores how modern and globalized forms of consumer capitalism have generated the growth of ethnic and "roots" celebrations. In the USA from the 1970s onwards, for example, companies started to turn away from mass advertising campaigns to focus on segmented marketing approaches and migrant shopping in particular. In migration shopping, academic ideas about multiculturalism in modern societies fuse together with the interests of the business sector. Thus, migrant groups were targeted as essential segments of modern consumers who, to a large extent, construct individual and group ethnic identities through their shopping. In the USA, such migrant shopping campaigns have targeted Jews, Irish Americans, Hispanics, and, more recently, Muslims, for example (Halter 2000). In US advertising and mass media, as well as in the new media environment of blogs, video, and social networks, Muslims and Islamic identity are taking center-stage (Hastings-Black 2009).

More specifically, these broader questions relate to globalized Islam post-9/11; shopping as a patriotic duty in mass culture; modern Islam as a discursive tradition; "the secular" as an epistemic category and "secularism" as a political doctrine; as well as Charles Taylor's idea that identities are partly given shape or denied by the recognition or non-recognition of others.

## Setting the scene: Muslim consumer culture in contemporary London

In 2006, the Office of National Statistics estimated that there were 1,558,890 Muslims in Britain. The two largest groups are Pakistani (43.2 percent) and Bangladeshi (16.55), while "Other Asians" account for 5.8 percent (www.statistics.gov.uk/cci/nugget.asp?id=954 and www.statistics.gov.uk/cci/nugget.asp?id=957, accessed November 12, 2009). The Muslim population in London is one of the largest in any European city and Islam is the second largest faith in London after Christianity. According to the 2001 census, 607,000 people living in London identified themselves as Muslims, that is, 8.5 percent of London's population. (www.london.gov.uk/gla/publications/equalities/muslims-in-london.pdf, accessed November 12, 2009).

London qualifies as a "global city" (Sassen 2002: 2) as it plays an important role in linking the national as well as European economy with global circuits of commodities, people, and ideas, and this is also the case with the Islamic marketplace. Muslim space-making or landscaping in London and comparable cities is the production of the social and cultural space of networks and identities created as Muslims interact with one another and with the larger community (Metcalf 1996: 2). The proliferation of Islamic markets contributes to social and cultural space-making in a city such as London. Often it is certain activities – shopping and eating, for example – that contribute to the creation of "Muslim space" (Metcalf 1996: 6). Another example is the display and transmission of the Arabic word *halal*, written in Arabic and/or Roman characters, and its involvement in the production, recognition, and contestation of *halal* space in London.

The spatial contexts of producing, displaying, selling, and shopping for Islamic commodities in the Western world have received modest attention. Shopping for Islamic commodities cannot be divorced from the context in which they are sold, that is, the spatial context of such consumption may in practice be just as significant as the qualities of the paraphernalia, food, or services. Hence, Islamic markets are not merely conditioning and conditioned by aesthetics and the religious self-understanding of Muslim consumers. They also reflect much more mundane understandings and practices, such as social aspects of chatting or socializing with the butcher in a *halal* butcher shop or customers in a convenience store. In recent years, *halal* spaces such as restaurants, butcher's shops, grocery and convenience stores, supermarkets and hypermarkets are proliferating in London. These Muslim spaces or landscapes often materialize in the interfaces between Islamic "paraphernalia" (using, for instance, plaques with Islamic calligraphy to evoke a form of Islamic authenticity), *halal* commodities (a growing number of Muslim consumers are concerned not only with traditional *halal* food requirements as stated in the Qur'an, but also contamination from *haram* ("forbidden") sources in products such as confectionary, toiletries, and medication), as well as Islamic organizations or "ethnic" consultancy firms that certify commodities or advise companies about proper Islamic branding and advertising.

In many parts of London, such as the Edgware Road, Finsbury Park, and Whitechapel Road, *halal* is a distinctive presence on signs and in butcher shops and restaurants. Lately, *halal* certified products have been appearing in large numbers in supermarkets such as Tesco (a UK-based international grocery and merchandising retail chain – Tesco is the largest British retailer by both global sales and domestic market share) and Asda (a British supermarket chain that retails both food and merchandise). In effect, the novel ubiquity of *halal* in some parts of London can be seen as a form of urban space-making (Metcalf 1996) and Islamic visibility (Esposito 1995: 195).

In itself, a city such as London can be said to be a charismatic entity (Hansen and Verkaaik 2009). Charisma is today being democratized in the marketplace, for example, and this has "entailed a measure of objectification – standardization, definition, and tangibility – and a commercial exchangeability of objects, attributes, and skills that are assumed to produce charisma" (Hansen and Verkaaik 2009: 7). The proliferation of Islamic markets in London is a good example of a particular type of urban exchangeability that is imbricated in the mundane practices of everyday shopping to effect charisma among Muslims.

## Islamic paraphernalia: of plaques and cell phones

In many of the grocery stores in the Edgware Road, a wide variety of Islamic paraphernalia is also sold. These Islamic commodities are no longer an expression of esoteric forms of production, trade, and consumption, but part of a huge and expanding globalized market marked by intensified flows of mass-produced commodities. Based on fieldwork among Muslim Sierra Leoneans living and working in Washington, DC, D'Alisera (2001) shows that a global trend in recent years has been the emergence of a thriving business in Islamic goods. Items from stickers, rugs, holiday cards, and plaques with Islamic calligraphy to special types of holidays aimed at Muslim audiences, watches displaying prayer (*salat*) times and other features, logos and ring tones on cell phones, clothes, etc. touch upon and "Islamicize" virtually every aspect of life (D'Alisera 2001: 97). At the same time, there has been a marked change from craft production to mass production of religious commodities (Starrett 1995). All these types of products are available in the Islamic marketplace in London.

D'Alisera's study explores in depth how and why Muslim Sierra Leoneans in Washington, DC inscribe religious identity onto their cars by means of a variety of Islamic commodities, such as bumper stickers displaying Qur'anic verses in Arabic. This type of decoration "serves to reflect the ways they bridge the gap between various, sometimes competing modes of reference, and thus define their place in the community" (D'Alisera 2001: 97). These forms of decoration, marking, or tagging of commodities or space are visible not only on the Edgware Road, but also in other areas of London that have sizeable Muslim populations.

When imported into Muslim homes, these religious commodities are highly visible manifestations of ways in which Islam can be domesticated, that is, given material expression in the intimacy of the home. The effect of this importation of Islamic paraphernalia is to individualize the house and thus transform it from being a mere commodity into a home. An example of this is that a plaque with Islamic calligraphy may serve a number of purposes. First, of course, it is an Islamic symbol or emblem seen as protecting the house and its inhabitants. Second, plaques or signs can also serve the purpose of marking Muslim space in public. A large part of my field-work took place in *halal* restaurants, particularly Malaysian ones, where I ate *halal* food and discussed *halal* with guests, restaurant owners, and *halal* traders. Several of the most popular Malaysian restaurants in London advertise themselves as "Malaysian (*halal*) cuisine" on signs. In one of these restaurants there are several tourist posters from Malaysia, but no visible Islamic paraphernalia, such as plaques with Islamic calligraphy. Another Malaysian restaurant in North London, which is part of a food court located in Oriental City Shopping Mall, likewise advertises itself as serving "*halal* Malaysian cuisine." Adjacent to the food court is an Asian supermarket that also sells fresh *halal* meat and a whole range of other *halal* products, as well as Islamic paraphernalia. In this restaurant in North London a plaque with Islamic calligraphy is visible behind the counter. In another Malaysian *halal* restaurant in Paddington, West London, plaques with Islamic calligraphy as well as the Malaysian national flag call attention to the focus on Malaysian Muslim *halal* cuisine.

Another dimension is the way in which cell phones and their widely marketed Islamic paraphernalia can be seen to inscribe technological equipment with some sort of "sacred" quality. Adding to this trend, in 2004 Ilkone Mobile, a Dubai company, launched an Islamic cell phone (www.ameinfo.com/43982.html, accessed November 12, 2009). Besides sending an SMS (Short Message Service) at prayer times, it can point to the exact location of Mecca from anywhere on the globe. On the one hand, the cell phone in itself is a quintessential example of a commodity that has been introduced fairly recently into the global market and also a relatively expensive commodity that some Muslims may conceptualize as a trendy and technologically advanced piece of Westernization or globalization. On the other hand, it is a social piece of equipment through which families can communicate in a rushed everyday life where both parents and children are often away from home.

London is a thriving market for a wide range of Islamic paraphernalia that can serve a number of purposes. This wide and growing range of commodities signifies intensified flows of goods in the era of globalization. During my periods of fieldwork in London, I spent a great deal of time in Muslim shops that sell Islamic paraphernalia and it was evident that these com-modities are imported from all over the world, eventually reaching London, where they can contribute to the marking of commodities and private/public spaces.

## The proper and improper dressing of Muslim bodies

The French concept of *laïcité* roughly translates as secularism. With particular reference to the question of why the law against religious signs in public schools was passed, Bowen concludes that the veil in France symbolizes rising Islamism, decaying social life, and "tracked" anxieties about the fraying of the Republic, as well as political Islam (Bowen 2007: 242).

The heated debate about religious signs in public, and Muslim women's dress in particular, is by no means limited to France. These questions are controversial in many European countries, including Britain. During my fieldwork in London, Muslim women's right to wear the *niqab* (a veil that covers the face) was criticized and questioned in the media. One headline read "This Veil Fixation Is Doing Muslim Women No Favours. We need an honest debate about women and Islam. But the current politically driven campaign is making that more difficult" (*Guardian*, October 19, 2006). Another headline was "Tribunal Dismisses Case of Muslim Woman

Ordered Not to Teach in Veil" (*Guardian*, October 20, 2006). Finally, in an article headed "White Pupils Less Tolerant, Survey Shows," the point was made that "Arguments about the Muslim veil in Britain are part of a wider debate taking place across Europe. Amid competing claims of religious freedom and official secularism, some argue that the debate is motivated by growing intolerance of Muslims" (*Guardian*, October 21, 2006). Thus, the veil is essentialized as "Muslim culture" and thought to establish a "community" with shared values despite ethnic, national, and linguistic diversity (Bauman 1996: 23).

Why is the dressing of Muslim women's bodies such a controversial question in a modern European context where bodies are constantly subjected to forms of experimentation in terms of dress, fashion, and plastic surgery? Human bodily existence can be seen as both the basis and the "model" of the constitution of the subject or the self. The body is essential in consumption as it is the site for often involuntary and revealing display. For Bourdieu, the most significant process of embodiment is the interaction that takes place between bodies, on the one hand, and the space structured around myth and ritual, on the other (Bourdieu 1977: 89). Dressing the body is "a means of symbolic display, a way of giving external form to narratives of self-identity" (Giddens 1991: 62). The main point here is that the dressing of the outer body is where the inner worlds of individuals and groups meet and/or conflict with the surrounding society. It is the overt dressing of Muslims that tends to generate intensifying debates about what is proper/ improper religious signification of public bodies.

Debates over Muslim dress have been explored in an extensive body of literature and it is not within the scope of this article to discuss or review all this literature. An example of an illuminating study (Tarlo 1995) of the *hijab* in Britain suggests that its adoption by middle-class Muslim women is often a product of the transcultural encounters they experience in a cosmopolitan urban environment. The article shows that the resonance of the *hijab* in Britain and elsewhere in the West is constantly being reshaped both through contemporary political events and their media coverage, as well as through the actions and campaigns of *hijab* wearers.

With reference to France and Britain, Werbner considers the ambiguities and ambivalences associated with the politics of embodiment surrounding veiling and honor killings comparatively, and the implications for ongoing debates on multiculturalism. She argues that the publicity surrounding symbolic practices of sexual intimacy in the context of modernity may come to be loaded with secondary symbolic connotations, often highly politicized, for both Muslims and Europeans, leading to "irresolvable conundrums" (Werbner 2007: 161).

In Turkey, secularists' fantasies about Islamists in public life have actively produced and maintained versions of Islamism (Navaro-Yashin 2002: 7). Consequently, Islamists' compulsions to gender segregation and veiling are not essential features of Islam. Rather, Islamists "began to know themselves and to take action upon the world in assuming, internalizing, reversing, and upholding what secularists had demonized" (Navaro-Yashin 2002: 42). The politics of identity within these groups has been deeply influenced by an expanding consumer market in the context of the globalization of the 1980s and 1990s. In this context, Islamists molded an Islamic consumer ontology emerging in this new market for identities (Navaro-Yashin 2002: 111). These controversies around the "veiling-fashion" are by no means resolved in modern Turkey and pose a latent field of tension (Gökarıksel and Secor 2009).

My fieldwork in London showed that some Malay Muslim women in London, but by no means all, wear the *tudung* (long headscarf). Based on my previous periods of fieldwork in urban Malaysia, it was clear that comparatively more women would be wearing the *tudung* in the Malaysian setting. This indicates that claims concerning piety and Islamic identities through dress for women in particular are not necessarily stronger in a diasporic context. Indeed, the diasporic context can be supportive of more relaxed sentiments compared with the homeland.

I suggest that, contrary to the tendency in much literature to see ethnic and religious traits reinforced in a diasporic context, the opposite effect is possible; that is, migrants may feel that in London, for instance, they can escape or negotiate what are seen to be dogmatic or conformist forms of religion in the homeland. Hence, the highly politicized discourses that again and again stress that Muslim women do not have a choice when it comes to dress are not necessarily backed by empirical evidence.

## *Halal* I: in and between bodies

*Halal* literally means "lawful" or "permitted." The Qur'an and the *Sunna* (the life, actions, and teachings of the Prophet Muhammad) exhort Muslims to eat the good and lawful food God has provided for them, but a number of conditions and prohibitions are imposed. Muslims are expressly forbidden to consume carrion, spurting blood, pork, and foods that have been consecrated to any being other than God himself, which are said to be *haram*. The lawfulness of meat depends on how it is obtained. Ritual slaughter, *dhabh*, requires that the animal is killed in God's name by making a fatal incision across the throat. In this process, the blood should be drained off as fully as possible. Among Muslim groups and individuals, the question of the stunning of animals prior to slaughter is highly contested; that is, some Muslims consider only meat from unstunned animals to be *halal*, while others accept that stunning is part of modern and ethical food production.

In spite of the fact that they are not mentioned in the Qur'an, consumption of a number of creatures has been forbidden by the *ulama'* (Denny 2006: 278). Another significant Islamic prohibition relates to wine and any other intoxicating drink or substance, all of which are, according to the majority of opinions, *haram* whatever the quantity or substance (Denny 2006: 279). Muslim dietary rules assumed new significance in the twentieth century, as some Muslims began striving to demonstrate how such rules conform to modern reason and the findings of scientific research. Another common theme in the revival and renewal of these dietary rules seems to be the search for alternatives to what are seen to be Western values, ideologies, and lifestyles. These re-evaluations of requirements and prohibitions are prominent, first, in post-colonial Islamic cultures such as Malaysia and, second, among diaspora groups, for whom *halal* can serve as a focal point for Islamic movements and identities (Esposito 1995: 376).

In the modern food industry around the world, a number of Muslim requirements have been taken into account, such as a recommendation to avoid substances that may be contaminated with porcine residues or alcohol, such as gelatine, glycerine, emulsifiers, enzymes, flavors, and flavorings (Riaz and Chaudry 2004: 22–5). Commenting on this area, an article in the *Guardian* (October 26, 2006), "Something Fishy in Your Pasta?," demonstrates that in some cases gelatine, among other things, is being "sneaked" into a variety of foods. The problem in certifying food and other products with regard to these substances is that they are extremely difficult to detect. For some Muslims, *halal* sensibilities necessitate that *halal* products be produced by Muslims only, and that this type of production be kept strictly separate from non-*halal* production – not unlike the way in which the proliferation of rules and taboos concerning food in orthodox Judaism excludes others as "unclean."

My study of modern *halal* in London demonstrated that many British Muslims and organizations call upon the state to help recognize and standardize *halal*. Contrary to the intense debate over veiling, there is no corresponding state discourse on *halal* in Britain. *Halal* in more and more commodities and contexts is becoming important for Muslim identities and bodies. At the same time, Islamic bodies or organizations in Britain try to certify and institutionalize *halal*, whereas state bodies are largely uninvolved. Apparently, secularism as a political doctrine defines the secular in everyday life in terms of overt dress codes or of Muslim bodies, whereas more covert *halal* consumption in these bodies is seen to be uncontroversial or unimportant (Fischer 2009b). What is more, the state plays a central role in the governance of London itself. Many Muslims in London consider the city a frontier wilderness that is in need of governance.

An EU-supported project "Religious slaughter: improving knowledge and expertise through dialogue and debate on issues of welfare, legislation and socioeconomic aspects" (DIALREL) explains that "religious slaughter has always been a controversial and emotive subject, caught between animal welfare considerations, cultural and human rights issues. There is considerable variation in current practices and the rules regarding religious requirements are still confusing." DIALREL "aims to gather this information by encouraging a constructive dialogue between interested parties" (ec.europa.eu/research/biosociety/food_quality/projects/168_en.html, accessed October 23, 2009).

As we saw it with regard to urban Muslim spaces or landscapes, *halal* is highly visible in signs and logos in the urban landscape. There are hundreds of *halal* butchers in London, that is, shops that mainly sell meat. They can be classified according to ethnicity and are often run by Pakistani, Indian, or Bangladeshi Muslims. In many cases *halal* meat is sold together with, for example, Mediterranean or Afro-Caribbean/Asian specialities.

The huge Tesco Extra store in Slough, outside London, a hypermarket, boasts of having the widest "Asian world foods" ranges, including *halal*, in Britain. Downstairs in the Tesco Extra store in Slough there is a more traditional *halal* butcher, operating as a concession selling fresh meat. Anecdotal evidence from my fieldwork in this area suggests that Tesco, by using this store in Slough as an entry into the *halal* market, has reduced sales among *halal* butchers in the surrounding area. Around the same time, in the Asda supermarket in North London, I found Halal Food Authority (HFA) certified chilled chicken and mutton; in other words, this shop too is undercutting the prices of local butchers. As I shall discuss in detail later on, the HFA is one of two Islamic bodies set up in 1994 to certify *halal* meat and other types of products. *Halal* is being lifted out of its traditional base in local *halal* butcher's shops to become part of "world food" ranges in major supermarkets.

Slaughter in accordance with Islamic law has been permitted in the UK under the Slaughter of Animals Act of 1933 (Charlton and Kaye 1985: 490; Lewis 1994; Vertovec 1996). The hostility to religious slaughter "heightened awareness of Islamic practice and a sense of self-identity among a growing number of British Muslims" (Ansari 2004: 355). There is an emerging literature on ritual slaughter and *halal* meat consumption in the West (Bergeaud-Blackler 2004, 2007; Bonne et al. 2007).

In this respect, the state has recognized religious needs and adapted policies to accommodate Muslim groups. However, as the understanding and practice of *halal* production, trade, and consumption are being transformed to involve more and more types of products, not unlike what has already happened with regard to kosher products, the state is called upon to help regulate these commodities. While the state in Britain recognizes traditional *halal* requirements, such as religious slaughter without stunning, it has virtually no authority to inspect, certify, or standardize *halal*. In the eyes of some British Muslims, this leaves consumers unprotected against growing commercial interest in *halal*. Hence, the more the culture of Islamic consumption asserts itself, the more the state's incapacity to define what is legitimately *halal* is felt. Contrary to the intense debate in Britain over veiling (overt and on bodies), for example, there is no corresponding state discourse on *halal* (covert and in bodies). Only recently has the established concept of *halal*, which largely focuses on ritual slaughter and pork and alcohol avoidance, been resignified and assumed new meanings in terms of what is pure, sacred, appropriate, or healthy.

## *Halal* II: "doubled in size for 2006"?

In November 2005, the Halal Exhibition at the major World Food Market (WFM) in London was held for the first time. In addition to the large number of booths displaying *halal* products, WFM also offered seminars on the business potential of *halal* in the rapidly expanding "ethnic food" or "world food" market.

The quotation in this heading is taken from a claim made in a pamphlet promoting the World Food Market held in 2006 in London that, compared with 2005, this event had "doubled in size for 2006." The exhibition may have "doubled in size," but the statement also reflects a broader *halal* hype in London. A large number of companies and Islamic organizations are represented at the Halal Exhibition, each with a particular understanding of what can be considered proper *halal* consumption. Companies at the Halal Exhibition also present a whole range of new products, such as chocolate and toothpaste, which can be subjected to divergent forms of standardization and certification. Supermarkets such as Tesco and Asda have introduced a *halal* chocolate bar (www.ummahfoods.com). Among other slogans, the advertising says, "Community & chocolate close to your heart? Isn't it time your chocolate bar did something more than just taste good?" The bar's label also carries the wording: "10% of net profit goes to charity." In addition to the large number of booths displaying *halal* products, WFM also offered seminars on the business potential of *halal* in the rapidly expanding "ethnic food" or "world food" market.

The controversial question of *halal* certification surfaced on the first day of the WFM seminars. A former director of environmental health and consumer affairs services, Dr. Yunes Teinaz, who was also an adviser to the London Central Mosque on *halal* questions, accused many of the companies present of promoting *halal* products that were not properly *halal* certified by an Islamic authority. For this adviser, the lack of a state body in Britain that is capable of inspecting the "totally unregulated" *halal* market has left this market open to fraud, corruption, and without any kind of standards, uniform certification, or legislation. This, in turn, is distorting the commercially promoted image of *halal* as healthy, pure, and modern food in an era of food scares. In the eyes of this adviser, as well as of many Muslims in London, the Jewish system of kosher certification is seen as a model for the institutionalization, standardization, and certification of *halal* in the gray zones between religious revivalism, the state, and consumer culture.

Present at WFM were, first, numerous Islamic organizations, groups, and individuals that understand and practice *halal* in divergent ways, including the HFA (www.halalfoodauthority. co.uk), set up in 1994 to certify *halal* meat.[2] Second, a number of government institutions, such as schools and hospitals, were represented in that they are experiencing an increase in *halal* sensibilities among Muslim groups. Third, several market research firms specializing in "ethnic markets" participated to provide in-depth understanding of the transformation of *halal*. Finally, a large number of confused Muslim consumers were there to learn how modern understandings and practices of *halal* are being transformed. In Ahmed's study of the marketing of *halal* meat in the UK between local shops and supermarkets, he concludes: "These issues and problems also have religious, traditional, ethical and industrial relations dimensions" (Ahmed 2008: 667). The emergence of *halal* as a global Islamic market evokes a whole range of social, moral, and religious questions. *Halal* lends itself well as examples of types of commodities to which certification as service is important.

## Islamic services: certification, ethnic business, and banking

We have seen above that Dr. Yunes Teinaz criticized products that were being promoted for not being properly certified. In front of a large audience at a WFM seminar in 2006, he made it clear that there are extensive opportunities for fraud and corruption within the *halal* trade as well as in the local certifying bodies such as HFA and the Halal Monitoring Committee (HMC) (www.halalmc.co.uk) – both represented in the audience at the seminar. He called for the Muslim community to "wake up" and "clean up their act," and finally declared that the state authorities might be willing to "take somebody to court" and "take enforcement action," but these bodies "feel that the Muslim community has not decided yet what the definition of halal is in the first place."

These views are supported by Dr. Yunes Teinaz, who has worked on illegal food and brought cases to court for ten years. As he explained to me, "You can easily buy certification if you pay for it. And they get away with it because there is no control, regulation or inspection from the state." The Muslim Council of Britain (MCB), an interest group, warns that up to 90 percent of the meat and poultry sold as *halal* in the UK may be being sold illegally and not slaughtered according to Muslim requirements. Consequently, several supermarkets are marketing their *halal* meat as 100 percent *halal* authorized by the HFA.

As *halal* and the aspect of religious slaughter increasingly infused Muslim identity in Britain, the need to establish a body of *halal* butcher shops was recognized. Consequently, in 1994 the HFA was set up with encouragement from the Muslim Parliament of Great Britain, a pan-Muslim interest group, and the HFA established a network of approved abattoirs and shops to provide the community with independently certified *halal* meat (Ansari 2004: 355). On the HFA's website the organization is described as a voluntary, non-profit-making organization (www.halalfoodauthority.co.uk). The HFA is "regulating, endorsing and authenticating" as well as "generating" its funds through fees paid for audit by slaughterhouses and cutting plants (www.halalfoodauthority.co.uk).

In contrast to the Jewish certification and institutionalization of kosher, the approach to *halal* among Muslims in Britain has been more fragmented and disunited, and "the broad range of emerging political demands may have served to dilute organizational effectiveness" (Kaye 1993: 251). Moreover, Muslim organizations in Britain claiming to represent the Muslim community are of relatively recent origin and often lack both resources and political experience (Kaye 1993: 247). What some Muslim groups call for is a national standard for *halal* that can mark a kind of British Muslim unity and identity. The central difference, of course, is that the secular state in Britain is reluctant to extend recognition of a relatively fragmented *halal* market beyond already existing regulation of food in general.

When I visited the HFA, there seemed to be a discrepancy between its visions, ambitions, and policies stated on the organization's website and the modest office facilities in London housing the organization's limited number of staff. My point here is that *halal* is a significant field for claiming recognition in a fragmented religious market, whereas practices of regulating *halal* are highly resource demanding. At WFM in 2005 and 2006, the HFA president Masood Khawaja was present, as was a representative from the HMC, Yunus Dudhwala. The HMC was established in 2003 in Leicester and, contrary to the HFA, is against the stunning of animals before slaughter. These two organizations can be seen as competitors with overlapping interests and claims to authority in the *halal* market.

Many of my informants saw the proliferation of *halal* in the UK as an overwhelmingly commercial endeavor for which Islam is a vehicle pragmatically employed by Islamic organizations, Islamic nations, and the *halal* industry. However, the HFA president objects to such commercialization of *halal* and maintains that there is also a distinctive religious or ethical aspect to *halal*. This is a significant point because, in the current *halal* market, a large part of the production and trade is carried out by non-Muslims, so maintaining that there is a definite religious aspect to *halal* is also a way of linking *halal* to Muslim groups and their interests. A large part of the research into *halal* and other forms of religious and ethnic marketing in the UK is carried out by "secular" market research companies such as Mintel (www.mintel.com) and Ethnic Focus (www.ethnicfocus.com), which are starting to recognize the commercial aspects of *halal*. The HFA president Masood Khawaja criticizes Mintel's overly commercial approach to *halal* but, at the same time, supermarkets in London such as Tesco and Asda require products that are *halal* certified by locally recognized bodies such as the HFA and HMC.

Islamic organizations in Britain claim authority through and compete over *halal* in the interfaces between expanding markets, the secular state, and the rights and demands of Muslim consumers. At the same time, these organizations push for a form of national *halal* standard, which could be seen as a sign of Muslim unity and identity. So far, these organizations have not been able to unite Muslim groups around a shared vision of standards. As more and more products appear in this expanding market, both Islamic organizations and commercial interests compete over standards and certification on the margins of the secular state. The emergence of this type of Islamic consumption draws attention to the state's incapacity to regulate *halal* and thus to recognize a Muslim "community."

In the Edgware Road you also find a branch of the Islamic Bank of Britain (www.islamic-bank.com), which promotes itself by saying: "As the first stand-alone, *shari'a* compliant, retail bank in the UK to be authorized by the Financial Services Authority we aim to provide a friendly, inclusive and personal service for all our customers." Based on fieldwork among participants in a local currency system in Ithaca, New York, as well as among Islamic banking practitioners in the USA, Indonesia, and elsewhere, Maurer (2005: 9) concludes that the modern "recuperation" of Islamic banking is not necessarily a reflection of its scriptural or medieval contractual forms of the past. In all this, the question of interest (*riba*) is essential.

The UK is one of the leading European countries in terms of Islamic banking. Compared with Islamic banking and finance (IBF) in Muslim countries, religious and political influences have been downplayed in the case of the UK, that is, "the emergence of Islamic banks in the United Kingdom is purely based on economic foundations" (Aldohni 2008: 198). Several factors have influenced London's status as a center for IBF: it is a global city; the attraction of oil wealth influenced the strategy of the financial authorities; the growing wealth of British Muslims represents a new source of funding that requires special facilities; it supports the aim to regulate Islamic banks to stop underground Islamic banking transactions (Aldohni 2008).

In much the same way as certification and ethnic/religious marketing/business can be seen to purify commodities and services, Islamic banking may be about controlling or purifying money. This point, I think, can also be applied to services such as certification and ethnic/religious marketing.

## Discussion: Islam, shopping, recognition

This final section will discuss some broader issues that arise from the previous discussions of the emergence of an Islamic market for identities in which paraphernalia, dress, *halal*, and services play an important role. In Faisal Devji's book *Landscapes of the Jihad: Militancy, Morality, Modernity* (2005) he argues that 9/11 has transformed Islam into both an agent and a product of globalization, making it a global phenomenon that demands an opinion about itself. Ironically, the demonization of Islam and Muslims that followed in the wake of 9/11 was complemented by the recognition that Muslims were also consumers with certain demands that were open to commercialization. It is in this context that the empirical material discussed above should also be seen, that is, modern Islamic markets are global in scope. This point also has salience in a global context of free markets and trade that may reinforce intensified flows of Islamic commodities and services.

Shopping has become a patriotic duty in mass culture (Fischer 2007, 2008; Zukin 2004: 14), especially now in times of an economic crisis that is felt globally. Therefore, a number of moral imperatives related to shopping link the shopping of individuals and groups with national sentiments and discourses. In this sense, shopping as a public activity is inescapably linked to the performance and spatial context of Islamic markets. Shopping is "the zero point where the whole economy of people, products, and money comes together" (Zukin 2004: 14). Of course, Muslim populations in the Western world are highly diverse. For example, a study of the Tatar minority in Poland shows that "Islamic" products are targeted at specific groups of Muslims with particular needs priorities (Górak-Sosnowska and Lyszczarz 2009). One way of conceptualizing Muslim diversity draws attention to the discourses about what Islam is or ought to be and the divergent responses produced by these controversies (Bowen 1993). In much the same manner, my research among Southeast Asian and British Muslims reflects the force of Islam as a discursive tradition, especially with regard to the way consumption is contested and debated in everyday life.

The following example from my research among middle-class Malays in London illustrates a specific point of tension or distinction between a modern Muslim puristic and a pragmatic orientation. While the moral stress on proper Muslim consumption with regard to paraphernalia, dress, *halal*, and services is morally given among a more puristically oriented group, pragmatic Muslims either reluctantly accept the imposition of this form of Islamic moralism or simply reject it as a material and thus shallow display of belief – as Islamic materialism or excess. An informant of mine, Nur, who was a woman in her thirties, clearly represented the more pragmatically inclined group. She explained the distinction between her personal position and "the other group," and emphasized that Islamic consumption in all its forms had become expressive of an unbearable moralism among those who, through proper Islamic consumption, tried to perform the role of perfectly pious Muslims. In other words, to Nur, this moralistic attitude was merely a public performance intended to display proper and balanced consumption and taste. Indicative of her more pragmatic stance, she concluded, "Islamic belief alone should be fine." Among Muslims in London, I found this form of discursive tension to be central.

Indeed, the idea of Islam as a discursive tradition is not recent, but rather an immanent feature of the history of Islam (Asad 1986: 14). Consumption or shopping as a point of debate in Europe and the USA can be seen to constitute such a new domain of contestation. The point here is that emerging Islamic markets may be just as contestable to some Muslims as they can be between groups of Muslims and non-Muslims, for example in the case of divergent understandings of proper/improper dress. In the end, social identity, Bourdieu maintains, is defined, asserted, and practiced through difference or distinctions (Bourdieu 1984: 172). As we saw in the case of distinctions between Islamists and secularists in Turkey, the politics of identity within these groups has been deeply influenced by an expanding consumer market in the context of the globalization of the 1980s and 1990s and this tendency, I would argue, has been accelerated in the new millennium.

Arguably, the "æsthetic motive" is endemic to religion (James 2002: 355), that is, "the visible world is part of a more spiritual universe from which it draws its chief significance" (James 2002: 375). For Muslims, the Islamic market may simultaneously be a manifestation of the visible and mundane world of shopping, on the one hand, and a spiritual universe, on the other hand, that helps shape both a moral and an aesthetic community. With respect to British Pakistanis as an aesthetic community, for example, this is intertwined with the moral community generating "moral conflicts about the legitimacy of aesthetic forms, or, indeed, of a morality which rejects these valorised forms" (Werbner 1996: 92). Theological aesthetics considers religion in relation to sensible knowledge, that is, sensation, imagination, and feeling (Viladesau

1999: 11). Islamic markets are good examples of the interplay between aesthetics and the more mundane, in the form of shopping that is also informed by convenience, thrift, and health, for example.

The proliferation and transformation of modern forms of *halal* in Britain shed light on the way in which *halal* as a theological concept is being resignified. Insightfully, Asad (2003: 1) asks what the connection is between "the secular" as an epistemic category and "secularism" as a political doctrine. A preliminary answer is that "the secular" comprises concepts, practices, and sensibilities that conceptually are prior to secularism (Asad 2003: 16). Modood writes that "political secularism can no longer be taken for granted but is having to answer its critics as there is growing understanding that the incorporation of Muslims has become the most important challenge of egalitarian multiculturalism" (Modood 2006: 37). Egalitarian multiculturalism builds on the idea that identities are partly given shape or denied by the recognition or non-recognition of others: "Due recognition is not just a courtesy we owe people. It is a vital human need" (Taylor 1994: 26). More specifically, there is a demand, as in the case of *halal* and dress, for example, for public institutions to acknowledge "ways of doing things" (Modood 2005: 134) privately as well as publicly; that is, while powerful political discourses and bodies regulate and discipline Islamic dress and banking, *halal* is largely outside state control.

The modern market for Islamic identities is sensitive to both excessive as well as insufficient regulation and control. In modern consumer societies such as Britain, the state plays a crucial role in trying to balance the forces of religion and markets. In shopping, the whole economy of people, products, and money comes together, but shopping and markets also generate debates about what Islam is or ought to be and divergent responses produced by these controversies. For some Muslims, the Islamic market may simultaneously be a manifestation of the visible and mundane world of shopping, on the one hand, and a spiritual universe, on the other, that helps shape both a moral and an aesthetic community. "The secular" plays an important role in balancing regulation, control, and the rights of consumers in modern societies. Modern citizens, religious or not, tend to be recognized as democratic consumers with rights in the interface between markets and the state.

## Conclusion

Many Western nations do indeed qualify as "consumers' republics" (Cohen 2004). The consumers' republic embodies a post-World War II strategy, emerging in order to reconstruct the nation's economy and to reaffirm its democratic values by promoting the expansion of mass consumption. Policy-makers, business, labor leaders, and civic groups all try to put mass consumption at the center of their plans for a prosperous nation. The health of the economy itself is measured according to indicators such as consumer confidence, spending, and housing construction (Cohen 2004: 401). In the Islamic market, identities, discourses, distinctions, the secular, and recognition tend to meet and be contested.

London has become a European center for Islamic markets during the last decade or so, and this has changed the Islamic business and entrepreneurial environment in Britain. Similar trends are recognizable on a global scale, that is, the global proliferation of Islamic commodities and services that are advertised as pure, pious, and wholesome are part of a market for identities. As a global city, London links the national as well as European economy with global circuits of commodities, people, and ideas, and this is also the case with the Islamic marketplace. Emerging Islamic markets reflect a particular type of urban exchangeability that is imbricated in the mundane practices of everyday shopping to effect charisma among Muslims.

In the eyes of some Muslims, the Islamic market is a way to control or purify money/shopping in everyday transactions. However, these ideals or practices are part of Islam as a discursive tradition, especially with regard to the way consumption is contested and debated in everyday life. Islamic markets, like any other market, are sensitive to both excessive as well as insufficient regulation and control by the state. In modern consumer societies such as Britain, the state is trying to balance the forces of religion and markets. In the end, modern citizens, religious or not, tend to be recognized as democratic consumers with rights in the interface between markets and the state.

An important theme was authority, particularly linked to the power involved in *halal* certification embedded in contemporary Malaysian and Islamic institutional discourses and practices. In a broader perspective, these ambiguities challenge the role religion and piety should or should not play in contemporary life among Muslims in the West. In the case of *halal* in Britain this was discussed as a sign of the state's unwillingness or incapacity to recognize the demands of religious consumers. Islamic organizations in Britain claim authority through and compete over *halal* in the interfaces between expanding markets, the secular, and the rights and demands of Muslim consumers. The state in Britain has virtually no authority to inspect, certify, or standardize *halal*. In the eyes of many of my informants, this leaves consumers unprotected against growing commercial interest in *halal*. At the same time, some of these Muslims feel that when the state or authoritative religious institutions are not involved this leaves *halal* open to excessive commercialization. This impotence of the state is reinforced, as more and more products appear in this expanding market in which both Islamic organizations and commercial interests compete over standards and certification on the margins of the secular state.

## Notes

1 Starting in 2005, I have visited London on several occasions. The extended period of fieldwork in London took place from July to December 2006, with one shorter stay in the spring of 2007. The methodology for this study was ethnographic, that is, I spent an extended period of time on research in London exploring, and I committed to adapt to this environment and to develop a sensitivity to the people I was learning from. During fieldwork in London, I spent a great deal of time in *halal* restaurants and butcher's shops, and in grocery stores, supermarkets and hypermarkets selling *halal* and other forms of Islamic products.
2 The Islamic Cultural Center (ICC) in Denmark is comparable to HFA, but on a smaller scale. It was founded in 1976 and is housed in a villa in the northwestern suburbs of Copenhagen, Denmark. ICC is privately run and houses a mosque, has a Qur'an school, and also arranges courses for local Danish Muslims, who for the most part are of Arab and Pakistani origin. ICC is the largest *halal* certifier of meat as well as non-meat products in Denmark. Denmark is a major exporter of both food and non-food products and thus *halal* is an important question for the state and companies.

## Bibliography

Ahmed, A. (2008) "Marketing of Halal Meat in the United Kingdom," *British Food Journal* 110(7): 655–70.
Aldohni, A.K. (2008) "The Emergence of Islamic Banking in the UK: A Comparative Study with Muslim Countries," *Arab Law Quarterly* 22(2): 180–98.
Ansari, H. (2004) *The Infidel Within: Muslims in Britain since 1800*, London: Hurst & Co.
Asad, T. (1986) *The Idea of an Anthropology of Islam*, Washington, DC: Georgetown University Center for Contemporary Arab Studies.
——(2003) *Formations of the Secular: Christianity, Islam, Modernity*, Stanford: Stanford University Press.
Bauman, G. (1996) *Contesting Culture: Discourses of Identity in Multi-ethnic London*, Cambridge: Cambridge University Press.
Bergeaud-Blackler, F. (2004) "Social Definitions of *Halal* Quality: The Case of Maghrebi Muslims in France," in Harvey, M., McMeekin, A., and Warde, A. (eds.) *Qualities of Food*, Manchester and New York: Manchester University Press.

——(2007) "New Challenges for Islamic Ritual Slaughter: A European Perspective," *Journal of Ethnic and Migration Studies* 33(6): 965–80.

Bonne, K., Vermeir, I., Bergeaud-Blackler, F., and Verbeke, W. (2007) "Determinants of Halal Meat Consumption in France," *British Food Journal*, 109(5): 367–86.

Bourdieu, P. (1977) *An Outline of a Theory of Practice*, Cambridge: Cambridge University Press.

——(1984) *Distinction: A Social Critique of the Judgement of Taste*, London: Routledge.

Bowen, J.R. (1993) *Muslims through Discourse: Religion and Ritual in Gayo Society*, Princeton: Princeton University Press.

——(2007) *Why the French Don't Like Headscarves: Islam, the State, and Public Space*, Princeton and Oxford: Princeton University Press.

Charlton, R. and Kaye, R. (1985) "The Politics of Religious Slaughter: An Ethno-religious Case Study," *New Community* XII(3): 490–502.

Cohen, L. (2004) *A Consumers' Republic: The Politics of Mass Consumption in Postwar America*, New York: Vintage Books.

D'Alisera, J. (2001) "I Love Islam: Popular Religious Commodities, Sites of Inscription, and Transnational Sierra Leonean Identity," *Journal of Material Culture* 6(1): 91–110.

Denny, F.M. (2006) *An Introduction to Islam*, Upper Saddle River, NJ: Pearson Prentice Hall.

Devji, F. (2005) *Landscapes of the Jihad: Militancy, Morality, Modernity*, London: C. Hurst & Company.

Esposito, J.L. (1995) *The Oxford Encyclopedia of the Modern Islamic World*, Oxford: Oxford University Press.

——(2003) *Modernizing Islam: Religion in the Public Sphere in the Middle East and Europe*, New Brunswick, NJ: Rutgers University Press.

Fischer, J. (2007) "Boycott or Buycott? Malay Middle-class Consumption post-9/11," *Ethnos* 72(1): 29–50.

——(2008) *Proper Islamic Consumption: Shopping among the Malays in Modern Malaysia*, Copenhagen: Nordic Institute of Asian Studies Press.

——(2009a) "Halal, Haram or What? Creating Muslim Space in London," in Pink, J. (ed.) *Muslim Societies in the Age of Mass Consumption: Politics, Religion and Identity between the Local and the Global*, Newcastle upon Tyne: Cambridge Scholars Publishing.

——(2009b) "Feeding Secularism: Consuming Halal among the Malays in London," *Diaspora* 18(1): 275–97.

——(2011) *The Halal Frontier: Muslim Consumers in a Globalized Market*, New York: Palgrave Macmillan.

Giddens, A. (1991) *Modernity and Self-identity*, Cambridge: Polity Press.

Gökarıksel, B. and Secor, A. (2009) "New Transnational Geographies of Islamism, Capitalism, and Sub-jectivity: The Veiling-fashion Industry in Turkey," in Pink, J. (ed.) *Muslim Societies in the Age of Mass Consumption: Politics, Religion and Identity between the Local and the Global*, Newcastle upon Tyne: Cambridge Scholars Publishing.

Górak-Sosnowska, K. and Lyszczarz, M. (2009) "(Un-)Islamic Consumers? The Case of Polish Tartars," in Pink, J. (ed.) *Muslim Societies in the Age of Mass Consumption: Politics, Religion and Identity between the Local and the Global*, Newcastle upon Tyne: Cambridge Scholars Publishing.

Halter, M. (2000) *Shopping for Identity: The Marketing of Ethnicity*, New York: Schocken Books.

Hansen, T. and Verkaaik, O. (2009) "Introduction – Urban Charisma: On Everyday Mythologies in the City," *Critique of Anthropology* 29(1): 5–29.

Hastings-Black, M. (2009) "American-Muslim Identity: Advertising, Mass Media+New Media," in Pink, J. (ed.) *Muslim Societies in the Age of Mass Consumption: Politics, Religion and Identity between the Local and the Global*, Newcastle upon Tyne: Cambridge Scholars Publishing.

James, W. (2002) *Varieties of Religious Experience: A Study in Human Nature*, London and New York: Routledge.

Kaye, R. (1993) "The Politics of Religious Slaughter of Animals: Strategies for Ethno-religious Political Action," *New Community* 19(2): 251–61.

Lee, R.L.M. (1993) "The Globalization of Religious Markets: International Innovations, Malaysian Consumption," *Sojourn* 8(1): 351–61.

Lewis, P. (1994) *Islamic Britain. Religion, Politics and Identity among British Muslims: Bradford in the 1990s*, London and New York: I.B. Tauris.

Maurer, B. (2005) *Mutual Life, Limited: Islamic Banking, Alternative Currencies, Lateral Reason*, Princeton: Princeton University Press.

Metcalf, B.D. (1996) "Introduction: Sacred Words, Sanctioned Practice, New Communities," in Metcalf, B. (ed.) *Making Muslim Space in North America and Europe*, Los Angeles and London: University of California Press.

Miller, D. (2009) *Stuff*, Cambridge: Polity Press.

Modood, T. (2005) *Multicultural Politics: Racism, Ethnicity and Muslims in Britain*, Edinburgh: Edinburgh University Press.

——(2006) "British Muslims and the Politics of Multiculturalism," in Modood, T. and Zapata-Barrero, R. (eds.) *Multiculturalism, Muslims and Citizenship*, New York and London: Routledge.

Navaro-Yashin, Y. (2002) *Faces of the State: Secularism and Public Life in Turkey*, Princeton: Princeton University Press.

Nielsen, J.S., Akgonul, S., Jeldtoft, N., Maréchal, B., and Moe, C. (eds.) (2010) *Yearbook of Muslims in Europe*, vol. 2, Leiden: Brill.

Pink, J. (ed.) (2009) *Muslim Societies in the Age of Mass Consumption: Politics, Religion and Identity between the Local and the Global*, Newcastle upon Tyne: Cambridge Scholars Publishing.

Riaz, M.N. and Chaudry, M.M. (2004) *Halal Food Production*, Boca Raton: CRC Press.

Sassen, S. (2002) *Global Networks, Linked Cities*, New York and London: Routledge.

Starrett, G. (1995) "The Political Economy of Religious Commodities in Cairo," *American Anthropologist* 97(1): 51–68.

Tarlo, E. (1995) "Hijab in London," *Journal of Material Culture* 12(2): 131–56.

Taylor, C. (1994) "The Politics of Recognition," in Gutman, A. (ed.) *Multiculturalism: Examining the Politics of Recognition*, Princeton: Princeton University Press.

Vertovec, S. (1996) "Muslims, the State, and the Public Sphere in Britain," in Nonneman, G., Niblock, T., and Szajkowski, B. (eds.) *Muslim Communities in the New Europe*, Reading: Ithaca Press.

Viladesau, R. (1999) *Theological Aesthetics: God in Imagination, Beauty and Art*, New York and London: Oxford University Press.

Werbner, P. (1996) "The Fusion of Identities: Political Passion and the Poetics of Cultural Performance among British Pakistanis," in Parkin, D., Caplan, L., and Fisher, H. (eds.) *The Politics of Cultural Performance*, Oxford and London: Berghahn Books.

——(2007) "Veiled Interventions in Pure Space: Honour, Shame and Embodied Struggles among Muslims in Britain and France," *Theory, Culture & Society* 24(2): 161–86.

Zukin, S. (2004) *Point of Purchase: How Shopping Changed American Culture*, New York: Routledge.

# Part 2.3

# Contributing to Islam

# 23

# A religious law for Muslims in the West

## The European Council for Fatwa and Research and the evolution of *fiqh al-aqalliyyat al-muslima*

*Uriya Shavit and Iyad Zahalka*

Dublin, famous for modernist literary genius and beer breweries and home to a population of no more than several thousand Muslims, is an unexpected location to spearhead a revolution in Islamic law. Yet its southern, pastoral suburb of Clonskeagh is the residence of the European Council for Fatwa and Research, a juristic panel that for over a decade has led the systemization of an audaciously pragmatic and hotly debated doctrine on the religious law of Muslim minorities (*fiqh al-aqalliyyat al-muslima*). According to Yusuf al-Qaradawi, a paramount contributor to its construction, the religious law of Muslim minorities is not a specific doctrine but the field of *fiqh* that addresses the unique conditions of Muslims living among non-Muslim majority societies (al-Qaradawi 2007: 32). However, while the doctrine on Muslim minorities propagated by the European Council (which was initiated by an American-based jurist, Taha Jabir al-'Alwani) is contested by other doctrines on Muslim minorities, the phrase *fiqh al-aqalliyyat al-muslima* is frequently used as a generic term for the Council's doctrine. The Council's relative liberalism reflects the attitudes of considerable numbers of devout Muslims in the West.

The Council's promotion of pragmatic juristic opinions for Muslim minorities constitutes an extension of the Sunni *wasati* (or "harmonizing middle ground") socio-juristic approach, which is associated mainly with al-Azhar graduates and Islamist activists. *Wasati* jurists base their ideology on Qur'an 2:143: "Thus We have appointed you a middle nation." They draw on the modernist tradition developed in the late nineteenth and early twentieth century by Jamal al-Din al-Afghani, Muhammad 'Abduh and Rashid Rida. *Wasati*s maintain that Islam, in its essence, harmonizes contrasts such as matter and spirit, individualism and communality, rationality and faith. They argue that modernity does not inherently contradict Islam, but that, in fact, modernity's virtuous aspects result from its interactions with Islam. In their juristic decisions, *wasati*s aim to find practical religious-juristic solutions, to make life easier where possible and enjoyable where permissible, and to make Muslims fond of their religion. They emphasize the need for Muslim societies to advance technologically and economically, and follow early Islamic modernists in arguing that compatibility exists between Islam and Western concepts and institutions, so long as the latter can be given an Islamic justification and are rid of components that *wasatis* deem un-Islamic. They also encourage greater participation of women in certain public spheres (al-Qaradawi 1973: 17–39; 2000; 'Imara 2007: 178–9, 197–8; Polka 2003: 39–64; Gräf 2009: 213–38).

Studying *wasati* jurisprudence on Muslim minorities enhances our understanding of Muslim minorities in the West as well as of contemporary *fiqh*. The European Council of Fatwa and Research aims to find religious-legal solutions that, while within the framework of *shari'a* as an all-encompassing system, and while encouraging the fortification of religious identity, enable Muslims in Europe to profess their religious beliefs without compromising their social and professional positions. In doing so, the Council expands the horizons for Muslim identity in the West, offering them a middle ground of sorts between "integration" and "introversion," but in the process also creates ethical and philosophical questions regarding identity, nationality, and law. Because abiding by the rules of the *shari'a* in the West presents some complex challenges that are not faced in majority Muslim countries, the studies issued by the Council on the general theory of *fiqh* and in response to specific queries of European Muslims represent the pinnacle of *wasati* innovation and daring, and thus also the potential and limitations for future transformations in the *fiqh* of majority Muslim societies.

The *wasati* approach to the religious law has been the subject of some academic attention, including works by Caeiro (2004, 2010), Fishman (2006), March (2007, 2009), Nafi (2004), Sisler (2009), and Shavit (2007, 2009, 2012). Most studies address the early years of *wasatis'* formulation of *fiqh al-aqalliyyat al-muslima*. This chapter, based on the analysis of several dozen studies and several hundred *fatwas* published by the Council and affiliated jurists, as well as on a number of interviews conducted by the authors with Council officials in Dublin in February 2012 (including with its secretary general, Hussein Halawa), aims to: (1) describe the Council's structure and form of activities from its initiation in 1997 to today; (2) analyze the ideology and the religious-legal methodology that direct the Council; and (3) explore several of the groundbreaking decisions undertaken by the Council and affiliated jurists on a variety of issues, from mortgages to electoral participation to marriage.

## Leadership and institutionalization of *wasati fiqh al-aqalliyyat*

Although mass migration of Muslims to the West, especially to Western European states, began in the late 1950s, the construction of a *wasati* approach that addresses the unique conditions of Muslim minorities did not begin until the late 1990s, when the permanent nature of Muslim presence in the West was already established. This process was led by two graduates of al-Azhar, the Egyptian Yusuf al-Qaradawi (b. 1926), who is the leader of the *wasati* approach in the Arab world, and the Iraqi Taha Jabir al-'Alwani (b. 1935), who made a name for himself mainly through his pioneering efforts in the field of minority jurisprudence.

Al-Qaradawi, a disciple of Hasan al-Banna, who twice (1973, 2004) rejected offers to become the general guide of the Egyptian Muslim Brothers, has been living since 1961 in voluntary exile in Qatar. He owes his status as a leading Islamic jurist in part to his sophisticated facilitation of advanced media technologies. Al-Qaradawi has had a career-long interest in Muslim minorities. When still a young jurist at al-Azhar, he was asked to participate in a project intent on providing introductory textbooks on Islam to Muslims living in Europe and America, as well as to non-Muslims. Al-Qaradawi met the challenge by writing a book that presented his *wasati* views on religious law, *al-Halal wa-l-Haram fi al-Islam* ("The lawful and the prohibited in

Islam"). The book, published in August 1960, became one of the century's bestsellers on Islamic religious law. It dealt with dozens of everyday issues faced by Muslims, but did not address the unique challenges faced by Muslim minorities. In the early 1970s, al-Qaradawi began visiting Western Muslim communities. By the late 1990s Muslim minorities had become his focal point, and in 2001 he systemized his *wasati* doctrine of *fiqh al-aqalliyyat al-muslima* in a book (al-Qaradawi 2007).

Al-'Alwani migrated to the United States in 1983 from Saudi Arabia, where he served as professor at Ibn Saud University. In 1986 he established the Fiqh Council of North America, a voluntary panel tasked with providing religious-legal decisions to Muslims in the United States and Canada. He has testified that he toiled to construct a religious-legal doctrine for Muslim minorities from the mid-1970s, after visiting the United States and meeting with American Muslims. However, his efforts to find prestigious jurists to join him continuously failed, and in the early 1990s he began to independently issue religious edicts based on the foundations of *fiqh al-aqalliyyat al-muslima* as he understood them (al-'Alwani 2004: 38–40). He systemized the doctrine in the form of a book only in 2000 (al-'Alwani 2000).

The European Council for Fatwa and Research was established in London in March 1997 on the initiative of an umbrella organization, the Federation of Islamic Organizations in Europe. Al-Qaradawi was appointed president, a position he still holds today, and a Lebanese Islamist, Faysal al-Mawlawi, was nominated as vice president, a position he held until his death, in 2011. Al-'Alwani did not join the Council, but has served on the consultative board of its journal. The Council's declared objective has been "achieving proximity and bringing together the scholars who live in Europe, and attempting to unify the jurisprudence views between them with regard to the main *fiqh* issues" (European Council for Fatwa and Research n.d.: 1). How-ever, since its initiation the Council has mainly served as a means to formulate and legitimize *wasati* views.

A majority of the jurists on the Council are based in European countries. Membership is contingent on the recommendation of a Council member; and once approved by the other members, it is for life. The Council does not employ any paid staff, nor does it operate an archive; the diffusion of its decisions is largely dependent on the individual efforts of jurists affiliated with it. Convening every year in June (until 2008 it was convened twice every year), the Council discusses the most challenging queries that arrive at its offices or at the offices of the committees for *fatwa* issuance it operates in France, Germany, and England, as well as queries directed from governmental bodies. The queries it addresses are initially deliberated on by its head sub-committee for the issuance of *fatwa*s, and some deliberations are based on studies commissioned by the Council. Decisions are established by absolute majority; al-Qaradawi does not have the final say. While in its early years the Council confirmed a general doctrine on *fiqh al-aqalliyyat al-muslima* and issued a number of *fatwa*s on hotly debated issues, in recent years it has generated fewer controversies. Sheikh Halawa told the authors that the Council has established itself as a *marja'iyya* – an authoritative reference – on religious law for Muslim minorities and that most Muslims in Europe, including those of Turkish descent, accept the Council's juristic approach and its decisions. 'Ali Salem, who worked as a translator for the Council, argued that most queries that arrived at its offices were in English, indicating that its reach is not limited to Muslims of Arab descent. The authors' qualitative field experience in European mosques suggests that while the Council's *fatwa*s are familiar to some European Muslims, they are unfamiliar to others, and that even among those who share its *wasati* outlook the Council is not regarded as an exclusive or binding authority. Some voices in the Council argue that greater efforts must be exerted to circulate and diffuse its views in Europe (al-Najjar 2009: 69–70).

## Ideology and methodology

The *wasati* approach to *fiqh al-aqalliyyat al-muslima*, as systemized in works published by the European Council for Fatwa and Research, emphasizes two objectives: *taysir* (facilitation, i.e. making life easier where possible) and *tabshir* (proselytizing, spreading Allah's truth). The two are tied to one slogan – *al-taysir fi al-fatwa wa-l-tabshir fi al-da'wa* (loosely translated as "facilitation in issuing *fatwa*s and the promotion of religion through proselytizing") (*Qararat wa-Fatawa* … n.d.: 26).

*Wasati*s believe *taysir* to be more than an option: It is a component of Islam, commanded by Allah through his Prophet. Relying on Qur. 5:6, 2:185, 4:28, *wasati*s hold that, at their heart, Allah's laws are intended to make life easier, not more difficult; relying on Qur. 22:78 and 21:107, they hold that Islamic law aims to relieve believers of hardship or dire straits (*haraj*) (*Qararat wa Fatawa* … n.d.: 16, al-'Alwani 2004: 22, 74–5). Based on this premise, they argue that issuance of *fatwa*s is not universally applicable but must accommodate, within the boundaries stipulated by Allah via his Prophet, the conditions in which one lives so as to ensure the facilitation of *fiqh* and the commitment of believers to obeying it (al-Qaradawi 2000: 28–9, 113). Al-Qaradawi suggests that in our era, given the weakness of religion in the hearts of Muslims and the (temporary) triumph of materialistic ideologies, exercising *taysir* is all the more essential (al-Qaradawi 2000: 28–30).

The *wasati* doctrine on the religious law of Muslim minorities is governed by the assumption that Muslims living in non-Muslim majority societies face some difficulties that are even graver than those faced by other Muslims. Thus, just as a sick person is entitled to considerations to which a healthy person is not, Muslims who live in non-Muslim majority societies are entitled to adjustments which Muslims who live in Muslim societies are not entitled to (al-Qaradawi 2007: 48–52; al-Najjar 2009: 105, 110).

Writings on *taysir* as a foundation of the religious law of Muslim minorities convey a sense of apologetics. Jurists emphasize that facilitation does not signify a break from the governing norms of *shari'a* but rather the application of these norms. Al-'Alwani stressed that the purpose of *taysir* is not to make things easier for minorities, but to allow them to be exemplary Muslims in their receiving societies (al-'Alwani 2000: 6; 2004: 49).

*Wasati*s legitimize Muslim residence in the West with a wide array of justifications, including one's need to provide for one's family, finding political shelter, and pursuing academic studies. The prospect of bringing non-Muslims to Islam serves as an additional justification, and is a foundational concept in *wasati* texts. As will be explored on pp. 371–6, while this prospect of *da'wa* rings triumphant, one of its ironic results is providing legitimization for the liberalization of Islamic laws.

Arguing that proselytization as a legitimate reason for Muslim migration is not an innovation. The issue of residence under non-Muslim rule became acute as early as the eleventh and eleventh centuries AD, following the Christian conquests of Sicily and of Muslim territories on the Iberian Peninsula, and resurfaced when Muslims lost additional lands. While jurists agreed that continued residence abroad could weaken faith and practice and strengthen non-Muslims in their wars against Islam, they held that it was permissible to live among infidels so long as Muslims are too weak physically or economically to migrate. Some held that residence in non-Muslim societies is permissible if the Muslim is able to practice his religion, and went as far as to suggest that if the latter condition is met, residence among the infidels is desirable because it has the potential to encourage non-Muslims to convert. Jurists of the Maliki school, which was dominant in the conquered lands, were more inclined toward a stricter opinion, whereas jurists of the Shafi'i and Hanafi schools were more inclined toward the lenient approach (Abu-Salieh 1996: 37–57; Abou el-Fadl 1994: 141–87).

The idea that Muslims in the West should engage in proselytizing entered *wasati* writings in the early 1980s and was fully integrated into some of the more systemized works on minority *fiqh* in the 2000s. In detailing the "duties of Muslims living in the West," al-Qaradawi (2006) wrote that they "ought to be sincere callers to their religion. They should keep in mind that calling others to Islam is not restricted to scholars and Sheikhs, but it goes far to encompass every committed Muslim. As we see scholars and Sheikhs delivering *khutba*s (sermons) and lectures, writing books to defend Islam, it is no wonder we find lay Muslims practicing *da'wa* while employing wisdom and fair exhortation."

Al-Qaradawi went so far as to state that, considering Islam's universal mission, on the one hand, and the West's current leadership of the world, on the other, Muslims must have a presence in the West and spread Islam there. Thus, if there had been no Muslim presence in the Western world, such a presence would have had to be created (al-Qaradawi 2007: 33). Similarly, al-'Alwani argued that any place where a Muslim is able to practice his religion can be regarded as *dar al-islam* and there he must stay, for his staying may result in the conversion of non-Muslims. Conversely, countries where Islam had not yet spread should be regarded as *dar al-da'wa* (realms of proselytizing). It is therefore obligatory for Muslims to create a presence in those countries and to bring to them the truth of Islam (Imam 1999: 26; al-'Alwani 2000: 16–19, 39–51; 2004: 84–85).

The notion that proselytizing is an essential aspect of *fiqh al-aqalliyyat al-muslima* was rejected by the European Council's secretary general, Hussein Halawa. In interviews with the authors, he emphasized that the doctrine does not seek the Islamizing of Europe and that it does not consider *da'wa* as an objective. He pointed to facilitation as the Council's greatest achievement and argued that the Council's jurisprudence made it possible for Muslims in Europe to live without *haraj* – that is, without being harmed due to their beliefs. Indeed, in the Council's more recent literature direct calls for *da'wa* have been largely neglected. The secretary general's comments indicate, perhaps, an appreciation of the sensitivity of the issue.

Essential to *wasati* jurisprudence in general, and specifically to the jurisprudence on minorities, is the widening of jurists' independence in interpreting the sources of law, or exercising *ijtihad*. Thus, *wasati*s emphasize that: (1) generalities (*kuliyyat*) that define the purposes of Islamic law can be derived from the Qur'an, have precedent over partialities (*juz'iyyat*), and should direct human behavior; (2) all sources of law, including the Prophetic traditions, must be read in light of the Qur'an, which is the supreme and ultimate guide; and (3), while Allah's guidance is eternal, the Qur'an's implementation was meant to constantly evolve in light of changing circumstances (al-Qaradawi 2000: 43, 50, 57, 70; al-'Alwani 2000: 24–5; 2004: 53–6, 70). Because the Qur'an is vague on many issues, certainly more than the immense body of Prophetic traditions (*hadith*), this point of view provides *wasati* jurists with greater discretion while endowing their decisions with legitimacy. A central point on the *wasati* agenda is the legitimacy of good relations between Muslims and non-Muslims who are not at war with Islam. The supremacy of the Qur'an over all other sources and the *wasati* interpretation of some Qur'anic verses play crucial roles in legitimizing this view. *Wasati*s extensively quote Qur. 60:8, which permits Muslims to honor and do justice with non-Muslims who do not fight against them, to reassert the permissibility of socializing with non-Muslims and constructively participating in their societies.

*Wasati*s broadly and liberally apply two already existing mechanisms of religious law to promote their ideological objectives. One is to search for the most suitable answer among all four Sunni law schools (*madhhab*) and beyond them. According to al-Qaradawi, crossing *madhhab* boundaries is essential for the *fiqh* of minorities (as it is for *fiqh* in general) because it provides jurists with greater discretion; a *madhhab* that is strict on one issue may be lenient on another, and rulings that have been neglected may be revived at the present time (al-Qaradawi 2007: 57–60; see also al-Qaradawi 2000: 35–9, 221–2; 1973: 11–12; al-Najjar 2009: 108). In explaining its methodology, the European Council for Fatwa and Research professed that "the four schools of law as well as all other people of *fiqh* knowledge are regarded as a resource of immense wealth" from which jurists should choose whatever is supported by "the correct and best evidence that achieves the best interest" (European Council for Fatwa and Research n.d.: 3). It cautioned against *madhhabi* fanaticism (European Council for Fatwa and Research n.d.: 31–4).

Another mechanism utilized by *wasati* jurists is *maslaha* (public or individual interest), which includes three categories: necessities (*darurat*), needs (*hajiyyat*), and improvements (*tahsinat*). This mechanism was developed by Abu Hamid al-Ghazali (d. 1111), who held that the purpose of the *shari'a* is the maintenance of religion, life, offspring, reason, and property, and that anything that is a necessity for the realization of these purposes may serve as an independent basis for a legal decision. In the twentieth century, Muhammad Rashid Rida developed the concept of *maslaha* as the principal means of effecting religio-legal change. Rida's primary goal was to show that Islamic law was intended to be a comprehensive legal structure for Muslim society. Central to this approach was his differentiation between *'ibadat* ("ritual devotion") and *mu'amalat* ("social transactions"). He argued that the latter are only of a general character, allowing for considerable adaptation by successive generations of Muslims in light of the demands of their worldly welfare (Kerr 1996: 187–90).

Al-Qaradawi's doctrine on Muslim minorities emphasized the use of *maslaha* in arguing that the religious law of Muslim minorities is realistic rather than idealistic, and that its realism, which characterizes the *shari'a* in general, is manifested in its recognition of individual and communal necessities (al-Qaradawi 2007: 55–6). Al-'Alwani suggested that, in accordance with the priorities of the Muslim nation, jurists dealing with Muslim minorities should broaden the list of objectives of the *shari'a* (al-'Alwani 2000: 27–8). In doing so, as well as in establishing (albeit not consensually) that "needs" can be regarded as "necessities" whether they are communal or individual, *wasati* jurists were able to invoke *maslaha* as justification for adjusting religious laws to the unique conditions of minorities on a number of critical issues.

A point that *wasatis* stress is that jurists must decide based on comprehensive knowledge of the situation of Muslims in the West. *Wasati* methods of determining what constitutes a necessity include the application of *fiqh al-muwazanat* – evaluating the benefit and the harm incurred by reaching a specific decision; *ma'alat al-af'al* – assessing the correlation between application of specific laws and materializing the purpose of *shari'a* in the context of the special circumstances faced by minorities; and the rephrasing of queries, so as to allow the answers to address the purposes of *shari'a* and lead to a beneficial result.

## *Wasati* fatwas in *fiqh al-aqalliyyat*

*Fatwa*s issued since the late 1990s by the Council and by jurists who share its convictions on *fiqh al-aqalliyyat al-muslima* addressed a variety of issues that are fundamental to the daily lives of Muslim minorities, and specifically to their prospect of integrating into majority societies while maintaining the *shari'a* as a binding, all-encompassing reference. In accommodating special conditions faced by minorities, a number of these *fatwa*s broke away from confirmed and long-held religo-legal opinions, including opinions based on unquestionable Qur'anic directives. *Fatwa*s testified to the centricity of the objectives of facilitation and proselytizing in *wasati* jurisprudence, as well as the utility of cross-*madhhab* search and broad application of *maslaha* in promoting those objectives.

## Participation in elections in Western countries

*Wasati* jurists issued decisions that permitted, and even obliged, Muslims living in non-Muslim countries to participate in elections. Legitimization relied mainly on application of *maslaha* based on *fiqh al-muwazanat*. This reflected an appreciation that Muslim communities will be able neither to advance their status nor to serve the greater interest of the "Muslim Nation" unless they gain political power.

One of the first jurists to deal with the matter was Sulayman Muhammad Tubulyak, a Bosnian who in 1996, at the University of Jordan, wrote, from a *wasati* perspective, a master's dissertation on political issues pertaining to the religious law of Muslim minorities. Applying the principles of *fiqh al-muwazanat* and *ma'alat al-af'al*, Tubulyak legitimized the formation of political parties by Muslims living as minorities as the only means for them to promote their rights and to spread Islam, noting that the experience of Muslim minorities from Britain to Bosnia testifies to the merit of establishing political parties. He also legitimized both their joining non-Muslim political parties when not given the right to establish Muslim ones and the alliance of Muslim political parties with non-Muslim parties if the alliance serves a *maslaha* and does not harm Islam or Muslims, for example by limiting their ability to spread their religion. He ruled that where a Muslim candidate does not run for office, Muslims are required to vote for the non-Muslim candidate or party list that is least hostile to Muslims. He cautioned that Islamic politics in non-Muslim societies must follow *shari'a* regulations; empty promises must not be made and personal attacks must be avoided. If elected, a Muslim member of parliament should not approve legislation that contradicts Islam or harms Muslims wherever they may be, and must champion the liberties and rights of Muslims everywhere. In swearing the oath of allegiance, a Muslim member of parliament must articulate that the purpose is to serve Islam and Muslims, and avoid uttering any words that contradict Islamic principles (Tubulyak 1997: 140–8).

Based on an application of *fiqh al-muwazanat*, the European Council, in its second session in 1998, issued a decision on a query about the permissibility of participation in municipal elections in Europe and about voting for a non-Muslim political party which "may not serve the interests of Muslims." The Council stated that "this matter is to be decided by Islamic organizations and establishments. If these see that the interests of Muslims can only be served by this participation, then it is permissible on the condition that it does not involve the Muslims making more concessions or losses than gains" (European Council for Fatwa and Research n.d.: 100).

In 1999, al-'Alwani ruled that it is not only permissible for Muslims in the United States to participate in American politics, it is their religious duty to do so in order to protect their rights, support their brothers in faith wherever they may be, spread the truth of Islam, and materialize its universality. Al-'Alwani emphasized that the minority's political participation constitutes a duty and is not optional because it is essential to protect the necessities, needs, and improvements of Muslim society in the United States. Thus, Muslims are encouraged to run for any public office that can benefit Muslims or protect them from harm, to endorse the election of the non-Muslim candidate who benefits Muslims more or harms them less than the contender, to aspire to gain American citizenship, and to register to vote. Al-'Alwani explained the mistake of those who think that legitimizing political participation in an infidel regime constitutes neglect of the duty to establish an Islamic regime. Establishing an Islamic regime, he wrote, is the duty of Muslims living in majority Muslim societies; the duty of Muslims living as a minority in the United States is different: It is to support Islam's presence in the country through participation in the general society and the building of a united community that would be able to bring the majority of society to Islam by convincing it of Islam's truthfulness. This process, through which an Islamic political order will be created in America, will take several centuries. The gradualist method, he argued, is in line with the path of the Prophet, who first established a community, then a society, then an Islamic system. Furthermore, any advancement of virtue and justice constitutes a brick in building an Islamic regime; thus, if Muslim political participation helps to outlaw abortion or drugs, then it should be considered a support for Muslim values even if it is not facilitated through Muslim political parties or slogans (Imam 1999: 26). In his 2000 systemization of *wasati fiqh al-aqalliyyat*, al-'Alwani asserted that it is the duty of Muslim minorities at large to be active in the politics of their societies in order to enhance Islam and materialize its universality (al-'Alwani 2000: 50).

In its seventeenth session in 2007, the European Council affirmed al-'Alwani's opinion that political participation is a necessity (al-Majlis al-urubi 2008: 511). In an interview with the authors, Sheikh Halawa presented a similar approach, arguing that it is not only the right, but the duty of Muslim minorities to be politically active. He stressed that the Council does not endorse candidates but calls on voters to determine for themselves who best enhances *maslaha*.

## Mortgages and student loans when no alternative is available

Qur. 2:275–7 prohibits usury (*riba*), and warns that Allah and his Prophet will wage war against those who do not obey this command. In modern economies, in which corporate and individual transactions often rely on interest-based loans, this prohibition creates a challenge. Islamic banking systems have developed several mechanisms that circumvent the prohibition on *riba*. In real estate, the most popular one is *murabaha*: the bank serves as an intermediary that buys a house at the request of a customer and then sells the house at a higher price, which the customer pays in installments (Lewis and Algaoud 2001: 52–5; Abdullah 1996: 76–95). In some Western countries Islamic banking systems are not available. Because most Muslim migrants in the West are not affluent and cannot afford to buy a house without a mortgage, the issue has become highly relevant.

Responding to this situation, at its fourth session, held on October 27–31, 1999, the European Council decided to legitimize mortgages. Its *fatwa* began with a reaffirmation of Islam's prohibition on usury. It encouraged Muslims in the West to find religiously legitimate alternatives to mortgages, such as the *murabaha* system offered by Islamic banks. It also encouraged Islamic organizations in Europe to ask European banks to adopt Islamic systems in order to attract Muslim customers. If, however, there is no alternative, then a Muslim living in Europe who does not own a house and does not have the means to purchase one without a loan is permitted to take a mortgage.

The Council based its argument on two notions. First it argued that a need (*haja*) can be regarded as a necessity (*darura*), whether the need is communal or individual. The *fatwa* explained that a "necessity" is something without which a Muslim cannot live and a "need" is something without which a Muslim would be put in a state of hardship (*haraj*). Qur. 22:78 and 5:6 state that Islam will not put Muslims in a state of hardship. Thus, certain needs can be regarded as necessities, and in addressing them it is possible to legitimize what is prohibited. While having a home (rented or owned) is a necessity for a Muslim family (as indicated in Qur. 16:80), owning a home is a need that can be regarded as a necessity because it is crucial for preserving Islamic identity and for promoting the spread of Islam. A Muslim in Europe who does not take a mortgage may be forced to pay rent to a non-Muslim landlord for many years without getting any closer to ownership and remaining under the threat of eviction, while a Muslim who is permitted to take a mortgage will be relieved of these concerns and will be able to choose a home that is close to a mosque and to an Islamic school. Buying homes may bring together Muslims living in non-Muslim majority countries, strengthen their ties, and enable them to create small Islamic enclaves within the larger society. Furthermore, mortgages advance proselytizing efforts, and thus constitute a communal need, in two ways: by becoming home-owners, Muslims will present a respectable face to non-Muslims; and relief from the financial burden of renting a house will make it possible for Muslims to pursue their duty to engage in *da'wa*.

The other argument presented in the *fatwa* draws on the *wasati* method of cross-*madhhab* search. The *fatwa* invoked the Hanafi opinion (endorsed by some Hanbalis) that contracts between Muslims and non-Muslims that are normally prohibited are permitted outside the Abode of Islam (*dar al-islam*). This opinion is based on two notions: first, while living among infidels, a Muslim is not obligated to follow the rulings of the *shari'a* on civil, financial, political and similar matters, because following them is beyond his ability, and Allah does not require people to do more than their ability; and, second, Islam seeks to strengthen its believers in all respects, including the elimination of financial hardship. The Council's *fatwa* criticized the argument of several Hanafi jurists, namely that Muslims in non-Muslim societies can charge interest, but not pay it, because they do not benefit from paying interest. The Council explained that no consensus was reached on this issue, and that by paying interest on a mort-gage the Muslim receives a benefit, because he will eventually own a home. The Council emphasized that it regards the Hanafi legitimization of mortgages in Europe merely as a sup-plement to its main argument, to wit, in the European context a mortgage may be considered a "need" that qualifies as a "necessity." It noted that jurists of all schools of law can permit mortgages based on its main argument (al-Qaradawi 2007: 174–9).

The Council's decision was opposed by several of its members. 'Abd Allah b. Bayya, a Mauritanian-born, Saudi-based jurist and politician (b. 1935), wrote that a "need" can be regarded as a "necessity" only in regard to Islam's weaker prohibitions and that a "need" by itself cannot legitimize usury (bin Bayya 2004: 93–145). Two other members of the Council – Denmark-based Muhammad al-Barazi, a Muslim Brother, and the England-based Pakistani Suhayb Hasan 'Abd al-Ghaffar – criticized the *fatwa* on two other grounds. First, they argued that the Council misinterpreted the Hanafi school in two ways: (1) Hanafis permit usury only in *dar al-harb*, a category that does not apply to contemporary European countries; (2) Hanafis allow Muslims in non-Muslim societies to take interest but not to pay (as mentioned above, the Council addressed this issue in its *fatwa*). Second, al-Barazi and al-Ghaffar asserted that the Council wrongfully applied the principle of a "need" becoming a "necessity" because the financial weakness experienced by Muslims in Europe is not the result of avoiding mortgages, but of disunity. It is therefore legitimate for a Muslim to take a mortgage only if he is unable to rent a home for an appropriate price or to purchase one in a religiously lawful way (al-Qaradawi 2007: 179–81).

Despite the criticism, al-Qaradawi reaffirmed the Council's legitimization of mortgages and its broad interpretation of the concept of necessity. More than one-quarter of al-Qaradawi's 2001 book on the religious law of Muslim minorities is dedicated to his Council's 1999 *fatwa*; clearly, al-Qaradawi felt that he needed to defend it. He conceded that in legitimizing interest-based loans for European Muslims he adopted a position that he had opposed his entire career (al-Qaradawi 1973: 230–3). He attributed his change of heart to the softness and confidence that comes with age (al-Qaradawi 2007: 169–70). In his response to al-Barazi and al-Ghaffar, al-Qaradawi stressed that to determine whether owning an apartment constitutes a "need" one should consult not only jurists but also non-religious experts as well as European Muslims who rent apartments (al-Qaradawi 2007: 182–3). In his defense of the *fatwa* he added several ele-ments to the Council's description of ownership as a condition for leading an Islamic life in the

West and promoting Islam. He argued that Muslims who own apartments have access to better education; reside in closer proximity to local mosques, Islamic centers, and other Muslims; enjoy better public services; enable their wives to walk around the house without being watched by neighbors (as is the case in rent-based residential areas); and gain the respect of all walks of society, from school teachers to drivers of garbage trucks. Al-Qaradawi hinted that the lateness of his juristic transformation on the matter had been harmful to the interests of the Muslim nation, noting that Muslims from the Indian subcontinent, who adhere to the Hanafi school and have taken mortgages, are some of the richest men in contemporary London (al-Qaradawi 2007: 154–61). Other *wasati* jurists have also defended the Council's stand on mortgages (Sidiqqi 2000).

Our interview with the secretary general of the Council revealed that more than a decade after its issuance the *fatwa* on mortgages remains a sensitive issue: When asked about the controversy the *fatwa* ignited, Sheikh Halawa passionately and apologetically read it to us, emphasizing that it opened with an assertion that usury is prohibited as well as with a call for European Muslims to find other alternatives. He also stressed that the *fatwa* permitted mortgages on a temporary basis, until the day comes when it is possible to purchase homes in Europe in line with Islamic regulations. Our qualitative field experiences in European mosques indicate that the *fatwa* is highly controversial, and that even some Muslims who identify with the *wasati* orientation do not approve of it.

In a study published by the Council's journal in 2009, student loans were legitimized based on justifications reminiscent of those invoked in relation to mortgages. Salim al-Sheikhi (b. 1964), a Libyan-born, Saudi-educated, and England-based jurist and member of the Council, argued that because Muslims in Britain do not have access to reliable Islamic-regulated interest-free loans, the principle that a need can be regarded as a necessity legitimizes the taking of interest-based student loans. The need is individual as well as communal. For individuals to find good jobs, academic education is required. Because most Muslims in the United Kingdom work in low-paying occupations, they will not be able to afford higher education if student loans remain prohibited. As for the communal need, unless student loans are legitimized the Muslim minority will be harmed, and Islamic law rejects such harm. Furthermore, to facilitate integration, Muslims are required to establish a presence in the public and private sector, and they can do so only if they have access to higher education. Al-Sheikhi concluded that, considering that the Council legitimized mortgages based on the notion that a need can be regarded as necessity, the legitimization of student loans is all the more justified, especially in considering that, unlike mortgages, student loans are matched to the rise in the consumer price index (and thus are considered by some jurists as legitimate in any case) (al-Sheikhi 2009: 445–53).

## Service in a Western military fighting against Muslims

Shortly after 9/11, as the United States was preparing to retaliate in Afghanistan, a Muslim chaplain in the American army, Muhammad 'Abd al-Rashid, presented al-'Alwani with a query on the permissibility of participation in a war against the perpetrators of the attacks. Al-'Alwani consulted with al-Qaradawi, who joined four jurists in approving of participation. Their decision was based on two considerations: first, the 9/11 attacks were terrorist acts, and Muslims should be united against those who terrorize innocents; second, applying *fiqh al-muwazanat*, they argued that if Muslim American military personnel were to resign their positions they would cause harm not only to themselves but also to millions of Muslim Americans, and this harm would be greater than that caused by participating in war. The jurists advised the questioner that he should ask to serve in a non-combat position, unless such a request would raise doubts about his allegiance or loyalty (Nafi 2004: 80–2).

Following the commencement of the war in Afghanistan in October 2001, in a *fatwa* responding to a query from Zaynab, a Canadian, on the permissibility of participation in the war, al-Qaradawi authorized military participation provided that the Muslim soldier does his best to avoid direct confrontation. His *fatwa* began by stressing that a Muslim who fights another Muslim has committed *kufr* (disbelief); several traditions on this matter were invoked, including one narrated by al-Ahnaf, in which the Prophet reportedly said that if two Muslims fight each other, not only the killer but also the killed is doomed to hell fire, because he was willing to kill his fellow Muslim. However, al-Qaradawi argued that a Muslim who is recruited to a non-Muslim army to fight against Muslims finds himself in a peculiar circumstance that demands special consideration. This Muslim might be a "helpless" soldier who has "no choice" but to yield to the orders of his commanders. If that is the case, the Muslim soldier can join the rear guard to help in military service, while avoiding combat confrontation to the extent possible. If he does participate in war against Muslims, the soldier should have an inner feeling of resentment, which is the "least of faith." As in the collective former *fatwa*, al-Qaradawi's approval was based on *fiqh al-muwazanat*, and specifically on concern for the future of proselytizing efforts. In his view the harm caused by avoiding the battle would be greater than that caused by participating in it, because if a Muslim soldier refused to fight other Muslims "the Muslim as well as the Muslim community may be accused of high treason. Such an accusation may pose a threat to the Muslim minority and this may also disrupt the course of *da'wa* that has been in full swing since tens of years ago [viz. for decades], and has started to reap fruits" (Group of Muftis 2001).

## Marriage to a non-Muslim husband

In his theorization on his approach to *fiqh al-aqalliyyat al-muslima*, al-Qaradawi brought the matter of female converts married to non-Muslims as one example of how cross-*madhhab* search enhances the implementation of the *taysir* which Allah wishes for humankind (al-Qaradawi 2007: 60). Islamic law allows men to marry Jewish and Christian women, but prohibits Muslim women from marrying non-Muslim men. The opinion among jurists of all four schools of Sunni law has been that if a woman converts to Islam and her husband does not follow in her footsteps, she must divorce him. That was also the original opinion held by al-Qaradawi, but, similarly to his change of heart and mind on mortgages, he revised his view on this matter, and made it permissible for female converts not to divorce their non-converted husbands (al-Qaradawi 2007: 105–6). His detailed deliberation demonstrated that in reading afresh into the depths of Muslim traditions, and classic interpretations of those traditions, it becomes clear that while there is unanimity on the impermissibility of a Muslim woman's marriage to a non-Muslim man there is no consensus regarding the obligation of a convert to terminate her marriage with a non-Muslim. Al-Qaradawi noted that the Prophet did not oblige married couples to divorce in cases in which only one of them became Muslim; neither did he rewrite their marital contract. The Prophet allowed women, including his daughter Zaynab, to wait, even a long time if necessary, for their husbands to embrace Islam as well, and then to resume marital relations. Following his example, the Khalifa 'Umar permitted women who converted to Islam to remain married to their unconverted husbands, with a similar expectation of a future conversion (al-Qaradawi 2007: 106–25).

Al-Qaradawi's opinion was embraced by the European Council for Fatwa and Research in its eighth session in a decision that followed three lengthy meetings and conveyed a greater sense of caution. The Council stated that while the four schools of law call on female converts to divorce their non-Muslim husbands, "some scholars" believe that it is permissible for female converts not to terminate the marriage and to maintain all their marital rights and duties so long as the husband does not limit their ability to profess their religion and so long as they aspire to bring their husbands into the fold of Islam. The Council justified this opinion by explaining that women should not to be deterred from embracing Islam. Sheikh Halawa told the authors that he deemed this decision as revolutionary as the one on mortgages, because it broke from a well-established consensus.

## Inheritance from non-Muslims

The four schools of law forbid Muslims to inherit from non-Muslims, and for non-Muslims to inherit from Muslims, based on the tradition according to which the Prophet said, "A Muslim does not inherit from the *kafir* ('infidel') nor does the infidel from a Muslim." This consensus seriously injures the financial prospects of Western converts to Islam whose parents did not convert, and serves as an obstacle to conversion efforts. Al-Qaradawi, relying on Ibn Taymiyya, broke from the consensus. He noted that Islam seeks to benefit the believers, and that the fear of losing the right to inherit their family's fortune is a major concern of people who contemplate conversion. Therefore, there is a *maslaha* to permit inheritance from non-Muslims (al-Qaradawi 2007: 126–31). The European Council adopted this view. It explained, as did al-Qaradawi, that the tradition that forbids inheritance from non-Muslims relates only to infidels who are in a state of battle with Muslims (European Council for Fatwa and Research n.d.: 148–9).

## Conclusion

The *fatwa*s discussed above demonstrate that in the scope of less than two decades the European Council for Fatwa and Research, and jurists associated with its *wasati* views, issued decisions that allow Muslims in the West greater integration into majority societies in various and crucial aspects of life. Decisions emphasize two points: facilitation – making the lives of Muslim minorities easier; and proselytizing – enhancing the prospect that non-Muslims convert to Islam. A "chicken and egg" question is unavoidable: Which is a means and which an end? Yet from the *wasati* point of view, facilitation and proselytizing are complementary rather than contradictory.

The European Council is located within a Muslim community that is on the periphery of Islam in Europe. Its juristic audacity is legitimized because it is headed by jurists situated at centers of authority in the Arab world. By formulating specific juristic decisions for minorities, it potentially contributes to the separation of Muslims in the West from their sending societies. Yet this process is made possible through a mechanism that asserts the authority of the center over the periphery.

## Bibliography

Abdullah, S. (1996) *Islamic Banking and Interest: A Study of the Prohibition of Riba and Its Contemporary Interpretation*, Leiden: Brill.

Abou el-Fadl, K. (1994) "Islamic Law and Muslim Minorities: The Juristic Discourse on Muslim Minorities from the Second/Eight to the Eleventh/Seventeenth Centuries," *Islamic Law and Society* 1(2): 141–87.

Abu-Salieh, S.A.A. (1996) "The Islamic Conception of Migration," *International Migration Review* 30(1): 37–57.

al-'Alwani, T.J. (2000) *Fi Fiqh al-Aqalliyyat al-Muslima*, 6th October City: Nahdat Misr li-l-Tiba'a wal-Nashr wa-l-Tawzi'.

——(2004) "Madkhal ila Fiqh al-Aqalliyyat," *al-Majalla al-'ilmiyya li-l-majlis al-urubi li-l-ifta' wa-l-buhuth* 4–5: 19–92.

al-Majlis al-urubi li-l-ifta' wa-l-buhuth (2008) "Al-Bayan al-Khitami lil-Dawra al-Sabi'a wa-l-'Ashra," *al-Majalla al-'ilmiyya li-l-majlis al-urubi li-l-ifta' wa-l-buhuth* 12–13: 399–513.

al-Najjar, 'A. al-M. (2009) *Fiqh al-Muwatana*, Dublin: al-Majlis al-urubi li-l-ifta' wa-l-buhuth.

al-Qaradawi, Y. (1973 [1960]) *al-Halal wa-l-Haram fi al-Islam*, Beirut: al-Maktab al-Islami.

——(2000) *Taysir al-Fiqh al-Mu'asar*, Beirut: Mu'assasat al-Risala.

——(2006) "Duties of Muslims Living in the West," Islamonline.net.

——(2007 [2001]) *Fi Fiqh al-Aqalliyyat al-Muslima*, Cairo: Dar al-Shuruq.

al-Sheikhi, S. (2009) "Hukm al-Qurud al-Tulabiyya fi-Uruba," *al-Majalla al-'ilmiyya li-l-majlis al-urubi li-l-ifta' wa-l-buhuth* 14–15: 411–58.

Bin Bayya, 'A.A. (2004) "al-Farq bayna al-Darura wa-l-Haja Tatbiqan 'ala ba'd ahwal al-Aqalliyyat al-Muslima," *al-Majalla al-'ilmiyya li-l-majlis al-urubi li-l-ifta' wa-l-buhuth* 4–5: 93–145.

Caeiro, A. (2004) "The Social Construction of Shari'a: Bank Interest, Home Purchase and Islamic Norms in the West," *Die Welt des Islams* 44(3): 351–75.

——(2010) "The Power of European Fatwas: The Minority Fiqh Project and the Making of an Islamic Counterpublic," *International Journal of Middle Eastern Studies* 42(3): 435–49.

European Council for Fatwa and Research (n.d.) *Fatwas of the European Council for Fatwa and Research*, translated by Anas Osama Altikriti and Shakir Nasif al-Ubaydi, Cairo: Islamic Inc.

Fishman, S. (2006) *Fiqh al-Aqalliyyat: A Legal Theory for Muslim Minorities*, Washington, DC: Hudson Institute.

Gräf, B. (2009) "The Concept of Wasatiyyah in the Work of Yusuf al-Qaradawi," in Gräf, B. and Skovgaard-Petersen, J. (eds.) *Global Mufti: The Phenomenon of Yusuf al-Qaradawi*, London: Hurst, pp. 213–38.

Group of Muftis (2001) "Ulama's Fatwas on American Muslim Participating in US Military Campaign," IslamOnline.net.

Imam, M. (1999) "Al-Hukm al-Shar'i fi Musharakat al-Muslimin fi al-Hay'a al-Siyasiyya al-Amrikiyya," interview with Taha Jabir al-'Alwani, *Al-Sharq al-Awsat*, November 13: 26.

'Imara, M. (2007) *al-Istiqlal al-Hadari*, 6th October City: Nahdat Misr li-l-Tiba'a wa-l-Nashr wa-l-Tawzi'.

Kerr, M.H. (1996) *Islamic Reform: The Political and Legal Theories of Muhammad 'Abduh and Rashid Rida*, Berkeley and Los Angeles: University of California Press.

Lewis, M. and Algaoud, L.M. (2001) *Islamic Banking*, Northampton, MA: E. Elgar Publishing.

March, A. (2007) "Islamic Foundations for a Social Contract in non-Muslim Liberal Democracies," *American Political Science Review* 101(2): 235–52.

——(2009) *Islam and Liberal Citizenship: The Search for an Overlapping Consensus*, Oxford: Oxford University Press.

Nafi, B.M. (2004) "Fatwa and War: On the Allegiance of American Muslim Soldiers in the Aftermath of September 11," *Islamic Law and Society* 11(1): 78–116.

Polka, S. (2003) "The Centrist Stream in Egypt and Its Role in the Public Discourse Surrounding the Shaping of the Country's Cultural Identity," *Middle Eastern Studies* 39(3): 39–64.

*Qararat wa-Fatawa al-Majlis min al-Dawra al-Thamina ila al-Dawra al-Khamisa 'Ashra* (n.d.) http://www.e-cfr.org.

Sisler, V. (2009) "European Courts' Authority Contested? The Case of Marriage and Divorce Fatwas On-line," *Masaryk University Journal of Law and Technology* 3(1): 51–78.

Shavit, U. (2007) "Should Muslims Integrate into the West?," Middle East Quarterly 14(4): 13–21.

——(2009) *The New Imagined Community: Global Media and the Construction of National and Muslim Identities of Migrants*, Brighton: Sussex Academic Press.

——(2012) "The Wasati and Salafi Approaches to the Religious Law of Muslim Minorities," *Islamic Law and Society* 20(4): 1–42.

Sidiqqi, M. (2000) "'Necessity' That Allows Buying a House on Mortgage," IslamOnline.net.

Tubulyak, S.M. (1997) *Al-Ahkam al-Siyasiyya li-l-Aqaliyyat al-Muslima*, Amman, Beirut: Dar al-Nafa'is, Dar al-Bayariq.

# 24

# Ethical questions in Western Islamic experience

*Francesca Forte*

In this contribution I focus on the current debate on fundamental ethical questions within the Islamic minorities of the United States of America. As the Islamic presence in the United States is extremely diverse and plural, both in ethnic and religious terms, and as it is a relatively old one (a fair chunk of the African American community chose Islam when they were able to self-determine their religious affiliation), the protagonists involved have to be clearly defined. In this context, getting a unitary picture may prove difficult. Besides, there is a problem of representation (who speaks on behalf of whom?). On the other hand, we are witnessing a unique workshop on coexistence and cultural mediation: in the USA, Muslims have to mediate between different positions and to tackle issues which are often absent in the public debate of many Muslim majority countries, particularly religious pluralism, tolerance and respect for different ways of living one's faith and for minority groups, matters of gender in the broadest sense of the word – not only rights of women but also of believers with a different sexual orientation – the human rights agenda, etc.

Given this context, I start analyzing the plurality of voices of American Muslim intellectuals and scholars who explicitly face the abovementioned ethical questions (human rights, gender, pluralism), and I give an account of the echo of their work within the Islamic community. I also make some brief notes on the comparison with the state of affairs and the intellectual debate in Europe.

## Islam says nothing … Muslims do

### The dialectic between universalism, pluralism, and the problem of authority

When discussing social ethics and the way Western rights are perceived by the Islamic minority, the dialectic between universalism and pluralism with reference to Islam should be dealt with. This is a central theme in one of the most recent works of the renowned philosopher Martha Nussbaum (2012). Compared to the European context, the American model of integration and coexistence of minority groups, based on respect for and preservation of differences, on shared ideals of citizenship rather than rights and obligations towards the State, clearly reveals the urgency of the issue of the identity of minorities, particularly the Islamic one. After 9/11, the fear of Islam exploded in the USA, and a reassessment of the models of integration of minorities has been required. For a part of the American public opinion, the attack on the Twin Towers has revealed that an actual *clash of civilizations* is taking place. Abou El Fadl, a scholar attentive to the changes within Islam and to radical and neo-fundamentalist currents, underlines that the premise of the Islam/West polarization is to be found in the undue association of some universal ethical values with one of the two parties:

> The terrorist attacks are symptomatic of a clash between Judeo-Christian civilization, with its values of individual freedom, pluralism, and secularism, and an amoral, un-Westernized, so-called "authentic Islam." Islamic civilization is associated with the ideas of collective rights, individual duties, legalism, despotism and intolerance.
>
> *(Abou El Fadl 2002: 3)*

Islamophobia has caused an alarming restriction on freedom and civil rights (Patriot Act) which jeopardizes historical achievements. In order to preserve the American pluralist model, Nussbaum proposes distinguishing between constitutional principles, which guarantee equal freedom in religion, and ethical norms. The author hopes that Europe may start a serious reassessment of the guarantees of religious freedom, which represent a shared ground in the United States (shared even by Sarah Palin, as noted by the author herself). On the other hand, given the growing climate of Islamophobia after 9/11, a strong need for reassessment of its role in the public debate has emerged within the Islamic community, along with a reflection on the problem of authority and representation.

The key issue seems to be the conciliation or assimilation within the Islamic culture of values which are perceived as Western. On this matter, attitudes vary considerably; Amina Wadud, mostly known for her studies on women in the Qur'an and for her strong stance against male supremacy within the community, points out that the globalization of some Western values is one of the causes of the identity crisis in Muslims:

> There's no getting around it. Muslims have been struggling through an identity crisis not only as a consequence of colonialism's infiltration and corruption of Muslim complacency, but also in response to the globalization of ideas like pluralism, Western secular human rights universals.
>
> *(Wadud 2006: 187)*

In the agenda of the *Progressive Muslims* (Safi 2003), the problem of the universalism of ethical values appears resolved by the assumption that the Islamic framework remains the fundamental ethical reference, and that it is possible to find in it values which are identical to those expressed by Western secular culture. Gender justice, respect for human dignity in all its aspects, social justice, and democracy are values that are not unknown to Islamic culture; on the contrary they represent its accomplishment and its fulfillment. The critique of the arrogance of modernity, shared by postmodernism, requires a new interpretative effort – *ijtihad* – which takes on the need for change against the neo-fundamentalist currents that impose a closed and violent view of Islam. "Our agenda has to be both progressive and Islamic" (Safi 2003: 8): it is thus necessary to take a stance that can mediate between neo-traditionalism and a modernism that refuses the confrontation with tradition and takes on uncritically so-called Western values. The action of Muslim intellectuals who agree with this agenda should be rapid and firm; as children of their time (*ibn al-waqt*), Progressive Muslims are called to act against any form of discrimination and oppression (both direct and indirect). It is obvious that the premise of Omid Safi's "manifesto" is the idea that some fundamental ethical values are universal, although they are articulated in different ways by different cultures: while in the West respect for the dignity of human beings has been the achievement of a reason-based law (natural foundation of rights), for Islam it is a duty towards all God's creatures, thus a religious duty:

> We do not grant this dignity to one another: it belongs to all of us simply because, as the Qur'an teaches us, all of us have the divine spirit breathed into us.
>
> *(Safi 2003: 26)*

The author's emphasis on the necessary reference to Islam is clearly polemical against the intellectuals who exploit it only to spread typically Western ideologies (Marxism, socialism, etc.); Islam provides the fundamental ethical framework, and a dialogue with the religious tradition (an intense and open dialogue) seems the only way to bring about the change. The Islamic message of social justice requires a transformation of society by means of a renewed *jihad*:

> For progressive Muslims, a fundamental for our struggle (*jihad*) to exorcise our inner demons and bring about justice in the world at large is to engage in a progressive and critical interpretation of Islam (*ijtihad*).
>
> *(Safi 2003: 8)*

The relationship with tradition is fundamental in the definition of identity and of the political agenda, as it clarifies the approach to religion: while fundamentalists and the Wahhabi crystallize tradition as a transcendental and untouchable entity, Muslims who want to act for change consider tradition as something in progress which answers and adapts to the needs of those who make it and question it, since "Islam says nothing … Muslims do" (Safi 2003: 22).

Criticism of such a rigid and essentialist idea of religious tradition, shared by the majority of intellectuals involved in the debate, has also been thematized by the African American intellectual Sherman Jackson, who writes about the need to unmask false universals, i.e. dehistoricized concepts such as those of *Islam* and *race*. In his seminal study on Blackamerican Muslims (Jackson 2005), the author makes an interesting methodological remark by referring to Ibn Taimiyya's critique of Greek logic: the Hanbalite theologian contrasted the Islamic concept of *fitra* (natural reason) with the ontological universals of the Greek philosophical tradition, by arguing Aristotelically that only the individuals are real. Ibn Taimiyya's critique aimed at showing the partiality of the Greek doctrine and of doctrines inspired by it, by referring to the value of the contingency of human experience and to an epistemology more open than the Greek logical paradigm.

This critique proves functional when applied to some contemporary false universals, such as the concept of Islam as something fixed and immutable in time and space: it is the religious idea maintained by the fundamentalist groups, and not only them, but also by immigrant Islam (as opposed to the indigenous Islam of black Americans). Jackson emphasizes that there is not a true and authentic Islam beyond the various forms it has taken throughout history: the problem of authenticity, then, is a false one, as it conceals logics of power and hegemony of a human group over other men. In the specific instance the reference is to the delegitimization suffered by the Islam of Blackamerican Muslims after the massive waves of immigration from the Middle East, starting from 1965. The aim of this methodological remark is to acknowledge the partiality of any point of view, be it that of immigrant Muslims or that of whites, in defining universal ethical standards:

The absolute man exists only as a mental concept. But the masterful conflation of this absolute human with the perspectives of the dominant group is what has established and sustains the power of white supremacy.

*(Jackson 2005: 15)*

As for the Blackamerican Muslims, the point at issue is not the acknowledgment of supposed Western values, which they helped to make universal through their fight against slavery and white supremacy, but the definition of religious identity in relation to the culturally dominant group (the immigrant Muslims). According to Jackson, the prospect for a third resurrection of the community is to "reconcile blackness, Americanness and adherence to Islam" (Jackson 2005: 19), and this can only be achieved through a reappropriation of the Tradition by Blackamerican Muslims. On the other hand, the basically open and anti-authoritarian features of the Sunni theological-legal tradition (infallibility of the community, flexible instruments of adaptation to various situations) give American Muslims the right and obligation to develop their own corpus of doctrines and to legitimate their positions by overcoming the self-alienation they found themselves in after immigrant Muslims had assumed religious authority.

Abou El Fadl, too, clearly defines the centrality of the issue of religious authority in order to get over the supremacist creed of the puritan groups. He underlines the fact that the contemporary Islamic world has experienced a considerable intellectual impoverishment due to the loss of centrality of the traditional religious authorities and a consequent *profound vacuum* (Abou El Fadl 2002: 7). In the past, religious authorities were relatively independent from political power and institutions were decentralized: theological-legal schools and doctrines developed all over the *dar al-islam*, and important figures such as the *fuqaha'* were acknowledged and respected. With colonialism and the birth of Nation-States the previous systems were replaced by centralized religious institutions which depended on governments, and pluralism ceased to be tolerated. Far from opening the gates to a renewal, the destruction of the institutions of knowledge and of the system of religious education has made room for a veritable anarchy where everyone feels legitimated to be the mouthpiece of Islam:

It was not so much that no one could authoritatively speak for Islam, but that virtually every Muslim was suddenly considered to possess the requisite qualifications to become a representative and spokesperson for the Islamic tradition, and even Shari'ah Law.

*(Abou El Fadl 2002: 47)*

S.H. Nasr, probably the most influential and best-known American intellectual in the Islamic world, reports the same danger: the Iranian-born author emphasizes that

anyone with an Arabic or Persian or Urdu or Turkish name can claim to be a "Muslim Thinker" ... There are many people who present themselves as authorities on Islam but are not.

*(Nasr 2003: 75)*

According to Abou El Fadl, to defeat the *cultural schizophrenia* to which contemporary Muslims have fallen victim, it is necessary to re-examine the tradition and to restore it against the temptation of bypassing it for a direct relationship with the – dehistoricized – sources. In this context the issue of historicity and of interpretative communities becomes central, as the sources are challenged by ever-changing points of view and answer moral standards which vary each time. Muslim intellectuals who criticize Islam from within in order to renegotiate the significance of religion in the contemporary world and to unmask the violent movements which use it as a flag, are accused of a lack of loyalty to Islam and are seen as servile imitators of the West. All attempts at criticism from the inside are labeled false Western universalism, and *puritan orientations* consider particular values to be the cultural result of the West, without recognizing their validity. The weakness of such a perspective is the inability to perceive values as cultural and historical constructions to which all civilizations have contributed throughout the centuries:

> this points to a basic and very serious fallacy, and that is the tendency, usually exhibited by religious fundamentalists and ideological purists, to presume that moral values have a pure lineage that can be precisely identified as Western or non Western. Whether Muslims or not, purists tend to classify particular values as squarely Judeo-Christian while others are Islamic.
>
> *(Abou El Fadl 2003: 42)*

The theme of the universalism of ethical values provides a backdrop for a reflection proposed by Abdullah an-Na'im, a jurist of Sudanese origin and a pupil of the well-known reformer Mahmud Taha: the Islamic reform proposed by this intellectual goes through a complete reassessment of *shari'a* and moves from the assumption that human rights, as they have been codified by international treaties, have universal value. His plan is to integrate the human rights agenda into the Islamic ethical-legal framework, purged of all that is openly in contrast with these standards. Nevertheless, the universality of human rights cannot be imposed, but

> has to be constructed through an internal discourse within and among different cultural and religious traditions, rather than simply proclaimed through International declarations and treaties. The objective of internal discourse is ... the deliberate promotion of cross-cultural consensus and solidarity on universal values.
>
> *(an-Na'im 2005: 40)*

In conclusion, the debate appears lively and open, and in some cases the conciliation between Islam and Western values becomes a search for foundations and religious legitimation of ethical norms that cannot be considered the exclusive property of the West. In some other cases (Blackamerican Muslims) it is a matter of reconciling the typically Western way of life of the black community with the religious standards imported by immigrant Islam. Beside this, there are intellectuals such as an-Nai'm who adopt altogether the universality and the validity of human rights: it is Islam that should adjust to ethical standards which are *de facto* universal (by means of a reform of the *shari'a*).

## Global Muslims: a comparison with Europe

Within the debate on the universalism of ethical values, the main problem seems to be that of religious authority (who is entitled to speak in the name of Islam?), the characteristics of which in the USA vary considerably compared to the extremely fragmented European context.

While in the United States the division within the Islamic minority is between the African American Muslim community and that of immigrants from Islamic countries, the most apparent break in Europe is between different generations of immigrant Muslims, which has been described as a division between ethnic Islam and global Islam (Cesari and Pacini 2005).

The issue of religious authority emerges in Western contexts as appropriation of leadership in the religious community. In Europe, different forms of religious authority correspond to different ways of experiencing the affiliation to Islam which have been developing on the Old Continent and which play a fundamental role in guiding believers' interpretations and in spreading a certain image of Muslims. We are actually witnessing the making of a new cosmopolitan elite (often educated in European universities) capable of meeting the requirements of the new believers (young people of the second and third generation who experience a deterritorialized Islam). One of these personalities who has become very popular with young European Muslims is the naturalized Swiss intellectual Tariq Ramadan, grandson of Hasan al-Banna. The problem of authority emphasizes that of the transmission of knowledge: who can convey the theological-religious knowledge required by the young Muslims (Ramadan 2003)?

The break within the Islamic community in Europe is predominantly generational, and two forms of religious affiliation can be distinguished: the former, mostly practiced by first-generation immigrants, is characterized by an ethnically differentiated adherence. This is why ethnic groups show a tendency to form communities whose habits are modeled on those of their home countries, and their religious practices are often mixed with and influenced by territorial traditions. This kind of religious adherence does not satisfy the religious needs of young people born or educated in Europe, or their search for identity. The answers to ethnic Islam are several: on the one hand a form of *secularized Islam* comes to the fore, which provides for the individualization of the religious-ethical sphere (faith is primarily seen as a private matter, not communal or a matter of identity); on the other hand there emerges a form of orthodox Islam which in its turn is articulated in *cosmopolitan Islam* and *fundamentalist Islam* (Cesari and Pacini 2005). In both cases ethnic Islam is overcome in favor of a religious affiliation experienced as global: the loss of power of national identities brings back the *ideal of the community of the faithful* (*umma*), even if only imagined or dreamed of. It is a kind of deterritorialized identity which coexists with other types of affiliation on the local level (political affiliation, associations, etc.). For young people of the second generation this type of religious affiliation, which purifies the message of faith of the elements of territorial tradition, provides a more convincing answer to their theoretical and identity needs.

The *globalized Islam* practiced by global Muslims (Roy 2002) leads to a *search for authenticity*: when the religious element is deterritorialized and loses its dimension of social norm (which is very evident in their home countries), it leaves room for a more intimate and authentic adherence to religious principles. A globalized Islam, which uses the web to communicate and to create transnational links among associations and believers, witnesses an uncontrolled proliferation of interpretations and readings of the doctrine. This interpretative anarchy is deplored by, amongst others, Abou El Fadl: without an authority which acts as the mouthpiece of orthodoxy, there is room and legitimation for the most diverse interpretations.

Although it shares similar problems, the context in the United States is different. Here immigrant Islam has made religion the basic identity element from the very beginning, leaving ethnic affiliation in the shade, while the African American community seems more attached to ethnic-racial identity. As Wadud clearly emphasizes, this element represents a factor of great division within the Islamic minority: the indigenous (African American) element came into contact with Islam through the experience of liberation from slavery and the relationship with *black religion*; blacks share a past made of struggles for liberation, and affiliation to the black community (beyond faith divisions) is a basic element of self-representation. Moreover, they feel part of American history, of which they have been active protagonists by contributing to the making of the modern idea of citizenship based on civil rights:

> African-American Muslims are intimately linked with other Americans through the history of horrific racial slavery in the Americas and with the development pains of American

pluralism in the period of Civil War, through the civil rights movement, and even up to the present. As a part of their collective heritage, slavery links all African-Americans, not just African-American Muslims, in a unique way and affects our identity and relationship to America.

*(Wadud 2003a: 280)*

The definition of citizenship current amongst the immigrant Muslims, for whom religious identity prevails over ethnic identity, is different. This globalized Islam emerged especially with the migration waves of the 1960s and 1970s, and corresponds to the assumption of leadership of the Arab element, which arose also through the creation of national organizations (the most influential being the Muslim Students' Association, followed by many others). The making of this global Islam seems to be a direct consequence of the failure of Arab nationalism and of the struggle for liberation inspired by Third World movements. Besides, the massive funding by Arab monarchies of rigorist and puritan movements which promote a strict interpretation of Islam has contributed to the creation of this break within the Islamic minority in the United States.

## Human rights in the Islamic agenda

The modern idea of human rights spread by the United Nation Charter of 1948 – and subsequent international treaties – presents two basic characteristics. It is universal and secular: universal, because it affirms rights and obligations which concern any human being (regardless of religion, race, sex, etc.); secular, because of the non-recognition of any religious base or legitimation for the rights. The debate which has always accompanied the signing of these international documents is linked to their true universality and to the fact that they have been built on the model of the Western white man, spreading values of the individualist and liberalist societies where they were born (Mutua 2001).

The theoreticians of universalism of rights (Ignatieff 2001) justify it on the basis of natural law, whose theoretical origins date back to Greek thought, although it is closely connected to the Roman concept of *jus gentium*. Natural law is based on the abstraction of a universal (cross-cultural and transhistorical) human nature and on the idea of the knowability of this nature without resorting to any kind of superior source (revelation or mystical intuition), with only the use of reason, another concept supposed universal and universally intelligible. Culturalist critique has expressed some perplexity about the value of individualism inherent in the international charters, which apparently contradicts the historical role that other cultures attach to the individual within a community (Cowan et al. 2001). Moreover, there is the risk of disguising, behind the exportation of rights and democracy, a precise, capitalist, economical-social model founded on rampant liberalism.

The Islamic world has been an active protagonist since the beginning (1948), expressing criticism and doubts: it has found a degree of common cause with the supporters of so-called Asian values (Dallmayr 2002), but it has above all intervened with regard to the issue of the foundation of rights, beginning from a different concept of law.

For Islam, religious law sets the limits of human intervention, with the purpose of protecting God's rights (to be worshipped, glorified, etc.) and to limit man's absolute freedom to act, by subjecting him to constraints with regard to other men. If man's rights are those established by God through revelation, they are evidently not natural, but mediated by the revealed word, or, rather, they are inborn to man as such, but mediated by revelation, therefore they concern the Muslim subject (the person who has access to Qur'anic revelation, who chooses to submit to the only God, etc.). This weakness in the notion of natural law makes it difficult for Islamic juridical thought to accept the concept of human rights which has become established in the West. Starting from these premises, several Muslim intellectuals have tackled tradition in order to trace a distinctive Islamic path towards human rights which, though not admitting a natural law basis, can find in some concepts of classical theology or in the reform of religious law the elements necessary to open up towards a modern idea of law, and the possibility of establishing a distinctively Islamic space for human rights.

I will now examine some particularly significant voices in the contemporary debate in the United States: first, the proposal for a reform of *shari'a* made by an-Na'im as long as twenty years ago and subsequently developed into a *cross-cultural perspective*; then the issue of rights with reference to gender, on the one hand taking into consideration the proposals of authoritative Muslim women scholars (Wadud, Mattson, Simmons) for a new reading of tradition which favors women's empowerment, and on the other hand analyzing the (still isolated) attempts at interpreting the sources with a particular attention to the rights of homosexual people in Islam (Kugle).

## The proposal of Abdullah an-Na'im

Jurist of Sudanese origin Abdullah an-Na'im is one of the contemporary intellectuals who have proposed a systematic reflection on the relationship between Islam and human rights. His reflection has been inspired by the hermeneutic proposal of Mahmud Taha, a Sudanese political activist and thinker executed in 1985 by the dictator of Sudan Nimayri (an-Na'im 1988): an-Na'im's discourse can't be understood without considering Taha's proposal of reading the sacred text of Islam by means of new interpretative tools.

According to Taha, *shari'a* remains the basic cornerstone which should inspire the Islamic peoples' actions, but it is a *shari'a* reinterpreted in the light of a new exegesis of the sacred text: it does not propose a weakening of the divine character of the law or its reduction to ethical principle (as his pupil will actually do); on the contrary Taha wants to affirm the divine origin of religious law, thus respecting its universal message. Its weakening is, instead, caused by a strict use of it, which does not consider its malleable and changeable character or its adaptability to all kinds of contexts.

Starting from this exegetic principle, an-Na'im embarks upon a road of reconciliation between Islam and human rights, accepting the assumption of the existence of universal values which can be and have to be integrated into differing cultural contexts. The Sudanese jurist goes so far as to deny the divine character of *shari'a*, emphasizing instead its completely human nature (as a result of man's interpretation and elaboration). Actually, in an-Na'im's proposal *shari'a* becomes an extralegal principle, a set of criteria regarding justice to which the norms of a positive legal system can be related.

Through a revival of *naskh*, the science of abrogation, an-Na'im advocates that the verses linked to the historical context of the first centuries (in practice the Medinan verses) are abrogated by the most universal ones (the Meccan ones), where there are fewer prescriptions which contrast with modern international human rights standards. He therefore proposes a new *ijtihad* (interpretative effort). Understanding who can claim such a task, which has been codified very precisely in classic law, remains a problem. An-Na'im takes up the challenge posed by Islam: everybody can question the text and carry out *ijtihad*, there is no dogma in Islam, and every believer should be allowed to directly approach the texts, so the Islamic community becomes an interpretative community in the true sense of the word. However, this attempt at reform encounters opposition even from those Muslim intellectuals who work on integrating human rights into the Islamic context: Ahmad Moussalli questions an-Na'im's choice of making a "minor" concept such as abrogation the methodology for changing the law, thus neglecting more important doctrines such as *shura* (consultation) and *ijma'* (consensus) to expand the historical meaning of *shari'a*. In practice an-Na'im considers historical *shari'a* unreformable and he takes it only as an ethical principle to be integrated into a secular normative context (Moussalli 2001: 8).

This interpretation of *shari'a* as an extralegal principle rather than a positive set of norms is (as has been said) functional to an integration of human rights into the Islamic cultural context, and, starting from reflections specifically regarding Islam, an-Na'im proposes an interpretation of human rights from a cross-cultural point of view, in order to overcome the opposition these might face in contexts different from the Western one:

> The universality of human rights should be seen as a product of a process rather than an established given concept and specific predetermined normative content to be discovered or proclaimed through International declarations and rendered legally binding through treatise.
>
> *(an-Na'im 2003: 2)*

Legitimation of the universal value of human rights can only be achieved through interaction and assimilation of these rights by the culture and values of a particular society, and in no way can it be imposed from above:

> The difficulty in achieving agreement – agreement among all communities – or a single foundation for human rights indicates that we should promote instead an overlapping consensus among multiple foundations.
>
> *(an-Na'im 2005: 57)*

The universal applicability of human rights implies their universal value within religious and philosophical cultural traditions. If the individuals do not accept these rights as binding from a cultural, religious, or philosophical point of view, they will never voluntarily conform to them in practice, nor will they ask their governments to respect and promote them in the execution of their official role. An-Na'im considers interdependence between human rights, religion, and secularism to be the cornerstone to promoting rights culture in differing contexts:

> Legitimating human rights in local cultures and religious traditions is a matter of vital importance for the survival and future development of the human rights paradigm itself. Religions must be also encouraged, from within, to provide moral underpinnings for fresh development of the paradigm in order to address emerging issues in differing contexts. The contribution of secularism to these critical developments must be provided the political stability and communal security essential for negotiating a unique dynamic relationship between human rights and region in every setting internationally.
>
> *(an-Na'im 2005: 68)*

According to the Sudanese jurist, it is possible to find within each cultural tradition a set of fundamental and universally shareable values where the original core of basic human rights can be recognized. The next step should be that of expanding this original nucleus, considering it not as a target but rather as a starting point for the elaboration of a real process of universalization.

In the specific case of Islam, *shari'a* itself, considered as an extralegal principle which should inspire positive law, and not a set of unchangeable norms, represents a resource within such a specific cultural context for integrating human rights values.

*Shari'a*, or rather its traditional interpretations, presents elements which are explicitly in contrast with human rights (male guardianship of women – *qiwama*; sovereignty of Muslims over non-muslims – *dhimma*; and violently agressive *jihad*). It is thus necessary to reassess the interpretation of religious law in order to make it an instrument of promotion and protection of rights:

> Significant Islamic reform is necessary to reformulate such problematic aspects of *shari'a*, but should not and cannot mean the wholesale and uncritical adoption of dominant Western theory and practice in these fields.
>
> *(an-Na'im 2008: 337)*

For example, the traditional concept of *dhimma* may evolve into a coherent and human principle of modern citizenship by referring to the Islamic principle of reciprocity (*mu'awada*), also known as the *Golden Rule*; this example shows that it is possible to find within the Islamic tradition the foundations for the promotion of a rights culture (an-Na'im 2010). An-Na'im's proposal of reform implies, therefore, the acceptance of a secularized legal context as a framework where every religious and cultural tradition may contribute to developing an ethos of rights and coexistence. The rational foundation of human rights is not questioned, while *shari'a* is weakened; this appears, in the view of the author, as a result of human exegetic practice:

> [*shari'a* is a] product of a very slow, gradual and spontaneous process of interpretation of the Qur'an and collection, verification and interpretation of Sunna during the first three centuries of Islam.
>
> *(an-Na'im 2008: 325)*

## Gender issues

### The gender *jihad*

The debate on women's rights and Islamic feminism in the USA, which involves various American women scholars who have been acting in the front line against gender discrimination in American society, and particularly within the Islamic minority, deserves specific attention.

The theme of the relationship between Islam and gender appears a very delicate one, as it risks leveling out differences experienced by Muslim women depending on the country they live in, the ethnic group they belong to, or their social status. Nevertheless, there are Islamic specificities demonstrated by the fact that in Muslim majority societies, and within religious minorities in the West, women's subordinate position is somehow favored by the religious element: religion plays an important part in defining and maintaining the position of gender roles (social constructions) and it often provides a justification for these roles. This is why introducing a female point of view in the field of theological studies, which has traditionally been a male prerogative, appears so important: Islamic feminism in all its forms intends to make the religious element and the new reading of the texts of tradition a factor of empowerment for Muslim women, in order to overcome social traditions and patriarchal and sexist habits, which have been unjustly associated with Islam. Scholars such as Amina Wadud (1992, 2003), Asma Barlas (2002), Khaled Abou El Fadl (2001), and Ingrid Mattson (2008) have opened new hermeneutic spaces for Qur'anic exegesis and proposed corresponding interpretations of *shari'a* and religion-based law to promote gender justice.

Against the criticism often directed towards these interpretations, which are accused of being excessively related to the personal experience of those who practice them, the African American scholar and activist Gwendolyn Simmons refers to the authority of Abd al-Karim Souroush, who talked of *experiential basis of religious knowledge*. Nevertheless, it appears undeniable that there is a textual basis for the sexist readings of the Qur'an: as an-Na'im has shown, it is not a matter of denying the discriminations present in the *shari'a*, but rather of considering them inapplicable to the modern context. This has already happened for the legal institution of slavery:

> Just a few Muslims would publicly advocate a return to the historical accepted practice of slavery, Muslims should no longer advocate discriminatory treatment of women. Muslims must begin to find such discrimination in all of its form as abhorrent as slavery.
>
> *(Simmons 2003: 208)*

Therefore a new Qur'anic hermeneutics which encourages women's empowerment appears necessary in order to reform not only Islamic societies, but also Muslim communities in the West. The American context is particularly interesting from this angle, and extremely varied. American women are often subject to a twofold discriminatory system: on the one hand, as women, they are subject to forms of discrimination within their communities, and do not have the instruments to appeal to American law, which protects them to a larger extent; on the other hand, as Muslims, after 9/11 they are seen as foreigners and dangerous. Besides, in the case of African American women there is also ethno-racial discrimination. Nevertheless, as Wadud (2006) emphasizes, in the USA women and Muslim believers in general show a more direct approach to the sacred text and religious sources: it is a quite unique condition, as the traditional interpretative apparatus which usually mediates between the faithful and the text is full of patriarchal and sexist readings. It is therefore a privileged position for embarking upon a new hermeneutics of the text in line with the requirements of modernity. However, as Abou El Fadl points out, this condition can prove dangerous because it may generate an uncontrollable *interpretative anarchy*. To avoid this risk, priority should be given to a historical perspective which clarifies the way in which some reforms have been introduced in existing contexts: historical contextualization allows one to see the progressive realization of the ultimate goal of *shari'a* – that is, social justice (Wadud 2003b: 193) – and to overcome the sexist point of view. Wadud therefore considers Qur'anic hermeneutics the necessary instrument to transform Islam from within, in order to recreate the relationship between Muslim men and women on an egalitarian basis. However, this is not sufficient and should be integrated with the implementation of social reforms. If it is true that Muslims cannot rewrite the Qur'an, because it is considered God's word, they can rewrite the law, *shari'a*, through *fiqh*. Moreover, it is a real duty:

> by rewriting legal codes, through distinguishing their sexist reflecting, we can achieve an Islamic reality more meaningfully reflecting Qur'anic principles in an harmonious equilibrium.
>
> *(Wadud 2006: 205)*

An interesting voice in the debate is that of the current president of the Islamic Society of North America (ISNA), the Canadian-born convert to Islam Ingrid Mattson. Just like Wadud, she does not define herself as a feminist because this word has too many connections with Western colonialism; moreover, its use might delegitimize her stances in the eyes of the Muslim community. Her reading of the Qur'an and of early Islamic history is not explicitly characterized by claims of gender equality, but the way she takes various ethical issues of the text shows her willingness to find in it the foundations of justice for women (Mattson 2008: 3). This scholar directs her attention to the way the revelation was inserted into the context of pre-Islamic Arabia, amending many discriminatory practices against the weakest subjects, women in particular; in the same way, the life of the prophet Muhammad is read with an emphasis on his positive and respectful attitude to women and to their role as religious guides in the early years of the community. One of the themes that unite Wadud and Mattson is indeed the reflection on female religious authority in historical and contemporary Islam; while Wadud made a strong gesture by breaking the taboo of leading the Friday prayer in front of the faithful in 2005, Mattson shows a more moderate approach and brings the question into the wider debate of religious leadership in Islamic communities by referring to the sources of the law:

> The majority of legal schools consider it "recommended" (*mandub* – a technical term indicating a religiously meritorious act) for women to pray together in congregation with one of them leading as imam, if they are not praying with the general (i.e., male inclusive) congregation.
>
> *(Mattson 2009)*

The scholar's conclusion is an appeal to the American Islamic community in its entirety to encourage an increase in and the spreading of religious education among its members, and also an appeal for the emergence of a leadership which represents and embraces its different components.

Fundamentalists and secular feminists do not share the premises of these exegetic approaches to the Qur'an and to tradition, as shown by the criticism and perplexities posed by a female scholar of Iranian origin, Haideh Moghissi:

> How could a religion based on gender hierarchy be adopted as the framework for struggle for gender democracy and women's equality with men?
>
> *(Moghissi 1999: 126)*

In the opinion of this scholar, religious Islamic law is based on explicit discrimination against women and minorities and for this reason cannot possibly provide the legal framework for promoting the rights of these categories of individuals. Why is Islamic feminism proposed nowadays as the only, and most authentically indigenous, ground on which the demand for women's rights can take root in Muslim societies? According to Moghissi, the problem lies in the fact that the secular discussion on the promotion of gender equality has been discredited as elitist, modernist, or white and pro-Western, delegitimizing every critical view.

It should not be forgotten that active feminists are divided in relation to their political orientations: an authoritative voice in the debate, that of the Egyptian writer Nawal El Saadawi, starting from an openly Marxist position, criticizes those feminists who do not take into adequate consideration class affiliation and access to economic resources as central elements in the subordination of Muslim women. It is a matter of what she defined a *double consciousness*, generated by subordination to and participation in the system of economic globalization and by imperialism, on the one hand, and religious conservatism, on the other: what is lacking is a strong political awareness which shows women that the systems of power (economical and patriarchal) are closely connected.

Compared to the United States, the European debate on Muslim women's rights appears more centered around the problem of the political model with respect to minorities: apart from Great Britain, where there is a model of strict multiculturalism, in other European countries the policy of integration of minority groups is still to be defined.

One of the issues which is being debated is the protection of cultural rights (including religious differences), which might confine women within consolidated discriminatory mechanisms. In Western democracies (particularly in the USA) multiculturalism has become the dominant theoretical approach to the theme of relationships between State and minority communities. This position, however, with its insistence on the necessity of respecting and tolerating diversity and differences, hides some problems which have been highlighted by some feminist scholars (Moller Okin 1999); the discussion on multiculturalism often tends to consider minority groups as homogeneous realities with no differences of class or gender. Therefore, power relations within the group, which originate precisely in the existence of such differences, are not recognized. In addition, this model can prove anti-democratic if the relations between state and minority groups are mediated by leaders who were never elected by anyone, who are men, and who are generally affiliated to socially conservative circles. The majority of these people come from the religious world, whose main interest is the protection of the family and of traditional values.

The so-called *affair du foulard* stirred up in France by a ruling of the Council of State which in practice forbids girls to wear the veil at school (Gaspard and Khosrokhavar 1995) typically represents the approach adopted by part of the States of the Union: the state intervenes to impose in the public sphere a kind of autonomy and equality greater than those apparently required by the concerned subjects themselves (Muslim girls), precisely referring to the dangers inherent in the culturalist model (Lévy and Lévy 2004). The French case has triggered a long and very lively debate in Europe, and the position of the well-known intellectual Tariq Ramadan seems to summarize the contradictions of the French choice: *if imposing the use of the veil is against Islam, forbidding it is a violation of human rights.*

We thus go back to the initial question: to what extent can different habits be tolerated without threatening the identity, and without considering violated the principles of equality and freedom of the individual which underlie the Western democracies? According to Nussbaum, the problem stems from the ideals of citizenship and of national identity, which in Europe have been built on an alleged cultural, linguistic, ethnic, and religious uniformity rather than on the sharing of ideals and political struggles (as in the USA, India, and Australia). In addition to approving of the multicultural model practiced in the USA as an instrument for the real promotion of equality and rights, Nussbaum's judgment points out the difficult definition of the model of integration of minority groups in Europe, particularly the Islamic minority, whose customs and habits apparently increase the fear of differences, bringing back old Orientalist prejudices.

## A sexuality-sensitive interpretation

To complete the picture of the American debate on gender issues, we should mention the studies of Scott Siraj al-Haqq Kugle on the Islamic culture's vision of homosexuality, and in general on the approach of Islamic sources to different sexual orientations. In the wake of feminist exegesis of the Qur'an, the American scholar hopes for a new *ijtihad*, which can introduce a more balanced perspective with regard to sexual orientation, as can be verified in the sources and attested to by Islamic history, rejecting as inauthentic sexist and patriarchal readings which present the heterosexual point of view as the only possible one. Kugle mentions a project in progress that so far has only been started and that requires huge interpretative work and an in-depth philological study of the sacred sources as well as of early Islamic history. The scholar starts from two basic assumptions: the positive vision of sexuality in Islam has been universally acknowledged, because it is linked to a form of spirituality and because sexual pleasure represents a positive element in itself; besides, the Qur'an, as shown by studies on pluralism in Islam, proclaims diversity as a value (cf. Qur. 49:13), and this can include gender relationships:

> With the Qur'an's vivid portrayal of diversity at so many levels of the natural and human world, it would be logical to assume that this diversity of creation plays out on the level of sexuality as well.
>
> *(Kugle 2003: 196)*

Amreen Jamel was the first to attempt a *sexuality-sensitive interpretation* of the Qur'an, as Kugle himself defines it, with his new reading of the story of the prophet Lut (Jamel 2001): in short, the story of this prophet does not appear centered on sexual acts at all, but rather on the meaning of his prophecy to the inhabitants of Sodom; there emerges a question of social ethics in Qur'anic history, and the divine condemnation of the city's inhabitants is due to their lack of generosity and to their failure to respect the sacred duty of hospitality towards foreigners (the weak subjects), rather than to their sexual acts. On the contrary, subsequent legal tradition has interpreted these Qur'anic episodes in order to prohibit and condemn homosexuality, although the same cannot be said of the whole intellectual history of Islam, where illustrious examples of authors and scholars who have shown a great sensitivity and respect toward all kinds of love relations can be found:

> As Ibn Hazm demonstrates many Muslim authors, ethicists and intellectuals saw hetero- and homoerotic love as being equally love.
>
> *(Kugle 2010: 27)*

The scholar proposes to start from Jamel's reading and to analyze the ancient sources, especially the literary genre of stories of the prophets, which are less strict than traditional *tafsir*, to show that it is far from certain that homosexuality was condemned at the time of the Prophet and in the early years of Islam. On the contrary, in Muhammad's life there is no trace of acts of violence or condemnation against people with a different sexual orientation, although these can be found in later traditions. The aim of Kugle's research is

> to separate what is imposed by culture from what is essential to faith, on the one hand, and to sift what is essential to faith from what is enshrined in religious tradition, on the other hand.
>
> *(Kugle 2010: 3)*

It is a hermeneutic project that is in continuity with the feminist exegesis of the Qur'an, to overcome the sexist and androcentric reading of the text, as well as with the attempt to release faith from the shackles of tradition and to propose a renewed approach to Islam. As Kugle himself points out, the process has only started, and it should be developed further in order for the political potential of sexual, emotional, and intimate life to emerge.

## Conclusion

The path outlined in this contribution began with the aim of giving an outline of the American debate on some ethically sensitive issues, and to make a comparison, where possible, with the European situation. For this reason, the first part has attempted to place the debate within a theoretical framework: through an analysis of the dialectic between pluralism and universalism, the assumptions and positions of some Muslim intellectuals with respect to the possibility of integrating so-called Western values within the Islamic framework have been clarified. While an intellectual such as Abou El Fadl has devoted various studies to the concept of tolerance and pluralism in the Islamic tradition, with the purpose of delegitimizing supremacist-puritan interpretations, Omid Safi proclaims the need for a new *jihad*, which Progressive Muslims have the duty to fight in order to renew the tradition and to achieve social justice, the ultimate goal of the Islamic message. On the other hand, the African American scholar Jackson warns against so-called false universals, stressing the need for a reappropriation of tradition by African American Muslims (Blackamerican Muslims), in order to make it a factor of empowerment within the Islamic minority as well as in the whole of American society. A central theme in this debate is that of religious leadership, a historically complex issue in Islamic culture, which is even more difficult to define in contemporary Western societies: it is necessary to rediscover pluralism and to abandon the strict vision of tradition of the radical groups (Abou al-Fadl), considering Islam as a set of diversified practices, expression of different interpretative communities. The same question has been debated in Europe with respect to the leadership of the community for the new generations of Muslims (Ramadan): the problem here is to find a leadership suitable for the new deterritorialized Islam experienced by young second- and third-generation Muslims who reject the ethnic Islam of the first immigrants.

The second part of this contribution focused on some specific questions of social ethics: in particular, I have tackled the issue of human rights on the Islamic agenda and, within this framework, the issue of the rights of women and of homosexuals. So-called Islamic feminism now has numerous women scholars who have devoted themselves to the exegesis of the Qur'an, tackling the issue of gender equality (Wadud, Barlas), or who work to bring out within Islamic history and tradition the often neglected role of women as religious guides (Mattson). Although an interpretation attentive to emotional and sexual aspects in its entirety is still to be defined, these studies are multiplying (Kugle). It is an extremely complex and varied picture; the plurality of voices examined represents just a small part of the intellectual debate, but the opinions of men and women active in the religious community, but who lack a recognized academic production, have had to be excluded. Nevertheless, the sensitivity of the authors who have been taken into account and their active role within the academic and religious community have made this gap less obvious, respecting as far as possible the idea that

> when we speak about the meaning of Islam today, we are really talking about the product of cumulative enterprises that have generated communities of interpretation through a long span of History.
>
> *(Abou El Fadl 2003: 39)*

## Bibliography

Abou El Fadl, K. (2001) *Speaking in God's Name*, Oxford: Oneworld.
——(2002) *The Place of Tolerance in Islam*, Boston: Beacon Press.
——(2003) "The Ugly Modern and the Modern Ugly: Reclaiming the Beautiful in Islam," in Safi, O. (ed.) *Progressive Muslims*, Oxford: Oneworld, pp. 33–77.
Ahmed, L. (1992) *Women and Gender in Islam: Historical Roots of a Modern Debate*, New Haven, CT: Yale University Press.

an-Na'im, A.A. (1988) "Mahmud Muhammad Taha and the Crisis in Islamic Law Reform: Implications for Interreligious Relations," *Journal of Ecumenical Studies* 25(1): 1–21.

——(1990) *Toward an Islamic Reformation: Civil Liberties, Human Rights and International Law*, Syracuse, NY: Syracuse University Press.

——(2003) "'Area Expressions' and the Universality of Human Rights: Mediating a Contingent Relationship," in Forsythe, D.P. and MacMahon, P.C. (eds.) *Human Rights and Diversity: Area Studies Revisited*, Lincoln: University of Nebraska Press, pp. 1–21.

——(2005) "The Politics of Religion and Morality of Globalization," in Juergensmeyer, M. (ed.) *Religion and Global Civil Society*, Oxford: Oxford University Press, pp. 23–48.

——(2008) "Shari'a in the Secular State: A Paradox of Separation and Conflation," in Bearman, P., Heinrichs, W., and Weiss, B.G. (eds.) *The Law Applied: Contextualizing the Islamic Shari'a*, London and New York: I.B. Tauris, pp. 321–41.

——(2010a) "Beyond *dhimmihood*: citizenship and human rights," in Hefner, R.W. (ed.) *The New Cambridge History of Islam, vol. 6: Muslims and Modernity, Culture and Society since 1800*, Cambridge: Cambridge University Press, pp. 314–34.

——(2010b) *Homosexuality in Islam*, Oxford: Oneworld.

Barlas, A. (2002) *Believing Women in Islam: Unreading Patriarchal Interpretation of the Quran*, Austin: University of Texas Press.

Cesari, J. and Pacini, A. (2005) *Giovani Musulmani in Europa*, Torino: Fondazione Agnelli.

Cowan, J.K., Dembour, M.-B., and Wilson, R.A. (eds.) (2001) *Culture and Rights: Anthropological Perspectives*, Cambridge: Cambridge University Press.

Dallmayr, F. (2002) "Asian Values and Global Human Rights," *Philosophy East and West* 52: 173–89.

Gaspard, F. and Khosrokhavar, F. (1995) *Le Foulard et la République*, Paris: La Découverte.

Ignatieff, M. (2001) *Human Rights as Politics and Idolatry*, Princeton: Princeton University Press.

Jackson, S. (2005) *Islam and the Blackamerican: Looking Toward the Third Resurrection*, New York: Oxford University Press.

Jamel, A. (2001) "The Story of Lut and the Qur'an's Perception of the Morality of Same-Sex Sexuality," *Journal of Homosexuality* 41(1): 1–88.

Kugle, S.S. al-H. (2003) "Sexuality, Diversity, and Ethics in the Agenda of Progressive Muslims," in Safi, O. (ed.) *Progressive Muslims*, Oxford: Oneworld, pp. 190–234.

——(2010) *Homosexuality in Islam: Critical Reflection on Gay, Lesbian, and Transgender Muslims*, Oxford: Oneworld.

Lévy, A. and Lévy, L. (2004) *Des Filles comme les autres : Au-delà du foulard, entretiens avec Véronique Giraud et Yves Sintomer*, Paris: La Découverte.

Mattson, I. (2008) *The Story of the Qur'an: Its History and Place in Muslim Life*, Oxford: Blackwell Publishing.

——(2009) *Can a Women Be an Imam?: Debating Form and Fuction in Muslim Women's Leadership*, macdonald.hartsem.edu/muslimwomensleadership.pdf.

Moghissi, H. (1999) *Feminism and Islamic Fundamentalism: The Limits of Postmodern Analysis*, London: Zed Books.

Moller Okin, S. (1999) *Is Multiculturalism Bad for Women?*, Princeton: Princeton University Press.

Moussalli, A. (2001) *The Islamic Quest for Democracy, Pluralism, and Human Rights*, Gainesville: University Press of Florida.

Mutua, M. (2001) "Savages, Victims and Saviors: The Metaphor of Human Rights," *Harvard International Law Journal* 42: 201–9.

Nasr, S.H. (2003) "American Islamic Intellectual Activity and the Islamic World," in Strum, P. (ed.) *Muslims in the United States*, Washington, DC: Woodrow Wilson Center for Scholars, pp. 75–85.

Nussbaum, M. (2012) *The New Religious Intolerance*, Cambridge, MA: Harvard University Press.

Ramadan, T. (2003) *Les Musulmans d'Occident et l'avenir de l'Islam*, Arles: Editions Actes sud.

Roy, O. (2002) *L'Islam mondialisé*, Paris: Seuil.

Safi, O. (ed.) (2003) *Progressive Muslims*, Oxford: Oneworld.

Simmons, G.Z. (2003) "Muslim Women's Experience as a Basis for Theological Interpretation in Islam," in Strum, P. (ed.) *Muslims in the United States*, Washington, DC: Woodrow Wilson Center for Scholars, pp. 203–12.

Wadud, A. (1992) *Qur'an and Women: Rereading the Sacred Text from a Women's Perspective*, Oxford: Oxford University Press.

——(2003a) "American Muslim Identity: Race and Ethnicity in Progressive Islam," in Safi, O. (ed.) *Progressive Muslims*, Oxford: Oneworld, pp. 270–85.

——(2003b) "The Role of Women in the American-Muslim Community and Their Impact on Perceptions of Muslim Women Worldwide," in Strum, P. (ed.) *Muslims in the United States*, Washington, DC: Woodrow Wilson Center for Scholars, pp. 191–201.

——(2006) *Inside the Gender Jihad: Women's Reform in Islam*, Oxford: Oxford University Press.

# 25

# Gender, feminism, and critique in American Muslim thought

*Juliane Hammer*

In early 2011, in the concluding paragraph of an essay entitled "Muslim Feminist Birthdays," Aysha Hidayatullah wrote the following in the *Journal of Feminist Studies in Religion*:

> Advancing gracefully will require that we face end points and forge new directions in our work without reinventing the wheel, failing to give each other credit, or falling prey to the divisive commercialism of the U.S. academy that exoticizes Muslim women and turns them into collectors' items of competing value. Our survival as Muslim feminist subjects will depend on our ability to remain accountable to our greater communities, foster a spirit of critical engagement, and maintain the momentum of a collective movement that continues to nourish new life.
>
> *(Hidayatullah 2011: 122)*

Hidayatullah, a scholar of Islamic studies, not only introduces us to the complexity of (American) Muslim feminist theology (her terminology), she also writes in response to Elisabeth Schüssler Fiorenza, a leading Catholic feminist theologian, and as part of a group of religious feminists who ponder the past, present, and future of religious feminist thought and practice. Her observation about this complexity as well as her charge for the future of Muslim feminist thought provide a suitable framework for this chapter on the roles of gender, feminism, and critique in American Muslim thought. I focus my presentation and analysis on American Muslim women scholars at the intersection of the American academy and American Muslim communities. I argue that their commitments as public intellectuals focus on meaningful change in their societies and communities which hinges on the possibility of multiple and nuanced critique as well as dynamics of power, authority, and interpretation. In other words, we can only critically and meaningfully analyze the works of American Muslim women scholars if we recognize them as products of historical circumstances, individual as well as collective agency, and part of the ongoing negotiation of Muslim religious tradition.

The group of scholars I focus on here deserves some further qualification. American Muslim women have participated in and contributed to scholarship in the traditional Islamic sciences as well as the more or less secular field of Islamic studies in the American academy. However, not all of them foreground their Muslim identity; not all of them carry out normative and/or prescriptive (sometimes called theological) work; and some women scholars do not identify with work that focuses on gender categories or changes in gender roles as central to their agenda. I focus on those Muslim women scholars who do identify with what has been called by some the "gender jihad" (Esack 1997: 239; Wadud 2006), a term that connotes specifically Muslim endeavors to approach Islamic textual sources, including the Qur'an, the *Sunna*, and the Islamic legal tradition, in ways that allow for reinterpretation of gender roles and societal change.

I hesitate to simply call them American Muslim feminist scholars because there has been much discussion and scholarship on Islamic and/or Muslim feminism (Badran 2009; Shaikh 2003; Hidayatullah 2009). While some of the scholars under discussion in this chapter apply the term feminist to themselves, others have rejected it as part of a hegemonic and colonial Euro-American enterprise. Yet others avoid identification with Western feminism because it potentially discredits their endeavors in the eyes of Muslim communities and thus weakens the potential for their recognition as religious and communal authorities and leaders, and thus the potential for change. Amina Wadud self-identified in 2006 as "pro-feminist, pro-faith" (Wadud 2006: 79), which might just be an acceptable middle ground. I avoid forcing the term feminist on American Muslim women scholars and their work, while I also acknowledge that it can be a useful shorthand for gender equality-focused projects and ideas.

My interest in gender-focused scholarship and Muslim women scholars is born out of my own experiences as a Muslim woman scholar in the American academy and more than a decade of research, discussion, and reflection on the dynamics of women's scholarship, feminist thought, and Muslim identities. The spotlight on gender-justice-focused Muslim women's scholarship runs many risks, among them patronizing forms of celebration, possible co-optation for liberal tolerance projects, criticism from Muslim communities about overemphasizing these particular scholars, and, not least, charges from the very scholars themselves of misreading or misrepresenting their work. Most of these cannot be entirely avoided. In what follows, however, I hope to offer a nuanced as well as critical portrait and analysis of the intellectual genealogies and faith struggles of women who are foremothers, colleagues, and in some cases friends. I engage in this scholarship both as an ongoing negotiation of my own positioning as a Muslim woman academic and as part of an equally ongoing push towards the full inclusion of gendered analysis into scholarship on Islam and Muslims. It is to this end that this chapter positions Muslim women scholars in a longer genealogy of gender thought in American Muslim intellectual endeavors while recognizing that the bulk of gender-justice-oriented work has indeed been carried out by Muslim women and not their more authoritative and influential male counterparts.

## Setting the stage

Women's roles in a society have been a litmus test for its modernness, provided they did not live in Euro-American countries, since the days of early colonialism. Many have described the unholy marriage between feminism and colonialism and the resulting judgment on non-Western societies as lower on the civilizational ladder and thus in need of "civilizing" and thus colonization. This is particularly the case for women's roles and status in Islam and in Muslim societies. The pervasive representation of Muslim women as oppressed, silent, and hidden behind veils (by Muslim men and Islam) is only rivaled in its mediatized power by the arguably more recent image of Muslim men as inherently violent (towards other societies as terrorists and towards their own women and children as abusers).

Modern Muslim reformist thought developed in response to the experiences of colonialism that affected most of the Muslim majority world directly or indirectly. It is thus no accident that reformers like Muhammad 'Abduh, Rashid Rida, Abu al-'Ala Mawdudi, and many others felt compelled to formulate their ideas on the status of women in their societies, typically with an eye towards equal rights gleaned from European discourses, regardless of whether those were in fact societal practice in those European model countries.

These representations, or rather stereotypes, have framed American Muslim community discourses on women and gender in Islam since the early twentieth century. American Muslims, diverse in ethnic and racial backgrounds, composed of Muslims from all Muslim majority countries as well as those born and raised in America, have always been thoroughly American and transnational at the same time. American Muslim attitudes to gender issues as well as the development of American Muslim thought have thus been grounded in the intersection of developments, values, and attitudes in Muslim majority societies and North America. As three waves of feminist theory and movement swept through North America and affected in myriad ways attitudes to gender roles and sexuality, Muslim societies from Morocco to Indonesia also negotiated, under the Western gaze, ideas about gender roles and changing economic, social, and political dynamics and Muslim religious adaptations to constantly changing societies.

## American Muslim thinkers and gender: the beginnings

It is important that the story of how American Muslim thinkers approached questions of gender roles should not start with Muslims who came to the United States as students and later scholars in the 1960s and 1970s. Part of the challenge lies in the ways in which scholars and/or intellectuals have been narrowly defined as engaged in higher education and the production of knowledge through institutions such as universities and research institutes. By that standard, leaders and intellectuals such as Elijah Muhammad, the long-term leader of the Nation of Islam (NOI), Malcolm X, the NOI's most iconic figure, and Warith Deen Mohammed, son of Elijah Muhammad, and heir as well as transformer of the Nation of Islam from the death of Elijah Muhammad in 1975 to his own death in 2008, would not be part of our purview here. Such exclusion would not only privilege American Muslim thinkers who came to the United States as immigrants; it also effectively marginalizes the thought and experiences of African American Muslims as somehow less important and not authentically Muslim.

Elijah Muhammad and Malcolm X both expressed most of their ideas through speech rather than writing, even though Elijah Muhammad's ideas have been published in many volumes of talks, lectures, and interviews. Malcolm X's thought is most often located primarily in his autobiography (as told to Alex Haley). Both had far-reaching and important ideas about gender – mainly traditional gender constellations in which men provided economic stability and moral norms for the family, while women were responsible for maintaining the household, raising the children, and nourishing Muslim family bodies through proper diet and religious practice. This model of gendered respectability was imparted to NOI members through NOI publications like *Muhammad Speaks*, as well as in lessons and lectures, to women and girls, and men and boys. Fulfilling these "traditional" gender roles was represented both as essentially Islamic and as a remedy to the damage slavery and slaveholder discourse had done to Black families and Black bodies. It is also worth remembering that the period from the 1940s to the 1960s, when these discourses were developed, was a time in American history when American women were advocating for suffrage, and that it was only from the 1960s onward that second-wave feminism came into its own with its critique of gender discrimination and its push towards equal rights. Elijah Muhammad and Malcolm X advocated for the right and responsibility of Black men to protect and defend their women against white assault and exploitation. In *Message to the Blackman in America*, Muhammad writes: "Islam will not only elevate your women but will also give you the power to control and protect them. We protect ours against all their enemies" (Muhammad 1965: 60). These views of ideal gender roles and programs for implementing them shaped several generations of members of the Nation of Islam and the broader African American Muslim community, which of course included other African American Muslim groups and movements, some of whom identified as Sunni and claimed more religious authenticity and grounding in traditional Muslim discourse than the NOI.

It was in the late 1950s that several prominent Muslim scholars of immigrant background came to North America. Three have been hailed as the most influential on the development of American Muslim thought and will thus be discussed here in some detail: Seyyed Hossein Nasr, a native of Iran, born in 1933; Ismail al-Faruqi, from Palestine (1921–86); and Fazlur Rahman (1919–88), a native of India/Pakistan. All three received education in both Muslim countries and Europe or the United States and (have) spent their scholarly and political careers as transnational Muslim scholars.

## Ismail al-Faruqi

Al-Faruqi studied at Indiana University and al-Azhar University in Cairo, and from the late 1950s until his untimely death in 1986 taught at McGill University in Montreal, at Syracuse University, and at Temple University. He also founded the International Institute of Islamic Thought as a conscious Islamic alternative to American higher education and the formation of an intellectual project he called the "Islamization of Knowledge." Al-Faruqi wrote about gender (without using the term) in some of his work, where he discussed Islamic concepts of the family and espoused a concept of equity that is based on the sexes as different but equal. Men and women in Islam, according to him, have complementary God-given abilities while enjoying equal religious and civil rights, duties and responsibilities (al-Faruqi 1992: 129–39). "The West" had undermined these clear gender roles and thus contributed to the breakdown of traditional societies and families. Al-Faruqi's ideas about women and gender were also taught by his wife, Lois Lamya al-Faruqi, who lectured extensively of the topic of women in Islam, representing versions of the complementary Islamic gender model in such lectures and her writings.

## Seyyed Hossein Nasr

Nasr attended school in the United States and later completed his college education and an MA at MIT and a Ph.D. at Harvard University. He taught in Iran until the Iranian Revolution in 1979, when he left for political reasons. He has taught at Temple University and, since 1984, at the George Washington University. A prolific writer and author of over fifty books on topics in Islamic studies, Nasr has only written one short piece that directly addresses questions of gender roles in Islam. Titled "The Male and the Female in the Islamic Perspective," it is a chapter in his book *Traditional Islam in the Modern World* (Nasr 1987: 47–58). In it, he presents as the Islamic perspective on gender roles and relations a model that is, similar to al-Faruqi's, based on complementarity. The male sex reflects the divine qualities of majesty and the absolute, while the female sex is a reflection of Divine beauty and infinity. Nasr asserts that discord and chaos in society have resulted from the revolt of modern people against these divine ordained principles, which have as their purpose to guarantee equilibrium in human society. In all his work, Nasr identified with perennialist and traditionalist thinkers, and leveled a general critique of modernity and its anti-religious movements and tendencies. The majority of his works present and analyze what he describes as the immutable Islamic tradition including Sufism, Islam and science, and cosmology.

## Fazlur Rahman

Perhaps the most directly influential male Muslim scholar of this generation (on the Muslim women scholars discussed here), Rahman focused his work on the necessity of reinterpretation of Islamic sources in order to maintain Islam as relevant for modern Muslims. While al-Faruqi could be characterized as a Muslim modernist, especially in his project of reconciling Western social sciences with Islamic principles, and Nasr as anti-modern in his intellectual and political pursuits, Rahman was a true and critical Muslim modernist reformer who early in his career also participated in educational politics in Pakistan. Educated in India and England, he initially taught at McGill, and, from 1969 until his death in 1988, at the University of Chicago. Rahman wrote several important books outlining his program for the reinterpretation and re-evaluation of Islamic textual sources, including *Islam* (1979), *Major Themes of the Qur'an* (1980), and *Islam and Modernity* (1982).

Rahman advocated for and carried out a thematic interpretation of the Qur'an, reflected in *Major Themes in the Qur'an*, as well as a historicized approach to the text which he called "the double movement":

> Whereas the first movement has been from the specifics of the Qur'an to the eliciting and systematizing of its general principles, values, and long-range objectives, the second is to be from this general view to the specific view that is to be formulated and realized *now*. That is, the general has to be embodied in the present concrete socio-historical context.
>
> *(Rahman 1982: 7)*

It is through these two hermeneutical strategies that Rahman became an important influence on American Muslim women scholars from the 1980s onward. Rahman also briefly mentions issues of gender, most notably in a chapter titled "Man in Society," in which he discusses polygamy as an example for his approach to achieving justice in human society. Rahman here advocates a move away from polygamy as incompatible with justice, and reinterprets verses of the Qur'an addressing the issue accordingly (Rahman 1980: 47–51). More curious perhaps is a move in the chapter on God in which Rahman, in 1980, opted to translate the word "*huwa*" in the Qur'an as him/her in Qur. 50:37, which indicates an attempt at and consciousness of the possibility of gender-inclusive translation/interpretation (Rahman 1980: 2).

During and after the intellectual "reign" of Nasr, al-Faruqi, and Rahman, there have of course been other Muslim scholars working in and around the American academy. Some, including, for example, Ebrahim Moosa and Farid Esack, both from South Africa, have contributed in meaningful ways to the development and discussion of progressive Muslim thought (especially on gender), as has Omid Safi. All three are represented alongside Khaled Abou El Fadl and Scott Kugle in a groundbreaking collection of essays edited by Omid Safi in 2003, *Progressive Muslims: On Justice, Gender, and Pluralism*. It is no coincidence that the title of the book includes both justice and gender and one of the three parts of the book is dedicated to gender justice. The volume set the tone for a generation of scholars and activists, and allowed for a sustained conversation on progressive reform in thought and practice. Khaled Abou El Fadl's thought is perhaps the second most important reference point for women's gender-justice-centered approaches to the Qur'an.

## Khaled Abou El Fadl

Born in 1963 in Kuwait, Abou El Fadl is professor of Islamic law at UCLA, holding degrees from Princeton University as well as more traditional Islamic legal training in Kuwait and

Egypt. Abou El Fadl has written extensively about authority and developments towards authoritarian discourse in modern Muslim discourse, and it is no accident that his most relevant work, *Speaking in God's Name*, takes women in Islamic law as its focus. Abou El Fadl argues for an approach to the Qur'an and the Islamic legal tradition that retains traditional methods and tools of *fiqh* while recognizing Qur'anic and legal interpretations from the Muslim past as framed by societal attitudes and thus a product of their time. It is, like in Rahman's work, the move from recognizing what in the Islamic sources is eternal and relevant for all times and places to distinguishing it from ideas and discourses that are historically determined and thus confined to a particular time. Abou El Fadl has argued for what he calls a "conscientious pause" in approaching the Qur'an, by which he means the possibility of acknowledging that particular passages in the Qur'an, at least on surface reading, may clash with the reader's values and thus her conscience, which then requires her to at least pause and then, possibly, follow her conscience and not the text (Abou El Fadl 2001: 94). Abou El Fadl has issued and published legal opinions on a variety of issues, thus participating in the production of contemporary American Muslim jurisprudential opinion. Abou El Fadl has also actively supported Muslim women scholars in a variety of ways.

There is acknowledged irony in opening a genealogy of the ideas of American Muslim women scholars with an overview of important male scholars and thinkers and their ideas on women and gender. However, the pages above provide a sense of the terrain into which Muslim women scholars stepped in the 1980s. They bring into sharp relief just how innovative and nothing short of revolutionary the ideas of scholars such as Riffat Hassan and Azizah al-Hibri in the 1980s, followed by those of Amina Wadud and Asma Barlas in the 1990s, and of Kecia Ali and Aysha Hidayatullah in the 2000s, truly were.[1] I have selected six women scholars from a larger group because of the ways in which they have propelled American Muslim thought on issues of gender justice forward through their extensive writing and various forms of activism. Elsewhere I have described the first and second generations of American Muslim women scholars as individual thinkers rather than part of a movement (Hammer 2012). Aysha Hidayatullah has described them as "a new cohesive field of scholarship on the Qur'an," the focus of her analysis (Hidayatullah 2011: 119). Approaching and reinterpreting the Qur'an was and is central to all Muslim reformist scholarship and has thus played a central role in the works of many Muslim scholars since the nineteenth century. The emphasis on a field of study rather than a movement is indicative of some of the issues and obstacles Muslim women scholars have faced and continue to face from various directions that have hampered their working collectively in the same direction. This will become clearer in my analysis below. Before proceeding to the analysis of such obstacles and challenges, as well as the patterns and dynamics of Muslim women's scholarship, it is prudent to present short sketches of the lives and works of the six scholars discussed here.[2]

## Riffat Hassan

Hassan was born in 1943 in Pakistan and educated in England. She came to the United States in 1972 and taught for thirty-three years at the University of Louisville in Kentucky. Since the 1980s, she has identified herself as a Muslim feminist theologian whose work focuses on feminist reinterpretation of the Qur'an. Hassan has emphasized the Qur'an as the only necessary framework for women's rights as human rights and has characterized the Qur'an as the "Magna Carta of human rights" (Hassan 1999: 248–50). Her readings of the Qur'an claim equality in God's creation of the sexes, which she argues needs to be translated into societal practices of gender equality. Most of her ideas were published in many articles she wrote from the 1980s to the early 2000s. Notably, Hassan published several pieces in collections of religious feminist writings, thus indicating her involvement with the religious part of the American feminist movement (Hassan 1991, 1999, 2006). Simultaneously, she has continuously been involved in NGO-based human rights work in Pakistan, campaigning for better protection for women by Islamic family law, including family planning and personal status law, as well as raising awareness of violence against women and the responsibility of the state and society in addressing these issues.

## Azizah al-Hibri

Al-Hibri was born and raised in Lebanon and educated at the American University in Beirut as well as in the United States. She taught at the law school of the University of Richmond from 1992 until her retirement in 2012. Her appointment in 1992 made her the first Muslim woman law professor in the United States. Al-Hibri is the founder of Karamah: Muslim Women Lawyers for Human Rights, a Washington, DC-based, globally operating organization advocating Muslim women's rights and their right to education and leadership. Karamah was founded in 1993 and positions al-Hibri together with Riffat Hassan as trailblazers and foremothers among American Muslim women scholars. Al-Hibri was also the founding editor of *Hypatia: A Journal of Feminist Philosophy*, which has been continuously published since the mid-1980s. The journal editorship as well as many articles in feminist journals and edited collections place al-Hibri, like Hassan, in the genealogy and history of American religious feminist thought and organization (al-Hibri 1982, 1999, 2001). Both started writing from their subject position as Muslim women at a time when most scholarship in Islamic studies was about Muslim women and not by them. Al-Hibri has argued that Islam at its core is gender just, and that Islamic law can and should be reinterpreted towards such gender equality where existing interpretations violate the divine requirement of justice. She has published scores of articles in law journals, Islamic studies journals, and edited collections but no book-length treatment of her ideas has appeared. In 2011, al-Hibri was appointed by President Barack Obama to the US Commission on International Religious Freedom.

## Amina Wadud

Wadud opened the door to a new era of Muslim women's scholarship in the 1990s and became the most important proponent of equality-centered reinterpretation of the Qur'an. She was born in 1952 to the family of an African American Methodist minister and converted to Islam during her college years at the University of Pennsylvania. She holds a Ph.D. in Islamic studies from the University of Michigan, and has also studied and worked in Egypt and Malaysia. From 1992 to 2008 she taught Islamic studies at Virginia Commonwealth University in Richmond, Virginia. Her two books, *Qur'an and Woman: Rereading the Sacred Text from a Woman's Perspective* (1999) and *Inside the Gender Jihad: Women's Reform in Islam* (2006), together with a large number of articles and book chapters, outline the trajectory and development of her thought and position her as the most important American Muslim woman scholar of the Qur'an to date.

Wadud has engaged in a thematic, gender-just reading of the Qur'an and developed her "Tawhidic paradigm of horizontal reciprocity," in which men and women in society can only be equal, in interchangeable positions, with God above (Wadud 2006). She has adopted Rahman's double movement and has furthered Abou El Fadl's call to a conscientious pause to argue that there are passages in the Qur'an that her conscience will not allow her to accept, regardless of how they are interpreted. Her first book, *Qur'an and Woman*, has been very widely read, including in Muslim countries and communities, and has been translated into many languages. Wadud gave a Friday *khutba* in 1994 in a South African mosque and led a mixed gender congregation Friday prayer, also offering a *khutba*, in 2005 in New York City (Hammer 2012). These acts of public and mediatized activism have brought her more attention and criticism from Muslims than any of her written work, unfortunately overshadowing her nuanced and deeply invested Qur'anic exegesis and its implications for change in Muslim societies and communities.

## Asma Barlas

Barlas was born in 1950 and educated in Pakistan and the United States. She was part of the Pakistani Foreign Service until concerns for her safety over criticism of the Pakistani government prompted her to apply for political asylum in the United States in 1983. She is professor of politics at Ithaca College in New York, and has been chair of the politics department as well as director of the Center for the Study of Culture, Race and Ethnicity. Her most central contribution to American Muslim thought on gender is her 2002 book *"Believing Women" in Islam: Unreading Patriarchal Interpretations in the Qur'an*. She has also published numerous articles and book chapters on related topics, as well as earlier work on the colonial legacy in South Asia and a more recent project on approaches to interfaith conversations. *"Believing Women"* has been translated into a number of languages and is widely read by students and scholars in American academia. Barlas argues that putting men in a hierarchically higher position than women in Muslim society violates the most basic principle of Islam, the oneness of God, the creator and omnipotent sovereign. Barlas acknowledges the possibility of multiple interpretations of the Qur'an, while arguing that no interpretation can violate the principle of justice in the Qur'an. Barlas is ambivalent about the designation feminist but extensively engages with feminist thought in her book. She has also written about Amina Wadud (Barlas 2004, 2006).

## Kecia Ali

Ali, born in 1971, was born and raised in the United States and converted to Islam during college. She holds a Ph.D. in Islamic studies from Duke University, and since 2006 has been teaching in the religion department at Boston University, where she is an associate professor. Ali is a specialist in Islamic law and ethics, and has focused her research, so far, on Islamic sexual ethics and marriage. Her 2006 book *Sexual Ethics & Islam: Feminist Reflections on Qur'an, Hadith, and Jurisprudence*, engages with the Islamic legal tradition regarding issues of gender and sexuality, including polygamy, homosexuality, dower, and divorce. In the book, Ali engages this historical tradition with contemporary reinterpretations, including the work of al-Hibri and Wadud, and thus begins to produce a new kind of conversation about gender justice that acknowledges as well as critiques past trajectories and ideas. Her second book, *Marriage and Slavery in Early Islam* (2010), continues her sustained engagement with Islamic law and furthers her argument that rather than rejecting the entire Muslim interpretative tradition as misogynist and patriarchal, which leaves Muslims with very little to hold on to, scholars and intellectuals interested in gender justice need to allow a critical look at Muslim knowledge and creatively apply what can be salvaged. Ali officiated at a Muslim wedding in 2006. She has been involved in feminist scholarly networks and self-identifies as a Muslim feminist.

## Aysha Hidayatullah

Hidayatullah was born in 1979 and thus belongs to the most recent generation of Muslim women scholars of note. She received her Ph.D. in Islamic studies from the University of

California, Santa Barbara, and teaches Islamic studies at the University of San Francisco, a Jesuit school in California. Hidayatullah's groundbreaking book, *Feminist Edges of the Qur'an* (2014), chronicles the approaches of Hassan, al-Hibri, Wadud, and Barlas to Qur'anic exegesis, and offers both a deep reflection on the nuances and trajectories of their interpretations and an important critique of their ideas. It is no accident that this chapter began with a reference to Hidayatullah's recent writing as she engages in the deeply painful task of honoring and critiquing her intellectual forebears. Hidayatullah's central contribution lies in her open acknowledgment that Muslim women's "feminist" theology has reached an impasse in interpreting the Qur'an in ways that cannot recognize textual limitations and reconcile the resulting tension with feminist commitments to justice and equality.

Ali and Hidayatullah, much more so than the older generation of American Muslim women scholars, operate as part of a network,[3] yet not a movement, of many more young Muslim women scholars and graduate students in the American academy, pointing to a future of American Muslim thought on gender justice and equality that may take surprising and unexpected turns in the future. In the second part of this chapter, I want to engage with the six scholars presented above with regards to how they negotiate the possibilities and challenges of multiple critique *vis-à-vis* feminist theory and practice, other Muslim scholars and their interpretations, and American liberal imperialism. I contextualize their ideas through a discussion of their claims to and investment with authority and their simultaneous marginalization in American (and transnational) Muslim communities, on the one hand, and the American academy, on the other.

## Multiple critique

In a much-cited essay published in 2000, and in her book *Women Claim Islam* (2001), miriam cooke coined the phrase "multiple critique" to describe what she saw as new forms of expression, debate, and activism among Arab Muslim feminists in the Middle East. She combined Moroccan cultural critic Abdelkebir Khatibi's "double critique" and African American sociologist Deborah K. King's "multiple consciousness" (cooke 2000: 100) to devise the term, which describes "Islamic feminists' critical rhetorical strategies" (cooke 2000: 99) in which they transcend their marking as victims and identify simultaneously with Islam, feminism, and other dimensions of their identity. These strategies of critique are based on multiple forms of consciousness and agency and enable Muslim women to recognize possibilities as well as dangers of alliances, networks, and co-optation. cooke's essay seems to have been born from widespread feminist puzzlement with Muslim women activists and thinkers in Muslim majority countries (as well as in America and Europe) who, unlike Western feminists and general public opinion, were not willing to locate the source of the oppression (which they did acknowledge as an issue) in Islam.

As part of a long and protracted intellectual debate about the term Islamic feminism[4] (which cooke embraces) and its (self-)ascription to particular Muslim women, Sa'diyya Shaikh has criticized the major assumption behind cooke's definition of the term as inviting "to consider what it means to have a difficult double commitment, on the one hand to a faith position, and on the other hand to women's rights both inside the home and outside" (cooke 2001: 59). Shaikh contends that cooke's construction of the opposition between their faith and women's rights is a false dichotomy and runs "contrary to the self-definitions of many Muslim feminists who see their feminism as emerging organically out of their faith commitment and whose contestation of gender injustice is more than simply the result of a post-colonial struggle" (Shaikh 2003: 155).

I would further argue that cooke's use of multiple critique is only useful if it transcends the dichotomy between Islam and feminism, the US and Muslim communities, the academy and the "real world." It is in their claim to simultaneous and legitimate critique of different actors, power dynamics, histories, and injustices that Muslim women scholars find moments on a spectrum of empowerment and marginalization. To that end, I present three of the many intersectional topics of negotiation in the works of American Muslim women scholars to illustrate how they negotiate critique and experience its impact. It is important to note here that "feminism," "academia," and "Islam/Muslims" are not discrete but overlapping and intersecting spheres the scholars negotiate in their work and life, thus creating powerful influences on Muslim women scholars' ideas, thoughts, and activism. The focus on how these intersecting and overlapping spheres have shaped American Muslim thought should also not overlook the varying and considerable degrees of agency Muslim women scholars exercise in their work. They do, however, present their ideas as dynamically produced in constant engagement with their surroundings, histories, and intellectual genealogies.

## Feminism: theory and practice

Despite reluctance and concern about adopting the term itself, it is clear from the scholar profiles above that Muslim women scholars have in multifaceted ways participated in feminist theory and practice. Whether in working with religious and secular feminist networks, like al-Hibri, Barlas, and Ali, or in the adoption of the ideas of leading feminist theoreticians which is evident in the works of all of the scholars discussed here, feminism has an enduring presence in these women's lives.

It is significant that some but not all of the scholars are also women of color, which makes it necessary to ground their negotiations of feminist theory and their participation in feminist practice in the trenchant critiques leveled by third-wave feminists. Third-wave feminism was and is characterized by critiques of second-wave feminist assumptions about femininity which are based on the experiences and values of white middle-class women, thus not reflecting the life-worlds of women outside that group. Feminist thinkers of color have called out power dynamics and abuse by white feminists and the differing interests of their doubly or more marginalized communities in North America. Reference to third-wave feminism is evident in the work of Amina Wadud, whose subject position as an African American Muslim woman convert has resulted in reflections on her marginalization and critiques of the structures that produce it (Wadud 2006).

Feminist thought has a complex and troubled history of dealing with religion, which produced a majority secular and often anti-religious stance in much of the feminist movement, whereby religions were dismissed as inherently patriarchal, products of patriarchal societies, and unredeemable for feminist transformation of society. Christian and later Jewish feminists (and occasionally others such as the Buddhist thinker Rita Gross) have carried out tremendous thought work in engaging their religious traditions as resources for feminist challenge and change in the USA while constantly negotiating their religious commitment *vis-à-vis* secular feminists, not to mention pushback from their religious communities and leaders (Sharma and Young 1999; Gross 1996).

Muslim women thinkers came into that conversation in the 1980s and have more often than not been treated as newcomers who can learn from their predecessors rather than full participants in the conversation. Wadud, Ali, and Hidayatullah have all discussed such experiences in different venues. They have thus engaged in multiple levels of critique as well as utilization of feminist discourse and practice. I have had my own recent experiences with presenting research on the limits of feminist inquiry for analyzing the arguments and programs of American Muslims engaged in work against domestic violence (Hammer 2013). I have been told that I am an apologist for conservative Muslims, men and women, as well as a traitor to feminist ideals. But mostly, I have had to contend with assumptions about Muslim women as oppressed by Islam, which I initially presumed to be a stereotype of the past. Feminists have of course historically participated not only in ideological justification of colonialism but, more recently, in military intervention in Muslim countries with the pretext of liberating Muslim women (Ahmed 1992; Weber 2001; Mahmood and Hirschkind 2002; Abu-Lughod 2002).

## Islam and Muslim communities

It is at the intersection of critical feminist commitments and perceptions of feminism as a product of and tool for continuing Western domination among many Muslims worldwide that Muslim women scholars negotiate their place within Muslim communities and their faith tradition. The intense struggle to interpret foundational Islamic texts in ways that reflect their commitment to gender justice (in itself not an unqualified notion) positions each and every one of them as Muslim and identifying with Islam. Wadud very clearly acknowledged the power struggle over definitions and boundaries of Islam or the Islamic tradition when she wrote: "I have moved to a new, albeit uncomfortable, reflection: neither their 'Islam' or my 'Islam' has ultimate privilege. We are all part of a complex whole, in constant motion and manifestation throughout the history of multifaceted but totally human constructions of 'Islam'" (Wadud 2006: 6).

Wadud, Barlas, and others are less willing to acknowledge the constructed nature of the Qur'an as the main source of divine self-disclosure and thus understanding of God's will. Wadud writes: "I come away from the Qur'an … with the sense that all the questions I have asked can be clarified therein" (Wadud 2006: 9). Kecia Ali and Aysha Hidayatullah have perhaps moved the furthest in recognizing that there may be limitations to reinterpreting the Qur'an that cannot be overcome by more sophisticated hermeneutical moves. Ali writes in 2009 that "there comes a point at which it becomes necessary to step outside the text" and goes on to say that the Qur'an could be read in conjunction with other materials, including *hadith*, *fiqh*, Sufi writings, and others, in order to provide "inspiration and a broader framework for ethical approaches to Muslim life. … An egalitarian ethics must be grounded in a theological approach to the Qur'anic text, and reformist thought in general must engage more explicitly with theological concerns. Ultimately, it is only at the level of discussions about God and God's relationship to humanity that key questions about basic principles can be addressed" (Ali 2009: 98).

Hidayatullah diagnoses the end of Muslim feminist theologians' relation to the Qur'an in a singular manner, and argues that they have "reached the end of the road" unless they are willing "to develop new ways of understanding their relationship to the Qur'an that account for the sexist elements of the literal text while also maintaining the sanctity and authority of their holy book as Muslims" (Hidayatullah 2011: 119). While this diagnosis and prescription for new paths to Muslim feminist engagement ring honest, painful, and true, especially in the work of Hidayatullah, they also move these scholars to the very fringes, if not outright outside, of the boundaries of Muslim communities.

With dwindling certainty about sources of Islamic religious authority, in what Khaled Abou El Fadl has described as a "crisis of authority" (Abou El Fadl 2005: 26), anyone can claim authority to interpret Islamic texts and derive guidelines for Muslim life. In his view, this crisis is linked to the systematic colonial destructions of Islamic institutions of jurisprudence while also allowing for new authorities, including public intellectuals (and women), to step into the vacuum created by the shifts in authority structures. More importantly for us, the weakening of traditional structures of Islamic legal authority has shifted the focus of many modern Muslims towards the Qur'an and the *Sunna* as the most authoritative sources for their life conduct. This has placed heightened responsibility on the shoulders of those who engage in their interpretation, but has also produced a situation of exegetical relativism in which every Muslim can interpret, the Qur'an especially, for her/himself. Contemporary American Muslim scholars assume and are invested with religious authority and are trusted, selectively, with guiding American Muslims in their religious affairs.

Muslim women exegetes thus not only challenge the authority of the Qur'an, when they move in that direction, they also challenge gender attitudes and practices that are not only deeply embedded in Muslim communal life but also often justified as authentically Islamic through the Qur'an and *Sunna*. In turn, their claims to authority are questioned, as has been the case for Hassan, al-Hibri, Wadud, Barlas, Ali, and Hidayatullah, as well as others. This rejection of either their qualifications for exegesis (including knowledge of Arabic and traditional Islamic training) or their authenticity as Muslims (convert status, wearing *hijab*, etc.) has left them vulnerable to attacks, which are often personal. More importantly, their interpretative stances have marginalized them within Muslim communities or, worse, have placed them outside Muslim communal networks altogether.

Active exclusion was most pronounced after Amina Wadud led the Friday prayer in 2005, when she received death threats and her university was petitioned to terminate her contract. There were accusations of her being an agent of American imperialism and Western feminism bent on feeding Islamophobia and destroying Islam from within. In response to such marginalization, Muslim women scholars have built and continue to build networks and alternative communities, as exemplified in the prayer event as well, and they continuously present their ideas to those open to them, thus building interpretative communities of their own. Wadud's (first) *hajj* trip to Mecca and Medina in 2010 demonstrated her claim to Islam and belonging to a Muslim community. Women scholars have also experienced silence as rejection. When their work is better known among American undergraduate students and in women's studies circles than among Muslim communities, and without the opportunity to discuss their ideas and convince Muslims of their merit, Muslim women scholars are under pressure to adjust their thoughts and negotiate their practical application. And, as Hidayatullah points out, some of their ideas can potentially even undermine years of grassroots activist effort to improve the lives of Muslim women globally (Hidayatullah 2011: 122).

And, not least, Muslim women scholars and their ideas also challenge the authority of male Muslim scholars and present competition in the marketplace of religious leadership and power. It is no coincidence that women scholars with less challenging ideas, such as Ingrid Mattson, the first woman president of the Islamic Society of North America (ISNA) and long-time professor of Islamic studies at Hartford Seminary, are considered authoritative and are not challenged in their ideas. This is because challenges to the gender role status quo in Muslim discourse and practice are perceived as a significant threat to communal stability despite the fact that sweeping changes and renegotiations have in fact taken place over the last century. On a more optimistic note, the work of Muslim women scholars such as Wadud, Barlas, and Ali has had a tangible impact on conversations about gender issues in Islam, whether Muslims are willing to acknowledge it or not. Even performances of mediatized activism like the 2005 prayer event have furthered conversation and mainstreamed gender discussions among Muslims (Hammer 2008).

Muslim women scholars are also involved in global Muslim feminist and activist networks, which has made some of them known (or infamous) beyond the boundaries of the United

States. Especially in the global "War on Terror" waged by the United States and its allies after September 11, 2001, certain American Muslim leaders have become representatives and spokespersons for the United States government and purported positive examples for Muslim moderation and American inclusion of Muslims in all spheres of American society. Muslim women's calls to reform Muslim societies and improve Muslim women's lives worldwide have in this vein sometimes been interpreted as part of American cultural imperialism and soft power, which bring/force progressive and liberal ideas onto Muslim societies for ulterior motives. This line of challenge is sometimes also adopted by American Muslim community leaders intent on undermining the authority of Muslim women scholars.

## Academia

There is probably a smoother way to connect Muslim community impact and debates with Muslim women scholars in the American academy, but one common denominator is the question of activism. It is the intersection of discourse and activist practice that also ties academic dynamics and scholarly authority to feminist ideas. All of the scholars discussed here, from Seyyed Hossein Nasr to Aysha Hidayatullah, have held or still hold teaching and research positions in American institutions of higher learning. How do they negotiate their commitments as scholars in secular academic institutions (even private religious universities and colleges have a commitment to liberal arts education) with their focus on prescriptive/normative work?

While scholars in the field of religion and later religious studies have engaged in debates about the blurry boundaries between faith commitments and secular analysis, normative versus analytical approaches to religions, and not least insider and outsider positions in the academic study of religion for many decades, the study of Islam has exhibited its own peculiar dynamics in this regard. When the American Academy of Religion (AAR) began to hold sessions on Islam in the 1970s, and even more so when the Study of Islam Section was founded as a major unit in the AAR in 1985, debates ensued about these forms of positionality that have continued into the present. How does one distinguish between teaching a religion and teaching about religion? How, in the spirit of liberal inclusion, can particular religious subject positions be accommodated without becoming forms of indoctrination and proselytization? This issue is more pronounced because of the Euro-American history of Orientalism, the study of non-Western societies in the service of colonial and neo-colonial domination so famously described by Edward Said in his book *Orientalism*, published in 1979.

The American academy has both marginalized and promoted Muslim women scholars, as evidenced in the positions they hold but also in their success in having their work published by mainstream academic presses. I claim simultaneous promotion and marginalization because it is the very dynamic of providing protected spaces for Muslim feminist inquiry while self-congratulating on one's tolerant inclusion of the liberal other that both creates opportunity and stifles it. Muslim women scholars who are critical of Muslim gender practices and call out the many injustices committed against Muslim women worldwide are always at risk of becoming poster children for simplistic as well as often imperial deconstruction of Muslim societies and Islam. Muslim women's scholarship has made few inroads in women's and gender studies, especially when it is religiously prescriptive, and Muslim women scholar activists have had to defend their investment and activism in their communities as undermining their scholarly authority as much as they have been included for the purpose of presenting American academia as open to new ideas and daring revolutionary thought.[5]

The tension between scholarship and activism, with one undermining the weight of the other, has been felt for decades by feminist scholars more generally. In addition, in academia as well, women scholars of color continue to experience multiple forms of marginalization and micro-aggression as well as hampered access to resources and positions unless they are willing to inhabit token positions. White privilege has allowed some Muslim women scholars access to better resources and less likelihood of being challenged for their activism and critique of academia. The unequal distribution of resources, positions of job security, and recognition has also divided Muslim women scholars and contributed to continued competition over cooperation. It requires continuous self-critical reflection as well as a willingness to challenge institutional structures that produce such inequality, at the risk of losing one's own professional security and/ or reputation.

## Conclusion: work and life, experience and struggle

In charting the intellectual trajectories of American Muslim thinkers, and Muslim women scholars especially, I have come to appreciate the complexity of their work but also their lives. Each in their own way has experienced faith struggles, challenges to authority, credibility, and communal belonging, and each has contributed to a growing body of American Muslim thought on gender. Their published works are a testament to the depth of their thinking and the complications and challenges in charting new paths towards their visions of more just Muslim communities and societies. Their writings incorporate, often seamlessly, their personal experiences and struggles into their scholarly ideas and expressions. To claim personal experience as politically and intellectually relevant, to admit pain as well as passion, means to open oneself to dismissal, ridicule, and more struggle.

However, foregrounding their experiences of challenge and struggle should not overshadow their myriad contributions to critique: of feminist theory and practice; of academic institutions, of Muslim communities, and American society; they lay bare the politics of knowledge production, the machinations of Islamophobia, bigotry, and discrimination in its many forms. They live intersectional lives and perform intersectional intellectual work as scholars, thinkers, public intellectuals, and leaders. They participate in intra-Muslim conversation and debate about gender, justice, tradition, and authority. And studying them and their thought(s) provides more than a passing glimpse into the dynamics of global and American Muslim thought; the forces of secularization and religious negotiation; and the continuing significance of gender analysis for understanding the past, present, and future of Islam.

## Notes

1 The six women scholars selected are arguably very significant but the selection is limited by the length of this chapter more than by a commitment to judging the relevance of some scholars over others. The list could and should have included, among others: Nimat Barazangi, Sa'diyya Shaikh, Debra Majeed, Gwendolyn Simmons, Asifa Qureishi, Hina Azam, Saadia Yacoob, and Mohja Kahf. Many more have been interlocutors for the women discussed here. One could even argue that more traditionally inclined Muslim women scholars, including Ingrid Mattson and Hadia Mubarak, have been part of an ongoing conversation about Muslim women's rights and roles in contemporary Muslim societies and the gendered nature of Islamic traditions.

2 Throughout this section I mention some of the works of the scholars which also appear in the list of references at the end. For a more complete list of each scholar's publications, see the bibliography of my book (Hammer 2012).

3 This is not to say that there have not been meetings, convergences, and instances of cooperation between Muslim women scholars from the 1980s to the 2000s. Books such as *Windows of Faith* (2000), edited by Gisela Webb, are testament to such cooperation and conversation; however, they are outweighed by a deep sense of lonely struggles in the works of Wadud, Barlas, and Hassan.

4 For the most thorough discussion of the various debates and positions, see Seedat (2013).
5 In 2010, Kecia Ali, Laury Silvers, Hina Azam, Aysha Hidayatullah, Fatima Seedat, Saadia Yacoob, and myself recognized the multiple forms of exclusion and marginalization Amina Wadud had experienced throughout her academic career, which resulted in our producing an alternative Festschrift for her, an edited collection of academic essays, personal reflections, and a painting by thirty-three contributors whose thought, work, and life have been touched by Wadud's work. The volume *A Jihad for Justice: Honoring the Work and Life of Amina Wadud* transcends the boundaries of academic publishing and is available as a free e-book: www.bu.edu/religion/files/2010/03/A-Jihad-for-Justice-for-Amina-Wadud-2012-1.pdf.

# Bibliography

Abou El Fadl, K. (2001) *Speaking in God's Name: Islamic Law, Authority and Women*, Oxford: Oneworld.
——(2005) *The Great Theft: Wrestling Islam from the Extremists*, San Francisco: Harper.
Abu-Lughod, L. (2002) "Do Muslim Women Really Need Saving? Anthropological Reflections on Cultural Relativism and Its Others," *American Anthropologist* 103(3): 783–90.
Ahmed, L. (1992) *Women and Gender in Islam: Historical Roots of a Modern Debate*, New Haven, CT: Yale University Press.
Ali, K. (2006) *Sexual Ethics & Islam: Feminist Reflections on Qur'an, Hadith, and Jurisprudence*, Oxford: Oneworld.
——(2009) "Timeless Texts and Modern Morals: Challenges in Islamic Sexual Ethics," in Vogt, K., Larsen, L., and Moe, C. (eds.) *New Directions in Islamic Thought*, London: I.B. Tauris, pp. 89–100.
——(2010) *Marriage and Slavery in Early Islam*, Cambridge, MA: Harvard University Press.
Ali, K., Silvers, L., and Hammer, J. (eds.) (2012) *A Jihad for Justice: Honoring the Work and Life of Amina Wadud*, ebook, www.bu.edu/religion/files/2010/03/A-Jihad-for-Justice-for-Amina-Wadud-2012-1.pdf.
Badran, M. (2009) *Feminism in Islam: Secular and Religious Convergences*, Oxford: Oneworld.
Barlas, A. (2002) *"Believing Women" in Islam: Unreading Patriarchal Interpretations of the Qur'an*, Austin: University of Texas Press.
——(2004) "Amina Wadud's Hermeneutics of the Qur'an: Women Rereading Sacred Texts," in Taji-Farouki, S. (ed.) *Modern Muslim Intellectuals and the Qur'an*, Oxford: Oxford University Press, Oxford, pp. 97–123.
——(2006) "Women's Readings of the Qur'an," in Dammen McAuliffe, J. (ed.) *The Cambridge Companion to the Qur'an*, Cambridge: Cambridge University Press, pp. 255–72.
cooke, m. (2000) "Multiple Critique: Islamic Feminist Rhetorical Strategies," *Nepantla* 1(1): 91–110.
——(2001) *Women Claim Islam: Creating Islamic Feminism Through Literature*, New York: Routledge.
Esack, F. (1997) *Qur'an, Liberation, and Pluralism: An Islamic Perspective on Interreligious Solidarity against Oppression*, Oxford: Oneworld.
Faruqi, I. al- (1992) *Al Tawhid: Its Implications for Thought and Life*, Herndon: International Institute of Islamic Thought.
Gross, R. (1996) *Feminism and Religion: An Introduction*, Boston: Beacon Press.
Haley, A. (1965) *The Autobiography of Malcolm X*, New York: Ballatine.
Hammer, J. (2008) "Identity, Authority and Activism: American Muslim Women's Approaches to the Qur'an," *The Muslim World* 98(4): 442–63.
——(2012) *American Muslim Women, Religious Authority, and Activism: More Than a Prayer*, Austin: University of Texas Press.
——(2013) "Men Are Protectors of Women: American Muslim Negotiations of Domestic Violence, Marriage, and Feminism," in Failinger, M., Schiltz, L., and Stabile, S. (eds.) *Feminism, Law, and Religion*, London: Ashgate, pp. 237–56.
Hassan, R. (1991) "Muslim Women and Post-Patriarchal Islam," in Cooey, P., Eakin, W., and McDaniel, J. (eds.) *After Patriarchy: Feminist Transformations of the World's Religions*, New York: Orbis Books, pp. 39–64.
——(1999) "Feminism in Islam," in Sharma, A. and Young, K. (eds.) *Feminism and World Religions*, Albany: State University of New York Press, pp. 248–78.
——(2006) "Islamic Hagar and Her Family," in Trible, P. and Russell, L (eds.) *Hagar, Sarah, and Their Children: Jewish, Christian, and Muslim Perspectives*, New York: Westminster Knox, pp. 149–70.
Hibri, A. al- (1982) "A Study of Islamic Herstory: Or How Did We Ever Get into This Mess?," *Women's Studies International Forum* 5(2): 207–19.

——(1999) "Islamic Law and Muslim Women in America," in Garber, M. and Walkowitz, R. (eds.) *One Nation under God? Religion and American Culture*, New York: Routledge, pp. 128–42.

——(2001) "Muslim Women's Rights in the Global Village: Challenges and Opportunities," *Journal of Law and Religion* 15(3): 37–66.

Hidayatullah, A. (2009) "Inspiration and Struggle: Muslim Feminist Theology and the Work of Elisabeth Schüssler Fiorenza," *Journal of Feminist Studies in Religion* 25(1): 162–70.

——(2011) "Muslim Feminist Birthdays," *Journal of Feminist Studies in Religion* 27(1): 119–22.

——(2014) *Feminist Edges of the Qur'an*, New York: Oxford University Press.

Mahmood, S. and Hirschkind, C. (2002) "Feminism, the Taliban, and Politics of Counter-Insurgency," *Anthropological Quarterly* 75(2): 339–54.

Muhammad, E. (1965) *Message to the Blackman in America*, Chicago: The Final Call.

Nasr, H. (1987) *Traditional Islam in the Modern World*, London: Kegan Paul.

Rahman, F. (1979) *Islam*, Chicago: Chicago University Press.

——(1980) *Major Themes of the Qur'an*, Minneapolis: Bibliotheca Islamica.

——(1982) *Islam and Modernity: Transformation of an Intellectual Tradition*, Chicago: University of Chicago Press.

Safi, O. (ed.) (2003) *Progressive Muslims: On Justice, Gender, and Pluralism*, Oxford: Oneworld.

Said, E. (1979) *Orientalism*, New York: Vintage.

Seedat, F. (2013) "When Islam and Feminism Converge," *The Muslim World* 103(3): 404–20.

Shaikh, S. (2003) "Transforming Feminisms: Islam, Women, and Gender Justice," in Safi, O. (ed.) *Progressive Muslims: On Justice, Gender, and Pluralism*, Oxford: Oneworld, pp. 147–62.

Sharma, A. and Young, K. (eds.) (1999) *Feminism and World Religions*, Albany: State University of New York Press.

Wadud, A. (1999) *Qur'an and Woman: Rereading the Sacred Text from a Woman's Perspective*, Oxford: Oxford University Press.

——(2006) *Inside the Gender Jihad: Women's Reform in Islam*, Oxford: Oneworld.

Webb, G. (ed.) (2000) *Windows of Faith: Muslim Women Scholar-Activists in North America*, Syracuse: Syracuse University Press.

Weber, C. (2001) "Unveiling Scheherazade: Feminist Orientalism in the International Alliance of Women, 1911–50," *Feminist Studies* 27(1): 125–57.

# 26

# Development and perspectives of Islamic economics (banking and finance) in the West

*Gian Maria Piccinelli*

About forty years ago, with the establishment in 1975 of the Islamic Development Bank in Jeddah, the new Islamic approach to banking operations took its first steps outside the Muslim world. From the 1980s and early 1990s, in particular, mainly as a consequence of the enormous increase in oil prices, along with the consciousness of a common religious and cultural identity, Islamic banking and finance has grown stronger and consolidated, becoming able to compete worldwide with conventional systems through "*shari'a* compliant" operations.[1]

The continuing growth of Islamic banking assets in global markets is forecast to exceed US$2 trillion by 2015. Considering that Islamic banks grew to US$1.3 trillion in 2011, we should notice an average annual growth of about 20–24 percent in the last three years. Moving from the Middle and Far East, through experiments in the West, forecasts of future establishment are projected in BRICS countries, from China to Brazil (see Ernst & Young 2012a). The birth of a system of banks, operating in compliance with Islamic legal principles, has been the first concrete result of a long debate covering the entire twentieth century. Islamic doctrine, in connection with the Qur'anic prohibition on usury (*riba*, Qur. 2:275), has discussed the legitimacy of banking interests applied by Western financial institutions operating in Islamic countries as well as the feasibility of specific instruments that are alternatives to interest (Saleh 1992).

The ethical-religious character assumed, today, by Islamic banks, with the intention of preserving consistency with the divine precept prohibiting any kind of usury, is itself part of a common historical heritage; early Western depositories and, later on, banks were born from the same cultural hummus. In Islam, the fundamental and constant dialectic between ethics and market clearly emerged in pre-capitalist times (see Rodinson 1968). The historical context, in which the relation between Qur'anic prohibition of usury and the financial demands of medieval trade surfaces, is that of the city of Mecca, flourishing as one of the most prosperous trade centers at the time of the Prophet, showing an indisputable understanding of such demands. The latter institutions appear, in more recent times, to have forgotten the ethical aspects connected to lending and, consequently, to so-called irregular deposits.

In Islam, on the other hand, prior to the nineteenth century – the period of codification and birth of nation-states – there was no theorization of autonomous rules and regulations with respect to religious *jus commune*, whereas this autonomous character of state law has mostly

411

meant a slavish adjustment to the civil and commercial normative models of colonial Western powers. For this reason, in the latter part of the twentieth century modern Muslim doctrine pursued the design of an Islamic economy newly founded on a more attentive reading of the prohibition of usury, imagining the possibility of building a valid "alternative" (from a Muslim perspective) to the social projects founded on capitalist liberalism and on socialist statism – an alternative founded, among other things, on the abolition of the pecuniary interest system, substituting it with a system based on profit- and risk-sharing.

Ancient associative contracts were thus recovered. This type of contract was (whether consciously or unconsciously) common to all traders in the Mediterranean *koiné*, itself active and in force already prior to the time of the Prophet Muhammad. These contractual instruments – such as the *mudaraba*, which already in the fifth and sixth centuries AD showed great affinity with coeval usury activity – were adopted by the Prophet, a skilled trader himself, and continue to be used by Muslims after him. The *mudaraba* is quite close to the medieval *commenda* (silent or limited partnership) and such development progresses in modern European corporate law; here, however, a progressive separation takes place, with the bank reaching, at the end, complete neutrality with respect to the risks involved in its clients' transactions. On the other hand, the ideological perspective founding the Islamic banking system has deliberately included and operatively reaffirmed the client–partner model, and it has developed, around this central core, increasing competitive ability through the elaboration of specific financial products in compliance with the values, principles, and ethical-juridical precepts of Islam.

The topicality of such a system, for a Western observer, resides first of all in the ethical challenge revolving around the modern meaning of the prohibition of *riba*, reinscribed in the light of the fundamental values of solidarity, cooperation, justice, and fairness in the social and economic realms. Such values should be the bases of financial and entrepreneurial activities, both private and public; a goal pursued, also in the West, by various bank initiatives, such as ethical banks, micro-credit, and renewed strength in cooperative credit. This reality and a (historical) convergence have been necessarily included and underlined in the following comparative analyses.

## From theory to practice: the client–partner model

With the first experiment, in 1966, of a "bank without interest" in Egypt (with many comparable elements in common with the rural banks and cooperative credit banks well known in European history), the Islamic economic system clearly opened the way for the adoption, in practice, of an associative relation between bank and client, thus representing an ethically licit alternative to the arithmetical calculation of interest both in giving and in taking.

The fundamental element in an Islamic bank is not so much the absence of interest in giving and taking (although this is a strongly distinctive aspect when compared with the Western bank experience), but rather – in theory at least – the implementation of the partnership scheme of sharing between bank and client in most transactions, both active and passive (see Anwar 2003). Being the subject that contributes the capital to the bank, the client cannot be alien to the company, but instead becomes a "partner," taking on the risks connected to such a position and, at the same time, gaining the right to receive possible benefits (profits) from the bank's economic activity, according to the typical pattern of profit- and loss-sharing which has demanded a quick and complex trial of innovative operational instruments, as well as the regulation of conventional tools.

Participation in financial risk legitimizes the profit both parties gain from the use of capital, and allows human activity to prevail on the gainful automatisms of capital. In theory, this frees the contractual relation of aleatory vexing and speculative elements, guaranteeing the highest possible equality for the two parties to the contract. It is in such a conceptual framework that the recovery of traditional types of capital and labor (such as *mudaraba*) or more typically corporate (such as *musharaka*) association must be analyzed, in which the profit shared among the partners is always the result of the activity of the enterprise, implemented with the contribution of both parties.

The profit- and loss-sharing model is applied to transactions of funds and savings management, as well as to unitization. More recently, this system was extended to insurance companies, with the aim of overcoming the limits imposed by the ban on aleatory contracts (*gharar*): a system similar to traditional mutual insurance was created using *takaful* – literally, "solidarity" – contracts, in which the element of solidarity prevails on the speculative-aleatory factor (see Archer et al. 2009).

In the Muslim tradition, the model for business is the *mudaraba*, a capital and labor association where the capitalist (*rabb al-mal*) entrusts his capital (*ra's al-mal*) to an agent (*'amil or mudarib*), to be managed and employed in generally determined trade operations. The agent agrees to return the capital when the transaction is complete, along with whatever profit has been agreed upon, while keeping the remaining amount of profit as compensation for his work. The financial risk is entirely assumed by the capitalist, while the agent is not charged with any refund if the deal fails for a reason not attributable to him. The combination of the elements of loan, mandate, and partnership (in which *intuitus personae* prevails) is the principal reason for the success this contract has attained throughout history.

Different types of financial instruments, without direct participation, have been implemented within the Islamic system through some asset-based transactions where the bank offers a financing facility to the client, buying and reselling goods, equipment, or real estate. Contracts like *ijara* (financial leasing) or *murabaha* (mark-up sale) are the most widespread transactions considering their short-term structure and the possibility for the bank to recover the funds rapidly.

The classification of deposits in Islamic banks is based on the consideration of the extent of profit- and loss-sharing management tools, like *mudaraba*. We find "call accounts," for which there is no participatory structure and therefore no form of profit, nor, generally, any charge. Deposit accounts (*al-hisab al-jari*) and savings accounts (*hisab al-tawfir*) are classified as call accounts. The bank may use the deposit funds (on the basis of a *wakala* – a mandate by the client) and guarantees the repayment of the entire amount of money at any given moment. Although there is no compensation conventionally agreed upon, at the end of every financial year, and at the bank's discretion, the clients who have opened large accounts may be rewarded through a payment in kind (*hadiyya*, *ikramiyya*), through small donations (*hiba*) in money, or with certain "privileged" conditions in access to credit (*tamwil*) for the sponsorship of small projects, or for installment purchases of durable or instrumental goods. The Islamic "call account" is no different in its structure from the non-Islamic one, except for the absence of remuneration based on interest. This is why, much more rigidly than in other systems, clients may take out money and write out checks only within the limits of their account or of the overdraft agreed upon. The same happens with the use of debit cards and ATM cards, while credit cards are not popular yet, due to the difficulty of accessing international circuits, based on interest-operation accounts.

"Savings accounts" (*hisabat al-tawfir*) and "investment accounts" (*hisabat al-istithmar*), on the other hand, have a sharing structure, with profits proportionally depending on the profits of the bank. In general, these are time deposits, the typology of which may vary significantly; they may be designed for a specific investment project, or reused by the bank for its ordinary financial activity, including common *mudaraba* or *musharaka* deposits managed by the bank. In this case, it may be necessary for the depositor to sign a mandate (*wakala*) for the bank, specifying the operations the funds may be used for. Without a specific mandate, the bank either uses the funds freely or establishes different specific investment funds.

This specific condition is designed to guarantee a broader transparency of management, allowing to both the client and the *shari'a* Control Councils – or other control bodies inside or outside the banks – strong control of the ethical-religious aspect of transactions. Theoretically, the consequence of the general implementation of the participatory principle and the consequent idea of risk permeating the entire activity of the Islamic bank is that no form of guarantee on the deposit is allowed, and the lack of an explicit obligation of reimbursement of the funds collected from the public may represent one of the main elements of "incompatibility" with the common Western bank discipline.

In this respect, a distinction is due between the protection of cost-free deposits and that relative to participation deposits. Only the latter can actually suffer losses potentially deriving from a negative sign in the bank operations balance and only if the bank capitals and reserves are insufficient to cover the losses.

## Islamic finance developments in Western countries

Islamic banks have constantly turned their attention to the possibility of entering Western banking systems, primarily as an answer to the requests of growing Islamic migrant communities. On the other hand, with reference to the position of Western countries in this respect, I would underline three main issues that are to be considered at the national and supranational level:

1. *The opportunity of attracting surplus liquidity from main Islamic countries and financial centers.* Such liquidity represents the most important factor in the growth of Islamic finance. Although in the last decade Islamic finance has been directly affected by the two main world crises, the market of Islamic capital seems to maintain a stronger profile than the conventional market. After the first two years of decrease following September 2001, Islamic investment funds recovered their losses at a ratio of more than 20 percent a year, and Islamic banks (including *takaful* funds) increased their assets by about 40 percent from 2006 to 2007. Furthermore, in the global financial crisis we are still experiencing, Islamic banks seem to be suffering less than many of their conventional rivals, with a more rapid recovery since the first months of 2010.
2. *The challenge of Islamic finance as an alternative method of investment*, which is less speculative and more likely to produce sustainable development in real economies. *Shari'a* compliant institutions invest in companies that charge no interest, do not engage in significant leverage, and avoid investments in derivatives and complex collateralized securities, which are at the heart of the present critical situation.
3. *Integration policies of Muslim communities in Europe* and the growing demand for compliant financial and banking services. Significant revenues could be obtained by retail banking services, donation management (coming from remittances and charity funds like *zakat* and *sadaqa*), consumer interest-free credit, small enterprise financing (even adopting micro-credit principles), home financing (through specific agreements). In innovating banking business, attention should be given to the relation between the *ethical label* and the *Islamic label*, where both can be perceived as a framework of religious and moral values that operates as a filter for choices concerning investments and the use of money in general.

## Great Britain

Since the early 1980s, European continental countries have contemplated very carefully the Islamic experiments conducted in Great Britain with Albaraka International Bank and other Islamic institutions. In general, according to the European principles of freedom of establishment, Islamic banks, together with every other bank with legal and administrative headquarters in a European country, may open branches in the territory of another country of the Union. So far, the European Central Bank (ECB) has never authorized the opening of Islamic branches at the European level. In this case, every Islamic bank established in Great Britain has not received the "passport" to Europe and has remained only English state chartered.

After the success of HBSC Islamic Loans (2003), a new season started in 2004 with the foundation of the Islamic Bank of Britain, headquartered in London and with branches in Birmingham, Leicester, and Manchester. With a majority of Qatari private shareholders, the Islamic Bank of Britain is the first and only retail bank offering *shari'a* compliant services to British Muslims (several types of deposits and accounts, mortgages and house purchase planning, investment funds, personal pension, *zakat* service, etc.). Other financial institutions, mainly as asset managers, have since been founded:

- HSBC Amanah Finance;
- European Islamic Investment Bank (2006);
- Bank of London and the Middle East (2007);
- Gatehouse Bank (2008);
- Qatar Islamic Bank – UK (2010 – awarded the "Best Asset Manager (Europe)" at the CPI Financial's 2012 Islamic Business and Finance Awards).

Other Islamic finance providers based in the UK, even as subsidiaries of foreign banks, are: ABC International Bank PLC, Ahli United Bank, Bank Negara Indonesia, Barclays Capital, Halal Financial Services Inc., HSBC Amanah Finance, Islamic Mortgages.

The wide space for an Islamic financial market encounters strong limitations deriving, first, from competition with conventional banks. Most British Muslims, in fact, continue to use high street banks, while Islamic operators continue to have high fixed costs in relation to customer numbers. As a consequence of the low income of Muslim families, deposits and investments from residents are too small to be involved in major financial activities. At the same time, the Islamic system is strengthening efforts to attract and accept deposits from other banks, including its Gulf-based relatives; and treasury activity largely involves commodity *murabaha*, which is a more expensive alternative to an Islamic money market.

## France

Also within continental Europe, a more critical approach towards Islamic finance appeared after 2001, along with the structural changes occurring in the EU economy: the introduction of a common currency, the EU monetary policy, the creation of the ECB and of the European System of Central Banks, the coordination of credit and oversight policies, the control of payment systems. Thus, while European operators have gained a wider knowledge of the Islamic system, the Islamic system has gained strength in the effort to achieve compatibility with international standard rules governing transparency as well as risk and capital management requirements.

After the British experience, France – a country with one of the largest Muslim communities in continental Europe – made the first steps in testing the progress of Islamic financial engineering. BNP Paribas and Société Générale are among the most engaged banks in the field. Thanks to the expertise of BNP Paribas Najmah, centered in Bahrain, BNP Paribas works in extra-European markets and it offers Islamic instruments for savings, credit, and investment: deposits, operations of *murabaha*, *sukuk*, *ijara*/leasing, asset management products, as well as FOREX with swap-free account and derivatives (about the last two operations there is no widespread acceptance by Muslim jurists). Investment funds are linked to the Dow Jones Islamic Market Index and to the FTSE Islamic Global Index.

Société Générale, through its controlled company SG Asset Management – Alternative Investments (SGAM AI), entered in the market between 2004 and 2006, launching the first protected capital products, which reached US$500 million at the end of 2007. SGAM also created a dynamically managed proprietary index (SGAM Baraka Index), based on an active selection from a basket of thirty Dow Jones Islamic Market Index stocks, appraised in advance by its *shari'a* Control Committee (Ratings Intelligence Partners).

These products are prepared using dynamic portfolio insurance (recognized as *halal* by some *shari'a* committees) combined with a *murabaha* contract (which is a pre-agreed mark-up sale) and an option ('arbun). They are mid-term protected investments that offer complete capital restitution or, if more positive, 85 percent of the highest market value obtained before stock maturity.

In 2008, SGAM AI launched a new passive index range, SGAM Index S&P Shariah, which seeks to track the performance of the 500 Islamic titles listed in the S&P Shariah indexes, within the SG unit trust in Luxembourg (in conformity with UCITS III European Directive). Such funds were approved by the French Autorité des marchés financières (AMF) in July 2007. Furthermore, Banque Française de Commerce (BFC) of the SG Group, launched SGAM AI Islamic products in the French territory of Réunion (with an average of about 7 percent of Muslim citizens). BFC has introduced a new short-term product named SGAM AI Shariah Liquidity with an eighteen-month maturity, which provides daily liquidity through a certificate managed in accordance with *murabaha* principles. The main obstacle to a wider introduction of Islamic financial transactions, in France and in most European civil law countries, has been represented by the need to adopt legislative revisions, following the model of English trust with the distinction between legal property and economic property, as well as with the opposability of the destination clause to third parties.

## United States

The development has almost been the same for Islamic banking and finance in the United States. The first institution, the LARIBA Finance House, in 1987 started offering home financing products according to the Islamic prohibition on usury and interest. LARIBA was located in California with the idea of using capital from individual American Muslims to provide home financing to other American Muslims (see Thomas 2001). Only after 1997 did a federal branch of the United Bank of Kuwait, under the National Bank Act, apply for a *shari'a* compliant *ijara* (lease-to-purchase) home financing program named Al-Manzil. In 1999 the program was approved to also offer *murabaha* (cost-plus-profit) home financing products in California. The program was closed after one year, having provided financing for sixty homes. The most important issue was the "customer training" required to educate customers about the special features of the Islamic operations.

Since then, no further authorization on Islamic products has been granted at US federal level. The events of September 11, 2001 had the effect of drawing stronger attention to Islamic finance, both for security issues and for a deeper Western presence in *shari'a* compliant affairs.

The University Islamic Financial Corp., founded in 2003 and controlled by University Bancorp (in Ann Arbor), offers different kinds of mortgages (home financing and commercial real estate financing) and savings accounts according to the profit- and loss-sharing scheme.

With the same goal of serving the American Muslim community, the Devon Bank (originally opened in Chicago in 1945 as the Devon North Town State Bank by local merchants who believed in the potential of community banks) has tailored its financial services to the particular demands of the local community. The bank began offering Islamic products in 2003, after receiving approval from Chicago-based Mufti Muhammad Nawal-ur-Rahman and the *shari'a* Supervisory Board of America, as well as in collaboration with the United Bank of Kuwait and the Institute of Islamic Banking and Insurance in London.

Nowadays, few state-chartered banks provide *shari'a* compliant products in the USA, whether for home financing or other financing facilities based on *ijara* and *murabaha*.

## Banking/mortgages

- Broadway Bank of Chicago (Chicago, IL)
- Devon Bank (Chicago, IL)
- Guidance Residential (West Falls Church, VA)
- United Trust Bank (Bridgeview, IL)
- University Bank (Detroit, MI)
- Zayan Finance (Chicago, IL)

## Wealth advisors/fund companies

- Allied Asset Advisors (Burr Ridge, IL)
- Azzad Asset Management (Falls Church, VA)
- Saturna Capital (Bellingham, WA)

## Investment banks

- Arcapita (Atlanta, GA)
- Overland Capital Group (Boston, MA)
- TransOcean Group (Boston, MA)
- UIB Capital (Chicago, IL)

The most interesting development in the USA has been the opening of the American multi-national banking industry to the Islamic system. Citi Islamic Investment Bank was incorporated in 1996 in Bahrain, as a subsidiary of Citicorp Banking Corporation, operating as the dedicated Islamic banking vehicle of CitiGroup. The core Islamic banking business of Citi Islamic Investment Bank has been the origination, structuring, and distribution of Islamic banking transactions in trade finance, structured trade finance, leasing, fund management, and Islamic securities. It also works as a "bridge" to introduce into the Islamic banking market other national companies of the group in Brazil, Korea, Turkey, Egypt, Mexico, South Africa, Pakistan, India, and Bangladesh.

## Islamic capital market

The Islamic capital market offers a wide range of funds: about 200 Islamic funds are currently operating at a national and/or international level. As a general trend, over 60 percent of such funds represent investments in stocks on the international, regional, and national markets: this is mainly due to the favorability of the *shari'a* compliant investment scheme for equity investment in the light of Qur'anic interdiction of *riba* and to the traditional inclination for risk-sharing forms of investment.

Since 1999, two key indexes contain stocks considered to be Islamic compliant, which are thus listed on international markets: the Dow Jones Islamic Market Index and FTSE Global Islamic Index. In recent years, other Islamic stock indexes have introduced further lists of companies based on *shari'a* compliant activities and detailed performance requirements. This success is also due to the preference for equity investment in the light of the Qur'anic system of *riba* and the traditional inclination towards risk-sharing forms of investment.

A number of criteria for the identification of companies operating in compliance with the Islamic precept were progressively developed. Such companies are periodically collected in national and international directories. In Malaysia, for example, the audit activity is carried out by the *shari'a* Supervisory Board, part of the Securities Commission, which in turn controls stock market operations. A similar directory is used in India, commissioned here by private groups (Parsoli IBF-Net Equity).

In recent years also the West has seen the emergence of stock directories containing stocks considered to be "compatible" and listed on international markets: the Dow Jones Islamic Market and FTSE Global Islamic Index. The Dow Jones Islamic Fund, created for Islamic equity funds in 2000, selects "compatible" companies among those listed in the Dow Jones Global Equity. The criteria on which stocks are considered compatible according to the *shari'a* may be summed up as follows:

- the main activities carried out by the company in question must not be involved in any of the following fields: swine breeding and swine food production; alcohol beverage production; conventional financial services (banks, insurance companies, etc.); entertainment (gambling, betting, pornography, cinema, music, etc.);
- the company balance must prove that: the total liabilities are not larger than 33 percent of the total assets; profit from bank interest is no higher than 5 percent of the total assets and must be used for social and charitable causes; collectable credits must not exceed 45 percent of the total assets.

With respect to the latter condition, it must be emphasized that the ratios are calculated on a venture capital basis, so that any estimate of loan interest is impossible in the ordinary activity. Islamic financial brokers have set up various types of *interest-free bonds* aiming to attract savings from Muslim communities and offering clients a wide variety of options. Among them we find *takaful* certificates and *sukuk* bonds.

The *takaful* contract is based on the Islamic principle of solidarity and offers a "mutual insurance." It is a pact amongst a group who agree to donate contributions to a fund that is used to jointly indemnify covered losses (in case of death, illness, or other negative events regarding life or health) incurred by the members of the fund. In conventional insurance, companies engage in investments that may derive income from interest and they accept anticipated premiums for future and uncertain claims. While the concept of *takaful* revolves around mutuality and is founded on a non-commercial basis, the operations and the funds are commonly managed by financial operators on a commercial basis through the classic schemes of *mudaraba* or *wakala*. According to the *mudaraba*, policyholders are owners of the fund and entitled to its profits, being at the same time both the insurer and the insured. Mutual guarantee means common liability in the financial result of the fund investment, sharing profits and losses arising from it. All investments must be *shari'a* compliant, through the use of instruments that are free of *riba* and are not involved in *haram* activities.

In the last few years, we have witnessed very fast growth of the *takaful* market, where some non-Muslim consumers also found appeal in the specific features of the products. In fact, *takaful* certificates seem to attract interest well beyond their "religious appeal." Ethically or socially responsible investors and consumers identify the market of *shari'a* inspired products as a full-potential and interesting sector of financial undertaking. Along this wave, the global expansion of *takaful* activities (excluding Saudi Arabia, which requires all insurance companies to operate under a cooperative business model; see Ernst & Young 2012b: 67) reached US$4 billion in 2012 (by comparison with US$0.9 billion in 2005–6), with a predicted further increase of about 15 percent in 2013.

On the other hand, *sukuk* (conventionally named Islamic bonds) are asset-backed or asset-based securities, deriving from the securitization of *ijara* and *murabaha* transactions, with the property of the asset divided into equally valued units and incorporated in the certificates. *Sukuk* cannot represent a debt (in Islam debt-selling is forbidden), as conventional bonds can; they must instead represent a property of a specific asset. The value of the *sukuk* thus remains connected to the value of the underlying asset. Some Muslim countries (i.e. Malaysia) are using *sukuk* as a substitute for public debt bonds.

The Accounting and Auditing Organization for Islamic Financial Institutions (AAOIFI) has so far issued standards for fourteen types of *sukuk*, the most widely spread of which is the *ijara sukuk*, which, as the name itself indicates, is linked to assets granted in leasing through a specific account, where the bond represents a quote of property rights.

The *sukuk* market has witnessed a rapid increase outside the *dar al-islam*, entering the global financial markets and attracting non-Muslim investors as well. For this reason, and considering the opportunities deriving from the presence of migrant communities, interesting experiments have been conducted in Western countries. For example, the German Saxony-Anhalt *sukuk al-ijara* (an asset-backed security based on leasing agreements) was issued in 2005 for US$100 million according to the following criteria:

- the underlying asset, consisting in buildings owned by the German Ministry of Finance, has been conferred on the Special Purpose Vehicle (SPV) (operating as a *mudaraba*) for 100 years;
- the SPV has handed the buildings over to the Ministry with a five-year leasing contract and an option to renew the lease;
- the benchmark has been set to one basis point above six months Euribor;
- the *sukuk* has been indexed on the Luxembourg stock exchange; the certificate's rating is AAA for Finch and AA- for Standard & Poor's.

In November 2012 FWU AG Group, a German financial services company, issued the first and largest private *sukuk* in Europe, with a size of US$55 million and a tenure of seven years remunerated by an annual profit rate of 7 percent. This is also the first *sukuk* to implement intellectual property rights under an *ijara* structure. FWU Group, which offers *takaful* solutions through strategic cooperation and distribution arrangements in Europe, the Middle East, and Malaysia, entered into the transaction through the Dubai branch of its subsidiary FWU Dubai Services GmbH. The ultimate financiers were GCC-based investors represented by *takaful* companies that have assisted FWU in raising funding through the leasing method. The *sukuk* were issued through a Luxembourg Issuer SPV incorporated using a Dutch *Stichting* (foundation) structure – first used in connection with the quasi-sovereign *sukuk* issuance by Saxony-Anhalt in 2005.

## Banking activity: a comparison between models

In order to verify the feasibility of the establishment of an Islamic bank or window operating in one or more European countries, first of all we must compare the fundamental notion of bank in both Islamic and European systems. As a consequence of its compliance with *shari'a* principles in banking activities, since its very beginning the Islamic system has applied two distinctive methods: the elimination of *riba* (money interest) from all transactions, as well as the choice of directly or indirectly participatory contracts – the so-called profit- and loss-sharing (PLS) – in most financial activities.

An Islamic bank can be defined as an institution that collects money (savings) from the general public and provides credit through interest-free transactions on both the asset and liability sides. At the same time, positively, we shall define Islamic banks as institutions operating through a system where profits and losses are shared between the parties of each transaction. PLS contracts are mainly an innovative result of the effort (*ijtihad*) to elaborate alternative financial instruments that could be competitive under the market profile and lawful (*halal*) from the religious point of view.

At present Islamic banks offer a wide range of deposit accounts, repayable on demand or with a term or call period; they operate as credit and investment intermediaries; they provide loans as well as private equity capital. Profit- and loss-sharing, as we have seen, is the main characteristic of most credit instruments in Islam. There is a distinction between directly participatory contracts, like *mudaraba* (limited partnership, joint venture) and *musharaka* (venture capital, project finance), and contracts with indirect participation, like *murabaha* (mark-up sale), *ijara* (leasing), *istisna'* (procurement, order to manufacture), etc. In the second group of contracts, the bank does not assume the role of partner of its own customer; it maintains instead a secondary economic risk in connection with the financial operation since the property of goods and equipment must necessarily be acquired by the bank before transferring it to the customer.

If we compare this model of banking activity with the current European concept we notice some relevant distinctive points. First of all, it is possible to denominate as "banks" only those enterprises whose main activity (so-called "banking activity") consists both in collecting repayable funds from the general public and in providing loans as well as all other financial activities (Italian Banking Law L. 385/1993 – art. 10.3). This specific activity is a requirement distinguishing Islamic brokers from other financial brokers. The activity of collecting funds produces the bank's obligation to repay and the depositor's right to be reimbursed, while it does not produce any duty of compensation on the deposited amounts.

The comparison between the two concepts of bank highlights the disparity, since in the Islamic system the different types of deposit do not produce a debt-based transaction between the depositor and the bank, but an equity-based transaction. Theoretically, as a consequence of the general implementation of the participatory principle and the consequent idea of risk, no guarantee on the deposit is allowed. The lack of an explicit obligation to reimburse may represent one of the first elements of "incompatibility" with European regulation. In this sense, according to the general European definition, Islamic banks cannot be considered banks. Nevertheless, in the domestic legislation of European countries the consideration may be different, as in the case of Great Britain.

With regard to financial cover on deposits, a distinction is made between cost-free on-demand accounts and participatory accounts: only the latter can actually suffer losses potentially deriving from a negative trend in the bank's balance sheet, and only when the bank's capital and reserves are insufficient to cover the losses. Apart from the abolition of capital remuneration based on interest and the introduction of the profit-sharing mechanism, Islamic and non-Islamic banks are equally subject to the general national legislation in force concerning, particularly, liquidity and reserve regulations. If the raising of the funds engenders some questions about repayment of deposits, the credit side operations require particular attention with regard to guarantees and fiscal profiles.

A specific arrangement is required for credit risk management (and insurance through the *takaful* scheme), which presents greater complexity since various degrees of borrower risk do not correspond to the application of different interest rates, but are congruent with different allocations of profit shares. For this reason, transparency-level analysis is largely suitable in relation to credit management under the profile of both the informative symmetry/asymmetry between the parties and credit monitoring tools and procedures by the bank. Furthermore, legislative reforms are required in European civil law systems in order to create an appropriate legal framework for new Islamic banking institutions or Islamic windows to be opened within existing banks or groups. Such reforms concern specific private law institutions:

- the law of trust in civil law systems with special regard to the opposability of beneficiary's rights to third parties (in Italy art. 2645 ter Civ.Code was introduced in 2006; in France the already mentioned project to modify art. 2011 *Code Civil* was approved by the National Assembly in October 2009 but currently enactment has been rejected by the Constitutional Council);
- the discipline of guarantees in the sale of goods (i.e. *no vice* guarantee or redhibitory fault guarantee) as well as guarantees relating to debt or credit transfer (i.e. debtor's performance guarantee) in consideration of the temporary nature of *murabaha* and *hawala* contracts;
- the leasing contract affecting goods or real estates, with special attention to installment payment conditions and to purchase options.

Further reforms are necessary also in fiscal legislation mainly in order to avoid double imposition in temporary purchase and sale transactions (such as *murabaha* financing and *musharaka* home financing agreements). In the case of non-profit purchase and sale *murabaha* agreements, the ideal fiscal system would provide for the allocation of sums paid in advance for publicity rights and registry rights on deferred payments, as well as neutralization of the impact of the fiscal rights platform (i.e. VAT) on the seller on credit, while distinguishing, in the final purchase price, the principal price of the cost of credit.

## Ethical banks vs. Islamic banks

A remarkable point is a certain parallelism between financial practices according to both the Islamic and the ethical viewpoint. Their collective investment schemes are equally defined by a process of selection of the listed company, based on both negative and positive criteria. The *shari'a* compatibility test excludes all those activities expressly violating Qur'anic precepts (alcoholic production, swine processing, pursuing of aims related to gambling and pornography) or conflicting with Islamic ethics deriving from the same precepts (some *entertainment* activities, but also tobacco, drugs, and weapon processing and manufacturing, projects aiming to create or maintain situations of poverty, or cases of exploitation and economic dependence).

In general, the criteria adopted in the ethical or "socially responsible" field appear to be less stringent because they do not directly depend on strict legal-religious provisions. The ethical pockets exclude all activities related to weapons, pornography, tobacco, drugs, alcohol, nuclear energy, animal testing, and, more recently, genetic manipulation and all those activities with a negative impact on the environment and development. At the same time, ethical investment should support sustainable economic development in emerging countries; as well as promote environmental sustainability, favoring renewable and clean energy, best practices in waste minimization and recycling, also taking into account energy efficiency. It should favor fair trade, good occupational health and safety practices, equitable industrial relations, gender equity.

In both cases a screening process of the pocket based on efficiency evaluation and company performance criteria is also implemented, with the aim of reassuring investors about the correct (from an ethical or Islamic point of view) practicality. From here, at least theoretically, derives a binding need for transparency and information disclosure, characterizing the two models of investment. Such a need directly regards the psychological security of each investor and calls for the principle of individual conscience to decide whether to follow an alternative route in investing money. In a case where, as frequently occurs, some of the activities emerge as not conforming with the theoretical model, it is necessary to activate a sort of "purification" of the investment returns, re-employing – all or part of – them in social or charitable or ethical targets.

If we read the bylaws of ethical banks, we will find aims and objectives certainly shared by Islamic operators. In ethical banks, savers renounce all or part of the interest, which is targeted at the financing of projects in the third sector with a strong social value. If stated in the bylaws, for an Islamic bank this practice could become an efficient way to purify the returns realized inside a system based on interest as the predominant instrument to compensate the financial risk at all levels of the market. Second, both systems share the necessity of carrying out most of their activity according to a "client–partner" model and, therefore, with the joint liability of the client in the decisions of the bank on the investment side. The cooperative typology of companies the ethical banks are based on in Italy offers the opportunity for an interesting convergence for *shari'a* compliant institutions who want to settle there. Although in the cooperative credit scheme there is no necessary coincidence between client and shareholder, the "partner–client" experience has on the other hand been widely developed, with the shareholder taking up the bank services. The widespread community of shareholders that characterizes cooperative and popular banks makes the transposition of the Islamic model easier and it represents an efficient means to customize clients.

This is relevant to institutions that make transparency and closeness to the client's needs (from the economic, social, and religious point of view) their point of strength. The activity directed towards the general public, in this case, should be limited to collecting repayable funds on demand accounts (fully repayable also in Islamic banks), in order to promote investments and asset-based credit activities providing the application of pre-agreed fees instead of interest rates. However, the additional burden of costs derived from the duties of both information and oversight remains particularly onerous for banks with an atomized shareholder community.

An interesting operational sector would be represented by instruments that channel donations managed by banking and financial mediators offering clients the opportunity to subsidize nonprofit organizations controlled through a (generally variable) part of the return on savings. Through an Islamic bank, we can also imagine the channeling of donations coming from payment of the *zakat*, the legal tax due annually from any pious Muslim on its patrimony with its mandatory (as written in the Qur'an) aim of solidarity; or donations derived from the *sadaqa*, voluntary alms to be devolved generally to humanitarian and philanthropic aims. The management of remittances to immigrants' countries of origin, furthermore, could find the proper space here. In all cases, religious clauses or conditions relating to services and procedures performed by an Islamic financial institution must be carefully evaluated in order to avoid any possible form of religious discrimination.

We should also contemplate the growth of demands for credit coming from so-called ethnic firms, the necessity to purchase real estate from newly stabilized immigrants, the growth of market sectors for production, transformation, and selling of "faith compatible" goods. In Western ethical institutions, it is structurally impossible to elude the fundamental duty to reimburse deposited capital, but this can be worked around with some formal correctives that make the obligations more acceptable from the *shari'a* point of view (such as, for example, compensation with the dividends eventually due to the saver-shareholder in his position of shareholder, maintaining the distinction between the deposited capital and the capital of the bank).

On the other hand, the "ethical" approach of the Islamic bank can actually represent a spur to the level of "bank customization" of Muslim communities, which in Italy, unlike in Great Britain and France, represent a prevalently poor economic bracket with low levels of saving and investment. Notwithstanding this issue, in some regions, like Emilia-Romagna, we find well-integrated communities in the economic-productive system and active under the entrepreneurial profile. In the meantime, the living reality of cooperative credit could become the basis for an ethical Islamic experiment. Domestic and European authorities should integrate with such elements the "sound and prudent assessment" required by European directives (2000/46 and 2004/39) in authorization procedures.

In this view of convergence, ethical institutions could certainly benefit from the wider experience of "Islamic financial engineering" and from the higher skills in resource allocation that we have seen are proper to Islamic finance. On the regulatory and organizational side, Islamic operators could benefit from the experience acquired by the system of cooperative banks in the Italian and European markets.

## Conclusion: complementarity vs. alternativeness

With respect to the Western approach to Islamic banking and finance, we should consider two different issues. The first concerns the impact of these types of operations and services at the national level. A significant development has been reached within Islamic countries and outside wide politically and economically integrated areas, where a possible encounter of supply and demand from Muslim communities has generated a positive process. BRICS countries are now attracting much investment from *shari'a* compliant institutions that are looking forward to opening local structures. Inside the European Union and the United States, noteworthy progress has been made in certain jurisdictions (namely in the UK, France, Ireland, Luxembourg, and in three or four American states) to broaden the value proposition of Islamic finance. This situation nevertheless remains limited and somewhat fragmented. Each of these countries has tended to focus on the promotion of Islamic finance from their national-state perspective. This is for different reasons: the concern of most European governments considering the Eurozone crisis and the partial lack of dedicated resources in Europe to promote competition and challenge between Islamic and conventional finance.

Furthermore, the solution to the request to use an *Islamic label* (i.e. the implementation of religiously compliant expressions in bank logos and trademark or contracts) is certainly complex, considering the different shades of meaning given to the idea of secularity. A fundamental role is to be played not only by the economies and foreign policies of the individual countries, but also by socio-economic integration policies and economic support for the stabilization of Islamic communities. Through these communities, the international image of a country can find significant promotion. The severity of performance challenge has prompted several institutions to initiate wide-ranging transformation programs concerning (Ernst & Young 2012a: 4):

- regulatory framework – involving compliance risk, capital optimization, integrated balance sheet management and liquidity management;

- risk management – around *shari'a* governance, single data management framework, segment specific risk models and fund transfer pricing capabilities;
- retail banking operations – strengthening the customer-centric operating model, channel integration and technology enablement: developing a "whole-customer" view of requirements and profitability will be an essential capability for Islamic banks to improve performance;
- supervisory uniform standards and transparency enhancements – harmonizing the interpretations coming from *shari'a* boards and building a new model of reliability towards the client/consumer.

The second and most important adaptation challenge is rising on a supranational level. From its beginning, Islamic economy (with its banking and financial operative tools) has been introduced as an ideal "alternative" to liberal and socialist ideas. Its alternativeness has also been its fortune. The possibility of attracting pious Muslims concerned about the payment of interest, along with creative and trustworthy financial engineering, has created a launchpad for entering both national and international markets.

Despite these developments, the "alternative" model is not always successful. Within Europe, as well as the USA, and their very strong and structured centralized banking systems, Islamic banking needs to seriously consider the opportunity of becoming a complement to conventional banking and capital markets, not a substitute. Given the valuable attributes of Islamic finance and its affinity with tangible economic assets, transparency, fairness and alignment with socially responsible investing, much more is feasible and can be expected.

The adaptation to the European environment needs to avoid overdependence on technical jargon and explore opportunities of connectivity with socially responsible investing (i.e. sustainable investments); and, in the case of *takaful*, to be aligned with mutual and cooperative insurance structures, finding a strong mix and balance between Islamic and conventional ethical finance. The financial innovation that the Islamic system has realized so far is questioning the West about the compatibility of existing rules not only from the technical-legal point of view, but also in the light of its financial and social policies.

Indeed, these are elements of strategic importance: we cannot forget the continuous adaptation and contamination amongst different social, economic, and legal cultures deriving from globalization and from their unavoidable dialog. Complementarity – without giving up its own ideal values – will be a challenge to the conventional banking and financial system, brought by Islamic banking, in order to contribute to a better integration of Muslim communities in the Western context and to further incorporate the Islamic economic pattern in the plural global market (Cattelan 2013: 228–9).

## Note

1 Islamic banking and finance, during the last decades, have shown themselves to be a very attractive issue for scholars and professionals. For a comprehensive bibliography on this subject, see Henry and Lamm 2010.

## Bibliography

Abdel Karim, R.A. and Archer, S. (2007) *Islamic Finance: The Regulatory Challenge*, Singapore: John Wiley & Sons (Asia).
Akram Khan, M. (2003) *Islamic Economics and Finance: A Glossary*, 2nd ed., London: Routledge.
Ali, S.N. and Ali, N.N. (2010 [1994]) *Information Sources on Islamic Banking and Economics: 1980–1990*, London: Routledge.

Anwar, M. (2003) "Islamicity of Banking and Modes of Islamic Banking," in *Arab Law Quarterly* 18: 291–308.

Archer, S., Abdel Karim, R.A., and Nienhaus, V. (eds.) (2009) *Takaful Islamic Insurance: Concepts and Regulatory Issues*, Singapore: John Wiley & Sons (Asia).

Cattelan, V. (ed.) (2013) *Islamic Finance in Europe: Towards a Plural Financial System*, Cheltenham: Edward Elgar.

Cekici, I.Z. and Weill, L. (2011) "Islamic Finance in France: An Emerging Market?," in Hassan, M.K. and Mahlknecht, M. (eds.) *Islamic Capital Markets: Products and Strategies*, Chichester: John Wiley & Sons, pp. 267–77.

Dylan Ray, N. (1995) *Arab Islamic Banking and the Renewal of Islamic Law*, London: Graham & Trotman.

Ernst & Young (2012a) *World Islamic Banking Competitiveness Report 2012–2013: Growing Beyond – DNA of Successful Transformation*, December, www.ey.com/EM/en/Issues/Issues—Middle-East-Issues—Perspectives (accessed February 12, 2014).

——(2012b) *World Takaful Report 2012: Industry Growth and Preparing to Regulatory Change*, April, www.ey.com/Publication/vwLUAssets/The_World_Takaful_Report_2012/$FILE/Ernst_&_Young's_The_World_Takaful_Report_2012.pdf (accessed June 2013).

Fahim Khan, M. and Porzio, M. (eds.) (2010) *Islamic Banking and Finance in the European Union: A Challenge*, Cheltenham: Edward Elgar.

Favali, L. (2004) *Qiràd Islamico, commenda medievale e strategie culturali dell'occidente*, Torino: Giappichelli.

Gonulal, S.O. (2013) *Takaful and Mutual Insurance: Alternative Approaches to Managing Risks*, Washington, DC: World Bank.

Hancock, M. (2013) "Islamic Finance in 2013: Beyond the Growth," *The Banker*, March 1, www.thebanker.com/Markets/Islamic-Finance/Islamic-finance-in-2013-beyond-the-growth (accessed June 2013).

Hassan, M.K. and Mahlknecht, M. (eds.) (2011) *Islamic Capital Markets: Products and Strategies*, Chichester: John Wiley & Sons.

Henry, C.M. and Lamm, J.E. (2010) *Islamic Finance: Oxford Bibliographies Online Research Guide*, Oxford: Oxford University Press, www.oxfordbibliographies.com (accessed June 2013).

Henry, C.M. and Wilson, R. (eds.) (2004) *The Politics of Islamic Finance*, Edinburgh: Edinburgh University Press.

International Business Publications (2010) *Islamic Financial Institutions (Banks and Financial Companies) Handbook*, 4th ed., Washington, DC: International Business Publications.

Kettel, B. (2011) *Case Studies in Islamic Banking and Finance*, Chichester: John Wiley & Sons.

Khan, J.A. (1995) *Islamic Economics and Finance: A Bibliography*, London: Mansell.

Khorshid, A. (2004) *Islamic Insurance: A Modern Approach to Islamic Banking*, London: RoutledgeCurzon.

Krichene, N. (2013) *Islamic Capital Markets: Theory and Practice*, Chichester: John Wiley & Sons.

Piccinelli, G.M. (1996) *Banche islamiche in contesto non islamico. Materiali e strumenti giuridici*, Rome: Istituto per l'Oriente.

——(2010) "The Provision and Management of Savings: the Client-partner Model," in Fahim Khan, M. and Porzio, M. (eds.) *Islamic Banking and Finance in the European Union*, Cheltenham: Edward Elgar, pp. 23–39.

——(2011) "La finanza islamica tra crisi globale e innovazione: la prospettiva europea," in *Il Libro e la Bilancia. Studi in memoria di Francesco Castro*, vol. 2, Naples: ESI, pp. 977–98.

Presley, J.R. (ed.) (2012 [1988]) *Directory of Islamic Financial Institutions*, London: Routledge.

Rodinson, M. (1968) *Islam and Capitalism*, London: Penguin.

Rosly, S.A. (2005) *Critical Issues on Islamic Banking and Financial Markets: Islamic Economics, Banking and Finance, Investments, Takaful and Financial Planning*, London: AutorHouse.

Saleh, N. (1992) *Unlawful Gain and Legitimate Profit in Islamic Law*, London: Graham & Trotman.

Schoon, N. (2009) *Islamic banking and Finance*, Bank of London and the Middle East, London: Spiramus Press.

Siddiqi, M.N. (1985) *Insurance in an Islamic Economy*, Leicester: The Islamic Foundation.

Thomas, A. (2001) "Methods of Islamic Home Finance in the United States," in *The American Journal of Islamic Finance*, www.shapefinancial.com/knowledgespace.html (accessed June 2013).

Vogel, F.E. and Hayes, S.L. (1998) *Islamic Law and Finance: Religion, Risk and Return*, The Hague, London, and Boston: Kluwer Law International.

# 27

# The production of Western Islamic knowledge

*Stefano Allievi*

## Islamic knowledge: approximations

Defining Islamic knowledge is far from an easy task. What Muslims define as properly Islamic is not something that holds general consensus. Islam is a living tradition that in practical terms refers to an orthodoxy and an orthopraxy. The idea of living tradition implies differences in views, opinions, and behaviors. In this sense, a single, unique, unified, homogeneous, universally accepted form of Islamic knowledge simply does not exist. What exists is a corpus that constitutes a set of references, in which differences, contradictions, and conflicts of interpretation, as well as consensus (*ijmaʿ*) and agreement, are intrinsic parts of the concept of tradition. A sociological concept, in this sense, not exactly equal to that of *taqlid*; and also a historical one: because, as Asad (1986) points out, tradition has (or, better, is) a history that refers to a past and redefines itself in respect to a future, through a relation with the present. In this sense we can speak of an Islamic discursive tradition, as the author does, in a broader sense: that is not only the common intellectual meaning of the word "discourse," but rather the etymological one, from the Latin *dis-currere* – "running (*currere*) here and there"; moving and changing, we might say.

We underline this aspect because, if in the rational process of deduction (which is the result of a merely intellectual approach) orthopraxy is the consequence of orthodoxy, in the process of socialization (in daily life) orthopraxy often comes before the reference to orthodoxy, and is more the outcome of a relational process. Islamic knowledge, in this sense, is much less the fruit of an intellectual activity than the result of a specific contextualization and of a set of interrelations. Orthopraxy is quicker in acknowledging change than orthodoxy: and often change in practices does not necessarily, and in any case not immediately, produce change in its reference to, interpretation of, and deduction from orthodoxy. What we mean here with Islamic knowledge, then, is whatever Muslims (and non-Muslims, in interrelation with Muslims, as we will see) consider to be the correct Islamic belief and practice: using both these words – belief and practice – in the widest possible sense, including also popular knowledge and embodied practices (van Bruinessen 2011). There is obviously no judgment, on our side, of what is correctly Islamic and what is not.

We also have to take into account that the word "Islamic" is often used too extensively, in analysis and, particularly, in debates in the public space about Muslims. Not everything Muslims do is Islamic; this is obvious. But in the meantime, most of what Muslims do, in such debates, is considered Islamic even when it is not, through a process of "over-Islamization of Muslims" (Al-Azmeh 2004) that involves both Muslims (particularly strict believers, 'ulama' and intellectuals, several social and political Islamic movements and organizations) and non-Muslims (in particular media, political actors – peculiarly anti-Muslim actors – but also, sometimes, academics, in the field of Islamic studies and Orientalism, religious studies, and political sciences, but also in sociology and anthropology). This process of over-Islamization is particularly visible in societal debates on individual and collective behaviors (wearing a *hijab*, for instance), or on deviating cases (to give an example, a husband beating his wife, or a father forcing his daughter into marriage), but also in more general debates on religion and politics, or religion and gender. To quote an example from family controversies: a violent husband or father from Morocco or Pakistan will often be considered by default as Muslim, and religion will be considered quite naturally as an obvious cause of his behavior; while in the case of a Greek or a Romanian nobody would search for the reason for his behavior in the Orthodox tradition, and in the case of a Danish or a Norwegian no one would consider Lutheranism the cause (even though in the early waves of migration to the United States and to northern Europe in the first half of the twentieth century the traditionalist Catholicism of Italians or Spanish was sometimes seen as a cause of "primitive" deviating behaviors).

This societal attitude also has implications in the process of production of Islamic knowledge.

## What does it change? Islamic knowledge in Western countries: specificities

We are not talking here of Islamic knowledge in general. In particular, we are not analyzing the process of producing Islamic knowledge in Muslim (or Muslim majority) countries. We are referring to the process of producing Islamic knowledge in non-Muslim countries, that is, in countries where Muslims are a minority. Even though there are interrelations and feedback effects, this process, in this context, has important specificities that it is necessary to underline from the beginning.

Islam in Western countries has very different characteristics from those in countries where Islam is the majority religion. Islam in these countries is a minority in a pluralistic and secularized context: an aspect whose consequences are rarely understood in all their dimensions. The process of secularization of Europe, the USA, and other Western countries, their progressive self-definition as plural societies, their being free and democratic countries, in which, even with certain limits occasionally concerning Muslims and immigrants more generally, individual and collective rights are in different ways recognized and protected and religious rights in principle guaranteed; all these things make the Western situation quite different from many others in which Muslims equally constitute a minority.

From the theological point of view – which is obviously crucial in the process of producing Islamic knowledge – the situation of Muslims in the West could be compared to the situation of Muslims in Mecca at the inception of Islam (see Allievi 2011, where the argument is more broadly treated). The importance of the passage from Mecca to Medina, the *hijra*, in 622 AD, is so evident that it has become the beginning of the Islamic calendar, the date of the birth of Islam. As Bernard Lewis (1996) noted, while Muhammad preached Islam in Mecca, in Medina he was able to practice it, also in its collective consequences. In Mecca, Islam was a minority religion (a marginal sect, in contemporary terms): during this period the Prophet Muhammad led a small group of followers and Muslims were excluded from power. In Medina Islam became a majority and, therefore, law and government (a state religion, in contemporary terms). And

Muhammad became for the whole city what in Mecca he was only for his few followers: prophet and envoy of God, but also religious, political, legislative, juridical, and even military authority. Only in Medina did Islam become *din wa-dunya wa-dawl*, as majority Islam is defined in politico-religious terms.

Present-day Western Islam is in a situation that in some crucial aspects is more similar to that which prevailed in Mecca than in Medina: a tolerated minority religion that is sometimes stigmatized and sometimes integrated and institutionalized; and being a minority has important sociological and theological consequences. Socially, it is a minority quite different from that of Mecca. In general terms, with some exceptions, the average Muslim in Europe is richer, more cultivated, freer, more entitled to individual rights than the average Muslim in the respective countries of origin; and this makes their situation different, in comparative terms (a situation that also has important and underestimated consequences in terms of feedback effects, at several levels). Conceptually, the problem is that, while Muslims in Mecca did not have a solid theology of community and power yet, Muslims in the West rely on a theology that is that of Medina. Much cultural production *on* Islam and much production that comes *from* Muslim countries implicitly refer to situations where Islam is hegemonic, dominant, in power. The same idea of *shari'a*, from many points of view (to quote an example, the majority/minority idea of society implicit in the concept of *dhimmi*) simply presupposes that Muslims are a majority. Incidentally, this also applies to religious structures: no legitimizing center exists that is able to issue licenses of orthodoxy or heterodoxy, and the dimension of legitimization is, for structural reasons, subject to the logic of *de facto* power of contestation and permanent regeneration.

Not only is Western Islam a minority; it is also internally pluralistic, as it reproduces in itself different cultural, national, theological, and juridical interpretations of Islam, to a degree that is hardly observable in Muslim majority countries and in other countries where the presence of Islam is not the result of a recent migration process. This characteristic of internal plurality is in fact far more accentuated in present-day Europe, in the USA, and in other Western countries. The origins of this are multiple: even in countries where there is – or there was – an identifiable dominant ethnic group, the process of internal pluralization and differentiation has weakened their strength. There is no single origin or an original center of power that can be easily identified as dominant and representative: as a consequence, it does make less sense to try to manage Islamic presence as a foreign politics issue, in collaboration with the countries of origin of immigrants, as happened particularly in the earlier waves of migration, and is still a common temptation, both for Western governments and for Islamic organizations. The observable panorama shows us a plurality of presences and contributions in terms of law schools (all coexisting, which makes them lose much of their traditional meaning), mystical confraternities (a far greater diversity of which can be encountered more easily in the West than elsewhere and whose boundaries are easier to cross in Europe), ethnic groups, religious denominations (Sunnis, Shi'is, Ismailis, Alevis, etc.), and languages (those of the countries of origin, and the dominant Western languages in the respective host countries, which, for newer generations, often become the main or only language Muslims have in common).

In many ways, the perception of the *umma* as uniting believers of all skin colors and languages is far more directly perceptible in Europe and America than in most countries of origin. Not only this: in Western countries the need to define themselves as Muslim, which in countries where Islam is a majority is simply obvious and pleonastic, becomes more urgent. Only on the occasion of the *hajj*, probably, can a Muslim experience the *umma* as a visible plural reality, in the same vivid way that the common believer can usually experience it in many mosques and Islamic organizations throughout Europe and Western countries (in the case of the *hajj*, obviously with more symbolical relevance, but probably with fewer practical consequences). The internal diversity among Muslims is, then, ordinarily, more evident in the West than in many countries of origin of Muslim immigrants. The *umma*, in its diversity, becomes a unifying concept as a reality – not only as a desire, as an emotion, or as a rhetorical tool – precisely because it is internally visibly divided; and Muslims know that.

This internal diversity has important consequences. A particularly relevant example is provided by law schools: all of the *madhhab* are present in the West; but the major difference from the situation in the countries of origin is that they mix much more easily, and individuals can find their way *through* them even more than *in* one of them. This is why Western Sunni Muslims are beginning to call the "minority" interpretative school now in progress the "fifth law school" of contemporary Sunni Islam: a new and different context, in which *fiqh* also needs to be produced differently, with specific tools of interpretation, different foundations, and inevitably new contents.

Internal plurality, as it is experimented with by common believers in many vivid ways, calls into question, even without doing so explicitly, traditional beliefs and behaviors, and produces self-reflexivity, in ways which in turn implement and accelerate the process of pluralization itself.

Our interest here is to show the processes by which Muslims acquire or produce Islamic knowledge in this context. The issue is even more important concerning young Muslims, for the majority of whom their country of origin is the Western country in which they were born and which they live in. This turn is crucial because in these cases we can talk of an autochthonous form of Islamic knowledge, which cannot be considered as imported, even if it can be heavily influenced by a more general and global process of production, diffusion, and discussion of Islamic knowledge.

Finally, we have to consider that the process of production of Islamic knowledge does not concern only Islamic institutions and authorized actors (such as '*ulama*', mufti, imam, and other religious authorities), but new emerging cultural and even economic actors (Haenni 2005), and even ordinary non-organized Muslim individuals (Jeldtoft and Nielsen 2012), in their process of interpretation and personal *ijtihad*. And this process is interrelated with the action of non-Muslim actors, as different as intellectuals, media, political parties, and also ordinary non-Muslim individuals, and their views and opinions on Islam.

## What are Muslims searching for?

The way Muslims in Western countries imagine their role and produce their self-image helps us to understand where they position themselves, between the connections they have and maintain with their multiple countries of origin, on the one hand, and their projections – including cultural and religious ones – in Western contexts, on the other: between where they come from (at least culturally and even mythologically, for those who were born in Western countries) and where they are going to. The success of their inclusion (or co-inclusion, Dassetto 2011) in Western societies largely depends – among other things – on the plausibility of this process. A process that is also crucial for the self-definition of host societies.

What kind of knowledge are Muslims in Western countries searching for? And are they all looking for some kind of Islamic knowledge? The answer cannot be other than approximate: but it is important to note, as an obvious but seldom considered starting point, that not every Muslim born or resident in a Western country is in search of some kind of knowledge about Islam. We can observe, among Muslim populations in the West, three main tendencies: which may vary in percentage from one country to another and in different periods.

A substantial part of the population from different ethnic Muslim backgrounds is simply being (or wants to be) progressively integrated, or, to put it differently, is and will be progressively increasingly similar to the autochthonous populations it is becoming part of: this happens also in matters that concern religious belief and practice. This does not mean that Muslims do not want to be Muslims anymore: but that they want to be Muslim in a way that is not different – in form, and in some ways in content – from other religious belongings, and particularly the dominant ones in the respective countries they live in. This means that among Muslims one can observe the same tendencies that are observable in every other religious milieu, where beliefs are passing through important transformations, and traditional practice is diminishing, while new forms of religious behavior are emerging. Only a minority of the Muslim populations of Europe actively practice their religion on a regular basis (the data depend on the behaviour observed): this means that the majority do not, and consequently do not seek (new, different) religious knowledge. This does not mean that they are not interested at all in Islamic knowledge: they may have a secondary interest in it, eventually as a tool of education and a heritage for their sons and daughters, but they are not involved in the active search for, and production and transmission of, religious knowledge. We might call them "low-profile Muslims" or secularized Muslims.

Another segment of the population from Muslim backgrounds is, for the opposite reason, not interested in the quest for (new) Islamic knowledge: because it identifies with the old one. These Muslims tend to identify with traditional beliefs and practices from their countries of origin. Culturally they often tend to lock themselves up in their religious and ethnic communities, sharing the same Islamic knowledge, through their mother language, with their imported imam and codes of behavior, with their cassettes and satellite programs, often with their transnationally arranged marriages, and so on, which they tend to replicate. This segment of the Muslim populations is primarily, though not exclusively, part of the first generation of migrants: destined to become smaller, even if each new wave of immigration results in a new "first generation." These "traditional Muslims" often constitute the most visible (though not necessarily the most conspicuous) segment of the Muslim population, and it receives disproportionate media attention. It is this segment in particular that is involved in clashes of cultural values that have led to incomprehension among the European public. Typically these Muslims continue to speak in their original languages, they tend to dress, eat, marry in the traditional way, and do not feel at ease or do not like at least some common Western values and practices, who more often produce incidents of miscommunication, and so on. This does not mean that the dimension of change is absent in this part of the Muslim population: a tree transplanted in a completely different ground and climate will not grow in the same way. In this sense what they go through it is not just cultural reproduction, but is in any case transformation, at least in its consequences: but this is more an unexpected secondary effect than a desire and a goal voluntarily achieved. These traditionalist attitudes, which are the consequence of specific forms of Islamic knowledge, are widespread, not only among the first generation, and they are strengthened by new forms of transnational communication, including the new electronic media (satellite TV, internet), and by transnational organizations. Transnationalism, in fact, does not only have innovative or progressive effects: it can simply be a new channel through which traditional views can be spread (as in the very un-innovative content of many Islamic websites, and of much Islamic – Neo-traditionalist and Salafi, for instance – literature in bookshops). Many of these traditional points of views are ineffective, and fail to offer explanations appropriate to the situation of Muslims in the West, for the precise reason that they come from very different situations and contexts, in which Muslims are by definition a majority, and the main if not the only admitted religious reference in the public space – Medinan situations, not Meccan ones.

There is, however, another part of the Muslim population that is actively searching for new interpretative tools, thus demanding new religious knowledge and actively promoting and producing it. This third segment does not constitute the majority, nor can it be considered in any sense – included statistically – more representative of Muslims than others. The quest for new interpretations is frequently related to efforts to integrate in the societies in which they live; in any case, it is their way of finding their place in Western societies, constructing their religious identities in different forms, that needs elaboration and, in many ways, a creative attitude. In their case, the production of Islamic knowledge can be a way of positioning themselves in the respective national public spheres, using the language of the country they live in (which from the second generation on is the language they know better). In this respect – and contrary to their fathers – they share the same interests, the same demands, and the same need for answers of converts (on which, see Allievi 1998; van Nieuwkerk 2006). They produce original contributions to emerging new discourses about Islam that are contextually Western (Dassetto 2000). The fact that they are the fruit and a consequence of Islamic presence in the West does not mean, in any sense, that the role they play and the knowledge they produce are necessarily progressive, secularized, pluralistic, democratic, tolerant, open-minded, etc. Neo-traditionalist, neo-Salafi, neo-conservative forms of Islamic knowledge are also part of this landscape. Their activity is visible in books, cassettes, magazines, radio and TV programs broadcast in and from Western countries, but also in *khutba*s, and in the discourses that can be heard in associations and NGOs. It is possible to observe in these various media how new contents that are specifically Islamic *and* Western – in a proactive, but also in a reactive way – are emerging. We could call all these groups the "new Western Muslims." Not only Muslims in the West, not only Muslims of the West, but Western Muslims that make their presence in the West – and in many ways their belonging to Western culture – the starting point of their reflection on Islam.

Altogether, secularized Muslims, traditional Muslims, and new Western Muslims constitute the multiple facets that, in their interrelations (internal to Muslim milieus and, external to them, with society at large), produce the new forms and the new images of Western pluralistic Islamic knowledge.

## Where does it happen? Places and examples

Where does change happen? Where is Islamic knowledge produced, and how is it transmitted and diffused? As we have already noted, it starts in individual and collective behaviors, in embodied practices and in the emergence of new orthopraxis. But it becomes more visible in the field of theology: the process of construction of a theology adapted to the Western situation of minority. A situation that, when acknowledged as different from that of Muslim majority countries, is already in itself a big step in the direction of change and, in Islamic terms, *ijtihad* (sometimes interpreted, from the traditionalist – and majority Muslim countries' theology – point of view, in the negative sense of *bid'a*). The effort Muslims make takes different directions. One is producing a sort of minority *fiqh*, as seems to be the case, among others, with the European Council for Fatwa and Research (Caeiro 2010, 2011), founded in Dublin in 1997, but also of many *fatwa*-online websites (Bunt 2003, 2009). Another one is trying to elaborate a theology of Islam in a situation of religious plurality (Islam and Muslim communities as part of a new and different society), which seems to be what religious intellectuals are attempting, among whom Tariq Ramadan (2004a, 2004b, 2010) is only the most well-known case (other examples include Amina Wadud and what is know as Islamic feminism, among others). Remaining on mere terms of principle and speculative analysis, without playing a social activist role, this attempt is also made by Muslim intellectuals coming from Muslim majority countries, often having fled to the USA or Canada or Europe, by choice or to escape from threats and menaces: to quote randomly, among others, Fazlur Rahman, Nasr Hamid Abu Zayd, Abdullahi an-Na'im, Abdolkarim Soroush, Ramin Jahan-begloo (on Muslim intellectuals of various tendencies see, among others, Benzine 1994, Esposito and Voll 2001, Campanini 2005, Donohue and Esposito 2007). In the form of adaptation of traditional *fiqh* to a different context, more than with the idea of a different *fiqh*, this is also the scope of some Muslim majority '*ulama*' (that do not play only a conservative role: Zaman 2002), preachers and clerks, of whom Yussuf al-Qaradawi is the best-known example (Graf and Skovgaard-Petersen 2009). Many popular tele-preachers have the same role – Amr Khaled is one of the best-known examples (see Mariani 2011) – as well as, occasionally, institutions like the International Union of Muslim Scholars (founded in London in 2004 and now based in Cairo). An important role is also played by Muslim origin secular intellectuals as different (also in their relation with Islamic knowledge) as Muhammad Arkoun or Bassam Tibi, and many others. At the opposite end of the spectrum from producers of Islamic knowledge, there are anti-Muslim actors from Muslim backgrounds, such as Ayaan Hirsi Ali, Chahdortt Djavann, Irshad Manji, Ibn Warraq, Magdi Allam, and many others, of local importance: their scope is to produce knowledge against Islam, giving legitimization to the prolific category of non-Muslim professional preachers of Islamophobic and anti-Muslim Western opinion (whose books are bestsellers in the West on Islam: their titles are regularly among the most sold books on Islam in Amazon, for instance). They are not at all popular among Western Muslims, but they play an important role in setting the agenda and the conditions of debate on Islam in the West.

Theology, theological interpretation, exegesis, hermeneutics are far from being the only means by which Western Islam emerges. Places and examples of production of Islamic knowledge in Western countries are many and various. Among others, they include: '*ulama*', muftis, *mujtahids*, preachers, intellectuals, but also scientists and humanists of various kind; Islamic associations (including those of women and youth), NGOs, social organizations, political parties, religious movements, Sufi orders; mosques, mosque committees, imams; Qur'anic schools, Islamic schools, religious higher education institutes, Muslim seminaries; Islamic websites, religious broadcasting and other media; and, of course, families and informal peer groups. We will not go through all of them in detail. It is enough to have in mind the richness and complexity of the panorama.

All these places are interconnected: they can mutually reinforce each other (families, mosques, Qur'anic schools, religious broadcasting, for instance), helping to build what Peter Berger (1967) has called significant "plausibility structures"; but they can also produce cognitive dissonance and conflict if they display, even implicitly, different forms and interpretations of Islamic knowledge.

They have variable importance, also depending on individual trajectories and phases of life. Altogether, they form a strong and relevant combination of institutions and references that become part of the "tool box" of the average Muslim (accepting that tools are not necessarily part of everyday experience: but usually we prefer to have the tools in our box, even if we do not use them often – just in case … ). One needs to acknowledge also the rapidity of the process that has led to their diffusion: in a few decades, a new religion (new for the context) has been able to expand and institutionalize in a bottom-up process particularly impressive for its strength and efficacy. Western countries – and, from many points of view, particularly European ones – cannot be understood anymore, in their social and political evolutions and tendencies, and in their symbolic, religious, and even institutional landscape, without taking into account their internal Islamic presence.

## What does it mean? Relevance and feedback effects

The process of the production of Islamic knowledge in the West does not happen in a vacuum, and does not concern only Western countries. Its relevance is enormous and equally underestimated, compared to its importance.

There is a common habit of depicting the process of diffusion of Islamic knowledge as if it were from a "there" (meaning Muslim countries, and in general the countries of origin of immigrant populations) to a "here" (meaning Western countries, and in general the host countries of immigrant populations). This might be partially true in the first wave of migrations: but things are far more complex. It is a question not only of the direction of these processes (often going in the opposite direction, from a "here" to a "there," as we will see), but of a completely different landscape. Cultural and religious feedback effects play an important role that has not yet been sufficiently analyzed by scholars and researchers. The production of Islamic knowledge in the West (as well as in Muslim countries) has effects both "here" and "there."

An important aspect of the religious and cultural processes concerning Islam in (and) the West is in fact their transnationalization (Allievi and Nielsen 2003; Mandaville 2011). Sometimes this process is labeled diaspora: but the word diaspora implies a center (a starting point and a symbolic – at least – reference) that sometimes is not so easy to define, and is in many ways a sort of extension of the concept of nation-state (Soysal 2000); and these social phenomena cannot be studied, observed, or measured by using the traditional approach of national-level case studies, marked by the borders of the different countries. We can probably better define it as the complex interrelation between the emerging importance of networks of all kinds and the existence of relatively open transnational spaces (Faist 2000). Processes involving communication flows, including the production and dissemination of Islamic knowledge, can only be properly understood if we adopt a transnational perspective. The links between Muslim communities and their countries of origin, as well as among Muslim communities within Europe and other Western countries, seem to be important elements in the current development of discourses concerning the social and political role of Muslim communities. They are also crucial to their theological status as minorities not living in Muslim countries, not exposed to an accepted common religious authority, and with no possibility of referring to a shared religious law. In this sense, plurality (which is not only internal to the West, representing diversities transplanted into the new context, but also external, transnational) constitutes an opportunity rather than an obstacle for the production of Islamic knowledge and its dissemination. It represents a source of different solutions to the problems encountered, rather than a problem in itself – even if religious representatives, whose starting point is often an implicit idea of internal homogeneity, do not always like to interpret it as such. This presumption of homogeneity, and the perception of internal and external diversity as a matter of pathology rather than physiology, incidentally, is not peculiar to Islam, and not even to religions only. It is a more general epistemological problem: we tend to start our understanding of cultural and social phenomena from a presumption of homogeneity, interpreting plurality as a sort of addition to an initial "one." But plurality as a starting point brings – and needs – a different logic, and presupposes a different way of reasoning.

A particular interest reveals the analysis of the feedback effects of the production of Islamic knowledge in the West: the feedback *to* – and not *from* – Muslim countries. It is a field which is difficult to research (the main indicators are not always easy to define, and it implies long qualitative research) and expensive to finance (it implies field research both "here" and "there"), but very promising in its results, also for its possible consequences, at the cultural, social, economic, political and religious level.

The feedback which is more easily identifiable is that at the economic level. It is not the focus of our interest here, but we can just mention the role of money transfers to countries of origin, which often represents a significant entry in the national balance sheet of many labor force exporting countries and an important percentage of their GNP. They concern individual and family transfers, which often represent crucial support for local economies, but also "Islamodollars". Even for funding religious organizations and also the construction of mosques and Qur'anic schools, or financing pious institutions, in an increasing number of cases the flows from Western countries to Muslim countries are higher than those coming from Muslim countries; and for several movements and Sufi confraternities, Western countries are becoming an important economic opportunity and support, if not the main one. Several Western countries (notably the City of London) are also among the main capitals of Islamic banking and finance, and some European local governments with significant Muslim populations have already issued Islamic bonds.

The political feedback is equally important. The rise of Western and particularly European Islamic leadership also has crucial effects in the public sphere in countries on the other side of the Mediterranean, and a particular impact in former colonies. It becomes a strategic tool in the increasingly religious dimension of international relations, and can influence significantly the development of Arab (and not only Arab) neo-democracies. The presence of political refugees (but with religious motivations) is a source of interest in the political and religious dimension of sending countries, and can offer in some cases important alternative leadership in the case of crisis and changes in government in those countries. They also play a key role in orienting Muslim populations both in the West and in respective countries of origin: an important source of information and activism also for Western diplomacies. Also increasing is the habit of involving Muslim religious personalities in Western diplomatic missions. Even more important is the political participation of Muslims in Western countries, and their social activism (in local associations, trade unions, NGOs, Muslim representative organizations, etc.), for two reasons. One is internal, because of their increasing numbers in municipal, regional, and national elected assemblies, where they acquire considerable experience in Western democracy, which can also have an effect in their countries of origin. The second reason is precisely external: an increasing number of Muslims, from Turkey to Senegal, from Tunisia to Pakistan, after an experience of engagement in social and political organizations in the West, have become leading figures in the politics of their countries of origin, becoming mayors, members of parliament, or even ministers and party leaders. But at a lower level, even political and religious internet discussion forums and social networks are interesting platforms in which members of the same organization or people discussing the same tendencies, living in their countries of origin or in the diaspora, intertwine continuously, elaborating transnational discourses concerning the role of Muslims and of Islamic knowledge in either the countries of origin or host countries.

The intellectual influence of Muslims in the West is increasing rapidly, and becoming more visible and pervasive. Cities like London and Paris are becoming intellectual capitals of the Arab world, and Berlin, Cologne, and Frankfurt are becoming important references for the Turkish context. The same is happening for other countries and situations elsewhere. The number of books written in Arabic or other languages of the Muslim world, for both internal and external markets, but published in Western countries, is increasing enormously, due to their openness in terms of markets and freedom of thinking. In Europe and the USA there is fertile theological production: many intellectuals born in the West, including Western converts, often teaching in Western universities, are regularly invited to lecture or speak at conferences in the Muslim world, and there is increasing awareness of the importance of their contribution. This is a major change in the traditional center–periphery dynamic, in which the Arab holy places and traditional intellectual institutions (al-Azhar, Zeytouna, etc.) were the center, where knowledge came from. New centers are now emerging, making these dynamics more complex. Agreements between universities (both American and European) are increasing in number, as are strategic projects, often with financing coming from Muslim countries, transnational Islamic institutions, and private foundations, with Islamic higher education offered in the West to students coming from Muslim countries. The increasing awareness on issues like the educational skills of imams in the West makes it a sector in which public institutions (including European governments) are directly or indirectly involved. Islamic quality instruction has become part of a subtle Muslim diplomacy by Western governments. Many knowledge networks that have no explicit religious content often have a sort of not-so-vague Muslim hint.

The mediasphere (Appadurai 1996) is of fundamental importance. Internet, web television, satellite television, but also religious press (newspapers, journals, and books), and even – still – video and audio cassettes are helping to a great extent to create a Muslim transnational public space, that includes the countries of origin of Muslim populations as well as Western countries, in which contributions and messages go in different directions. The web is particularly important in building a transnational public space, creating interrelations in various languages, but particularly in English, which has become the main "Muslim" language worldwide.

Forms and occasions for interreligious dialog are also an important way to create transnational links, as well as institutional occasions such as those created by the different exchange programs of the European Union and other projects related to media, education, development, etc.

But probably the main religious feedback effect, in terms of efficacy, is the least studied and the most informal one: personal interrelations, family ties, travel to the countries of origin for holy days, religious festivals, family encounters, to arrange marriages, for import–export activities, etc. The development of communications and the diffusion of low-cost travel have had an enormous, though under-evaluated, impact in the reframing of transnational issues.

## Future actors of religious knowledge

One of the emerging issues, and one of the most interesting changes we can observe in the field of production of Islamic knowledge, is the increasing number of actors and places in which it is elaborated, and of the channels through which it is diffused, discussed, and disseminated. It is a change that is not only due to the ICT revolution (Eickelman and Anderson 1999; on the Muslim debates on media, see Larsson 2011); it is something that involves the ways in which religion is referred to, perceived, and practiced, particularly in the West. It is not something specific to Islam only; but the characteristics of Western Islam, and the quick contemporary changes to which it is subject, make it a particularly significant example of this transformation, for at least two main reasons, which, acting together, reinforce each other: the fact of being a minority rather than a majority – with the subsequent theological implications – and the passage from the first generation of migrants to the second and third generations born in a different context, which also includes a change in the language through which Islam is questioned that often precludes access to an entire corpus of traditional interpretation and exegesis.

This change has several consequences: the emergence of new Islamic actors, with a background in Islamic studies and curricula progressively different from traditional ones; the development of new places of elaboration and debate; the increasing influence of new and different media; the growing importance of new fields of study and research; the reduced importance given to traditional boundaries, that lose importance in the Western context (belonging to a specific *madhhab* or entering in a *tariqa* coming from a completely different context: to quote but one example, a Moroccan second-generation Muslim entering a Sufi group coming from India or Turkey and now based in Europe); the interrelation of all these factors, and their feedback with different but equally important changes taking place in Muslim countries.

Form and content of religion are both involved in this transformation, which for Islam takes the shape of profound processes of personal and collective *ijtihad* (for a vision from within Islam, see Khan and Ramadan 2011).

We can resume these transformations with two quotations from Muslim actors interviewed in the field (which are part of the materials collected for Maréchal et al. 2003).

The first one, concerning *madhhabs*, comes from an African Muslim of Yemeni origin based in London: "I am a Shafi'i, but I have to follow the most common *madhhab* here, which is the Hanafi one. Personally, as far as the *hajj* is concerned I am a Hanafi, for *jihad* I am a Maliki, for the conception of minority I am a Hanbali."

The second one, on *ijtihad*, is part of a dialogue with another Muslim, during a gathering of believers on the occasion of one of the frequent European conference tours of Yusuf al-Qaradawi, followed by the usual question and answer session. To my observation on the fact that the questions were always more or less the same, my interlocutor answered: "Do you know why they always ask the same questions? Because they always hope for a different answer."

## Two interpretative problems: exceptionalism and Islamophobia

The role of the perception of Islam in Western countries and of the production of Islamic knowledge by non-Muslim actors is significant not only for Western populations, but also for the feedback effects it has on Muslim actors. We will consider it briefly: starting with two key interpretative problems.

The first one is the tendency – of media, public institutions, political parties – to give, to the presence of Islam, specific and contextual answers, finding specific solutions, even when the issues raised, if correctly interpreted, could be compared and comparable to the issues raised by other religious (and even non-religious) groups.

We might define this tendency as exceptionalism, that is to say a tendency to see Islam and Muslims as an exceptional rather than standard case, one that does not fall within the cases relating to religious pluralism, and therefore requires specific bodies, actions, and specific targeted reactions, unlike those used for other groups and other religious minorities. Examples of exceptionalism include the forms of representation of Islam in various European countries, which vary from case to case but also differ with respect to the recognized practices of relations between states and religious denominations in general. The most symbolic case is the creation in various European countries of collective bodies of Islamic representation. Other cases concern the approval of laws banning specific dress (such as various forms of *hijab*, *niqab*, and *burqa*, even if often such laws are couched so that they do not seem specifically related only to Muslims, even when they are applied only or mainly to them) or buildings (minarets in some regions of Austria – Carinthia and Vorarlberg – and Switzerland, with a referendum), or the introduction of specific questions or conditions when applying for citizenship.

Forms of exceptionalism from a legal, political, and social perspective are, however, present in many other fields, following a pervasive trend: they even include, in some countries, the language used about Islam and Muslims, and the creation and increasing impact of political parties for whom fighting against the presence of Islam and Muslims in Europe is becoming a central point of their agenda.

These politics and policies concerning Islam and Muslims often contradict the principles of non-interference in the internal affairs of religious communities on which relations with other denominations and religious minorities are grounded. And their conceptual foundation is neither equality of treatment nor religious freedom: exceptionalism seems to be constructed in these cases as a (problematic) third way. Even the media perception of Islam, by default in conflictual terms, can be considered a form of exceptionalism; and conflict a specific way of understanding Islam.

Islamophobia is a specific case of exceptionalism, to which it is necessary to pay a certain amount of attention (Geissier 2003; Allen 2010; Helbling 2012). The word became widespread with the report *Islamophobia: A Challenge for Us All*, published by the Runnymede Trust in 1997. A first empirical survey came out in 2002 with the *Summary Report on Islamophobia in the EU after September 11*. A significant form of "officialization" of the term appeared with the seminar organized at the United Nations, at the highest level, on "Confronting Islamophobia: Education for Tolerance and Understanding" in December 2004. Following on from this, other agencies joined in, among them the Organization of the Islamic Conference (OIC), which set up an observatory on Islamophobia, and since 2008 has been producing monthly bulletins and an annual report on the subject. In recent years various websites have also dedicated themselves to this subject (among which www.islamophobia.org and www.islamophobia-watch.com), and practically all Islamic information sites, especially European and American ones, now have a section of documentation dedicated to Islamophobia.

Despite its institutionalization and its entry into the language and literature on the Islamic presence at an international level, the term has stirred up much criticism, also in spheres that could certainly not be suspected of anti-Islamic attitudes, because, among other reasons, it reduces all phenomena of reaction to Islam to the same kind, ending up by constructing the object of analysis instead of defining it correctly.

Nevertheless, Islamophobia as a phenomenon exists: in media and intellectual debates, and particularly among political entrepreneurs of Islamophobia. The political parties that take Islamophobia as a central part of their program, and as an efficient method of gaining consensus, are expanding strongly in several European countries and in other Western contexts. Islamophobia is not used only to target Islam, but also to attack multicultural politics and inclusive policies. On the other hand, anti-multiculturalist discourses often mask with general arguments a specific scope, having Islam as a hidden target.

## Interrelations: views on Islam and Muslims, and their effects on Muslim populations

The evolution of a tradition is the fruit of interrelation between internal and external actors. As Alasdair MacIntire points out,

> A tradition is an argument extended through time in which certain fundamental agreements are defined and redefined in terms of two kinds of conflict: those with critics and enemies external to the tradition who reject all or at least key parts of those fundamental agreements, and those internal, interpretative debates through which the meaning and rationale of the fundamental agreements come to be expressed and by whose progress a tradition is constituted.
>
> *(MacIntire, quoted in Zaman 2012: 34)*

We might add that external observers are not necessarily critics, but can also be sympathetic and positive towards a tradition.

Thus, the perception of the Islamic presence in Western countries, and specifically the attention paid to its intellectualization, plays an important role in the global perception of its Muslim presence, and also in the perception of Islam in general, not only Western Islam. From this point of view it is important to understand the role and the effects – also on Muslims themselves – of debates *on* Islam in the public space, which includes, among others, what is discussed in the media, in the political arena, and in the intellectual production.

Discourses about Islam are not only, and not even mainly, the product of Muslim interlocutors and social actors. There is a significant production of discourses about Islam that are becoming discourses about Muslims, and particularly Muslims in the West, that are produced by non-Muslims, but have important effects also on Muslims and on the production of Islamic knowledge.

The common lack of a socio-historical perspective and of a diachronic dimension (examples of which are the implicit assumption that nothing relevant has changed in the countries of origin, the common neglect of the rupture between the first and second generation in the host country, and so on), as well as the fact that links with the country and culture of origin are considered obvious, unidirectional, and not subject to reinterpretation, are but a few illustrations of this way of thinking. The selective perception of what is important and what is not in what happens in Muslim communities (very different between Muslims and non-Muslims) has other important effects: highlighting specific issues (notably the most controversial ones: the *hijab*, polygamy, female circumcision, gender roles and relations, separation between politics and religion, the whole issue of security, fundamentalism, and terrorism) and forgetting others; choosing between different aspects of Islam; pushing interpretation in one direction or another; or simply not seeing certain aspects of Islam and changes in Islamic knowledge that are less visible in the public space (popular religious practices, for instance; or processes of de-Islamization and secularization).

The role of selective perception in shaping the image of Muslim social, cultural, and religious actors is decisive also for its feedback effects on the actors themselves, who are obliged to deal with this image, take it into account, and often react to it, implicitly or explicitly.

The image of Islam and Muslims in the West is also produced by Western scholars and academics specializing in issues related to their presence, whose texts and research have a great impact – on societies and on Muslims themselves – in defining the frame, setting the agenda, and legitimizing policies. The outcome of their activity can be found in local and national researches, in collections of essays, in interpretative synthesis (more concerned with Europe, see Nielsen 1992; Dassetto 1996; Cesari 2004; Roy 2004; Klausen 2005; Jenkins 2007, and many others; on the American context, among the more recent, are Ahmed 2010; Bilici 2012), and as the outcome of comparative research (Maréchal et al. 2003); but also in less public activities including confidential reports, politicians' counseling, legal advice, training of public officials at different levels (including security agencies and police forces), etc. Together with the media, political parties, social and religious organizations, they are one of the main actors influencing the respective Western contexts (on the social, cultural, religious, political, institutional, jurisdictional level), particularly important in terms of legitimization (of political action and of public discourse): a key factor in favoring open processes of construction and recognition – but also transformation – of identities or, on the contrary, creating obstacles to them (Klausen 2005; Ferrari and Pastorelli 2012; Laurence 2012).

It is sufficiently clear that these processes are not only inherent in and internal to the respective identities – whose boundaries are not so easy to define and not so stable in time. They include interrelations with other identities, and imply transformation and change, also through forms of *métissage* and cultural syncretism: not only as a possible destiny, but as a necessity and, in the end, as a sign of vitality, on both sides of the coin: Muslim individual and collective actors, and society at large.

## Bibliography

Ahmed, A. (2010) *Journey into America: The challenge of Islam*, Washington, DC: Brookings Institution Press.
Al-Azmeh, A. (2004) *L'Obscurantisme postmoderne et la question musulmane*, Paris: Sindbad-Actes Sud.

Allen, C. (2010) *Islamophobia*, Burlington: Ashgate.

Allievi, S. (1998) *Les Convertis à l'islam. Les nouveaux musulmans d'Europe*, Paris: L'Harmattan.

——(2011) "Muslim Voices, European Ears: Exploring the Gap between the Production of Islamic Knowledge and Its Perception," in van Bruinessen, M. and Allievi, S. (eds.) *Producing Islamic Knowledge: Transmission and Dissemination in Western Europe*, Abingdon and New York: Routledge, pp. 28–46.

Allievi, S. and Nielsen, J. (eds.) (2003) *Muslim Networks and Transnational Communities in and across Europe*, Leiden: Brill.

Appadurai, A. (1996) *Modernity at Large: Cultural Dimensions of Globalization*, Minneapolis: University of Minnesota Press.

Asad, T. (1986) *The Idea of an Anthropology of Islam*, Washington, DC: Center for Contemporary Arab Studies, Georgetown University.

Benzine, R. (1994) *Les Nouveaux Penseurs de l'islam*, Paris: Albin Michel.

Berger, P. (1967) *The Sacred Canopy: Elements of a Sociological Theory of Religion*, New York: Anchor Books.

Bilici, M. (2012) *Finding Mecca in America: How Islam Is Becoming an American Religion*, Chicago: Chicago University Press.

Bunt, G. (2003) *Islam in the Digital Age. E-Jihad, Online Fatwas and Cyber Islamic Environments*, London: Pluto Press.

——(2009) *iMuslims: Rewiring the House of Islam*, Chapel Hill: University of North Carolina Press.

Caeiro, A. (2010) "The Power of European Fatwas: The Minority Fiqh Project and the Making of an Islamic Counterpublic," *International Journal of Middle East Studies* 24(3): 435–49.

——(2011) "Transnational Ulama, European Fatwas and Islamic Authority: A Case Study of the European Council for Fatwa and Research," in van Bruinessen, M. and Allievi, S. (eds.) *Producing Islamic Knowledge: Transmission and Dissemination in Western Europe*, Abingdon and New York: Routledge, pp. 121–41.

Campanini, M. (2005) *Il pensiero islamico contemporaneo*, Bologna: Il Mulino.

Cesari, J. (2004) *When Islam and Democracy Meet: Muslims in Europe and in the United States*, Macmillan: Palgrave.

Dassetto, F. (1996) *La Construction de l'islam européen. Approche socio-anthropologique*, Paris: L'Harmattan.

——(2000) *Islamic Words: Individuals, Societies and Discourses in Contemporary European Islam*, Paris: Maisonneuve & Larose

——(2011) *L'Iris et le croissant. Bruxelles et l'islam au défi de la co-inclusion*, Louvain: Presses Universitaires de Louvain.

Donohue, J.J. and Esposito, J.L. (eds.) (2007) *Islam in Transition: Muslim Perspectives*, New York and Oxford: Oxford University Press.

Eickelman, D.F. and Anderson, J.W. (eds.) (1999) *New Media in the Muslim World: The Emerging Public Sphere*, Bloomington: Indiana University Press.

Esposito, J.L. and Voll, J.O. (eds.) (2001) *Makers of Contemporary Islam*, Oxford: Oxford University Press.

Faist, T. (2000) *The Volume and Dynamics of International Migration and Transnational Social Spaces*, Oxford: Oxford University Press.

Ferrari, S. and Pastorelli, S. (eds.) (2012) *Religion in Public Spaces: A European Perspective*, Burlington: Ashgate.

Geissier, V. (2003) *La Nouvelle Islamophobie*, Paris: La Découverte.

Graf, B. and Skovgaard-Petersen, J. (eds.) (2009) *The Global Mufti: The Phenomenon of Yusuf al-Qaradawi*, London: Hurst & Co.

Haenni, P. (2005) *L'Islam de marché. L'autre révolution conservatrice*, Paris: Editions du Seuil.

Helbling, M. (2012) *Islamophobia in the West: Measuring and Explaining Individual Attitudes*, London and New York: Routledge.

Jeldtoft, N. and Nielsen, J.S. (eds.) (2012) *Methods and Contexts in the Study of Muslim Minorities: Visible and Invisible Muslims*, Abingdon and New York: Routledge.

Jenkins, P. (2007) *God's Continent: Christianity, Islam and Europe's Religious Crisis*, Oxford: Oxford University Press.

Khan, L.A. and Ramadan, H.M. (2011) *Contemporary Ijtihad: Limits and Controversies*, Edinburgh: Edinburgh University Press.

Klausen, J. (2005) *The Islamic Challenge: Politics and Religion in Western Europe*, Oxford: Oxford University Press.

Larsson, G. (2011) *Muslims and the New Media: Historical and Contemporary Debates*, Farnham: Ashgate.

Laurence, J. (2012) *The Emancipation of Europe's Muslims: The State's Role in Minority Integration*, Princeton: Princeton University Press.

Lewis, B. (1996) *Cultures in Conflict: Christians, Muslims and Jews in the Age of Discovery*, Oxford: Oxford University Press.

Mandaville, P. (2011) "Transnational Muslim Solidarities and Everyday Life," *Nations and Nationalism* 17(1): 7–24.

Maréchal, B., Allievi, S., Dassetto, F., and Nielsen, J. (2003) *Muslims in the Enlarged Europe: Religion and Society*, Leiden: Brill.

Mariani, E. (2011) "Cyber-Fatwas, Sermons and Media Campaigns: Amr Khaled and Omar Bakri Muhammad in Search of New Audiences," in van Bruinessen, M. and Allievi, S. (eds.) *Producing Islamic Knowledge: Transmission and Dissemination in Western Europe*, Abingdon and New York: Routledge, pp. 142–68.

Nielsen, J. (1992) *Muslims in Western Europe*, Edinburgh: Edinburgh University Press.

Ramadan, T. (2004a) *To Be a European Muslim*, Leicester: Islamic Foundation.

——(2004b) *Western Muslims and the Future of Islam*, Oxford: Oxford University Press.

——(2010) *The Quest for Meaning: Developing a Philosophy of Pluralism*, London: Allen Lane.

Roy, O. (2004) *Globalised Islam: The Search for the New Ummah*, London: Hurst & Co.

Soysal, Y.N. (2000) "Citizenship and Identity: Living in Diasporas in Post-war Europe?," *Ethnic and Racial Studies* 23(1): 1–15.

van Bruinessen, M. (2011) "Producing Islamic Knowledge in Western Europe: Discipline, Authority and Personal Quest," in van Bruinessen, M. and Allievi, S. (eds.) *Producing Islamic Knowledge: Transmission and Dissemination in Western Europe*, Abingdon and New York: Routledge, pp. 1–27.

van Nieuwkerk, K. (2006) *Women Embracing Islam: Gender and Conversion in the West*, Austin: University of Texas Press.

Zaman, M.Q. (2002) *The Ulama in Contemporary Islam: Custodians of Change*, Princeton: Princeton University Press.

——(2012) *Modern Islamic Thought in a Radical Age: Religious Authority and Internal Criticism*, Cambridge: Cambridge University Press.

# 28

# Islam, Sufism, and the postmodern in the religious melting pot

*Francesco Alfonso Leccese*

## Sufism: stereotypes and globalization

In recent decades new modalities of transmission of Islamic knowledge, in particular of its mystical trend, Sufism, have given birth to original religious movements from the traditional Islamic key concepts. The process of globalization, quickened in recent years by the great technological innovations in transport, communication, and information, has also brought about a transformation in the way Islamic knowledge is transmitted on a global scale. As already stated, the numerous economic, political, and cultural changes that have occurred in the last two centuries do not allow a clear distinction between the Islamic and the Western world anymore (Ernst 2004). For example, the "discovery" of Sufism by the West and the emergence in the Western mainstream culture of capital figures of classical Sufism, such as Muhyi al-Din Ibn 'Arabi (1165–1240) and Jalal al-Din Rumi (1207–73), has been linked to the "rediscovery" of Sufism in Islamic countries since the second half of the twentieth century.

Sufism had been first introduced into the Western culture in the nineteenth century by some British Orientalists who had undertaken research projects on the Indian subcontinent about some of the most fascinating aspects of what they classified as "Oriental" culture – Sufi poetry, dance, and rituals. Even though those elements were among the most genuine expressions of the Islamic tradition, they did not suit the earlier Orientalists' idea of Islam. Therefore they created the academic concept of Sufism, presented as a mystical current strongly influenced by Hinduism and different from Islam. Their interpretation has greatly affected Western mainstream opinion about Sufism, perceived as a universal "spiritual" doctrine. Other research carried out in the same period on the branches of some Sufi brotherhoods in North African French colonies gave rise to a series of stereotypes – useful for legitimizing the *mission civilisatrice*[1] – which showed Sufis as conservative and incompatible with the project of modernization of the imperial powers (Sirriyeh 1999; Ernst 2011). Those stereotypes turned out to be so influential that even the new Muslim elite, who had been educated in European schools and who would lead the nationalist movements against colonial rule in the first decades of the twentieth century, accepted them. Sufism and its institutionalized aspects, such as brotherhoods and their practices, were rejected as elements of backwardness, responsible for the decay of the Islamic civilization and of the colonial penetration into Muslim countries.

## René Guénon and the Traditional movement

It was only at the beginning of the twentieth century that actual Sufis began to appear in the West as a result of translated texts and research by some European – and later American – scholars on the esoteric doctrines of the East. The most important of them was undoubtedly René Guénon (1886–1951), whose works on the spiritual doctrines of some Oriental traditions such as Islam, Hinduism, and Taoism – interpreted as parts of a unique Tradition – exerted a strong influence on Sufi movements and researchers, not only in the West, but even in Muslim countries. Guénon was initiated into Sufism by Ivan Aguéli (John Gustaf Agelii) (1869–1917), a Swedish painter and intellectual of Tatar-Finnish origin, who had embraced Sufism and taken the name 'Abd al-Hadi. Aguéli contributed to *Il Convito – Al-Nadi*, an Italian Arab review published in Cairo from 1904 to 1910, and to *La Gnose*, a journal published in Paris from 1909 to 1912, whose main promoter and contributor was Guénon himself ('Abdul-Hâdî 1988).

Aguéli put Guénon in contact with an Egyptian branch of the Shadhiliyya, the 'Arabiyya Shadhiliyya, whose *shaykh* was 'Abd al-Rahman Elish al-Kabir (d. 1929). Guénon dedicated to the Egyptian master one of his most important works, *Le Symbolisme de la Croix* (1931), to underline the strong influence of his teachings on his own spiritual research, even though they had never met. In 1930 Guénon decided to move to Cairo, where he lived for the rest of his life known as *shaykh* 'Abd al-Wahid Yahya. In those years he kept in touch with the disciples of the Hamidiyya Shadhiliyya, a Sufi brotherhood founded by Sidi Salama al-Radi (1866–1939) (Gilsenan 1973). The key themes of Guénon's thought are criticism of the Western modern world, the contrast between East and West and between traditional and modern sciences, the rediscovery of Tradition – that he believed was still alive in some Oriental spiritual paths – and the search for a self-realization that in his view was strictly linked to formal adhesion to an Oriental way of initiation. He did not suggest any particular spiritual path, but many of his readers considered Sufism the best way Westerners could follow to achieve spiritual progress. Even though Guénon neither created a new school of thought nor led a religious movement, he had a profound impact on his contemporaries as well as on subsequent generations, and today he is recognized as one of the seminal figures of the Traditional School, based on the belief that the world's great religions all share the same origin. Guénon was the major inspiration behind *Études traditionnelles* (1935–92), a French journal that was exclusively dedicated to the esoteric and metaphysical doctrines of East and West. It contributed also to arousing interest in Sufism in Europe and in the United States with the first translations of and commentaries on a series of treatises by Ibn 'Arabi and texts by other Sufi masters that up to then had been available only in their original languages. The journal published writings by Guénon himself and his collaborators and correspondents, such as Frithjof Schuon (1907–98), Titus Burckhardt (1908–84), Martin Lings (1909–2005), and Michel Vâlsan (1911–74).

In 1933 Frithjof Schuon affiliated to the 'Alawiyya Shadhiliyya, an Algerian Sufi brotherhood whose eponymous *shaykh* was Ahmad al-'Alawi (1869–1934), one of the most charismatic Sufi masters of his time, widely known in Europe and in the United States thanks to the study *A Sufi Saint of the Twentieth Century* (1961) by Martin Lings. Al-'Alawi had founded his order in Mostaganem, Algeria, his birthplace, and then spread it throughout Algeria and other parts of North Africa, Syria, and Yemen. His brotherhood was one of the first to establish a presence in Europe, especially among Algerians in France and Yemenis in Wales. Ahmad al-'Alawi was highly considered in Europe for his open-minded approach to the dialog relations between Sufism and Christianity. In 1926 he was invited to Paris to lead the first communal prayer at the inauguration ceremony of the newly built Great Mosque in the presence of the French President.

After the death of Ahmad al-'Alawi in 1934 and the appointment of 'Adda Bentounes (1898–1952) as his successor at the head of the order, Schuon performed a spiritual retreat, *khalwa*, in the *zawiya* of Mostaganem, followed by a disputed claim (Sedgwick 2004a: 88) of having received an *ijaza* (license) as a *muqaddam* (deputy) of the 'Alawiyya, with permission to admit disciples to the 'Alawiyya order. The first *zawiya* of the 'Alawiyya under Schuon's guidance was founded in Basel, soon followed by others settled in Amiens, Paris, and Lausanne.

Schuon was an important representative of the Perennial Philosophy,[2] a school of thought which claims that permanent and universal metaphysical truths underlie the diverse religions, whose written sources are in the revealed Scriptures as well as in the writings of the great spiritual masters. In this perspective a new direction in Schuon's thought resulted from his deep interest in the religious traditions of the Native Americans.

Schuon had been attracted by American Indians since he was a child but his interest became more serious in 1946, when he asked his followers and admirers to be put in touch with a Native American "elder." Joseph Epes Brown (1920–2000), an anthropologist at the University of Indiana affiliated to the 'Alawiyya, sent him John Neihardt's *Black Elk Speaks* (1932), a sort of autobiography – which had been heavily edited – of Black Elk, a Lakota speaking Oglala Sioux, a leader and *wichwasha wakan* (holy man), who had taken part in the battles of Little Big Horn and Wounded Knee. Schuon appreciated the book so much that he began to discuss Native American spirituality in his correspondence with Guénon and asked Brown to contact Black Elk to do a research project about Native American religion. After spending one year between 1947 and 1948 with Black Elk, in 1953 Brown published *The Sacred Pipe: Black Elk's Account of the Seven Rites of the Oglala Sioux* – a work he wrote in Lausanne with Schuon's intellectual support (Sedgwick 2004a: 123). In 1959 Schuon visited the United States for the first time and lived for several months with the Plains Indians, coming into contact with their religious traditions. He was adopted into the Sioux and participated in a number of Native American rituals (Sedgwick 2004a: 123).

In 1948 the turning point in Schuon's thought gave rise to a sharp dispute with Guénon about the correct nature of a Traditional Sufi brotherhood. Guénon denounced the risks of falling into a sterile syncretism as in his opinion esoteric practice was complementary to an exoteric framework. He also thought that a European Traditional Sufi brotherhood should not differ from a Sufi brotherhood rooted in Islamic countries, just as European Islam should not differ from its original interpretation. On the contrary, Schuon paid less attention to the exoteric framework, focusing on the esoteric practice instead. Schuon's departure from the model of a Traditional Sufi brotherhood became more evident in the 1960s, when he changed the name of his *tariqa* into 'Alawiyya Maryamiyya – generally shortened to Maryamiyya – from Schuon's visions of the Virgin Mary (in Arabic *Maryam*). This change was not perceived by Schuon's followers as a departure from Islam, even though a short prayer to the Virgin Mary was added to the daily litany.[3] During the 1960s and 1970s, various Maryamiyya *zawiya*s were present in Europe, Argentina, and the United States. The main American *zawiya* was established in 1967 in Bloomington, Indiana, by Victor Danner (1926–90), a professor of religious studies at Indiana University, which became an important center for the diffusion of Schuon's Perennialism among a group of intellectuals and bestselling writers like Thomas Merton, Houston Smith, and Sayyed Hossein Nasr. In 1981 Schuon moved to Indiana, where a new Schuonian community of sixty to seventy disciples had settled at Inverness Farm. He lived there for the rest of his life and introduced Native American rituals into the spiritual practices of his community.

Within the Traditional movement, René Guénon and Frithjof Schuon can be regarded as representatives of two different trends that in the second half of the twentieth century would be peculiar to Western Sufism. On the one hand René Guénon focused on Sufi doctrine and, even though he lived in Cairo from 1930 until his death, he influenced the spread of traditional Sufi thought in the West. He had an intensive correspondence with some European intellectuals who had embraced Sufism and who favored the birth of European branches of various Sufi orders that claimed their indissoluble connection with Sufism, viewed as the inner aspect of Islam. They put an emphasis on Islamic external law (*shari'a*) as a complementary but functional way to grasp the inner reality of existence (*haqiqa*), and on the transmission of spiritual teaching through a Sufi genealogical tree (*silsila*). The most important among those orders were the 'Alawiyya, guided by Michel Vâlsan, and the Darqawiyya, whose leader was Roger Maridort.

In 1950 Michel Vâlsan, who had been the Paris *muqaddam* of the Schuonian 'Alawiyya branch for ten years, wrote a twenty-five-page open letter to announce his decision to distance himself from Schuon and denounce his departure from Islam into universalism (Chacornac 1958). Some years later Vâlsan, who was an accomplished scholar and a collector of Ibn 'Arabi manuscripts, which he edited and published in French, emerged as the independent master of another European branch of the 'Alawiyya. He based most of his teachings on Akbarian[4] thought and had among his disciples Michel Chodkiewicz and Charles-Andrés Gilis, eminent experts of Ibn 'Arabi's doctrines.

Roger Maridort (1903–77) received an *ijaza* from the Moroccan Darqawi *shaykh* Muhammad al-Tadhili (d. 1952) and settled his own branch in Turin, Italy, by 1961. Roger Maridort and his disciples devoted themselves to spreading Guénon's work, classical Sufi texts, and Traditional writings through their publishing house, Edizioni Studi Tradizionali, and the journal *Rivista di Studi Tradizionali*, the Italian equivalents of the French Éditions Traditionnelles and *Études Traditionnelles*.

On the other hand, Schuon was a charismatic master who succeeded in creating his own Sufi order in the West. Schuon's attempt to combine Sufi practice with various Oriental spiritual ideas and techniques in some cases resulted in a sort of universal Sufism. Today, the Maryamiyya's membership still consists mainly of a circle of intellectuals and academics – some of them are Schuon's older disciples – who are preserving the perennialist teaching of their master, trying at the same time to underline its Islamic essence (Aymard and Laude 2004: 92–4).

## Universal Sufism and forerunners of the New Age

While the Traditional movement was bringing Sufi doctrines to the West thanks to the influence of charismatic intellectuals and to the translations of classical Sufi texts, some Eastern Sufi masters began to travel across the West presenting Sufism as part of an Oriental timeless wisdom without any formal link with Islam. The most influential among them was Hazrat Inayat Khan (1882–1927), an Indian classical musician who was linked to the Nizami school of the Chishtiyya brotherhood – one of the most popular Sufi brotherhoods of the Indian subcontinent. In 1910 he left India for a music tour in the United States, and later in Europe, during which he began to transmit Sufi teachings and practices. Despite the fact that he was affiliated to the Chishtiyya, he did not spread Chishtiyya's doctrine and rituals but created his own way, the Sufi Order of the West, now Sufi Order International. Hazrat Inayat Khan focused his doctrine on the Divine Unity and on the inner aspect of six religions – Islam, Christianity, Judaism, Zoroastrianism, Buddhism, and Hinduism – that involved the conception of a universal Sufism. The reference texts of this movement were a collection of the abovementioned six religions and the creation of a practice characterized by a new kind of meditative technique that mixed up ritual elements of Islam and Hinduism with others inspired by Christianity. This belief implied that Sufism did not necessarily require conversion to Islam, since in Khan's opinion Sufism was an inner religion without any link with its exterior form. Initially, Inayat Khan spread his movement in the United States. His first female disciple was Rabia Ada Martin, previously Ada Ginsberg (1871–1947), a woman of Russian-Polish Jewish origin who he designated as his spiritual successor at the head of the Sufi Order. This appointment resulted in a dispute on the succession that gave rise to a series of independent offshoots, whereas the leadership of the Sufi Order passed to the founder's son, Pir Vilayat Inayat Khan (1916–2004), and later to his grandson Zia Inayat Khan, current master of the Order.

In the 1940s Rabia Ada Martin began a correspondence with the Indian guru Meher Baba[5] (1894–1969), who had attracted many followers during his visits to the United States and who would later publicly declare himself the Avatar – in Hinduism the direct manifestation of the Divine Being – of the Age. When Rabia Ada Martin died, the designated successor, Ivy Oneita Duce (1895–1981), a former businesswoman, handed over that Inayat Khan's branch to Meher Baba, who created Sufism Reoriented (Hammer 2004). In the late 1960s one of Inayat Khan's disciples, Samuel Lewis (1896–1971), an American mystic and dance teacher who had collaborated with Rabia Martin in the guidance of the Sufi Order branch in the United States, formulated the Dances of Universal Peace (www.dancesofuniversalpeace.org), that is, exhibitions of "psychic purification" and "moral development." Lewis combined the dance of the Mevlevi whirling dervishes with meditative techniques derived from 500 different spiritual traditions, as a method to promote peace through the arts. Lewis, who was called Murshid SAM (Sufi Ahmad Murad) by his disciples, spent the last years of his life traveling through Asia and the Middle East, and after returning to the Unites States – shortly before he died – he founded his own Sufi group in San Francisco, the Sufi Islamiyya Ruhaniat Society, later Sufi Ruhaniat International (Lewis 2008; Hermansen 2004). Lewis was one of the leading figures of the New Age movement in the United States, to the extent that the book which contains a series of ten lectures he gave from July to September 1970 was titled *This Is the New Age, in Person* (Lewis 1973).

Lewis was not the first to show Westerners the Sufi whirling dances since a decontextualized form of whirling dance had already been introduced into the West by Georges Ivanovič Gurdjieff (1872–1949). Born in Alexandropoul, Transcaucasia, between the late 1890s and the early 1910s he traveled through the Middle East and Central Asia and was initiated into the alleged Sarmoun Brotherhood, a secret Sufi order rooted in quite an inaccessible area of Afghanistan which he described in his *Meetings with Remarkable Men* (1963), one of his most successful works. Gurdjieff developed a peculiar teaching method that he called the *Fourth Way*, which was based on a syncretic combination of the spiritual teachings he had derived from different religious traditions of the East, especially from Sufism. He spread his teachings in the main cities of Europe and the United States – London, Paris, and New York – through the Institute of the Harmonious Development of Man, founded in 1919. Gurdjieff also taught his disciples a complex meditative dance inspired by the whirling dervishes' ritual and the various movements of the Islamic and Sufi rituals, such as the ritual prayer (*salat*) and the invocation of God (*dhikr*). Gurdjieff and his followers presented their *movements* in theater performances in front of an enthusiastic audience – completely unaware of their meaning and origin – for the first time in Paris in 1923 and some months later in New York (Lewis 2008: 515).

Peter Brook (b. 1925), the famous English theater and film director,[6] showed some of those movements in his movie adaptation of *Meetings with Remarkable Men* (1978), on which Jeanne de Salzmann (1889–1990), one of Gurdjieff's closest disciples, collaborated as a consultant. The movements are choreographically perfect, even though they may appear rather mechanical if compared to the original Sufi rituals. Sufism's seminal contribution to the teachings of Gurdjieff is attested to by the research carried out by one of his disciples, John G. Bennett

(1897–1974), a British scientist and philosopher. He identified the roots of the principles and techniques of Gurdjieff's method in the wisdom of the *Khwajagan*,[7] Sufi masters who lived between the eleventh and thirteenth centuries in Central Asia. Two centuries later their spiritual heritage was adopted by the Naqshbandiyya order and formally expressed through the eleven principles of the order itself (Bennett 1995 [1977]).

Another forerunner of the New Age was Idries Shah (1924–96). Born in India of an Afghan father and a Scottish mother and raised in England, Idries Shah had a large following in the West for his interpretation of Sufism as a psychological method for self-realization rather than a spiritual path rooted in the Islamic tradition. He neither spread the teachings and ritual techniques of a specific Sufi brotherhood nor asked his disciples for formal adherence to Islam, but he represented a kind of non-traditional Sufi who, like Inayat Khan and Gurdjieff before him, made proselytes mainly in the Western intellectual sphere. Idries Shah was a prolific writer and among his works we can find some of the most successful texts on Sufism published in the West, such as *The Sufis* (1964) and *The Exploits of the Incomparable Mulla Nasrudin* (1966). The main promoter of Shah's Sufism is Robert Ornstein (b. 1942), a psychology professor at Stanford University who has translated Sufi themes into a psychotherapeutic language, meeting with an enthusiastic reception in the American academic community of psychologists. His academic essays, among which *The Psychology of Consciousness* (1972) is the most famous, have played an active role in the spreading of universal Sufism in the United States with a marked therapeutic imprinting (Lewis 2008; Hermansen 2004).

## Sufism and the 1960s counterculture movement

The discovery of Sufism by Westerners was also linked to some aspects of the American and British counterculture that emerged in the 1960s, that is, interest in Oriental traditions and the search for the disclosure and the nurture of "the authentic self," which often took the "journey to the East" (Taji-Farouki 2007: 3).

Even if the New Age eludes a univocal definition, its main themes are the centrality of the concept of self-spirituality and a de-traditionalized and anti-authoritarian character melted up with a perennialist inclination. A leading figure in the British alternative culture of the late 1960s was Bulent Rauf (1911–87), a Turkish intellectual settled in London in 1966, who played an important role in the spreading of Ibn 'Arabi's thought through the Beshara movement, founded in 1971. This movement was the long-time result of his encounter with Reshad Feild (b. 1934), previously Tim Feild, an Englishman of aristocratic origins who had been previously involved in pop music as a member of the British folk trio the Springfields. He joined the Sufi Order of Pir Vilayat Khan after receiving initiation by spiritual masters of different orientations, from both the East and the West. Reshad Feild was designated by Vilayat Khan as the representative of his order in the UK and was among the founders of the charitable trust that on Bulent Rauf's suggestion was called Beshara (from the Arabic original word *bishara*, "good news"). In 1971 the Beshara Trust purchased Swyrne Farm in the Cotswolds, England, and under the guidance of Reshad Feild it became the first center of the Sufi Order in the UK. Meditation sessions – based on Chishti techniques, *dhikr* from other Sufi traditions, and Mevlevi whirling dances – were organized there, initially addressing young people who were linked to the hippie movement, and later Oxbridge graduates[8] as well. In 1972 *The Twenty-nine Pages*, a summary of Ibn 'Arabi's metaphysical teachings collected by Bulent Rauf himself, was introduced in the study sessions, and the following year Rauf took over from Feild as the guide of the Beshara movement. In 1974 the Beshara Trust began to organize seminars at the Crisholme house, in Scotland, as well as residential courses. They were focused on intellectual exercises based on the study of Ibn 'Arabi's texts, on meditation and spiritual practice (*dhikr* and *wazifa*), and on service, such as kitchen and garden work.

In the following years, the Beshara movement spread outside Britain, with the establishment of new study circles in France, the Netherlands, Canada, the United States, and Australia. Alongside those circles, an academic organization, the Muhyiddin Ibn 'Arabi Society, was founded in 1977 with the aim of promoting the metaphysical doctrine of the Andalusian Sufi master in Europe and in the United States. Since then the Society has organized annual symposia in the UK and in the United States, and has produced translations and editions of Ibn 'Arabi's texts. Twice a year it publishes the *Journal of Muhiyddin Ibn 'Arabi Society*, which contains the contributions of eminent scholars from all over the world.

In 1973, after leaving Inayat Khan's Sufi Order and the leadership of the Sufi community of Swyrne Farm, Reshad Feild began to travel across Central and North America, and later created centers for spiritual and psychological development in Mexico, Canada, and California. In his successful autobiography *The Last Barrier* (1976) he gave an account of the teachings he had learned from the many Sufi masters he had met, like Bulent Rauf and the Konyan Mevlevi *shaykh* Suleyman Loras Dede (1904–85). Even though Reshad Feild brought the traditional Mevlevi line to the West at the request of *shaykh* Suleyman Loras Dede, with whom he had a lifelong relationship, he did not consider himself a Sufi, but rather – as he himself said – a true seeker with no labels (Feild 2002 [1976]: ix).

Bulent Rauf did not even regard himself as a traditional Sufi master, and although his family was rooted in Ottoman Sufism – his grandfather having been buried in Ibn 'Arabi's mausoleum in Damascus – he was not formally affiliated to any Sufi lineage. He always conceived the Beshara movement as a medium to popularize the teaching of Ibn 'Arabi, one of the most difficult authors of Sufism.

Since his death, the Beshara school, under the leadership of Peter Young, one of his first students, has continued to promote a perennialist interpretation of Ibn 'Arabi's texts, organizing a wide variety of courses, seminars, reading weeks, and educational events around the world. The courses provided by the Beshara are a balanced program of study – often focused on a particular text by Ibn 'Arabi or Jalal al-Din Rumi – work, meditation, and devotional practice, aimed at achieving spiritual self-realization of the students, regardless of their backgrounds (Taji-Farouki 2007; Jeffery-Street 2012).

Bulent Rauf developed his universal approach to Sufism over the years. While in the early years he promoted relations with and visits to the Mevlevi and the Jerrahiyya-Khalwatiyya orders in Turkey, he gradually distanced the Beshara movement from traditional Sufism until he interrupted any formal contacts with the traditional Sufi background in the late 1970s. Nowadays the Beshara continues to organize visits to the saints' tombs in Turkey as part of the school program, and trips to Andalusia and Anatolia – *In the Footsteps of Ibn 'Arabi* – to visit the places where Ibn 'Arabi lived. This emphasis on Sufism's cultural heritage is present in *Turning* (Cilento 1973), a documentary film made in Turkey to commemorate the 700th anniversary of Jalal al-Din Rumi. It was directed by the Australian actress Diane Cilento, who also acted as narrator in the first part of the film, while Bulent Rauf, her consultant, was narrator in the second part, in which he "provides a concise commentary on the cosmology expressed through the geometry of the movements" (Beshara). This documentary film was probably the first made by Westerners to show the Mevlevi dervishes' rituals to a Western audience (Taji-Farouki 2007; Jeffery-Street 2012).

A role in the discovery of Sufism by exponents of the counterculture in the late 1960s was also played by a branch of a Moroccan Sufi order, the Habibiyya Darqawiyya, which had settled in London exactly in those years.

In that period the British branch was led by 'Abd al-Qadir al-Sufi (b. 1930), previously Ian Dallas, a Scottish intellectual and scriptwriter who had also starred in Federico Fellini's *8½* (1963) as Maurice, the mind reader. Ian Dallas had been initiated into Sufism in 1967 by the Moroccan *shaykh* Muhammad ibn al-Habib al-Darqawi (1876–1971), who would later appoint him as his *muqaddam* in the UK. Dallas gathered around himself a group of European and American intellectuals and artists, who met in the three main Western *zawiya*s of the order settled in London, Cordova, and Berkeley, California (Whiteman 2012).

Among the first group of British followers of this Habibiyya branch, there were three members of the psychedelic rock band Mighty Baby, Ian Whiteman (b. 1945), Roger Powell (b. 1949), and Mike "Ace" Evans (1944–2010), who, in 1972, after an extensive journey made to Morocco a year before, recorded and released an album, *If Man But Knew*, as the Habibiyya. This work, one of the earliest pieces of world music ever recorded in Britain and the Habibiyya's sole album, was the result of their encounter with Sufism. They had been profoundly affected, both spiritually and musically, by the traditional Sufi music and singing they had heard in the Habibiyya *zawiya*s of Fez and Meknes. Moroccan Sufism inspired the lyrics of *If Man But Knew*. They were sung in Arabic and focused on the Divine and on love for the Prophet. The texts were taken directly from traditional Sufi orations and from the *qasida*s (Sufi poems traditionally chanted in the Sufi rituals and gatherings) collected in the *Diwan* of the Habibiyya *shaykh* Muhammad ibn al-Habib al-Darqawi (d. 1971). After their return from Morocco, they made the recordings in London with the contribution of two multi-instrumentalists from Northern California, Conrad and Susan Archuletta, who were disciples of the order themselves. The album was deeply influenced by Sufi practice – the musicians fasted for three days before recording, said their prayers and meditated for an hour before each session – and was mostly extemporized.[9] The result was a combination of the common instruments of modern, Western music (acoustic guitar, drums, piano, organ, viola, flute, and so on) with more exotic instrumentation (such as *bina organ*, *koto*, *shakuhachi*, zither, *nay* flute, *mandola*, and all kinds of percussion) and an Eastern-influenced hypnotic psychedelic music (Vernon 2008; Whiteman 2007). This project was somewhat unique because it was not an ethnomusicological work,[10] but probably the first album ever made by a group of European Sufi musicians and an example of the mediating role played by music in the discovery of Sufism by the 1960s counterculture. The front cover photograph of the album was evocative as it showed a *sibha*, the Sufi rosary, while on the back cover were the turbaned faces of the band members. The man who took the photos was Peter Sanders, one of London's key photographers of rock musicians in the mid-1960s, a member of the British Habibiyya order himself.[11]

In 1973 another musician, Richard Thompson (b. 1949), a songwriter and former member of the British folk-rock band Fairport Convention – one of the greatest guitarists of all time, according to *Rolling Stone* magazine – joined the Habibiyya order. Thompson had read a lot about Sufism as a teenager, but he had had no way of finding any practitioners until they almost arrived on his doorstep when the church hall in Belsize Park – about 200 meters from his house – was one day rented for a Sufi meeting. So he went down there and looking around he realized that he knew four of the people in there, all musicians he had done session work with. They were members of the British branch of the Habibiyya order, which had its *zawiya* in Bristol Gardens, Maida Vale, London (Thompson 2012). Thompson was struck by that Sufi group's great background mix from all classes and different countries, and subsequently he spent a few sabbaticals in Morocco and Algeria "listening to the wisdom of old guys" (Adams 2010). He transferred this spiritual experience to the album *Pour Down Like Silver* (1975), made with his first wife Linda Thompson. The cover photographs show the Thompsons dressed in traditional Muslim clothes, while the lyrics were a sign of their new ascetic direction.

The Western Habibiyya branch was characterized by a countercultural membership from the British rock scene and artists of the San Francisco Bay Area, like Conrad and Susan Archuletta and the poet and painter Daniel Moore (b. 1940), who joined the Habibiyya order in 1970. He had made his mark in 1964 with his first poetry collection, *Dawn Visions*, published by Lawrence Ferlinghetti's the City Lights Books, San Francisco. From 1966 to 1969 Daniel Moore wrote and directed ritual theater for his Floating Lotus Magic Opera Company, in Berkeley, California.[12]

After his conversion, Daniel Moore began traveling extensively in Europe and North Africa, renouncing written poetry for about ten years. In 1980 he published three books of poetry in Santa Barbara, California, and in the following years he organized poetry readings for the Santa Barbara Arts Festivals. In 2005 he created Ecstatic Exchange, his personal publishing company specializing in contemporary Sufi poetry. Today Daniel Moore continues to give public readings, often accompanying himself on specially tuned zithers.

In about 1977, 'Abd al-Qadir al-Sufi (b. 1930) began to consider himself an independent master in the line of the Habibiyya and consequently he created his own movement, the Murabitun, In its etymology, the word "Murabitun" evokes the Sufis who inhabited the *ribat*s (fortifications built along the frontier of the *dar al-islam*) and, historically, the Almoravid dynasty that in the eleventh and twelfth centuries ruled in North Africa and Spain (al-Andalus). The Murabitun Movement was characterized by the militant imprinting given by 'Abd al-Qadir, who focused his teaching on political and economical issues, promoting the study of the *Muwatta'* – the first written collection of *hadith* comprising the subjects of Muslim Law, compiled and edited by Malik ibn Anas (715–96) – among his disciples. 'Abd al-Qadir al-Sufi considered the *Muwatta'* the foundation of an ideal legal and social system. His perspective implied a total rejection of the Western capitalist banking system, to be replaced by an Islamic one based on the *zakat*, on the abolition of bank loans, and on the re-establishment of a *halal* currency. Consequently 'Abd al-Qadir advocated the restoration of the Islamic gold *dinar* and of the silver *dihram*, used in the age of the caliphate, and later a system of *e-dinars* on the internet (www.dinarshops.com) and within the Murabitun communities around the world to avoid paper money, considered *haram* (forbidden).

The new direction in 'Abd al-Qadir's thought resulted on the one hand in the abandonment of his order by a great deal of earlier Western converts from an alternative background (Sanders 2007 [2002]), on the other in "the most far-reaching and successful Islamic *da'wa* (the proselytizing of Islam) in the twentieth century" (www.shaykhabdalqadir.com/content/bio.php). In Spain the Murabitun were involved in the various political initiatives promoted by Spanish Muslim organizations and foreign donors that brought about the construction of Granada Mosque in 2003. The missionary activities of the movement have concentrated on regions with intense social conflicts, such as the Mexican state of Chiapas, where in 1996 the Murabitun took part in the Zapatista uprising,[13] and South Africa, where, during the 1980s newly converted Zulus were recruited (Hermansen 2005: 483–9; Garvin 2005; Hermansen 2009: 34–6). Today South Africa is the main center of the Marabitun Movement as its leader himself currently lives there. In 2004 'Abd al-Qadir founded the Cape Town Dallas College with "the function of educating and producing a new generation with the capacity for leadership at the national and international level" (Dallas College, Leadership for Young Muslims, www.dallas collegect.com/?page_id=2).

The Murabitun has emerged as a movement without parallel in any Western Sufi order; some researchers even liken it to the Islamist movements. As a matter of fact, while a lack of interest in political issues is generally peculiar to Western Sufi orders, the Murabitun's political involvement – though criticized by other Western Sufi brotherhoods – can be traced back to a typology of militant Sufism having occurred in particular historical contexts, such as the anti-colonial movements led by Sufi masters during the nineteenth century (Cook 2005: 73–92).

## Sufi ideas in the postmodern

Nowadays, at the third stage of its rooting in the West, Sufism appears as a cultural category, in some cases even a "consumption good". As we have seen, the first stage, the introduction of Sufi doctrines and techniques into the West in the first half of the twentieth century, was characterized by an intellectual and spiritual interest in Oriental traditions which resulted in two main directions: the Traditional movement and universal Sufism. In the former, the reference figures for European and American Muslim converts were the Traditional movement leading figures, Western intellectuals, or Western Sufi masters. In the latter, Eastern masters created a new orientation: Sufi traditions melded with Oriental spiritual trends, giving life to a Sufi universalism. Separated from its Islamic roots, Sufism addressed – as generic Oriental wisdom – a wide range of Western spiritual seekers and led sometimes to new religious movements.

The second stage of the spread of Sufism in the West – between the 1960s and the 1980s – was characterized by the *discovery* by Westerners of Sufi masters and brotherhoods in their countries of origin. Traditional Sufi orders recruited disciples among Westerners, and their masters began to travel extensively across European and American countries trying to settle a traditional Sufism in completely different contexts.

Among the orders that settled their branches in the West in those years we have to mention the Naqshbandiyya Haqqaniyya, the Burhaniyya Dusuqiyya Shadhiliyya, and last – in chronological order – the Qadiriyya Budshishiyya.

Muhammad Nazim al-Haqqani (b. 1922), Cypriot master of the Haqqaniyya, made his first visit to London in 1973 and in a few years he spread his order in the UK and later in the USA, continuing to visit periodically his communities scattered in Western countries. In Europe and in the USA the Haqqani Naqshbandi Sufi Order increased the number of its adherents also thanks to some charismatic figures present in the order. The best known of these is the German convert Burhanuddin Herrmann, famous for his ability in telling traditional Sufi stories (Herrmann 2006) and for the seminars on Sufi traditions he organizes for contemporary seekers all over the world. A prominent exponent of the Haqqani Naqshbandi Sufi Order in the United States, the Lebanese American *shaykh* Muhammad Hisham al-Kabbani, is the founder and chairman of the Islamic Supreme Council of America. Through this organization that promotes the activities of the order in the United States he aims to play a leading role in a more general Muslim framework.

The Burhaniyya Dusuqiyya Shadhiliyya is a Sudanese order revitalized by Muhammad 'Uthman Abduhu al-Burhani (1901–83), its charismatic *shaykh*, who succeeded in spreading it from Sudan to Egypt. Since the 1980s, the Burhaniyya has taken root throughout Europe, especially in Germany, with communities of disciples consisting mainly of European converts as that country was not involved in Egyptian or Sudanese migrations. In the following years – also thanks to its strong centralized organization – the Burhaniyya settled branches in other European countries, in the Middle East, and in the United States. The close link between the present master of the Burhaniyya, *shaykh* Muhammad ibn Ibrahim – the grandson of the founder of the order – and the German disciples is underlined not only by the fact that he spends long periods of the year with them in their country, but also by his marriage to a German convert.

The Qadiriyya Budshishiyya, mainly rooted in Morocco, expanded under the guidance of Abu al-'Abbas al-Mukhtar (d. 1971) and nowadays is led by his son, Hamza ibn Abu al-'Abbas al-Budshishi al-Qadiri. In recent years the Budshishiyya has also been spreading in some European non-francophone countries such as the United Kingdom and Spain, but it is in France that, under the guide of the local *muqaddam* Fouad Skali, it has gained the largest number of adherents not only among Maghrebi migrants but also among French Muslim converts. Fouad Skali, a Moroccan intellectual, is also director of the Fez Music Soul Festival, which has hosted traditional music groups of different religious backgrounds from all over the world since 1994.

The abovementioned Sufi brotherhoods share an emphasis on the role of their masters, thus confirming the old Sufi saying: "the master is the path, and the path is the master." Yet the global diffusion of these orders is due not only to the charisma of their masters but also to some ritual innovations they have introduced. For example, the aspiring disciples do not, as they had to in the past, have to overcome a long trial period before taking the bond of allegiance (*bay'a*) with their master, nor do they have to face a long spiritual retreat. Nowadays this practice, the *khalwa*, is not considered indispensable in these brotherhoods and is replaced by a meditation practice that allows the disciple a retreat from everyday life without a total withdrawal from society.

For these reasons, while in the West other *globalized* brotherhoods – like the Senegalese Muridiyya and the Indian Chistiyya – recruit their disciples above all among migrants coming from the original countries of the brotherhoods themselves, the Haqqaniyya, the Burhaniyya, and the Budshishiyya have succeeded in proselytizing not only among natural-born Muslims but also – or mainly – among Westerners.

In the third stage of the rooting of Sufism in the West, the internet has played a decisive role, not only as a medium of proselytizing but also because for the first time in the history of the Sufi orders a disciple can be virtually in touch with his/her master twenty-four hours a day, while in the past a disciple could spend years – traveling long distances – in search of his/her own Sufi master. In fact the esoteric teaching that was once restricted to an inner circle of disciples or to the elite in a brotherhood has today become accessible on global scale to whoever has a connection to the internet at his/her disposal.

The paradox of the divulgation of inner teachings is in the advertising character of the various Sufi orders' websites, making them appear just like a *product* on the religious global market and risking misinterpretation of the religious message (Ernst 2009).

As a matter of fact, in the present religious melting pot many New Age followers adopt the word "Sufi" as a label and appropriate Sufi iconic symbols, like the whirling dervishes, to promote their activities, giving birth to decontextualized forms of Sufism. The mystification of Sufism and its New Age interpretation can be easily seen in the cultural and commercial operation made about the Persian Sufi poetry by Jalal al-Din Rumi (Ernst 2009) and Hafez (Loloi 2004: 49–78). In particular, American pop culture has appropriated Rumi's figure and poems, and distorted his spiritual teaching.

The bestselling versions of Rumi's poems, edited by some American poets – Robert Bly and Coleman Barks are the best known among them – have succeeded in presenting Rumi's teaching as timeless wisdom with no reference to its original Islamic framework, and as suitable to satisfy the spiritual need of the many who do not identify with the traditional religions but are in search of personal development.

As a reaction against this religious melting pot and the degeneration of some Sufi orders – primarily their economical and political involvement – some Western Sufi intellectuals and scholars argue for the historical existence of Sufism before and outside its organized forms. In their opinion, a real and effective transmission of Sufi teaching can be preserved only under the guidance of a Sufi master in a restricted circle of disciples, without necessarily affiliating to an order (Chodkiewicz 1996; Geoffroy 2003: 290–3).

These two antithetical trends remind us of the elusive nature of Sufism expressed by a tenth-century Sufi *shaykh*: "Sufism once was a reality without a name; it is now a name without reality." Even though used over the centuries by the detractors of Sufism against its historical developments, this paradoxical aphorism represents the undeniable complexity of the relation that exists between the signifier and the signified. As a matter of fact the practical and historical dimensions of Sufi thought are the glow of a Spiritual ideal that is unattainable except by a few.

## Notes

1 The main aim of the French *littérature "de surveillance"* was the census of Algerian Sufism through information about the doctrines and practices of the different Sufi brotherhoods, about their *zawiya*s, their organization, and their political role (Rinn 1884; Petit 1899; Depont and Coppolani 1897).

2 Even though Schuon's disciples do not consider Aldous Huxley a "true" representative of the Perennial Philosophy, the fame of this movement in the mainstream culture is exactly due to Huxley's work *The Perennial Philosophy* (2009 [1945]) (Oldmeadow 2010: 272–5).

3 A collection of small texts written by Schuon himself, the *Book of Keys*, inspired by Islamic, Sufi, and Hindu sources, was introduced as the main text of Schuon's Maryamiyya.

4 Akbarian is an adjective that derives from the epithet given to Ibn 'Arabi by his disciples: *al-shaykh al-akbar*, "the greatest master."

5 Meher Baba is popularly associated with the sentence "Don't worry, be happy," which he often used to encourage his disciples and which is reproduced on one of his standard portraits. It inspired the famous song by Bobby McFerrin (1988) that gave the motto a worldwide diffusion.

6 Peter Brook was heavily influenced by Gurdjieff. The direct Sufi heritage in his work is perceivable in the theater adaptation of the classical Sufi text *The Conference of the Birds* (1979) of Farid al-Din 'Attar (1142–1220) and in the theater adaptations of Amadou Hampâté Bâ's *Vie et enseignement de Tierno Bokar: Le sage de Bandiagara* (1957): *Tierno Bokar* (2004) and *11 and 12* (2009) (Nicolescu 1985, 1997; Gibbson 2010).

7 *Khwajagan* means "Masters" in Persian. The most important masters of the Naqshbandiyya genealogical tree in that period were Khwaja 'Abd al-Khaliq (d. 1220) and Yusuf Hamadani (1048–1141).

8 "Thousands of seekers came all over the world to spend weeks, or even months living in the community" (Feild 2002: xiv).

9 The underlying "theory was that the meditation would get the egos out of the way, so the music could become truly spontaneous … At the end of that we would just play, as if we were instruments being played, not the players" (Whiteman 2007).

10 This is the case of *Islamic Liturgy: Song and Dance at a Meeting of Dervishes* (1960) an 'Alawiyya *hadra* recorded by the ethnomusicologist John Levy (1910–76) in London, enriched by a detailed annotation by Martin Lings with transcriptions and translations of the litanies and recitations.

11 In 1970 Sanders made a photo report in the holy cities of Mecca and Medina, as he was among the few professional photographers who had access to the holy cities of Islam. In the following years he has become a specialist in reportages on the Muslim world (Sanders 2002).

12 *The Walls Are Running Blood* and *Bliss Apocalypse* were the two major musical ritual dramas presented during those years. The theater company consisted of amateurs, painters, musicians – such as Conrad and Susan Archuletta – or artists in different fields, and their inspiration was primarily Zen Buddhism. Each performance was played at night using only Coleman lanterns for illumination.

13 Today the Murabitun of San Cristobal forms a community of indigenous and non-indigenous Mexicans, as well as other Latin American and European converts.

## Bibliography

'Abdul-Hâdî (1988) *Écrits pour La Gnose. Comprenant la traduction de l'arabe du Traité de l'unité*, Milan: Archè.

Adams, T. (2010) "Why Richard Thompson Is Keeping the Faith," *Observer*, April11, www.guardian.co.uk/music/2010/apr/11/richard-thompson-faith-feature.

Aymard, J.-B. and Laude, P. (2004) *Frithjof Schuon: Life and Teachings*, New York: State University of New York Press.

Bennett, J.G. (1995 [1977]) *The Master of Wisdom*, London: Bennett Books.

Biasotti, D. (2007) *The Habibiyya: If Man But Knew*, CD booklet of the Remastered Expanded Edition of 1972, Sunbeam Records.

Brown, J.E. (1989 [1953]) *The Sacred Pipe: Black Elk's Account of the Seven Rites of the Oglala Sioux*, Norman: University of Oklahoma Press.

——(2003 [1953]) *Les Rites secrets des Indiens sioux*, Paris: Editions Le Mail.

Chacornac, P. (1958) *La Vie simple de René Guénon*, Paris: Editions Traditionnelles.

Chodkiewicz, M. (1996) "Le Soufisme au XXe siècle," in Popovic, A. and Veinstein, G. (eds.) *Les Voies d'Allah. Les ordres mystiques dans le monde musulman des origines à aujourd'hui*, Paris: Fayard.

Cilento, D. (dir.) (1973) *Turning*, Cheltenham: Beshara Publications.

Cook, D. (2005) *Understanding Jihad*, London: University of California Press.

Depont, O. and Coppolani, X. (1897) *Les Confréries religiouse musulmane*, Algiers: A. Jourdan.

Ernst, C.W. (2004) *Following Muhammad: Rethinking Islam in the Contemporary World*, 2nd ed., Edinburgh: Edinburgh University Press.

——(2005) "Ideological and Technological Transformations of Contemporary Sufism," Cooke, M. and Lawrence, B.B. (eds.) *Muslim Networks: From Hajj to Hip-hop*, Islamic Civilization and Muslim Networks Series, 2, Chapel Hill: University of North Carolina Press, pp. 198–207.

——(2009) "Sufism, Islam, and Globalization in the Contemporary World: Methodological Reflections on a Changing Field of Study," *In Memoriam: The 4th Victor Danner Memorial Lecture*, Bloomington: Department of Near Eastern Languages and Cultures.

——(2011) *Sufism: An Introduction to the Mystical Tradition of Islam*, Boston: Shambhala Publications; originally published as *The Shambhala Guide to Sufism*, Boston: Shambhala, 1997.

Feild, R. (2002 [1976]) *The Last Barrier. A Journey into the Essence of Sufi Teachings*, Great Barrington: Lindisfarne Books.

Garvin, N. (2005) "Conversion and Conflict: Muslims in Mexico," *ISIM – International Institute for the Study of Islam in the Modern World – Review* 15: 18–19.

Geaves, R., Dressler, M., and Klinkhammer, G. (eds.) (2009) *Sufis in Western Society: Global Networking and Locality*, London and New York: Routledge.

Geoffroy, E. (2003) *Initiation au soufisme*, Paris: Fayard.

——(2010) *Introduction to Sufism: The Inner Path of Islam*, translated by Roger Gaetani, Bloomington: World Wisdom.

Gibbson, F. (2010) "The Prayers of Peter Brook," *Guardian*, January 17, www.guardian.co.uk/stage/2010/jan/17/peter-brook-eleven-twelve.

Gilsenan, M. (1973) *Saint and Sufi in Modern Egypt: An Essay in the Sociology of Religion*, Oxford: Clarendon Press.

Guénon, R. (1931; 3rd ed. 1957) *Le Symbolisme de la Croix*; trans. Angus Macnab (1958; 3rd ed. 1996) *Symbolism of the Cross*, London: Luzac & Co. Ltd.

Hammer, O. (2004) "Sufism for Westerners," in Westerlund, D. (ed.) *Sufism in Europe and North America*, New York: RoutledgeCurzon.

Hermansen, M. (2000) "Hybrid Identity Formations in Muslim America: The Case of American Sufi Movements," *The Muslim World* 90: 158–97.

——(2004) "What's American about American Sufi Movements?," in Westerlund, D. (ed.) *Sufism in Europe and North America*, New York: RoutledgeCurzon.

——(2005) "The 'Other' Shâdhilis of the West," in Geoffroy, E. (ed.) *Une Voie soufie dans le monde: La Shâdhiliyya*, Paris: Maisonneuve & Larose/Espace du Temps Présent/Editions Aïni Bennaï.

——(2009) "Global Sufism 'Theirs and Ours'," in Geaves, R., Dressler, M., and Klinkhammer, G. (eds.) *Sufis in Western Society: Global Networking and Locality*, London and New York: Routledge.

Herrmann, B. (2006) *Il cammello sul Tetto. Discorsi Sufi. Una guida mistico-pratica alla Via dei Dervisci*, Milan: Armenia. Spanish trans. (2008) *El camello sobre el tejado: enseñanzas sufies para al vida cotidiana: una guía místico-práctica hacia la vía de los* derviches; German trans. Judith Elze (2010) *Das Kamel auf dem Dach: Weisheiten und Ratschläge einen modernen Derwischs*.

Huxley, A. (2009 [1945]) *The Perennial Philosophy*, New York: HarperCollins.

Jeffery-Street, I. (2012) *Ibn 'Arabi and the Contemporary West: Beshara and the Ibn 'Arabi Society*, Sheffield: Equinox.

Lewis, F.D. (2008) *Rumi. Past and Present. East and West. The Life, Teachings and Poetry of Jalâl al-Din Rumi*, Oxford: Oneworld.

Lewis, M.S.L. (1973) *This Is the New Age, in Person*, San Francisco: Sufi Ruhaniat International.

Lings, M. (2006 [1961]) *A Sufi Saint of the Twentieth Century: Shaikh Ahmad al-'Alawi – His Spiritual Heritage and Legacy*, Cambridge: The Islamic Texts Society.

Loloi, P. (2004) *Hafiz Master of Persian Poetry: A Critical Bibliography*, New York: I.B. Tauris.

Malik, J. and Hinnels J. (eds.) (2006) *Sufism in the West*, New York: Routledge.

Moore, D. (1964) *Dawn Visions*, San Francisco: City Lights Books.

Neihardt, J. (1932) *Black Elk Speaks*, New York: William Morrow & Company.

Nicolescu, B. (1985) "Peter Brook et la pensée traditionnelle," in Banu, G. (ed.) *Les Voies de la création théâtrale: XIII Brook*, Paris: CNRS Editions, pp. 143–61.

——(1997) "Theatre, Determinism and Spontaneity," *English in Contemporary Theatre Review* VII: 11–23.

Oldmeadow, H. (2010) *Frithjof Schuon and the Perennial Philosophy*, Bloomington: World Wisdom.

Petit, L. (1899) *Les Confréries musulmane*, Paris: Librairie Bloud et Barral.

Raudvere, C. and Stenberg L. (eds.) (2009) *Sufism Today: Heritage and Tradition in the Global Community*, New York: I.B. Tauris.

Rinn, L. (1884) *Marabouts et Khouans: étude sur l'islam en Algérie avec une carte indiquant la marche, la situation et l'importance des ordres religieux musulmans*, Algiers: A. Jourdan.

Sanders, P. (2007 [2002]) *In the Shade of the Tree: A Photographic Odyssey through the Muslim World*, London: Inspiral Books.

Sedgwick, M. (2004a) *Against the Modern World: Traditionalism and the Secret Intellectual History of the Twentieth Century*, New York: Oxford University Press.

——(2004b) "In Search for Counter-Reformation: Anti-Sufi Stereotypes and the Budshishiyya's Response," Browers, M. and Kurzman, C. (eds.) *An Islamic Reformation?*, Oxford: Lexington Books.

Sirriyeh, E. (1999) *Sufis and Anti Sufis: The Defence, Rethinking and Rejection of Sufism in the Modern World*, London: Curzon.

Taji-Farouki, S. (2007) *Beshara and 'Ibn Arabi: A Movement of Sufi Spirituality in the Modern World*, Oxford: Anqa Publishing.

Thompson, R. (2012) "Sufism," email, October 3–11.

van Bruinessen, M. and Day Howell, J. (eds.) (2007) *Sufism and the "Modern" in Islam*, London: I.B. Tauris.

Vernon, J. (2008 [2006]) *The Tapestry of Delights: The Comprehensive Guide to British Music of the Beat, R&B, Pychedelic and Progressive Eras 1963–1976*, London: Borderline Productions.

Westerlund, D. (ed.) (2004) *Sufism in Europe and North America*, New York: RoutledgeCurzon.

Whiteman, I. (2007) *The Habibiyya: If Man But Knew*, CD booklet of the Remastered Expanded Edition of 1972, Sunbeam Records.

——(2012) "Music and Sufism," email, October 10.

# Index

Manow, P. 307
Mantovan, C. 314
Manzano Moreno, E. 21, 23–4
Marazzi, F. 55
March, A. 366
Marco of Toledo 31
Maréchal, Brigitte 6, 93, 95, 97, 436, 438
Margaret of Navarra 63–4
marginal identities 98, 221
marginalization 237, 280, 407–8
Mariani, E. 432
Maridort, Roger 444
Marín Guzmán, R. 156, 165
Marín, M. 22, 27
Marques, V. L. M. 176
Marr, T. 130
marriage 281; migration 88, 164, 274; religious law 375–6
Marsala 65–6
Marti, M. 312
Martin, R. 165
Martin, Rabia Ada 445
Martinello, M. 91
Martínez Montiel, Luz Maria 156
Martínez Ruiz, Juan 45
Martinez-Vazquez, H. A. 268
Marvin X 325, 329
masculinity issues 275–7
Masjid-i Qurtuba 33
maslaha 370–2, 376
Massey, D. B. 276
masters and disciples 451
Matar, N. 261–2, 273
material culture 348–60
materialsim 98, 117
Matthew of Aiello 60, 64
Mattson, I. 148, 385, 387, 389, 406
Maurer, B. 357
Maurici, F. 62
Maussen, M. 309
Mavelli, L. 186, 194, 272
Mawdudi, Abu al-'Ala 397
Maya Indians 160
Meakin, B. 33
Mecca 427–8; pilgrimage 62, 94
Mecca Cola 338
Mecca2Medina 338
media 231–2, 435
Medina 158, 289, 294, 296, 299–301, 427–8
Meegan, R. A. 276
Meer, N. 223, 231
Mekka Foods 338
melting pot experiments 144, 451
Méndez, N. 174
Mendoza 177
Mendus, S. 218–19
Menem, Carlos 174

Merkel, Angela 186, 223
Merton, Thomas 443
Messina 61–2, 65–6
mestizos 160, 163
Metcalf, B. D. 4, 349–50
Metcalfe, A. 55, 63, 262
Mevlevi order 447
Mexico 8, 110, 154–64, 167, 173, 175–6, 449
Mexico City 157–9
Meyer, B. 336
Mezquita Al Dawah Islámica 165
Mezquita Omar ibn al-Khattab 176
Middle East 113, 118, 216, 274
Mighty Baby 448
migration 76, 88, 216, 308, 368; anti-immigrant racism 91–2, 272; Balkans 79–80; Britain 273–4; Central America 156–7, 159, 164–6; Ismailis 249–51; labor 87, 282, 305; marriage and 88, 164, 274; and radicalization 272–4; South America 171–5, 177; USA 118, 137, 140–1, 201, 282, 325–6; Western Europe 86–9, 91, 199–203, 263
Milan 304
Miles, R. 275
militant mobilization 86
military service 374–5
Miller, Daniel 348
Millî Görüş 306, 312
Million Man March 134
Milton, John 218
Minaret of the Messiah 301
minarets 289–91, 293
minority status 76–8, 199–203, 275, 281, 427–8, 435–6
Mintel 357
Miquel, A. 3
Mirdal, G. M. 200
missionary activities 89, 158–9, 163, 176, 323 see also proselytizing
mixed marriage 375–6
mobilization 86, 89–90, 93–9, 140, 142, 314, 316; contrastive 94–7; cultural 97–9; symbolic 97–9
models for Islamic architecture 289–91
modernism 208, 399; architecture 294–7
modernity 191, 232, 352, 365–6, 379; Aga Khan and 253–5; Ismaili communities 246, 253–5; Muslim modernities 245–7
modernization 78, 187, 261, 441
Modood, T. 219–21, 223, 231, 359
Moghissi, Haideh 389
Mohriez, Mohamed 115
Molénat, J.-P. 25, 27
Moller Okin, S. 390
Moncada, Ramón 28
Monk, Thelonious 323
Montenegro 70, 72, 74
Montenegro, S. 176–7